Assessment of Intellectual Functioning

Second Edition

PERSPECTIVES ON INDIVIDUAL DIFFERENCES

CECIL R. REYNOLDS, *Texas A&M University, College Station*
ROBERT T. BROWN, *University of North Carolina, Wilmington*

A Continuation Order Plan is available for this series. A continuation order will bring delivery of each new volume immediately upon publication. Volumes are billed only upon actual shipment. For further information please contact the publisher.

Assessment of Intellectual Functioning

Second Edition

Lewis R. Aiken

Pepperdine University
Malibu, California

Plenum Press • New York and London

Library of Congress Cataloging-in-Publication Data

Aiken, Lewis R., 1931-
    Assessment of intellectual functioning / Lewis R. Aiken. -- 2nd
  ed.
        p.   cm. -- (Perspectives on individual differences)
    Includes bibliographical references and index.
    ISBN 0-306-45152-2
    1. Intelligence tests.   I. Title.   II. Series.
  BF431.A49   1996
  153.9'3--dc20   95-26038
                                                                   CIP

Front cover photo of Alfred Binet courtesy of Culver Pictures, Inc.

ISBN 0-306-45152-2

© 1996 Plenum Press, New York
A Division of Plenum Publishing Corporation
233 Spring Street, New York, N. Y. 10013

10 9 8 7 6 5 4 3 2 1

The first edition of this book was published by Allyn and Bacon, Inc.,
Newton, Massachusetts, 1987

Printed in the United States of America

Psychological tests are a little like firearms; used carefully by someone with appropriate training, they can be very valuable, but in the hands of the incautious or inexpert, they are potentially dangerous.

—Robert M. Thorndike

Preface

This book is a comprehensive, basic text on the assessment of intellectual abilities in children and adults. Emphasis is placed on the rationale and techniques for measuring intellectual functioning in educational, clinical, and other organizational contexts. Detailed descriptions of the most widely used procedures for administering, scoring, and interpreting individual and group intelligence tests are provided.

In addition to describing many different individual and group tests of cognitive abilities, the book provides sufficient coverage of psychometric concepts and methods to serve as a framework for interpreting test results and guiding students, practitioners, and researchers in the appropriate selection and usage of these instruments and procedures. Theoretical conceptions of the nature of cognitive abilities and research on their origins and relationships to other variables are also considered. The thirteen chapters, three appendixes, and three indexes are sufficiently detailed and integrated for the book to serve either as a text for upper undergraduate and beginning graduate-level courses on intellectual or cognitive assessment or as a sourcebook for practicing psychologists in schools, clinics, and other organizational settings. Case materials and associated psychological testing reports are presented to facilitate understanding and application of the tests and other procedures.

Unlike certain related volumes on intellectual assessment, this text covers the entire chronological age range from infancy through later life. Special problems encountered in examining individuals in different age, sex, ethnic, and socioeconomic groups are considered. In addition, an entire chapter is devoted to research on individual and group differences in mental abilities, another chapter to ability tests and testing in other countries and cultures, and a third chapter to theories and issues. Standardized tests of intelligence are featured, but a variety of tests and procedures are discussed. The fact that test scores must be interpreted with respect to other behavioral and background data is emphasized.

An effort has been made to include the latest facts, figures, and ideas on intellectual assessment, a field of research and application that has weathered numerous storms but continues to flourish. Significant in this development are publication of a professional journal, *Intelligence*, an international newsletter, *Human Intelligence*, and an *Encyclopedia of Human Intelligence*, devoted to research reports, features, news, and announcements concerning the measurement, meaning, development, and correlates of intellectual abilities. Furthermore, new theories of cognition and new approaches to psychological measurement have contributed to the development of a variety of tasks and other psychometric instruments. Among these are the Kaufman Assessment Battery for Children, the Differential Ability Scales, the Stanford-Binet Intelligence Scale: Fourth Edition, the WISC-III, and the Bayley Scales of Infant Development (2nd ed.).

Among those individuals who deserve special thanks for their constructive criticisms, suggestions, and recommendations with respect to the second edition of this book are Cecil R. Reynolds, Robert T. Brown, and Eliot Werner. Valuable assistance in copyediting and attention to the many additional details involved in producing a textbook were provided by Cecilia Secor, Herman Makler, and Robert T. Brown.

LEWIS R. AIKEN

Contents

Contents

Chapter 1

Foundations and Definitions

Intelligence, a popular term today, was rarely used before the latter part of the nineteenth century. Certain philosophers in ancient Greece, such as Plato and Aristotle, and medieval scholastics such as Thomas Aquinas (1225–1274) referred to a unitary coordinating "mental faculty" that was similar to the modern conception of intelligence. Aquinas described this general faculty as the ability to detect similarities and dissimilarities among things and thus to combine and separate them. However, systematic efforts to study and measure "intelligence" did not actually begin until the second half of the nineteenth century. During that time the philosopher Herbert Spencer and the gentleman-scientist Francis Galton introduced the Latin-derived term *intelligence* in their writings.

Galton, a cousin of the famous naturalist Charles Darwin, whose theory of evolution is a cornerstone of modern biology, was greatly influenced by Darwin's ideas on the origin of species differences. But rather than concentrating on differences among species, Galton decided to investigate the nature and origin of variations within a particular species: homo sapiens. The intraspecies difference of greatest interest to Galton was mental quickness or general mental ability, which he believed to be an inherent, measurable human characteristic distinct from special abilities. Unlike Herbert Spencer, who was content to philosophize about the

1

nature of "intelligence," Galton devised many tests and procedures for assessing and investigating this psychological construct.

HISTORICAL ANTECEDENTS OF INTELLIGENCE TESTING

Galton's research on human abilities, which is described in detail later in this chapter, is representative of the general interest in individual differences that permeated scholarly discussions during his time. Although scientific interest in individual differences was not great before the 1800s, this does not mean that people had previously been unaware of differences in mental abilities and personality. Certainly it does not require a great deal of observational skill to see that human beings, and other animals as well, differ in their abilities to learn and understand their environments. For thousands of years stories and anecdotes have described events in which individual differences in abilities and personality were observed and exploited.

Testing in Antiquity

As indicated in Table 1-1, the roots of formal psychological assessment go back at least as far as ancient China (2200 B.C.). At that time, administration of a series of oral tests was instituted by the Chinese emperor to determine a candidate's fitness for performing governmental duties. This system, according to which officials were reexamined every three years, was continued by later Chinese emperors (Bowman, 1989). In addition, a number of biblical passages indicate that the ancient Jews were aware of the value of questions and observations for assessing mental abilities and personality. For example, in Judges 7:3–7, God says to Gideon:

> You have too many men for me to deliver Midian into their hands. In order that Israel may not boast against me that her own strength has saved her, announce now to the people: "Anyone who trembles with fear may turn back and leave Mount Gilead." So twenty-two thousand men left, while ten thousand remained.
>
> But the Lord said to Gideon, "There are still too many men. Take them down to the water, and I will sift them for you there. If I say, 'This one shall go with you,' he shall go; but if I say, 'This one shall not go with you,' he shall not go."
>
> So Gideon took the men down to the water. There the Lord told him, "Separate those who lap the water with their tongues like a dog from those who kneel down to drink." Three hundred men lapped with their hands to their mouths. All the rest got down on their knees to drink.
>
> The Lord said to Gideon, "With the three hundred men that lapped I will save you and give the Midianites into your hands. Let all the other men go, each to his own place."

Recognizing the importance of individual differences, God presumably surmised that men who lapped like dogs while drinking were more alert or wary and hence a few hundred of them would be as effective as a much larger fighting force.*

---

*Even older than the water-lapping test of Judges is the apple-eating test in Genesis. This test was concerned with whether Adam and Eve would eat of the tree of knowledge of good and evil, a test that they reportedly failed.

Recommendations for using psychological tests to assess individual differences among people are also found in the writings of Plato and Aristotle (fourth century B.C.). To the ancient Greeks, tests designed to assess mastery of both intellectual and physical skills were part of the educational process (Doyle, 1974). In a sense, the Socratic method of instruction, in which students are induced to "discover" the solution to a problem by being asked a series of leading questions, can be construed as a type of testing. But even with their enlightened educational system and democratic ideals, the ancient Greeks were not invariably humane in their treatment of persons of low mental ability. "Inferior" infants were often put to death, a practice condoned by no less a personage than Aristotle (Peterson, 1925).

From the Middle Ages to the French Revolution

The Middle Ages (A.D.400–1400) was not a time when great value was placed on human life, or the victory of human abilities over nature was encouraged. The study of individuality was held back by the same social and religious forces that restricted progress in art and science. The Middle Ages, which lasted approximately from the fall of the Roman Empire (A.D. 476) until the fifteenth century, was, for most people, a time of unquestioning faith and a struggle to survive and do one's duty. Augustine and other theologians emphasized turning inward and introspective reflection, while materialism and science were viewed as enemies of the church.

Scholarly concern with individual differences was almost nonexistent in medieval Europe. Limitations on activities were prescribed by the social class into which one was born, and little freedom was allowed for personal expression or individual pursuits. Consequently, no progress and even setbacks in the assessment of individual differences characterized this period of history. For more than a thousand years, tradition and conformity held sway. Human earthly existence was viewed as transitory, insignificant, and merely a time of preparation for the life to come.

Owing to a combination of social and economic forces, the influence of the Roman Catholic Church began to diminish during the fifteenth century. The rise of a middle class and the emphasis on individual freedom and choice that begin during the Renaissance and was fueled by the Protestant Reformation had powerful political and intellectual consequences in European society during and after the fifteenth century.

By the sixteenth century, European society had become more capitalistic, less doctrinaire, and more receptive to the idea that all people are unique and entitled to express their natural gifts and improve their lives. The spirit of individualism, which had flourished in ancient Greece and was reawakened in Renaissance Europe, found expression in art, science, government, and other cultural pursuits. These effects were quite evident in the political and scientific arenas during the eighteenth century. The winds of change and the emphasis on individual freedom and dignity were particularly strong in eighteenth-century France, which exploded in revolution at the end of the century.

The French Revolution was a harbinger of political and social changes that were to occur throughout the European continent and eventually the rest of the world. Among the effects of particular importance to the study and measurement of

TABLE 1–1 **Significant Events in the History of Mental Testing**

2000 B.C.	Mandarins set up civil-service testing program in China.
A.D. 1219	First formal oral examinations in law held at the University of Bologna.
C. 1500	Early test of mental ability, including counting 20 pence, telling one's age, and identifying one's father, proposed by Fitzherbert.
1575	Juan Huarté publishes book, *Examinen de Ingenios,* concerned with individual differences in mental abilities.
1837	Edouard Seguin devises Seguin Formboard to test mentally retarded children.
1838	Jean Esquirol distinguishes between mental illness and mental retardation.
1866	Edouard Seguin writes the first major text on the assessment and treatment of mental retardation.
1869	Francis Galton authors *Classification of Men according to Their Natural Gifts,* stimulating investigations of the hereditary basis of mental ability and studies of individual differences.
1884	Francis Galton opens Anthropometric Laboratory for International Health Exhibition in London.
1888	J. M. Cattell opens testing laboratory at the University of Pennsylvania.
1890	J. M. Cattell introduces the term *mental tests* into the psychological literature.
1893	Joseph Jastrow displays sensorimotor abilities tests at Columbian Exhibition in Chicago.
1896	Alfred Binet and Victor Henri ouline a theoretical program for the development of a test of intelligence.
1897	Hermann Ebbinghaus devises tests of arithmetic, memory span, and sentence completions to assess intelligence.
1901	Clark Wissler discovers that Cattell's mental tests have essentially zero correlation with college grades.
1904	Charles Spearman proposes a two-factor theory of intelligence; Karl Pearson formulates the theory of correlation.
1905	Alfred Binet and Theophilé Simon develop the first practical test of intelligence.
1908	Revision of Binet-Simon Intelligence Scale published.
1909	Henry Goddard translates Binet-Simon scales from French into English.
1912	Wilhelm Stern proposes concept of mental (intelligence) quotient (IQ).
1916	First Stanford-Binet Intelligence Scale published, authored by Lewis Terman.
1917	First group intelligence tests, Army Alpha and Army Beta, used in selection of military recruits.
1919	Psychological Examination for College Freshmen constructed by Louis Thurstone.
1920	National Intelligence Scale published.
1921	First major psychological test publishing company, The Psychological Corporation, established.
1923	Kohs Block Design, a test of nonverbal reasoning, published; Pintner-Cunningham Primary Mental Test first published.
1926	Florence Goodenough publishes Draw-A-Man Test.
1928	Arthur Point Scale of Performance, first nonverbal intelligence test battery, published.
1933	Louis Thurstone proposes a multifactor theory of intelligence.
1936	Edgar Doll publishes the Vineland Social Maturity Scale, for use in evaluating level of functioning of mentally retarded individuals.
1937	Revision of Stanford-Binet Intelligence Scale published.
1938	Publication of Gesell Maturity Scale, a product of Arnold Gesell's research on intelligence in infants; L. L. Thurstone proposes theory that intelligence consists of seven primary mental abilities; J. C. Raven publishes Raven Progressive Matrices, a nonverbal reasoning test designed to measure Spearman's *g* factor.
1939	Wechsler-Bellevue Intelligence Scale published.

(continued)

TABLE 1–1   (*Continued*)

1949	Beginning of attacks on intelligence tests as culturally biased. Wechsler Intelligence Scale for Children published.
1954	*Technical Recommendations for Psychological Tests and Diagnostic Techniques* published by the American Psychological Association.
1959	J. P. Guilford proposes structure of intellect model based on the results of applying factor-analytic methods to test scores.
1960	Form L-M of Stanford-Binet Intellligence Scale published.
1962	Raymond Cattell proposes theory of fluid and crystallized intelligence.
1967	Wechsler Preschool and Primary Scale of Intelligence (WPPSI) published , revised in 1989; court rules in *Hobson v. Hansen* against use of group tests of ability to "track" students on grounds that these tests discriminate against children in minority groups.
1969	Arthur Jensen's controversial paper on ethnic group differences in IQ published in the *Harvard Educational Review*; Bayley Scales of Infant Development published.
1971	U.S. Supreme Court rules that tests used in personnel selection must be shown to be valid for the specific jobs involved.
1975	Public Law 94-142, the Education for All Handicapped Children Act, passed by U.S. Congress.
1979	Court rules in *Larry P. v. Riles* that standardized IQ tests are culturally biased against black children.
1980	Court rules in *Parents in Action of Special Education v. Hannon* that standardized IQ tests are not racially or culturally biased.
1981	Wechsler Adult Intelligence Scale—Revised published.
1983	Kaufman Assessment Battery for Children published.
1984–85	Court rules in *Marshall v. Georgia* that assigning students to special classes for the mentally retarded is for their benefit.
1985	*Standards for Educational and Psychological Testing* published; Vineland Adaptive Behavior Scales published.
1991	Wechsler Intelligence Scale for Children—Third Edition published.
1992	Eleventh edition of *The Mental Measurements Yearbook* published; Judge Robert Peckham lifts his ban on IQ testing in California public schools.

individual differences were improvements in the treatment of the mentally ill and the mentally retarded and the beginnings of compulsory public education. Philippe Pinel had already instituted a movement for humane treatment of the mentally ill when he "struck the chains from the limbs of the insane" at La Bicêtre Asylum in Paris in 1787. Subsequently, under the leadership of Napoleon Bonaparte, a system of public education was developed. It was not until 1881, however, that school attendance was made compulsory for French children. The enactment of this law brought mentally retarded children, who had formerly been educated away from public scrutiny at home, to the attention of school and government officials.

Idiocy and Individual Differences

Interest in the mentally retarded and the mentally ill antedates the eighteenth and nineteenth centuries. In ancient Greece, Hippocrates, known as the "father of medicine," was very much aware of mental disorder and disability. Although little progress in the treatment of the mentally ill was made in Christian Europe during the Middle Ages, physicians in Moslem countries (e.g., Ibn Sina) gained some insight into the identification and treatment of mental disorders.* However, the fact that a single term, idiocy, was still used as late as the early 1800s to refer to both mental disorders and mental retardation indicates the slowness of progress in understanding human behavior.

Esquirol

It was not until 1838 that another Frenchman, Jean Esquirol, made a clear distinction between idiocy (mental incapacity) and mental derangement. He observed that, although mentally deranged people have lost the abilities they once possessed, idiots never had those abilities to start with:

> Idiocy is not a disease but a condition in which the intellectual faculties are never manifested or have never been developed sufficiently to enable the idiot to acquire such amount of knowledge as persons of his own age reared in similar circumstances are capable of receiving.

Esquirol pointed out that the way in which an individual uses language is the best method for distinguishing between idiocy and mental illness as well as the most dependable index of intellectual ability. He also noted, however, that intellectual ability is not an all-or-none affair; rather, it exists on a continuum extending from idiocy to genius. In this regard, Esquirol's descriptions of the verbal characteristics of various levels of idiocy may be viewed as one of the very first tests of mental ability.

Seguin

Another pioneer in the diagnosis and treatment of mental retardation was Eugen Seguin, a contemporary and countryman of Esquirol. Seguin founded the first school devoted exclusively to educating mentally retarded children, and many of the sense-training and muscle-treating techniques that he devised (Seguin, 1886/1907) are still in use. Another of Seguin's contributions was the formboard, a board containing cutout recesses into which examinees are asked to insert appropriately shaped blocks. In the twentieth century, the Seguin Formboard became one of the tests selected by Lewis Terman for inclusion at the 2- to 3-year level of the Stanford-Binet Intelligence Scale.

Maskelyne and Kinnebrook

During 1796, Nevil Maskelyne, the royal astronomer at the Greenwich Observatory in England, experienced some difficulty with his assistant Kinnebrook. One

---

*Unlike Christians, who tended to see science as a danger to religion, Muslims were encouraged not to abdicate their reason but to look at the world attentively and with curiosity. It was this attitude that enabled them to build a fine tradition of natural science when medieval Europe was still in intellectual darkness (Armstrong, 1993).

of the tasks assigned to Kinnebrook was to measure the time that it took the planet Venus to pass between two lines on a telescope lens. Unfortunately, Kinnebrook's time measurements were 0.8 seconds longer than those of Maskelyne, so poor Kinnebrook was fired. Some years later this incident came to the attention of certain German scientists and mathematicians, who interpreted the discrepancy between the measurements made by Kinnebrook and Maskelyne as an illustration of differences in the response times of two people. The interest taken by these eminent persons in individual differences in response times (the so-called *personal equation*) did much to stimulate systematic research on the topic in the fledgling discipline of experimental psychology.

Cattell and Galton

The fact that people differ not only in their response times but in a host of other sensory, motor, and mental abilities subsequently became the topic of many psychological research investigations. At the forefront of those psychologists who were interested in the measurement of individual differences were the Englishman Sir Francis Galton and the American J. McKeen Cattell. Cattell was a student of Wilhelm Wundt, the German physiological psychologist who had launched the first formal psychological laboratory in the world at Leipzig, Germany, in 1879. The story is told that when the young Cattell announced to Professor Wundt that he wanted to do his doctoral research project on individual differences in reaction time, Wundt reluctantly agreed but labeled the proposal as *"ganz amerikanisch"* (entirely American). After receiving his Ph.D. at Leipzig, Cattell stopped over in England on his way back to the United States. There he became acquainted with the "mental tests," as he later called them, that Sir Francis Galton had been using in his own research on individual differences.

Galton, a highly gifted member of a prominent English family, had originally devoted his efforts to investigating and writing about the hereditary basis of genius. His studies of family trees had convinced him that heredity plays an important role in the formation of many psychological characteristics, including genius (Galton, 1869). Believing that genius is to a large extent inherited, he employed statistical analysis to estimate the number of geniuses that could be expected in a random sample of people.

Consistent with the philosophy of empiricism, which holds that "mind" is the result of experience, Galton (1883) maintained that

> the only information that reaches us concerning outward events appears to pass through the avenues of our senses; and the more perceptive the senses are of difference, the larger is the field upon which our judgment and intelligence can act. (p. 27)

Consequently, Galton argued that a person's intelligence is a product of the speed and refinement of his or her responses to environmental stimuli.

To measure the speed and refinement of individual responses to stimuli, Galton invented a number of simple sensorimotor tests. Included among these test instruments were the Galton bar for measuring visual discrimination and the Galton

FIGURE 1-1 Francis Galton. The designated "father of individual psychology," Galton initiated the study of intelligence and its origins. (The Bettmann Archive)

whistle for measuring auditory discrimination; measures of reaction time, weight discrimination, muscular strength, and sensitivity to touch and pain; memory for visual forms and for consonants; and more direct physical measurements such as breathing capacity and head size. An estimated 9,000 visitors to Galton's "anthropometric laboratory," which was set up at London's South Kensington Museum in 1882, paid threepence to take the series of tests that presumably measured their mental abilities.

The extensive amount of empirical data obtained from Galton's research was analyzed by various statistical methods, including the method of "corelations" developed by Galton and his statistician-student Karl Pearson. Among the conclusions suggested from these data was that persons who had been independently diagnosed as "idiots" had lower than normal capacity to discriminate between sensory stimuli (such as heat, cold, and pain). Generalizing to the other end of the intellectual spectrum, Galton concluded that the ability to discriminate among sensory stimuli should be greatest among people who are intellectually most capable (Galton, 1883). It was found, however, that certain measurements (such as strength of grip) were unrelated to others and that many measures (such as head size) did not discriminate between eminent scientists and ordinary individuals.

It is now generally recognized that the statistical procedures (correlation and regression, in particular) and other research methods and devices (rating scales, word associations, test batteries, twin-method in inheritance studies, etc.) introduced by Galton were actually more valuable than his tests of mental ability. Be that as it may, Galton's failure to design practical tests of mental abilities served as a stimulus to Alfred Binet and other psychologists to construct better mental tests.

From today's viewpoint, Galton's belief that intelligence can be measured by simple sensorimotor tests and physical measurements may seem like a rather naive assumption for such an intellectually gifted individual to have made. But judging our predecessors from the perspective of our own time is a facile exercise in conceit. Galton's reasoning becomes more comprehensible when one realizes the influence that was exerted on nineteenth-century thinking by the philosophy of association-ism or empiricism. According to this philosophy, all knowledge, and hence mind itself, comes about by mental associations among sensory impressions. Such was the position of numerous British thinkers, from the time of John Locke in the seventeenth century down through John Stuart Mill in Galton's own time. In this sense, Galton's expectation that differences in intelligence are reflections of differ-ences in sensorimotor capacity was merely a logical consequence of the dominant British philosophy of empiricism.

To test the supposition that scores on simple sensorimotor tests of the sort that Galton had devised were related to performance on tasks that presumably required substantial mental capacity, J. M. Cattell administered a series of such tests individu-ally to students at the University of Pennsylvania and subsequently at Columbia University. The tests included measures of movement speed (speed of moving the hand 50 centimeters), muscular strength (pressure exerted on a dynamometer), two-point touch sensitivity, pain sensitivity (amount of pressure on the forehead required to produce pain), weight discrimination (just noticeable differences in heaviness), reaction time to sound, time to name colors, time judgment (10-second period), bisection of a 50-centimeter line, and simple memory (number of letters remembered after one presentation).

The Failure of Sensorimotor Tests

In a manner reminiscent of Galton's display of his own tests at the International Exposition in London in 1884, Joseph Jastrow, another psychologist of the time, set up a series of tests of sensory, motor, and perceptual abilities at the Chicago World's Fair in 1893. Visitors were invited to take these tests of "mental anthropometry" for a small fee and compare their performance with the test norms. Unfortunately, neither Jastrow nor Cattell was successful in demonstrating that his test had a significant degree of validity as a measure of intelligence. Not only did scores on the various tests have low relationships (corelations) with each other, but they had almost no relationships to school marks or other accepted criteria of intellectual functioning.

Additional negative results were not long in coming. A study of 250 freshmen and 35 senior girls conducted by Clark Wissler (1901) at Barnard College found very low relationships between grades in courses and measures of reaction time, color naming, and speed of canceling the letter *a* in written material. He also found near zero correlations among the various tests, indicating that they were measuring nothing in common. On the other hand, he found that grades in most school subjects, even gymnasium, correlated fairly well with grades in other subjects, suggesting that some common ability, which the tests failed to measure, underlay academic performance. Wissler interpreted the results as indicating that the tests were measuring only special abilities and that there was no functional relationship between them. These findings and Wissler's interpretation of them were consistent with the results of a similar investigation of a small sample of Cornell University graduate students conducted by Stella Sharp (1898).

The findings of Cattell, Wissler, Sharp, and others (e.g., Franz Boas and J. Gilbert), which at the time were considered to have disproved Galton's and Cattell's hypothesis that sensorimotor tests are measures of intellectual ability, were subsequently criticized as being based on poorly designed tests and unrepresentative samples of examinees. For example, more recent research (Eysenck, 1984; Jensen, 1985) has suggested that psychologists may have been too hasty in rejecting reaction time as a measure of intelligence. Stronger relationships between intelligence test scores and various measures of response time than those reported by Wissler have been obtained when better research methodology is employed. Be that as it may, the negative results obtained with the Galton–Cattell tests led psychologists and educators to turn away from simple sensorimotor tests and toward what proved to be one of the most important products in the history of psychological testing: the mental age scale of Alfred Binet.

Efforts to assess intellectual ability during the late nineteenth century were not limited to the tests devised by Galton, Cattell, and their students. For example, Emil Kraeplin, the famous psychiatrist whose system of classifying mental disorders served as the basis for the modern system of psychiatric diagnosis, and his student A. Oehrn (1895) employed a variety of tests of perceptual, motor, and memory functions in their investigations. Hermann Ebbinghaus, a psychologist who became famous for his research on memory, also devised a variety of tests (among them memory span, arithmetic computations, and sentence completions) to measure mental ability. On Ebbinghaus's sentence completion test, examinees were asked to fill in as many blanks in sentences as they could within a 5-minute period. Other early investigators who devised questions and other verbal materials to assess mental functioning were Carl Wernicke and T. Ziehen. With the exception of sentence completions, however, none of these tests proved to be significantly related to the scholastic achievements of children.

Guicciardi and Ferrari (1896) constructed other physiological and psychological tests to measure not only simpler psychophysiological functions such as motor ability and perceptual apprehension but also more complex mental functions such as picture interpretation. However, almost all of the tests devised by Galton, Kraeplin, Ebbinghaus, and other researchers of the time were rejected by Alfred Binet (Binet & Henri, 1896) as measures of intelligence. To Binet, the available tests tended to be too simple, too specialized, and too sensory in nature to serve as measures of such a complex mental function as intelligence.

BINET AND HIS SUCCESSORS

Of all the early scholars who theorized about intelligence and conducted research on the topic, the most deserving of the title "father of intelligence testing" is Alfred Binet. Binet was something of a Renaissance man, having been a lawyer, a playwright, a hypnotist, and an experimental psychologist who conducted research on fantasy and other topics before becoming interested in intelligence testing. This versatility undoubtedly contributed to his flexibility and creativity. Whereas Galton, Cattell, and others were tied to the past in their conceptions of intelligence measurement, Binet was able to break with tradition and develop a new approach to the measurement of mental abilities. Receptive to criticism and willing to change, he was an empirical scientist of the first order.

Binet did not arrive at his new approach to intelligence measurement in a sudden flash of insight. Rather, his first practical intelligence test was a product of trial and error, and eventually trial and success. Binet and Victor Henri, his co-worker in the 1890s, investigated many different tests as potential measures of intelligence. These included not only sensorimotor tasks such as tactile discrimination but more complex tasks such as recalling a series of digits, mental addition, suggestibility, and moral judgment, and even cranial capacity, lines in the palm, and handwriting.

Also characteristic of Binet's thinking about intelligence is that he was not wedded to a specific theory of mental abilities. To be sure, in their 1896 paper Binet and Henri did suggest ten "mental functions" of intelligence: memory, imagery, imagination, attention, comprehension, suggestibility, aesthetic appreciation, moral sentiments, muscular force (willpower), and motor skill. But they recognized the tentativeness of this list of functions, and in no way did it restrict their later research on mental measurement. Rather than being a confirmed theorist, Binet was basically an empiricist and a pragmatist who was willing to discard a test or approach that did not work and experiment with something new and different.

FIGURE 1-2 **Alfred Binet**. With Theophilé Simon, Binet constructed the first practical intelligence test in 1905. (The Bettmann Archive)

Binet-Simon Scales

The beginning of what proved to be Binet's most outstanding contribution to the study of individual differences occurred in 1904. The overcrowded conditions in the Paris school system of the time led the minister of public instruction to make what was basically an economic decision: to remove from the regular classroom children who were unable to learn satisfactorily. Then, it was argued, more of the teacher's time and attention could be devoted to children who would profit most from instruction.

To find a means of identifying and training these "mentally retarded" children, the minister appointed a commission to devise appropriate diagnostic and instructional procedures. The commission, one member of which was Alfred Binet, decided to start by administering educational and medical examinations to identify retarded children in the public schools. Children who were screened out of the regular classrooms in this manner were then supposed to be given special instruc-

---

TABLE 1–2   The Thirty Tests on the 1905 Binet-Simon Intelligence Scale

1. Visual coordination
2. Prehension provoked tactually
3. Prehension provoked visually
4. Cognizance of food
5. Seeking food under difficulty
6. Execution of simple orders
7. Cognizing objects by name
8. Cognizing pictured objects by name
9. Naming objects designated in a picture
10. Comparison of supraliminally different lines
11. Auditory memory for three digits
12. Comparisons of supraliminally different weights
13. Suggestibility
14. Definitions of familiar objects
15. Memory for sentences
16. Differences between familiar objects recalled in memory
17. Memory for pictures
18. Drawing from memory
19. Auditory memory for more than three digits
20. Resemblances between familiar objects recalled in memory
21. Discrimination of lines
22. Arrangement of five weights
23. Detection of the missing weight
24. Rhymes
25. Missing words
26. Sentence building
27. Replies to problem questions
28. Interchange of the clock hands
29. Drawing from a design cut in a quarto folded paper
30. Distinction between abstract terms

tion. Based on the existing classification system, the commission differentiated among three grades of subnormal intelligence: the lowest level was *idiocy*, the intermediate level was *imbecility*, and the highest level was *moronity*.

1905 Binet-Simon Scale

To assist in identifying mentally retarded children between the ages of 3 and 13 years, Binet and his physician coworker Theophilé Simon constructed a test consisting of thirty problem-type tasks arranged in order of difficulty (Table 1-2). The subtests consisted of tasks such as memory for digits and sentences and identifying objects and parts of the body. Subtests were administered in order of ascending difficulty, and the examinee's performance on each task was recorded and evaluated.

In devising their first intelligence scale, Binet and Simon assumed that intelligence is a composite of many abilities and that its nature changes with age. A variety of test tasks were tried out, the majority being simple problems of the sort included in schoolwork (memory, reasoning ability, numerical facility, comprehension, time orientation, object comparison, knowledge, combining ideas into wholes, and so forth). The final arrangement of tasks was determined by administering the scale to fifty normal children aged 3, 5, 7, 9, or 11 years, in addition to a sample of mentally retarded children and adults. Using the method of age-graded norms introduced by Damaye (1903, cited in Wolf, 1973), Binet and Simon designated items on the scale according to the age at which an average child could complete the task. This process also made possible the diagnosis of different degrees of mental retardation in adulthood. Passing item 6 on the scale was considered the upper limit for adult idiots, passing item 16 the upper limit for adult imbeciles, and passing item 23 the upper limit for adult morons. Passing item 24 or 25 on the scale ruled out a diagnosis of mental retardation in an adult.

1908 Scale

The 1905 scale, which had no standard directions for administration and no objective procedures for determining a total score, was intended by Binet to be a preliminary test for the identification of mental retardation in children. A revision of the Binet-Simon Scale, consisting of more and better subtests to measure a wider range of mental abilities in children, was published in 1908 (Table 1-3). Like its predecessor, the 1908 scale emphasized judgment, comprehension, and reasoning with verbal and perceptual materials, but especially the former. Subtests on this revised scale were grouped into age levels on the basis of the performance of 300 normal children aged 3-13 years. A subtest was included at a particular age level only if it was passed by 67-75 percent of a representative sample of children of that age and also by a smaller percentage of younger children and a larger percentage of older children. The effect of applying these criteria to the selection of subtests for inclusion in the scale was that an increasing percentage of children passed each subtest at each successive age level.

TABLE 1–3 Sample Items from the 1908 Version of the Binet-Simon Scale

Age level 3 (five items)
   1. Point to various parts of a face
   2. Repeat two digits forward

Age level 4 (four items)
   1. Name familiar objects
   2. Repeat three digits forward

Age level 5 (five items)
   1. Copy a square
   2. Repeat a sentence containing ten syllables

Age level 6 (seven items)
   1. State age
   2. Repeat a sentence containing sixteen syllables

Age level 7 (eight items)
   1. Copy a diamond
   2. Repeat five digits forward

Age level 8 (six items)
   1. Recall two items from a passage
   2. State the differences between two objects

Age level 9 (six items)
   1. Recall six items from a passage
   2. Recite days of the week

Age level 10 (five items)
   1. Given three common words, construct a sentence
   2. Recite months of the year in order

Age level 11 (five items)
   1. Define abstract words (for example, *justice*)
   2. Determine what is wrong with absurd statements

Age level 12 (five items)
   1. Repeat seven digits forward
   2. Provide the meaning of pictures

Age level 13 (three items)
   1. State the differences between pairs of abstract terms

Another improvement in the 1908 scale was the introduction of the concept of *mental age*, an easily understood concept that contributed to the popularity of intelligence testing. An examinee's mental age on the test corresponded to the chronological age, in years and months, of a group of normal children who performed at the same level as the examinee.

Administration of the scale, which took 30–85 minutes, began with the determination of the *basal age*—the highest age level at which the examinee passed all subtests. Testing continued until the *ceiling age*, the lowest age at which the examinee failed all subtests, was reached. Then the examinee's mental age was computed as the sum of his or her basal age plus a credit of one year for every five subtests passed beyond the basal age. Fractional year credits were not given for passing fewer than five subtests. The fact that the scale was heavily loaded with verbal-type tasks and contained relatively few subtests of perceptual–motor functioning was also considered a drawback.

1911 Scale

A further revision of the Binet-Simon Scale was published in 1911 (Table 1-4), the year of Binet's untimely death. Five subtests were included at each age level (except age 4, which had four subtests), and partial year credits were assigned for passing fewer than five subtests. The scale was also extended to include an adult level, for which new tests were devised. Had Binet lived longer, there is every reason to believe that he would have made further improvements and revisions in the scales. He was especially interested in developing and adding tests of special

TABLE 1–4   The Fifty-Four Tests on Binet's 1911 Mental Age Scale

Age 3
Points to nose, eyes, and mouth
Repeats two digits
Enumerates objects in a picture
Gives family name
Repeats a sentence of six syllables

Age 4
Gives own sex
Names key, knife, and penny
Repeats three digits
Compares two lines

Age 5
Compares two weights
Copies a square
Repeats a sentence of ten syllables
Counts four pennies
Unites halves of a divided rectangle

Age 6
Distinguishes between morning and afternoon
Defines familiar words in terms of use
Copies a diamond
Counts thirteen pennies
Distinguishes pictures of ugly and pretty faces

Age 7
Shows right hand and left ear
Describes a picture
Executes three commands given simultaneously
Counts the value of six sous, three of which are double
Names four cardinal colors

Age 8
Compares two objects from memory
Counts from twenty to zero
Notes omissions from pictures
Gives day and date
Repeats five digits

Age 9
Gives change from twenty sous
Defines familiar words in terms superior to use
Recognizes all the (nine) pieces of money
Names the months of the year in order
Answers or comprehends "easy questions"

Age 10
Arranges five blocks in order of weight
Copies two drawings from memory
Criticizes absurd statements
Answers or comprehends "difficult questions"
Uses three given words in not more than two sentences

Ages 12
Resists suggestion as to length of lines
Composes one sentence containing three given words
Names sixty words in 3 minutes
Defines three abstract words
Discovers the sense of a disarranged sentence

Age 15
Repeats seven digits
Finds three rhymes for a given word in 1 minute
Repeats a sentence of twenty-six syllables
Interprets pictures
Interprets given facts

Adult
Solves the paper-cutting test
Rearranges a triangle in imagination
Gives differences between pairs of abstract terms
Gives three differences between a president and a king
Gives the main thought of a selection read

aptitudes to the Binet-Simon Scale to permit a more complete assessment of the mental abilities of children.

English Translations and Revisions of Binet-Simon Scale

Interestingly enough, the Binet-Simon Intelligence Scale was greeted more enthusiastically in the United States than in Binet's native France. By the beginning of the twentieth century, many states had enacted laws requiring school attendance to the age of 13 or 14 years, and an intelligence test proved useful in identifying children who could not profit sufficiently from instruction in regular classrooms.

Several translations, revisions, and extensions of the Binet-Simon scales appeared in the few years after the initial publication of the test. Although his efforts were not entirely successful, Henry Goddard, director of research at Vineland Training School in New Jersey, produced an English version of the 1905 scale in 1908 and a translation and standardization of the 1908 scale in 1910. Other English translations of the Binet-Simon Intelligence Scale included those of Huey (1910), Whipple (1910), Kuhlmann (1912), and Herring (1922). The Kuhlmann version, one of the first attempts to measure the intelligence of infants and toddlers, extended the 1908 scale downward to 3 months; it was revised in 1922 and again in 1930.

It is assumed in constructing an age scale that significant behaviors appear for the first time at different points in human development. Therefore, items that are passed by the great majority of children of a particular chronological age are placed at that age level. Then a child's score on a test constructed in this way depends upon what other children of his or her age-group are able to do. Unlike an age scale, on a *point scale* the quality and degree of correctness of an examinee's responses determine how many points he or she receives. The items on a point scale measure specific cognitive functions, which are assumed to be present at all age levels covered by the test. Consequently, the same kinds of items, but of a greater difficulty level than those below, appear at both higher and lower age levels. This situation contrasts with that of an age scale, on which the types of items vary more across age levels.

Not content merely to translate and extend the Binet-Simon Scale, Robert Yerkes and his colleagues rejected the concept of an age scale and published a point-scale version of the test in 1915. Scoring of this Yerkes, Bridges, and Hardwick Point Scale, which was revised and extended downward in 1923, involved assigning points, or numerical weights, rather than years' or months' credit, to correct responses. Items having similar content were grouped together and arranged within groups in order of difficulty, a procedure also followed by David Wechsler a quarter-century later in designing the Wechsler-Bellevue Intelligence Scale. The relative merits of the age-scale and point-scale methods have been debated frequently, but contemporary psychometricians consider the point scale to be more flexible.

The most popular and enduring of all adaptations and revisions of the Binet-Simon Scale was made by Lewis Terman. Terman and Childs had published a preliminary revision of the scale in 1912 (Terman & Childs, 1912), and in 1916 a modification and extension called the Stanford Revision and Extension of the Binet-Simon Intelligence Scale was published. It incorporated Wilhelm Stern's concept of an intelligence quotient (IQ)—the ratio of mental age to chronological age in months. Later known as the Stanford-Binet Intelligence Scale, Terman's revision of the Binet-Simon Scale served as a standard for intelligence testing throughout the world for over two decades. The scale was revised in 1937, again in 1960, and lastly in 1986.

For years, many school and clinical psychologists were characterized as "Binet testers," who traveled frequently from place to place with their Stanford-Binet testing kits. This activity, as much as any other, was the source of the comment that testing had become the "bread and butter" of psychology. Thus, it was by administering and interpreting tests such as the Stanford-Binet that many psychologists discovered they could make a living outside the classrooms and laboratories of academic institutions.

Group Testing during World War I

To make certain that the those whom he trained to administer and score the Stanford-Binet received sufficient practice, Lewis Terman required students in a graduate course at Stanford University to give the test to several dozen examinees of various ages and circumstances. The story goes that one of these students, Arthur Otis, fell behind in administering the required number of Stanford-Binets and in desperation devised a multiple-choice form of the test. This test could be administered to many people at the same time, and hence Otis was able to complete the assignment on schedule. Whether the story is fact or fantasy, Otis is credited with devising the first intelligence test designed for simultaneous administration to a group of people.

When the United States entered World War I during 1917, there was a pressing need for thousands of competent officers and men in the army. To meet that need, a group of psychologists under the leadership of Robert Yerkes convened at a New York City hotel to discuss possible military selection and screening procedures. It was at this week-long meeting that Terman described Otis's work on group intelligence testing and the possibility of adapting it for military screening purposes. Not long afterward, the Army Alpha—the first group intelligence test to be administered on a mass basis—was ready for use. Because many recruits at that time could not read, a nonverbal measure of intelligence was also needed. The result was a second group test, the Army Beta. Another intelligence test developed during World War I—the Army Performance Scale Examination—consisted of tasks that came to be used as diagnostic devices by psychologists in clinics, schools, and hospitals in the coming years. Among these were the Picture Completion, Picture Arrangement, Digit Symbol, and Object Assembly tests later adopted by David Wechsler and other clinical psychologists.

After World War I

Experience with the Army Alpha and Army Beta during World War I increased the enthusiasm of psychologists for the value and promise of mental testing. As stated by Goddard (1920, pp. 28-29) during the immediate postwar period:

> With this army experience it is no longer possible for anyone to deny the validity of mental tests, even in case of group testing; and when it comes to an individual examination by a trained psychologist, it cannot be doubted that the mental level of the individual is determined with marvelous exactness. The significance of all of this for human progress and efficiency can hardly be appreciated

at once. Whether we are thinking of children or adults it enables us to know a very fundamental fact about the human material. The importance of this in building up the cooperative society such as every community aims to be, is very great. The mechanical engineer could never build bridges or houses if he did not know accurately the strength of materials, how much of a load each will support.

Of how infinitely greater importance is it then when we seek to build up a social structure that we should know the strength of our materials. Until now we have had no means of determining this except a few data on the physical side such as a man's strength, ability to bear burdens, and so forth, and on the mental side a rough estimate born of more or less experience with him. How inadequate all this has been is indicated by the large proportion of failures that are continually met with in society.

After the war, Otis and other psychologists turned their military experience with intelligence testing to civilian use in schools, clinics, and industrial contexts. For example, in 1919 Louis Thurstone developed a group-administered, intelligence-type examination for selecting college freshmen. Two years later, the first major test publishing company—The Psychological Corporation—was established. Thus the 1920s saw the rapid expansion of psychological and educational testing, including not only paper-and-pencil, group-administered, and verbal-type examinations but also individually administered, single-task tests (e.g., Kohs Block Design in 1923) and performance test batteries (e.g., Arthur Point Scale of Performance in 1928). One indication that intelligence testing was to become a multimillion-dollar enterprise is that by 1922 the Stanford-Binet Intelligence Scale was "being given in the United States at the rate of a quarter of a million a year" (Terman et al., 1922, p. 2). During that same year the entire yearbook of the National Society for the Study of Education consisted of a detailed, rather flattering discussion of intelligence testing (National Society for the Study of Education, 1922; Osgood, 1984).

The growth of intelligence testing, and the questionable assumptions on which it was based, did not go unnoticed. Critics such as the journalist Walter Lippmann (1923) were quite vehement in some of their pronouncements and questions concerning the validity and social repercussions of psychological testing. Lippmann (1922, p. 247) maintained that

> The intelligence test ... is an instrument for classifying a group of people, rather than a "measure of intelligence." People are classified within a group according to their success in solving problems which may or may not be tests of intelligence.... The tests are all a good deal alike. They all derive from a common stock, and it is entirely possible that they measure only a certain kind of ability.... We must remember, too, that the emotional setting plays a large role in any examination. To some temperaments the atmosphere of the examination room is highly stimulating ... other people cannot do themselves justice under the same conditions.... We cannot measure intelligence when we have not defined it.

If the 1920s were a time of unchecked growth in psychological testing, the 1930s were characterized by the application of statistical procedures and other rigorous techniques to the analysis of test scores. What is now referred to as classical test theory, and the associated concepts of test reliability and validity, was developed during the late 1920s and 1930s by Truman Kelley, Clark Hull, and others. Factor-analytic methods, initiated by Charles Spearman around 1904, were applied to scores on groups of tests to determine the number of mental factors or separate variables being measured by those tests. Spearman maintained that general intelligence consists of a single general mental ability factor (g) plus a number of specific subsidiary or satellite abilities (s's). Contrasting with Spearman's viewpoint was that of Louis Thurstone, whose factor-analytic research at the University of Chicago during the 1930s led him to posit seven mental abilities or factors (see Chapter 12). Subsequent research showed, however, that the two positions, and indeed those of other factor analysts, were not irreconcilable.

Despite its many competitors and detractors, the supremacy of the Stanford-Binet Intelligence Scale was not successfully challenged until 1939, when the Wechsler-Bellevue Intelligence Scale (WB-I and WB-II) was published by David Wechsler. This scale and its extensions and successors—the Wechsler Intelligence Scale for Children (WISC), the Wechsler Preschool and Primary Scale of Intelligence (WPPSI), and the Wechsler Adult Intelligence Scale (WAIS)—gradually dethroned the test that had ruled for decades. A fourth version of the Stanford-Binet (SB-IV) was published in 1986, but it now seems certain that it will never match the popularity and prestige of previous editions of the test.

DEFINITIONS AND TESTS

Despite their success in measuring intelligence, early mental testers were not completely clear about what it was they were measuring. The eminent journalist Walter Lippmann (1923) was particularly troubled by the fact that psychologists were claiming to measure something they could not even define. To Lippmann, it seemed as if the measurement of a psychological characteristic such as intelligence should begin with a clear definition.

Early Definitions

There was certainly no scarcity of definitions of intelligence in the late nineteenth and early twentieth centuries. The faculty psychologists of the late nineteenth century considered intelligence to be a collection of "mental faculties," a point of view to which Alfred Binet initially subscribed. Later Binet and Simon (1905, p. 196) emphasized mental judgment in their definition of intelligence as "the ability to judge well, to comprehend well, to reason well." Many other definitions were proposed in a symposium held in 1921 ("Intelligence," 1921). While admitting that there were other components of intelligence, Lewis Terman preferred to characterize it primarily as the ability to "carry on abstract thinking." Two other psychologists stressed the importance of learning and adjustment in their definitions of intelligence as "learning or the ability to adjust oneself to the environment" (S. S. Colvin) and "acquiring capacity" (Herbert Woodrow). Among the more biologically based definitions were "general modifiability of the nervous system"

(Rudolf Pintner) and the "biological mechanism by which the effects of a complexity of stimuli are brought together and given a somewhat unified effect in behavior" (Joseph Peterson). Among more global definitions of intelligence were the "power of good response from the point of view of truth or fact" (E. L. Thorndike) and a "group of complex mental processes traditionally defined … as sensation, perception, association, memory, imagination, discrimination, judgment, and reasoning" (M. E. Haggerty).

Although participants in the 1921 symposium did not completely agree on how intelligence should be defined, there was obvious unanimity on the fact that the concept is not a "thing." Rather, it is a multifaceted psychological construct referring to (1) problem-solving ability, or adaptability to new situations; (2) the ability to deal with symbols, concepts, and relationships; and (3) the ability to learn or profit from experience. Not all of these facets are uniformly measured by all intelligence tests, but well-designed tests in this category attempt to tap most of them. Furthermore, abstract thinking and problem solving—and hence intelligent behavior—are not limited to human beings. Many other animal species, such as porpoises, dogs, and apes, are able to form concepts, carry on abstract reasoning of a sort, and solve problems (see Box 1-1 and Coren, 1994).

Two other features of intelligence that were emphasized by Binet are what might be called "planning ability" and "mental flexibility." An intelligent person can find and maintain a definite direction or purpose, adjust his or her strategy and behavior to achieve that purpose, and criticize the strategy in order to make necessary adjustments in it. Binet felt that *autocriticism*, the ability to observe or monitor one's own behavior to determine when it is inadequate or inefficient, and to improve it, is an important earmark of intelligent behavior. Mentally retarded individuals manifest a pronounced deficiency in autocriticism.

Later Definitions and Meanings

The definitions of intelligence proposed by later psychologists are not demonstrably superior to earlier ones, but they do combine several features of the earlier definitions. David Wechsler (1958, p. 7) suggested a holistic definition of intelligence as "the aggregate or global capacity of the individual to act purposefully, to think rationally and to deal effectively with his environment." Alexander Wesman (1968, p. 273) proposed a less abstract definition of intelligence as "the sum total of all the learning experiences [an individual] has uniquely had up to any point in time." Perhaps the simplest definition was proposed by E. G. Boring (1923), who suggested that intelligence should be (operationally) defined as "what the intelligence tests test" (p. 35). As appealing as this definition may seem, it is inadequate: different intelligence tests do not measure exactly the same thing.

Attempting to achieve some consensus on the meaning of intelligence is obviously a problem of some difficulty. The situation is rather like the fable of the blind men of Indostan who attempted to describe an elephant while each was touching a different part of the animal. But elephants are entities, whereas intelligence is an abstraction with many connotations or meanings. Three such connotations or uses of the term are (Vernon, 1969): (1) the innate capacity of individuals, that is, their genetic makeup; (2) behavior involved in learning, thinking, and problem solving; and (3) scores obtained on intelligence tests that measure various abilities (verbal, nonverbal, mechanical, etc.).

It is no longer considered fruitful to spend a great deal of time attempting to formulate a universally acceptable definition of intelligence. The emphasis has shifted from "What is it?" to "How can it be used?" The change from a "what" to a "how" question implies that the major concern is pragmatic: Is the concept helpful, in the sense that it assists in efforts to predict and understand behavior? Stated in this way, the question refers to both research and application. There is certainly no lack of disagreement on the ability of intelligence tests to predict and explain behavior, but the position taken in this text is that the concept of general mental ability, or intelligence, has both theoretical and practical utility. The concept of intelligence and the various methods of assessing it contribute not only to solving practical problems and making decisions about people; they also assist in our basic understanding of cognitive behavior and development.

OVERVIEW OF THE BOOK

In many ways, today's psychological examiners are faced with a more complex task than their predecessors. There are now so many tests of general intelligence and special abilities—individually and group-administered, verbal and nonverbal, single level and multilevel, single test and test battery—that it is difficult for an inexperienced examiner to know which test or tests to administer in a specific situation. Tests of mental abilities can provide useful information in academic, vocational, and personal counseling contexts, but the results must be administered and interpreted with caution and with an appreciation for their consequences and limitations. Today's psychological examiners must also be aware of the legal requirements and ramifications associated with psychological testing and assessment, problems with which psychologists in previous generations did not have to contend.

One of my purposes in writing this textbook was to provide sufficient information concerning the criteria for good tests and procedures for administering, scoring, interpreting, and reporting the findings so that clinical, school, or industrial psychologists would feel competent and comfortable in using them. Some familiarity with a wide range of instruments, both general and special purpose, is needed in order to function effectively as an educational and/or psychological diagnostician and counselor. Without attempting to provide a substitute for the manual accompanying every test, I have tried to clarify and supplement the procedural descriptions presented in various test manuals. Because test administration is a tedious, time-consuming exercise unless the findings are communicated and applied, detailed suggestions for reporting and using test results are also presented. Finally, the proper use of tests of mental abilities requires some knowledge of selected concepts in psychological measurement and statistics. The next chapter is designed to provide students and professionals with basic information of this kind.

Box 1–1

Animal Intelligence

Differences in mental abilities of various animal species have interested philosophers and scientists since antiquity. Over two thousand years ago, Aristotle tried to rank different animal species on a scale of intelligence, a so-called scala natura. Although the seventeenth-century philosopher René Descartes maintained that there was no resemblance between the minds of animals and the minds of humans, Charles Darwin, G. J. Romanes, and other nineteenth-century scientists used observation and anecdote to argue for the presence of humanlike character in much animal behavior and the continuity of mental ability across phyla and species. These researchers were guided by their belief in the theory of evolution and the principle of encephalization. The latter principle holds that the degree of development of animals proceeds as they ascend the phyletic scale, a development that is especially pronounced in the growth of the brain and hence should be reflected in interspecies differences in intelligence.

Romanes, the father of comparative psychology, made many cross-species comparisons of learning ability and other psychological characteristics. The American psychologist E. L. Thorndike also studied a variety of species, including crab, fish, turtle, dog, cat, monkey, and human baby. He concluded that the intellects of these animals are similar in that they are subject to the laws of exercise and effect (Thorndike, 1898/1911). In his early work Thorndike was most concerned with animal learning, an aspect of cognitive ability that subsequently became of great interest to experimental psychologists. However, interspecies comparisons of the ability to think, solve problems, and perform other mental activities have also been undertaken by psychologists and biologists.

A seemingly insurmountable difficulty in such investigations has been to devise standard measures or tasks that are suitable tests of ability across a wide range of species. Different species possess different sensory, perceptual, and motor capacities, and are adapted to meet different situations (Tinbergen, 1951). Hence it may be these differences rather than variations in intelligence or learning ability that are reflected in scores on the test tasks. Although a species may appear deficient in the ability defined by a particular test, this deficiency can be compensated for in the animal's natural habitat by the development of other abilities (Hinde, 1970).

Among the tasks that have been used to test the general mental abilities of animals are classical and instrumental conditioning, habituation to stimuli that are unimportant to the animal, serial maze learning, resistance to extinction of a conditioned response, stimulus and response generalization and discrimination, delayed responding, discrimination learning (e.g., the four-door problem), concept formation (e.g., oddity problems, conditional matching, and rule learning), reasoning or problem solving (including detour problems and double alternation maze), modeling the behavior of other animals, reversal learning, and the formation of learning sets.

Perhaps the most useful of these tasks has been the learning sets procedure, a special kind of positive transfer test in which an animal is examined on its ability to "learn how to learn" (Harlow, 1949). In a typical learning sets task for monkeys, a tray bearing two objects varying in some aspect(s) (such as size, color, or shape) is presented; food is contained in a shallow well under one of the objects. The animal's task is to select the object designated as correct by the experimenter, that is, the object under which the food is located. On a given trial, the experimenter raises a door in the animal's cage and exposes the stimuli; the animal makes its choice of the two objects, then the door is closed until the next trial. In a typical experiment, the animal must learn to discriminate between a whole series of different pairs of objects. The interesting fact is that the number of trials needed for the animal to solve a discrimination problem decreases as a function of the number of problems that it has solved previously; that is, it has established a *set to learn*, or has learned how to learn.

Rhesus monkeys, chimpanzees, and gorillas show rapid improvement on a learning sets task, but squirrel monkeys and marmosets show considerably less improvement (Harlow, 1958). Rats, cats, squirrels, tree shrews, and racoons are markedly inferior to primates, revealing little improvement after hundreds of trials (Koronakos & Arnold, 1957). Learning sets data are considered one of the most satisfactory sources of evidence on differences in learning ability between primates and other mammals (Hinde, 1970), but certain animals perform better than their phyletic level of development would suggest. Thus, cats, ferrets, marmosets, blue jays, mynas, and pigeons do about as well as squirrel monkeys, but crows show little improvement (Plotnik & Tallarico, 1966; Zeigler, 1961).

The assumption that intelligence is qualitatively more or less the same both within and across species had a profound impact on the measurement of intelligence and research on learning during the first half of the twentieth century. This assumption, however, became more and more questionable after 1950. Discouraged by the scarcity of empirical evidence for a unitary trait of intelligence that varies in amount on an orderly scale from species to species, certain researchers elected to search for qualitative differences in mental abilities. Bitterman (1965, 1975) argued, for example, that one should look not for differences in the rate of learning among various species but rather in the ways they learn. Such a species-specific abilities approach has been stimulated by the research of ethologists and other naturalists who have

(*continued*)

SUMMARY

   As witnessed by folktales, literature, and art, people in ancient times were
aware of individual differences in mental abilities. Though formal efforts to measure
general intelligence as a psychological construct were not made until the nineteenth century, simple verbal and performance tests have been used for thousands
of years to differentiate between mental ability and disability.

   During the early nineteenth century, the research and writings of French
physicians and educators such as Esquirol and Seguin led to a distinction between
mental retardation and mental illness and to improved methods of educating and
training mentally retarded children. The interest shown by nineteenth-century
mathematicians, physicists, and biologists in the normal law of errors, as exem-
plified by individual differences in perceptions and responses, helped provide a
climate for later research on mental abilities. Darwin's theory of evolution, which
proposed that differences among animal species occur through natural selection,
stimulated comparative research on interspecies and intraspecies differences in
behavior.

   Galton focused on individual differences in intelligence, which he believed to
be inherited. However, the efforts of Galton, Cattell, and others to devise useful
sensorimotor tests of intelligence were unsuccessful. The first successful test of
intelligence, in the sense that it proved to be a practical method for identifying

mentally retarded individuals and forecasting achievement in school-type tasks, was constructed by Binet and Simon in 1905. Two revisions of the 1905 Binet-Simon Intelligence Scale were published, in 1908 and 1911. All three versions were age scales, yielding a mental age equivalent to the examinee's performance. Several American translations and revisions of the Binet-Simon scale were made. The most popular and influential of these was the Stanford-Binet Intelligence Scale, which was constructed by Lewis Terman and his associates.

The first group intelligence tests, the Army Examination Alpha for literates and the Army Examination Beta for illiterates, were administered to nearly two million men during World War I. Immediately after the war, intelligence testing, and psychological testing in general, expanded rapidly. Dozen of tests of intelligence, achievement, special abilities, interests, and personality appeared in the 1920s and 1930s. Unfortunately, many of these instruments were poorly designed and provided ammunition for critics of psychological tests and testing practices. During the 1930s, statistical methods for analyzing test scores became more refined, a trend that has continued to the present day. The intervening years have also led to an ever-increasing number of intelligence tests (see Appendix A and Tables 9–1 and 10–1).

Intelligence is a term having multiple meanings and a variety of definitions, ranging from the operational to the highly abstract. It is important to remember that intelligence is not an entity but a hypothetical construct used to refer to a wide range of behaviors labeled as "intelligent." Intelligent behavior is characterized as adaptive, problem solving, reasonable, autocritical, and productive. Despite criticisms of the concept of intelligence and attempts to measure it, the position adopted in this book is that it is a useful psychological concept. A similar statement can be made with regard to the utility of intelligence tests, which contribute to understanding behavior and assist in making decisions about people.

QUESTIONS AND ACTIVITIES

1. Define each of the following terms used in this chapter:

age scale	imbecility
basal age	intelligence
ceiling age	mental age
holistic	moronity
idiocy	personal equation

2. Describe the contribution(s) of each of the following persons to intelligence testing:

Alfred Binet	Eugen Seguin
J. McKeen Cattell	Stella Sharp
Hermann Ebbinghaus	Lewis Terman
Jean Esquirol	David Wechsler
Francis Galton	Clark Wissler
Henry Goddard	Robert Yerkes
Arthur Otis	

3. What prompted the development of the first intelligence tests during the turn of the century, and what were their principal uses?
4. What assumptions and/or theories underlay Galton's approach to intelligence? What kinds of tests did he develop? What practical purposes did they serve?
5. Why were Terman's efforts to develop an American version of the Binet-Simon scale more successful than those of other psychologists?
6. Describe the construction of the first group intelligence test, and how it was used. Why was it necessary to construct both a verbal and a nonverbal group test?
   Describe the various ways in which the construct *intelligence* has been defined and how successful or useful these definitions have been.
7. Take the following Inventory of "Attitudes toward Intelligence Testing" yourself, and then administer it to several of your friends and classmates. Compare your responses with theirs. Save your results.

ATTITUDES TOWARD INTELLIGENCE AND INTELLIGENCE TESTING

Directions: Write the letter(s) indicating the strength of your agreement or disagreement with each of the following statements concerning intelligence and intelligence testing opposite the number of the item:

SA = Strongly Agree
A = Agree
U = Undecided
D = Disagree
SD = Strongly Disagree

1. Scores on standardized intelligence tests are determined mostly by heredity.
2. It is appropriate to use intelligence test scores for diagnostic purposes in clinical, counseling, and educational contexts.
3. Intelligence tests are biased against people of lower socioeconomic status and non-white ethnic groups.
4. Intelligence testing fosters democratic ideals by rewarding people according to their abilities.
5. Intelligence tests are not valid measures of a person's ability to perform in school or on the job.
6. Intelligence tests have proven useful in the diagnosis of mental retardation in children and adults.
7. Scores on intelligence tests should not be used for purposes of selection and promotion in employment contexts.
8. Intelligence tests measure what a person has learned in the past rather than what he or she is capable of learning in the future.
9. It is fair to use intelligence tests in selecting students for admission to colleges, universities, and professional schools.
10. It is inappropriate to use intelligence tests for academic and/or vocational counseling purposes.

SUGGESTED READINGS

Chapman, P. D. (1988). *Schools as sorters: Lewis M. Terman, applied psychology, and the intelligence testing movement, 1890-1930*. New York: New York University Press.

Coren, S. (1994). *The intelligence of dogs: Canine consciousness and capabilities*. New York: Free Press.

Forrest, D. W. (1974). *Francis Galton: The life and work of a Victorian genius*. London: Elek.

French, J. L., & Hale, R. L. (1990). A history of the development of psychological and educational testing. In C. R. Reynolds & R. W. Kamphaus (Eds.), *Handbook of psychological and educational assessment of children: Intelligence & achievement* (pp. 3–28). New York: Guilford Press.

Hilgard, E. R. (1989). The early years of intelligence measurement. In R. L. Linn (Ed.), *Intelligence: Measurement, theory, and public policy* (pp. 7–28). Urbana: University of Illinois Press.

Minton, H. L. (1988). *Lewis M. Terman: Pioneer in psychological testing*. New York: New York University Press.

Thorndike, R. M. (1990). Origins of intelligence and its measurement. *Journal of Psychoeducational Assessment, 8*, 223–230.

von Mayrhauser, R. T. (1992). The mental testing community and validity: A prehistory. *American Psychologist, 47*, 244–253.

Wolf, T. H. (1973). *Alfred Binet*. Chicago: University of Chicago Press.

Chapter 2

Measurement Concepts and Methods

The results of administering an intelligence test or other psychometric instrument (achievement or aptitude test, interest or personality inventory, etc.) are typically expressed in numerical form. Scores on such instruments are computed as the sum of the points given to the examinee's responses to all items. These points, or item weights, are usually integers ranging from 0 to some maximum (perfect answer) value. In the case of objective test items, such as multiple-choice or true-false questions, a perfect answer is almost always assigned a weight of 1. On standardized group tests, a correction for guessing, in which a portion of the wrong answers is subtracted from the right answers, is sometimes used to compute a corrected total test score.

ITEM ANALYSIS AND TEST STANDARDIZATION

One of the first steps after administering and scoring a newly constructed test is to analyze the items that make up the test. Like any other assessment instrument, an intelligence test consists of a series of questions or items. However, not all items contribute to the overall goals of the test. The purpose of an item analysis is to determine whether the individual items contribute to those goals by functioning as they are supposed to. An item analysis reveals which items are not working properly and consequently should be revised or discarded.

Item analysis procedures vary with the type of test and the preferences of test designers, but any such analysis begins by designating an internal or external criterion with which item scores can be compared. In conducting an item analysis of a scholastic achievement test, the criterion is usually an internal one: total scores on all items making up the test. To be judged an effective measure of performance in the specified content area, an achievement test item must differentiate between high and low scorers on the test as a whole.

Item Analysis of an Intelligence Test

Unlike the internal criterion used with an achievement test, an item analysis of an intelligence test requires an external criterion such as chronological ages, school marks, scores on another intelligence test, or some other index or correlate of intellectual status and growth. The designers of certain intelligence tests decided, for example, that older children are brighter than younger ones, and hence that chronological age was a reasonable criterion of intellectual ability. Consequently, the standard for accepting an item for inclusion on those intelligence tests was that the item should distinguish between children of different chronological ages. In other words, the percentage of children passing the item should increase with chronological age. This was the method employed by Alfred Binet and his successors in constructing Binet-type intelligence tests.

Because the procedure for selecting intelligence test items and determining their effectiveness in distinguishing between people having different amounts of mental ability varies with the specific test, more detailed discussion of the topic is reserved for the chapters in which those tests are covered at length. The topic is an important one because the effectiveness of a test as a whole—in other words, its validity—depends on the extent to which the individual items making up the test measure what they are supposed to measure.

Test Standardization

Even after the test items have been prepared and administered, the raw scores for all examinees have been determined, and the items analyzed, the work of test construction is not over. This is true even in the case of a teacher-made achievement test. Scores on nonstandardized tests are usually interpreted somewhat informally by comparing them with maximum possible scores, with scores obtained by other examinees, or against someone's subjective judgment or expectation of how a particular group should perform on the test. Interpreting scores on a standardized test, which has set directions for administration that should be closely followed and has been administered to an appropriate *standardization group*, is, however, a more formal process. The raw scores on standardized tests are compared with the test performance of the standardization (norm) group by converting test scores to some type of *norm*. Norms serve not as criteria of desirable performance, but rather as a frame of reference for interpreting the raw scores on a test.

The extent to which norms serve as an adequate standard for evaluating and interpreting test scores depends on how representative the test standardization group (the *norm group*) is of the population of examinees for whom the test is intended (the *target population*). Some intelligence tests are standardized on samples of individuals who are not truly representative of the population of people for whom the test was designed. For example, the standardization sample for the 1916 version of the Stanford-Binet Intelligence Scale consisted primarily of children living in California. This was a convenient sample for a test constructed in California, but it was hardly representative of the wide range of American children to whom the test was eventually administered. In other instances, the sample as a whole may be fairly representative of the target population, but a given subgroup is not representative of the same group in the population. Such was the case with the older adult (60+ years) sample of people used in standardizing the Wechsler Adult Intelligence Scale. That sample consisted of older adults living in metropolitan Kansas City, who were assumed to be a microcosm of the entire U.S. elderly population but were subsequently found not to be (Doppelt & Wallace, 1955).

The extent to which a test standardization sample is representative of a specified target population varies with the method of selecting the sample. Various sampling procedures, including random sampling, systematic sampling, cluster sampling, stratified sampling, and stratificd random sampling, have been employed. Of these, the last is most likely to yield a sample that accurately represents the target population. In *stratified random sampling*, the target population is first divided into a number of strata on characteristics known to be related to the variable measured by the test. Demographic characteristics on which a test standardization sample may be stratified include sex, chronological age, grade level, socioeconomic status, ethnicity, parental education and occupation, geographic region or urbanicity of residence, type of school attended, and even handicapping conditions. Estimates of the total number and percentage of people in each stratum are obtained from national census information or other available sources. Once the relevant strata are specified and estimates of the total number of people in each stratum are determined, a sample that is proportional to the total number of people in the specified stratum is selected at random from that stratum. *At random* means that every person in the stratum has an equal chance of being selected.

It is frequently impossible or impractical in large-scale test standardizations to select individual examinees at random from the entire target population or even from specified strata within that population. In such cases, a larger sampling unit, such as schools, may be employed. Once the schools have been selected at random from a stratum of schools having specified characteristics in common, all students—or at least a random subset of students in the appropriate grade levels in each school—are tested. In particular, the standardization of group tests of intelligence on many thousands of school children has involved such a *block* or *cluster*,

sampling procedure. Standardization of individual intelligence tests, in which people are tested individually rather than in groups, typically involves much smaller
samples.

DESCRIPTIVE STATISTICS

After everyone in the standardization sample has been tested, the resulting
scores are grouped in the form of a *frequency distribution*. To illustrate this
process, consider the following intelligence test scores obtained by thirty school
children:

102	107	88	114	94	110
98	102	119	99	120	112
109	96	108	91	100	108
108	101	106	116	104	111
115	111	105	104	99	92

A frequency distribution constructed from these scores is given in Table 2-1. The
following steps were followed in constructing this distribution:

1. The score range was computed by subtracting the lowest score (88) from
   the highest score (120). range = 120 − 88 = 32.
2. The range was divided by an appropriate number of intervals (usually 10 to
   20; in this case, 10), and the resulting quotient was rounded to the nearest
   integer: 32/10 = 3.
3. The intervals were set up from lowest to highest, starting with the lowest
   limit of the lowest interval and continuing through the upper limit of the
   highest interval. (The lower limit of the lowest interval should not be an
   actual score, and, if possible, it should be an even multiple of the interval

TABLE 2–1 **Frequency Distribution of
Thirty Test Scores**

Interval	Midpoint	Tallies	Frequency (f)
120–122	121	1	1
117–119	118	1	1
114–116	115	111	3
111–113	112	111	3
108–110	109	11111	5
105–107	106	111	3
102–104	103	1111	4
99–101	100	1111	4
96–98	97	11	2
93–95	94	1	1
90–92	91	11	2
87–89	88	1	1

width.) For these data, the lower limit of the lowest interval was selected
as 87.

4. The scores falling in each interval were tallied and converted to frequencies.

Averages

Inspection of the thirty scores and the frequency distribution in Table 2-1
provides an indication of the average and variability of the scores. The computation
of appropriate statistics, however, yields more accurate estimates. Three measures
of the average, or most representative, score are the mode, the median, and the
arithmetic mean. The *mode*, which is the score occurring the greatest number of
times, is the simplest average to determine. Since 108 occurs three times, more
often than any other score, the mode is 108 in this case.

The *median* of a group of scores is determined by ranking them from highest
to lowest and finding the middlemost score when the number of scores is odd or
one-half the two middlemost scores when the number of scores is even. Ranking
the scores from highest to lowest yields:

120	112	108	105	101	96
119	111	108	104	100	94
116	111	108	104	99	92
115	110	107	102	99	91
114	109	106	102	98	88

The number of scores in the example is an even number (30), so the median is
the sum of the 15th and 16th scores divided by 2: $(105 + 106)/2 = 105.5$.

The *arithmetic mean* ($\bar{X}$) of a set of raw scores is also easy to compute: the
scores are added, and the sum is divided by the number of scores. For the thirty
scores in the example, the arithmetic mean is $\bar{X} = 3149/30 = 104.97$.

The three averages—mode, median, and arithmetic mean—can also be computed from a frequency distribution such as the one in Table 2-1, but the corresponding values turn out to be a bit different from those computed from the raw
scores. The mode of a frequency distribution is the midpoint of the interval
containing the greatest number of scores (109 in Table 2-1). To calculate the mean
of a frequency distribution, first multiply the interval midpoints by the corresponding frequencies, sum the resulting products, then divide the sum of the products by
the total number of scores. For the example, this yields $\bar{X} = 3153/30 = 105.1$. Since
the median is the fiftieth percentile, that is, the score below which 50 percent of the
scores fall, the computation of the median of a frequency distribution is discussed
later in the chapter under the topic of percentiles and percentile ranks.

Variability

The variability of a set of scores is the extent to which they are spread out or
dispersed. The simplest measure of variability is the *range* of the scores (highest

score − lowest score), which has already been determined to be 32 for the thirty scores of the example. Unfortunately, the range is not a representative or stable measure of the variability of the scores; it is affected greatly by one extremely small or extremely large score. Less influenced by extreme scores are the variance and its square root, the standard deviation.

The *variance* (s^2) of a set of scores is obtained by (1) subtracting the arithmetic mean from each score, (2) squaring the resulting differences, (3) adding the squared differences, and (4) dividing the sum of the squared differences by the number of scores. In symbols,

$$s^2 = \Sigma(X - \bar{X})^2/n,$$

where Σ (sigma) means "take the sum of all values of the following expression." The variance of the thirty scores of the example is $s^2 = 1954.97/30 = 65.1657$, and the *standard deviation* $s = \sqrt{65.1657} = 8.07$.

The variance can also be computed from a frequency distribution by (1) subtracting the mean from the midpoint of each interval, (2) squaring the resulting differences, (3) multiplying the squared differences by the corresponding interval frequencies, (4) summing the resulting products, and then (5) dividing this sum by the number of scores. For the frequency distribution in Table 2-1, the variance (s^2) is 66.69, and the standard deviation (s) is 8.17. These values are close but not identical to those obtained with the ungrouped scores.

Other characteristics of a frequency distribution of a set of scores, such as indexes of *skewness* (degree of asymmetry) and *kurtosis* (degree of steepness or flatness), can also be computed, but these measures are seldom used in describing test scores.

Percentile Ranks and Percentiles

Interpreting a set of test scores is facilitated by first converting the scores to percentile ranks. A *percentile rank* is the percentage of the total number of scores falling at or below a particular score. Computation of the percentile ranks corresponding to a series of scores begins by ranking the scores from highest to lowest. To find the percentile rank (PR) of a score, first count the number of scores (cf) falling below the score; then to the value of cf add half the number of times the given score occurs ($\frac{1}{2}f$). Finally, dividing this sum by the total number of scores (n) and multiplying by 100 yields the formula PR = $100(cf + \frac{1}{2}f)/n$.

For example, to determine the percentile rank of a score of 99 in the above set of thirty scores, we note that there are six scores below a score of 99, and two 99s. Therefore, the percentile rank of a score of 99 is PR = $100(6 + 2/2)/30 = 23.33$ percent. This means that approximately 23 percent of the scores fall below the midpoint of a score interval ranging from 98.5 to 99.5. As another example, the percentile rank of a score of 105 is $100(14 + 1/2)/30 = 48.33$. Consequently, approximately 48 percent of the scores fall below the midpoint of the score interval ranging from 104.5 to 105.5.

The problem can also be worked backward: we can find the score (*percentile*) corresponding to a given percentile rank. For example, to find the 50th percentile (*median*), the score below which 50 percent of the scores fall, we begin by multiplying the total number of scores (*n*) by .50, so .50(30) = 15. Then we count up to the 15th score—105 in this case. Since the interval containing 105 actually extends from 104.5 to 105.5—its *real limits*—the 15th score is the upper real limit of the interval, namely 105.5. If the desired percentile does not fall on an upper real limit of a score interval, then it is necessary to interpolate within the interval. For example, to find the 75th percentile—the score below which 75 percent of the scores fall—we begin by multiplying *n* by .75: .75 × 30 = 22.5. Therefore, we need to find the value of the 22.5th score. Now 22 scores fall below 110.5, and another .5 of a score is needed from the two scores in the next interval (110.5 to 111.5). So the 22.5th score, or the 75th percentile, is 110.5 + .5/2 = 110.75.

Percentile ranks and percentiles can also be computed from a frequency distribution having any convenient interval width. To find the percentile ranks of the midpoints of the intervals in Table 2-1, for example, first determine how many scores fall below the interval (*cf*). Then add one-half the frequency on the given interval (*f*/2) to *cf*, multiply the resulting sum by 100 and divide the product by *n* (the total number of scores); in symbols, PR = 100(*cf* + *f*/2)/*n*. The percentile ranks of the midpoints of all twelve intervals in Table 2-1 are given in the third column of Table 2-2.

TEST NORMS

The percentile ranks corresponding to a set of test scores or score interval midpoints are referred to as *percentile norms*. A table of percentile norms for a test

TABLE 2–2   Percentile Ranks, *z* Scores, *T* Scores, and Stanines of Interval Midpoints of Frequency Distribution in Table 2–1

Interval midpoint	Frequency	Percentile rank	*z*	*T*	Stanine
121	1	98.33	1.95	69	9
118	1	95.00	1.58	66	8
115	3	88.33	1.21	62	7
112	3	78.33	.84	58	7
109	5	65.00	.48	55	6
106	3	51.67	.11	51	5
103	4	40.00	−.26	47	4
100	4	26.67	−.62	44	4
97	2	16.67	−.99	40	3
94	1	11.67	−1.36	36	2
91	2	6.67	−1.73	33	2
88	1	1.67	−2.09	29	1

gives the percentages (percentile ranks) of the sample of examinees in the standard-ization group whose scores on the test fall below each score or score midpoint.

Grade and Age Norms

Because they are fairly easy to understand, percentile norms are very popular among test users. However, they do have their drawbacks and are not the only types of test norms. Among the other types of norms are grade norms, age norms, and standard score norms.

A *grade norm* is the median test score obtained by examinees (in the test standardization group) at a given grade level. Grade norms are expressed in grades and tenths of a grade (3.4, 5.1, 7.3, etc.); it is assumed that growth in the ability or other characteristic that is being measured is inconsequential during the two summer months. For example, the range of grade norms for the sixth grade is 6.0 to 6.9, in one-month intervals from the first to the last month of the school year. Although a table of grade norms is more commonly found in an achievement test manual, grade norms of a sort, known as *mental age grade placements*, or *intelligence grade placements*, are included in some intelligence test manuals. Such grade-equivalent scores, which are computed like any other grade norms, are indexes of the grade levels at which examinees are functioning intellectually.

Similar to a grade norm, an *age norm*, which is appropriate for children but not for adults, is the median test score obtained by examinees of the same chrono-logical age. Age norms for intelligence tests are sometimes referred to as *mental ages*. The mental age corresponding to a given test score is equal to the chronologi-cal age, in years and months, of the segment of the test standardization sample whose median score on the test was equal to the given score. The possible mental ages for the eighth year, for example, range from 8-0 to 8-11 in one-month intervals.

Grade and age norms have often been used in computing *quotients*, but the practice has almost disappeared. A *ratio IQ*, which was used to designate perfor-mance on older intelligence tests, was obtained by dividing the examinee's mental age (MA) in months, determined from his intelligence test performance, by his or her chronological age in months and then multiplying the result by 100. Further-more, dividing a person's educational age (age norm on an achievement test) by his or her chronological age yielded an *educational quotient*. Finally, dividing the educational quotient by the intelligence quotient yielded an *accomplishment quo-tient*.

Despite their popularity, percentile, grade, and age norms have serious short-comings. A major problem with all three types of norms is that the units in which they are expressed are not equal across the entire range of scores. For example, although the numerical difference between 50 and 55 is equal to the difference between 90 and 95, the difference in ability between a person who scores at the 50th percentile and one who scores at the 55th percentile on an intelligence test is actually much less than the difference in ability between a person who scores at the 90th percentile and one who scores at the 95th percentile. Likewise, in terms of mental ability, the difference between the 50th and 55th percentiles is much less than the difference between the 5th and 10th percentiles. This is so because the unit of measurement becomes progressively larger from the center to the left and right extremes of the percentile rank scale.

The magnitudes of grade- and age-equivalent units of measurement also vary with grade level and chronological age, respectively. Because children tend to grow, learn, or otherwise change less in succeeding grades or years, the unit of measurement typically becomes progressively smaller with each age or grade. The assumption in using mental age units is that growth in ability is uniform across childhood. But mental growth is actually greater during early childhood than middle childhood and greater during middle than later childhood. Consequently, the difference between mental ages of 5-2 and 6-2 is not the same as the difference between mental ages of 10-2 to 11-2. The problem of unequal units of measurement has led specialists in psychological and educational measurement to advocate a type of norm that does not suffer from this shortcoming but rather has a more nearly constant unit of measurement across the entire range of scores. These are the z, T, deviation IQ, and stanine scores, known collectively as *standard scores*.

Standard Score Norms

Of all types of norms, standard scores are the best candidates for measurement at something higher than an *ordinal scale*. Numbers on an ordinal measurement scale (e.g., first, second, third, fourth, etc.) represent only rank orders and not true magnitudes. On the next higher level of measurement, an *interval scale*, equal numerical differences imply equal differences in the characteristic or attribute being measured. For example, assume that scores on an intelligence test are interval-level measurements. Then if George's score is 120, Frank's score is 100, and Paul's score is 80, the difference in intelligence between George and Frank is equal to the difference in intelligence between Frank and Paul. If the three scores had been only ordinal scale measurements, all that could have been said is that George is more intelligent than Frank and Frank is more intelligent than Paul—but not how much more.

The most basic type of standard score is a z score, computed as $z = (X - \bar{X})/s$. In this formula, X is a raw score, $\bar{X}$ the mean, and s the standard deviation of the scores. The fourth column of Table 2-2 gives the z scores corresponding to the interval midpoints of the frequency distribution in Table 2-1, based on a mean of 105.1 and a standard deviation of 8.17.

The mean and standard deviation of a set of z scores are 0 and 1, respectively; consequently, z scores are positive and negative decimal numbers. The negative numbers and the decimals, which are a nuisance, can be eliminated by multiplying each z score by 10, adding 50 to the product ($10z + 50$), and rounding the result to the nearest whole number. The resulting T scores, which are listed in column 5 of Table 2-2 for the midpoints of those intervals, have a mean of 50 and a standard deviation of 10.

There is nothing sacred about multiplying each z score by 10 and adding 50;

other numbers may do just as well. In computing stanine scores, the z scores are multiplied by 2 and 5 is added to the resulting products. The stanine scores for the interval midpoints in Table 2–2 are given in column 6 of the table. The mean and standard deviation of deviation IQs (DIQs) on Wechsler intelligence tests are 100 and 15. These and other standard score scales are depicted in Figure 2–1. Another type of standard score that is becoming increasingly more popular is the normal curve equivalent (NCE) scale. Like T scores, the mean of the NCE scale is 50, but the standard deviation is 21. Therefore, the effective range of NCEs is approximately 0 to 100.

It is assumed when using T scores or stanine scores that the frequency distribution of scores is normal (bell-shaped), like the theoretical distribution shown in Figure 2–1. Consequently, the use of T scores and stanines with the data in Table 2–1, which is clearly not a normal distribution, is somewhat misleading. Procedures for "normalizing" a frequency distribution and then computing the T scores and stanines of the transformed distribution are available (see Aiken, 1994, ch. 4), but the normalization procedure is not commonly applied with test scores.

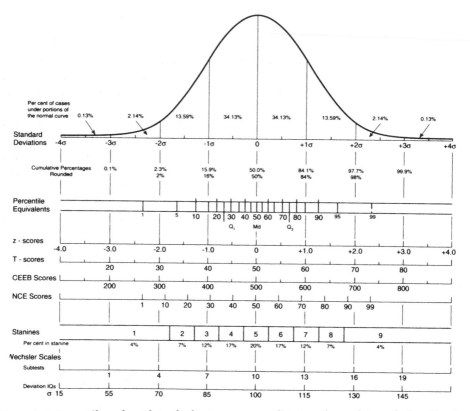

FIGURE 2–1 **Percentile ranks and standard scores corresponding to various points on the baseline of a normal distribution of scores.** (H. G. Seashore, "Methods of Expressing Test Scores," The Psychological Corporation *Test Service Bulletin*, No. 48, 1955.)

The frequency distribution of the intelligence test scores (IQs) of a large representative sample of the American population tends to be fairly normal. But rather than being a perfect bell-shaped curve, there is frequently a hump at the lower end of the IQ curve. This hump is produced by the low test scores of an disproportionately large number (relative to the normal curve) of individuals with very low IQs. The underlying cause is generally some specific organic condition, either environmental or genetic, which has led to brain damage. Such individuals are described as "organic retardates," in contrast to those "familial retardates" whose low intelligence runs in families and is not due to any demonstrable organic factor (Zigler, 1967). Furthermore, although the frequency distribution of the intelligence test scores of a large, heterogeneous group of people is usually fairly normal in shape, rather than being this way by nature it is influenced by the fact that the test constructors designed and scored the test in such a way that the score distribution would be normal.

RELIABILITY AND VALIDITY

It is important for a test to be standardized on a representative sample and the scores expressed in terms of norms that can serve as a frame of reference for interpreting them. However, no matter how adequately a test is standardized or how elaborate the test norms are, the scores are meaningless unless they are reliable and valid.

Reliability

According to classical test theory, a test of ability or any other human characteristic is said to be *reliable* if the scores are relatively free from random, unsystematic errors of measurement. That is, when a test measures reliably the scores are close in numerical value to the examinees' "true scores" on the variable measured by the test. Since these true scores can never be known precisely, the reliability of the scores on a test must be estimated in some way. Because reliability may vary with the situation in which the test is administered, the kinds of people to whom it is given, and the particular items or questions on the test, all of these factors should be considered when estimating reliability. Various methods have been devised to study the effects on reliability of temporal and situational factors, test content, and the nature of the group tested. Among these are the methods of stability, equivalence, and internal consistency.

Method of Stability

An estimate of the consistency or stability of test scores over a period of time provides one kind of reliability information. The procedure for determining a reliability coefficient in this case is simple. The test is administered to the same people twice, with a specified time interval (such as one week, one month, or one year) between administrations. Then the coefficient of correlation between the two sets of scores is computed. The reliability coefficient will decrease somewhat as the test–retest interval increases, because people change with time and different people change by different amounts.

Computation of the Pearson product-moment correlation coefficient (r), an index number ranging from -1.00 to 1.00, is outlined in Table 2–3. The closer the correlation (coefficient of stability) is to 1.00, the higher the reliability of the test; the closer the correlation is to $.00$, the lower the reliability. The method of stability, sometimes referred to as the test–retest method, is convenient, but it takes into account only one source of measurement error: that related to different times of administration of a test.

Method of Equivalence

A second method for determining reliability, the *equivalent* or *parallel forms method*, takes into account another source of measurement error: that due to different samples of items making up the test. Preparing an equivalent or parallel form of a test is a tedious process involving construction of a set of items that are parallel but not identical to those on the first form. Because this procedure is more difficult with intelligence tests than achievement tests, parallel forms of intelligence tests are seldom constructed.

TABLE 2–3   **Computation of the Product-Moment Correlation Coefficient**

Examinee	X(IQ)	Y(GPA)	X^2	Y^2	XY
1	88	2.32	7,744	5.3824	204.16
2	119	2.96	14,161	8.7616	352.24
3	109	2.88	11,881	8.2944	313.92
4	106	2.72	11,236	7.3984	288.32
5	105	2.64	11,025	6.9696	277.20
6	114	3.68	12,996	13.5424	419.52
7	99	2.52	9,801	6.3504	249.48
8	91	3.36	8,281	11.2896	305.76
9	116	3.88	13,456	15.0544	450.08
10	104	3.44	10,816	11.8336	357.76
Sums	1,051	30.40	111,397	94.8768	3,218.44

$$r = \frac{n\Sigma XY - (\Sigma X)(\Sigma Y)}{\sqrt{[n\Sigma X^2 - (\Sigma X)^2][n\Sigma Y^2 - (\Sigma Y)^2]}}$$

$$= \frac{10(3218.44) - (1051)(30.4)}{\sqrt{[10(111397) - 1051^2][10(94.8768) - 30.4^2]}}$$

$$= \frac{234}{\sqrt{(9369)(24.608)}} = \frac{234}{480.1587} = .4873$$

An equivalent forms reliability coefficient (*coefficient of equivalence*) is determined by administering both forms of the test to a large sample of people and computing the correlation coefficient between their scores on the two forms. Combining the procedure for determining a coefficient of stability with that of finding a coefficient of equivalence permits computation of a *coefficient of stability and equivalence*. Such a coefficient takes into account errors due to different times of administration and different samples of test items.

Method of Internal Consistency

It is possible, under certain conditions, to obtain an estimate of equivalent forms reliability without actually administering two separate forms of a test. This procedure, which is referred to as the *method of internal consistency*, is based on the idea that a test of, say, fifty items actually consists of many different equivalent pairs of twenty-five-item tests.

An internal consistency coefficient for a test on which items are scored either 0 (wrong) or 1 (right) may be computed by using one of the *Kuder-Richardson formulas*:

$$r_{11} = \frac{k[1 - \Sigma p_i(1 - p_i)/s^2]}{k - 1}$$

or

$$r_{11} = \frac{k[1 - \bar{X}(k - X)/(ks^2)]}{k - 1}.$$

In these two formulas, known as the Kuder-Richardson (K-R) formulas 20 and 21, respectively, k is the number of items on the test, $\bar{X}$ is the mean, and s^2 the variance of total test scores, and p_i is the proportion of examinees who answered item i correctly. In applying the second formula, it is assumed that all items are of equal difficulty. The second formula also yields a more conservative (lower) estimate of reliability than the first.

In the case of multipoint or multiscore items, an appropriate measure of a test's internal consistency reliability is provided by *coefficient alpha*. The computation of coefficient alpha begins by determining the individual variances (s_i^2) of the k items on the test and the variance (s_t^2) of total test scores. The k item variances are then summed, and coefficient alpha is computed as

$$r_{11} = \frac{k(1 - \Sigma s_i^2/s_t^2)}{k - 1}.$$

The method of internal consistency requires less time and effort than the other two methods of estimating reliability, but it has serious limitations. The resulting reliability coefficients are based on the assumption that the various items on the test measure the same thing and that examinees have ample time in which to complete the test. Thus, the internal consistency method does not provide an accurate estimate of the reliability of a speeded test, a test consisting of a long series of easy items that few examinees can be expected to finish in the allotted time.

Standard Error of Measurement

The reliability coefficients of carefully designed intelligence tests, both individual and group, are usually in the high .80s or .90s. A correlation as high as this is required for interpreting individual scores, although tests with lower reliabilities may be used with considerable skepticism or for reporting group results. A high reliability coefficient indicates that scores on the test are relatively free from random errors of measurement. The average amount of this error, which is estimated by a statistic known as the *standard error of measurement* (SM), can be determined from the formula $SM = s\sqrt{1 - r}$, where s is the standard deviation of the obtained test scores and r is the reliability coefficient.

Knowing the standard error of measurement of a test permits the determination of a range of values (a *confidence interval*) within which we can be fairly certain that an examinee's true score on the test falls. Using normal probability theory, it can be said that the true scores of approximately 95 percent of a group of examinees who make the same test score (X) will fall within 1.96 standard errors of measurement of that score. For example, suppose that John, a 14-year-old ninth grader makes a raw score of 20 on the Verbal subtest and a raw score of 15 on the Nonverbal subtest of the Otis-Lennon School Ability Test (sixth edition). The manual for Form G of this test gives values of 2.7 and 2.6, respectively, for the standard errors of measurement of the Verbal and Nonverbal subtests in the standardization sample of 14-year-olds (Otis & Lennon, 1989). Consequently, it can be estimated that 95 percent of all 14-year-olds in the target population making a Verbal score of 20 will have true Verbal scores falling between $20 - 1.96(2.7) = 14.71$ and $20 + 1.96(2.7) = 25.29$. It can also be estimated with 95 percent confidence that the same group of students will have Nonverbal scores falling between $15 - 1.96(2.6) = 9.90$ and $15 + 1.96(2.6) = 20.10$. Therefore, we can be fairly certain that a member of this group, such as John, will have a true Verbal score between 15 and 25 and a true Nonverbal score between 10 and 20. It is assumed in drawing these conclusions that the test was administered according to the standard procedure and that the examinees were ready, willing, and able to respond to the best of their ability.

On tests that yield IQs, the standard error of measurement is usually 5 points or less. Consequently, in most instances an examinee's true IQ can be expected to fall within 10 points of his or her obtained IQ. This means that, on the average, scores on an IQ test are relatively stable from one administration of the test to the next or from one form to another when the test is properly administered to people who are motivated to take it.

Standard Error of Measurement of Score Differences

Many individual and group intelligence tests consist not of a single test yielding only one score but of two or more separately scored subtests. The reliabilities, and hence the standard errors of measurement, of the several subtests making up the test may vary substantially. Furthermore, a major reason for administering such a *test battery* is to compare an examinee's performance on the various subtests. By assessing different intellectual functions, the subtests permit a diagnosis of the examinee's areas of intellectual strength and weakness. Such a diagnosis requires calculating the differences between the examinee's scores on the various subtests and then determining which differences are significant.

To determine whether a person's scores on two different tests or subtests (1 and 2) are significant, we begin by computing the standard error of measurement of the test score differences (SMD) by the formula:

$$\text{SMD} = \sqrt{(s_1^2 + s_2^2 - 2r_{12}s_1s_2)(2 - r_{11} - r_{22})/[2(1 - r_{12})]},$$

where s_1^2 and s_2^2 are the variances of the two subtests, r_{11} and r_{22} are their reliabilities, and r_{12} is the correlation between subtests 1 and 2. To illustrate the use of this formula, assume that, for the sample of 14-year-olds on whom the Otis-Lennon School Ability Test was standardized, the standard deviations of the Verbal and Nonverbal subtests are 6.3 and 5.9 and the reliability coefficients of the two subtests are .82 and .80. If the correlation between the two subtests is .60, then

$$\text{SMD} = \sqrt{[6.3^2 + 5.9^2 - 2(.60)(6.3)(5.9)](2 - .82 - .80)/[2(1 - .60)]} = 3.77.$$

Multiplying this value by 1.96 gives 7.39. This is the minimum difference between the two subtest scores that is required in order to be 95 percent confident that the difference between the examinee's scores on the two subtests is not due to chance.

Validity

A reliable test is not useful unless it is also valid. Scores on a test or other psychometric device may be relatively free from random (unsystematic) errors of measurement—in other words, "reliable"—and yet be systematically deflated or inflated by errors of measurement in a particular direction. *Validity*, the extent to which a test or other psychometric instrument measures what it was designed to measure, refers to relative freedom from *both* unsystematic and systematic errors of measurement. Since reliability is affected only by the unsystematic errors, it is possible for a test to be reliable and still not be valid. On the other hand, a test cannot be valid without being reliable; the upper limit of a test's validity coefficient is the square root of its equivalent forms reliability. Compared with reliability, validity is also more situation specific, in that it is more affected by the specific situation in which it is determined. For example, a particular test may be valid in an employment context but not in an academic one. Consequently, a more appropriate question than "Is this test valid?" is "For what purpose and under what conditions is this test valid?"

Content Validity

As with reliability, there are several types of validity, or rather several methods of obtaining information about the validity of a test. Perhaps the most direct method is to have experts carefully inspect the content of the test to determine whether it corresponds to the detailed specifications of what it should measure. *Content validity* is of greatest concern with respect to measures of knowledge, skills, and other *achievements*, although it is also relevant to the validity of intelligence tests and other psychometric devices.

Criterion-Related Validity

A second type of validity, which is of foremost concern to psychologists who use testing procedures to select and place people in employment or educational contexts, is criterion-related validity. An index of the *criterion-related validity* of a test is the correlation between scores on the test and scores on some standard reference measure, or *criterion*, of performance. The most popular criteria for validating intelligence tests are measures of academic performance or achievement, such as course grades, scores on achievement tests, and speed of learning. Criterion-related validity can be broken down into two types, depending on whether the criterion information is available immediately (*concurrent validity*) or later (*predictive validity*). Predictive validity is of greatest relevance to intelligence testers because good criteria of performance in schools and other situations where intelligence tests are used are typically not available until some period of time after the test has been administered.

One index of the predictive validity of an intelligence test is a correlation coefficient. This coefficient, which typically ranges from about .50 to .80 when predicting achievement test scores, is usually a *Pearson product-moment coefficient*, or *r*. It is a signed decimal number ranging from -1.00 (perfect negative correlation) to $+1.00$ (perfect positive correlation). Knowing that two variables such as intelligence (IQ) and grade-point average (GPA) are significantly correlated enables one to predict GPAs from IQs. As illustrated in Table 2–3, the procedure for computing *r* is fairly straightforward. In this case $r = .4873$, which is not very high but may contribute something to the prediction of GPA from IQ.

We can use *r*, as well as the means and standard deviations of the predictor (*X*) and criterion (*Y*), to find a linear regression equation for predicting GPA from IQ. Letting *X* stand for IQ and *Y* stand for GPA, the equation for predicting GPA from IQ is

$$Y_{pred} = r(s_y/s_x)(X - \bar{X}) + \bar{Y}.$$

Substituting $r = .4873$, $\bar{X} = 105.1$, $\bar{Y} = 3.04$, $s_x = 9.6794$, and $s_y = .4961$, $Y_{pred} = [.4873(.4961)/9.6794] (X - 105.1) + 3.04 = .025X + .415$. To predict the GPA of a person having an IQ of 100, we enter the person's IQ into this regression equation and compute $Y_{pred} = .025(100) + .415 = 2.915$. Although 2.915 is the examinee's predicted GPA, it does not mean that the person's actual GPA will be exactly equal to this value. To estimate a range of values (a *confidence interval*) within which the person's actual GPA is likely to fall, we must first compute a statistic known as the *standard error of estimate* (SE) where $SE = s_y\sqrt{1 - r^2}$. In this formula s_y is the standard deviation of the *Y* variable (GPA) and *r* is the correlation between *X* and

Y. For the data in Table 2–3, SE = $.4961\sqrt{1 - .4873^2}$ = .4332. Therefore, it can be concluded that, whatever the examinee's actual GPA may be, we are 95 percent confident that it is within 1.96 standard errors of estimate of his or her predicted GPA. Thus, we are 95 percent confident that the examinee's GPA will be between $2.915 \pm 1.96(.4332)$ = 2.07 and 3.76.

Construct Validity

The most comprehensive of all types of validity, in that it encompasses information from both content validity and criterion-related validity studies, is *construct validity*. A "construct" such as intelligence, achievement, or anxiety is obviously not a concrete "thing," but rather an abstraction that presumably facilitates understanding and predicting events with which a particular scientific discipline is concerned. Every scientific discipline has its own constructs, which are intangible but hopefully tied to reality in some observable manner. Information on the construct validity of a test or other psychometric procedure indicates the extent to which scores on the test are related to observable behavior in situations where the particular psychological construct is operating. Construct validity is of concern in all psychological assessments, including intelligence testing.

Information pertaining to construct validity is not obtained by a single procedure. Various kinds of evidence may be used: analysis of the content of the test, correlations between scores on the test and other measures of the same construct, and comparisons of the scores of people who are recognized as possessing different amounts of the construct. As we shall see throughout this book, various kinds of information may have a bearing on the question of whether a certain test is a valid measure of the construct of intelligence.

A test that has construct validity should not only correlate highly with other tests or measures of the same characteristic (*convergent validity*) but it must also have low correlations with measures of different characteristics (*discriminant validity*). Four types of correlations are of interest in this regard. These are the correlations between measures of (1) the same trait by the same method, (2) different traits by the same method, (3) the same trait by different methods, and (4) different traits by different methods. Using this *multitrait–multimethod approach* (Campbell & Fiske, 1959), supporting evidence for construct validity is obtained when correlations between the same trait measured by the same and different methods are higher than the correlations between different traits measured by either the same or different methods. However, the actual results are often different from what is expected: correlations between different traits measured by the same method are sometimes higher than correlations between the same trait measured by different methods. When this occurs, it means that the method by which the characteristic or trait was measured had a more consistent effect on the examinee's responses than the hypothesized trait itself. Such a result may cast doubt on the importance of that characteristic as a stable determinant of behavior. Be that as it may, tests of general intelligence typically possess satisfactory construct validity. They usually have correlations in the .80s and .90s with each other and correlations between .40 and .80 with measures of academic achievement (Pellegrino & Varnhagen, 1985).

Validity Reconsidered

Traditional approaches to validity determination—content, criterion-related, construct—are all concerned more with the *inferences* made on the basis of test scores than with the *actions* taken as a result of the scores. Thus, testers usually focus on selecting and expertly administering the best tests for specific diagnostic or predictive purposes, and consider their job done when the results have been interpreted and explained, and specified predictions made on the basis of them. Messick (1988, 1989) has argued, however, that in considering the validity of a test we should also think about the value implications of the scores and the actual and potential social consequences of using them for specified purposes. Following this approach, for example, one should take into account not only the accuracy with which performance in school or on the job can be predicted from intelligence test scores but also whether it is valuable to predict these criteria and the social consequences of doing so. Furthermore, according to Messick we should consider whether the social consequences associated with using a particular test are a reflection of the test or the actual phenomenon being measured. Although adoption of Messick's proposals would undoubtedly cause mental testers to consider values more carefully in the selection of tests and criteria, the approach is somewhat controversial. Science is, of course, not "value free," but, like beauty, values are in the eyes of the beholders.

FACTOR ANALYSIS

One type of information pertaining to the construct validity of a test consists of the results of a factor analysis of the scores on the test and other measures of the same construct. Factor analysis is a statistical procedure introduced during the early part of this century by Charles Spearman, who used it to support his belief that all intelligence tests measure a general mental ability (*g*). Factor analysis has been developed extensively since Spearman's time, and now there are many techniques of factor analyzing a set of tests, subtests, or test items. The aim of all these techniques is the same: to determine the factor composition of the tests or items— that is, how many psychological dimensions, or factors, the tests or items are measuring and what weight (loading) each item or test has on each factor.

Factoring and Rotation

Every factor analysis consists of two general stages: *factoring* and *rotation*. The aim of the factoring stage is to determine the number of factors needed to account for the relationships between the various tests and provide preliminary estimates of the numerical loadings of each test on each factor. The purpose of factor rotation is to make the factors more interpretable by producing a configuration in which only a few tests have high loadings and the majority of tests have low loadings on any given factor.

Factor Analysis of the WISC-III

One way to begin a factor analysis of the scores of a large group of people on a set of tests is to compute the correlations among all the test scores and arrange them in the form of a matrix. This has been done in Table 2-4 with the average correlations for all ages on the subtest scaled scores of the Wechsler Intelligence Scale for Children—Third Edition (WISC-III). Notice that the matrix is symmetric; that is, the correlations in a given row are identical to those in the corresponding column. In addition, there are no entries on the major diagonal of the matrix.

The question of what values to place on the diagonal of the correlation matrix—the reliabilities of the tests, estimates of their common-factor variances (*communalities*), or all 1.00's—depends on the particular factor-analysis procedure or theory followed by the researcher. In one factoring procedure, Thurstone's *centroid method*, estimates of the communalities of the tests are placed on the diagonal of the correlation matrix. On the other hand, the *principal axis method* requires the diagonal entries to be 1.00's. The choice of what values to place on the diagonals is an important one, in that it affects both the number of factors that are extracted and the obtained weights (*factor loadings*) of each test on each factor.

Factoring the Correlation Matrix

The initial result of a typical factor analysis is an original (unrotated) factor matrix such as the one in columns A, B, and C of Table 2-5.* In this case the factor-analytic procedure has reduced the number of variables or psychological dimensions from thirteen, the total number of subtests on the WISC-III, to three, the number of common factors extracted. The decimal numbers in each column of the factor matrix are the loadings of the thirteen WISC-III subtests on that factor. For example, the Information subtest has a loading of .779 on factor A, a loading of −.330 on factor B, and a loading of .026 on factor C. Each factor loading is the correlation between a particular subtest and one of the factors. The square of the loading of a given subtest on a factor is the proportion of total variance of the subtest scores accounted for by that factor. Thus $(.779)^2 = .607$ means that 60.7 percent of the variance of the Information subtest scores can be accounted for by factor A. Only $(−.33)^2 = .109$, or 10.9 percent, of the variance on this subtest can be accounted for by factor B, and only $(.026)^2 = .0007$, or less than 1 percent, by factor C.

---

*The correlation matrix in Table 2-4 was factored by the principal axis procedure using the SPSS/PC+ computer program FACTOR. Varimax (orthogonal) rotation of the resulting factor matrix (columns A, B, and C of Table 2-5) produced the rotated factor matrix in columns A′, B′, and C′ of that table.

Table 2–4 Matrix Average Intercorrelations among WISC-III Subtests

Subtest	1	2	3	4	5	6	7	8	9	10	11	12	13
1. Information		.66	.57	.70	.56	.34	.47	.21	.40	.48	.41	.35	.18
2. Similarities	.66		.55	.69	.59	.34	.45	.20	.39	.49	.42	.35	.18
3. Arithmetic	.57	.55		.54	.47	.43	.39	.27	.35	.52	.39	.41	.22
4. Vocabulary	.70	.69	.54		.64	.35	.45	.26	.40	.46	.41	.35	.17
5. Comprehension	.56	.59	.47	.64		.29	.38	.25	.35	.40	.34	.34	.17
6. Digit Span	.34	.34	.43	.35	.29		.25	.23	.20	.32	.26	.28	.14
7. Picture Completion	.47	.45	.39	.45	.38	25		.18	.37	.52	.49	.33	.24
8. Coding	.21	.20	.27	.26	.25	.23	.18		.28	.27	.24	.53	.15
9. Picture Arrangement	.40	.39	.35	.40	.35	.20	.37	.28		.41	.37	.36	.23
10. Block Design	.48	.49	.52	.46	.40	.32	.52	.27	.41		.61	.45	.31
11. Object Assembly	.41	.42	.39	.41	.34	.26	.49	.24	.37	.61		.38	.29
12. Symbol Search	.35	.35	.41	.35	.34	.28	.33	.53	.36	.45	.38		.24
13. Mazes	.18	.18	.22	.17	.17	.14	.24	.15	.23	.31	.29	.24	

Rotating the Factors

To simplify the interpretation of the obtained factors by increasing the number of high and low positive loadings in the columns of the factor matrix, a procedure known as *factor rotation* is applied to the original factor matrix. Depending on the particular rotation method, either uncorrelated factors (*orthogonal factors*) or correlated factors (*oblique factors*) can be obtained. Certain factor analysts prefer orthogonal rotation, whereas others like oblique rotation. The rotated factor matrix in columns A′, B′, and C′ of Table 2-5 was generated by orthogonal rotation of the

Table 2–5 Original and Rotated Factor Matrices

Subtest	Original (unrotated) factor matrix			Rotated factor matrix		
	A	B	C	A′	B′	C′
Information	.779	−.330	.026	.805	.247	.089
Similarities	.777	−.337	.022	.807	.246	.081
Arithmetic	.737	−.099	.117	.647	.262	.283
Vocabulary	.789	−.342	.101	.833	.193	.135
Comprehension	.704	−.294	.145	.747	.138	.164
Digit Span	.507	−.018	.285	.450	.056	.364
Picture Completion	.661	.014	−.346	.434	.606	.020
Coding	.442	.548	.542	.097	.087	.879
Picture Arrangement	.597	.164	−.080	.340	.447	.271
Block Design	.745	.181	−.261	.411	.664	.215
Object Assembly	.664	.216	−.360	.310	.708	.142
Symbol Search	.615	.480	.302	.228	.322	.738
Mazes	.367	.420	−.450	−.060	.706	.106

original factor matrix in columns A, B, and C, so factors A′, B′, and C′ are not correlated with each other.

Interpreting the Factors

After all statistical computations required by factoring and rotation have been made, the researcher or test designer faces the task of interpreting the factors. This is accomplished by inspecting the pattern of high and low loadings of each test on the different factors, remembering that the higher the loading, the more important the factor is on the given test. As shown in Table 2-5, the first five subtests have loadings of over .60 on factor A′. Because all of these subtests are on the Verbal Scale of the WISC-III, an appropriate name for this factor is "verbal comprehension." On the other hand, the Picture Completion, Block Design, Object Assembly, and Mazes subtests are the only ones with loadings of over .60 on factor B′. Since these four subtests are all on the Performance Scale of the WISC-III, an appropriate label for this factor is "perceptual–motor performance ability." Finally, only the Coding and Symbol Search subtests have high loadings on factor C′; inspection of these two subtests suggests that they are both measures of "processing speed and attentiveness," which may be an appropriate name for factor C′.

Communality and Specificity

The total variance of a test is equal to the sum of the variance due to common factors, specific factors, and errors of measurement. The portion of the total variance that is due to factors that the test has in common with other tests is the test's *communality*, and the portion due to factors specific to the test itself is the test's *specificity*. The second column in Table 2-6 lists the communalities of the thirteen WISC-III subtests. The communality of a subtest is computed as the sum of squares of the factor loadings on that subtest. For example, the communality of the Information subtest is $(.805)^2 + (.247)^2 + (.089)^2 = .717$, so approximately 72 percent of the variance of scores on the Information subtest can be accounted for by factors A′, B′, and C′. Reliability estimates for the thirteen WISC-III subtests are given in the third column of Table 2-6. Subtracting the communalities of the subtests from their reliabilities gives the specificities listed in the last column of the table. For example, the specificity of the Information subtest is $.84 - .72 = .12$. This means that 12 percent of the total variance of the Information subtest scores can be accounted for by factors specific to that subtest.

SUMMARY

Procedures for analyzing test scores vary with the characteristics and purposes of the test, but a first step is usually some form of item analysis. Item analysis is concerned with determining the extent to which each item contributes to the assessment or prediction of a criterion of whatever the test was designed to mea-

TABLE 2–6   Communalities, Reliabilities, and Specificities of WISC-III Subtests

Subtest	Communality	Reliability[a]	Specificity
Information	.72	.84	.12
Similarities	.72	.81	.09
Arithmetic	.57	.78	.21
Vocabulary	.75	.87	.12
Comprehension	.60	.77	.17
Digit Span	.34	.85	.51
Picture Completion	.56	.77	.21
Coding	.79	.79	.00
Picture Arrangement	.39	.76	.37
Block Design	.66	.87	.21
Object Assembly	.62	.69	.07
Symbol Search	.70	.76	.06
Mazes	.51	.70	.19

Source: D. Wechsler, 1991. Wechsler Intelligence Scale for Children—Third edition manual (p. 166). San Antonio, TX: The Psychological Corporation.
[a]These are averages of the reliabilities of eleven age groups.

sure. The criterion may be either an internal one, such as total test scores, or an external one. In the case of an intelligence test, the criterion against which test items are validated is typically external to that test itself, such as grades in school, scores on an academic achievement test, or chronological age.

Interpretation of test scores can be facilitated by comparing them with norms. A set of norms for a test consists of derived scores computed from the distribution of raw scores on the test obtained by a representative sample of the population for whom the test is targeted. Various sampling methods may be used to select a test standardization group, but stratified random sampling usually yields a sample that is most representative of the target population. In stratified random sampling, the population is divided into a series of subgroups or strata on one or more relevant variables, and a proportional sample is selected at random from each stratum.

The most common types of norms are age, grade, percentile, and standard score norms. Tables of age and grade norms give the average score on the test obtained by children of specified ages (in years and twelve monthly intervals) or grade levels (year and ten monthly intervals). A table of percentile norms lists the percentage of people in the standardization group who scored at or below each test score (or selected scores). Standard score norms—z scores, T scores, deviation IQs, stanines, etc.—are the only norms measured on an interval scale. Basic to all standard score norms are z scores; other standard scores are linearly transformed z scores.

Statistics such as measures of the average (mode, median, arithmetic mean) and variability (range, variance, standard deviation) of a set of grouped or ungrouped scores and measures of the relationships between two sets of scores (product-moment correlation coefficient) are used extensively in the analysis of test data. The correlation coefficient is especially useful in that it provides a numerical index of how reliable or valid a test is.

Reliability refers to the extent to which scores on a test are relatively free from errors of measurement. Four methods may be used to obtain information about a test's reliability: stability (test–retest reliability), equivalent forms (parallel forms reliability), stability and equivalence (test–retest on parallel forms), and internal consistency (Kuder-Richardson reliability or coefficient alpha).

A test is considered valid if it measures what it was designed to measure, but it need not be valid merely because it is reliable. Reliability is a necessary but insufficient condition for validity. Three types of validity, the use of which varies with the nature of the test, are content validity, criterion-related validity, and construct validity. Determining the content validity of a test entails an analysis of the test's content by an expert in the subject matter with which the test deals. In criterion-related validity, scores on a test are correlated with performance on an acceptable criterion of what the test is supposed to measure. Criterion data may be available immediately after the test is administered (concurrent validity) or some-time later (predictive validity). The use of a linear regression equation to predict criterion scores from test scores requires that the test and criterion measure be significantly related. Determining the construct validity of a test involves a network of research investigations to ascertain whether the test sorts people in the same way as known methods or procedures for observing the functioning of the particular psychological construct. Especially helpful in determining construct validity is an analysis of the correlations between scores on a test and other measures of the same construct (psychological variable) obtained by the same or different methods, as well as correlations of the test with measures of different constructs obtained by the same or different methods (multitrait–multimethod approach). Various values— efficiency, monetary, personal satisfaction and happiness, ethical, etc.—play a role in assessing the validity of a test and the selection of appropriate performance criteria.

Factor analysis is a statistical procedure designed to identify the common dimensions, or factors, underlying the scores of a large sample of people on a collection of measurements. Many different factor-analytic procedures are available, but all involve factoring a matrix of correlations or covariances among scores on a number of tests or other measures. The resulting factor matrix is then rotated to simplify the factor structure and facilitate interpretation of the factors. Factor interpretation involves an analysis of the loadings that indicate the weight each test has on each factor. Each test's communality, or the proportion of total variance on the test that is due to common factors and hence shared with the other tests, and the test's specificity, or the proportion of the total test variance not shared with the other tests, may also be referred to in the factor interpretation process.

QUESTIONS AND ACTIVITIES

1. How many of the following terms from this chapter can you identify?

accomplishment quotient	age norm
achievement	arithmetic mean

block (cluster) sampling	multitrait–multimethod approach
centroid method	normal curve equivalent (NCE)
coefficient alpha	norms
coefficient of equivalence	oblique factors
coefficient of stability	ordinal scale
communality	orthogonal factors
concurrent validity	Pearson product-moment coefficient
confidence interval	percentile
construct validity	percentile norms
content validity	percentile rank
convergent validity	predictive validity
criterion	principal axis method
criterion-related validity	random sample
deviation IQ (DIQ)	ratio IQ
discriminant validity	reliability
educational quotient	specificity
equivalent (parallel) forms method	speeded test
factor rotation	standard deviation
factor loadings	standard error of estimate
factor analysis	standard error of measurement
frequency distribution	standard scores
grade norm	standardization group
intelligence grade placements	stratified random sampling
internal consistency	T scores
interval scale	target population
intelligence quotient (IQ)	test battery
Kuder-Richardson formulas	test–retest method
median	validity
mode	variance

2. Suppose that Frank makes a raw score of 75 on a test having a mean of 60 and a standard deviation of 5, but he makes a raw score of 90 on another test having a mean of 85 and a standard deviation of 10. What are Frank's z scores, T scores, and stanine scores on each test?

3. Construct a frequency distribution of the following fifty IQ scores, using an interval of 3, and then prepare a table showing the percentile rank, z, T, and stanine scores corresponding to the IQ interval midpoints.

102	105	90	111	95	108	98	102	105	99	99	116	110
107	97	107	93	100	116	130	106	101	105	113	104	109
112	109	104	107	103	99	94	120	101	104	118	103	113
113	98	112	109	111	100	101	115	125	114	100		

4. The following table indicates whether each of twenty people answered each of ten items on a four-option multiple-choice group intelligence test right (+) or wrong (−). Total scores on the test are given in the extreme right column of the table. Compute the internal consistency reliability of the test, using Kuder-Richardson formulas 20 and 21 and coefficient alpha.

	Item										
Examinee	1	2	3	4	5	6	7	8	9	10	Score
1	+	+	+	+	+	+	+	+	+	+	10
2	+	+	−	+	+	+	−	+	+	+	8
3	+	−	+	+	−	+	−	+	+	+	7
4	−	+	+	+	+	+	−	+	+	−	7
5	−	−	+	+	+	+	+	+	−	+	7
6	−	+	−	+	+	+	+	−	+	+	7
7	+	−	+	−	+	−	+	−	+	+	6
8	+	+	−	+	+	+	+	−	−	−	6
9	+	−	+	−	−	+	−	+	+	+	6
10	+	+	−	+	−	+	+	−	+	−	6
11	−	+	−	+	−	+	−	+	+	−	5
12	+	−	+	−	+	−	−	+	+	−	5
13	+	−	+	−	−	+	+	−	−	−	4
14	−	+	−	+	−	+	−	−	+	−	4
15	−	−	−	+	−	−	+	−	+	−	3
16	−	−	+	−	−	+	−	+	−	−	3
17	+	−	−	−	−	−	−	+	−	+	3
18	−	−	−	−	−	+	+	−	−	−	2
19	−	+	−	−	−	−	+	−	−	−	2
20	−	−	−	−	−	+	−	−	−	−	1

5. Why are standard score norms better than age norms, grade norms, and percentile norms?
6. Compute the standard error of measurement of a test having a standard deviation of 5 and an equivalent forms reliability coefficient of .84. Use the computed value of the standard error of measurement to find the 95 percent and 99 percent confidence intervals for the true scores corresponding to obtained scores of 70, 80, and 90.
7. What is the standard error of estimate for predicting grade-point average (GPA) from an intelligence test if the standard deviation of the GPA is .5 and the correlation between test and GPA is .60? Interpret the result.
8. Describe the optimal procedure for standardizing a test.
9. What is the purpose of conducting a factor analysis of the scores on several tests? Do the results contribute to an understanding of the reliability or validity of the scores on the test?

SUGGESTED READINGS

Aiken, L. R. (1994). *Psychological testing and assessment* (8th ed., pp. 77–104). Needham Heights, MA: Allyn & Bacon.

Golden, C. J., Sawicki, R. F., & Franzen, M. D. (1990). Test construction. In G. Goldstein & M. Hersen (Eds.), *Handbook of psychological assessment* (2nd ed., pp. 21–40). New York: Pergamon Press.

Lyman, H. B. (1991). *Test scores and what they mean* (5th ed.). Englewood Cliffs, NJ: Prentice-Hall.

Messick, S. (1989). Meaning and values in test validation: The science and ethics of assessment. *Educational Measurement, 18*(2), 5–11.

Pagano, R. R. (1994). *Understanding statistics in the behavioral sciences* (4th ed.). St. Paul, MN: West.

Ree, M. J., & Earles, J. A. (1992). Intelligence is the best predictor of job performance. *Current Directions in Psychological Science, 1*, 86–89.

Chapter **3**

Test Administration, Scoring, and Interpretation

The purpose of this chapter is to provide a comprehensive overview of the administration, scoring, and interpretation of measures of intellectual abilities in general and to describe the preparation of psychological examination reports. Procedures for administering and scoring specific tests of intellectual abilities will be discussed in later chapters, and details that are omitted can be found in the manuals accompanying the tests.

STANDARDS FOR STANDARDIZED TESTS

No matter how carefully constructed and standardized a test may be, the results will be useless if it is not administered and scored properly. In fact, a *standardized test* is defined as one that is administered with standard directions and under standard conditions. The test must be scored as objectively as possible, and the results interpreted according to standard procedures.

The importance of having a set of guidelines for administering and scoring tests, and for interpreting and reporting test results, is recognized by all professional

organizations concerned with psychological testing. Such guidelines are incorporated in the *Standards for Educational and Psychological Testing*, a booklet
prepared by representatives of the American Educational Research Association, the
American Psychological Association, and the National Council on Measurement in
Education (1985). Also concerned with standards for administering, scoring, and
interpreting tests are the *Guidelines for Computer-Based Tests and Interpretations*
(American Psychological Association, 1986) and the *Principles for the Validation
and Use of Personnel Selection Procedures* (Society for Industrial and Organizational Psychology, Inc., 1987).

The proper use of psychological tests can be controlled to some extent by a
code of ethics to which professional testers and publishers subscribe. Both the
American Psychological Association (APA) and the American Personnel and Guidance Association (APGA) have ethical codes pertaining to test administration and
other psychological services. These codes cover many of the same matters of test
administration, standardization, reliability, and validity as the *Standards for Educational and Psychological Testing* (American Educational Research Association et
al., 1985). In particular, they stress the importance of considering the welfare of the
examinee or client and guarding against misuses of assessment instruments.

With regard to evaluation and assessment, the "Ethical Principles of Psychologists and Code of Conduct" (American Psychological Association, 1992) emphasizes
that evaluation and diagnosis should be provided only in a professional context by
trained, competent test users who administer appropriate psychometric instruments. Emphasis is also placed on the applications of scientific procedures for
designing and selecting tests and techniques that are appropriate for specified
populations, the thoughtful interpretation of test results, the careful use of test
scoring and interpretative services, the clear but sensitive explanation of assessment findings, and the need for maintaining test security.

The availability of high-quality psychometric instruments and a set of standards
or principles with which test publishers, distributors, and consumers are asked to
comply does not guarantee that these instruments will be administered and interpreted properly. The responsibility for using tests correctly lies with the test
administrators and interpreters themselves, a responsibility that has been increasingly recognized and accepted by professional psychologists. Unfortunately, the
skills and knowledge possessed by many counselors, clinicians, and other professionals are inadequate for administering certain instruments. Therefore, psychological examiners must be made aware of the limitations of their professional
qualifications, the necessity for further training, and the need to rely on other
professionals and up-to-date sources of information for assistance. Furthermore,
examiners must be able to make sound ethical judgments by being sensitive to the
needs of examinees, the institutions or organizations by which they are employed,
and society as a whole.

TEST ADMINISTRATION

Procedures for administering standardized tests depend on the type of test
(individual or group, verbal or performance, and so on) and the nature of the

examinees to whom the test must be administered (e.g., young or old, handicapped or nonhandicapped). Whatever the examinee's status may be, factors such as the extent of their preparation for the test, sophistication in test taking, motivation, anxiety, and feelings of fatigue or illness can affect test performance. Testing time and the number of individuals who can be tested simultaneously also vary with the age and self-sufficiency of the examinees. Young children require shorter testing periods and are tested in smaller groups than older children. Young or handicapped children usually require more attention and encouragement from the examiner than those who are older or not handicapped.

Examiner Characteristics and the Testing Situation

Because procedures for administering tests vary with the nature of the test and the examinees, the amount and type of training required by the examiner also depend on these factors. The particular test to be administered is frequently a matter of the examiner's preference. Many different instruments may be selected, depending on the purpose of the examination, the time allotted to it, and the characteristics of the examiner. Consequently, a well-prepared psychological examiner, whether employed by a school, a clinic, or in an organizational/industrial situation, should have a variety of tests available and be aware of their strengths and weaknesses as well as their usefulness and appropriateness in specific situations. The Non-Discriminatory Testing and Evaluation paragraph of the Education for All Handicapped Children Act (Public Law 94-142) requires that

> the tests and procedures used to evaluate a child's special needs must be racially and culturally non-discriminatory in both the way they are selected and the way they are administered, must be in the primary language or mode of communication of the child, and no one test or procedure can be used as the sole determinant of a child's educational program. (Children's Defense Fund, 1976, pp. 4–6)

In the case of a child or adult who is referred for testing from some outside agency or person (e.g., a physician or court judge), the tests and other diagnostic procedures that may be administered depend on the purpose of the referral or specific information requested by the referral source. For example, more detailed testing procedures may be required when the referral is concerned with the question of organic brain disorder or a personality disorder than when the only question is whether the child is mentally retarded. In any case, the examiner should make an effort to have the referral source specify the precise purpose of the referral and what questions concerning the examinee's abilities and behavior need to be answered.

Psychological examiners should be thoroughly familiar with the tests they administer and the kinds of individuals for whom the tests are appropriate. A greater degree of skill, involving more extensive training, is needed to administer individual than group tests and to administer tests to handicapped rather than nonhandicapped persons. The characteristics of a good examiner include not only a thorough knowledge of the test and the procedure for administering it, but also an appropriate attitude and style. The examiner should be warm and friendly, skilled in eliciting information from the person who is being examined, and in every way a *professional.* He or she should be authoritative without being authoritarian, appropriate in manner and dress, and in charge of the situation.

Although the skill and personality of the examiner are important in obtaining valid test scores, apparently neither the sex nor the race of the examiner has a consistently significant influence on performance (Graziano, Varca, & Levy, 1982; Jensen, 1980, p. 596ff.; Samuels, 1977; Sattler & Gwynne, 1982). Certain studies have found that female examiners elicit higher test scores than male examiners, but the findings are not consistent (Black & Dana, 1977; Bradbury, Wright, Walker, & Ross, 1975).

Well-prepared examiners—male and female, black and white—should be equally effective in test administration. An examiner's vocabulary and expressions should be appropriate to the age and educational level of the examinee, but not condescending or grammatically incorrect. Simple words and a nonthreatening manner, but not baby talk or childish mannerisms, are appropriate when testing young children.

Examiners should be aware of any physical handicaps or emotional problems of examinees and should make allowances and provisions for them. In administering a group test, it is best to assume a businesslike but friendly attitude. Even in a one-to-one testing situation, the relationship between examiner and examinee should not be overly personal or unprofessional.

It seems reasonable to suppose that a good relationship between examiner and examinee, a condition of *rapport*, would contribute to the latter's best performance on the test, but it is not essential to spend a great deal of time becoming acquainted. In a study of first and fifth graders, Irons (1981) found that the amount of time spent in establishing familiarity with the examiner had no significant effect on children's intelligence test scores.

Before the Test

Before administering an individual test it is customary to obtain the consent of the test taker or, in the case of a minor, the parents or guardian. As stated in the *Standards for Educational and Psychological Testing* (American Educational Research Association et al., 1985, p. 85):

> Informed consent should be obtained from test takers or their legal representatives before testing is done except (a) when testing without consent is mandated by law or governmental regulation (e.g., statewide testing programs); (b) when testing is conducted as a regular part of school activities (e.g., schoolwide testing programs and participation by schools in norming and research studies; or (c) when consent is clearly implied (e.g., application for employment or educational admissions). When consent is not required, test takers should be informed concerning the testing process.

The term *informed consent* in this standard is an agreement made by an individual or his or her legal representative with an agency or another person to permit use of test scores or other personal information for specified legal purposes. The requirement is usually satisfied by the signature of the examinee, a parent, or other legal representative on a standard form used by the school district or other agency. The form should clearly indicate the purposes of the testing, the uses that will be made of the obtained information, and the parent's or other guardian's rights and procedures for obtaining a copy of the report and an explanation of the results (Figures 3-1 and 3-2).

When a group test is to be administered, examinees should be informed well in advance when and where the test will be given and what sort of examination it will be. Conscientious examiners make it a point to be thoroughly familiar with the test and preferably even take the test or a portion of it themselves in order to understand the examinees' task more thoroughly. The examiner should study the directions for administration carefully in advance and review them just prior to administering the test. In addition, all testing materials, including answer sheets, booklets, pencils, and any other apparatus or objects needed for the test, should be checked carefully to make certain they are on hand.

A quiet, comfortable, well-lighted, and adequately furnished room should be reserved and a sign posted on the door indicating that testing is in progress. Appropriate restroom facilities and exits adequate for the size of the group being tested should be available. Special provisions (wheelchair ramps, wide doors, left-handed desks) must also be made for physically handicapped or physically different individuals.

I, _____ voluntarily give my consent to serve as a participant in a psychological examination conducted by _____. I have received a clear and complete explanation of the general nature and purposes(s) of the examination and the specific reason(s) why I am being examined. I have also been informed of the kinds of tests and other procedures to be administered and how the results will be used.

I realize that it may not be possible for the examiner to explain all aspects of the examination to me until it has been completed. It is also my understanding that I may terminate my participation in the examination at any time without penalty. I further understand that I will be informed of the results and that the results will be reported to no one else without my permission. At this time, I request that a copy of the results of this examination be sent to:

_____

_____

Examinee's Name	Signature of Examinee
Date	Signature of Examiner

FIGURE 3-1 **Form for Obtaining Informed Consent for a Psychological Examination.**

| Date Signed
Assessment
Plan is Received
Date IEP to be held | LOS ANGELES UNIFIED SCHOOL DISTRICT
Division of Special Education
ASSESSMENT PLAN AND PARENTAL CONSENT FOR ASSESSMENT | Procedural Safeguards
Due Process Procedures
( )Given ( )Mailed
To Parent on:

By: |

TO THE PARENT/GUARDIAN OF: _____   Date: _____

Birthdate: _____   _____   Primary Language: _____
      Mo.   Day   Yr.   School

English Proficiency_____   Measured by Instrument (Specify)_____   Date:_____

WE REQUEST YOUR CONSENT FOR ASSESSMENT OF YOUR SON/DAUGHTER WHO ( ) MAY BENEFIT FROM SPECIAL EDUCATION OR ( ) IS ALREADY RECEIVING SPECIAL EDUCATION AND ADDITIONAL ASSESSMENT IS NEEDED.

QUALIFIED PROFESSIONALS WHO MAY CONTRIBUTE TO THE MULTIDISCIPLINARY ASSESSMENT ARE INDICATED BELOW BY THEIR INITIALS AND TITLES SUCH AS PSYCHOLOGIST, RESOURCE SPECIALIST, PHYSICIAN, SPEECH SPECIALIST, ADAPTIVE P.E. TEACHER, EDUCATIONAL AUDIOLOGIST, SCHOOL NURSE/PHYSICIAN, SPECIAL EDUCATION TEACHER AND OTHERS. REPRESENTATIVE TYPES OF TESTS ARE LISTED ON THE BACK OF THIS PLAN.

PLEASE REVIEW THE PLAN AND INDICATE IN THE PARENT CONSENT SECTION BELOW WHETHER OR NOT YOU CONSENT TO THIS ASSESSMENT. IF YOU HAVE ANY QUESTIONS ABOUT THE PLAN OR THE PROCEDURAL SAFEGUARDS/DUE PROCESS PROCEDURES YOU RECEIVED WITH THE PLAN, PLEASE CONTACT:

                                                                   (   )
        NAME   TITLE   PHONE

PROPOSED SPECIAL EDUCATION ASSESSMENT PLAN

TYPE AND PURPOSE OF ASSESSMENT	ASSESSMENT RESPONSIBILITIES (Indicate Initials and Title)
ACADEMIC/PREACADEMIC ACHEIVEMENT - To assess basic reading skills and reading conprehension, mathematics calculation and reasoning, spelling, written expression and, if appropriate, pre-reading skills	
COGNITIVE LEVEL - To assess specific skills, learning rate and problem solving ability NO STANDARDIZED INTELLIGENCE (I.Q.) TESTS WILL BE GIVEN.	
COMMUNICATION/LANGUAGE FUNCTIONING - To measure the ability to understand, relate to and use language/speech clearly and appropriately	
SOCIAL/EMOTIONAL STATUS - To assess level of social maturity, ability to function independently and inter-personal skills	
MOTOR ABILITIES - To assess the coordination of body movements in large and small muscle activities	
MEDICAL - To assess general physical condition by a history and physical examination	
AUDIOLOGICAL ASSESSMENT - To measure the nature and degree of possible hearing loss.	
OTHER Purpose _____	

PARENT CONSENT FOR ASSESSMENT
PLEASE INDICATE BY A CHECK MARK AND YOUR SIGNATURE

1. ( ) I CONSENT TO THE ASSESSMENT PLAN

2. ( ) I DO NOT CONSENT TO THE ASSESSMENT PLAN

SIGNATURE _____   _____   (   )   (   )
             Parent/Guardian   Date   Home Phone   Work Phone

In addition, I wish to submit a written report(s) from the following person(s) who has evaluated my son/daughter:

_____   _____
         Name   Title

27 805B (Rev 6/88)   RETURN THE WHITE COPY AS INDICATED IN THE COVER LETTER. KEEP THE YELLOW COPY FOR YOUR RECORDS

STUDENT FILE COPY

FIGURE 3-2 Los Angeles Unified School District: Assessment Plan and Parental Consent Form for Assessment. (Reprinted by permission of the Los Angeles Unified School District.)

When testing groups in rooms equipped with public address systems for public announcements and fire drills, whenever possible these activities should be suspended during the test. Although research has shown that low-level noises or other minor disturbances do not greatly affect test performance, this is probably less true for younger than for older examinees (Trentham, 1975).

Whatever the reasons may be, when one is unprepared for a test it is tempting to try to avoid a poor mark by gaining improper access to answers or by other means deceiving or misrepresenting one's knowledge of the test material. Everyone knows that some people cheat, and some people believe that almost anyone cheats at some time. With respect to the frequency and circumstances of cheating, information on how often, under what circumstances, and by what means cheating on tests occurs can be empirically determined (Aiken, 1991).

According to the *Standards for Educational and Psychological Testing* (American Educational Research Association et al., 1985, p. 83), "reasonable efforts should be made to assure the validity of test scores by eliminating opportunities for test takers to attain scores by fraudulent means." For example, paying some attention to seating to minimize cheating during a test is necessary; seating examinees one seat apart or in such a way that cheating is made difficult is recommended. If possible, the seats should be desks or tables rather than arm chairs. At least one proctor in the case of small groups, and several proctors with large groups, should be on hand to assist in distributing and collecting test materials, to answer questions concerning procedure, and to discourage cheating and unruliness during a test. The need for a certain number of proctors and other procedures designed to guard against cheating is taken quite seriously in administering secure standardized tests such as the Scholastic Aptitude Test and the Graduate Record Examinations. *Secure tests*, each copy of which is assigned a serial number, are inventoried before and after administration and administered under conditions of close supervision (e.g., examinees must show proper identification) to make certain that the specific content of the test does not become generally known.

Not only the conveniences and accommodations of the physical context but psychological aspects of the environment, such as its familiarity, may also influence test performance. Strange or unfamiliar situations create a certain amount of tension or anxiety in almost anyone, and if the unfamiliarity of the situation and the resulting stress are great enough test scores may be lower than they would be in more familiar surroundings.

When scheduling a test, whether individual or group, the examiner should take into account not only the conditions of the testing environment but also other activities in which examinees usually engage at that time. Thus, it is unwise to schedule a test during lunchtime, playtime, or when other enjoyable activities usually take place, are being anticipated, or have recently occurred (e.g., immediately before or after a holiday). Furthermore, the testing period should seldom be longer than an hour when testing elementary school children or one and a half hours when testing secondary school students. In the case of preschool and primary children, thirty minutes is typically about as long as the examinees can remain attentive to an intelligence test. Therefore, longer tests such as the Wechsler

Preschool and Primary Scale of Intelligence—Revised (WPPSI-R) should probably be administered in two sessions.

During the Test

Individual testing should be conducted in a private room with only the examiner and examinee present; if necessary, one additional person, such as a parent or guardian, may be present. On both individual and group tests, directions concerning the method of presenting the test materials, the phrasing of the test questions, and the time limits for responding must be followed carefully. Test directions should be read slowly and clearly, after making certain that the examinees are paying attention. On an individual test, repeating or rephrasing questions may be permitted (the examiner should consult the test manual), but going beyond the directions printed in the manual is against the rules. As indicated in the *Standards for Educational and Psychological Testing* (American Educational Research Association et al., 1985, p. 83):

> In typical applications, test administrators should follow carefully the standardized procedures for administration and scoring specified by the test publisher. Specifications regarding instructions to test takers, time limits, the form of item presentation or response, and test materials or equipment should be strictly observed. Exceptions should be made only on the basis of carefully considered professional judgment, primarily in clinical applications.

Departure from the standard directions for administration given in the test manual results in a different task being presented to examinees than the test designers had in mind. Consequently, if the directions deviate from those given to the group on which the test was standardized (the *norm group*), examinees' scores may not have the same meaning as those of that group. The outcome will be the loss of a valuable frame of reference for interpreting scores.

Often more important than the physical environment in which a test is administered, particularly an individual test, is the psychological environment. For example, even a smile from the examiner occasionally provides enough encouragement to improve an examinee's test performance. The examiner should convey enough interest and warmth (*rapport*) to put the examinee at ease, while also convincing the examinee that he or she should respond honestly and to the best of his or her ability. This implies not only courtesy, patience, and acceptance, but also seriousness of purpose on the part of the examiner. Finally, the examiner should note and record the examinee's responses as unobtrusively as possible on the test record form.

Although examinations for general intelligence and specific cognitive abilities are not usually tape recorded, in certain cases electronic recording may be helpful if the consent of the examinee and/or his legal guardian has been obtained. For example, having another qualified examiner listen to the recording might be helpful in dealing with difficult cases. In addition, a recording can provide feedback to the examiner on his or her own performance (e.g., Were the test directions read properly? Does the examiner sound bored?).

Encouragement and positive reinforcement during the test may result in higher test scores and therefore yield a better index of *maximum performance*. For example, one research investigation of mentally retarded black children found that, compared with a nonreinforcement condition, both tangible reinforcements (candy) and culturally relevant social reinforcement (verbal praise such as "good work, young blood," "nice job, little brother," "good work, young soul") led to higher intelligence test scores in mentally retarded black children (Terrell, Terrell, & Taylor, 1981). In another study, giving verbal praise to black and white mentally retarded children for their responses to items on the Wechsler Intelligence Scale for Children—Revised resulted in higher scaled scores on five subtests, as well as higher Verbal, Performance, and Full Scale IQs (Saigh, 1981). Because failures on test items are rather common, praise for effort may be even more effective than praise or rewards for the results of effort (Sattler, 1988).

With respect to performance feedback, intelligence test manuals usually caution against giving too much information to examinees about how well they are doing while the test is in progress. Rather than informing a person as to whether he or she answered a test item correctly, it is recommended that the examiner tell the person that it is against the rules. It is advisable, however, to temper this statement with the reassurance that no one is expected to get every question right and that the examinee is performing satisfactorily and should keep trying to do his or her best.

Not only the examinee's mental abilities but also his or her feelings and attitudes can affect test performance. When administering an individual test, the examiner has a better opportunity to observe the examinee than in a group testing situation and is therefore more likely to detect low motivation, distractibility, and anxiety. Efforts can then be made to cope with these potentially debilitating influences or at least take them into account in interpreting test scores. On a group test, where personal interaction with every examinee is unlikely, the examiner is understandably more limited in observing low motivation or emotional disturbance.

Special Considerations and Circumstances

A test is typically a tension-provoking situation, and occasionally an examinee becomes quite upset. In this case the examiner needs to be sympathetic and understanding, as well as adept at handling the emotional disturbance. Testing very young, mentally disordered, physically handicapped, or culturally disadvantaged individuals also presents special problems of administration. The examiner is seldom prepared to handle every emergency that may occur (such as an epileptic seizure or a psychotic reaction), but experience in a variety of testing situations is important in developing the skills needed to cope with such problems.

Some flexibility is usually permitted in administering nonstandardized instruments and even certain standardized tests, but as recommended by the *Standards for Educational and Psychological Testing* (American Educational Research Association et al., 1985, pp. 83–84):

In school situations not involving admissions and in clinical and counseling applications, any modification of standard test administration procedures or scoring should be described in the testing reports with appropriate cautions regarding the possible effects of such modifications on validity.

The manual of administration for a test should make clear to what extent deviations from standard procedure are permissible and what effects such deviations may have on score interpretation.

Typically, relatively few variations from standard directions or procedure are permitted because their effects on test scores are not completely predictable. However, the examiner can usually take the following steps without seriously jeopardizing the meaning of the scores:

1. Allow sufficient practice on sample or practice items.
2. Provide the maximum time allotted for examinees to respond to the test material.
3. Use relatively shorter testing periods with very young and/or handicapped persons.
4. Watch out for fatigue and anxiety, and take them into account when interpreting the test results.
5. Be aware of and make provisions for visual, auditory, and other sensory and perceptual–motor deficits.
6. Do not try to force examinees to respond to test items when they repeatedly decline to do so.

Although the speed with which a person responds to a test question is often indicative of intellectual ability, speed of responding is also a personality characteristic. Some individuals, whether they know the answers or not, respond quickly and often impulsively to test items, whereas others are more reflective or slower in reacting. The importance of allowing sufficient time for responding and even encouraging examinees to delay responding was revealed in an investigation of sixty 8-year-old children (Walker, 1981). The Matching Familiar Figures Test was used to divide the children into two groups of thirty each, labeled "Reflectives" and "Impulsives." The children were tested on four subtests of the Wechsler Intelligence Scale for Children–Revised under two conditions of administration: normal delay and forced delay. No difference was found in the mean scores of the Reflectives under the two conditions, but the mean subtest scores of the Impulsives were higher under the forced delay condition than under the normal delay condition. Making impulsive children wait before responding improved their scores.

After the Test

After administering an individual test, the examiner should collect and secure all test materials. The examinee should be reassured concerning his or her performance, perhaps given a small reward in the case of a child, and returned to the appropriate place. In clinical testing, it is usually important to interview a parent or other person who has accompanied the examinee, perhaps both before and after the test. Some information on what will be done with the results and how they are to be used can be provided to the examinee and/or the accompanying party. The examiner will promise to report the results and interpretations to the proper person(s) or agency and to recommend what further action may be advisable.

Following administration of a group test, the examiner should collect the necessary materials (booklets, answer sheets, scratch paper, pencils, and so on). In the case of a standardized test, the booklets and answer sheets should be counted and collated and all other materials checked to make certain that nothing is missing. Only then are the examinees dismissed or prepared for the next activity and the answer sheets arranged for scoring.

Adaptive Testing by Computer

Computers have been used for many years to assist in the development of tests by determining norms, derived scores, and reliability and validity coefficients, and in conducting item analyses. Tests can also be administered by computer, as in *adaptive testing*. Adaptive testing works in the following manner. Applying an appropriate statistical model, a pool of test items scaled in terms of their difficulty levels, discrimination indexes, and percentage guessing indexes is assembled for administration. An estimate of the examinee's ability level determines which item(s) will be administered first; subsequent presentation of additional items is dependent on the examinee's responses to previous items. Testing continues until an estimate of error or level of accuracy in the examinee's responses reaches a specified level. Then the test score is determined not merely by counting the number of items that are answered correctly but by taking into account the difficulty level and other statistical characteristics of the items.

By making the decision concerning which items to administer contingent on the examinee's response(s) to the previous item(s), adaptive testing makes possible, with no loss of information and equal reliability and validity, administration of only a fraction of the number of items required by the traditional testing practice in which all examinees attempt every item. A disadvantage of adaptive testing is that examinees are not permitted to review and perhaps change their answers after making their initial choices.

So far the uses of adaptive testing in assessing general intelligence and special abilities have been limited, but Educational Testing Service, the U.S. Army, and various other organizations have experimented with the interactive, adaptive administration of ability tests, such as the Scholastic Aptitude Test (SAT), the Armed Services Vocational Aptitude Battery (ASVAB), and the Graduate Record Examination (GRE), by computer. Computer-based administration of the SAT and other college admissions, job qualification, and military selection tests has also been implemented at sites throughout the world. The Educational Testing Service's Computerized Placement Test, a computer-adaptive placement battery for assessing written communication, learning skills, and mathematical skills, became commercially available in the late 1980s. Currently, the use of graphics, modems, and other input–output devices such as voice encoders and decoders is being improved and expanded to increase the flexibility and ease with which computer-based tests can be administered.

In addition to the method (conventional, adaptive, and others) used to select items for a test, certain cautions concerning the equipment for presenting the test stimuli should be exercised in administering a test by computer. Six of the recommendations made in the *Guidelines for Computer-Based Tests and Interpretations* (American Psychological Association, 1986, pp. 11–12) are:

1. The environment in which the testing terminal is located should be quiet, comfortable, and free from distraction.
2. Test items presented on the display screen should be legible and free from noticeable glare.
3. Equipment should be checked routinely and should be maintained in proper working condition.
4. Test performance should be monitored, and assistance to the test taker should be provided, as is needed and appropriate.
5. Test takers should be trained on proper use of the computer equipment.
6. Reasonable accommodations must be made for individuals who may be at an unfair disadvantage in a computer testing situation.

TEST SCORING

Machines for scoring objective tests have been in use for most of this century, and the increased availability of computers since the 1950s has made test scoring much more rapid and flexible. The *Standards for Educational and Psychological Testing* (American Educational Research Association et al., 1985, p. 84) recommends that test-scoring services document the procedures they follow to ensure accurate scoring and to monitor and report scoring error rates. The *Standards* also recommends that whenever important decisions, such as those concerned with educational admissions or professional licensing, depend on test scores, examinees should be provided with a means of verifying their scores. Finally, corrected score reports should be distributed when errors in reporting are detected.

Computers have also made possible the automated interpretation of test scores. Computerized scoring and interpretation are not limited to group-administered, multiple-choice tests; programs have been devised for administering, scoring, and interpreting individually administered tests as well.

Despite the importance of computerized test scoring, the majority of individual intelligence tests are still scored by hand. Much of the scoring of responses to the items on these tests can be done while the test is being administered, but final scoring and the conversion of raw scores to norms (standard scores, intelligence quotients, etc.) should wait until the examinee has been dismissed. Scoring during the test must be done as unobtrusively as possible, and at no time should the scores be visible to the examinee. It is appropriate to say "Good," "Very good," and the like when an examinee makes a good effort, whether successful or not, but neither the score nor whether the answer was right should be revealed.

Human beings are not always entirely objective when scoring tests. Considering the fact that the scoring directions or guidelines for many items on tests such as the Stanford-Binet and Wechsler intelligence series are not completely clearcut, it is not surprising that a wide range of scores may be assigned to the same response. In an investigation of students' errors in administering and scoring the Wechsler Intelligence Scale for Children—Revised (WISC-R), Slate and Jones (1990) found that failure to record responses correctly, judgmental and mechanical errors in scoring, failure to question ambiguous responses, and generosity in scoring were common and difficult to eliminate without extensive training. One might hope that such errors would be restricted to inexperienced student examiners, but they are also made by experienced testers. Franklin and Stillman (1982) found, for example, that both item scoring and administration errors on subtests of the Wechsler Adult Intelligence Scale (WAIS) occurred in a sample of school psychologists and graduate students. Some errors were even serious enough to result in misplacement in special programs or incorrectly excluding individuals from those programs. In another investigation (Ryan, Prefitera, & Powers, 1983), nineteen professional psychologists and twenty graduate students scored a revised edition of the WAIS (the WAIS-R) that had been administered to two vocational counseling students. Scoring errors by both groups resulted in Verbal, Performance, and Full Scale IQ variations of 4 to 18 points.

Intelligence tests are rarely scored blindly, in the sense that the only information available to the scorer, other than the test responses, are the examinee's chronological age and sex and the date on which the test was given. More commonly, the scorer has enough additional information to form a distinct impression or attitude concerning the examinee. Unfortunately, this impression, which may be positive or negative, can affect the scoring of the test and lead to higher or lower scores than warranted.

The expectations of scorers, whether they consider the examinee to be bright or dull, may also affect scores on intelligence tests. Sattler and his coauthors (Sattler, Hillix, & Neher, 1970; Sattler & Wingit, 1970) found that student scorers tended to assign more credit when they were told that the test takers were bright than when told they were dull. Nevertheless, the halo effect of giving higher scores to examinees who are perceived as or reported to be bright is less common when the tests are scored by the examiners themselves and when the scorers or examiners are more experienced testers (Schroeder & Kleinsasser, 1972; Sneed, 1976).

With respect to the influence of the scorer's knowledge of the ethnic group membership of the examinee, the findings are mixed. In a carefully designed study of the Stanford-Binet protocols of examinees ranging from 5 to 8 years of age, the effects on obtained IQs of knowing the examinee's ethnic group were found to be nonsignificant (Mishra, 1983). These findings are consistent with the results of the great majority of studies showing that the race of the examiner has an insignificant effect on the intelligence test scores of black and white children (Costello & Dickie, 1970; Sattler & Gwynne, 1982).

TEST INTERPRETATION AND REPORTING

A substantial amount of training is needed to interpret the results of any intelligence test, and especially an individual test. Not only must the examiner consider the subscores, the overall scores, and their norm equivalents, but this information must be combined with the results of behavioral observations and interviews with the examinee and other significant persons. Consequently, the examiner should not only be proficient in administering the test(s) but also alert and sensitive. Because these skills cannot be attained without considerable training, in most states a psychological examiner is required to be licensed or certified as a school psychologist, a counseling psychologist, or a clinical psychologist in order to administer individual intelligence tests. Improper practice, leading to a violation of the ethical code of the American Psychological Association, can result in revocation of the license or certificate.

Observing and Interviewing

Important information that serves as a frame of reference in interpreting the results of a psychological examination can be obtained from observations and interviews. Observations made in testing situations are usually uncontrolled, quickly recorded notes of incidents or impressions, but the examiner should be careful to differentiate between the actual observed behavior and the interpretation of that behavior. The ability to make accurate observations is a skill acquired only by experience, and experience teaches that observations should be made and recorded as unobtrusively as possible. Clearly one should not stare at the examinee or interviewee in a calculating way or remain coldly aloof while watching his or her every move. It is also important to remember that observing is a two-way street, an interactive process in which the person being observed is also observing the observer and adjusting his or her behavior accordingly.

Because interviewing is a complex interpersonal skill that is to some extent a function of the personality of the interviewer, effective interviewing, like accurate observation, cannot be easily taught. Attending to the following suggestions can, however, improve one's interviewing skills. Professional interviewers are usually friendly but neutral, impartial, and not prying in responding to the interviewee. In diagnostic interviews designed to determine the causes and correlates of a person's disability or other problems, it is recommended that the interviewer:

- Convey a feeling of interest and warmth (rapport).
- Try to put the interviewee at ease.
- Assure the interviewee of confidentiality of the interview.
- Encourage the interviewee to express his or her thoughts and feelings freely.
- Adjust the questions to the cultural and educational background of the interviewee.
- Listen without overreacting emotionally.
- Be courteous, patient, and accepting.

- Take notes or make a recording as inconspicuously as possible.
- Attend not only to what is said but also to how it is said.

The Psychological Report

Psychological evaluation is often prompted by a referral from an agency or person, and as such there is usually an accompanying referral question or several questions: Is this person mentally retarded? Is this person brain damaged? What are the chances that this person will succeed in a certain educational or vocational program? What are the chances that a specified therapeutic intervention will be effective with this person? In such instances the primary goal of the report is to answer the referral question. Whether or not there is a formal, specific referral question, the overall goals of an intelligence examination include: (1) educational selection, classification, placement, or remediation; (2) diagnosis of behavioral or organic disorders; (3) determination of vocational competency; and (4) research on cognitive abilities. Whatever the purposes and goals of the examination may be, some form of written report of the findings is usually required.

The content and style of a psychological report vary with its purposes, the readers for whom it is intended, and the background and theoretical orientation of the preparer. The outline given in Figure 3–3 is representative. Perhaps the most important part of the report is the "Recommendations" section, because this is the end result of all the evaluating and diagnosing. If the recommendations are not sound and sensitive, the entire process of psychological evaluation and the time and efforts of many people will have been wasted.

An example of a report of a comprehensive intellectual evaluation is given in Report 3–1. The recommendations given at the end of the report are an illustration of "intelligent testing," to use Kaufman's (1994) term. An intelligent tester organizes and interprets the examinee's specific strengths and weaknesses and translates this information into appropriate suggestions for intervention.

In preparing a report of a psychological examination, the writer should keep clearly in mind the questions that need to be answered about the cognitive and personality functioning of the examinee, including dynamics, development, and probable outcomes (prognosis). The examinee's characteristics and their interrelationships should be described as fully and specifically as possible, avoiding vague generalizations, stereotypes, and banalities. In particular, stigmatizing or uninformative categories, such as "moron," "antisocial," or "underachiever," should be avoided. As indicated in the *Standards for Educational and Psychological Testing* (American Educational Research Association et al., 1985, p. 86):

> When score reporting includes assigning individuals to categories, the categories chosen should be based on carefully selected criteria. The least stigmatizing labels, consistent with accurate reporting, should always be assigned.

In preparing a psychological report it is also important to have a theory of personality or behavior, or at least some framework, to serve as a basis for interpreting the results of the examination.

Name of Examinee _____

Age _____ Birth Date _____ Education _____

Examiner _____

Place of Examination _____ Date _____

Tests Administered. List the names, including forms and levels, of all tests and inventories that were administered.

Referral and Background Information. Why was the examinee referred for psychological testing? What was the purpose of the referral, and what person or facility made it? What background information relevant to the case was obtained from other sources (school records, interviews, etc.)? Give the examinee's own story, as well as that of other observers if available. Describe the examinee's physical and psychological history and characteristics, educational and employment situation. In the case of children in particular, information on the home and family (social status, characteristics of parents, siblings, etc.) is important. Serious sensory or psychomotor handicaps, as well as the presence of emotional disorder, should also be noted.

Appearance and Behavioral Characteristics. Describe the appearance and behavior of the examinee during the examination. Describe the examinee's characteristics, his or her approach to the tasks, level of motivation and emotionality, and any other factors that might have influenced the results. What behaviors on the part of the examinee were symptomatic of particular physical, cognitive, or affective conditions or characteristics?

Test Results and Interpretations. Give a detailed description of the results of the tests or other instruments administered and how they may be interpreted. If the examiner is interpreting the results according to a particular theory of personality or behavior, make certain that the reader understands the language and assumptions of that theory. Be as specific and individualized as possible in interpreting the results.

Conclusions and Recommendations. Describe the conclusions (descriptive, dynamic, diagnostic) stemming from the observational, interview and standardized or unstandardized test data. What recommendations are warranted by the results? Include appropriate interpretative cautions, but don't "hedge" or deal in generalities. Additional psychological assessment (be specific), neurological or other medical examinations, counseling or psychotherapy, special class placement and training, vocational rehabilitation and institutionalization are among the recommendations that might be made. If a handicap or disability exists, is it remediable?

_____

Name and Signature of Examiner

FIGURE 3–3 Format of a Psychological Examination Report.

Reporting Style

A report of a psychological examination should be written in a succinct, clear style that is comprehensible to the reader. Unfortunately, many psychological reports are too abstract, ambiguous, overgeneralized, awkward in wording, and go beyond the objective results. A report is of little value if it is not understood or not read by persons who can use the information to help make decisions about the examinee's life and well-being.

The aim of psychological reporting is efficient communication of the results of tests and other instruments, as well as observational and interview findings. Thoughtful writers always keep their potential readers in mind, attempting to bridge the gap between the mind of the writer and the minds of the readers in the most straightforward manner. Consequently, wordiness, alliterations, poetic expressions, mixed metaphors, and other circumlocutions or distractions are inappropriate. Colloquialisms, clichés, and vulgar expressions are also bad form, as is jargon. A basic rule of professional communication is that if there is more than one way to say something, one should always choose the simplest way. This does not mean that only a terse, telegraphic style of writing is acceptable. It is possible to write economically but interestingly, avoiding abrupt transitions and choppy wording.

Every well-structured paragraph in an integrated report contains a topic sentence and one or more additional statements elaborating on the theme. As in the case of each paragraph, the report as a whole is well integrated; the writing flows or glides from paragraph to paragraph in an organized, goal-oriented manner. The writer knows where he or she is going and communicates this to the reader. Jumping from topic to topic—within or between paragraphs—is avoided, as are misspellings, grammatical errors, and other irregular, nonstandard constructions.

Computer-Based Reports

Psychological reports prepared by computers have become quite popular in recent years. The first computer test interpretation programs were developed at the Mayo Clinic, the Hartford Institute of Living, and the University of Alabama during the early 1960s (Glueck & Reznikoff, 1965; Swenson & Pearson, 1964; Rome et al., 1962). These programs were designed to score, profile, and interpret responses to the Minnesota Multiphasic Personality Inventory (MMPI). Subsequently, more complex programs for automated interpretation of the MMPI and other measures of personality and mental abilities became available.

Today a variety of organizations provide computer test scoring and interpretation services and market microcomputer software for interpreting intelligence tests such as the Stanford-Binet and the Wechsler series. A sample report generated by one computer package is shown in Report 4–1. In addition to providing a printout of standard scores, score confidence intervals, and tests of significance of the differences among scores, interpretative verbal statements are made in computer-based test reports. It should be emphasized that a computer-based report is not

Report 3–1

Psychoeducational Evaluation

Confidential
For Professional Use Only

Name: John Johnson	**School**: Center Elementary
C.A. 8–9	**Grade**: 2
Date of Testing: Nov. 9	**Examiner**: Jamey Roy

Tests Administered. Wechsler Intelligence Scale for Children—Revised (WISC-R), Kaufman Assessment Battery for Children (K-ABC)

Referral and Background Information.   John was referred for testing by his teacher, who is concerned by his lack of progress in second grade and the extreme anxiety he exhibits when called upon to speak in class. He is in the average group in reading after having repeated first grade. He is repeating the same reader this year and there appears to be very little carryover. Skills development tests indicate specific problems with sequencing and drawing conclusions. His teacher reports seeing "concern in his eyes." He is reported to be quite artistic, aggressive with other kids, and "squirmy—off in his own world." The teacher indicated that he does not daydream when doing independent work, only when she is giving directions. Self-esteem is a concern of the parents as well as of his teacher. Mr. and Mrs. Johnson feel this may be caused in part by his repeating the first grade. John has two sisters, ages 6 and 14.

A review of the cumulative records indicate that all his teachers have been concerned not only about his reading but about his poor work habits and use of class time as well. He has participated in remedial reading programs the past 2 years, but with little reported success. His Stanford Achievement Test percentile ranks in May of this calendar year for reading, mathematics, and listening were 56, 30, and 38, respectively. The reading percentile showed an increase from the 25th percentile in May of 1987. Mathematics was not listed as a problem area on the referral or in past conference notes, and he is reported to be doing satisfactorily in the average group.

Appearance and Behavioral Characteristics.   John is a handsome 8½-year-old Caucasian male with dark hair and brown eyes. He is neat in appearance and of average build. Rapport was easily established and maintained during the testing sessions. The examiner has had numerous occasions to interact with John and his entire class in group guidance sessions. He stated that he liked mathematics best and reading least of all his subjects. As an icebreaker and to get some indication of his feelings toward himself and his family, he was asked to draw his family. He spent 16 minutes absorbed in the task. His drawings were appropriate, but he erased many times, appearing to be quite perfectionistic.

John exhibited much more confidence on items that did not require him to give a verbal response. His body posture and facial expression visibly altered when response requirements changed from a motor to a verbal one. He was quick to give up when verbal responses were called for, and he did not respond to encouragement. He seldom gave incorrect verbal responses; rather, he gave no responses. He was eager to attempt tasks requiring a motor response. He frequently asked for reinforcement in the form of questions such as "Did I get it right?" "Are they in the right order?" and so on. The most verbalizing he did was on a task requiring him to complete some mazes. He encouraged himself on these and even displayed a sense of humor after attempting the last one by saying, "Whew! I sure hope there's no number 10."

Test Results and Interpretation. John was given the WISC-R and the K-ABC. On the WISC-R he obtained a Full Scale IQ of 93, placing him in the Average range of intellectual functioning and at the 32nd percentile for children his age. The chances are 90 percent that his true Full Scale IQ is in the 88–98 range. On the K-ABC he earned a Mental Processing Composite Standard Score (MPC) of 97 ± 6 (with 90% confidence), which also places him in the Average range.

On the WISC-R, John's Performance IQ of 104 ± 7 indicates average abilities when he expresses himself by manipulating nonverbal concrete materials, whereas his Verbal IQ of 86 ± 6 reveals below-average abilities when he is required to given verbal response to oral questions. On the K-ABC, John obtained an Achievement standard score of 88 ± 4, indicating below-average success on tasks that rely heavily on acquired knowledge and school-related skills. This score is nine points lower than his score on the MPC, supporting the low Verbal and high Performance profile on the WISC-R.

On the K-ABC, John obtained an average to high-average range score of 109 ± 7 on the Simultaneous Processing Scale (73rd percentile), while receiving a well-below-average to below-average range score of 80 ± 8 on the Sequential Processing Scale (ninth percentile). This significant difference suggests much better functioning when integrating many stimuli at once than when manipulating one stimulus at a time in serial fashion. This pattern was also evidenced by the WISC-R. On both intelligence tests, John performed much better on tasks demanding usage of several stimuli, such as finding the missing part of a picture, assembling several identical triangles into an abstract pattern to match a model, and placing photographs of an event in chronological order (86th percentile on the average) than he did on tasks

(continued)

Report 3–1

(*Continued*)

requiring sequential processing of information such as repeating digits in the same order presented, touching a series of silhouettes of common objects in the same sequence as the examiner said the names of the objects, and performing a series of hand movements in the same sequence as the examiner performed them (17th percentile). Many of these tasks also indicate a weak, generalized short-term memory, as does a low score on a task asking him to rapidly copy abstract symbols paired with numbers. On this last task, John was unable to memorize the pattern quickly, although he could reproduce the simple designs motorically. John's weakness in sequential processing and short-term memory may be an answer to his poor math and listening scores on standardized achievement tests. In these testing sessions, he had a difficult time solving oral arithmetic problems with and without visual cues. Virtually all of John's lower scores are greatly influenced by feelings of anxiety. This is certainly consistent with the "concern in his eyes" reported by the teacher and the behaviors observed by the examiner. John's high level of anxiety could well have depressed many of his scores.

    Summary and Recommendations.   John is an 8-year-old male who was referred for testing by his second-grade teacher, who is concerned by his lack of progress in second grade and the extreme anxiety he exhibits in class. He repeated first grade. He scored in the average range of intellectual functioning on both the WISC-R, with a Full Scale IQ of 93, and the K-ABC with an MPC of 97. John's ability to deal with verbal comprehension and school-related tasks, as shown with a Verbal IQ on the WISC-R of 86 and a K-ABC Achievement Standard Score of 88, are significantly lower than his ability to

---

necessarily better than, or even as good as, a report prepared by a professional psychologist. Because of the shortcomings of many computer-based test interpretation programs, in the future it will probably be necessary to arrange for something like an official "seal of approval" for these programs.

Informed Consent and Confidentiality

    In recent years there has been a great deal of concern about improper disclosure of test data, especially data identified by the names of examinees. The expanding use of computers and associated data banks has increased the need for

express his intelligence through manipulation of nonverbal concrete materials in a holistic manner. This is evidenced by his Performance IQ of 104 on
the WISC-R and his Simultaneous Processing Standard Score of 109 on the
K-ABC. His ability to deal with stimuli in a serial fashion is significantly below
his simultaneous abilities and is shown in his Sequential Processing Standard
Score of 80. John's feelings of anxiety were clearly evident throughout the
testing sessions.

Recommendations are as follows:

1. Use teaching materials that John, a simultaneous learner, can see and
   manipulate. His performance is best when visual integration of stimuli is
   required and verbal responses are not demanded.
2. Keep instruction short and review instruction over time in an effort to
   accommodate his memory difficulty.
3. John's feelings of anxiety, especially toward verbalization, need to be
   addressed.
   a. The school counselor might wish to include him in some individual
      and group sessions to deal with his anxiety. Play therapy using sand
      and clay may be a good choice for him. In a group, requiring him to
      verbalize should be increased as gradually as possible.
   b. His teachers should be sensitive to his feelings and try to let his re-
      sponses be as nonverbal as possible until he is more comfortable.
   c. Oral reading in class should be kept to a minimum.
   d. Praise of any verbal efforts should be low-key and sincere.
4. His academic progress should be closely monitored. If he does not begin
   to perform in a solidly average manner, he might need to be considered for
   some remedial help in a small group setting.

SOURCE: Reprinted with permission from Kaufman, A. S., & Ishikuma, T. (1993).
Intellectual and achievement testing. In T. H. Ollendick & M. Hersen (Eds.), *Handbook of child and adolescent assessment* (pp. 203–205). Boston: Allyn & Bacon.

vigilance in ensuring that test scores maintained in electronic files in particular are
protected against improper disclosure. As indicated by the *Standards for Educational and Psychological Testing* (American Educational Research Association et
al., 1985, p. 85):

> Test results identified by the names of individual test takers should not be
> released to any person or institution without the informed consent of the test
> taker or an authorized representative unless otherwise required by law. Scores
> of individuals identified by name should be made available only to those with a
> legitimate, professional interest in particular cases.

Not only do examinees have a legal right of access to the findings in their own examination reports, but they can arrange for transmittal of their scores to educational, clinical, or counseling agencies for any appropriate purpose:

> In educational, clinical, and counseling applications, when test scores are used to make decisions about individuals, the affected person or legal representative should be able to obtain transmittal of this test score and its interpretation for any appropriate use. (American Educational Research Association et al., 1985, p. 86)

At the same time, every effort must be made to maintain confidentiality of the scores and other personal information. The Family Educational Rights and Privacy Act of 1974 specifies, for example, that test results and other student records maintained by educational institutions that are recipients of federal funds can be made available in a personally identifiable way to other people only with the written consent of the student or his or her parents. This act also permits parents and school personnel with a "legitimate educational interest" to review student records, as does Public Law 94-142 in the case of handicapped children.

Consultations and Conferences

A written report is only one way in which the results of a psychometric evaluation are communicated to those who have a legitimate right to know. Parent–teacher and parent–counselor conferences in the school situation and clinical-case conferences or consultations in mental health contexts may occur before and after a psychological examination. When conducting a posttesting conference with a person who is unsophisticated in psychological testing, such as a typical parent, the counselor should describe, in language appropriate to the listener, the test results and whatever conclusions can reasonably be drawn from them. In general, qualitative rather than quantitative descriptions and interpretations should be employed. The purpose and nature of the tests, why these particular instruments were selected, and the limitations of the tests and results should also be discussed. In describing the results of an intelligence test, it is particularly important to dispel the myth that an IQ is a fixed, indelible measure of cognitive ability or worth that the examinee is stuck with for the rest of his or her life. It is advisable to report descriptive categories of intelligence rather than numerical IQs. If numbers must be reported, it is best to provide a range of values (a 68 percent or 95 percent confidence interval) for a scaled score or IQ rather than a single number.

When reporting and explaining test results to examinees and/or their parents, a counselor should make certain that facilities for counseling persons who become angry or otherwise emotionally upset during the session are available. In any event, the consultation involves a discussion of options and decisions—for treatment remediation, rehabilitation, or other interventions—and information on referral sources will be provided. Following the consultation, the examiner sends a copy of the examination report to the parents or other responsible individuals as well as the appropriate agency (school, social service department, and so forth). The examiner also retains a copy of the test protocol and the written report, as well as any notes from observations and interviews (American Educational Research Association et al., 1985).

Case Study

A complete case study requires more than the administration of psychological tests, an interview, and a series of objective observations of the person being evaluated. Details of the background and other characteristics are obtained from the examinee and significant other persons; follow-up data are also collected over a period of time. Information in all of the following categories may be obtained in a case study:

- *The family*: persons in the home, home attitudes
- *The culture*: cultural group, cultural deviation and conflict
- *Medical history*: medical examinations, physical development, physical conditions, sex development
- *Developmental history*: prenatal period and birth, early developmental signs, cognitive development, language development, emotional development, social development
- *Educational history*: school progress, educational achievement, school adjustment, educational aspirations and plans
- *Economic history*: for older children and adults, occupation, occupational history, vocational plans and ambitions
- *Legal history*: delinquencies, arrests
- *The person's life*: life routines, interests, hobbies, recreations, fantasy life, sex life, social adjustments

This information is then combined with the psychometric results, and a detailed report of the findings and recommended treatments or other intervention procedures is prepared.

SUMMARY

Psychological and educational tests should be administered according to standard directions, scored as objectively as possible, and interpreted according to available norms and other systematically obtained information and procedures. Sections of the *Standards for Educational and Psychological Testing* (American Educational Research Association et al., 1985) provide guidelines for test administration, scoring, and interpretation that should be followed by people and organizations concerned with marketing and using psychological tests.

In addition to cognitive abilities, numerous personal and environmental circumstances can affect test scores. Whether an individual or group test is administered, the responsibility for controlling many of these factors rests squarely on the shoulders of the psychological examiner. The examiner is responsible for being thoroughly familiar not only with the test and procedures for administering it but also with the characteristics and behavior of the age-, social, and cultural group to which the examinee belongs. Furthermore, the examiner must make certain that the testing conditions are conducive to the best performance of the examinees. Among these conditions are a comfortable physical and psychological testing environment that is free from unnecessary distractions. The examiner's behavior during the test should be professional, cordial, and helpful. Other characteristics of the examiner, such as his or her ethnicity and sex, are less important than experience and professionalism in test administration.

A psychological examiner needs to make many preparations before administering a test. In addition to studying the test directions carefully and making certain that all test materials (booklets, answer sheets, pencils, stopwatches) are ready and in good working order, arrangements must be made for a suitable room, desks or chairs, and the possibility of unexpected disturbances such as fire alarms, announcements over an intercom, and problems with examinees. On group tests, enlisting the help of a sufficient number of proctors also needs to be attended to.

During the test the examiner is alert but skillful in interacting with the examinee(s). The test directions are read slowly and clearly, but the examiner does not go beyond what is permitted according to the test manual. Although some scoring of an individual test can take place while it is being administered, examinees are not permitted to see their scores or, in most instances, even be told whether their answers are right or wrong.

Although it is appropriate to encourage examinees to do their best and to give verbal reinforcement or praise to them on occasion, it is advisable to praise effort rather than correct responses. Furthermore, except under very special circumstances (such as when conducting research or testing very difficult children), candy and other physical rewards should not be given for performance on standardized tests. The examiner should be alert to sensory or motor handicaps and signs of fatigue or illness on the part of the examinee. Such circumstances, together with any deviations from standard testing procedure, must be carefully noted and reported. It is particularly important with young and/or physically handicapped children to be encouraging but patient and to provide sufficient time for them to respond.

After the examination is over, the examiner needs to leave the examinee in a good frame of mind and to return him or her to the appropriate place. When testing a child, the parent or guardian may be interviewed to supply background information for interpreting the child's scores. The responsible individual will be told when a report on the test results can be expected and what will be done with the findings. Arrangements for a posttesting conference and other follow-up procedures can be made at this time.

Although adaptive testing with a computer depends more on a machine than a human examiner, it is not completely examiner independent. Adaptive testing is more efficient than conventional testing because fewer test items are usually presented. The questions asked are dependent on the estimated ability and the answers given by the examinee to previous questions. Consequently, the examinee's rate of progress through the test depends on his or her own competencies.

Standardized tests can be scored by machine, but most individual intelligence tests are still scored by hand. Although group intelligence tests are completely objective in terms of their scoring, many answers to individual intelligence test items must be evaluated in a semiobjective manner. Consequently, scoring individual intelligence tests requires substantial training. Additional information about the examinee, which may be obtained from observations, interviews, or other reports and tests, can affect the manner in which a particular response to a test item is scored.

Interpreting the results of an intelligence test is even more subjective than the scoring process. Score interpretation takes into account direct behavioral information obtained from observing the examinee and background data obtained by interviewing the examinee and other significant persons (e.g., parents or guardian). A description of this information, with the test results, forms the basis of a psychological test report. Identifying data, the reason for referral, observational and interview findings, and test results and interpretations should all be included in the report of a psychological examination. Another important section of the report consists of conclusions and recommendations for intervention (remedial treatment or institutionalization, for example). An even more detailed report is necessary when conducting a case study of an individual. In preparing the report of a psychological examination or case study, the writer should keep clearly in mind the purposes of the examination or case study and the needs and comprehension level of the persons for whom the report is intended.

As computer technology and software have become more sophisticated and less expensive, computer-based reports of a variety of psychological tests have become more popular. Among the individual intelligence tests that can be scored and interpreted by computer are the Stanford-Binet Intelligence Scale-IV, the Wechsler Adult Intelligence Scale—Revised, the Wechsler Intelligence Scale for Children—Third Edition, and shorter instruments such as the Slosson Intelligence Test.

Pretest and posttest conferences involving the psychological examiner and other concerned individuals (parents, teachers, school authorities) are held to plan the assessment procedure, describe and discuss the results, and make decisions concerning what action should be taken in the light of the test result and posttest consultations. Informed consent of the parents, the guardian, or other legal representatives must be obtained not only to administer an individual intelligence test and certain other psychological assessment instruments but also to use the obtained information in a specified way.

QUESTIONS AND ACTIVITIES

1. Identify the following terms discussed in this chapter:

adaptive testing	norm group
halo effect	rapport
informed consent	secure tests
maximum performance	standardized test

2. Interview any one of the following professional persons concerning his or her activities and in particular what intelligence tests, if any, the person has administered as one of those activities.

> school psychologist
> school counselor
> clinical psychologist in private practice
> clinical psychologist in an organizational or institutional setting
> counseling psychologist (other than in school setting)
> personnel psychologist or other test administrator in a business or industrial setting

3. Most departments of psychology and education keep on file materials for administering individual and group intelligence tests. In the case of a group intelligence test, these materials include test booklets, answer sheets, scoring keys, manuals, and perhaps other interpretive materials. Using an outline such as the following, prepare a review of a group intelligence test. Wherever possible, you should fill in this outline from information obtained by reading the test manual and examining the test itself. Wait until you have completed your own reviews before consulting published reviews of the test in the *Mental Measurements Yearbooks*, *Test Critiques*, or other sources.

    Content. List the title author(s), publisher, date and place of publication, forms available, type of test, and cost. Give a brief description of the sections of the test, the kinds of items of which the test is composed, and the mental operations or characteristics the test is supposed to measure. Indicate how the test items were selected and whether the construction procedure or theory on which the test is based is clearly described in the manual.

    Administration and Scoring. Describe any special instructions, whether the test is timed, and, if so, the time limits. Give details concerning scoring: as a whole, by sections or parts, and so on. Indicate whether the directions for administration and scoring are clear.

    Norms. Describe the group(s) (demographic characteristics, size, and so on) on which the test was standardized and how the samples were selected (systematic, stratified random, cluster, etc.). What kinds of norms are reported in the test manual or technical supplements? Does the standardization appear to be adequate for the recommended uses of the test?

    Reliability. Describe the kinds of reliability information reported in the manual (internal consistency, parallel forms, test–retest, and so on). Are the nature and sizes of the samples on which reliability information is reported adequate with respect to the stated uses of the test?

    Validity. Summarize the available information on the validity (content, predictive, concurrent, construct) of the test given in the manual. Is the validity information satisfactory in terms of the stated purposes of the test?

    Summary Comments. Give a summary statement of the design and content of the test, and comment briefly on the adequacy of the test as a measure of what it was designed to measure. Does the manual provide satisfactory descriptions of the design, content, norms, reliability, and validity of the test? What further information and/or data are needed to improve the test and its uses?

4. Obtain a matrix of intercorrelations between a selected group of intelligence tests or between the subtests constituting a particular individual or group test. Such matrices may be found in the manuals accompanying specific tests and in journal articles or other reports dealing with the tests. Perform a factor analysis of the data using one of the

available statistical programs at your college or university computing center (SPSS/PC+, SAS, BMDP, etc.). Alternatively, you may obtain a computer printout of the results of a factor analysis of a set of intelligence test scores from your instructor. In either case, you will need to enlist the help of your instructor or another knowledgeable person to interpret the results of the factor analysis and rotation.

5. Examine the *Reader's Guide to Periodical Literature* and the *New York Times Index*, and other popular media sources, for the past year or two and record on note cards every reference to intelligence or intelligence testing that you can find. Draw appropriate conclusions concerning the nature of the articles about intelligence and intelligence testing that appear in the popular magazines and newspapers. What issues or other matters pertaining to the topics of intelligence and intelligence testing are discussed most frequently in the articles?

6. Prepare a short paper on "Intelligence Testing and the Law" or "Legal Aspects of Intelligence Testing," including a discussion of legal statutes pertaining to the use of intelligence tests in education, business and industry, clinical and mental institutions, government, and other organizations. Obviously, appropriate library sources should be consulted before beginning the paper.

SUGGESTED READINGS

Aiken, L. R. (1980). Problems in testing the elderly. *Educational Gerontology, 5*, 119–124.

Airasian, P. W., & Terrasi, S. (1994). Test administration. In T. Husén & T. N. Postlethwaite (Eds.), *International encyclopedia of education* (2nd ed., Vol. 9, pp. 6311–6313). New York: Wiley.

American Psychological Association. (1992). Ethical principles of psychologists and code of conduct. *American Psychologist, 47*, 1597–1611.

Franklin, M. R., & Stillman, P. L. (1982). Examiner error in intelligence testing: Are you a source? *Psychology in the Schools, 19*, 563–569.

Graziano, W. G., Varca, P. E., & Levy, J. C. (1982). Race of examiner effects and the validity of intelligence tests. *Review of Educational Research, 52*, 469–498.

Groth-Marnat, G. (1990). The psychological report. In *Handbook of psychological assessment* (2nd ed., pp. 395–443). New York: Wiley.

Lautenschlager, G. J., & Flaherty, V. L. (1990). Computer administration of questions: More desirable or more social desirability? *Journal of Applied Psychology, 75*, 310–314.

Sandoval, J., & Irvin, M. G. (1990). Legal and ethical issues in the assessment of children. In C. R. Reynolds & R. W. Kamphaus (Eds.), *Handbook of psychological & educational assessment of children: Intelligence & achievement* (pp. 86–104). New York: Guilford Press.

Stewart, K. J., Reynolds, C. R., & Lorys-Vernon, A. (1990). Professional standards and practice in child development. In C. R. Reynolds & R. W. Kamphaus (Eds.), *Handbook of psychological & educational assessment of children: Intelligence & achievement* (pp. 105–126). New York: Guilford Press.

Individual Testing of School-Age Children I: SB-IV and WISC-III

The first intelligence tests were designed primarily for educational purposes: to identity children who were below average in their ability to learn school-type tasks and to place such students in special classes or instructional programs geared to their abilities and needs. Subsequently, these tests were also used to enrich school curricula for mentally gifted children and to assess children within the so-called normal range of abilities so their parents, teachers, and other caregivers would be better able to instruct and guide them. Intelligence tests were originally developed and employed primarily for educational purposes, but they have been used in counseling and clinical contexts to assist in understanding and treating children with emotional problems.

The two men who are featured in this chapter—Lewis Terman and David Wechsler—represent these two arenas, the educational and the clinical. The instruments stemming from the work of Terman and Wechsler have been the most popular of all individually administered tests of intelligence. Over the years, the tests that they developed have been used to evaluate the intellectual abilities of children and adults having a broad range of abilities and in a wide variety of circumstances.

This chapter and the next one focus on school-age children, because this is the age group with which individual intelligence tests such as the Stanford-Binet Intelligence Scale and the Wechsler Intelligence Scale for Children have been used extensively. In subsequent chapters this age range is extended to the adult and preschool levels by considering tests that are most appropriate for individuals in those age groups.

STANFORD-BINET INTELLIGENCE SCALE

The first intelligence tests were administered individually to one examinee at a time. Even today, clinical, counseling, and school psychologists prefer individual testing for evaluating the intellectual abilities of children and adults. The most enduring of all individual tests has been the Stanford-Binet Intelligence Scale. For most of the years since it was first published, the Stanford-Binet and its author, Lewis Terman, played central roles in the drama of psychological and educational testing on the American scene. The Stanford-Binet has not lacked competition, but many of its competitors owe much to the pioneering test development and research efforts of Terman and his associates.

Lewis Terman was a bright, midwestern farm boy who attended an Indiana Normal School. He later enrolled at Clark University, where he studied under the pioneering psychologist G. Stanley Hall. Terman spent his early career as a teacher and principal in the public schools, experiences that prepared him well for developing an intelligence test for children and adolescents. In 1910, a few years after moving to California, he joined the staff of the School of Education at Stanford University and during that same year began adapting and revising the 1908 Binet-Simon Intelligence Scale for American children. This established his career direction for life, a career that spanned nearly five decades and influenced numerous graduate students, professional psychologists, and the field of psychology in general.

First Edition of the Stanford-Binet

In revising the Binet-Simon Scale, Terman adhered fairly closely to the guidelines provided by Alfred Binet. Like Binet, Terman was interested in designing a test of general mental ability. The test had an age scale format, in which items were grouped according to the age levels at which a majority of examinees passed those items. Binet's concepts of basal age, ceiling age, and mental age were also retained, but Terman wished to go beyond Binet's emphasis on identifying mentally retarded individuals. His goal was to devise a test more difficult and broader in scope than the Binet-Simon Scale so that differentiations could be made among people of various degrees of intellectual ability in a normal population. Such a test, Terman argued,

FIGURE 4-1 Lewis M. Terman. (Courtesy of News Service, Stanford University.)

could be used not only to identify and forecast the abilities of retarded children but to predict scholastic performance and related criteria of success in normal children and even adults.

Although the first American revision of the Binet-Simon scale in which Terman participated appeared in 1912 (Terman & Childs, 1912), a version of the scale that had been subjected to the standardization process did not appear until 1916. The items on this test, the Stanford Revision and Extension of the Binet-Simon Intelligence Scale, were, as on the Binet-Simon scales, grouped according to age levels. However, the test, which became known as the Stanford-Binet Intelligence Scale, was superior to the Binet-Simon scales in a number of ways. The Stanford-Binet Intelligence Scale was designed to measure the intelligence of children from ages 3 to 16 years. It was carefully constructed and was standardized, in that standard directions for administration and scoring, as well as norms, were provided. The number of tests was increased from the fifty-four on the Binet-Simon Scale to ninety on the Stanford-Binet. Not only were items on the Stanford-Binet test selected (and some discarded) from the Binet-Simon Scale, but many new items representing a wider range of tasks were added.

In constructing the first edition of the scale, Terman made an effort to include tasks that were not so dependent on specific learning experiences in school. This goal was consistent with his belief that intelligence tests should consist of tasks dealing with experiences that are common to children in the dominant culture. More than Binet, Terman stressed the genetic nature of intelligence and therefore that an intelligence test should measure hereditary potential. Terman realized that hereditary potential cannot be measured directly by a psychological test, but he argued that if an intelligence test deals with culturally common experiences, in that all children in the culture are exposed to those experiences and thereby have an equal opportunity to learn from them, brighter children should benefit more than duller children and consequently earn higher test scores.

The concept of *age differentiation*, which was applied in deciding whether to include a particular test on the scale, was that an increasing percentage of children should pass the test at each successively higher chronological age level. In order for the numerical units in which overall performance on the scale was expressed to remain fairly constant across chronological age levels, the percentage-passing requirement was lower for items at higher age levels than for those at lower age levels. The percentage passing each item varied from 67 to 75 percent, depending on the age level at which the item was placed.

A suggestion made by Wilhelm Stern to express scores on intelligence tests as the ratio of mental age to chronological age was adopted by Terman in scoring the Stanford-Binet scale. Terman introduced the term *intelligence quotient (IQ)* into the English language. This *ratio IQ*, computed as

$$IQ = (MA/CA) \times 100,$$

was Stern's coefficient multiplied by 100 to get rid of the decimal point. In this formula, MA is the mental age (in months) obtained on the Stanford-Binet scale, and CA is the child's chronological age to the nearest month.

An MA on the Stanford-Binet was the total months credit earned for each subtest passed by the examinee. The MA was calculated by adding to the *basal age* (the highest year level at which the examinee passed all subtests) the appropriate number of months credit for all subtests passed up to the *ceiling age* (the lowest year level at which the examinee failed all subtests).

Second Edition of the Stanford-Binet

The first edition of the Stanford-Binet scale had a number of shortcomings. Two major problems were the low validities of certain items and the nonrepresentativeness of the norms. Recognizing the problems and limitations of the 1916 scale, Lewis Terman and his associate Maud Merrill began revising it in 1926. The two alternate forms (L and M), which were published eleven years later, bear the initials of the authors' first names.

Similar to the first edition, three criteria were applied in deciding whether to include an item on the second edition of the scale: (1) the item must be judged to be a measure of intelligent behavior; (2) the percentage of children passing the item must increase with chronological age; and (3) the mean mental age of children who pass the item must be significantly greater than the mean mental age of children who fail the item. The six to eight subtests included at each level were grouped at half-year intervals from Year II through Year V, at year intervals from Year VI through Year XIV, and at an Average Adult and three Superior Adult (I, II, III) levels.

Testing with the revised Stanford-Binet began, as with the first edition of the scale, by finding the examinee's basal age, and continued until his or her ceiling age was reached. The examinee's mental age was then computed by adding to the basal age the total number of months credit obtained for all subtests passed up to the

ceiling age. Finally, the MA and CA were converted to months and the corresponding ratio IQ found by the formula or from a special table.

Third Edition of the Stanford-Binet

Modern Western culture does not stand still, and by the mid-1950s it was
obvious that the second edition of the Stanford-Binet needed revising and updating.
Compared with the more recently published Wechsler intelligence scales, many of
the items on the second edition seemed outmoded. Terman and Merrill felt the
need to maintain continuity with the 1937 scale by developing not a totally new
instrument but one that incorporated the best features of the former instrument. An
extensive amount of research and statistical analysis had been conducted with the
second edition of the scale, and the product of efforts to produce a completely new
scale might have been a test that was conceptually related to its predecessor but
was functionally inadequate. Consequently, the decision was made to compromise
between the two aims of maintaining continuity with the two forms of the second
edition and developing an instrument having more contemporary content and
scoring.

Published in 1960, the third edition of the Stanford-Binet, like forms L and M,
was designed to measure the intelligence of individuals ranging in age from 2 years
to the adult level. It consisted of an updating of the best items from forms L and M of
the second edition and contained the same number of subtests at each level as the
second edition. There were six subtests at each half-year level from Year II through
Year VI, six subtests at each year level from Year VI through Year XIV, eight subtests
at the Average Adult level, and six subtests at each of the three Superior Adult levels
(Superior Adult I, Superior Adult II, and Superior Adult III). An alternate subtest, for
use when one of the basic subtests was not or could not be administered correctly,
was also provided at each level. Subtests at lower age levels consisted of perceptual–motor or simple verbal tasks, but the content of subtests at the higher age
levels was more verbal and abstract. Among the mental abilities tapped by the tests
were memory, judgment, interpretation, and abstract reasoning.

As with the second edition, in administering the third edition of the scale
(Form L-M) it was crucial for the examiner to be adept at establishing a friendly but
professional relationship (rapport) with the examinee so the latter would be motivated to score as well as possible. It was also important for the examiner to have
sufficient familiarity with the test to keep the examination moving rapidly enough
to retain the examinee's interest. Furthermore, the examiner was expected to
follow the directions in the manual carefully, not paraphrasing or reciting them
from memory. Only the test materials that were being used were exposed during
testing; the remaining materials were kept out of sight so they would not distract
the examinee from the task at hand.

Total testing time varied not only with the examiner's skill but also with the
age, ability level, and motivation of the examinee. Average testing time was approximately 1 hour, ranging from as little as 30 minutes for preschool or mentally
retarded children to as long as 1½ hours for older children of average or superior

ability. In addition to recording and scoring responses, the examiner was expected to make notes and/or ratings of the examinee's affective behavior (emotional expression, signs of interest or disinterest, etc.) during the examination. Specific deficiencies or proficiencies in language, arithmetic, problem solving, fund of information, and other areas were also revealed on certain subtests. Family background, specific school experiences, and other information that could be relevant in evaluating test performance was also obtained from other sources, as well as from the examinee's statements and nonverbal behaviors.

Adherence to the scoring criteria given in the manual was required, with the examiner exercising sound professional judgment when the exact responses given by the examinee were not listed in the manual. Because the decision to administer subtests at higher (or lower) levels depended on whether specified subtests were passed, responses were scored immediately after they were made. This meant that the examiner had to understand the test directions and scoring standards thoroughly and be discrete in the scoring and note-taking process so that it did not influence the examinee's motivation or other aspects of the examination. After the test had been administered and scored, a report was usually prepared and transmitted to the appropriate persons (school or other agency officials, parents, etc.).

A significant change in scoring Form L-M was the expression of overall performance in terms of a *deviation IQ*. A ratio IQ, like any other age norm, does not really satisfy the requirements of equality of age units. For this reason, direct comparisons of ratio IQs at different age levels are not meaningful. A ratio IQ of 90 at age 5, for example, is not directly comparable to a ratio IQ of 90 at age 15. In addition, the concept of ratio IQ is meaningless when applied to adults. It was never clear what CA figure was most appropriate in the denominator of the MA/CA ratio when testing adults. Fourteen, 16, and 18 years were all suggested at various times when it was felt that these were the CAs at which mental growth stops. Because of such problems in determining the ratio IQ, Terman decided to change from a ratio IQ to a deviation IQ scale having a mean of 100 and a standard deviation of 16. The older ratio IQ was still reported on occasion, and tables for computing it were supplied in the manual.

Form L-M of the Stanford-Binet scale was not restandardized before its release in 1960, and therefore the MA scores were still expressed in terms of the results obtained with the norm group for the second edition of the scale. The standardization group for Form L-M consisted of 4,500 children aged 2½ through 18 years who had taken either Form L or Form M of the second edition between 1950 and 1954. Realizing the need for updated norms, the publisher arranged for the test to be administered in 1972 to a stratified national sample of 2,100 children (100 children at each half-year interval from age 2 through 5½ and at each year interval from age 6 through 18). The sample was more representative than earlier normative samples of the general U.S. population. Based on the 1972 standardization, a revised manual for the third edition was published (Terman & Merrill, 1973). According to the manual, the test-retest reliability coefficients of the deviation IQs were over .90. And, as with the first two editions of the scale, moderate correlations between IQs and school grades and achievement test scores (.40 to .75) were reported.

Fourth Edition of the Stanford-Binet

The fourth edition of the Stanford-Binet Intelligence Scale (SB-IV) was authored by Robert Thorndike, Elizabeth Hagen, and Jerome Sattler in 1986. This test was constructed with a focus on the needs of clinical, school, and other psychologists who use intelligence test information. It maintained historical continuity with the older versions of the scale in that some item types from previous editions were retained. Still, in terms of its theoretical and psychometric foundations, content, and testing procedure, the fourth edition of the Stanford-Binet was a distinct departure from its predecessors. As is true of many modern tests, item-response theory (Rasch scaling), ethnic bias analysis, and other sophisticated psychometric procedures were employed in constructing SB-IV. The goal was to develop a psychometric instrument that would not only assist in identifying mentally retarded and mentally gifted individuals but also provide diagnostic information concerning specific learning problems or disabilities (e.g, clinical indicators of brain damage). With respect to sex and ethnic bias, items judged to be unfair or that showed atypical statistical differences between the sexes or different ethnic groups were not included on the test.

Theoretical Model

A three-level hierarchical model constitutes the theoretical basis of SB-IV. The model consists of a general intelligence factor (g) at the first level, three broad factors (crystallized abilities, fluid-analytic abilities, and short-term memory) at the second level, and three factors (verbal reasoning, quantitative reasoning, and abstract/visual reasoning) at the third level. The verbal and quantitative reasoning factors at the third level compose the crystallized abilities factor at the second level, and the abstract/visual factor at the third level composes the fluid-analytic abilities factor at the second level (see Figure 4–2).

Descriptions of the Tests

As with previous editions of the Stanford-Binet, the fourth edition purports to measure intelligence from age 2 to adulthood. There are fifteen tests, including three to four tests in each of the three broader categories of Level 3 plus four Short-Term Memory tests. Each test is arranged in a series of levels consisting of two items each, providing sufficient range to measure intelligence ranging from that of a below-average 2-year-old to that of an intellectually superior adult. Almost all of the tests have sample items to introduce and familiarize examinees with the nature of the specific test task.

The fifteen tests on SB-IV are the following:

Test 1: Routing and Vocabulary. This test consists of forty-six vocabulary words to be identified or defined (tell the meaning of). Items 1–14 are Picture Vocabulary, and items 15–46 are Oral Vocabulary. The test is administered first to all examinees (ages 2–18+ years); the starting point (entry level) varies with the

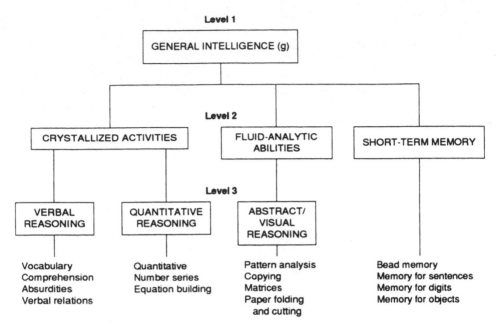

FIGURE 4-2 **Theoretical model and tests for Stanford-Binet IV.** (Courtesy Riverside Publishing Company.)

examinee's CA. As on all fifteen tests, items are scored 0 (fail) or 1 (pass). The total Vocabulary score is used for routing purposes—to determine at what level (entry level) to begin the other fourteen tests—and as a part of the Verbal Reasoning score.

Test 2: Bead Memory. The materials on this updated version of a test appearing on earlier editions of the Stanford-Binet consist of a set of beads varying in shape and color, a bead stick, and pictures of bead arrangements. The examinee is directed to look at the picture of a bead layout for a few seconds and then construct the layout from memory by arranging the beads on the stick.

Test 3: Quantitative. The thirty-four items on this test are designed to measure quantitative skills and concepts. They range from simple counting to tasks requiring an understanding of arithmetic concepts and operations.

Test 4: Memory for Sentences. The examiner reads a sentence, and the examinee attempts to repeat it from memory. The sentences vary from two to twenty-two words, depending on the examinee's age and ability.

Test 5: Pattern Analysis. This test consists of six sample items and thirty-six timed items (items 7–42). The examinee uses cubes to copy a picture of a cube pattern (items 25–42). The examiner mixes up the cubes before going on to the next pattern. Pattern Analysis is the only SB-IV test with time limits.

Test 6: Comprehension. On the first six items of this test, the examinee is asked to point to various body parts on a child card. The facial features, dress, and hair of the child figure have been drawn to minimize race and gender so all ethnic groups and both boys and girls can identify with it. Items 7–42 require a verbal response in which the child provides reasons for certain actions or conditions. The items are read but not shown to the child on items 7–20; they are both read and shown on items 21–42. Example: "Why should people be quiet in a hospital?"

Test 7: Absurdities. For each of the thirty-two items on this test, the examinee tells why a picture or certain parts of a picture are absurd.

Test 8: Memory for Digits. After listening to the examiner read a series of digits aloud, the examinee attempts to repeat them forward on part I (Digits Forward) or backward on part II (Digits Reversed). The total score on this test is the sum of scores on the two parts.

Test 9: Copying. At levels A through F of this test, the examinee attempts to duplicate designs made by the examiner from blocks, either built up (items 1–3) or laid flat on the table (items 4–12). At levels G through N, the examinee copies sixteen designs, such as a diamond or two overlapping circles, in the record booklet. The copied designs are scored pass or fail, according to five criteria: shape, size or number of elements, orientation, proportion, and integration. To be scored pass, the response to an item must meet all five criteria.

Test 10: Memory for Objects. The examinee is shown a series of pictures on cards, one picture per second, and then required to identify the pictures in the order in which they were shown from a card containing all the pictures.

Test 11: Matrices. On the four sample items and items 1–22 of this test, the examinee selects the correct multiple-choice option to fill in an incomplete matrix. On items 23–26, the examinee fills in an incomplete matrix. The items on this test are especially useful with examinees whose native language is not English.

Test 12: Number Series. The examinee lists the next number in a series according to an identified rule.

Test 13: Paper Folding and Cutting. The examiner folds and cuts a piece of paper in a certain way. The examinee identifies, from a set of choices, how the paper will look when it is unfolded.

Test 14: Verbal Relations. For each of the eighteen items on this test, the examinee tells what is similar about the first three things (words) that is not true of the fourth thing (e.g., Shoes, Socks, Sandals, not Gloves).

Test 15: Equation Building. The examinee is required to arrange numbers and mathematical signs in a specified way to form number sentences.

Administering the Tests

As on any other psychological test, it is important to spend a brief period of time at the beginning establishing rapport so the examinee will be encouraged to do his or her best. Under certain conditions, it is permissible to repeat a question or to query a response as indicated in the test manual. However, the directions for each test should be followed closely and read rather than recited from memory.

With the exception of most of the Pattern Analysis items, the tests consist of untimed, power-type items. Total testing time for the entire scale is approximately 75 minutes, varying with the age of the examinee and the number of tests taken. The Vocabulary, Comprehension, Quantitative, Pattern Analysis, Bead Memory, and Memory for Sentences tests are administered to all examinees (2–18+ years); the Number Series, Matrices, Memory for Digits, and Memory for Objects tests to examinees aged 5–18+ years; the Verbal Relations, Equation Building, and Paper Folding and Cutting tests to examinees aged 8–19+ years; and the Absurdities and Copying tests to examinees aged 2–9 years.

The adaptive or multistage nature of SB-IV calls for giving the routing (Vocabulary) test first to determine the entry level on the other tests. The entry level on the routing test is determined by the examinee's chronological age (CA) and the basal level is the highest level at which the examinee passes both items at two consecutive levels. Administration of the routing test continues until the examinee fails three or four items at two consecutive levels, the higher of which is the critical level. The entry level for the remaining fourteen tests is determined from a table by a combination of the critical level on the routing test and the examinee's CA. Administration of each of these tests begins at the entry level, continuing downward until both items are passed at two consecutive levels and continuing upward until three or four items are failed at two consecutive levels. The higher of these levels is the examinee's *ceiling age* for that test.

Directions and some stimulus materials for the tests in each of the four areas are given in four booklets. The booklets are placed open on an easel so the test instructions are on the page closest to (and hence visible only to) the examiner, while the printed stimulus material is on the page closest to (and hence visible to) the examinee. The examinee's response to each item is recorded in a forty-page record booklet; the test, area, and composite scores are recorded on the front page of the booklet (see Figure 4–3). In addition to listing the raw and standard scores in section D of the front page, identifying data are listed in sections A and B, and ratings of behavior that may have affected test performance are listed in section C.

Scoring

The raw score on each of the fifteen tests consists of the number of items passed. Raw scores on each test are converted, within each age group, to a standard age score (SAS) scale having a mean of 50 and a standard deviation of 8. Raw scores on the four areas (Verbal Reasoning, Abstract/Visual Reasoning, Quantitative Reasoning, Short-Term Memory), which are the sum of the raw scores on the three or four tests making up that area, are converted to standard scale scores (area SAS's) having a mean of 100 and a standard deviation of 16. Finally, an overall score consisting of the sum of the four area scores is converted to a standard score (composite SAS) scale having a mean of 100 and a standard deviation of 16. The range of the overall composite scores is 36 to 164, which is equivalent to a z-score range of -4 to $+4$.

RECORD BOOKLET				9-74539

STANFORD-BINET INTELLIGENCE SCALE

RECORD BOOKLET
Stanford-Binet Intelligence Scale: Fourth Edition

Name *John C.*

Sex *M*

Ethnicity NA H B (W/NH) O/AA PI Other _____

	YEAR	MONTH	DAY
Date of Testing	94	6	29
Birth Date **B**	80	1	18
Age	14	5	11

School *Hillview High School*

Grade *9th* **A**

Examiner *Robinson*

Father's Occupation: *Civil engineer*

Mother's Occupation: *Social worker*

FACTORS AFFECTING TEST PERFORMANCE
Overall Rating of Conditions **C**

Optimal	Good	Average	Detrimental	Seriously detrimental

D

	RAW SCORE	STANDARD AGE SCORE *
Verbal Reasoning		
1 Vocabulary	27	47
6 Comprehension	39	61
7 Absurdities *(Est. ceiling)*	31	57 (Est.)
14 Verbal Relations		
Sum of Subtest SAS's ③		165
Verbal Reasoning SAS		(111)
Abstract/Visual Reasoning		
5 Pattern Analysis	40	56
9 Copying		
11 Matrices	14	48
13 Paper Folding & Cutting		
Sum of Subtest SAS's ②		104
Abstract/Visual Reasoning SAS		(105)
Quantitative Reasoning		
3 Quantitative	19	39
12 Number Series	6	37
15 Equation Building		
Sum of Subtest SAS's ②		76
Quantitative Reasoning SAS		(73)
Short-Term Memory		
2 Bead Memory	28	51
4 Memory For Sentences	32	60
8 Memory For Digits *(Est. basal)*	12	47 (Est.)
10 Memory For Objects	9	55
Sum of Subtest SAS's ④		213
Short-Term Memory SAS		(108)
Sum of Area SAS's		397

	COMPOSITE SCORE *
Test Composite	(97)
Partial Composite	109
Partial Composite based on *VR, A/VR, STM*	

* Be sure that all Standard Age Scores (SAS's) are based on the tables in the *Guide* with the number 9-74502 on the cover.

	1	2	3	4	5	
Attention						
a) Absorbed by task				✓		Easily distracted
Reactions During Test Performance						
a) Normal activity level				✓		Abnormal activity level
b) Initiates activity			✓			Waits to be told
c) Quick to respond		✓				Urging needed
Emotional Independence						
a) Socially confident			✓			Insecure
b) Realistically self-confident				✓		Distrusts own ability
c) Comfortable in adult company			✓			Ill-at-ease
d) Assured				✓		Anxious
Problem-Solving Behavior						
a) Persistent				✓		Gives up easily
b) Reacts to failure realistically			✓			Reacts to failure unrealistically
c) Eager to continue			✓			Seeks to terminate
d) Challenged by hard tasks			✓			Prefers only easy tasks
Independence of Examiner Support						
a) Needs minimum of commendation				✓		Needs constant praise and encouragement
Expressive Language						
a) Excellent articulation			✓			Very poor articulation
Receptive Language						
a) Excellent sound discrimination			✓			Very poor sound discrimination

Was it difficult to establish rapport with this person?

Easy	✓					Difficult

The Riverside Publishing Company

Robert L. Thorndike
Elizabeth P. Hagen
Jerome M. Sattler

FIGURE 4-3 Front cover of record booklet of the Stanford-Binet Intelligence Scale: Fourth Edition. (Reproduced with permission of the Riverside Publishing Company from p. 7 of *Stanford-Binet Intelligence Scale Examiner's Handbook: An Expanded Guide for Fourth Edition Users* by E. A. Delaney and T. F. Hopkins. Copyright © 1987, The Riverside Publishing Company.)

Standardization, Reliability, and Validity

SB-IV was standardized on 5,013 individuals between the ages of 2 years and 23 years, 11 months in forty-seven states and the District of Columbia. The standardization sample was selected, using U.S. Census figures for 1980, by geographic region, community size, ethnic group, age group, and gender. The sample was 48 percent male and 52 percent female, 75 percent white, 14 percent black, 6 percent Hispanic, 3 percent Asian/Pacific Islander, and 2 percent other ethnic groups. Student examinees were also stratified according to their relative standing in their school class. Despite efforts to select a standardization sample that was truly representative of the U.S. population, the sample contained disproportionate numbers of individuals at the upper socioeconomic and educational levels. An attempt was made to correct for this problem in scoring the test by differential weighting of individual scores in computing norms, but it was not completely successful. In addition, there are no norms for persons over age 23.

With respect to the reliability of SB-IV, the internal consistency coefficients are mostly in the .80s and .90s, averaging .88 for the four area scores and .95 for the composite score (Thorndike, Hagen, & Sattler, 1986b). However, many of the test–retest coefficients for the area and subtest scores are appreciably lower. Because the reliability coefficients are somewhat lower at younger than at older age levels, the standard error of measurement and the confidence interval around the obtained score are larger in the case of younger children. For example, the 95 percent confidence interval for a composite SAS of 120 obtained by a 6-year-old is 114 to 126, whereas it is 116 to 124 for a 14-year-old and 117 to 123 for a 17-year-old with the same SAS.

Evidence for the construct validity of SB-IV has been obtained from factor analyses, correlations with other tests, and differentiations among groups of people of known abilities. The results of factor analyses of scores on the fifteen tests point to a strong general intelligence factor. The area and composite scores have high correlations with scores on other cognitive abilities tests (Carvajal, Gerber, Hewes, & Weaver, 1987; Carvajal, Hardy, Smith, & Weaver, 1988; Knight, Baker, & Minder, 1990; Laurent, Swerdlik, & Ryburn, 1992; Smith, St. Martin, & Lyon, 1989; Thorndike, Hagen, & Sattler, 1986b). In addition, groups of gifted children obtained higher composite scores and groups of mentally retarded children obtained lower composite scores on SB-IV than the standardization group. Thus, it would seem that the SB-IV is an excellent test for diagnosing mental retardation and predicting academic achievement. Unfortunately, there are problems with the test and its standardization.

Critique of SB-IV

Cohen, Swerdlik, and Smith (1992) fault the SB-IV manual for not including interscorer reliability coefficients, although internal consistency and test–retest coefficients are reported. In addition to the low reliabilities of some of the subtests, particularly at younger age-groups, the theoretical structure underlying the SB-IV has been questioned. Thus, the results of several factor analyses do not clearly support the separation of the fifteen subtests into four areas (Reynolds, Kamphaus, & Rosenthal, 1988; see Thorndike, 1990, for a response). Furthermore, the factor structure of the SB-IV is not constant across chronological age-groups. A strong general factor (g) underlies the subtest scores at all ages, but the group factors change with age level. Below age 10 the factors seem to represent verbal and nonverbal abilities, between ages 10 and 17 they may be labeled reasoning and memory, and between ages 17 and 32½ the appropriate factor labels are general reasoning, quantitative, and possibly nonverbal reasoning. One reason why the meanings of the area scores and the factor structure vary with the age of the examinee is that younger children do not take the same subtests as older children; consequently, their scores are based on different tasks. Because of the ambiguity surrounding the area scores, Sattler (1988) recommends using factor scores in interpreting performance on the test.

Perhaps the most serious criticism of the SB-IV was made by Reynolds (1987), who noted the serious consequences of failing to stratify the standardization sample by socioeconomic status, in addition to age, sex, race, geographic region, and community size. Reynolds maintains that the scaling of the area scores was improper, in that they were scaled according to the *number*, as opposed to the *type*, of subtests administered. Because the correlations between the various subtests, as well as correlations between area scores, are unequal, the composite scores and IQs are inaccurate whenever fewer than all the age-appropriate subtests are administered.

WECHSLER INTELLIGENCE SCALE FOR CHILDREN

Following its initial publication by David Wechsler in 1939, it was not long before the Wechsler-Bellevue Intelligence Scale became the principal individual intelligence test for adults. Meanwhile, the Stanford-Binet Intelligence Scale maintained its position as the foremost intelligence test for children. With the publication of the Wechsler Intelligence Scale for Children (WISC) in 1949, however, the Stanford-Binet faced strong competition. The WISC, a downward extension of the Wechsler-Bellevue Intelligence Scale (WB-I), was designed to assess the intellectual functioning of children ranging in age from 5 years through 15 years, 11 months. The fact that many of the WISC items were merely simplifications of items on the WB-I resulted in its content being criticized for being too adult oriented. In addition, it seemed somewhat inconsistent that David Wechsler, whose initial motivation for constructing a new intelligence test was the inadequacy of available tests for measuring adult intelligence, should simplify his adult-level test to measure the intelligence of children.

The Stanford-Binet was able to maintain its position in competition with the WISC for some years, but during the 1960s and 1970s the original WISC and a revised edition gained in popularity. The Wechsler Intelligence Scale for Children — Revised (WISC-R), which was published in 1974, was designed for children aged 6 through 16 years, 11 months, 30 days. While much of the content of the WISC-R consisted of new or modified items designed to make the scale less adult oriented and more child oriented, over two-thirds of the items were carried over, intact or with only slight modifications, from the WISC. During the late 1980s the WISC-R itself was revised, yielding the Wechsler Intelligence Scale for Children—Third Edition (WISC-III) (Wechsler, 1991).

There are thirteen subtests on the WISC-III, six on the Verbal Scale and seven on the Performance Scale. These subtests, in the order in which they are typically administered, are:

1. Picture Completion	8. Vocabulary
2. Information	9. Object Assembly
3. Coding	10. Comprehension
4. Similarities	11. (Symbol Search)
5. Picture Arrangement	12. (Digit Span)
6. Arithmetic	13. (Mazes)
7. Block Design	

Subtests 1, 3, 5, 7, 9, 11, and 13 are on the Performance Scale, and subtests 2, 4, 6, 8, 10, and 12 are on the Verbal Scale. The subtests in parentheses are supplementary subtests that can be given when one of the other subtests has been administered incorrectly or a handicap prevents the child from taking a given subtest. Digit Span may be substituted for any Verbal subtest and Mazes for any Performance subtest other than Coding; Symbol Search may be substituted for Coding. Some items similar to those on the WISC-III are illustrated in Figure 4-4.

Scores on only ten subtests are typically used in calculating WISC-III IQs, but all thirteen subtests should be administered if time permits. The three supplementary subtests provide additional quantitative and qualitative information about abilities and behavior. Note that the Performance and Verbal subtests are administered in alternating order, starting with a performance subtest (Picture Completion) and ending with a verbal subtest (Comprehension) or with Mazes when all thirteen subtests are administered.

Descriptions of WISC-III Subtests

Descriptions of the thirteen subtests and some details concerning administration follow:

Picture Completion. The material on this subtest consists of thirty cards on which pictures are printed. An important part is missing from each picture, and the child is given 20 seconds to indicate (say or point to) what is missing. The sample item is administered first to children of all ages. Testing proper begins with item 1 for children aged 6-7 (or older children suspected of being mentally retarded), with item 5 for children aged 8-9, with item 7 for children aged 10-13, and with item 11 for children aged 14-16. Responses are scored 0 (fail) or 1 (pass), and testing is discontinued when five consecutive items are failed. The Picture Completion

Information

How many legs do you have?
What must you do to make water freeze?
Who discovered the North Pole?
What is the capital of France?

Similarities

In what way are pencil and crayon alike?
In what way are tea and coffee alike?
In what way are inch and mile alike?
In what way are binoculars and microscope alike?

Arithmetic

If I have one piece of candy and get another one, how
  many pieces will I have?
At 12 cents each, how much will 4 bars of soap cost?
If a suit sells for 1/2 of the ticket price, what is the cost of
  a $120 suit?

Vocabulary

ball   poem
summer   obstreperous

Comprehension

Why do we wear shoes?
What is the thing to do if you see someone dropping his
  packages?
In what two ways is a lamp better than a candle?
Why are we tried by a jury of our peers?

Digit Span

Digits Forward contains seven series of digits, 3 to 9
  digits in length (Example: 1-8-9).
Digits Backward contains seven series of digits, 2 to 8
  digits in length (Example: 5-8-1-9).

Picture Completion

The task is to identify the essential missing part of the
picture.
A picture of a car without a wheel.
A picture of a dog without a leg.
A picture of a telephone without numbers on the dial.
An example of a Picture Completion task is shown below.

Picture Arrangement

The task is to arrange a series of pictures into a meanii
ful sequence.

Block Design

The task is to reproduce stimulus designs using four o
nine blocks. An example of a Block Design item is show1
below.

Object Assembly

The task is to arrange pieces into a meaningful object. An
example of an Object Assembly item is shown below.

Coding

The task is to copy symbols from a key (see below).

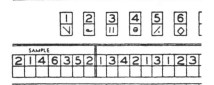

Mazes

The task is to complete a series of mazes.

FIGURE 4-4 Some items like those on the WISC-III. (Copyright © 1949, 1955, 1974, 1981, and 1989 by
The Psychological Corporation. Reproduced by permission. All rights reserved.)

subtest was designed to measure visual alertness, memory, and attention to details. Scores are affected by poor attention and concentration, as well as anxiety.

Information. This subtest consists of thirty general information questions, arranged in order of difficulty and answered with a few words or a number. Testing begins with item 1 for children aged 6-7 years, with item 5 for children aged 8-10, with item 8 for children aged 11-13, and with item 11 for children aged 14-16. Responses are scored 1 (correct) or 0 (incorrect), and testing is discontinued when the child fails five consecutive items. The Information subtest measures long-term memory, or fact acquisition and retrieval. Compared with other subtests, scores on this subtest are affected more by familial and cultural background, as well as by intellectual motivation.

Coding. This subtest consists of two parts: Coding A is for children who are 6-7 years old and Coding B for children aged 8-16. The materials on Coding A consist of a sample (key) composed of five shapes (star, circle, triangle, cross, square), each containing a specific mark (a vertical line, two horizontal lines, a horizontal line, a circle, and two vertical lines, respectively). Below the key, in mixed order, are several copies of each of the five shapes; five of the sixty-four items are samples used for practice purposes. The child is given a graphite pencil without an eraser and directed to fill in each shape with the appropriate mark, as illustrated in the key. The maximum time permitted for Coding A is 120 seconds. One point is given for each correct response, and a time bonus is awarded for perfect performance. On Coding B, the child is directed to fill in the bottom part of each of seven sample (practice) double boxes and 119 test double boxes with the appropriate coded symbol corresponding to a single-digit number appearing in the upper part of the double box. A key consisting of nine correctly marked double boxes is given above the sample and test boxes. The time limit for Coding B is 120 seconds, and one point is given for each correct response. The Coding subtest measures speed and accuracy of simple visual-associative encoding and responding, in addition to visual discrimination and freedom from distractibility.

Similarities. Nineteen items of the type "In what way are 'A' and 'B' alike?" make up this subtest. The items are presented in order of ascending difficulty until the child fails four in a row. Responses to items 1-5 are scored 0 or 1, and, depending on the quality and degree of understanding shown in the response, items 6-19 are scored 0, 1, or 2. The Similarities subtest was designed to assess verbal, abstract concept formation or to differentiate concrete, functional, and abstract thinking processes. A concrete response to the question "How are a plum and a peach alike?" is "They both have skins." A functional response to the same question is "You eat them both," and an abstract response is "They're both fruit." Abstract responses earn higher scores than concrete or functional responses. Low scores on this subtest point to a rigidly concrete mode of thinking and sometimes private or distorted conceptual thinking.

Picture Arrangement. The materials on this subtest are fifteen sets of cards (including a sample set), each containing a small picture. The examiner lays out each set of cards in a standard sequence and asks the child to put the pictures in the "right" order to tell a sensible story. After presenting the sample item, testing begins with item 1 for children aged 6–8 years or item 3 for children aged 9–16 years. Responses to items 1 and 2 are scored 0, 1, or 2, depending on whether the examinee gets the item right on the first or second trial. Three additional time bonus points are given on items 3–14. The test is discontinued when the child fails three consecutive items. The Picture Arrangement subtest measures ordering or sequencing ability and the ability to anticipate, as well as social sensitivity and a sense of humor. Low scores are indicative of problems in nonverbal planning.

Arithmetic. This subtest consists of twenty-four arithmetic problems in order of increasing difficulty. Problems 1–18 are presented orally by the examiner, and the child reads problems 19–24 aloud before attempting to solve them. Testing begins with item 1 for 6-year-olds (or older children suspected of being mentally retarded), item 6 for children aged 7–8 years, item 12 for children aged 9–12 years, and item 14 for children aged 13–16. Thirty seconds is allowed on problems 1–17, 45 seconds on item 18, and 75 seconds on items 19–24. Responses are scored 0 or 1, and a bonus point is given on items 19–24 for answering correctly within 10 seconds. The Arithmetic subtest measures elementary knowledge of arithmetic, together with the ability to concentrate and reason quantitatively. Low scores are indicative of low attention span or distractibility, possibly caused by anxiety.

Block Design. The materials on this subtest are nine red and white blocks and a booklet containing twelve red and white printed designs. The child is instructed to duplicate each design with four or nine blocks. Testing begins with item 1 for children aged 6–7 (or older children suspected of being mentally retarded) and with item 3 for children aged 8–16 years. The time limits are 30 seconds for design 1, 45 seconds for designs 2–5, 75 seconds for designs 6–9, and 120 seconds for designs 10–12. Designs 1–3 are scored 0, 1, or 2 points, depending on whether the examinee gets the item right on the first or second trial. Designs 4–12 are scored 0, 4, 5, 6, or 7, depending on how quickly the examinee arranges the blocks in the correct pattern. Testing is discontinued when two consecutive designs are failed (receive 0 points). The Block Design subtest was constructed to measure the ability to perceive and analyze a visual pattern into its component parts. Low scores indicate perceptual problems and poor spatial conceptualization or, in adolescents, a reflective or unhurried approach to problem solutions. As seen in its high correlations with Performance Scale and Full Scale IQs, Block Design is considered to be the best Performance subtest for measuring general mental ability.

Vocabulary. This subtest requires the child to explain what is meant by each of thirty words, listed in order of ascending difficulty. Testing begins with item 1 for children aged 6–8 years (or older children suspected of being mentally retarded), with item 3 for children aged 9–10 years, with item 5 for children aged 11–13 years, and with item 7 for children aged 14–16 years. Responses to each word are scored 0, 1, or 2 points, depending on the extent of understanding of the word shown by the child. Testing is discontinued when five consecutive words are failed. The Vocabulary subtest was designed to measure knowledge of words, a skill that is closely related to general mental ability. In fact, Vocabulary is considered the best single WISC-III subtest for predicting scholastic performance. High scores are indicative of good integration into the mainstream culture and schooling. Low scores are usually indicative of limited educational and familial background, although they may be due to verbalization problems rather than ignorance.

Object Assembly. The materials on this subtest consist of five jigsaw puzzles presented in a standard layout, with directions to put the pieces together to make something (a girl, a car, a horse, a ball, a human face). For children of all ages, testing begins with the sample item (an apple). Then all five test items are administered to every child. The time limits are 120 seconds on item 1, 150 seconds on items 2 and 3, and 180 seconds on items 4 and 5. The score for each puzzle is determined by the number of cuts that are correctly joined, together with bonus points for rapid, perfect performance. Point scores range from 0 to 8 on items 1–3 and 0–10 on items 4 and 5. The Object Assembly subtest was designed to measure visual-perceptual organization (the ability to visualize a final form from its parts), but scores are affected by attention and persistence. Low scores are indicative of poor planning ability, and very low scores point to perceptual-motor deficiencies.

Comprehension. This subtest is composed of eighteen questions, in order of ascending difficulty, requiring detailed answers that reveal an understanding of specific situations or problems. Testing begins with item 1 for all children and continues until the child fails (scores 0) on three consecutive items. The Comprehension subtest assesses practical knowledge, social judgment, and the ability to organize information. High scores point to broad experience, social maturity, and a superior ability to organize practical knowledge. Low scores indicate limited practical coping ability or overly concrete thinking.

Symbol Search. This supplementary subtest is divided into two parts—Symbol Search A for children aged 6–7 years and Symbol Search B for children aged 8–16 years. Each part contains forty-five paired items, and each pair consists of a target group and a search group of symbols. On every pair, the child is told to scan the two groups of symbols and indicate whether or not a target symbol appears in the search group. Total time limit is 120 seconds per part. Scores range from 0 to 45; high scores indicate attentiveness or freedom from distractibility and rapid mental processing speed and low scores the reverse.

Digit Span. This supplementary subtest consists of two sets of numerical digits, to be recited forward (in the order in which they are pronounced by the examiner) or backward (in reverse order to that in which they are pronounced by the examiner). The Digits Forward set contains eight series (two to nine digits long); the Digits Backward set contains seven series (two to eight digits long). The child is instructed to repeat each series immediately after the examiner has finished reading it. Two trials (two different sets of digits of the same length) are given on each series. Testing on Digits Forward continues until the child fails both trials of a series or succeeds in repeating nine digits forward. Testing on Digits Backward continues until the child fails both trials of a series or succeeds in repeating eight digits backward. The score on each series of Digits Forward or Digits Backward is 0 (both trials failed), 1 (one trial passed), or 2 (both trials passed). Total score on the Digit Span subtest is the sum of the scores on Digits Forward and Digits Backward. This subtest was designed to measure immediate rote memory but scores are affected by attention span, comprehension, and (freedom from) distractibility.

Mazes. This supplementary subtest requires the child to draw a line through a printed maze, from start to finish, without entering a blind alley (block). There are ten mazes in order of increasing difficulty, plus a sample maze. Children aged 6–7 start with the sample, and children aged 8–16 start with maze 4. The time limits are 30 seconds on mazes 1–4, 45 seconds on maze 5, 60 seconds on maze 6, 120 seconds on mazes 7 and 8, and 150 seconds on mazes 9 and 10. Scores are determined by the number of errors that the child makes in traversing the maze; scores range from 0–2 on mazes 1–6, 0–3 on maze 7, 0–4 on mazes 8 and 9, and 0–5 on maze 10. Testing is discontinued when two consecutive mazes receive scores of 0. The Mazes subtest is considered to be primarily a measure of perceptual organization and planning (foresight), although freedom from distractibility is also an important factor with younger children.

The manual should be followed closely in administering and scoring the WISC-III, but a certain amount of flexibility is permitted. The Verbal subtests are usually easier to administer and more difficult to score than the Performance subtests. However, mistakes can be made in administering or scoring the subtests on either scale. The scoring criteria for all subtests are listed in the same section of the manual as the directions for administration, but the examples do not exhaust the possible answers. For this reason, experience and judgment are required in order to apply the scoring criteria accurately. Concerning the matter of scoring items when errors in administration are made, items that are presented early in a subtest and should not have been administered are given full credit. When items past the discontinuance criterion are mistakenly administered, they are not credited in the score.

Scaled Scores, IQs, and Factor Scores

After scoring each of the ten (or thirteen) WISC-III subtests, the examiner records the raw scores on all administered subtests in the appropriate column of the record form (section C in Figure 4–5). The subtest raw scores are converted to scaled scores by referring to the 4-month table appropriate for the child's chronological age in Table A.1 of the WISC-III manual (Wechsler, 1991). The subtest scaled scores, which are standard scores having a mean of 10 and a standard deviation of 3, are recorded in the appropriate row and column (Verbal or Performance) of the upper left-hand section (section C of Figure 4-5) of the record form. These are age-corrected scaled scores, in that they are specific to the particular 4-month age group. The subtest scaled scores may also be plotted in profile form, as shown in the graph in the lower left-hand section (section E) of Figure 4–5.

WISC-III IQs

Scaled scores on the five nonsupplementary Verbal subtests are summed to yield a Verbal Scale score, scaled scores on the five nonsupplementary Performance subtests are summed to yield a Performance Scale score, and the Verbal and Performance Scale scores are added to yield a Full Scale score. When only four subtests on

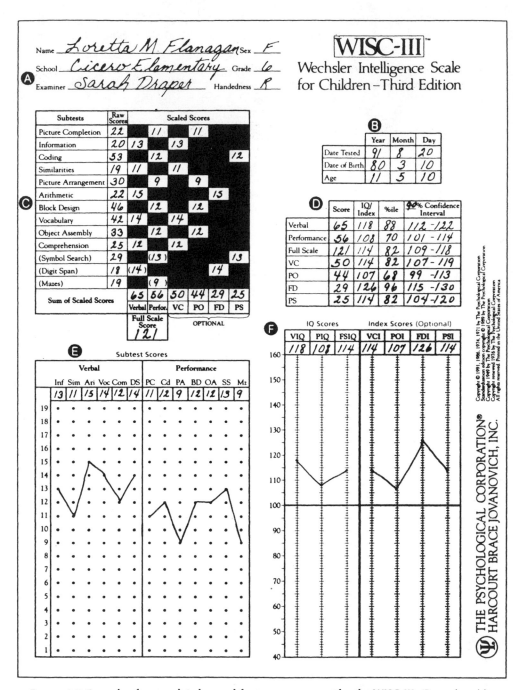

FIGURE 4-5 Example of a completed record form summary page for the WISC-III. (Reproduced by permission from the Wechsler Intelligence Scale for Children—Third Edition. Reproduced by permission. Copyright © 1990 by The Psychological Corporation. All rights reserved.)

either the Verbal or Performance Scale are administered, the sum of the subtest scaled scores on that scale is prorated to five subtests. In any case, the Verbal, Performance, and Full Scale scores are converted to deviation IQs by referring to Tables A.2, A.3, and A.4 of the WISC-III manual. These IQs are recorded in the upper right-hand section (section D) and plotted in the lower right-hand section (section F) of the record form (Figure 4–5).

Each of the three IQ scales was designed to have a mean of 100 and a standard deviation of 15 in the standardization sample. The lowest and highest IQs attainable on the WISC-III are 46 and 155 on the Verbal and Performance Scales and 40 and 160 on the Full Scale. Although this somewhat limited range may be considered a shortcoming of the WISC-III, David Wechsler did not intend it to differentiate precisely between the various levels of either mental retardation or mental giftedness.

Test Ages

In addition to the scaled scores for each subtest, test ages equivalent to the subtest raw scores can be determined from a special table in the WISC-III manual (Table A.9). The *test age* corresponding to a child's raw score on a given subtest is the expected chronological age of a person for whom that raw score corresponds to a subtest scaled score of 10. The mean of a child's test ages on all WISC-III subtests is roughly equivalent to his or her mental age, a concept that Wechsler originally perceived as misleading. Test ages were not included in the original WISC manual but were added in later printings because of user demand for scores equivalent to mental ages. In any event, mean test ages on the WISC-R have sometimes been compared with mental ages on the third edition of the Stanford-Binet Intelligence Scale and are used for the same purpose.

Index Scores

The results of factor analysis of subtest scores on the WISC-III have produced evidence for four factors: Verbal Comprehension (VC), Perceptual Organization (PO), Freedom from Distractibility (FD), and Processing Speed (PS). The loadings of the thirteen WISC-III subtests on these four factors vary substantially. The Information, Similarities, Vocabulary, and Comprehension subtests have high loadings on the Verbal Comprehension (VC) factor; the Picture Completion, Picture Arrangement, Block Design, and Object Assembly subtests have high loadings on the Perceptual Organization (PO) factor; the Arithmetic and Digit Span subtests have high loadings on the Freedom from Distractibility (FD) factor; and the Coding and Symbol Search subtests have high loadings on the Processing Speed (PS) factor. As shown in the upper left-hand corner of Figure 4–5, the scaled scores on the subtests having high loadings on the corresponding factor can be added to yield a sum of scaled scores for each of the four factors. By referring to Tables A.5 to A.7 in the WISC-III manual, these factor scores can then be converted to Index Score Equivalents and recorded in section D of the record form. Note that the percentile ranks and the 90 percent confidence limits for the IQs and Index Score Equivalents are also listed in section D of the record form.

Psychometric Characteristics of the WISC-III

The sample on which the WISC-III was standardized consisted of 2,200 children between the ages of 6 and 16, 100 boys and 100 girls in each of eleven age groups. The sample was selected, on the basis of 1988 United States Census data, from the four geographic regions (Northeast, West, North Central, South) of the country. To ensure the accuracy of item statistics, other groups of black and Hispanic children were also tested. Additional groups of children were tested for comparisons between different tests in the Wechsler series, resulting in a total of approximately 4,500 test administrations. In addition to being stratified by age, the sample was stratified by parental occupation and race. The ethnic composition of the sample was 70.09 percent white, 15.34 percent black, 10.81 percent Hispanic, and 3.76 percent other. Table 4-1 lists the percentages of children in the standardization sample whose Full Scale IQs on the WISC-II placed them in the respective intelligence categories.

Reliabilities of Subtest, IQ, and Factor-Based Scores

The split-half reliabilities of all subtests except Coding and Symbol Search for the eleven age groups in the standardization sample range from .61 to .91, with the Verbal subtests being somewhat more reliable than the Performance subtests. Test–retest reliability coefficients of the subtests, based on a group of 353 children who were retested after an interval ranging from twelve to sixty-three days, are somewhat lower than the split-half coefficients but still acceptable (mostly in the .70s and .80s). The reliability coefficients of the Verbal, Performance, and Full Scale scores are, as might be expected of composite scores, even higher than those of the subtest scores. The split-half coefficients averaged .95 for Verbal, .91 for Perfor-

TABLE 4–1   Classfication of WISC-III Full Scale IQs and Percentages of Standardization Sample in Each Category

IQ	Classification	Percent in sample
130 and above	Very superior	2.1
120–129	Superior	8.3
110–119	High average	16.1
90–109	Average	50.3
80–89	Low average	14.8
70–79	Borderline	6.5
69 and below	Intellectually deficient	1.9

Source: D. Wechsler, 1991. *Wechsler Intelligence Scale for Children— Third Edition manual* (p. 32). Reprinted by permission of The Psychological Corporation.

mance, and .96 for Full Scale scores; the test–retest coefficients averaged .94 for Verbal, .87 for Performance, and .94 for Full Scale scores. The reliabilities of the four factor (index) scores average .94 for VC, .90 for PO, .87 for FD, and .85 for PS; the corresponding test–retest coefficients are .93, .87, .82, and .64. A separate study revealed that there is a high degree of consistency in scoring, even in the case of those subtests requiring more scorer judgment (Similarities, Vocabulary, Comprehension, and Mazes). The interrater reliability coefficients of these four subtests are all in the .90s (Wechsler, 1991).

With respect to score differences, the WISC-III manual provides, by age group, a table (B.1) of differences between Verbal and Performance IQs or between any two factor-based index scores required for statistical significance at the .15 or .05 level. Also in the manual is a table (B.3) of differences between single subtest scaled scores and average subtest scaled scores on the subtests of a scale required for statistical significance at the .15 and .05 levels, and a table (B.4) of differences between subtest scaled scores required for statistical significance at these two levels. These two tables, which provide the same kind of information for the factor-based index scores, may be useful in the interpretation of score profiles like those in sections E and F of Figure 4–5.

Validity

Various kinds of information concerning the validity of the WISC-III is presented in Chapter 6 of the WISC-III manual, including: (1) findings from factor-analytic studies of the internal validity of the WISC-III; (2) correlations between WISC-III scores and scores on other Wechsler tests and on other intelligence tests; (3) correlations between WISC-III scores and scores on neuropsychological tests, achievement tests, and school grades; (4) the results of studies of special groups of children such as the gifted and mentally retarded, as well as children with learning disabilities, attention-deficit hyperactivity disorder, severe conduct disorders, epilepsy, speech/language delays, or hearing impairment. To obtain validity data within the Wechsler series, the WISC-III and WAIS-R were administered to 200 16-year-olds, the WISC-III and WPPSI-R to 200 6-year-olds, and the WISC-III and WISC-R to 200 children across the age range. In addition, as noted above in the discussion of reliability, over 300 children were tested and then retested with the WISC-III over a 4- to 8-week period. The clinical validity data were based on a study of approximately 400 special children (conduct disordered, attention disordered, hearing impaired, mentally retarded, emotionally dysfunctional, epileptic, gifted, etc.) in eighteen sites. As a whole these data provide substantial support for the validity of the WISC-III as a measure of intellectual functioning in children.

Interpreting Scores on the WISC-III

As with any other psychological test, scores on the WISC-III should not be interpreted blindly without considering the child's sociocultural background and his or her behavior during the examination. In interpreting and reporting the results of administering a multiscore test such as the WISC-III, the examiner often follows a successive-levels approach of examining the IQs first, the subtest scaled scores second, responses to specific subtest items third, and qualitative responses last.

Kaufman (1994) provides a seven-step approach to organizing and interpreting scores derived from the WISC-III subtests and the factor indices. As with all approaches to interpreting WISC-III scores, the purpose of these steps is to understand the child's specific strengths and weaknesses and to translate them into appropriate suggestions for intervention.

Usually the first matter of interest in interpreting the WISC-III is the Full Scale IQ. If the test has been administered properly and the child has cooperated, the Full Scale IQ provides an overall measure of the child's cognitive ability. Table 4-1 provides a basis for classifying any WISC-III Verbal, Performance, or Full Scale IQ, and the percentile rank corresponding to the IQ may be obtained from Table A.2 of the WISC-III manual. The classification categories and percentile ranks corresponding to all three IQs may be included in a psychological test report.

One problem regarding Full Scale IQs on the WISC-III is that they are generally a few points lower than those obtained by the same children on the WISC-R, a difference attributable mostly to scores on the Performance Scale rather than on the Verbal Scale. Because, on the average, WISC-III IQs are 5.69 points lower than those on the WISC-R, it is difficult to explain to parents whose children have taken both the WISC-R and the WISC-III why their children's IQs are lower on the WISC-III than the WISC-R. Weiss (1995) recommends explaining to these parents that the children on whom the WISC-III was standardized were smarter than those on whom the WISC-R was normed, so a child has to do better on the WISC-III than the WISC-R to make an average score.

Verbal–Performance IQ Differences

Depending on the specific age group tested, the correlations between Verbal and Performance IQs on the WISC-III standardization group range from .57 to .76. Because these are less than perfect correlations, it is not surprising that significant differences between Verbal and Performance IQs are fairly common. Although Verbal–Performance IQ differences are, to some extent, explicable by the fact that the two scales are less than perfectly reliable, the differences can also be due to the fact that the two scales do not measure the same abilities. Consequently, large differences in the two IQs may be diagnostically meaningful.

There is some evidence that large differences between Verbal and Performance IQs are related to localized cerebral dysfunction. For example, Rourke (1975) concluded that right-hemisphere brain damage in middle childhood is associated with a significantly higher Verbal than Performance IQ, and left-hemisphere brain damage is associated with a significantly higher Performance than Verbal IQ on the WISC. With the exception of organic brain damage, certain sensorimotor handicaps, and cultural deficits, the use of these IQ differences in diagnosing psychological disorders remains controversial. The value of the Verbal–Performance IQ difference required for statistical significance varies with the child's chronological age and the significance level. As a general rule, one can interpret a difference of 10 points or more as statistically significant, although not necessarily as meaningful or diagnostically useful.

Differences among Subtest Scaled Scores

It was Wechsler's hope that differences among scaled scores on the WISC would be useful in diagnosing psychopathology and learning disorders. Wechsler and certain other psychologists believed that specific psychopathological conditions were associated with characteristic profiles of subtest scaled scores or that high scores on certain subtests and low scores on others might be useful diagnostic signs. Unfortunately, a survey of studies concerned with identifying psychological disorders in children found that neither Verbal–Performance Scale differences nor differences among subtest scaled scores on the WISC-R reliably differentiated among mentally retarded, emotionally disturbed, learning disabled, and minimally brain-injured children (Gutkin, 1979).

Not all research findings concerned with the diagnostic significance of WISC and WISC-R subtest score scatter have been negative (Burstein, 1976; Dean, 1977; Naglieri & Harrison, 1979). Bannatyne (1974) provided some interesting, if controversial, suggestions for identifying reading and learning disabilities from children's WISC-R scores. Such children were said to have strong spatial ability, medium verbal conceptualization ability, weak sequencing ability, and limited acquired knowledge. If so, they should have high scores on Picture Completion, Object Assembly, and Block Design, medium scores on Similarities, Vocabulary, and Comprehension, and low scores on Arithmetic, Digit Span, and Information.

Although research on subtest scatter analysis continues, the findings thus far are inconsistent. Kaufman (1982, p. 167) concluded that "the failure of scatter in WISC-R profiles to distinguish, in a meaningful way, between normal and clinical samples militates against its value in diagnosis." McDermott, Fantuzzo, and Glutting (1990) apparently concur with and reinforce Kaufman's assertion, as seen in their conclusion that "until preponderant and convincing evidence shows otherwise, we are compelled to advise that psychologists just say 'no' to subtest analysis" (p. 299).

Although analyzing subtest scaled score scatter is not as popular as it once was, school and clinical psychologists continue to make subjective interpretations of differences in performance on the various WISC-III subtests. By focusing on the description of what each subtest is supposed to measure and comparing it with what other subtests purportedly measure, hypotheses concerning the areas of an examinee's strength and weakness are proposed. These hypotheses should be treated as suggestions that may be confirmed or disconfirmed by the results of other tests or by additional sources of behavioral information concerning the examinee.

Computer-Based Scoring and Interpretation

Examiners who are interested in computer-based scoring and interpretation of the WISC-III should become familiar with The Psychological Corporation's WISC-III Writer software. A portion of a sample printout of this program is given in Report 4–1. The system that prepared this report converted the raw scores on the WISC-III

Report 4–1

Interpretive Report of WISC-III Testing
(The Psychological Corporation)

Name: William (Bill) Johnson   **Report Date**: 02/24/95
Age: 7 years 7 months   **Examiner**: Dr. Teresa Jones
Date of Birth: 07/05/85   **Title**: School Psychologist
ID: 22054   **Lic/Cert**: 123456
Gender: Male   **Test Site**: MLK Elementary
Grade: 2   **Ethnicity:** African American
Test Administered: WISC-III (02/10/93)

Subtest Scores Summary

Verbal Subtests	Raw Score	Scaled Score	PR
Information (IN)	8	8	25
Similarities (SI)	12	12	75
Arithmetic (AR)	10	7	16
Vocabulary (VO)	19	11	63
Comprehension (CO)	17	14	91

Performance Subtests	Raw Score	Scaled Score	PR
Picture Completion (PC)	21	16	98
Coding (CD)	28	6	9
Picture Arrangement (PA)	24	14	91
Block Design (BD)	25	12	75
Object Assembly (OA)	28	14	91
(Symbol Search SS)	14	6	9

WISC-III Scale	Score
Verbal (VCI)	107
Performance (POI)	124
Full Scale	109

Reason for Referral

Bill was referred for an evaluation by his teacher, Mrs. Calderon, because of attention problems and behavior problems.

Home

Bill is a 7-year-old child who lives with his parents. There is one other child in Bill's home. His living arrangement has been in effect for less than one year. His mother completed high school and his father completed between one and three years of college or technical school.

Development

According to Bill's mother, he was born prematurely and spent time in a neonatal intensive care unit. Bill's mother reported that he reached the following milestones within the expected age ranges: speaking first words and speaking short sentences. Finally, others were reached later than expected: sitting alone and crawling.

Health

Bill's visual screening revealed that he has normal visual acuity. Also, a hearing test showed normal auditory acuity. In addition, his mother stated that Bill has been diagnosed as suffering from severe allergies and asthma. Also, his mother said that he currently is taking medication for allergy symptoms and asthma.

School

As for his conduct in school, at this time he is having frequent disciplinary problems and he had an exemplary conduct record in the past.

Interpretation of WISC-III Results

Bill's general cognitive ability is within the average range of intellectual functioning, as measured by the Wechsler Intelligence Scale for Children—Third Edition. His overall thinking and reasoning abilities exceed those of approximately 73% of children his age (Full Scale IQ = 109; 90% confidence interval = 104–113).

He performed significantly better on nonverbal than on verbal reasoning tasks. Such differences in performance, however, are not especially unusual among children in general. His verbal reasoning abilities are most appropriately characterized by his score on the Verbal Comprehension Index, which is average and above those of approximately 68% of his peers (VCI = 107; 90% confidence interval = 101–112). His nonverbal reasoning abilities are best described by his score on the Perceptual Organization Index, which

(continued)

Report 4–1

(*Continued*)

is superior and above that of approximately 95% of students Bill's age (POI = 124; 90% confidence interval = 115–129).

   Processing visual material quickly is an ability that Bill performs poorly as compared to his nonverbal reasoning ability. Processing speed is an indication of the rapidity with which Bill can mentally process simple or routine information without making errors. Bill's speed of information processing abilities are within the low average range and better than those of approximately 9% of his age-mates (Processing Speed Index = 80; 90% confidence interval = 75–91).

   Compared to his mean score for all of the verbal reasoning tasks, Bill's performance was significantly better on the Comprehension subtest and significantly weaker on the Arithmetic subtest. His strong performance on the Comprehension subtest was better than that of most students his age. His weak performance on the Arithmetic subtest was below that of most of his peers. The Comprehension subtest required Bill to provide oral solutions to everyday problems and to explain the underlying reasons for certain social rules or concepts. This subtest provides a general measure of verbal reasoning. In particular, this subtest assesses his comprehension of social situations and social judgment as well as his knowledge of conventional standards of social behavior (Comprehension scaled score = 14).

   Bill was required to mentally solve a series of orally presented problems on the Arithmetic subtest. A direct measure of his numerical reasoning

---

to scaled scores and IQs and generated descriptions of Verbal and Performance functioning. The descriptive information in the first part of the report is followed in the second part by statements concerning confidence intervals for the deviation IQs, the significance of the difference between Verbal and Performance IQs, and a table of deviations (and their significance) of subtest scores from the mean subtest scaled scores. The third part of the report consists of an interpretation of the child's scores and score differences. A fourth (optional) section can be prepared to include case-specific comments, observations, recommendations, and additional data provided by the examiner at the time when the report-generating computer program is run.

   Another useful computer program is the WISC-III Compilation (available from Slosson), designed to facilitate the preparation of assessment reports and individu-

abilities, the subtest requires attention, concentration, short-term memory, and mental control (Arithmetic scaled score = 7).

Bill's performance was significantly better on the Picture Completion subtest than his own mean score for all nonverbal reasoning tasks. Further, he performed much better than most of his age-mates, thus demonstrating very strong abilities on the Picture Completion subtest. The Picture Completion subtest required Bill to identify the missing part in each of a series of pictures of common objects and scenes. An indication of his ability in visual discrimination, the Picture Completion subtest assesses the abilities to detect essential details in visually presented material and to differentiate them from nonessential details. Performance on this task also may be influenced by an individual's general level of alertness to the world around him and long-term visual memory (Picture Completion scaled score = 16).

Summary

Bill is a 7-year-old child who completed the WISC-III. He was referred by his teacher due to attention problems and behavior problems. His general cognitive ability, as estimated by the WISC-III, is average (FSIQ = 109). Bill's general verbal abilities were in the average range (VCI = 107), and general nonverbal abilities were in the superior range (POI = 124).

This report is valid only if signed by a qualified professional:

_____

Dr. Teresa Jones
School Psychologist

_____

alized education plans (IEPs). Long-term goals, short-term objectives, as well as resources and materials for remediation of cognitive deficits are identified.

SYSTEM OF MULTICULTURAL PLURALISTIC ASSESSMENT

During the late 1970s and early 1980s there was a great deal of enthusiasm among educational psychologists and special educators for one particular application of the Wechsler series of tests for children, that of being a part of the System of Multicultural Pluralistic Assessment (SOMPA) (Mercer & Lewis, 1979). The authors of SOMPA maintained that minority children often score low on standardized tests because the tests are culturally biased, or loaded with culture-specific materials. A more accurate picture of a child's potential, they argued, could be obtained by using a multifaceted battery of tests rather than a single test of intelligence.

Description of SOMPA

SOMPA, which is available from The Psychological Corporation, was designed for children between the ages of 5 and 11 years. It consists of two parts. One part, the Student Assessment Materials, follows the *medical model* that health and perceptual-motor development are related to learning disabilities. The battery of tests making up the Student Assessment Materials includes measures of weight by height, visual acuity (measured by a Snellen Chart), auditory acuity (measured by an audiometer), a test to assess perceptual-motor development and detect neurological impairment (Bender Visual Motor Gestalt Test), and a physical dexterity test consisting of ambulation (walking on tiptoes), equilibrium (counting aloud with arms raised and eyes closed, stepping forward before command, pause in counting, and others), placement (index finger to nose, eyes open), fine motor sequencing (finger tapping, one hand), finger–tongue dexterity (opening and closing hands alternately, tongue placement—left cheek), and involuntary movement (arms extended, eyes closed).

A second part of SOMPA is the Parent Interview, which may be conducted in English or Spanish. The Parent Interview is an assessment tool of the *social system model*, which views learning difficulties as related to the child's behavior in adapting to social situations (family, school, community). It consists of three measures: Adaptive Behavior Inventory for Children (ABIC), the Sociocultural Scales, and the Health History Inventories. Sample items from each of these measures are shown in Figure 4–6.

The Student Assessment Materials and the Parent Interview comprise the *pluralistic model* of SOMPA. The various measures employed in the pluralistic model are interpreted by comparing the examinee's performance with that of other children having a similar sociocultural background. Intelligence test scores are analyzed by taking into account the child's position on four sociocultural scales: family size, family structure, socioeconomic status, and urban acculturation. Scores on the WISC-R (or WPPSI) are "corrected" with reference to these measures to produce an *estimated learning potential* (ELP). In contrast to an IQ score, which predicts the effects of instruction in mainstream public school classes, the ELP is designed to predict the extent to which a child will benefit from an educational program that takes his or her sociocultural background into account (Mercer & Lewis, 1979).

Criticisms of SOMPA

Among the criticisms of the SOMPA approach is that it excludes many minority children from the special instruction they require. According to Clarizio (1979), the use of ELPs, or "corrected" Wechsler scores, would result in large numbers of black,

---

Adaptive Behavior Inventory for Children (ABIC)

How often does _____ completely dress himself/herself, including putting on shoes?

1 some of the time,   2 most of the time,   or 0 never (M)

Does _____ go places around the neighborhood (farm) with a group of children his/her own age

2 frequently,   1 occasionally,   or 0 never? (P)

When _____ runs errands where he/she has to carry money or bring back change, does he/she usually go

2 alone or with friends his/her own age,   1 with an older person, or 0 doesn't he/she do this? (E)

Sociocultural Scales

How many persons live in the household?
What is the chief source of income for the family?
What is _____'s relation to the head of the household?

Health History Inventories

Was _____ born earlier than he/she was expected? How many weeks early?
Has _____ ever had a temperature of 104 degrees or higher for more than a few hours?

FIGURE 4-6 **Sample items from the SOMPA Parent Interview.** (Reproduced by permission from the System of Multicultural Pluralistic Assessment. Copyright © 1977 by The Psychological Corporation. Reproduced by permission. All rights reserved.)

Chicano, and Native American children being ineligible for the special educational services and programs that they need.

SOMPA has also been criticized for its limited ELP norm tables, which were computed on a limited sample of California school children. In one study, ELPs based on the regression formula derived by Mercer from the California norms data were 7 to 8 points different from those based on data obtained in Austin, Texas (Oakland, 1979). Other reviewers of SOMPA (Humphreys, 1985; Reynolds, 1985; Sandoval, 1985) have also been critical of the approach. Among their criticisms are that the assumptions on which SOMPA is based are more a matter of opinion than fact, that the claims for SOMPA have not been substantiated, that certain aspects of the approach are not technically sound, that it emphasizes classification rather than intervention, and that it provides little assistance with the development of individualized educational programs.

SUMMARY

The first edition of the Stanford-Binet Intelligence Scale, published in 1916, was designed by Lewis Terman and his associates to differentiate among people within the entire range of general intelligence. Like the Binet-Simon Scale, it was an age scale that retained the concepts of basal age, ceiling age, and mental age. A criterion used in selecting test items for the Stanford-Binet was that an increasing percentage of children at each successive chronological age level should pass the item. Scoring included the concept of an intelligence quotient (ratio IQ), computed as 100 times mental age divided by chronological age.

The second edition of the Stanford-Binet, which consisted of two forms (L and M) and had greater floor and ceiling than its predecessor, was published in 1937. The standardization sample for the second edition was more representative of U.S. children in general than that of the first edition, though only native-born white Americans were included. In general, the IQ scores were highly reliable and their variance had substantial overlap with a general intelligence factor (g).

The third (1960) edition of the Stanford-Binet (Form L-M) was not a new test but a composite of the most reliable and valid items from Forms L and M of the second edition. As was the case with previous editions, testing on Form L-M began by determining the basal age (highest age level at which all subtests were passed) and continued to the ceiling age (lowest age level at which all subtests were failed). The concept of the deviation IQ was introduced as a way of expressing overall performance on the scale. Form L-M was standardized in 1972 on a sample of children selected from seven U.S. communities.

The fourth edition of the Stanford-Binet (SB-IV), which was published in 1986, represented a major departure from previous editions of the scale. The construction of SB-IV involved more sophisticated psychometric procedures and provided for separate scores on fifteen tests and four cognitive abilities areas, as well as a composite score. In designing SB-IV emphasis was placed not only on identifying mentally retarded and gifted children but also on providing information for diagnosing specific causes of learning disabilities.

For many years the earlier editions of the Stanford-Binet served as a standard against which other intelligence tests could be compared. During the past four decades, however, the Wechsler intelligence scales have become increasingly popular. The first Wechsler test designed specifically for school-age children was the Wechsler Intelligence Scale for Children (WISC); the WISC-III is the latest (third) edition of that test. The thirteen subtests of WISC-III are appropriate for children 6 through 16 years, 11 months. Scores on only ten subtests—five Verbal and five Performance—are typically used in determining IQs; scores on Symbol Search, Digit Span, and Mazes, which are supplementary subtests, are not generally included in the computation of IQs.

Raw scores on the WISC-III subtests are converted to subtest scaled scores by referring to a table of score equivalents appropriate for the examinee's age; the subtest scaled scores have a mean of 10 and a standard deviation of 3. The sum of the scaled scores on the five verbal subtests is converted to a Verbal IQ, the sum of the scaled scores on the five performance subtests is converted to a Performance IQ, and the sum of the scaled scores on all ten subtests is converted to a Full Scale IQ. Scaled scores and Index Score Equivalents on four factors—Verbal Comprehension, Perceptual Organization, Freedom from Distractibility, and Processing Speed—may also be computed.

The WISC-III was standardized on a carefully selected national sample of 200 children (100 boys and 100 girls) in each of eleven age groups. Other stratification variables used in selecting the sample were parental education and race. The split-half and test–retest reliability coefficients of the WISC-III subtest scaled scores, the three IQs, and the four factor scores are all satisfactory. The results of validation studies indicate that the scale has a great deal of construct validity.

The System of Multicultural Assessment (SOMPA) was designed to take the child's sociocultural background as well as his or her performance on the WISC-R or WPPSI into account in determining an estimated learning potential (ELP). SOMPA is no longer employed as extensively as it was in the late 1970s and early 1980s.

QUESTIONS AND ACTIVITIES

1. Review the following terms described in this chapter:

abstract response	intelligence quotient (IQ)
basal age	medical model
basal level	pluralistic model
ceiling age	rapport
concrete answer	ratio IQ
critical level	routing test
deviation IQ	SAS
estimated learning potential (ELP)	social system model
functional response	test age

2. Trace the development of the Stanford-Binet Intelligence Scale from the first through the fourth edition.
3. What is the ratio IQ of a child who is 8 years, 9 months if his or her mental age on the Stanford-Binet Form L-M is equal to a mental age of 6 years, 5 months?
4. Why are deviation IQs considered to be psychometrically superior to ratio IQ scores?
5. What are some of the criticisms of the fourth edition of the Stanford-Binet, and why should a review of these criticisms lead Reynolds (1987) to conclude that the use of the SB-IV is like playing IQ roulette and that the test should *requiescat in pace* (rest in peace)?
6. Compare the WISC-III with the older and newer editions of the Stanford-Binet in terms of age range, types of abilities measured, fairness of the test to physically or culturally disadvantaged people, and other pertinent features.
7. What are the z score and percentile rank equivalents of the following Full Scale IQs on the

WISC-III: 70, 80, 90, 100, 110, 120, 130? Use a table of normal curve percentages from any elementary statistics book to find the percentile ranks.

8. What are some of the shortcomings of the approach to assessing the cognitive abilities of disadvantaged children represented by the System of Multicultural Pluralistic Assessment (SOMPA), and what is the current status of SOMPA?

SUGGESTED READINGS

Carter, A. (1990). A new Binet, and old premise: A mismatch between technology and evolving practice. *Journal of Psychoeducational Assessment, 8,* 443–450.

Chapman, P. D. (1988). *Schools as sorters: Lewis M. Terman, applied psychology, and the intelligence testing movement, 1890–1930.* New York: New York University Press.

Glutting, J. J., & Kaplan, D. (1990). Stanford-Binet Intelligence Scale, Fourth Edition: Making the case for reasonable interpretations. In C. R. Reynolds & R. W. Kamphaus (Eds.), *Handbook of psychological & educational assessment of children: Intelligence & achievement* (pp. 277–295). New York: Guilford Press.

Laurent, J., Swerdlik, M., & Ryburn, M. (1992). Review of validity research on the Stanford-Binet Intelligence Scale: Fourth Edition. *Psychological Assessment, 4,* 102–112.

Matarazzo, J. D. (1990). Psychological assessment versus psychological testing: Validation from Binet to the school, clinic, and courtrooms. *American Psychologist, 45,* 999–1017.

McDermott, P. A., Fantuzzo, J. W., & Glutting, J. J. (1990). Just say no to subtest analysis: A critique on Wechsler theory and practice. *Journal of Psychoeducational Assessment, 8,* 290–302.

Reynolds, C. R. (1987). Playing IQ roulette with the Stanford-Binet, 4th ed. *Measurement and Evaluation in Counseling and Development, 20,* 139–141.

Zachary, R. A. (1990). Wechsler's Intelligence Scales: Theoretical and practical considerations. *Journal of Psychoeducational Assessment, 8,* 276–289.

Individual Testing of School-Age Children II: K-ABC, DTLA, and DAS

The three instruments discussed in this chapter—the Kaufman Assessment Battery for Children (K-ABC), the Detroit Tests of Learning Aptitude (DTLA-3), and the Differential Ability Scales (DAS)—are alike in a number of ways. All three intelligence test batteries consist of a large number of subtests (sixteen for the K-ABC, eleven for the DTLA-3, and twenty for the DAS) having a wide age range. All three instruments yield a number of part scores on subtests that presumably measure different mental processes, as well as a total score. Thus, they are designed to diagnose strengths and weaknesses in specific cognitive functions and to provide clues for instructional remediation. However, the three instruments have as many differences as similarities. The K-ABC is based on several theories of intelligence or cognition and has been subjected to a large number of validation studies. The DTLA-3, on the other hand, is a revision of an older (1935) instrument that has nowhere near the extensive research foundations of the K-ABC. Finally, the DAS, which is a revision and restandardization of the British Ability Scales, is based on a hierarchical, developmental theory of intelligence.

KAUFMAN ASSESSMENT BATTERY FOR CHILDREN

A more recent American entry into the individual intelligence test market than the Stanford-Binet and Wechsler tests is the Kaufman Assessment Battery for Children (K-ABC). Developed by Alan S. Kaufman and Nadeen L. Kaufman, the K-ABC was designed for use in educational and clinical settings. The Kaufmans maintained that intelligence tests such as the Stanford-Binet and the Wechsler Intelligence Scale for Children—Revised (WISC-R) result in too many minority students being placed in special classes. Consequently, they planned an instrument that would be fairer to minorities, provide separate measures of intelligence and achievement, and serve the following purposes: psychological and clinical assessment, psychoeducational evaluation of learning-disabled and other exceptional children, educational planning and placement, minority group assessment, preschool assessment, neuropsychological assessment, and research investigations. They recognized, however, that the K-ABC would not be a measure of innate or immutable ability, a neurological test battery, or the complete test battery (Kaufman & Kaufman, 1983b). The Kaufmans proposed to construct a set of tests that would measure intelligence from a theoretical perspective, include novel tasks, be easy to administer, be sensitive to the characteristics of preschool, minority, and exceptional children, distinguish between problem-solving skills and knowledge acquisition, and yield scores that could be translated into educational interventions.

Theoretical Background

The theoretical perspective from which the K-ABC was developed incorporated ideas from a variety of sources, in particular the neuropsychological model of brain functioning proposed by Aleksandr Luria and adapted by J. P. Das and his colleagues. Although Luria's theory distinguished among the arousal, planning, and sequential–simultaneous problem-solving functions of the human brain, only the last of these played a role in the development of the K-ABC. According to Luria (1966), the frontal and temporal lobes of the cerebral cortex control successive, or sequential, mental scanning processes, whereas the parietal and occipital lobes control simultaneous reasoning processes.* An example of a sequential task is attempting to recall a series of numbers; the successful completion of this task requires the examinee to order a set of stimuli serially or temporally. A simultaneous reasoning task, such as interpreting a partially complete picture, requires the ability to synthesize and integrate information into a whole (*gestalt*).

Rather than adhering to Luria's specific brain localization of simultaneous and successive processes, Kaufman and Kaufman preferred Roger Sperry's (1968) split-

---

*See Chapter 12 for another approach to intelligence testing based on Luria's research—the PASS cognitive processing model.

brain interpretation of the two processes as being functions of the right and left cerebral hemispheres, respectively.* Unfortunately, the empirical evidence for separate brain centers that are responsible for simultaneous and successive processing is skimpy at best, and the Kaufmans' use of this distinction in the development of the K-ABC has been criticized (Bracken, 1985; Das, 1984; Herbert, 1982; Lichtenstein & Martuza, 1984). A. S. Kaufman (1984) responded at length to the critics, and, as we shall see, the results of research on the K-ABC offer support for the simultaneous–successive distinction between mental tasks. These findings, however, do not prove that the two mental functions are located in specific hypothesized brain areas. An equally probable explanation is that they are complex functions involving several areas of the brain.

The Kaufmans criticized other intelligence tests, such as the Stanford-Binet and Wechsler series, as being primarily measures of knowledge acquisition (achievement) rather than intelligence. Maintaining that problem solving and information processing are different functions from knowledge acquisition, the Kaufmans recognized the predictive and diagnostic value of achievement tests. Consequently a separate series of Achievement subtests was included on the K-ABC. The items on these subtests were derived from rational and logical considerations rather than from a theoretical base such as that which guided the development of the Mental Processing scales. The K-ABC Achievement subtests contain items similar to those found on conventional tests of achievement and/or intelligence (reading, verbal concepts, vocabulary, arithmetic, and general information), as opposed to the problem-solving tasks of the Mental Processing subtests. Items were selected on the basis of their difficulty and discrimination indexes, goodness of fit to a one-parameter latent trait model, and freedom from sex and ethnic bias.

A set of subtests on the K-ABC also forms a separate Nonverbal Scale. The subtests on this scale can be administered in pantomime and responded to motorically by children with language handicaps. Thus the sixteen subtests on the K-ABC are grouped in various combinations to yield four scales: Sequential Processing, Simultaneous Processing, Mental Processing Composite (Sequential + Simultaneous), and Achievement. Scores on a fifth, Nonverbal Scale can also be obtained to provide intelligence estimates for linguistically or culturally handicapped children. The items on all scales were reportedly designed to be as fair as possible to children of both sexes and different sociocultural backgrounds. Whether the effort to create an unbiased test resulted in poorer predictive validity and less effective measurement of general intelligence (g) than competing batteries is a matter of dispute (see Jensen, 1984).

Descriptions of the K-ABC Subtests

The sixteen subtests of the K-ABC are described below. Three of the sixteen subtests (Magic Window, Faces and Places, and Reading/Understanding) are novel tasks, and four subtests (Face Recognition, Hand Movement, Gestalt Closure, and

*Sperry's cerebral specialization theory differentiates between analytic-sequential and gestalt-holistic processes controlled by the left and right hemispheres, respectively.

Word Order) were adapted from neuropsychological research. The remaining nine subtests are modifications of subtests or tasks on other intelligence tests.

Sequential Processing Subtests

3. Hand Movements. The twenty-one items on this subtest were designed for ages 2½ years to 12 years, 5 months. The examiner makes a series of hand movements, and the examinee tries to repeat them in the same sequence. Hand Movements is usually the first subtest administered to children aged 5 years and over.

5. Number Recall. The nineteen items on this subtest were designed for ages 2½ years to 12 years, 5 months. The examiner says a series of numbers, and the examinee tries to repeat them orally in the same sequence as they were presented.

7. Word Order. The twenty items on this subtest were designed for ages 4 years to 12 years, 5 months. The examiner says a series of words (names of common objects) and then exposes a page containing silhouettes of the objects. The examinee's task is to point to the silhouettes of the objects in the same order as the examiner named them.

Simultaneous Processing Subtests

1. Magic Window. The fifteen items on this subtest were designed for ages 2½ years to 4 years, 11 months. The examiner rotates a disk to expose continuous segments of a picture through a narrow slit or window, making the picture only partially visible to the examinee at any time. The examinee attempts to name the object pictured without having seen it in its entirety.

2. Face Recognition. The fifteen items on this subtest were designed for ages 2½ years to 4 years, 11 months. The examiner exposes for 5 seconds a photograph with one or two faces pictured. Then the examinee tries to select the face(s) from a second photograph of a group of people.

4. Gestalt Closure. The twenty-five items on this subtest were designed for ages 2½ years to 12 years, 5 months. The examiner exposes a partially completed inkblot drawing, and the examinee tries to name the object that is pictured.

6. Triangles. The eighteen items on this subtest were designed for ages 4 years to 12 years, 5 months. The examiner supplies the correct number of identical triangles; the examinee must assemble the triangles to construct an abstract design matching a model.

8. Matrix Analogies. The twenty items on this subtest were designed for ages 5 years to 12 years, 5 months. The examiner exposes a visual analogy with one element missing. The examinee's task is to select the picture or design that best completes the analogy.

9. Spatial Memory. The twenty-one items on this subtest were designed for ages 5 years to 12 years, 5 months. The examiner exposes a page of one or more pictures for 5 seconds. On the following page, the examinee must demonstrate memory of the placement of the pictures by pointing to a series of boxes indicating the positions of the pictures shown on the preceding page.

10. Photo Series. The seventeen items on this subtest were designed for ages 6 years to 12 years, 5 months. The examiner places before the examinee a set of photographs of an event in a specific, nonchronological order. The examinee tries to stack the pictures in the examiner's hand in a logical chronological order.

Achievement Subtests

11. Expressive Vocabulary. The twenty-four items on this subtest were designed for ages 2½ years to 4 years, 11 months. The examiner shows a photograph to the examinee, who tries to name the object pictured.

12. Faces and Places. The thirty-five items on this subtest were designed for ages 2½ years to 12 years, 5 months. The examiner shows a photograph or illustration of a well-known person, a fictional character, or a place to the examinee, who attempts to name it.

13. Arithmetic. The thirty-eight items on this subtest were designed for ages 3 years to 12 years, 5 months. The examiner shows a picture and asks a question to assess the examinee's ability to solve mathematical tasks using math concepts, counting, and computational skills.

14. Riddles. The thirty-two items on this subtest were designed for ages 3 years to 12 years, 5 months. The examiner reads a list of characteristics, and the examinee tries to give the name of the concrete or abstract concept indicated by the characteristics.

15. Reading/Decoding. The thirty-eight items on this subtest were designed for ages 5 years to 12 years, 5 months. The examiner exposes letters and words, and the examinee attempts to name the letters and read the words aloud.

16. Reading Understanding. The twenty-four items on this subtest were designed for ages 7 years to 12 years, 5 months. The examiner exposes a sentence telling the examinee to do something; the examinee must demonstrate reading comprehension by acting out the command.

Administration and Scoring

For those who have administered individual intelligence tests such as the Sanford-Binet and Wechsler series, it is fairly easy to learn to give the K-ABC. You should read the *K-ABC Administration and Scoring Manual*, especially Chapter 3, for complete details on administering and scoring the battery. Administration time ranges from an average of 45 minutes for preschoolers to 70–75 minutes for school-age children. The test materials are included in three easels and other packets of materials.

Seven to thirteen of the sixteen subtests are administered, the specific subtests varying with the chronological age of the examinee. When a subtest is spoiled or otherwise omitted, Table 9 of the *K-ABC Administration and Scoring Manual* can be used to estimate the sum of subtest scaled scores. Starting and stopping points on a specific subtest, shown in the Individual Test Record booklet, also vary with the age of the child. Testing is continued past the stopping point—the last unit for an examinee's chronological age—only when the child passes all items in that unit. Testing is discontinued before the last unit only if every item in a preceding unit is failed.

Rules for Starting and Stopping Subtest Administration

The starting and stopping rules for the K-ABC subtests are the following (Kaufman & Kaufman, 1983a):

1. On the Mental Processing subtests, administer the sample item first, teaching (demonstrating its solution) if necessary.
2. On all subtests, begin testing with the item designated for the child's age. Teach the first two scored items on a Mental Processing subtest but not on an Achievement subtest if they are failed.
3. On all subtests, stop testing at the item designated for the child's chronological age in the second booklet unless the criterion for discontinuing has been met or unless the child passes all items in the last unit for the age group. In the latter case, continue testing on that subtest until the child fails an item.
4. On all subtests, stop testing before the designated stopping point if the child fails all items in a unit. However, if the child fails all items in the first unit for his or her age-group, go back to item 1 of that subtest and test with successive items until the criterion for discontinuing has been met.

Testing a child at a different level from his or her chronological age (*out-of-level testing*) is permissible in two cases: a mentally retarded child whose chronological age is 5 years through 5 years, 11 months, may be tested at the level for 4-year-olds, and a mentally gifted child aged 4 years, 6 months to 4 years, 11 months, may be tested at the 5-year level.

Scoring

In determining the total raw score on a subtest, the number of errors (items scored 0) is subtracted from the ceiling item (highest item administered). The raw score on each Mental Processing subtest is then converted to a standard score scale (scaled score) having a mean of 10 and a standard deviation of 3 (see "Mental Processing Subtests" in the lower-left section of Figure 5–1. Percentile ranks specific to the examinee's sociocultural group (low, medium, high), which are referred to as "Sociocultural Percentile Ranks," are also available for recording and interpreting. These norms were obtained from testing students in three socioeconomic, or socioeducational, categories. Other norms, such as age equivalents, may also be recorded on the Mental Processing and Achievement subtests.

Scores on five Global Scales (Sequential, Simultaneous, Mental Processing Composite, Achievement, Nonverbal) are listed in the lower right section of the Individual Test Record (Figure 5–1). In this case, not all subtests on the Nonverbal Scale were given to the examinee (Mary B.), so the converted Nonverbal scores are

K·ABC Kaufman Assessment Battery for Children
by Alan S. Kaufman and Nadeen L. Kaufman

INDIVIDUAL TEST RECORD

Name _Mary B._ Sex _F_

Parents' names _Rita and James_

Home address _807 S. Lincoln_

Home phone _782-4602_

Grade _4_ School _Central Elementary_

Examiner _Norma Ehrhardt_

SOCIOCULTURAL INFORMATION (if pertinent)

Race _black_

Socioeconomic background _Mather finished 3rd grade, housewife; father finished 6th grade. construction worker_

	YEAR	MONTH	DAY
Test date	94	10	17
Birth date	83	11	12
Chronological age	10	11	5

Achievement Subtests X = 100; SD = 15	Standard score – band of error 90 % confidence	Nat'l %ile rank Table 4	Socio-cultural %ile rank Table 5	S or W Table 11	age eq. Other data	grade eq
11. Expressive Vocabulary	⊥		/////			
12. Faces & Places	87 - 8	19	35		8-9	
13. Arithmetic	92 - 8	30	70		9-6	
14. Riddles	99 - 9	47	90	S	10-6	
15. Reading/ Decoding	73 - 8	4	10	W	7-6	2.4
16. Reading/ Understanding	67 - 8	1	5	W	7-3	1.9
Sum of subtest scores	418		Transfer sum to Global Scales Sum of subtest scores column			

Mental Processing Subtests X = 10; SD = 3	Scaled Score			Nat'l %ile rank Table 4	S or W Table 11	age eq. Other data
	Sequential	Simultaneous	Non-verbal			
1. Magic Window	/////		/////			
2. Face Recognition	/////					
3. Hand Movements	10	/////		50		11-9
4. Gestalt Closure	/////	14		91	S	above 12-6
5. Number Recall	11	/////		63		above 12-6
6. Triangles	/////	8		25		8-0
7. Word Order	6	/////	/////	9	W	6-6
8. Matrix Analogies	/////	9		37		9-9
9. Spatial Memory	/////	7		16		8-3
10. Photo Series	/////	9		37		9-9
Sum of subtest scores	27	47		Transfer sums to Global Scales. Sum of subtest scores column		

AGS ®

© 1983, American Guidance Service. Inc
Circle Pines, Minnesota 55014

No part of this test record may be photocopied or otherwise reproduced

Global Scales X = 100; SD = 15	Sum of subtest scores	Standard score – band of error 90 % confidence Table 2	Nat'l %ile rank Table 4	Socio-cultural %ile rank Table 5	age eq. Other data
Sequential Processing	27	93 - 8	32	50	11-9
Simultaneous Processing	47	95 - 6	37	80	9-9
Mental Processing Composite	74	93 - 6	32	70	9-9
Achievement	418	81 - 4	10	30	8-9
Nonverbal		-			

Global Scale Comparisons

Indicate ·· or		Circle the significance level
Sequential ≈ Simultaneous (Table 10)	NS	05 01
Sequential ≈ Achievement (Table 10)	NS	05 01
Simultaneous > Achievement (Table 10)	NS	05 (01)
M.P.C. > Achievement (Table 10)	NS	05 (01)

FIGURE 5-1 Front page of Individual Test Record form of Kaufman Assessment Battery for Children. (Kaufman Assessment Battery for Children, by Alan S. Kaufman and Nadeen L. Kaufman. © 1983 American Guidance Service, Inc., 4201 Woodland Road, Circle Pines, Minnesota 55014-1796. Reproduced with permission of the Publisher. All rights reserved.)

not listed. Scores on the Global Scales are converted to standard scores having a mean of 100 and a standard deviation of 15, to national percentile ranks, to socio-cultural percentile ranks, and to age-equivalent scores appropriate for the child's chronological age. Other data listed in Figure 5-1 are explained later in the chapter.

Interpretation and Reporting

Chapter 4 of the *K-ABC Administration and Scoring Manual* (Kaufman & Kaufman, 1983a) outlines the steps in scoring and score interpretation. The inter-pretation process consists of comparing scores on the Global Scales, as well as determining significant strengths and weaknesses on the Mental Processing and Achievement subtests.* This involves determining, from Table 10 of the *K-ABC Administration and Scoring Manual*, the standard score difference between two specific Global Scales (Sequential versus Simultaneous, Sequential versus Achieve-ment, Simultaneous versus Achievement, Mental Processing Composite versus Achievement) required for significance at the .05 or .01 levels for the examinee's chronological age level. In the case of a 10-year-old child, these differences are 12, 13, 11, and 10, respectively, at the .05 level and 16, 17, 13, and 12, respectively, at the .01 level. The standard scores obtained by Mary B. on the four Global Scales are 93, 95, 93, and 81, so the obtained differences are 2, 12, 14, and 12 (see Figure 5-1). The third and fourth differences (Simultaneous versus Achievement and Mental Processing Composite versus Achievement) are significant at the .01 level. The significant differences in these comparisons indicate that Mary B. is not achiev-ing up to her intellectual potential.

Interpreting Subtest Scores

After scores on the Global Scales have been compared, significant strengths and weaknesses on the subtests should be examined. Table 11 of the *K-ABC Admin-istration and Scoring Manual* gives the minimum scaled score differences re-quired to be significantly different (.05 or .01 level) from the scaled score average. The average score on the eight Mental Processing subtests administered to Mary B. is 9.25. The scaled score differences from this average required for significance at the .05 level at Mary's age are listed in Table 11 of the manual as 4 for Gestalt Closure and Number Recall and 3 for the other six subtests. The score of 14 on Gestalt Closure is significantly higher, and the score of 6 on Word Order is signifi-cantly lower than the mean of Mary's scaled scores on the Mental Processing subtests. These are the significant differences to be emphasized in the report of subtest scores. In interpreting differential strengths and weaknesses on the various subtests, the examiner should refer to pages 36–57 of the *K-ABC Interpretive Manual* (Kaufman & Kaufman, 1983b), where the background and psychological analysis of each subtest are described.

*Report 3-1 in Chapter 3 is a narrative case report of performance on the K-ABC, integrated with scores on other psychological tests and behavioral observations.

Table 11 of the manual includes a list of differences between standard scores on the Achievement subtests that are required for statistical significance. The procedure for determining on which subtests or scaled scores the examinee has significant strengths and weaknesses is the same as with the Mental Processing subtests. Averaging Mary B.'s standard scores on the Achievement subtests yields a mean of 83.6. Table 11 of the manual shows that at age 10 a minimum difference of 12 points (from a base figure of 83.6) for the Riddles subtest and 11 points (from 83.6) on the other four subtests is required for significance at the .05 level. Notice that the obtained score of 99 on Riddles is significantly higher than 83.6 and is therefore a strength (S). Similarly, the score of 67 on Reading/Understanding, which is significantly lower than 83.6, is interpreted as a weakness (W).

Score Profile

A profile of scaled scores on the various subtests and the Global Scales, plotted on the last page of the Individual Test Record form, provides a graphical summary of the examinee's overall performance (Figure 5-2). Notice that for the Achievement subtests and the Global Scales, a band of error at the 68 to 99 percent confidence level is drawn below the bar representing the scaled score. The numerical equivalents of these error bands, obtained from Table 2 of the *K-ABC Administration and Scoring Manual*, are listed to the left of the score profile bars in Figure 5-2. Each band spans a range of values within which one can be 90 percent confident (in this case) that the examinee's (Mary B.'s) true score on the subtest or scale falls.

Psychometric Characteristics of the K-ABC

The K-ABC was standardized in 1981 on a sample of 2,000 children at 34 testing centers in 24 states. In addition to being stratified by age group (100 children at each half-year age level between 2½ and 12 years, 5 months), the sample was stratified by sex, geographic region, socioeconomic status (educational attainment of parents or adults in home), ethnic group (white, black, Hispanic, other), community size, and educational placement of the child (normal or special classes). The proportion of examinees represented at almost all levels of the stratification variables was based on the 1980 U.S. Census. The norms are expressed as standard scores, percentile ranks, and age equivalents.

Sociocultural Norms

Subsequent to testing the national standardization group, samples of 496 black and 119 white children were tested between November 1981 and March 1982. The scores obtained from these supplemental samples were combined with those obtained from 311 black children and 1,450 white children in the national standardization group, yielding a total sociocultural norms sample of 807 black and 1,569 white children. Norms for the combined group were computed on the Global

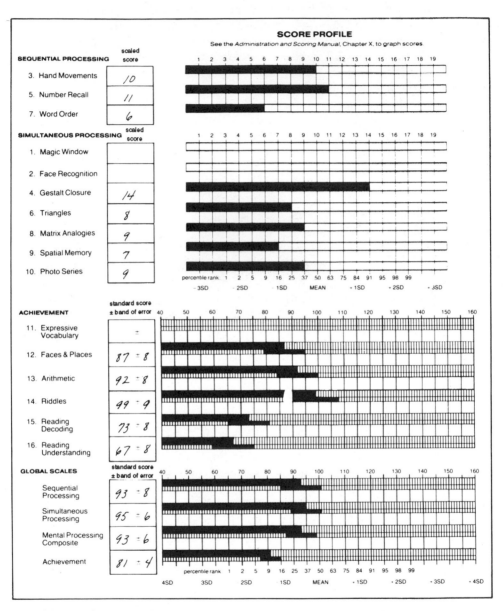

FIGURE 5-2 Back page of Individual Test Record form of Kaufman Assessment Battery for Children.
(Kaufman Assessment Battery for Children, by Alan S. Kaufman and Nadeen L. Kaufman. © 1983
American Guidance Service, Inc., 4201 Woodland Road, Circle Pines, Minnesota 55014-1796. Repro-
duced with permission of the Publisher. All rights reserved.)

Scales, the Nonverbal Scale, and all the Achievement subtests except Expressive Vocabulary. The sociocultural norms were determined separately by ethnic group (black versus white) and socioeconomic status (three parental educational levels). The norms, expressed as sociocultural percentile ranks for the twelve groups (two races × two ages × three parental educational levels) are listed in Table 5 of the *K-ABC Administration and Scoring Manual*. These norms are interpreted similarly to the estimated learning potential (ELP) of the System of Multicultural Pluralistic Assessment (SOMPA) (see Chapter 4), taking the sociocultural status of the child into account in interpreting his or her scores. Unlike the ELPs of SOMPA, however, separate norms on the K-ABC are not provided for Hispanics and Native Americans.

Out-of-Level Norms

Supplementary norms for out-of-level testing of children in the 4½- to 5-year age bracket are also given in the *K-ABC Administration and Scoring Manual*. The norms on three subtests—Matrix Analogies, Spatial Memory, and Reading/Decoding— were extended downward from age 5 to 4 years, 1 month. Similarly, the norms on three other subtests—Magic Window, Face Recognition, and Expressive Vocabulary— were extended upward from age 4½ to 5 years through 5 years, 11 months. These out-of-level norms, given in Table 8 of the manual, were derived by psychometric estimation procedures based on the national sample rather than actual out-of-level testing of 4- and 5-year-old children.

Reliability

Split-half and test–retest reliability coefficients for various subtests and the Global Scales are given in Chapter 4 of the *K-ABC Administration and Scoring Manual*. Split-half coefficients for the subtests range from .72 for Magic Window to .88 for Number Recall at the preschool level and from .71 for Gestalt Closure to .85 for Matrix Analogies at the school level. The split-half coefficients of the Achievement subtests range from .77 for Faces and Places at the preschool level to .92 for Reading/Decoding at the school level. The split-half coefficients for the Global Scales range from .86 (Simultaneous Processing) to .93 (Achievement) for preschool children and from .89 (Sequential Processing) to .97 (Achievement) for school-age children. The split-half coefficients for the Mental Processing Composite and the Achievement Scale average in the .90s at all age levels.

Data on the test–retest reliability of the Global Scales were obtained by retesting 246 children in the 2½- to 12½-year age range after an interval of 2 to 4 weeks. The test–retest coefficients, which increase with age, range from .75 to .85 for most Mental Processing subtests and from .85 to .95 for the Achievement subtests. Test–retest coefficients for the Global Scales range from .77 to .97, being lowest for Sequential Processing and highest for Achievement. Alternate forms coefficients ranging from .83 to .95, based on a sample of forty-one 4- to 5-year-olds, are also reported in the manual.

Validity

Evidence for the construct, predictive, and concurrent validity of the K-ABC is described in Chapter 4 of the *K-ABC Interpretive Manual*. Support for the construct validity of the simultaneous and successive processing dimensions is found in the results of confirmatory factor analyses of the K-ABC scales in large, heterogeneous groups of examinees. Each subtest of the Simultaneous Processing Scale has its highest loading on the Simultaneous factor, and subtests on the Sequential Processing Scale generally have their highest loadings on the Sequential factor. Factor analyses and other research findings also support separation of the Achievement subtests from the Mental Processing Composite subtests.

Moderately high correlations (.60s and .70s) have been obtained between the K-ABC Mental Processing Composite (MPC) and scores on the SB-IV Test Composite, the WISC-R Full Scale IQ, and scores on other intelligence tests (Bloom et al., 1988; Hayden, Frulong, & Linnemayer, 1988; Krohn & Lamp, 1989; Krohn, Lamp, & Phelps, 1988; Smith, St. Martin, & Lyon, 1989). Also noteworthy is that MPC scores tend to be about 5 points lower than WISC-R Full Scale IQs. This may mean either that the two tests measure different characteristics or that the norm group for the K-ABC was not comparable to that on which the WISC-R was standardized. In any case, the findings demonstrate that the MPC is not identical to or interchangeable with WISC-R IQs.

Concerning the correlations of the K-ABC with standardized achievement tests such as the Iowa Tests of Basic Skills or the California Achievement Test, in normal samples scores on the K-ABC Achievement subtests correlate between .58 and .80 with these tests. Representative of the concurrent validity of MPC scores is a correlation of .63 with the Woodcock Passage Comprehension Test (592 children aged 6 to 12½ years) and correlations in the .50s with scores on various standardized reading tests (Kaufman & Kaufman, 1983b).

Regarding its factor structure, the K-ABC appears to tap three factors. Two of these factors are interpreted as sequential and simultaneous processing, but the third factor has been variously described as verbal comprehension and reading achievement (Good & Lane, 1988), achievement and reading ability (Kaufman & McLean, 1986), or reading achievement and verbal reasoning (Keith & Novak, 1987).

Applications and Criticism

One of the major uses for which the K-ABC was designed is the identification and diagnosis of learning disabilities in children, which might suggest specific remediation programs. The last section of Chapter 4 of the *K-ABC Interpretive Manual* contains profiles of scores based on testing of learning-disabled, mentally retarded, behaviorally disordered, physically handicapped, high-risk (preschool children), hearing-impaired, and gifted children. Many of these profiles, however, are tentative and await more extensive research to confirm their accuracy. A number of other studies using the K-ABC have been concerned with learning diagnosis and remediation for deaf children (Martin, n.d.), word-finding disorders (German, 1983), learning-disabled children (Naglieri & Haddad, 1984), and developmental dyslexia (Hooper & Hynd, 1982).

In the K-ABC, the Kaufmans have constructed an intelligence test battery based on a quasi-theoretical foundation, according to fairly sophisticated psychometric procedures and freer from ethnic group bias than many of its competitors. Black–white score differences in the standardization sample are smaller than those on the Stanford-Binet and WISC-R.

Criticisms of the K-ABC

Despite its advantages, the K-ABC is not without shortcomings. In a critical review, Bracken (1985) faulted the test battery for being an imperfect match with its theoretical foundations, having a disproportionate contribution of the Simultaneous Processing subtests to the Mental Processing Composite, the manner in which the specific variance of the subtests was computed and is used in interpreting scores, problems with prorating scores when fewer than the usual number of subtests are administered, and the utility of the test with various exceptional populations. Also in a critical vein, Sattler (1988) complained of (1) misleading use of the term *mental processing* for some subtests and *achievement* for other subtests, (2) more emphasis in the Mental Processing Composite placed on Simultaneous Processing subtests than on Sequential Processing subtests, (3) a lack of verbal comprehension or reasoning items on the Mental Processing Composite, (4) heavy reliance on short-term memory and attention tasks, (5) use of the term *processing* to characterize some subtests and not others, (6) ambiguity in the use of the terms *simultaneous processing* and *sequential processing*, (7) improper use of the K-ABC in classifying mental retardation over the entire age range of the scale, (8) limitations in its use with gifted children because of the low ceiling of the K-ABC, (9) difficulty in evaluating the effectiveness of instructional strategies based on a child's K-ABC profile, and (10) major sampling problems with the test standardization group.

Although it can be adapted to testing hearing-handicapped children, the highly visual nature of the test materials makes the K-ABC less useful with visually handicapped children than instruments having greater verbal–auditory content. Some of the materials may also be difficult for orthopedically handicapped children to manipulate. In addition, the K-ABC shares with other intelligence tests the problems of insufficient floor and ceiling; it measures less accurately at the extremes of the ability and age ranges. The limited verbal demands of the test may also make it less clinically useful than the Stanford-Binet and Wechsler scales (Lichtenstein & Martuza, 1984).

Kaufman (1984) denied that the K-ABC was designed specifically to minimize racial differences, but Jensen (1984) alleged that the inclusion of many tests that rely heavily on short-term memory and circumvent language skills—tests that have a research history of producing small mean score differences between blacks and whites—is responsible for the smaller racial differences found with the K-ABC than with conventional intelligence tests. Because of the "heavy memory demands" of the Simultaneous Processing Scale in particular, Sternberg (1984) challenged the validity of the K-ABC as a whole.

In addition to revealing smaller racial discrepancies, the K-ABC Mental Processing scales predict scholastic achievement less accurately than the Stanford-Binet and WISC-R. Kaufman (1984) acknowledged this criticism but argued that if one's sole purpose is to predict school achievement, then a measure of school achievement rather than intelligence should be employed. He maintained that conventional intelligence tests predict achievement better than the K-ABC because they are basically tests of achievement. The K-ABC, on the other hand, is a measure of the child's approach to problem solving and learning.

Instructional Planning

Other criticisms of the K-ABC include its reliance on an outmoded neuropsychological theory of brain functioning (Herbert, 1982) and whether, as the Kaufmans maintain, the scores can be used to design educational plans and teaching strategies. Kaufman, Kaufman, and Goldsmith (1984) provide recommendations for teaching based on K-ABC scores. Materials consisting of a *Leader's Guide*, a set of transparencies, and a cassette tape–recorded interview were designed to train teachers in the interpretation and application of the sequential–simultaneous processing dichotomy. The emphasis in workshops employing these materials has been on adapting instructional programs or strategies to student abilities defined by scores on the K-ABC. For example, it is recommended that students who score high on sequential processing should be taught by the guidelines for sequential processing (see Report 3–1). Despite its intuitive appeal, this testing–teaching approach has yielded mixed results.

Lichtenstein and Martuza (1984) concluded that the claim that the K-ABC can be applied to the planning of instructional strategies matched to the abilities measured by the test battery is at best only tentatively supported by research evidence. According to these critics the guidelines and examples provided by the Kaufmans for teaching reading, spelling, and arithmetic to children having sequential or simultaneous processing strengths and/or weaknesses must be evaluated on an individual case basis rather than being adopted as an overall blueprint for educational intervention. A review of the above criticisms and other matters pertaining to clinical and research applications of the K-ABC is given in the book by Kamphaus and Reynolds (1987).

DETROIT TESTS OF LEARNING APTITUDE

The first edition of the Detroit Tests of Learning Aptitude (DTLA) was published in 1935, and a revised manual was published in 1967 (Baker & Leland, 1967). A second, completely restandardized edition of the test (DTLA-2) was published in 1985 (Hammill, 1985), and a third edition (DTLA-3) in 1991 (Hammill, 1991). DTLA-3, which is designed for children between six and 17 years old, consists of the eleven subtests listed in Table 5–1. The subtests on a primary edition (DTLA-P:2) (by D. D. Hammill & B. R. Bryant; pro.ed), designed for children between the ages of 3 and 9 years, are listed in Table 5–2. The subtests on an adult version of the tests, the Detroit Tests of Learning Aptitude—Adult (DTLA-A) (by D. D. Hammill & B. R. Bryant) are listed in Table 5–3.

Administration and Scoring

The entire series of eleven DTLA-3 subtests takes from 50 to 120 minutes to administer, but the primary edition (DTLA-P:2) requires only 15 to 20 minutes. As with the Stanford-Binet, administration of the DTLA-3 subtests involves determining a basal level and a ceiling level. On subtests 2, 4, 5, 6, 10, and 11, testing begins with item 1; on subtests 1, 3, 7, 8, and 9 it begins with the entry point items listed in the manual (Hammill, 1991). There is no ceiling age on subtests 2, 4, 5, and 10; on subtests 1, 3, 7, 8, 9, and 11, the ceiling age is five consecutive misses, and on subtest 6 the ceiling age is reached when three consecutive items are missed. Items on subtests 1, 2, 3, 4, 5, 7, 8, 9, and 11 are scored 0 or 1 point; items on subtest 6 are scored 0, 1, 2, or 3 points, and items on subtest 10 are scored 0 to 5 points.

Raw scores on the subtests are converted to standard scores having a mean of

---

TABLE 5–1   Subtests on the Detroit Tests of Learning Aptitude (DTLA-3)

1. *Word Opposites.* The examiner says a word, and the examinee responds with a word that means just the opposite.
2. *Design Sequences.* The examinee is shown a series of designs for 5 seconds. The picture is then removed from view, and the examinee is given a group of cubes that have designs on all sides. The examinee then arranges the cubes to reproduce the previously shown design sequence.
3. *Sentence Imitation.* The examiner says a sentence, and the examinee repeats it verbatim.
4. *Reversed Letters.* The examiner says a series of letter names. The examinee then writes each letter in a small box, reversing the presentation order of the letters.
5. *Story Construction.* The examinee makes up three stories about three different topics (basketball game, field trip, and space activity). The stories are scored for thematic content.
6. *Design Reproduction.* The examiner shows a design for 5 seconds. Once it is removed from view, the examinee draws the design from memory.
7. *Basic Information.* The examinee responds to questions concerning commonly known facts.
8. *Symbolic Relations.* The examinee is shown a visual problem involving geometric or line drawings and is then asked to point to the correct answer, which is embedded among six pictured possibilities.
9. *Word Sequences.* The examiner says a series of unrelated and isolated words to the examinee, who then repeats the sequence.
10. *Story Sequences.* The examiner shows a series of cartoonlike pictures to the examiee, who then indicates the meaningful order of the pictures by placing numbered chips in boxes below the pictures.
11. *Picture Fragments.* The examinee is asked to say aloud the names of common objects depicted in a series of pictures that are printed with various elements missing.

Reprinted by permission of pro.ed.

TABLE 5–2   Subtests on Detroit Tests of Learning Aptitude—Primary (DTLA-P:2)

Articulation. The child repeats a stimulus word exactly as the examiner has articulated it.

Conceptual Matching. The child points to the response choice that best goes with a set of stimulus pictures.

Design Reproduction. The child copies a design that is shown by the examiner.

Draw-A-Person. The child draws a picture of a boy or girl and receives credit for including specified body parts.

Letter Sequences. The child either points to or writes a series of letters that matches the stimulus sequence.

Motor Directions. The child imitates motor patterns produced by the examiner.

Object Sequences. The child either points to or notes with a pencil the order of objects shown by the examiner.

Oral Directions. The child performs paper-and-pencil tasks in response to a verbal command.

Picture Fragments. The child identifies a picture that has some of its parts missing.

Picture Identification. The child identifies a picture of a common object.

Sentence Imitation. The child repeats sentences spoken by the examiner.

Reprinted by permission of pro.ed.

10 and a standard deviation of 3; percentile ranks and age equivalents corresponding to raw scores may also be determined.*

The standard scores on various combinations of the eleven subtests are summed to yield four types of composite scores. These composite scores ("quotients") are based on a mean of 100 and a standard deviation of 15. An Overall Composite score is determined by combining scores on all eleven subtests. An Optimal Level Composite, which is considered to be the best estimate of the examinee's overall cognitive "potential," is obtained by combining the four highest standard scores on the eleven subtests. The third class of composites, the Domain Composites, is subclassified into the following six composite scores:

- *Verbal Composite.* Knowledge of words and their use.
- *Nonverbal Composite.* Does not involve reading, writing, or speech.
- *Attention-Enhanced Composite.* Emphasizes concentration, attending, and short-term memory.
- *Attention-Reduced Composite.* Emphasizes long-term memory.
- *Motor-Enhanced Composite.* Emphasizes complex manual dexterity.
- *Motor-Reduced Composite.* Relatively motor free.

The last class of composites, the Theoretical Composites, is formed by assigning the eleven subtests to appropriate categories in various theoretical conceptions of intelligence. These include Cattell and Horn's model of fluid and crystallized intelligence, Jensen's model of associative and cognitive levels, Das's model of simul-

*A Software Scoring and Report System for DTLA-3, DTLA-P:2, and DTLA-A is available from pro.ed. The computer software for DTLA-3 converts raw scores to standard scores, percentile ranks, and age equivalents, and generates composite scores. Significant differences among the converted scores are determined, and comparisons are made between performance on the DTLA-3 and achievement tests.

TABLE 5–3   Subtests on Detroit Tests of Learning of
Aptitude—Adult (DTLA-A)

1. *Word Opposites.* Vocabulary.
2. *Form Assembly.* Creating a whole, given its parts.
3. *Sentence Imitation.* Grammar.
4. *Reversed Letters.* Oral recall, auditory.
5. *Mathematical Problems.* Solving word problems.
6. *Design Sequences.* Visual discrimination and memory.
7. *Basic Information.* Knowledge of commonly known facts.
8. *Quantitative Relations.* Abstract numeric problem solving.
9. *Word Sequences.* Repeating words.
10. *Design Reproduction.* Drawing from memory.
11. *Symbolic Relations.* Visual reasoning.
12. *Story sequences.* Organizational concept ability.

Reprinted by permission of pro.ed.

taneous and successive processing, and Wechsler's model of verbal and performance scales.

Standardization, Reliability, and Validity

The DTLA-3 was standardized on 2,587 students in thirty-six states. The DTLA-
P:2 was standardized on 2,217 children from thirty-six states and two Canadian
provinces, and the DTLA-A was standardized on 1,000+ adults from over twenty
states. The demographic characteristics of the normative samples for the DTLA-3
and DTLA-A corresponded to the 1990 Census data relative to gender, geographic
region, ethnicity, race, and urban-rural residence.

The average internal consistency reliabilities of all three DTLA batteries are
mostly above .80 for the subtests and above .90 for the composites. Test–retest
coefficients for DTLA-3 exceed .70 for the subtests and .80 for the composites.
Evidence for the criterion-related validity of DTLA-3 is found in correlations with
the WISC-R, the Kaufman Assessment Battery for Children, the Scholastic Aptitude
Test, and the Woodcock-Johnson Psycho-Educational Battery—Revised. Evidence
for the construct validity was demonstrated by correlations of DTLA-3 scores with
chronological age and with scores on the Science Research Associates (SRA)
Achievement Series, the Diagnostic Achievement Test for Adolescents—Second
Edition, and the Wide Range Achievement Test—Revised.

The psychometric characteristics of the DTLA-3 are a definite improvement
over those of the DTLA-2. The norm groups are more representative of the target
population, and the internal consistency and test–retest reliabilities are higher. The
manual (Hammill, 1991) is clearer with respect to administration procedures and
provides more information concerning the psychometric characteristics of the test.
In particular, evidence for the construct and criterion-related validity of the instru-

ment is much more detailed than for DTLA-2. In sum, DTLA-3 represents a much improved, thorough revision of DTLA-2.

DIFFERENTIAL ABILITY SCALES

Somewhat reminiscent of another adaptation of a foreign-born, individually-administered intelligence test (the Binet-Simon Intelligence Scale) for American school children are the Differential Ability Scales (DAS). The DAS, which was designed by Colin Elliott and published by The Psychological Corporation in 1990, is a revision and restandardization of the British Ability Scales (BAS). The basic purpose of the DAS, like that of the BAS, is to provide ability profiles for analyzing and diagnosing children's learning difficulties, to assess changes in abilities over time, and to identify, select, and classify children (ages 2½ to 17 years) with learning disabilities.

Description

The DAS consists of seventeen cognitive and three achievement subtests for assessing the multidimensional nature of abilities in children and adolescents. The subtest tasks, which are colorful, interesting, and varied, were designed to have homogeneous content and good reliability so examinees' profiles could be analyzed for strengths and weaknesses. A hierarchical model of intelligence, with a general conceptual ability at the top level, general verbal and general nonverbal abilities at a second level, and the individual (verbal and nonverbal) subtests at a third level, was used in designing the DAS.

As shown in Table 5–4, the preschool level subtests are grouped into three ability areas: Verbal Ability, Nonverbal Reasoning Ability, and the Diagnostic subtests. The subtests at this age level, which can be administered to children aged 2.6 to 6 years, measure reasoning, verbal, perceptual, and memory abilities. Subtests at the school-age level are grouped into four areas: Verbal Ability, Nonverbal Reasoning Ability, Spatial Ability, and the Diagnostic subtests. These subtests can be administered to children aged 7 to 17.11 years.

Administration

Typically, eight to twelve ability subtests, with a total time of approximately 35 minutes at the preschool level and 90 minutes at the school-age level, are administered. Testing begins with items that are easy enough to measure low ability. For each subtest, starting and stopping points based on the child's age are recommended. The particular items that are administered are adapted or tailored to the examinee's responses to previous items, reducing overall testing time. In addition to the subtests of cognitive abilities, three achievement subtests (Word Reading, Spelling, and Basic Number Skills), requiring a total time of 15–20 minutes, are included in the battery. Grade equivalents, grade percentiles, and age-based stan-

TABLE 5-4   Preschool and School-Age Level Subtests on the DAS

Ability area	Subtests	
	Preschool level	School-age level
Verbal Ability	Verbal Comprehension Naming Vocabulary	Word Definitions Similarities
Nonverbal Reasoning Ability	Picture Similarities Pattern Construction Copying Early Number Concepts	Matrices Sequential and Qualitative Reasoning
Spatial Ability		Recall of Designs Patterns Construction
Diagnostic subtests	Block Building Matching Letterlike Forms Recall of Digits Recall of Objects Recognition of Pictures	Recall of Digits Recall of Objects Speed of Information Processing

dard scores (mean of 100 and standard deviation of 15) are determined on the three achievement subtests.

Scoring

The sum of scores on the Verbal and Nonverbal Ability subtests at the pre-school level or the Verbal, Nonverbal, and Spatial Ability subtests at the school-age level is converted to a General Conceptual Ability (GCA) score having a mean of 100 and a standard deviation of 15. Separate standard scores on Verbal Ability and Nonverbal Ability at both levels and on Spatial Ability at the school-age level (mean of 100 and standard deviation of 15) are also determined. Finally, the subtest scaled scores have a mean of 50 and a standard deviation of 10.

Performance on the Diagnostic subtests provides information for diagnosing the child's strengths and weaknesses in cognitive abilities. Separate percentile ranks and standard scores on Verbal Ability, Nonverbal Reasoning Ability, and Spatial Ability are reported for the diagnostic subtests, including measures of perceptual and memory skills.

Standardization and Norms

The cognitive abilities and achievement subtests on the DAS were standardized on a sample of 3,475 children selected to match the 1988 U.S. Census figures and stratified according to age, gender, race/ethnicity, parent education, geographic region, and educational preschool enrollment. The cognitive and achievement measures were developed and normed together to permit measurement and interpretation of ability–achievement differences. In addition to normal children, the standardization sample included children with learning disabilities, speech and language impairments, mental retardation, emotional disturbance, and mild visual, hearing, or motor impairments. Items biased against blacks and Hispanics were identified by bias analysis of the performance of large samples of children in these ethnic categories. The provision of out-of-level norms on the achievement tests permits the evaluation of children within a broad range of abilities.

Reliability and Validity

With respect to the reliability of the DAS, test–retest coefficients range from .85 to .94 for the GCA score and from .79 to .95 for the Verbal and Nonverbal Ability scores. Interrater reliability estimates for subtests that require subjective reasoning (Copying, Recall of Designs, Similarities, Word Definitions) are all in the .90s.

The results of factor analyses of the subtest scores indicate that the DAS measures one factor (GCA) at ages 2 years, 6 months to 3 years, 5 months, two factors (Verbal Ability and Numerical Ability) at ages 3 years, 6 months through 5 years, 11 months, and three factors (Verbal Ability, Nonverbal Reasoning Ability, and Spatial Ability) at ages 6 years through 17 years, 11 months. Comparisons of DAS scores with scores on other measures of ability and achievement in handicapped and nonhandicapped children attest to the validity of the test as a measure of both cognitive ability and achievement. However, the samples on which the validity data were obtained were relatively small.

SUMMARY

The three individual intelligence test batteries discussed in this chapters—the Kaufman Assessment Battery for Children (K-ABC), the Detroit Tests of Learning Aptitude (DTLA-3, DTLA-P:3, DTLA-A), and the Differential Ability Scales (DAS)— are similar in a number of ways. All three batteries include a large number of subtests containing a variety of content and are appropriate for a wide range of chronological ages. The K-ABC and the DAS are also similar in being based on a theory of intelligence and in including a set of achievement measures as well as ability tests. With respect to differences between the three test batteries, the K-ABC and the DAS differ from the DTLA-3 in being based on a definite theory of intel- ligence, in relying on sophisticated psychometric procedures in test development, and in their greater freedom from sex and ethnic bias. Other differences between the three batteries include a larger number of subtests on the K-ABC and the DAS, but a wider age span on the DTLA-3, and the greater body of research conducted on the K-ABC than the DTLA-3 and the DAS. Overall, the K-ABC and the DAS are more carefully constructed and standardized instruments than the DTLA-3 although not without shortcomings.

The sixteen subtests on the K-ABC, a maximum of thirteen of which are administered to a child within the chronological age span of the test (2½ to 12½ years), are grouped into three categories: three Sequential Processing subtests, seven Simultaneous Processing subtests, and six Achievement subtests. The Sequential and Simultaneous Processing subtests are combined as ten Mental Processing subtests, in addition to a group of six Nonverbal subtests. Scaled scores on the various subtests are combined and converted to yield scores on the five Global Scales (Sequential Processing, Simultaneous Processing, Mental Processing Composite, Achievement, and Nonverbal). Scores on the first three Global Scales assess a child's ability to solve problems requiring simultaneous and sequential mental processes, whereas the Achievement Scale measures acquired skills in reading and arithmetic. The Nonverbal Scale is employed less frequently but is useful in providing an estimate of the functioning intelligence of language-handicapped children.

The gamelike subtests of the K-ABC can be administered to a preschool child in 30–50 minutes or to a school-age child in 50–80 minutes. The K-ABC was standardized on a stratified sample of 2,000 American children, in addition to supplementary samples of minority and exceptional children. Separate percentile norms by race and by socioeconomic level for white and black children are reported in the manual. Both split-half and test–retest reliability coefficients for the Global Scales and subtests are similar to those obtained with other individual tests of intelligence. In addition, over forty validity studies are reported in the K-ABC 1983 interpretive manual, and dozens of additional studies have been conducted subsequently.

Despite its obvious good features, the K-ABC has been criticized for a number of reasons, including its reliance on a questionable theory of brain functioning (the Das-Luria neuropsychological theory), the large number of memory subtests (which may account for smaller differences in mean scores between blacks and whites), the lower predictive validity of the Mental Processing Composite score than IQs on other tests, and applications of the simultaneous–sequential distinction in determining teaching strategies.

The second individual intelligence test discussed in this chapter, the DTLA-3, is a revision of an older and longer series of tests published originally in 1935 and revised in 1984. The eleven subtests on the DTLA-3 were designed primarily for school-age children, the age range of the 1984 standard score norms being at six-month intervals from age 6 to 17 years, 11 months.

The eleven subtest scaled scores on the DTLA-3 may be combined to yield nine composite scores, including an Overall (General Intelligence) Composite consisting of scores on all eleven subtests, an Optimal Composite, six Domain Composites, and eight Theoretical Composites. The internal consistency reliabilities of the subtests and composite scores are comparable to those of other intelligence tests, but the test–retest reliability and validity statistics provided in the manual are meager. Furthermore, the modest reliabilities of the differences between scores on the pairs of aptitudes constituting each of the four domains make the use of these scores for differential diagnosis questionable.

The third individual intelligence test battery discussed in this chapter, the DAS, is an adaptation and restandardization on American children of the British Ability

Scales. The battery contains seventeen subtests of cognitive abilities and three achievement subtests. The cognitive abilities subtests are grouped into two ability areas—Verbal and Nonverbal—at the preschool level and into three ability areas—Verbal, Nonverbal Reasoning, and Spatial—at the school-age level. Subtests are scored separately as well as in combination to obtain the area scores and a General Conceptual Ability (GCA) score. The norms and reliability coefficients for the subtest, area, and GCA scores are satisfactory. The results of factor analyses of the DAS provide support for its construct validity, but empirical evidence for the validity of this instrument is, like that for the DTLA-3, somewhat scanty.

QUESTIONS AND ACTIVITIES

1. Define each of the following terms used in this chapter:

gestalt	overall composite score
mental processing	sequential processing
optimal level composite	simultaneous processing
out-of-level testing	

2. Compare the Kaufman Assessment Battery for Children (K-ABC), the Detroit Tests of Learning Aptitude (DTLA-3), and the Differential Ability Scales (DAS) in terms of age range, types of abilities measured, fairness to physically handicapped and culturally disadvantaged children, and other relevant characteristics.
3. What are the principal assets and liabilities of each of the three individual intelligence tests described in this chapter?
4. On what neuropsychological theory of brain functioning is the K-ABC based, and how valid is the theory?
5. Which of the three intelligence tests described in this chapter would be most appropriate for testing the cognitive abilities of: (1) normal school children, (2) mentally retarded children, (3) physically handicapped children, (4) culturally disadvantaged children, (5) children with specific learning disabilities, (6) "normal" adolescents, (5) mentally disordered adults?
6. Kaufman argues that traditional intelligence tests such as the Stanford-Binet and Wechsler series are actually tests of achievement and therefore it is not surprising that scores on such tests correlate more highly with school grades than the mental processing composite of the K-ABC. Are most intelligence tests really tests of achievement? Is that all they are? If so, why not just use achievement test scores to select applicants for admission to academic programs?
7. During the first two weeks of school, psychologists were hired by a public elementary school in an affluent neighborhood to administer the K-ABC to all entering kindergarten and first-grade children. Was this procedure desirable and/or useful? Why or why not?
8. Why did Kaufman consider it necessary to include an achievement test in addition to simultaneous and successive processing scales on the K-ABC?
9. The Differential Ability Scales were originally developed in Great Britain as the British Intelligence Scales. Even though they were restandardized on American children, can the DAS really be considered a fair measure of the cognitive abilities of children in what is a rather different culture from that of Great Britain?

SUGGESTED READINGS

Conoley, J. C. (1990). Review of the K-ABC: Reflecting the unobservable. *Journal of Psycho-educational Assessment, 8,* 369–375.

Elliott, C. D. (1990). The nature and structure of children's abilities: Evidence from the Differential Ability Scales. *Journal of Psychoeducational Assessment, 8,* 376–390.

Elliott, S. N. (1990). The nature and structure of the DAS: Questioning the test's organizing model and use. *Journal of Psychoeducational Assessment, 8,* 406–411.

Kamphaus, R. W. (1990). K-ABC theory in historical and current contexts. *Journal of Psychoeducational Assessment, 8,* 356–368.

Kamphaus, R. W., Kaufman, A. S., & Harrison, P. L. (1990). Clinical assessment practice with the Kaufman Assessment Battery for Children (K-ABC). In C. R. Reynolds & R. W. Kamphaus (Eds.), *Handbook of psychological & educational assessment of children: Intelligence & achievement* (pp. 259–276). Norwood, NJ: Ablex.

Keith, T. Z. (1985). Questioning the K-ABC: What does it measure? *School Psychology Review, 14*(1), 9–20.

Chapter 6

Individual Testing of Adolescents and Adults: Wechsler Adult Intelligence Scale

---

CHAPTER OUTLINE

Two of the test batteries described in the last chapter—the DTLA-3 and the DAS—in addition to the WISC-III, are appropriate for adolescents up through ages 16 or 17. In addition, the Stanford-Binet-IV can be used with adolescents and adults. Less widely known individual intelligence tests for adolescents and adults are the Detroit Tests of Learning Aptitude-Adult (DTLA-A), the Kaufman Brief Intelligence Test (K-BIT), and the Kaufman Adolescent and Adult Intelligence Test (KAIT). Like the K-BIT, the KAIT (from American Guidance Service) is based on R. B. Cattell's theory of fluid and crystallized intelligences (see Chapter 12). The core battery of the KAIT consists of three tests (Auditory Comprehension, Double Meanings, Definitions) making up the Crystallized Scale and three tests (Rebus Learning, Mystery Codes,

Logical Steps) making up the Fluid Scale. Four additional tests (Memory for Block Designs, Famous Faces, Rebus Recall, Auditory Recall) are also administered in the expanded battery. Global scores on fluid, crystallized, and composite intelligence ($\bar{X} = 100$, $s = 15$) and scaled scores on the ten subtests ($\bar{X} = 10$, $s = 3$) are calculated. The KAIT is new and noteworthy, but the most popular intelligence test for adolescents and adults has been the Wechsler Adult Intelligence Scale.

BACKGROUND AND EARLY TESTS

Among the thousands of young men who were inducted into the U.S. Army during the First World War was one whose name became a household word in psychological testing: David Wechsler. Wechsler's primary job in the military was to administer the new group intelligence tests—the Army Examinations Alpha and Beta—to inductees. Those who failed these group-administered tests were given the individually administered Stanford-Binet Intelligence Scale and/or the Yerkes, Bridges, and Hardwick Point Scale. His army testing experiences made Wechsler aware of some of the limitations of the Stanford-Binet, particularly as a test for adults. The development of a better test for assessing adult intelligence had to wait, however, for another twenty years.

Wechsler held several professional positions during the 1920s. He was a psychologist at the New York Bureau of Child Guidance and at the Brooklyn Jewish Social Service Agency. He also served as secretary of The Psychological Corporation, a commercial testing organization founded in 1921 by J. McKeen Cattell, E. L. Thorndike, and Robert Woodworth (Wechsler, 1981a). In the early 1930s Wechsler

FIGURE 6-1 **David Wechsler.** (From J. D. Matarazzo, 1972. *Wechsler's measurement and appraisal of adult intelligence,* 5th ed., Baltimore: Williams & Wilkins. Used by permission of the author.)

became chief psychologist at Bellevue Hospital in New York City, an institution whose name combined with his became the shortened title (Wechsler-Bellevue) of the most famous test of adult intelligence. It was a test that, because of its suitability for adults and its clinical emphasis, became one of the foremost assessment devices in clinical psychological testing during and after World War II.

As in any other hospital that attempts to diagnose and treat acutely and chronically disturbed mental patients, the psychologists at Bellevue Hospital cooperated with physicians in identifying specific disorders and recommending treatment. The task was not easy; the patients represented a variety of diagnostic conditions: transient or milder emotional disorders, schizophrenia, manic-depressive psychosis, disorders associated with organic brain damage, mental retardation, illiteracy, and others. Even determining the functioning intelligence of such adult patients was not simple. Most of the patients had little formal education, and many could not read or write English at a basic level. This made valid administration of the Stanford-Binet Intelligence Scale, a highly verbal test designed primarily for children, difficult.

From his experiences at Bellevue Hospital, Wechsler concluded that there was a need for an intelligence test that was less heavily loaded with verbal material, composed of tasks more suitable for adults, and which would place less emphasis on time limits. Like the Stanford-Binet, such a test would consist of many different types of items. Unlike the Stanford-Binet, in addition to an overall score, separate scores would be provided on various subtests. Wechsler hoped that by yielding separate subtest scores, the scale would also prove useful in diagnosing mental disorders.

Conceptions of Intelligence

Wechsler's aim was to design an instrument that would be different in many ways from Lewis Terman's Stanford-Binet Intelligence Scale. Wechsler's ideas differed from Terman's—for one, his definition or conception of intelligence. In all fairness, Terman surely recognized that performance on the Stanford-Binet was influenced by both heredity and environment. But to a greater extent than Binet, Terman tried to design a test that measured genetic potential. Wechsler, on the other hand, candidly admitted that the Wechsler-Bellevue scale was not a measure of inherited potential independent of experience. To Wechsler, performance on an intelligence test was the result of a complex interplay between biological development and personal experiences. Not only did he recognize the role of experience but also that noncognitive variables play a significant role in determining how well a person does on an intelligence test.

Wechsler's definition of intelligence changed somewhat over the years, and he never seemed entirely clear about what his tests were measuring. In 1958 he defined intelligence as the "aggregate or global capacity of the individual to act purposefully, to think rationally, and to deal effectively with his environment" (Wechsler, 1958, p. 7). By 1975 he had revised the definition of intelligence to the "capacity of an individual to understand the world about him and his resourcefulness to cope with its challenges" (Wechsler, 1975, p. 139). The common core of meaning in these definitions is the ability to cope or effectiveness in dealing with the environment. Clearly, however, coping with the environment involves more than cognitive skills; affective (emotional) and conative (motivational) factors are also important in determining intelligent behavior. Thus Wechsler's definition of intelligence is not restrictively cognitive; it involves other aspects of personality in a more holistic way. For example, how well one performs on an intelligence test, and in solving life's problems in general, depends not only on cognitive abilities but on attentiveness to the task and the dedication with which a solution is pursued.

In sum, David Wechsler viewed general intelligence as multifaceted, multi-determined, and a function of personality as a whole. He considered an intelligent person to be one who is able to deal effectively with life's challenges—abstract, practical, or social. Therefore, differentiating between more intelligent and less intelligent persons requires a multifaceted measure of cognitive, affective, and conative behaviors. Intelligent people behave more intelligently in the sense that they are likely to be aware of the consequences of their actions, and those actions tend to be more rational, worthwhile, and meaningful (Wechsler, 1975).

Wechsler-Bellevue Intelligence Scales I and II

Wechsler's first intelligence test, the Wechsler-Bellevue Intelligence Scale (Wechsler-Bellevue Form I), was published in 1939 (Wechsler, 1939). In developing this scale, Wechsler rejected Binet's concept of mental age in favor of Yerkes's point-scale method of scoring. On a point scale, numerical weights or points are assigned to each item; the number of points awarded depends on the level of sophistication of the examinee's response. Unlike the Stanford-Binet, on which items were grouped into age levels, items on the Wechsler-Bellevue I were grouped into sub-tests according to content. Within each of the eleven subtests, items were arranged in order of increasing difficulty.

The six Verbal subtests (Information, Comprehension, Arithmetic, Similarities, Vocabulary, Digit Span), which required responding in words or sentences, were administered first in the order listed. The five Performance subtests (Picture Completion, Picture Arrangement, Block Design, Object Assembly, Coding), which required pointing (Picture Completion), arranging cards in order (Picture Arrangement), constructing designs with blocks (Block Design), putting puzzles together (Object Assembly), and writing symbols (Coding), were administered after the Verbal subtests and in the order listed.

Grouping test items into Verbal and Performance scales made possible the calculation of three intelligence quotients: a Verbal IQ derived from the sum of scaled scores on the six Verbal subtests; a Performance IQ derived from the sum of scaled scores on the five Performance subtests; and a Full Scale IQ derived from the sum of scaled scores on all eleven subtests. All three intelligence quotients were deviation IQs having a mean of 100 and a standard deviation of 15. The Wechsler-Bellevue I was standardized on 1,081 whites in New York City and surrounding areas. Although the standardization sample was selected according to the U.S. Census figures by age (10–60 years), education, and occupation, it was not truly representative of the adult population of the United States.

Performance scales such as the Arthur Point Scale of Performance Tests, the Leiter International Performance Scale, and the Pintner-Paterson Scale of Performance Tests had been available for some years prior to publication of the Wechsler-Bellevue I and had proved their value in assessing intelligence in children having linguistic, educational, or cultural handicaps. However, what made the Wechsler-Bellevue I unique was the incorporation of Verbal and Performance scales within the same test battery and the standardization of the battery on adults. This made possible the testing of a wider range of individuals—for example, those with linguistic or sensorimotor handicaps. Furthermore, a comparison of the Verbal and Performance IQs, as well as the pattern of scores on the eleven subtests, provided clues for diagnosing clinical disorders and learning disabilities. Unfortunately, Wechsler profiles were and continue to be overinterpreted in many cases.

Appearing as it did on the eve of World War II, in addition to its civilian uses the Wechsler-Bellevue I was employed extensively for testing military personnel and veterans. A second form of the scale, the Army Wechsler, was devised in 1942. After the war (1946), a modified and extended version of the Army Wechsler was published as the Wechsler-Bellevue Intelligence Scale Form II.

Wechsler Adult Intelligence Scale

The inadequate standardization of the Wechsler-Bellevue Intelligence Scale was remedied in 1955 with the publication of the Wechsler Adult Intelligence Scale (WAIS). The WAIS was designed to test the intelligence of adults from ages 16 to 75 years; a correction for "deterioration" was applied to the scores of examinees at the upper end of the age range. Similar to the Wechsler-Bellevue I and II, the WAIS consisted of six Verbal and five Performance subtests. The eleven subtests were administered in the same order as those on the Wechsler-Bellevue I: all the Verbal subtests first and then all the Performance subtests. Items within each subtest were arranged in order of increasing difficulty, and testing on a particular subtest was discontinued when the examinee failed a specified number of items in succession. It took approximately 1 hour to administer the Full Scale (all eleven subtests).

Although the Full Scale WAIS provided measures of the examinee's functioning in a wide range of cognitive tasks, it was not possible to administer all eleven subtests to handicapped persons. When there were severe visual or motor handicaps, for example, it was sometimes necessary to omit the Performance Scale entirely and administer only the Verbal Scale. The reverse (administration of the Performance Scale alone) was recommended in the case of examinees having severe language handicaps. However, an authorized Spanish-American edition of the WAIS—the Escala de Inteligencia Wechsler Para Adultos—was made available for testing Spanish-speaking adults. This Spanish translation was standardized in Puerto Rico in 1965. Unfortunately, the standardization sample was not selected in such a way that the norms could be considered representative of the Puerto Rican population. The WAIS was also translated into several other languages, but the translations were not properly standardized.

In scoring the WAIS, the raw score on each subtest was converted to a standard score scale having a mean of 10 and a standard deviation of 3. The sum of scaled scores on the six Verbal subtests was then converted to a Verbal IQ, the sum of scaled scores on the five Performance subtests was converted to a Performance IQ, and the sum of scaled scores on all eleven subtests was converted to a Full Scale IQ. Tables for these conversions, which varied with the chronological age group, were given in the WAIS manual.

The standardization sample for the WAIS consisted of 1,700 adults, including equal numbers of men and women 16 years and over, divided into seven age-groups. The sample was carefully selected to be representative of the U.S. population, according to statistics obtained from the 1950 Census, in terms of geographic location, urban versus rural residence, race (white versus nonwhite), occupational level, and education. One institutionalized mentally retarded person of each sex was included at each age level in the standardization sample.

An additional sample of persons aged 60 years and over was used in developing supplementary old-age norms for the WAIS. This sample consisted of fifty men and fifty women in each of four age groups (60–64, 65–69, 70–74, 75 and over), but the number of cases in each age–sex group on which the IQ tables were based was considerably smaller. Furthermore, the old-age groups were selected by quota-sampling procedures from metropolitan Kansas City, which was described as a typical U.S. city. For these and other technical reasons, the sample used in computing the IQ tables on the WAIS for age 60 and above was not truly representative of U.S. citizens in that age group. Recognition of this fact was seen in the provision for more representative sampling of older adults in the development of the Wechsler Adult Intelligence Scale—Revised (WAIS-R).

CONTENT, ADMINISTRATION, AND SCORING OF THE WAIS-R

A generation after publication of the WAIS, it was evident that the scale needed revising and restandardizing. Approximately four-fifths of the items, unmodified or in slightly modified form, were retained in the new edition, the WAIS-R, published in 1981. The remaining WAIS items were omitted because of datedness or poor psychometric characteristics, and new items were designed to replace them. In addition, arrangement of the items and the scoring of some of them were changed. Two new subtests, a test of spatial ability and a level of aspiration measure, were considered for inclusion on the WAIS-R; however, experimental tryouts of these two subtests led to a decision not to include them on the new scale.

One of the most significant changes made in revising the WAIS was the order of administering the subtests. Unlike the procedure of giving all WAIS Verbal subtests first and then all Performance subtests, the six WAIS-R Verbal and five Performance subtests are administered in alternating order, as follows:

> Information (V)
> Picture Completion (P)
> Digit Span (V)
> Picture Arrangement (P)
> Vocabulary (V)
> Block Design (P)
> Arithmetic (V)
> Object Assembly (P)
> Comprehension (V)
> Digit Symbol (P)
> Similarities (V)

Experience had suggested that alternating the administration of Verbal and Performance subtests creates greater variety and interest and decreases boredom and fatigue.

Descriptions of Subtests

Information. The material on this subtest consists of thirty-three general information questions to be answered in a few words or numbers. The questions are arranged in easy-to-difficult order. Testing begins with item 5; items 1 to 4 are administered if the examinee fails either item 5 or 6. Testing is discontinued when the examinee fails seven items in a row. Responses are scored 0 or 1, and are affected by familial and cultural background.

Picture Completion. The material on this subtest consists of twenty-seven pictures on cards, each having a part missing. The examinee is allowed 20 seconds per picture to indicate what is missing. Testing begins with item 1 and is discontinued when the examinee fails seven consecutive items. Responses are scored 0 or 1. The subtest was designed to measure visual alertness, memory, and attention to details.

Digit Span. On this subtest, seven series of digits are to be recited forward and seven series are to be recited backward. Testing on "Digits Forward" begins with three digits read aloud (one digit per second) by the examiner. The examinee is told to repeat each series as soon as the examiner has finished. Two trials are given on each series length (two different sets of digits). Testing on "Digits Forward" continues until the examinee fails both trials of a series or succeeds on nine digits forward. On "Digits Backward" the examinee is told to say the digits backward after the examiner has finished saying them forward. Testing begins at two digits backward and continues until the examinee has failed both trials of a series or succeeded on eight digits backward. The score on each set of "Digits Forward" or "Digits Backward" is 0, 1, or 2; total score is the sum of part scores on "Digits Forward" and "Digits Backward." This subtest was designed to measure immediate rote memory, but scores are affected by attention span and comprehension.

Picture Arrangement. The material on this subtest consists of ten sets of cards, with each card in a set containing a small picture. The examinee is directed to arrange the pictures in each set of cards into a sensible story. The time limits are 60 seconds on sets 1 to 4, 90 seconds on sets 5 to 8, and 120 seconds on sets 9 and 10. Testing is discontinued when the examinee fails five consecutive sets. Responses are scored 0, 1, or 2, depending on their accuracy. This subtest measures ordering or sequencing ability, as well as social planning, humor, and the ability to anticipate.

Vocabulary. On this subtest thirty-seven words to be defined are presented in order of ascending difficulty. Testing starts with item 1 for examinees having poor verbal ability, otherwise with item 4. Testing is discontinued when the examinee fails six words in a row. Responses to each word are scored 0, 1, or 2, depending on the degree of understanding of the word that is expressed. The subtest was designed to measure knowledge of words, a skill that is highly related to general mental ability.

Block Design. The materials on this subtest are ten red-and-white geometric designs on cards and nine red-and-white blocks. The examinee is instructed to duplicate each design with four or nine blocks. Two attempts are permitted on the first two designs, and one attempt on each succeeding design. Testing is discontinued when four designs in a row are failed. Base scoring is 0, 1, or 2 points on designs 1 and 2, and 0 or 2 points on designs 3 to 10; bonus points are given for rapid, perfect performance. The subtest was designed to measure the ability to perceive and analyze a visual pattern into its component parts. In terms of its correlations with total scores on the Performance Scale and scores on the test as a whole, "Block Design" is considered to be one of the best performance tests of intelligence.

Arithmetic. On this subtest fifteen arithmetic problems are presented in order of increasing difficulty. Testing begins with item 3 and is discontinued after five consecutive failures; items 1 and 2 are given if items 3 and 4 are failed. Fifteen seconds is allowed on problems 1 to 4, 30 seconds on problems 5 to 10, 60 seconds on problems 11 to 14, and 120 seconds on problem 15. Responses are scored 0 or 1; bonus points are given for rapid, perfect performance on certain problems. This subtest measures elementary knowledge of arithmetic, together with the ability to concentrate and reason quantitatively.

Object Assembly. The materials on this subtest consist of four cardboard picture puzzles presented to the examinee in a prearranged format, with directions to put the pieces together to make something. All four puzzles are presented; the time limits are 120 seconds on puzzles 1 and 2 and 180 seconds on puzzles 3 and 4. The score for each puzzle is determined by the number of "cuts" that are correctly joined; bonus points are given for rapid, perfect performance. The subtest was designed to measure thinking, work habits, attention, persistence, and the ability to visualize a final form from its parts.

Comprehension. On this subtest eighteen questions requiring detailed answers are presented in order of ascending difficulty. The questions are asked until the examinee fails six consecutive items. The responses are scored 0, 1, or 2, depending on the quality and degree of understanding expressed. The subtest measures practical knowledge, social judgment, and the ability to organize information.

Digit Symbol. On this subtest the examinee is directed to fill in each of ninety-three boxes with the appropriate coded symbol for the number appearing above the box. Testing begins with a practice series, after which the examinee is given 90 seconds to fill in the ninety-three blank boxes with the correct symbols copied from a key listed above. The score range is 0 to 93 points. The subtest was designed to measure attentiveness and persistence in a simple perceptual-motor task.

Similarities. The materials on this subtest are fourteen items of the type "In what way are A and B alike?" The items are presented in order of ascending difficulty until the examinee fails five in a row. The responses are scored 0, 1, or 2, depending on the quality and degree of understanding expressed. The subtest is designed to measure logical or abstract thinking—the ability to categorize and generalize.

Administration and Scoring

Total testing time for the full WAIS-R battery ranges from 60 to 90 minutes, but the time is considerably less when only the Verbal or Performance Scale or an abbreviated version of the test is administered. As with any other psychological test, the WAIS-R should be administered in a quiet, well-lighted, properly ventilated room. A number of other factors, including the examinee's anxiety level, the examiner's expectations, and the relationship between the examiner and examinee, can affect performance on the test. Although a mild amount of test anxiety is not necessarily a handicap, severe anxiety has a debilitating effect on test performance. Similarly, the examiner's expectations (how well or how poorly the examinee is expected to do) can affect test performance. Prior knowledge, obtained from other sources, of the examinee's abilities can influence these expectations. The biasing effects of the examiner's expectations are particularly significant on verbal tests (Schroeder & Kleinsasser, 1972).

Other factors that might be expected to affect test performance are the language in which the test is administered, whether the examiner and the examinee are of the same or different sex, the training of the examiner, and how the examinee feels about the examiner and the test itself. Whether examinees are tested in their native language appears to have an effect on Verbal but not Performance Scale scores (De Jesus, 1978; Tsushima & Bratton, 1977). However, the question of whether test scores are affected if the examinee and the examiner are members of different ethnic, sex, or socioeconomic groups has not been answered conclusively. In any case, the examiner should be thoroughly trained in the administration and scoring of the WAIS-R. An attempt should also be made to establish rapport with the examinee by introducing oneself and asking a few questions about the examinee's background and experiences.

Examinees should be told why they are taking the test and be able to verbalize the reason to the examiner. To facilitate this understanding, the examiner may make some general statement concerning the nature of the test—for example, that the questions will range from easy to difficult and that although the examinee should do as well as possible on all of them, no one is expected to perform perfectly on every item. Once testing has begun, the examiner should encourage and reassure the examinee but refrain from indicating whether an answer is right or wrong. Test materials that are not in use should be kept out of sight so they will not distract the examinee from the task at hand.

On every item, whether answered correctly or incorrectly, some mark should be made in the Record Form to indicate the examinee's response. Wechsler (1981b) suggested that the following marks be made: "Q" for "question," when the examiner asks a question to get a clearer response; "DK" for "don't know," when the examinee says "I don't know" or in some other way does not finish in the time limit allotted; "NR" for "no response," when the examinee answers neither verbally nor by gesturing; "P" for "portion," when the examinee points to the right place on the Picture Arrangement subtest and "PX" when the wrong place is pointed to.

Scaled Scores and IQs

An examinee's raw score on each of the WAIS-R subtests is converted to a standard score scale having a mean of 10 and a standard deviation of 3. Either Table 19 of the WAIS-R manual or the Table of Scaled Score Equivalents on the first page of the WAIS-R Record Form (Figure 6-2) may be used for the conversion. Subtest scaled score norms for all examinees are based on the responses of a reference sample of 500 examinees ranging from 20 to 34 years of age. The six scaled scores on the Verbal Scale are added to give a Verbal sum of scaled scores, the five scaled scores on the Performance Scale are added to give a Performance sum of scaled scores, and the scaled scores on all eleven subtests are added to give a Full Scale sum of scaled scores. Each of the three sums of scaled scores is then converted to a deviation IQ—Verbal, Performance, Full Scale—by referring to the section of Table 20 of the WAIS-R manual appropriate for the examinee's chronological age-group. Each of the three deviation IQ scales has a mean of 100 and a standard deviation of 15 within the examinee's age-group. Because of the presumed decline of certain mental abilities with age, the sum of scaled scores need not be as high for older examinees as for younger ones to obtain the same IQ. A separate table of age-scaled scores, based on norms for the examinee's age group but not used in the determination of IQs, is also given in the WAIS-R manual. This table permits direct comparisons of an examinee's subtest scaled scores with those of his or her own chronological age group (see numbers in last column of Summary section of Figure 6-2).

Short Forms of the WAIS-R

Although desirable, it is not always possible to administer all six Verbal subtests and all five Performance subtests. If a single subtest is spoiled or for some other reason cannot be given, the sum of scaled scores can be prorated by using Table 23 of the WAIS-R manual. By referring to this table, the sum of scaled scores on five Verbal subtests can be prorated to six subtests, and the sum of scaled scores on four Performance subtests can be prorated to five subtests.

NAME _James L. Clark_ AGE _24_ SEX _M_
MARITAL STATUS _Single_ HANDEDNESS _Right_
OCCUPATION _Shoe Clerk_ EDUCATION _H.S. Graduate_
PLACE OF TESTING _Midwest Testing Center_
TESTED BY _Paul T. Johnson, Ph.D._
REFERRED BY _Frank Miller, Counselor_
REASON FOR REFERRAL _Career Planning_

WAIS-R® EXPANDED RECORD FORM

	Year	Month	Day
Date Tested	1994	4	10
Date of Birth	1970	1	15
Age	24	2	25

TABLE OF SCALED SCORE EQUIVALENTS*

Scaled Score	VERBAL SUBTESTS						PERFORMANCE SUBTESTS					Scaled Score
	Information	Digit Span	Vocabulary	Arithmetic	Comprehension	Similarities	Picture Completion	Picture Arrangement	Block Design	Object Assembly	Digit Symbol	
19	—	28	70	—	32	—	—	—	51	—	93	19
18	29	27	69	—	31	28	—	—	—	41	91-92	18
17	—	26	68	19	—	—	20	20	50	—	89-90	17
16	28	25	66-67	—	30	27	—	—	49	40	84-88	16
15	27	24	65	18	29	26	—	19	47-48	39	79-83	15
14	26	22-23	63-64	17	27-28	25	19	—	44-46	38	75-78	14
13	25	20-21	60-62	16	26	24	—	18	42-43	37	70-74	13
12	23-24	18-19	55-59	15	25	23	18	17	38-41	35-36	66-69	12
11	22	17	52-54	13-14	23-24	22	17	15-16	35-37	34	62-65	11
10	19-21	15-16	47-51	12	21-22	20-21	16	14	31-34	32-33	57-61	10
9	17-18	14	43-46	11	19-20	18-19	15	13	27-30	30-31	53-56	9
8	15-16	12-13	37-42	10	17-18	16-17	14	11-12	23-26	28-29	48-52	8
7	13-14	11	29-36	8-9	14-16	14-15	13	8-10	20-22	24-27	44-47	7
6	9-12	9-10	20-28	6-7	11-13	11-13	11-12	5-7	14-19	21-23	37-43	6
5	6-8	8	14-19	5	8-10	7-10	8-10	3-4	8-13	16-20	30-36	5
4	5	7	11-13	4	6-7	5-6	5-7	2	3-7	13-15	23-29	4
3	4	6	9-10	3	4-5	2-4	3-4	—	2	9-12	16-22	3
2	3	3-5	6-8	1-2	2-3	1	2	1	1	6-8	8-15	2
1	0-2	0-2	0-5	0	0-1	0	0-1	0	0	0-5	0-7	1

¹Scaled score equivalents of raw scores for a specific age range(see Manual, Table 21). Not to be used for determination of IQ.

*Clinicians who wish to draw a profile may do so by locating the examinee's raw scores on the table above and drawing a line to connect them. See Chapter 4 in the Manual for a discussion of the significance of differences between scores on the subtests.

SUMMARY

	Raw Score	Scaled Score	Age Scaled Score¹
VERBAL SUBTESTS			
Information	20	10	11
Digit Span	12	8	8
Vocabulary	44	9	10
Arithmetic	13	11	11
Comprehension	15	7	7
Similarities	18	9	9
Verbal Score		54	
PERFORMANCE SUBTESTS			
Picture Completion	13	7	7
Picture Arrangement	6	6	6
Block Design	27	8	8
Object Assembly	28	8	7
Digit Symbol	45	7	7
Performance Score		37	

	Scaled Score	IQ	Percentile Rank	Classification
Verbal Score	54 †	94	34	Average
Performance Score	37 ‡	80	9	Low Average
Full Scale Score	91	86	18	Average

†Prorated from 5 subtests, if necessary.
‡Prorated from 4 subtests, if necessary.

FIGURE 6-2 **WAIS-R Record Form.** (Reproduced by permission from the Wechsler Adult Intelligence Scale—Revised. Copyright © 1981, 1955 by The Psychological Corporation. Reproduced by permission. All rights reserved.)

The situation becomes more complicated when several subtests are omitted. If all subtests on either the Verbal or Performance Scale are omitted, then obviously only the Performance or Verbal IQ, respectively, can be obtained. An abbreviated scale consisting of selected Verbal and Performance subtests can also be administered under special circumstances, as when testing time is short or when the most reliable and valid results are not required. A short form might be useful, for example, in determining the likelihood that a person is retarded and therefore that more extensive testing is necessary.

Silverstein (1982b) proposed as a screening device a two-subtest short form of the WAIS-R consisting of the Vocabulary and Block Design subtests, as well as a four-subtest short form consisting of Vocabulary, Block Design, Arithmetic, and Picture Arrangement. Tables of Full Scale IQ equivalents of the sums of scaled scores on these two short forms are provided by Silverstein (1982b). The estimated IQ on the four-subtest short form is within 9 points of the actual IQ about two-thirds of the time. Silverstein recognized, however, that the tabled values are only estimates of Full Scale IQs. Because they are based on WAIS-R standardization data in which all eleven subtests were administered, the tables do not take into account differences in testing conditions and possible corresponding differences in results when only two or four subtests are administered to independent groups of examinees. Because of their limited reliability, the conclusion of King and King (1982, p. 433) that "while Wechsler short forms may be useful as research instruments, their clinical applications are extremely limited at this time," would still seem to apply. Whenever shortened or abbreviated versions of the WAIS-R are administered, they should be viewed as rough screening devices that do not provide the same opportunity as administration of the Full Scale for making qualitative observations of the examinee's behavior.

PSYCHOMETRIC CHARACTERISTICS OF THE WAIS-R

The WAIS-R was standardized on a carefully selected national sample of 1,880 adults in nine age groups: 16–17, 18–19, 20–24, 25–34, 35–44, 45–54, 55–64, 65–69, and 70–74 years. The subsample for each of these age-groups contained equal numbers of men and women, including 100 persons of each sex in the first three groups, 150 persons of each sex in the fourth group, 125 of each sex in the fifth and sixth groups, and 80 of each sex in the seventh through ninth age groups (Wechsler, 1981b).

The 16–17 and 18–19 year age-groups in the standardization sample were not really representative of these age groups in the total population. This is probably the main reason why the WAIS-R scores of these two age-groups are substantially lower than those of the 20–24 year age-group. As a consequence of this problem, the WAIS-R normative data led to overestimates of the actual intellectual abilities of examinees under age 20 (Kaufman, 1983).

More recent norms for the elderly through age 97 were developed by a team of researchers at the Mayo Clinic and published in the June 1992 (volume 6) supplement to *The Clinical Neuropsychologist*. A computer program for these norms is also available from The Psychological Corporation.

Standardization of the WAIS-R differed principally from that of the WAIS in the stratification of the sample by race and the provision for more representative sampling of older adults. Each age group subsample was stratified not only by race (white, nonwhite) but also by geographic region (Northeast, North Central, South, West), by education (five educational levels), and by occupation (six occupational groups). The number of persons selected from each stratum was proportional to the total number falling in that stratum according to the 1970 U.S. Census data, updated by later reports. Other characteristics, such as urban versus rural residence, were controlled for but did not serve as stratification variables. All persons selected in the standardization sample, who were tested between May 1976 and May 1980 at 115 centers located in thirty-nine states and the District of Columbia, were "normal" adults. Excluded from the sample were institutionalized mental defectives, persons known to have brain damage or severe emotional problems, and persons whose physical defects limited their ability to complete the test.

Score Distribution

A percentage distribution of Full Scale IQs and the corresponding classifications in the standardization sample are given in Table 6-1. These percentages are quite close to those expected in a normal distribution of IQs having a mean of 100 and a standard deviation of 15.

The sum of scaled scores on the Verbal and Performance scales changes with chronological age. The mean sum of scaled scores on both the Verbal and Performance scales increases up to the middle or late 20s, and then declines fairly steadily in middle age and late adulthood. The age-related decline is more pronounced for the Performance Scale than for the Verbal Scale, the drop in Performance Scale scores being caused primarily by declines on certain subtests. The largest age

TABLE 6-1 **Classification of WAIS-R Deviation IQs and Percentage of Standardized Sample in Each Category**

IQ	Classification	Percentage included in standardization sample[a]
130 and above	Very superior	2.6
120–129	Superior	6.9
110–119	High average	16.6
90–109	Average	49.1
80–89	Low average	16.1
70–79	Borderline	6.4
69 and below	Mentally retarded	2.3

[a]The percentages shown are for Full Scale IQs and are based on the total standardization sample (N = 1,880). The percentages obtained for Verbal IQ and Performance IQ are essentially the same.

decrements occur on Picture Arrangement, Block Design, and Digit Symbol, all of which are Performance subtests requiring quick responses. The smallest age decrements occur on Information, Vocabulary, and Arithmetic, all of which are Verbal subtests. Information and Vocabulary have no time limits, but a bonus for very quick, accurate responses can be earned on a few of the Arithmetic subtest items.

Concerning the psychometric characteristics and utility of the WAIS-R, Matarazzo (1985) concluded that "no other test … is as reliable, valid, or clinically useful for assessing the measurable aspects of adult intelligence." Matarazzo's evaluation was supported by Parker, Hanson, and Hunsley (1988), who concluded that the WAIS-R has acceptable reliability and validity.

Reliabilities of Scales and Subtests

With one exception, the split-half reliabilities (Spearman-Brown formula) obtained with the standardization sample on the Verbal, Performance, and Full Scale IQs are in the .90s. The exception is a split-half coefficient of .88 on Performance IQ at ages 16–17. Because Digit Span and Digit Symbol are speeded tests, the split-half procedure is inappropriate with these subtests. The WAIS-R manual reports test–retest coefficients in the .70s and .80s at four age levels for these two subtests.

Test–retest (stability) coefficients are also reported at two age levels (25–34 and 45–54) for all eleven subtests, as well as Verbal, Performance, and Full Scale IQs. These coefficients were obtained by administering the WAIS-R twice, over an interval of 2–7 weeks, to seventy-one individuals in the 25–34 year range and forty-eight individuals in the 45–54 year range. Test–retest coefficients for the Verbal, Performance, and Full Scale IQs range from .89 for the Performance Scale at ages 25–34 to .97 on the Verbal Scale at ages 45–54. The test–retest coefficients for single subtests are somewhat lower, ranging from .67 for Object Assembly to .94 on Information at ages 45–54.

Both the internal consistency (split-half) and test–retest (stability) reliabilities tend to be higher for the individual Verbal subtests and the Verbal IQ than for the individual Performance subtests and the Performance IQ. As with the reliability coefficients, the standard errors of measurement of the subtest scaled scores have an appreciable range—from .61 on the Vocabulary subtest to 1.54 on the Object Assembly subtest. The average standard errors of measurement are reported as 2.74, 4.14, and 2.53 for the Verbal, Performance, and Full Scale IQs, respectively.

Validity

The WAIS-R manual contains no validity data as such, but there is ample evidence for the validity of the WAIS—and by extension the WAIS-R—as a predictor of academic performance and other criteria (Matarazzo, 1972; Wechsler, 1958; Zimmerman & Woo-Sam, 1973). Understandly, the correlations between Verbal IQs and academic-type criteria are usually higher (.40–.50) than those between these criteria and either Full Scale or Performance IQs. Supporting the case for the construct validity of the WAIS-R is the fact that white-collar workers tend to make higher Verbal than Performance IQs, but the reverse is true for skilled workers (Phares, 1992). As expected, correlations between WAIS-R IQs and school grades are significant, although less so than with the Stanford-Binet—a more highly verbal test at the adult level. The fact that the correlations between scores on the Stanford-Binet and educational criteria tend to be higher than the correlations between WAIS-R IQs and these criteria is a reflection not only of the differing content of the two instruments. The differential validity of the two instruments is also a result of the different age groups for which the two tests are appropriate. In the case of adults, for whom the WAIS-R is a more appropriate measure than the Stanford-Binet, motivation and experience are usually more important determinants than intelligence of performance in college and on the job.

Correlations with Other Tests

Both WAIS and WAIS-R IQs are significantly related to scores on other intelligence tests, but the correlations are not uniformly high (Cooper & Fraboni, 1988). For example, Thorndike, Hagen, and Sattler (1986b) found a correlation of .91 between the WAIS-R and Stanford-Binet IQs of forty-seven normal examinees. In mixed groups of psychiatric patients, Ryan and Rosenberg (1983) found moderately high correlations between WAIS-R IQs and scores on the Wide Range Achievement Test. In general, there is a strong relationship between WAIS-R IQs and educational attainment, including not only school grades but years of school completed and other indicators of academic performance (Kaufman, 1990).

With respect to its relationship to other tests in the Wechsler series, correlations between WAIS-R IQs and IQs on the WISC-R are quite high (.76–.80), and the corresponding mean IQs of the two tests are very similar (1 to 2 points difference). Furthermore, correlations of .91 for Verbal IQs, .79 for Performance IQs, and .88 for Full Scale IQs have been found between the WAIS and the WAIS-R (Wechsler, 1981b). Despite these high correlations and the similarity between the content of the WAIS-R and that of the WAIS (80 percent item overlap), the two tests do not yield identical IQs. On all three scales, WAIS-R IQs tend to be lower than WAIS IQs for the same individuals. WAIS-R IQs are 6 to 7 points lower on the Verbal Scale, 5 to 8 points lower on the Performance Scale, and 5 to 8 points lower on the Full Scale (Mishra & Brown, 1983; Wechsler, 1981b). Thus, the WAIS-R is a more difficult test than the WAIS.

Factor Analyses

The results of factor analyses of the eleven WAIS-R subtests are relevant to the question of the validity of the WAIS-R as a measure of intelligence. A classic factor-analytic investigation of the WAIS was Cohen's (1957) analysis of several age groups in the WAIS standardization sample. Cohen labeled the resulting three factors Verbal Comprehension, Perceptual Organization, and Memory. In order to compare Cohen's WAIS results with those obtained from the WAIS-R standardization sample, the author conducted a principal axis factor analysis of the average intercorrelations given in the WAIS-R manual between the subtest scores for nine age groups. The three factors obtained in this analysis were subjected to varimax rotation. The resulting loadings of the eleven WAIS-R subtests on the three rotated factors, in addition to the communalities of the subtests, are given in Table 6-2. The highest loadings on Factor A are, similar to Cohen's Verbal Comprehension factor, those of the Information, Vocabulary, Comprehension, and Similarities subtests. The highest loadings on Factor B, similar to Cohen's Perceptual Organization factor, are those of the Picture Completion, Block Design, and Object Assembly subtests. The highest loadings on Factor C, which appears to be a Numerical or Attention-Concentration factor rather than a pure Memory factor as labeled by Cohen, are those of the Digit Span, Arithmetic, and Digit Symbol subtests.

In general, factor analyses of the WAIS-R have confirmed the observation that the test measures a strong general factor of intelligence. In addition, there are at least two group factors, one of which is predominantly verbal in nature. The results of factor analysis also confirm the Verbal–Performance distinction postulated in designing the several instruments in the Wechsler series (Geary & Whitworth, 1988; Kaufman, 1975b; Wallbrown, Blaha, & Wherry, 1973).

PSYCHODIAGNOSTIC APPLICATIONS OF THE WAIS-R AND ASSOCIATED TESTS

In designing the Wechsler Bellevue-Intelligence Scale and its successors, David Wechsler planned to measure more than an examinee's "aggregate or global capacity ... to act purposively, to think rationally, and to deal effectively with his environment" (Wechsler, 1958, p. 7). Like any other psychologist who has worked in a psychiatric hospital, he observed that general intelligence is negatively related to psychopathology—that serious mental disturbance tends to be accompanied by below-average intellectual functioning (Gaines & Morris, 1978). Wechsler also reasoned that different kinds of psychiatric disorders have different effects on various cognitive functions and consequently that analysis of the differences between Verbal and Performance IQs and the differences between subtest scaled scores might be of assistance in the differential diagnosis of psychiatric disorders.

Difference between Verbal and Performance IQs

Despite the failure of research to confirm many of Wechsler's hypotheses concerning the diagnostic significance of score differences on his tests, large differences between Verbal IQ (VIQ) and Performance IQ (PIQ) have been found to be of some diagnostic value. Obviously, deficiencies in language, education, and other cultural experiences can lead to lower VIQs than PIQs. With respect to the diagnosis of organic brain damage, the research findings of Reitan (1966) and his coworkers indicated that a VIQ significantly lower than a PIQ is a diagnostic indicator of left-hemisphere damage and that a PIQ significantly lower than a VIQ points to right-hemisphere damage. If Rapaport, Gill, and Schafer (1968) were

TABLE 6–2   Factor Loadings and Communalities for WAIS-R
Subtests

Subtest	Factor loadings			Communality
	Factor A	Factor B	Factor C	
Information	.81	.21	.29	.78
Digit Span	.27	.11	.83	.77
Vocabulary	.82	.22	.34	.84
Arithmetic	.49	.28	.59	.67
Comprehension	.79	.23	.26	.74
Similarities	.75	.30	.25	.72
Picture Completion	.48	.64	.11	.65
Picture Arrangement	.51	.49	.13	.52
Block Design	.26	.72	.38	.73
Object Assembly	.14	.85	.19	.78
Digit Symbol	.23	.37	.61	.56

correct in their assertion that Performance subtests are more affected than Verbal subtests by emotional disorders, then one should expect to find VIQs significantly higher than PIQs in emotionally disturbed individuals. But what is the evidence? Although chronic schizophrenics usually have higher VIQs than PIQs, violent sociopaths tend to have higher PIQs than VIQs (Kunce, Ryan, & Eckelman, 1976; Matarazzo, 1972). The latter finding, however, may be due to the poor reading ability of sociopaths, lowering their scores on several of the Verbal subtests (Henning & Levy, 1967). Also of interest is a report of significantly higher Verbal than Performance IQs in male homosexuals (Willmott & Brierley, 1984).

Despite years of research on the matter, findings concerning the diagnostic utility of VIQ–PIQ differences are not clear-cut. The WAIS-R manual indicates that a VIQ–PIQ difference of 7 IQ points is required for significance at the .15 level and a difference of 10 points at the .05 level. Wechsler recommended that a VIQ–PIQ difference of 15 points be investigated for its diagnostic significance. Naglieri (1982) provided additional tables of statistically significant differences between scores on the WAIS-R scales and subtests.

Subtest Scaled Score Scatter

Even more detailed than attempts to relate VIQ–PIQ differences to psychopathology are techniques for analyzing the pattern, scatter, or differences among scaled scores on the eleven WAIS-R subtests. Analysis of the peaks and valleys in a WAIS-R profile has been approached both qualitatively and quantitatively. However, interpretation of the individual scaled scores for the various subtests should probably only be done using the age-scaled scores (see scores in parentheses in the last column of Figure 6–2).

Among the clinical observations concerning the association between subtest scaled scores and psychopathology are those relating low Information scores to hysteria; poor Digit Span to anxiety, and poor ability on Digits Backward to chronic schizophrenia; low Arithmetic scores to sociopathic personality, psychotic depression, and simple schizophrenia; low Similarities scores to brain injury and mental retardation; and low Block Design subtest scores to test anxiety and depression (Boor & Schill, 1968; Edwards, 1966; Hodges & Spielberger, 1969; Matarazzo, 1972). When a significant drop in overall performance on the WAIS-R occurs because of brain damage or severe emotional disturbance, one of the last subtests to be affected is Vocabulary. Also on Vocabulary, as well as Similarities, responses marked by idiosyncratic definitions and concepts are often seen in schizophrenia.

On the quantitative side, Zimmerman and Woo-Sam (1973) recommended computing numerical values consisting of the ratio of the sum of scaled scores on certain "hold" subtests to other "don't hold" subtests. The resulting *deterioration quotients* (DQs) are computed as ratios of subtest scaled scores that remain fairly constant to those in which the patient's disorder results in a distinct impairment in cognitive performance. The lower the DQ, the greater the impairment in performance. Among the DQs described by Zimmerman and Woo-Sam are:

Brain damage (male): $(S + D + DS + BD)/(I + A + PC + OA)$
Brain damage (female): $(S + D + DS + PA)/(I + V + BD + OA)$
Depression: $(DS + PC + PA + OA)/(I + C + A + V)$
Schizophrenia: $(D + DS + PA + BD + OA)/(I + C + S + V + PC)$
Neurotic and personality disorder: $(A + DS + BD + OA)/(C + S + V + PC)$*

A DQ that is significantly lower than 1.00 is considered to be consistent with the particular diagnosis. The DQ approach to WAIS-R subtest scaled score analysis has, however, been largely discredited and is now primarily of historical interest only.

Despite continuing research efforts, Matarazzo's (1972, pp. 429–430) conclusion that "alas, hundreds upon hundreds of studies in the use of profile, pattern, or scatter analysis with the Wechsler scales conducted between 1940 and 1970 failed to produce reliable evidence that such a search would be fruitful" has not greatly changed even today. This does not necessarily imply that the search for diagnostic patterns has been abandoned; some success in using the WAIS-R in the diagnosing of brain damage and other pathological conditions has been achieved. It is recognized, however, that the problem of analyzing subtest scaled score scatter and VIQ–PIQ differences is more complex than previously believed.

One reason for the difficulties experienced in attempting to place people in specific psychiatric categories is that these categories themselves are not very reliable or distinctive. Another problem in making such differential diagnoses on the basis of relatively short subtests such as those on the WAIS-R is that the scores are not highly reliable and in many instances are substantially correlated with each other. As a consequence, the difference between an examinee's score on two given subtests must be fairly large before it can be viewed as significant or meaningful.

*A = Arithmetic, BD = Block Design, C = Comprehension, D = Digit Span, DS = Digit Symbol, I = Information, OA = Object Assembly, PA = Picture Arrangement, PC = Picture Completion, S = Similarities, V = Vocabulary.

Wechsler (1981b) stated that the difference between the scaled scores on two WAIS-R subtests is significant if it is at least 3 points. Silverstein (1982a) noted, however, that this rule does not take into account the fact that the clinician, in inspecting the profile for subtests having at least 3-point differences in scaled scores, is actually making multiple comparisons of all subtest score differences.

The approach recommended by Silverstein (1982a), which entails using the values listed in Table 6–3, is statistically more sophisticated than Wechsler's. After scoring all subtests and converting the raw scores to subtest scaled scores, the examiner calculates the mean of scaled scores on the six Verbal subtests, the mean of scaled scores on the Performance scale, and the mean of scaled score on all eleven subtests. Next, the difference between the scaled score on each subtest and the mean scaled score (on the Verbal Scale for the verbal subtests, on the Performance Scale for the performance subtests, and on the Full Scale for all subtests) is determined. The differences that are equal to or greater than those listed in Table 6–3 are significant at the stated probability level (.05 or .01).

To illustrate the use of Table 6–3, we begin by computing the mean scaled scores on the Verbal, Performance, and Full Scale data given in Figure 6–2 as 9, 7.4, and 8.3, respectively. Although it is possible to subtract the mean scaled score on all eleven subtests (8.3) from each subtest scaled score and compare the resulting differences with the significant values in the "All subtests" columns of Table 6–3, Silverstein maintained that this procedure gives a false impression of the examinee's strengths and weaknesses and is less sensitive than the following alter-

TABLE 6–3   Minimum Differences Required for Significance When Comparing Each WAIS-R Subtest Scaled Score with a Mean Subtest Scaled Score

	Subtest scaled score compared with mean of:					
	Verbal subtests		Performance subtests		All subtests	
	Probability		Probability		Probability	
Subtest	.05	.01	.05	.01	.05	.01
Information	2.4	2.8			2.6	3.1
Digit Span	2.9	3.5			3.4	3.9
Vocabulary	1.8	2.1			1.9	2.2
Arithmetic	2.8	3.3			3.1	3.7
Comprehension	2.9	3.4			3.3	3.8
Similarities	3.0	3.5			3.4	4.0
Picture Completion			3.0	3.5	3.4	4.0
Picture Arrangement			3.2	3.9	3.8	4.4
Block Design			2.5	3.0	2.8	3.2
Object Assembly			3.4	4.2	4.1	4.8
Digit Symbol			3.0	3.5	3.5	4.0

Source: A. B. Silverstein, 1982a. Pattern analysis as simultaneous statistical inference. Journal of Consulting and Clinical Psychology, 50, p. 237. Copyright © 1982 by the American Psychological Association. Adapted with permission.

native. The alternative is to subtract the mean scaled score on all Verbal subtests (9.0) from each Verbal subtest scaled score and compare the resulting differences with those in the "Verbal subtests" columns of Table 6–3. Similarly, the mean scaled score on the Performance subtests (7.4) is subtracted from each Performance subtest scaled score and compared with the values in the "Performance subtests" columns of Table 6–3. Using this method, none of the Verbal Scale differences (1, −1, 0, 2, −2, 0) and none of the Performance Scale differences (−.4, −1.4, 1.6, .6, −.4) is significant at the .05 level. Because the examinee in this case fell in the reference group of 20- to 34-year-olds, it was reasonable to use the scaled scores based on that group. In any case, if we use the age scaled scores rather than the scaled scores based on the reference group we also fail to obtain any significant differences between subtest scaled scores in this case.

Qualitative Observations

A sensitive clinician does not rely on numerical indexes alone in attempting to understand and diagnose an examinee's problem(s). The test-related and nontest-related behavior of an examinee during a testing session can provide clues of an impressionistic sort that suggest certain problems or characteristics. Mannerisms and other nonverbal behaviors (squirming, tremors, hesitating, sighing, scowling, avoiding eye contact, volume and tone of voice, etc.) frequently reveal more than numbers about the personality and problems of an individual. With respect to verbal behavior, answers to specific items on the WAIS-R reflect cultural background, anxiety level, and other characteristics. Responses that are overelaborate (include irrelevant details), overinclusive (too general), evasive (indirect), self-referent (reflecting self-involvement), or bizarre (idiosyncratic associations) are especially suggestive of psychopathology. In response to the Similarities item "In what way are a dog and a lion alike?" posed by the author, a patient answered: "They use sound to tame them both, and they're using it to try and tame me too!" Matarazzo (1972) provided numerous illustrations of responses given by patients having different psychiatric diagnoses to items on the WAIS. He suggested that slow responding and self-disparagement are associated with depression; hesitation, suspiciousness, and a tendency to see personalized meanings in the items are associated with paranoid conditions; flip, self-centered responses are characteristic of psychopaths; and bizarre, overinclusive responses indicate the presence of a thought disorder (schizophrenia).

In addition to scrutinizing such qualitatively distinct responses, errors and correct answers can be analyzed for possible insight into the cognitive styles or problem-solving strategies of examinees (Anastasi, 1988). The subtest scaled scores and deviation IQs obtained from administering the WAIS-R, as with any other intelligence test, provide a certain kind of information. But administering a test should also be viewed as a chance to make observations in a controlled situation, an opportunity that can provide a great deal of extratest information and data to confirm or disconfirm hypotheses about the examinee's mental status and personality functioning.

Wechsler Memory Scale and WAIS-R NI

One of the most frequent accompaniers of organic brain damage due to cerebral trauma, toxins, microorganisms, and aging is a deterioration in the ability to remember. Such deterioration occurs in both short-term and long-term memory, but in most cases it is more noticeable in the former. The decline in recall memory, especially free recall, is also more pronounced than the decline in recognition memory. Because individual intelligence tests typically focus on free recall, a brain-damaged patient is often at a disadvantage and appears more impaired on such tests than may be warranted. Measures of recognition or identification memory often reveal less deficit in memory and other psychological functions than is shown by tests of free recall. In any event, the ability to remember is usually one of the first neuropsychological assessments to be made in cases of suspect brain damage or deterioration.

One popular test of memory is the Wechsler Memory Scale—Revised (WMS-R), which consists of thirteen brief verbal and nonverbal subtests requiring a total of 50 minutes testing time. These subtests are designed to measure memory for verbal and figural stimuli, meaningful and abstract material, in both delayed and immediate recall modes. In scoring the WMS-R, subsets of weighted subtest scores are added and converted to Composite Index Scores to provide measures of general memory, attention/concentration, verbal memory, visual memory, and delayed recall. Norms for the WMS-R, which were obtained in the mid-1980s, are based on nine age-groups ranging from 16 to 74 years.

A more comprehensive assessment of the behavioral effects of organic brain damage may be obtained from a modification of the WAIS-R known as the "WAIS-R as a Neuropsychological Instrument" (WAIS-R NI). Focusing on the process, or "how," as opposed to the product, or "what," of behavioral performance, the additional subtests on the WAIS-R NI were designed for individuals who are suspected of having neuropsychological problems. The subtests on the WAIS-R NI consist of those on the WAIS-R (with some modifications such as three new Object Assembly puzzles), plus the following six subtests: Information Multiple Choice, Arithmetic Paper and Pencil, Similarities Multiple Choice, Sentence Arrangement, Spatial Span, and Symbol Copy. After administering the Information, Vocabulary, and Similarities subtests, an additional multiple-choice test is given to permit a finer assessment of the patient's spared and impaired cognitive functions. Examinees who are minimal free responders or who have difficulty accessing their store of knowledge are presumably benefited by the use of the multiple-choice (recognition memory) testing format. In addition, the Arithmetic Paper and Pencil subtest provides an alternate method of administration that helps the examiner identify problem areas such as memory, reasoning, computation, and visuo-spatial deficits in solving arithmetic items. The Symbol Copy task is a purer measure than the Digit Symbol subtest of the examinee's speed in copying, providing a better understanding of the visuo-spatial processes than the Digit Symbol subtest. A visual analogue of the Digit Span subtest is provided by the ten cube Spatial Span subtest, and a verbal analogue to the Picture Arrangement subtest is provided by the Sentence Arrangement subtest. In addition to a comparison of scores on the various subtests, an analysis of errors made by the examinee is conducted to identify problems that may underlie impaired performance. In addition, documenting the behavioral strategies employed by the examinee in solving problems on the test can lead to recommendations for the rehabilitation of diagnosed performance deficits.

The Beat Goes On

In studying the material in this chapter, the reader may well wonder why a test that was standardized in the late 1970s and published in 1981 has not been revised and restandardized. Although it is not considered necessary to publish a new edition of a general intelligence test as often as a revision of a standardized achievement test, it is admittedly time to consider the development of a revised WAIS-R. According to representatives of The Psychological Corporation, a new edition of the test, the WAIS-III, is being planned for publication in June 1997. WAIS-III will not be a brand-new test, but rather an updating and restandardization of its predecessor. As was true when the WAIS was revised as the WAIS-R, at least half of the items on the WAIS-R will probably be retained in the WAIS-III. Particular attention will be paid to the revision of verbal subtests such as Information, Vocabulary, and Comprehension, which are subject to cultural changes and consequent datedness. The biggest problem, and the most work, in devising the new edition will be the restandardization process—identifying a representative standardization sample, administering the WAIS-III to all individuals in this group, and analyzing the results.

SUMMARY

David Wechsler's interest in intelligence testing began during World War I when he was a psychometrist in the U.S. Army, but his ideas for constructing an intelligence scale for adults were not developed until years later when he became chief psychologist at Bellevue Hospital. The Wechsler-Bellevue Intelligence Scale, which was published initially in 1939, was designed to be less highly loaded with verbal material and composed of tasks more suitable for adults than the Stanford-Binet; it also placed less emphasis on speed of responding. Wechsler hoped that in addition to providing a measure of global intelligence, the Wechsler-Bellevue I would be useful in the differential diagnosis of psychiatric disorders. He recognized not only that scores on the test are determined by a complex interaction of biological development and experience but also that affective as well as cognitive variables play an important role in test performance.

The Wechsler-Bellevue I and its successors (Wechsler-Bellevue II, WAIS, WAIS-R) are point scales on which item scores depend on the level of sophistication revealed in responses to the items. The items are grouped according to content into subtests, which are organized into a Verbal Scale consisting of six subtests and a Performance Scale of five subtests. On the most recent version of the test (the Wechsler Adult Intelligence Scale—Revised, or WAIS-R), Verbal and Performance subtests are administered in alternate order. The raw score on each subtest of the WAIS-R is then converted to a scaled score, based on a mean of 10 and a standard deviation of 3 in the reference group (20- to 34-year-olds). By referring to a table of norms appropriate for the examinee's age, the sum of scaled scores on the WAIS-R Verbal Scale is converted to a Verbal IQ, the sum of scaled scores on the Performance Scale is converted to a Performance IQ, and the sum of scaled scores on all subtests is converted to a Full Scale IQ.

Among the factors affecting performance on the WAIS-R are the physical surroundings in which the test is administered, the examinee's anxiety level, the examiner's expectations of how well the examinee should do, whether the test is administered in the examinee's native language, and the psychological relationship (rapport) between the examiner and the examinee. The WAIS-R typically takes about 1½ hours to administer, depending on the ability level and age of the examinee and on other conditions. It is possible to administer an abbreviated form of the test to serve as a rough screening measure of intellectual functioning, but the scores are not as reliable as those on the full test. Shortening the testing time also provides less opportunity to make qualitative observations of the examinee's behavior.

The WAIS-R was carefully standardized between 1976 and 1980 on a national sample of 1,880 adults in nine age-groups. Equal numbers of men and women were tested in each age-group, stratified by race, geographic region, and occupation according to 1970 U.S. Census figures. Other variables, including urban versus rural residence, were controlled for in the standardization sample. The norms show that scores on the Verbal and Performance scales change with age; the age-related decline is especially noticeable on certain Performance Scale subtests. Age decrements are greatest on the Picture Arrangement, Block Design, and Digit Symbol subtests and least on the Information, Vocabulary, and Arithmetic subtests.

The split-half and test–retest reliabilities of the WAIS-R Verbal, Performance, and Full Scale IQs are in the high .80s and .90s; the reliabilities of the subtest scores are substantially lower. Scores on the WAIS-R are significantly correlated with scores on other intelligence tests; evidence from factor-analytic and prediction studies also indicates that the WAIS-R is a valid measure of general intellectual ability.

The question of the diagnostic meaning and utility of WAIS-R subtest scaled score differences continues to receive equivocal answers. There is evidence for the diagnostic significance of large differences in Verbal and Performance IQs in cases of organic brain damage, but the classification of psychiatric disorders by means of subtest scaled score scatter remains dubious.

Qualitative observations made during the process of administering the WAIS-R are frequently of diagnostic value. The examiner should be alert for nonverbal as well as verbal indicators of emotional disorders, organic disturbances, or educational and cultural differences that should be considered in interpreting scores on the WAIS-R. Significant differences between Verbal and Performance IQs or between subtest scaled scores and mean subtest scaled scores should be evaluated against a background of data from observations and other sources of information about the examinee.

Supplements to the WAIS-R used in the diagnosis of neuropsychological problems include the Wechsler Memory Scale—Revised and the WAIS-R as a Neuropsychological Instrument (WAIS-R NI). Finally, a new edition of the Wechsler Adult
Intelligence Scale, the WAIS-III, is planned for 1997. Rather than being a completely
new test, the WAIS-III will represent an updating and restandardization of the WAIS-
R.

QUESTIONS AND ACTIVITIES

1. How is a point scale like the WAIS-R or WISC-III different from an age scale like the
   Stanford-Binet? Which type of scale is psychometrically superior? Which one results in a
   test with greater practical utility?
2. Distinguish between the Verbal IQ, the Performance IQ, and the Full Scale IQ on the WAIS-
   R in terms of the subtests composing each scale, what they measure, and how the scaled
   scores and IQs are computed.
3. What are age-scaled scores and how are they different from scaled scores based on the
   reference group for the WAIS-R?
4. How reliable are the scaled scores on the Verbal, Performance, and Full scales of the WAIS-
   R? How reliable are the subtest scaled scores?
5. How useful are Verbal–Performance IQ differences on the WAIS-R in diagnosing organic
   and functional mental disorders? What does it mean when the Verbal IQ is significantly
   higher than the Performance IQ? When the Performance IQ is significantly higher than the
   Verbal IQ?
6. What are some of the reasons why an intelligence test such as the WAIS-R should be
   administered? Has it lived up to David Wechsler's goal of providing an intelligence test that
   would be useful in clinical diagnosis? Why or why not?
7. What are deterioration quotients (DQs), and how useful are they in detecting differential
   decline in cognitive abilities in specific diagnostic groups?
8. What are some of the qualitative responses given by examinee's during administration of
   the WAIS-R that might be useful for psychodiagnostic purposes?
9. Every year The Roper Center for Public Opinion Research conducts a General Social
   Survey for The Natiional Opinion Research Center on a large representative sample of
   adult Americans (Davis & Smith, 1994). The following correlation coefficients were
   computed on data collected in the 1994 survey. The correlations are between total scores
   on an eight-item similarities test, similar to the Similarities subtest of the WAIS-R, and
   responses to questions on chronological age, educational level, health status, 1991 income, a socioeconomic index, and sex (gender).

Variable	Correlation with similarities test score
Age	−.142
Education	.409
Health	.077
Income	.214
Socioeconomic	.268
Sex	.001

The sample size was 2072, so all of the correlation coefficients except the one between
similarities score and sex are statistically significant (.01 level). What do these results

mean? What confounding variables might have affected the magnitude of the correlations?

SUGGESTED READINGS

Forster, A. A., & Matarazzo, J. D. (1990). Assessing the intelligence of adolescents with the Wechsler Adult Intelligence Scale—Revised (WAIS). In C. R. Reynolds & R. W. Kamphaus (Eds.), *Handbook of psychological & educational assessment of children: Intelligence & achievement* (pp. 166–182). New York: Guilford Press.

Geary, D. C., & Whitworth, R. H. (1988). Dimensional structure of the WAIS-R in a simultaneous multi-sample analysis. *Educational and Psychological Measurement, 48,* 945–959.

Kaplan, E., Fein, D., Morris, R., & Delis, D. C. (1991). *WAIS-R as a neuropsychological instrument.* San Antonio, TX: The Psychological Corporation.

Kaufman, A. S. (1983). Test review: WAIS-R. *Journal of Psychoeducational Assessment, 1,* 309–319.

Kaufman, A. S. (1990). *Assessing adolescent and adult intelligence.* Boston: Allyn & Bacon.

Matarazzo, J. D. (1985). Review of the Wechsler Adult Intelligence Scale—Revised. In J. V. Mitchell (Ed.), *The ninth mental measurements yearbook* (pp. 1703–1705). Lincoln: The Buros Institute of Mental Measurements, University of Nebraska.

Parker, K. C. H., Hanson, R. K., & Hunsley, J. (1988). MMPI, Rorschach, and WAIS: A meta-analytic comparison of reliability, stability, and validity. *Psychological Bulletin, 103,* 367–373.

Ryan, J. J., Paolo, A. M., & Brungardt, T. M. (1990). WAIS-R reliability and standard errors for persons 75 to 79, 80 to 84, and 85 and older. *Journal of Psychoeducational Assessment, 8,* 9–14.

Sprandel, H. Z. (1985). *The psychological use and interpretation of the Wechsler Adult Intelligence Scale—Revised.* Springfield, IL: Charles C Thomas.

Chapter 7

Individual Testing of Preschool Children and Infants

CHAPTER OUTLINE

Interest in assessing the mental abilities of young children is as old as intelligence testing itself. During the first two decades of this century, Alfred Binet, Frederic Kuhlmann, Cyril Burt, Robert Yerkes, and Lewis Terman developed intelligence tests that extended down into the preschool years. These early instruments were not designed exclusively for preschoolers, nor did they reach down as far as infancy (birth to 1½ years). In the 1920s and 1930s, however, many psychometric scales for measuring the intelligence of young children were published, some designed specifically for infants and other preschoolers. Since that time dozens of new intelligence tests and revisions of older instruments have been published, either as parts of multilevel intelligence test batteries or exclusively for infants and other young children.

Stimulated to some extent by compensatory educational programs for culturally disadvantaged preschool children and by research on child development, during the past two or three decades there has been an upsurge of interest in tests designed to measure the cognitive abilities of young children. In fact, testing of cognitive abilities in infancy and early childhood is more prevalent today than at any other time in this century. Concern for the development of children who are medically and/or environmentally "at risk" has resulted in the passage of laws, such as the Americans with Disabilities Act (PL 101-336) and the Individuals with Disabilities Act (PL 101-476). These laws provided funds for the implementation of multidisciplinary systems of screening and assessment of children who are experiencing developmental delays in cognitive, linguistic, motoric, socioemotional, and adaptive skills, as well as interventions with such children.

Table 7-1 is a representative but by no means an exhaustive list of available tests for assessing the cognitive development of infants and young children. These instruments have been, and continue to be, employed for a variety of purposes, including adoptive placement decisions, determination of readiness for school, treatment and other intervention procedures, and research on child development. This chapter begins by focusing on the most carefully designed tests for preschoolers (1½–6 years), after which intelligence tests and related developmental scales designed specifically for infants (birth–1½ years) are discussed.

A common problem shared by preschool and infant tests is the fact that young children usually have a shorter attention span and a tendency to tire more easily than school-age children. The distractibility, low test-taking motivation, and limited verbal ability of most preschoolers contribute to the lower reliabilities and validities of intellectual assessment in this age group than in older children and adults. The use of colorful toys, novel tasks, and other stimulating materials and procedures assists in maintaining the young child's interest and attention. But if the tasks are greatly different from those used in testing older children, the skills and abilities that are measured may not be the same in the different age-groups.

The skills required by psychological examiners of young children are also somewhat different from those needed for testing older children and adults. The great majority of tasks on intelligence tests for infants and young children require oral responses and/or the manipulation of various objects by examinees. Consequently, the examiner must be alert and active. The context of testing is also different from that in testing older children. Rather than confronting a well-behaved, mannerly person seated at a table, the examiner may be faced with a highly distractible, socially shy or frightened youngster supported in a parent's lap or, in the case of a neonate, lying down.

Not only should examiners of infants and other preverbal children be thoroughly familiar with the test materials and procedures; they must be adaptable, flexible, enthusiastic, and empathic, using simple words and demonstrating to the child to a greater extent than when testing older individuals. In addition to administering the test and recording responses to the items, the examiner should observe the child's actions and utterances in the testing situation closely and interview the

TABLE 7–1   Individual Intelligence Tests and Developmental Scales for Young Children and Infants

AGS Early Screening Profiles (EAP), by P. Harrison et al.; © 1990; ages 2–6.11; American Guidance Service.

Arthur Adapation of the Leiter International Performance Scale, by G. Arthur; © 1952; ages 3.0 to 7.11; Western Psychological Services.

Bayley Scales of Infant Development, Second Edition, by N. Bayley; © 1993; ages 1 to 42 months; The Psychological Corporation.

Brazelton Neonatal Behavioral Assessment Scale (NBAS), by T. B. Brazelton; © 1973, 1984; 3 days to 4 weeks; J. B. Lippincott.

Cattell Infant Intelligence Scale, by P. Cattell; © 1940–1960; ages 3 to 30 months; The Psychological Corporation.

Coloured Progressive Matrices, by J. C. Raven; ages 5 to 11 years and mentally retarded adults; The Psychological Corporation.

Columbia Mental Maturity Scale, Third edition, by B. B. Burgemeister, L. H. Blum, and I. Lorge; © 1954–1974; ages 3½ to 1 year, 11 months; The Psychological Corporation.

Denver Developmental Screening Tests, by W. K. Frankenburg et al., 1975, 1981; 3 months to 5 years. LADOCA Publishing Foundation.

FirstSTEP: Screening Test for Evaluating Preschoolers, by L. J. Miller; © 1993; ages 2.9 through 6.2; The Psychological Corporation.

Gesell Developmental Schedules, by H. Knobloch and B. Pasamanick, 1974; ages 2½ to 6 years.

Gesell Preschool Test, by J. Haines et al.; © 1980; ages 2.5 to 6 years; Programs for Education.

Goodenough-Harris Drawing Test, by D. B. Harris; © 1963; ages 3–5 years; The Psychological Corporation.

Hess School Readiness Scale, by R. J. Hess; © 1975; ages 3–7 years; Mafex Associates.

Kahn Intelligence Test: 1975 Revision, by T. C. Kahn; © 1975; ages 1 year and over; Psychological Test Specialists.

Kaufman Assessment Battery for Children (K-ABC), by A. S. Kaufman &. N. L. Kaufman; © 1983; ages 2½ to 12½ years; American Guidance Service.

Kaufman Developmental Scale, by H. Kaufman; © 1972–1974; infants through age 9 years; Stoelting.

Kent Infant Development Scale, by L. Katoff, 1970; birth to 14 months; Stoelting.

Leiter International Performance Scale, by R. G. Leiter; © 1929–1952; ages 2 years and over; Stoelting, Western Psychological Services, and Psychological Assessment Resources.

McCarthy Scales of Children's Abilities (MSCA), by D. McCarthy; © 1979–1972; ages 2.6 to 8.6 years; The Psychological Corporation.

Merrill-Palmer Scale, by R. Stutsman; © 1926–1948; ages 18 months–4 years; Stoelting.

PACE, by L. K. Barclay & J. R. Barclay; © 1986, 1988; computer-based diagnostic-prescriptive intervention program for preschool children; MetriTech.

Peabody Picture Vocabulary Test—Revised (PPVT-R), by L. M. Dunn; © 1981; ages 2½ to 18 years; American Guidance Service.

Pictorial Test of Intelligence, by J. L. French; © 1964; ages 3 to 8 years; Riverside Publishing Co.

Quick Screening Scale of Mental Development, by K. M. Banham; © 1963; ages 6 months to 10 years; Psychometric Affiliates.

Ring and Peg Tests of Behavioral Development, by K. M. Banham; © 1975; ages birth to 6 years; Psychometric Affiliates.

Slosson Intelligence Test for Children and Adults, by R. L. Slosson; © 1961–1964; ages ½ month and over; Slosson Educational Publications.

Smith-Johnson Nonverbal Performance Scale, by A. J. Smith & R. E. Johnson; © 1977; ages 2–4 years; Western Psychological Services.

Stanford-Binet Intelligence Scale: Fourth Edition (SB-IV), by R. E. Thorndike, E. Hagen, & J. Sattler; © 1986; ages 2 years to adulthood; Riverside Publishing Co.

Uzgiris-Hunt Scales, by I. C. Uzgiris & J. McV. Hunt; © 1975; ages 2 weeks to 2 years; Uzgiris, 1976, 1983; Uzgiris & Hunt 1975.

Wechsler Preschool and Primary Scale of Intelligence—Revised (WPPSI-R), by D. Wechsler; © 1993; ages 4–6½ years; The Psychological Corporation.

parents or other caretakers in depth about the child's typical behavior at home and in other situations. A standard developmental inventory such as the AAMD Adaptive Behavior Scales (CTB/McGraw-Hill), the Vineland Adaptive Behavior Scales (American Guidance Service), or the Minnesota Child Development Inventory (Behavior Science Systems) can also provide helpful background information for interpreting the performance of a young child on an intelligence test.

WECHSLER PRESCHOOL AND PRIMARY SCALE OF INTELLIGENCE— REVISED

One of the most popular tests for measuring the intelligence of young children is the Wechsler Preschool and Primary Scale of Intelligence—Revised (WPPSI-R). In constructing this revision of the WPPSI, the content was expanded, certain technical refinements were made, and the standardization was more extensive than that of its predecessor. The WPPSI-R is designed for children aged 3 to 7 years, 3 months, and has a total testing time of approximately 75 minutes. This is a rather lengthy period for preschoolers, so it may be necessary, and it is permissible, to administer the test in two sessions. In addition to the ten basic subtests, there is an optional Sentences subtest on the Verbal Scale and an optional Animal Pegs (formerly "Animal House") subtest on the Performance Scale. The Sentences subtest, which may be substituted for any of the Verbal subtests, is basically a measure of short-term memory. It serves the same function as the Digit Span subtest on the WAIS-R or WISC-III, using meaningful verbal stimuli instead of numbers. Animal Pegs, which may be substituted for any of the Performance subtests, requires the child to place pegs of the correct colors in holes below a series of pictured animals. It is similar in function to the Digit Symbol subtest of the WAIS-R or the Coding subtest of the WISC-III.

Descriptions of the WPPSI-R Subtests

The subtests on the WPPSI-R are described below, in order of administration, with alternating Verbal (V) and Performance (P) subtests.

Object Assembly (P). Pieces of a puzzle arranged in a standard configuration are presented to the child, who is required to fit them together to form a meaningful puzzle within a specified time limit.

Information (V). Requires the child to demonstrate knowledge about events or objects in the environment. On lower-level items the child points to a picture to answer a question. On other items the child responds verbally to brief oral questions about commonplace objects and events.

Geometric Design (P). On one type of item on this subtest, the child looks at a simple design and points to one exactly like it from an array of four designs. On another type of item, the child draws a geometric figure from a printed model.

Comprehension (V). Items on this subtest require the child to express an understanding of the reasons for actions and the consequences of events.

Block Design (P). This subtest requires the child to analyze and reproduce patterns made from flat, two-colored blocks within a specified time limit.

Arithmetic (V). Items on this subtest require the child to demonstrate his or her understanding of basic quantitative concepts. The subtest begins with picture items, progresses through simple counting tasks, and ends with more difficult word problems.

Mazes (P). This subtest requires the child to solve paper-and-pencil mazes of increasing difficulty within a specified time period.

Vocabulary (V). This subtest consists of two parts. On the first part, the child is required to name a pictured object. On the second part, the child is asked to give verbal definitions for words presented orally.

Picture Completion (P). This subtest requires the child to identify a missing part in pictures of common objects or events.

Similarities (V). On the first part of this subtest the child points to the object in a set of several pictured objects that is most similar to a group of objects sharing a common property. On the second part, the child completes an orally presented sentence reflecting a similarity or analogy between two things.

Animal Pegs (P). On this subtest the child is required to place pegs of the correct colors in holes below a series of pictured animals.

Sentences (V). The child is asked to repeat verbatim a sentence read aloud by the examiner.

Determining Scaled Scores and IQs

By referring to the section of a table (Table 25) in the WPPSI-R manual (Wechsler, 1989) appropriate for the child's age, the raw score on each subtest can be converted to a scaled score having a mean of 10 and a standard deviation of 3. The scaled scores on the five Verbal subtests are then summed and converted, using Table 27 of the manual, to a Verbal IQ; the scaled scores on the five Performance subtests are summed and converted to a Performance IQ, and the scaled scores on all ten basic subtests are summed and converted to a Full Scale IQ. The three WPPSI-R IQs, like those on the WISC-III and the WAIS-R, are deviation IQs having a mean of 100 and a standard deviation of 15.

The somewhat restricted range of IQs on the WPPSI (55–155) was extended to 41–160 in the WPPSI-R. Since the most frequent use of the test in school settings is identification of children for special education categories involving mental retardation, the lower "floor" of the revised version of the test is a definite improvement. However, the fact that—compared with its predecessor—WPPSI-R IQs are somewhat lower for most children who are tested can affect classification decisions.

Standardization of the WPPSI-R

The WPPSI-R was standardized during 1987–1989 on a representative sample of 1,700 American children (850 boys and 850 girls) ranging in age from 3 years, 0 months through 7 years, 3 months. The age breakdown of the sample was 100 boys and 100 girls at each half-year interval from 3 to 7 years and 50 boys and 50 girls from

7 years, 0 months to 7 years, 3 months. In addition to being stratified by age and sex, the sample was stratified according to 1986 U.S. Census data by geographic region, ethnicity, and parental education and occupation. The percentage of children in the standardization sample in each of seven Full Scale IQ categories is given in Table 7–2. Notice that the distribution of WPPSI-R IQs is very similar to what would be expected in a normal distribution of IQs.

Reliability of the WPPSI-R

Table 9 of the WPPSI-R manual (Wechsler, 1989) lists reliability coefficients for the twelve subtests and the three IQs at successive half-year age levels from 3 to 7 years. Average values of the subtest reliabilities, which, with the exception of Animal Pegs, are split-half coefficients, are given in this table. Because Animal Pegs is a speeded test, a test–retest coefficient was computed for this subtest. The average split-half reliabilities of the subtests range from .63 for Object Assembly to .86 for Similarities. Average split-half coefficients for the Performance, Verbal, and Full Scale IQs are .92, .95, and .96, respectively. A separate study of the stability of WPPSI-R scores in a group of 175 children who were tested twice over a period of 3 to 7 weeks yielded test–retest coefficients for the subtests ranging from .52 for Mazes to .82 for Picture Completion and .88, .90, and .91 for the Verbal, Performance, and Full Scale IQs, respectively. Interscorer reliability coefficients ranging from .88 to .96 for the Comprehension, Vocabulary, Similarities, Mazes, and Geometric Design subtests have been reported by Gyurke (1991).

Significant Score Differences

The magnitude of the difference between scaled scores on two WPPSI-R subtests that is required for statistical significance varies with the subtest and the desired statistical significance level. With the exception of the Object Assembly

TABLE 7–2 Classfication of WPPSI-R Deviation IQ Categories and Percentage of Standarization Sample Falling in Each Category

IQ	Classification	Percentage in standardization sample
130 and above	Very superior	2.7
120–129	Superior	6.5
110–119	High average	17.3
90–109	Average	49.4
80–89	Low average	15.7
70–79	Borderline	6.4
69 and below	Intellectually deficient	2.0

subtest, for which it is somewhat larger, the critical difference is around 3 points for the 15 percent level and around 4 points for the 5 percent level. The statistically significant difference between scaled scores on individual subtests and the average subtest score is 3–5 points. And, as shown in Figure 7–1, the statistically significant difference between Verbal and Performance IQs ranges from 7.27 at age 3 to 10.06 at age 7 for the 15 percent level and from 9.90 at age 3 to 13.70 at age 7 for the 5 percent level.

Validity of the WPPSI-R

Evidence for the validity of the WPPSI-R has been obtained from factor-analytic studies, concurrent validity studies, score profiles for special groups, and predictive validity studies. Factor analyses of WPPSI-R subtest scores have yielded both a general factor corresponding to the Full Scale IQ and two separate factors corresponding to the Verbal and Performance subtests (Gyurke, Stone, & Beyer, 1990; Wechsler, 1989). Correlations between the WPPSI (and by extension, the WPPSI-R) with other intelligence tests are reported in the manual. The scores are also

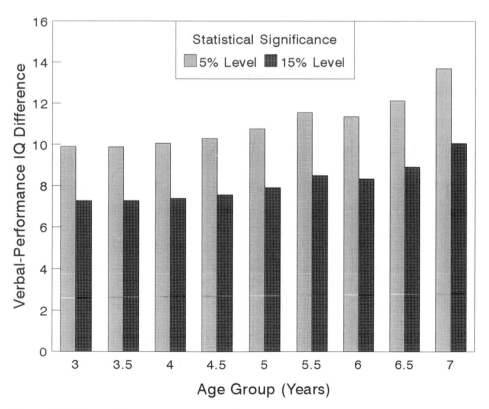

FIGURE 7-1 Difference between WPPSI-R Verbal and Performance IQs required for significance at the 15 and 5 percent levels. (Data from Wechsler, 1989, p. 137.)

positively correlated with socioeconomic status, occupational status of the father, academic achievement, and other criteria.

Reviews of the WPPSI-R (e.g., Buckhalt, 1991; Delugach, 1991) have been quite positive. The test has been praised for its technical sophistication and state-of-the-art design, clear administrative directions and procedure, and representative standardization. If there is any shortcoming in this and other tests in the Wechsler series, it is the failure of the designers to take into account theories and research on cognitive psychology. Like the WISC-III and the WAIS-R, the WPPSI-R is an empirically rather than theoretically based instrument. But perhaps the decision to make it so was a wise one, considering the uncertain status of current psychological theories of intelligence and cognition and that attempts to apply cognitive research findings do not invariably result in demonstrable improvements over straightforward empirical procedures.

MCCARTHY SCALES OF CHILDREN'S ABILITIES AND OTHER PRESCHOOL TEST BATTERIES

Somewhat dated but still viewed as well-designed and standardized is the McCarthy Scales of Children's Abilities (MSCA). Extending further in each age direction than the WPPSI-R, the MSCA provides appropriate measures of the cognitive, perceptual, and motor development of children between the ages of 2.6 and 8.6 years.

Administration time for the entire battery of eighteen tests on the MSCA is 45–50 minutes for children under 5 and 1 hour for children aged 5 years and over. Scores on the separate subtests are summed to yield scores on the five scales listed in Table 7–3.

Raw scores on the Verbal, Perceptual-Performance, Quantitative, Memory, and Motor scales are transformed to a scale index having a mean of 50 and a standard deviation of 10. The raw scores on the General Cognitive Scale are converted to a General Cognitive Index (GCI), having a mean of 100 and a standard deviation of 16.

Standardization of the MSCA

The MSCA was standardized on a national sample of 1,032 children, 100–106 individuals in each of ten age groups at half-year steps from 2½ to 5½ and 1-year steps from 5½ to 8½ years. The sample of children was stratified, proportional to data from the 1970 U.S. Census, by race, geographic region, father's occupation, and urban versus rural residence. Although sex was not one of the stratification variables, significant sex differences in MSCA scores have not been found.

Reliability and Validity of the MSCA

The MSCA manual (McCarthy, 1972) reports split-half reliability coefficients for the GCI averaging .93 and a standard error of measurement for the index averaging

TABLE 7–3   Subtests on the McCarthy Scales of Children's Abilities

Verbal Scale (V) (measures verbal expression and verbal conceptualization):
   3. Pictorial Memory
   4. Word Knowledge
   7. Verbal Memory
   15. Verbal Fluency
   16. Opposite Analogies
Perceptual-Performance Scale (P) (measures ability to conceptualize and reason without words):
   1. Block Building
   2. Puzzle Solving
   6. Tapping Sequence
   8. Right–Left Orientation
   12. Draw-A-Design
   13. Draw-A-Child
   18. Conceptual Grouping
Quantitative Scale (Q) (measures numerical aptitude):
   5. Number Questions
   14. Numerical Memory
   15. Counting and Sorting
Memory Scale (Mem) (measures alertness and immediate recall of words, numbers, pictures, and tonal
      sequences):
   3. Pictorial Memory
   6. Tapping Sequence
   7. Verbal Memory
   14. Numerical Memory
Motor Tests (Mot) (two tests from the Perceptual-Performance Scale for measuring fine motor ability plus
      three tests of gross motor development not included in the General Cognitive Scale):
   9. Leg Coordination
   10. Arm Coordination
   11. Imitative Action
   12. Draw-A-Design
   13. Draw-A-Child
General Cognitive Index (GCI) (all 15 tests on the V, P, and Q scales).

approximately 4 points for the ten age-groups. The average split-half reliabilities reported for the remaining five scales range from .79 to .88 across age groups. Test–retest reliabilities obtained over 1 month for three different age groups are .90 for the GCI and .69 to .89 for the other five scales.

Evidence for the construct validity of the General Cognitive Index is found in correlations of the GCI with Stanford-Binet IQs ($r = .81$), WPPSI Full scale IQs ($r = .71$), and scores on the Metropolitan Achievement Tests ($r = .34$ to $.54$). Although the correlations of the GCI with Stanford-Binet, WPPSI, and WISC-R IQs are high, they are far from perfect. Thus the MSCA does not measure precisely the same variables as those three intelligence tests. For example, social intelligence and problem-solving tasks of the sort that appear on the Wechsler tests are not adequately represented on the MSCA. In addition, GCI scores are substantially lower than IQs obtained from other intelligence tests, a fact that makes caution advisable in using the MSCA for placing children in special programs.

Evidence for the construct validity of the MSCA scales is found in the results of factor analyses of scores on the eighteen tests. Appearing throughout the ten age levels covered by the test are five factors: Verbal, Motor, General Cognitive, Memory, and Perceptual-Performance (Kaufman, 1975a). The factor analysis results are similar for black and white children (Kaufman & DiCuio, 1975), but black and white children do not score alike on the separate scales. Kaufman and Kaufman (1975) found that blacks in the lowest age-group (4–5½ years) scored higher than whites on the Motor scale, but whites in the highest age-group (6½–8½ years) scored higher than blacks on the other five scales. The researchers felt that socioeconomic status was an important confounding variable in these ethnic group differences. Furthermore, later studies have found that the obtained factors do not always correspond to those proposed by McCarthy (Forns-Santacana & Gomez- Benito, 1990; Keith & Bolen, 1980; Purvis & Bolen, 1984; Trueman, Lynch, & Branthwaite, 1984).

In interpreting differences between scores on the five MSCA scales, McCarthy (1972) recommended that a 15-point difference between Verbal and Memory, Perceptual-Performance and Motor, and Quantitative and Memory scaled scores be viewed as significant. According to Ysseldyke and Samuel (1973), however, differences as low as 10 points are meaningful. Other guidelines for interpreting scores on the MSCA may be found in Kaufman and Kaufman (1977).

Merrill-Palmer Scale and Extension

One of the oldest preschool intelligence test batteries is the Merrill-Palmer Scale. Designed as a predominantly nonverbal substitute for the Stanford-Binet Intelligence Scale in testing children 1½ to 4 years of age, the thirty-eight tests on the Merrill-Palmer involve a variety of tasks. The tests include forms or other objects to be manipulated, as well as copying, remembering words and sentences, and matching or discriminating between forms. The tests are ranked according to difficulty level, and take about 45 minutes to administer.

The Merrill-Palmer Scale was standardized on 331 boys and 300 girls between the ages of 18 and 77 months. Most of the test–retest reliabilities are fairly modest, ranging from .39 to .92. The test was designed to serve as a substitute for or supplement to the Binet, but correlations with the Stanford-Binet are relatively modest (.22 to .79).

The Extended Merrill-Palmer Scale—1978 Version consists of sixteen tasks designed to evaluate the cognitive abilities of children aged 3 to 5 years. The test tasks assess both the content (the material processed) and the process (the way the material is processed) of children's thinking. Following J. P. Guilford's structure-of-intellect model, two content and two process categories are combined to yield measures on four dimensions of children's thinking: Semantic Production, Figural Production, Semantic Evaluation, and Figural Evaluation. Each dimension is measured by four tasks. The four dimensions are scored according to percentile bands, which are provided at 6-month intervals from 3 years to 5 years, 11 months.

Unfortunately, the Extended Merrill-Palmer Scale was not adequately standardized. The standardization sample consisted of only white preschool children ($N =$ 1,124), aged 36–71 months, from New York and Ohio. In addition to being poorly standardized, the reliability and validity data provided for the scale are meager.

BRIEF SCREENING TESTS

Rather than administering an abbreviated version of the Stanford-Binet or WPPSI, psychological examiners of young children often prefer to give one of the many brief screening tests of intelligence. Such instruments can be useful when time is short or the child's reading skills are limited. A brief screening test may also be used as a supplement to a longer intelligence test or as a quick test of vocabulary knowledge, drawing skill, or the ability to traverse mazes or construct designs with blocks.

Single-Task Tests

A number of instruments for assessing intelligence exclusively employ pictures as test stimuli. Examples of these pictorial intelligence tests are the Columbia Mental Maturity Scale, the Full-Range Picture Vocabulary Test, the Peabody Picture Vocabulary Test, the Quick Test, and the Pictorial Test of Intelligence.

Other single-task measures of intelligence include performance tests such as the Goodenough-Harris Drawing Test, the Porteus Maze Test, and the Stanford-Ohwaki-Kohs Block Design Intelligence Test. These instruments provide for rapid screening of young children on mental ability, although they do not give a complete picture of cognitive functioning. The most adequately standardized of the three tests is the Goodenough-Harris Drawing Test. This test (from The Psychological Corporation) is a revision of the Goodenough Draw-a-Man Test, together with a similar Draw-a-Woman and an experimental Self-Drawing scale. Appropriate for children from 3 to 15 years of age, the Goodenough-Harris requires the examinee to draw pictures of a man, a woman, and the self. The child's drawings are scored by comparing them with twelve model drawings and for the presence of seventy-three specific characteristics.

Slosson Intelligence Test—Revised

The widest age range of all quickly and individually administered tests of intelligence is covered by the Slosson Intelligence Test—Revised (SIT-R). Designed to provide IQs equivalent to those on the Stanford-Binet from infancy to adulthood, the SIT-R can be administered in 10–20 minutes. It contains a variety of items taken from the Stanford-Binet Intelligence Scale and Gesell Developmental Schedules, and, like the Stanford-Binet, is heavily loaded with verbal or linguistic tasks. Learning to administer the SIT-R is fairly simple, a fact which, along with its brevity, contributes to its popularity.

The SIT-R was standardized on 1,800 individuals from thirty-one states stratified to approximate a contemporary U.S. census, and expanded norms tables were prepared in 1991. The IQ range is 36 to 164, based on a mean of 100 and a standard deviation of 16. Kuder-Richardson reliabilities of .90 or higher are reported across all age groups, and the correlation of Slosson IQs with Full Scale IQs on the WISC-III is listed as .863.

Assessing Developmental Delays in Preschoolers

Compliance with the Individuals with Disabilities Education Act (IDEA) has become a requirement for tests that purport to screen accurately large numbers of children for developmental delays and serve as a precursor for in-depth diagnostic testing. Two instruments that fulfill the IDEA requirements are FirstSTEP: Screening Test for Evaluating Preschoolers and the AGS Early Screening Profiles.

FirstSTEP was designed as a developmental screening test for preschool children. Three levels—Level 1 (ages 2.9–3.8), Level 2 (ages 3.9–4.8), and Level 3 (ages 4.9–6.2)—cover the age range from 2.9 through 6.2 years. Administered in a total time of only 15 minutes, the twelve subtests on FirstSTEP are divided into three of the five IDEA domains: Cognition, Communication, and Motor. Interpretation of the child's performance on the twelve subtests, as indicated by a composite score, leads to three classification categories: "within acceptable limits," "caution" (mild to moderate developmental delays), or "at risk" (for developmental delays). The accuracy of the interpretation and classification may be enhanced by the use of optional rating scales and checklists. An optional Social-Emotional Rating Scale and a Parent/ Teacher Rating Checklist are used to assess the fourth IDEA domain (Attention/ Activity Levels, Social Interactions, Personal Traits, and Serious Behavior Problems). An optional Adaptive Behavior Checklist assesses the fifth IDEA domain (Activities of Daily Living, Self-Control, Relationships and Interactions, and Functioning in the Community). Training in the administration of FirstSTEP may be acquired by viewing two specially prepared videotapes or from certified trainers.

The AGS Early Screening Profiles (ESP) consists of three basic components, called profiles, supplemented by four surveys. The profiles are administered in less than 30 minutes, and the surveys in 15–20 minutes. The first profile—Cognitive/ Language Profile—consists of tasks to assess reasoning skills, visual organization and discrimination, receptive and expressive vocabulary, and basic school skills. The second profile—Motor Profile—assesses both gross and fine motor skills, such as walking a straight line, imitating arm and leg movements, tracing mazes, and drawing shapes. The third profile—Self-Help/Social Profile—is a questionnaire, completed by one of the child's parents or another caretaker, to assess the child's typical performance in the areas of communication, daily living skills, socialization, and motor skills.

The four surveys are on the ESP are the following:

Articulation Survey: Measures the child's ability to pronounce twenty words for identifying common articulation problems in the initial, medial, and final word positions.

Home Survey: Asks the parent questions about the child's home environment.

Health History Survey: The parent checks any health problems the child has had.

Behavior Survey: The examiner rates the child's attention span, frustration tolerance, response style, and other behaviors during administration of the Cognitive/ Language and Motor profiles.

At Level I of ESP, profile scores are converted to screening indexes to determine which children need further assessment. At Level II, standard scores, percentile ranks, and age equivalents are provided to determine the need for further assessment.

INFANT INTELLIGENCE TESTING: EARLY DEVELOPMENTS

Long before the first formal intelligence tests appeared, parents and other observers of infant behavior kept anecdotal records and diaries to describe signs of mental brightness and dullness in infants. Some of the most famous baby diaries, such as those kept by Charles Darwin and Jean Piaget, undoubtedly provide a picture of infant intelligence in the superior rather than the average or retarded category. Nevertheless, baby diaries and anecdotal records paved the way for more systematic and representative scientific studies of infant abilities.

S. E. Chaille (1887) should perhaps be given credit for devising the first test of infant intelligence, but it was the 1905 Binet-Simon Intelligence Scale that, extended downward to the first year of life, became the stimulus and model for later infant tests. The second edition of the Kuhlmann-Binet Scale, which was basically a 1922 revision of the 1908 Binet-Simon Intelligence Scale, represented the first serious attempt to provide a psychometrically sound measure of infant mental development (Brooks-Gunn & Weinraub, 1983). The Kuhlmann-Binet included five items at each of five age levels during the first 2 years of life (2, 6, 12, 18, and 24 months); these items were tests of coordination, speech, imitation, and recognition. Unfortunately the Kuhlmann-Binet was poorly standardized and infrequently administered. Another infant test published in the 1920s (Linfert & Hierholzer, 1928) was more carefully standardized than the Kuhlmann-Binet but also lacked popularity.

During the 1920s and 1930s, research projects on infant development began at several locations throughout the United States. Among the instruments stemming from these studies were the Gesell Developmental Schedules, the California First Year Mental Scale, and the Iowa Tests for Young Children. All these tests were subsequently revised or discontinued, but they deserve recognition for the care with which they were constructed.

Gesell Developmental Schedules

Research begun by Arnold Gesell at the Yale Clinic of Child Development in the 1920s led to an extensive series of investigations of infancy and early childhood that continued for 40 years. A guiding assumption of these studies was that human development follows an orderly, sequential pattern of maturation. Normative data on motor development, language development, adaptive behavior, and personal-social development from birth to age 6 were collected. Detailed information on each child was obtained by various methods: home record, medical history, daily record, anthropometric measurements, material observations, reports of the child's behavior at the clinic, normative examination, and developmental ratings. The following excerpt is characteristic of the normative behavioral descriptions provided by Gesell and his coworkers (Gesell & Amatruda, 1941, p. 41):

> The baby can reach with his eyes before he can reach with his hand; at 28 weeks a baby sees a cube; he grasps it, senses surface and edge as he clutches it, brings it to his mouth, where he feels its qualities anew, withdraws it, looks at it on withdrawal, rotates it while he looks, looks while he rotates it, restores it to his mouth, withdraws it again for inspection, restores it again for mouthing, transfers it to the other hand, bangs it, contacts it with the free hand, transfers, mouths it again, drops it, resecures it, mouths it yet again, repeating the cycle with variations—all in the time it takes to read this sentence.

Scores on the Gesell Developmental Schedules, determined from the presence or absence of specific behaviors characteristic of children at certain ages, were summarized in terms of a *developmental age* (DA). As with the ratio IQ, a child's DA could be further converted to a *developmental quotient* (DQ) by the formula DQ = 100 (DA/CA [chronological age]). However, Gesell did not in any way consider the DQ as equivalent to an IQ.

The Gesell Developmental Schedules have probably been used more by pediatricians than by psychologists to identify infants and children at risk for neurological impairment and mental retardation. Psychologists, particularly those with a strong psychometric or statistical orientation, have criticized the Gesell schedules as being too subjective and poorly standardized. However, a later version of the scales provided more objective observational procedures and acceptable reliability (Bernheimer & Keogh, 1988; Knobloch & Pasamanick, 1974; McTurk & Neisworth, 1978).

The age range on the revised scales is 4 weeks to 5 years, and five behavioral categories are covered: adaptive (alertness, intelligence, constructive exploration), gross motor (balance, sitting, locomotion, postural reactions), fine motor (manual dexterity), language (facial expression, gestures, vocalizations), and personal-social (feeding, playing, toilet training). Knobloch and his coauthors (Knobloch & Pasamanick, 1974; Knobloch, Stevens, & Malone, 1987) provided detailed instructions for making and interpreting observations on the revised Gesell Developmental Schedules. Norms for small groups of preschoolers (2½ to 6 years) by half-year intervals, but not for infants, have also been published (Ames et al., 1979). However, the norm group was not representative of the general population of infants, being biased toward individuals of northern European descent living in the Northeast. Some evidence for the validity of the Gesell has been reported (e.g., Williamson et al., 1990), but an overall judgment is that it falls short of acceptable psychometric standards.

California First-Year Mental Scale

In the late 1920s, Mary Shirley at the University of Minnesota (Minnesota Infant Study) and Nancy Bayley at the University of California (Berkeley Growth Study) began collecting research data and constructing tests of infant development. The tests devised by Shirley were not widely used, but the California First Year Mental Scale, published by Bayley in 1933, was the forerunner of one of the most carefully designed and representatively standardized of all tests of infant development.

The California First Year Mental Scale, designed for infants and toddlers from birth to 3 years, consisted of 185 items. Only 115 of these items—measures of adaptive behavior, language comprehension, and social responsiveness—were appropriate for infants (0–1½ years). Like Gesell, Bayley did not view the items on her test items as measuring the same abilities as those assessed by the Stanford-Binet or other intelligence tests administered at later ages. As she stated (Bayley, 1933, pp. 74, 82):

> Behavior growth in the early months of infant development has little predictive relation to the later development of intelligence…. We have measured at successive ages varying components of more or less independent functions; not until the age of 2 years do these composites exhibit a significant degree of overlapping with the aggregations of traits constituting "intelligence."

Although well researched and more carefully standardized than most tests at the time, a shortcoming of the California First Year Mental Scale was that it was standardized primarily on upper-middle-class children.

Cattell Infant Intelligence Scale

Among the many infant intelligence tests and developmental scales published or already in use during the 1940s and 1950s were the Northwestern Intelligence Test, Griffith's Mental Development Scale, and the Cattell Infant Intelligence Scale. A major function of all these tests was to provide early diagnostic information for purposes of adoptive placement of infants. The Northwestern Intelligence Test consisted in large measure of items borrowed from the Gesell Developmental Schedules. The reliability of the Northwestern was satisfactory, but validity information was scanty and the test was not considered superior to other infant tests of the time. Griffith's Mental Development Scale, viewed by many people as an improvement over existing tests in terms of standardization, reliability, and validity, was developed in England and seldom administered in the United States.

Only one of the three tests listed above, the Cattell Infant Intelligence Scale, is still commercially available. Also borrowing heavily from items on the Gesell Developmental Schedules, the Cattell was designed as a downward extension of the Stanford-Binet Intelligence Scale, Form L, and patterned after that instrument. Thus, an item was included on the Cattell scale only if the percentage of children passing it increased steadily with age in the range of the test (3–30 months), the item was easy to administer and of interest to young children, it required no cumbersome apparatus or the use of large muscles, and it was not greatly dependent on home training. Five items were included at each 1-month interval from 2–12 months and at each 2-month interval from 12–36 months. Among the test items included at the earliest levels were following objects with the eyes and attending to the human voice; such tasks as manipulating objects and forms were introduced at later age levels.

The Cattell Infant Intelligence Scale, which can be administered in 20–30 minutes, was standardized on a small sample ($N = 274$) of children at 3, 6, 9, 18, 24, and 30 months of age. The split-half reliabilities of the scale increase with age, ranging from .56 at 3 months to .90 at 30 months; the test–retest reliabilities follow a similar trend. Unfortunately, as with other infant intelligence tests, the predictive validities of the Cattell are low. Of interest is the fact that low scores on the scale appear to have greater predictive validity than high scores, particularly when the child has an unfavorable medical history or an impoverished social environment (Damerin, 1978).

INFANT INTELLIGENCE TESTING: LATER DEVELOPMENTS

The problem of low predictive validity continued to plague infant intelligence tests published during the 1960s and 1970s. Scores on tests administered during the first 2 years of life typically had fairly low correlations (.10 to .50) with scores on tests administered to the same children when they reached school age (Bayley, 1949; Hindley, 1965; MacFarlane, 1953). The younger the age of initial testing and the greater the interval between tests, the lower the correlation between scores on infant and childhood tests proved to be (see Figure 7–2).

One reason for the low correlations between tests administered in infancy and tests given at a later age is that the kinds of tasks on infant tests are not identical to those on tests for older children. Infant intelligence tests are primarily measures of sensorimotor development, such as the ability to lift and turn the head, follow a moving object with the eyes, and reach for or grasp an object. In contrast, tasks on Binet-type tests of the sort administered after infancy are more linguistic or verbal in nature. Obviously, the behavior repertoire of a preschool child is markedly greater than that of an infant. In addition to communicating with the examiner, a child of preschool age can walk and sit at a table while manipulating the test materials.

Not only do infant tests have relatively low predictive validities, but their reliabilities are also lower than those of tests administered during later preschool years. The greater distractibility or inattentiveness of infants in the testing situation obviously contributes to the lower reliabilities of infant tests, but bona fide changes in cognitive abilities also seem to occur in the young child from testing to testing. Thus, despite the earlier belief that intellectual growth is continuous and unitary throughout childhood, qualitative as well as quantitative changes in abilities take

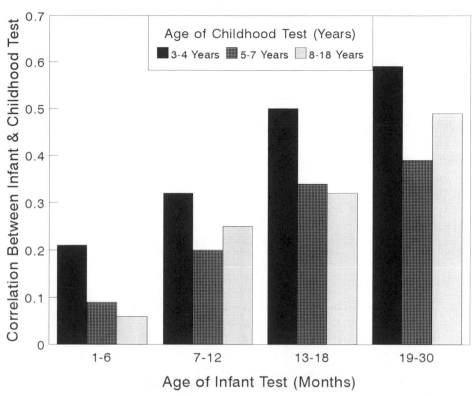

FIGURE 7-2 **Median correlations between infant test scores and childhood IQs.** (From McCall, R. B. [1979]. The development of intellectual functioning in infancy and the prediction of later IQ. In J. D. Osofsky (Ed.), *Handbook of infant development.* New York: Wiley. Reprinted by permission of John Wiley & Sons, Inc.)

place as the infant becomes a child and the child becomes an adolescent. Children are not only more attentive and motivated than infants in the testing situation, but their cognitive abilities appear to be of a different quality. Preschoolers are much more interested in words and social interactions than when they were infants. As one mother said of her toddler, "He now seems like a real person to me rather than just a living thing."

Despite low correlations with later test results, infant tests are still useful in diagnosing mental retardation and organic brain disorder. Studies of retarded or neurologically impaired children reveal that the test scores of these children during infancy are significantly prognostic of later intellectual status (Ames, 1967; Simon & Bass, 1956). The results of such studies indicate that infant tests can contribute to an understanding of child development and even to practical decisions about infants. However, information from infant tests must be combined with and interpreted in the light of other information about the infant and with an awareness of the limitations of the tests. With these cautions in mind, the remainder of this chapter considers infant tests that have been developed during the past two or three decades. Three of these tests—the Brazelton Neonatal Behavioral Assessment Scale (Brazelton, 1973, 1984), the Bayley Scales of Infant Development—Second Edition (Bayley, 1993), and the Infant Psychological Development Scale (Uzgiris, 1983; Uzgiris & Hunt, 1975)—are described in some detail.

Human beings are assessed or evaluated in many ways, formal and informal, throughout their lifetime and in some instances even before they are born. The Rochester Obstetrical Scale, for example, consists of a prenatal scale, a delivery scale, and an infant scale. A common procedure for evaluating the neonate, or newborn child, is the Apgar score. This score, which is determined at 1 minute and at 5 minutes after birth, is derived from measurements of heart rate, respiration, muscle tone, reflexes, and color (Chinn, Drew, & Logan, 1975). The three best known neonatal tests are the Graham/Rosenblith Behavioral Examination of Neonates (Rosenblith, 1961), the Prechtl Neurological Examination (Prechtl & Beintema, 1964), and the Brazelton Neonatal Behavioral Assessment Scale.

Brazelton Neonatal Behavioral Assessment Scale (NBAS)

The NBAS was designed to assess the quality and organization of the newborn's neurological, behavioral, and social functioning (Brazelton, 1973, 1984). Having an age range of 3 days to 4 weeks, the scale is composed of items for assessing twenty elicited reflexes (Moro, Babinski, rooting, etc.) and twenty-seven behavioral items in two categories: attractiveness and need for stimulation. The aim of the NBAS is to assess the infant's ability to elicit, participate in, and sustain interactions with other people. Illustrative items include hand–mouth coordination, habituation to sensory stimuli, startle responses, reflexes, stress responses, motor maturity, and cuddliness. The attractiveness category refers to the infant's ability to elicit and sustain social interactions; the need for stimulation category refers to the organizing or disorganizing effect of the examination procedure on the infant's behavior.

Administering and scoring the NBAS is somewhat complex, relatively difficult, and not completely standardized. The examination takes about 20 minutes and begins while the baby is asleep. The equipment includes a pocket flashlight, an orange rubber ball, a paper clip, some popcorn kernels, and other similar materials. Lack of standardization undoubtedly contributes to the modest reliability coefficients of the NBAS (Sameroff, 1978; Sostek, 1978). Its interrater reliability varied from .85 to .90 after ten or more practice sessions by the raters (Sostek, 1978). The scale has been used as a diagnostic tool and in a variety of research investigations, including studies of cocaine use during pregnancy (Chasnoff, Burns, & Burns, 1987), prenatal alcohol exposure (Coles, Smith, & Falek, 1987), environmental agents (Tronick, 1987), parent–infant attachment (Beal, 1991), and high-risk neonates (Emory, Tynan, & Dave, 1989).

Reviews of the NBAS by Als and his coauthors (Als, 1984; Als et al., 1979) are quite positive, and the scale has considerable merit as a research tool. Nevertheless, the lack of norms and little or no information on the predictive and construct validity counsel the need for caution in using this instrument as a test of infant intelligence. Although not unique in this regard, the NBAS has not been found to be useful in predicting later intelligence test scores (Tronick & Brazelton, 1975). Despite its shortcomings, the NBAS is a popular test and research instrument. Emphasizing the individuality of the infant, who actively interacts with the mother and other features of the environment from the moment of birth, this test will probably continue to be used by pediatricians and child psychologists. But more research is needed to clarify the meaning and implications of the scores (Beal, 1991).

Bayley Scales of Infant Development

Perhaps the most carefully designed and widely administered of all American infant developmental scales are the Bayley Scales of Infant Development. A product of the extensive longitudinal program of the Berkeley Growth Study, the Bayley Scales are an extension and refinement of the California First-Year Mental Scales. The second edition of the Bayley Scales (Bayley-II), which was published in 1993, is designed for children between the ages of 1 and 30 months who are at risk or suspected of being at risk. Working time is 25–35 minutes for children under 15 months old and up to 60 minutes for children over 15 months old.

There are three parts to Bayley-II: a Mental Scale (yielding a Mental Development Index), a Motor Scale (yielding a Psychomotor Development Index), and a Behavior Rating Scale used to supplement information from the Mental and Motor scales. Abilities measured by the Mental Scale include: sensory/perceptual acuities, discriminations, and the ability to respond to them; acquisition of object constancy; memory, learning, and problem solving; vocalization, beginning of verbal communication; early evidence of the basis of abstract thinking, habituation, mental mapping, complex language, mathematical concept formation. The skills assessed by the Motor Scale include: degree of control of the body; coordination of the large muscles; finer manipulative skills of the hands and fingers, dynamic movement; dynamic praxis; postural imitation; stereognosis. The four factors measured by the Behavior Rating Scale include attention/arousal, orientation/engagement, emotional regulation, and motor quality.

Bayley-II was standardized on a stratified random sample of 1,700 children selected from all four geographic regions of the United States, paralleling the 1988 U.S. Census statistics on age, gender, region, ethnicity, and parental education. The manual for the test contains data on a variety of clinical samples, including children who were born prematurely, children with HIV antibody, children exposed to drugs prenatally, children asphyxiated at birth, and children who are developmentally delayed, or who have frequent otitis media, are autistic, or have Down's syndrome.

A companion product to the Bayley-II is the Bayley Infant Neurodevelopmental Screen (BINS), which is appropriate for children between the ages of 3 and 24 months. The BINS is composed of items that assess basic neurological functions, auditory and visual receptive functions, and social and cognitive processes. It was standardized on 600 cases matched to U.S. demographic percentages for racial/ethnic groups, geographic region, and parental educational level. Cut scores on the BINS are provided for infants born prematurely, asphyxiated at birth, or who experienced intraventricular hemorrhage, apnea, patent ductus arteriosus or seizures.

Psychometric Instruments Based on Piaget's Theory

According to the Swiss psychologist Jean Piaget, cognitive development takes place in a series of stages or periods. Beginning with the sensorimotor stage, progressing through the preoperational and concrete operations stages, and ending with the stage of formal operations, the child becomes more knowledgeable and sophisticated in his or her interactions with the environment. From the simple assimilations and adaptations of the early stages, the child progresses to the concrete and abstract problem-solving of later stages. Piaget's theory of cognitive development is discussed in more detail in Chapter 12.

Concept Assessment Kit–Conservation and Montreal Tests

Many researchers and test designers have been influenced by Piaget's conceptions of cognitive development. For example, Laurendeau and Pinard (1962, 1970) constructed a series of tests at the University of Montreal to assess the 2- to 12-year-old child's concepts of causality and space. Two other psychologists devised the Concept Assessment Kit–Conservation (M. L. Goldschmid & P. M. Bentler, EdITS) to measure the extent to which young children (4–7 years old) understand the physical principle of conservation. According to Piaget, when the child comes to realize that the physical properties (weight, volume, number, and so forth) of objects remain unaltered when their shape, position, or other attributes are changed, he or she understands the principle of conservation. In Piaget's stage theory, the child's initial appreciation of this principle is characteristic of the transition from the preoperational to the concrete operational stage of thinking.

The Concept Assessment Kit–Conservation was standardized on 560 Los Angeles children between the ages of 4 and 8 years. Forms A and B of the test, which consist of six conservation tasks (Two-Dimensional Space, Number, Substance, Continuous Quantity, Weight, Discontinuous Quantity) are equivalent and highly correlated ($r = .95$). Form C, which assesses conservation of area and length, has lower correlations (.74–.76) with the other two forms.

Both the University of Montreal Tests and the Concept Assessment Kit–Conservation were designed for children aged 4 years and above. Several Piagetian-type scales have also been developed exclusively for the sensorimotor stage of cognitive development. Among these scales are the Albert Einstein Scales of Sensorimotor Development, the Casati-Lézine Scale, and the Uzgiris-Hunt Scales. The research programs underlying the development of these instruments took into account Piaget's division of the sensorimotor stage into six substages: use of reflexes, primary circular reactions, secondary circular reactions, coordination of secondary schemata and their application to new situations, tertiary circular reactions, and invention of new means through mental coordination.

Uzgiris-Hunt Scales

Perhaps the most popular of the Piagetian instruments for infants, at least from a research perspective, are the Uzgiris-Hunt Scales (Uzgiris, 1976, 1983; Uzgiris & Hunt, 1975). These scales were designed to assess an infant's abilities on several subscales, each consisting of a series of ordinal steps in the development of the specific ability measured by the subscale. The subscales are: Visual Pursuit and Permanence of Object (14 steps), Development of Means-Ends (13 steps), Vocal Imitation (9 steps), Gestural Imitation (9 steps), Development of Operational Causality (7 steps), Construction of Object Relations in Space (11 steps), and Development of Schemes for Relating to Objects (10 steps). Although the interobserver and test–retest reliabilities of the scales appear satisfactory, and the correlations with chronological age are fairly high (Uzgiris, 1976), the procedure for administering the scales is insufficiently standardized, and the norms are inadequate. Furthermore, correlations between scale scores and later IQs are quite low until the examinees are at least 18 months old (Kahn, 1983; Wachs, 1975).

Piagetian scales are generally more time-consuming and difficult to administer than other individual intelligence tests, but it can be argued that the reward is commensurate with the effort. At least in infancy and early childhood, Piagetian scales often provide a more detailed picture than other tests of what young children can and cannot do. These instruments are also in tune with the contemporary focus on mental ability as a collection of specific skills rather than a unitary capacity. The Piagetian approach recognizes the dynamic nature of cognitive abilities in early childhood, abilities that change qualitatively and quantitatively as the child matures and interacts with the environment.

SUMMARY

The formal assessment of intelligence in infants and young children began with the first Binet-Simon Intelligence Scale (1905), but not until the 1920s and 1930s did the development of such instruments become intensive. Among the most popular intelligence test batteries designed specifically for young children are the Wechsler Preschool and Primary Scale of Intelligence—Revised and the McCarthy Scales of Children's Abilities. Multilevel intelligence tests that are also appropriate for preschoolers include the Stanford-Binet IV, the Slosson Intelligence Test—Revised, and the Detroit Tests of Learning Aptitude-P:2 (see Chapter 5). Single-task measures used for screening purposes, including the Columbia Mental Maturity Scale, the Peabody Picture Vocabulary Test, the Goodenough-Harris Drawing Test, the Porteus Maze Test, and the Stanford-Ohwaki-Kohs Block Design Intelligence Test, are also suitable for young children. More extensive screening tests that comply with the requirements of the Individuals with Disabilities Education Act (IDEA) in assessing developmental delays in young children include FirstSTEP and the AGS Early Screening Profiles.

Testing infants and young children requires special skills and materials. Pre-schoolers are less able to sustain attention, less motivated, and more easily fatigued than older children in testing situations, so the examiner must be alert, enthusiastic, patient, and flexible, as well as thoroughly familiar with the test materials and procedures.

Anecdotal records and baby diaries were forerunners of formal intelligence tests and developmental scales for infants. The first serious attempt to provide a psychometrically sound measure of infant mental development was the second edition of the Kuhlmann-Binet Scale. Research programs begun by Arnold Gesell, Nancy Bayley, Charlotte Buhler, Mary Shirley, and others during the 1920s led to the design of many more infant scales. The Gesell Developmental Schedules, result-ing from the research of Arnold Gesell at Yale University, and the California First Year Mental Scale, a product of the research of Nancy Bayley and the Berkeley Growth Study, are the two best examples of infant scales refined during the 1930s. Other tests, such as the Cattell Infant Intelligence Scale, Griffith's Mental Develop-ment Scale, and the Northwestern Intelligence Test, were published during the 1940s and 1950s. Among the infant scales published from 1930 to 1960, only the Gesell Developmental Schedules and the Cattell Infant Intelligence Scale have survived.

More recently published developmental scales for infants include the Brazelton Neonatal Behavioral Assessment Scale (NBAS), the Bayley Scales of Infant De-velopment—Second Edition (Bayley-II), and the Uzgiris-Hunt Scales. The NBAS is a somewhat folksy test for assessing the physical and mental functioning of infants during the first 2 weeks of life. It is not a very well standardized instrument and rather difficult to administer, but it remains popular with pediatricians. The Bayley-II, designed for infants and toddlers from 3 to 30 months of age, is one of the most carefully constructed and standardized of all measures of infant development. The Uzgiris-Hunt Scales consist of seven categories of ordinal-level measurements based on Piaget's theory of cognitive development. Like other ordinal-scale instruments, it has been used primarily as a research tool.

Scores on intelligence tests or developmental scales administered during the first 2 years of life have rather low correlations with scores on intelligence tests administered to the same children at school age. The magnitudes of the correlations increase as the interval between tests decreases and the age at which the first test is administered increases. A significant reason for the low correlations between scores on tests administered in infancy and scores on tests administered later is the difference in materials and tasks appearing on the tests. Tests for infants and young preschoolers are heavily loaded with sensorimotor-type tasks, whereas those for older preschoolers and school-age children place greater emphasis on language and social skills.

Evidence for a general factor of intelligence, at least at later age levels, is sub-stantial, lending support to the argument that intelligence is a unitary capacity. However, qualitative as well as quantitative changes occur in cognitive abilities as infants mature into preschoolers and preschoolers become school-age children.

QUESTIONS AND ACTIVITIES

1. Define each of the following terms, as they are used in this chapter:

conservation	General Cognitive Index (GCI)
developmental age (DA)	IDEA
developmental delay	infant intelligence test
developmental quotient (DQ)	need for stimulation
developmental schedule	screening test

2. Why are the correlations of scores on infant intelligence tests with scores obtained by the same children on intelligence tests taken at a later age so low? Is it due to the low reliability of infant intelligence tests, the fact that infant intelligence tests measure different factors than tests administered in childhood, inadequate administration of infant intelligence tests, or what?

3. Describe Piaget's theory of cognitive development. Why do you think this theory has been so influential in the development of preschool and early school educational programs?

4. Collect as much information as you can on the provisions of various laws concerned with the identification, diagnosis, and intervention programs with children who are medically and/or environmentally "at risk." Focus on PL 94-142, PL 99-457, PL 101-476 (IDEA), PL 101-336 (ADA), and PL 102-119 in particular.

5. What characteristics and skills make for a good examiner of infants and young children? How are these characteristics and skills different from those required in testing older children and adults? How are they the same?

6. List and describe the three currently available tests in the Wechsler series of intelligence tests, including the age range for which each is appropriate and the subtests on each scale.

7. Compare the Bayley Scales of Infant Development—Second Edition with the McCarthy Scales of Children's Abilities in terms of: number and composition of subtests, age range for which each test is appropriate, method of scoring, standardization, reliability, and validity.

8. One of the most widely administered of all intelligence tests is the Slosson Intelligence Test—Revised. Despite its brevity and wide age range, the reported reliability coefficients of this test are quite respectable. How can this be so?

9. Compare FirstSTEP with the AGS Early Screening Profiles in terms of purpose, composition, and scoring categories.

SUGGESTED READINGS

Bracken, B. A. (Ed.). (1991). Wechsler Preschool and Primary Scale of Intelligence (WPPSI-R) [Special issue]. *Journal of Psychoeducational Assessment, 9*(3).

Buckhalt, J. A. (1991). Wechsler Preschool and Primary Scale of Intelligence—Revised. *Journal of Psychoeducational Assessment, 9,* 271–279.

Goodman, J. F. (1990). Infant intelligence: Do we, can we, should we assess it? In C. R. Reynolds & R. W. Kamphaus (Eds.), *Handbook of psychological & educational assessment of children: Intelligence & achievement* (pp. 183–208). New York: Guilford Press.

Gyurke, J. S. (1991). The assessment of children with the Wechsler Preschool and Primary

Scale of Intelligence—Revised. In B. A. Bracken (Ed.), *The psychoeducational assessment of preschool children* (2nd ed., pp. 86–132). Needham Heights, MA: Allyn & Bacon.

Lewis, M., & Sullivan, M. W. (1985). Infant intelligence and its assessment. In B. B. Wolman (Ed.), *Handbook of intelligence: Theories, measurements, and applications* (pp 505–599). New York: Wiley.

Rosetti, L. M. (1990). *Infant-toddler assessment: An interdisciplinary approach*. Austin, TX: pro.ed.

Valencia, R. R. (1990). Clinical assessment of young children with the McCarthy scales of children's abilities. In C. R. Reynolds & R. W. Kamphaus (Eds.), *Handbook of psychological & educational assessment of children: Intelligence & achievement* (pp. 209–258). New York: Guilford Press.

Chapter **8**

Individual Testing
of the Handicapped

The grandfather of modern intelligence tests, the Binct-Simon Intelligence Scale, was designed primarily for testing mentally handicapped children. The term *handicapped*, however, has been used in a more general way to refer to persons with physical, mental, cultural, or even emotional handicaps. Because the procedures employed in testing nonhandicapped individuals are often unsuitable or unfair for testing the handicapped, special methods and tests were devised. In this chapter we shall consider a representative sample of tests of intelligence and certain other abilities that have been constructed to evaluate children and adults having various handicaps. It has become customary to refer to such children—those with physical

191

or mental handicaps—as *special children*, but *special* also refers to children of above-average ability.

The Stanford-Binet and Wechsler tests, or adaptations of them, have been used to test the intelligence of both nonhandicapped and handicapped persons. The fact that the Wechsler Adult Intelligence Scale—Revised (WAIS-R) and the Wechsler Intelligence Scale for Children—Third Edition (WISC-III) contain separate verbal and performance scales makes these tests more suitable than the Stanford-Binet for examining individuals with physical, language, and cultural handicaps. For example, the Wechsler performance scales tend to be more accurate measures of intellectual functioning in hearing-impaired and culturally different children, whereas the Wechsler verbal scales are more valid measures for the blind and partially sighted.

Despite the usefulness of conventional intelligence tests, adaptations of them are not always suitable and have not always been available for testing handicapped people. Consequently, numerous special-purpose instruments have been devised over the years. Among the earliest single-task performance tests that were administered to persons with language handicaps were block design tests, formboards, and mazes of various kinds.

One of the oldest nonverbal tests, the Seguin Formboard, was introduced in 1866. It was not until the early part of the twentieth century, however, that Knox, Porteus, and other psychologists made serious efforts to standardize such tests. Many types of formboards, which were eventually combined as the Seguin-Goddard Formboards (available from Stoelting) and also included in several test batteries, were investigated and standardized. Other nonverbal tests of intelligence included puzzles of various kinds, sequential tapping of cubes, matching problems, block designs, and mazes.

Mazes have been employed extensively in psychological laboratories and clinics and were included on a number of standardized tests. The Porteus Mazes, viewed by its designer, S. D. Porteus, as a measure of foresight and planning ability, was introduced in 1914. This test, which is distributed by The Psychological Corporation, consists of a series of mazes arranged in order of increasing difficulty. On each maze the examinee is directed to draw the shortest path between the start and finish points without lifting the pencil or entering a blind alley. The Porteus is particularly suitable as a brief test (25 minutes) for the verbally handicapped and has been employed in a number of anthropological studies. It is also reported to be sensitive to brain damage, but, as is true of scores on intelligence tests in general, Porteus scores are affected by education and experience.

Another nonverbal performance task for testing the handicapped consists of a set of block designs such as those on the Wechsler scales and the Differential Ability Scales. One of the earliest of these tests, the Kohs Block Design, was designed by S. C. Kohs. The materials on the Kohs, which takes up to 40 minutes to administer, consist of sixteen colored cubes and seventeen cards with colored designs to be duplicated by the examinee. The Kohs Block Design is considered to be especially appropriate for language- and hearing-handicapped children between the ages of 3 and 19 years. The materials are also included on performance test batteries such as the Merrill-Palmer Scale and the Arthur Point Scale of Performance. Other batteries of performance tests, such as the Knox tests developed in 1914 (available from Stoelting) and the Pintner-Paterson Scale of Performance Tests published in 1917, were also designed for persons with English-language handicaps. These tests minimized the importance of speed and could be administered without language.

Today many individual intelligence tests designed exclusively for handicapped persons are available; the list in Table 8–1 is representative. Some of these are single-task tests, others are test batteries, and still others are extensions or adaptations of conventional intelligence tests such as the Stanford-Binet and Wechsler series.

In addition to special intelligence tests for physically handicapped people, a number of sensorimotor or perceptual-motor tests have been devised. Scores on intelligence tests are affected by sensory acuity and discrimination, as well as by psychomotor skills in the case of certain tasks. Consequently, instruments such as

---

TABLE 8–1   Individual Intelligence Tests for Handicapped Persons

Arthur Adaptation of the Leiter International Performance Scale, by G. Arthur; © 1952; ages 2–12 years; Stoelting, Western Psychological Services.

Arthur Point Scale of Performance Tests, Form 1, by G. Arthur; © 1925–1943; ages 4 years to adult; Stoelting.

Blind Learning Aptitude Test (BLAT), by T. E. Newland; © 1971; blind, ages 6–20 years; U.S. Department of Education & University of Illinois Press.

Columbia Mental Maturity Scale (CMMS), 3rd ed., by B. B. Burgemeister, L. H. Blum, & I. Lorge; © 1954–1972; ages 3½–10 years; The Psychological Corporation.

Extended Merrill-Palmer Scale, by R. Stutsman Ball, P. Merrifield, & L. H. Stott; ages 3–5 years; 45 mins.; Stoelting.

Full-Range Picture Vocabulary Test, by R. B. Ammons & H. S. Ammons; © 1948; ages 2 years and over; Psychological Test Specialists.

Haptic Intelligence Scale, by H. C. Shurrager & P. S. Shurrager; © 1964; Stoelting.

Hiskey-Nebraska Test of Learning Aptitude, by M. S. Hiskey; © 1966; ages 3–18; from Marshall S. Hiskey, 5640 Baldwin, Lincoln, NE 68507.

Kahn Intelligence Test: 1975 Revision, by T. C. Kahn; © 1975; ages 1 year and over; Psychological Test Specialists.

Kohs Block Design Test, by S. C. Kohs; ages 6 years and over; Stoelting.

Leiter Adult Intelligence Scale, by R. G. Leiter; © 1949–1964; adults; Stoelting.

Leiter International Performance Scale, by R. G. Leiter; © 1929–1952; ages 2 years and over; Stoelting, Western Psychological Services.

Matrix Analogies Test, by J. A. Naglieri; © 1985; ages 5–17 years; expanded and short forms; The Psychological Corporation.

Merrill-Palmer Scale, by R. Stutsman; ages 1½–4 years; 45 mins.; Stoelting.

Peabody Picture Vocabulary Test—Revised (PPVT-R), by L. M. Dunn; © 1981; ages 2½ to adult; American Guidance Service.

Perkins-Binet Tests of Intelligence for the Blind, by C. J. Davis; © 1980; blind and partially sighted; ages 3½–18 years; Perkins School for the Blind.

Quick Test, by R. B. Ammons & C. H. Ammons; © 1958–1962; ages 2 to adults; Psychological Test Specialists.

Smith-Johnson Nonverbal Performance Scale, by A. J. Smith & R. E. Johnson; © 1977; ages 2–4 years; Western Psychological Services.

Test of Nonverbal Intelligence, 2nd ed. (TONI-2), by L. Brown, R. J. Sherbenou, & S. K. Johnsen; ages 5 through 85; 10–15 mins.; Stoelting.

TABLE 8–2   Perceptual, Motor, and Memory Tests

Auditory Continuous Performance Test, by R. Keith; © 1994; ages 5–11 years; 10 mins.; Psychological Corporation.

Bender Visual Motor Gestalt Test, by L. Bender; © 1938, 1946; ages 4–adult; no time limit; Psychological Corporation.

Benton Visual Retention Test, 5th ed., by A. B. Sivan; © 1991; ages 8 years to adult; 5 mins; Psychological Corporation.

Boston Diagnostic Aphasia Examination, by H. Goodglass & E. Kaplan; © 1983; adults; untimed; Psychological Corporation.

Bruininks-Oseretsky Test of Motor Proficiency, by R. H. Bruininks; © 1978; ages 4½–14½ years; complete battery 45–60 mins., short form 15–20 mins., American Guidance Service.

Fuld Object-Memory Evaluation, by P. A. Fuld; ages 70–90 years; 16 mins.; Stoelting.

Goldman-Fristoe-Woodcock Auditory Skills Test Battery, by R. Goldman, R. Fristoe, & R. W. Woodcock; © 1974, 1975, 1976; age 3 to adult; 15 mins. per test; American Guidance Service.

Goldman-Fristoe-Woodcock Test of Auditory Discrimination, by R. Goldman, M. Fristoe, & R. W. Woodcock; © 1970; ages 4 and above; 20–30 mins.; American Guidance Service.

Memory Assessment Scales (MAS), by J. M. Williams, © 1990; ages 18–90; 40–45 mins.; PAR.

Memory for Designs Test, by F. Graham & B. Kendall; © 1960; ages 8½ through 60; Psychological Test Specialists.

Minnesota Test for Differential Diagnosis of Aphasia, by H. Schuell; © 1973; adult; 45–120 mins.; American Guidance Service.

Multilingual Aphasia Examination, by A. I. Bendon & K. DeS. Hamsher; © 1989; ages 6–69 years; 20–25 mins. in nonaphasic subjects; The Psychological Corporation.

SCAN: A Screening Test for Auditory Processing Disorders, by R. W. Keith; © 1986; ages 3 through 11 years; 20 mins.; Psychological Corporation.

SCAN-A: A Test for Auditory Processing Disorders in Adolescents and Adults, by R. W. Keith; © 1993; ages 12 through adult; 25 mins.; Psychological Corporation.

Test of Memory and Learning (TOMAL) , by C. R. Reynolds & E. D. Bigler; ages 5–19 years; less than 45 mins.; Stoelting.

Visual Aural Digit Span Test, by E. M. Koppitz; © 1977; ages 5.6 to 12 years, 10 mins.; Psychological Corporation.

Western Aphasia Battery, by A. Kertresz; © 1982; adolescent through adult; approx. 1 hour; Psychological Corporation.

Wide Range Assessment of Memory and Learning, by W. Adams & D. Sheslaw; ages 5–17 years; 45 mins. total, 15 mins. for brief memory screening; Stoelting.

---

those listed in Table 8–2 are often combined with intelligence tests to provide a clearer picture of a person's cognitive abilities and any perceptual-motor deficits that might account for low intelligence scores. In addition to the more complex perceptual-motor tests listed in Table 8–2, many simpler measures of visual and auditory acuity (such as a sight screener, an audiometer, and a color visual test) serve as sensory screening tests. As we shall see later in the chapter, scores on a combined battery of tests of cognitive and perceptual-motor abilities often provide insight into neurological disabilities.

In order for a test score to be a valid indicator of an individual's functioning intelligence, it is necessary to adhere closely to the directions for administration and scoring. If this is not done, the examiner cannot rely on the test norms in interpreting performance. Unfortunately, the directions on conventional tests of intelligence cannot always be followed precisely when testing handicapped persons. Inattentiveness, lack of test-taking motivation, inability to see or hear well, clumsiness or awkwardness in moving and manipulating objects, and even extreme shyness or fear on the part of the examinee may make it impossible to administer the test correctly. In such cases, the examiner can: (1) adapt the test to the person's abilities and behavior or administer only those items on which the person will not be at a disadvantage; (2) administer a test designed specifically for individuals with such handicaps; (3) collect data on the examinee's functioning intelligence by informal observation or by interrogating other observers (such as parents); or (4) give up. The last alternative is not necessarily final because a child may be more receptive to being tested tomorrow or next week, or perhaps by another examiner.

Certain matters, such as determining whether the examinee can see, hear, and manipulate the test materials appropriately, should be checked before formal testing is begun. This kind of information can be obtained from the parents or other caretakers, from the examinee's case history or referral form, by observing the examinee carefully before beginning the test, or by administering one or more simple sensorimotor tests.

The examiner must judge whether special adaptations of, or deviations from, standard testing procedure invalidate the test results. Permitting alternative response modes (such as pointing or pantomiming rather than answering verbally), providing ample time for responding, and scheduling more than one testing session are provisions that will not invalidate the results on many intelligence tests. Other helpful suggestions in testing handicapped persons are to allow sufficient practice on sample items; to be alert for signs of anxiety, fatigue, and other disruptions and take them into account in deciding whether to continue and how to interpret the test results; and to employ a sufficient amount of encouragement and social reinforcement (e.g., "Good!") when the examinee exhibits good effort, whether the answer is right or wrong. Disapproval of wrong answers or punishment in any form should be avoided, and the examinee should not be forced to respond when he or she repeatedly refuses to do so.

TESTING VISUALLY IMPAIRED PERSONS

Procedures for testing individuals with visual defects depend upon the amount of (corrected) usable vision possessed by the person. According to the American Medical Association (Connor et al., 1975, p. 240).

> A person shall be considered blind whose central visual acuity does not exceed 20/200 in the better eye with correcting lenses or whose visual acuity, if better than 20/200, has a limit in the center field of vision to such a degree that its widest diameter subtends an angle of no greater than twenty degrees.

Of course, many individuals who fit this description, although legally blind, retain sufficient sight to utilize vision as their primary learning sense; they are referred to as partially sighted.

Regarding methods of administering psychological tests to visually handicapped persons, Bauman (1974) proposed a three-category taxonomy of visual impairment. Included in the first category are totally blind individuals and those who can distinguish between light and dark or even distinguish shapes but only when the shapes are placed between the eyes and the light source. The second category includes people who have enough usable vision to assist them in handling large objects, to locate pieces in a work space, or to follow the examiner's hand movements, but who are unable to read even enlarged ink print. Such individuals must be tested with materials that require an appropriate combination of vision and touch rather than relying exclusively on vision. The third category of visual impairment consists of people who can read ink print but may need large type, people who hold the page very close to their eyes, and those who use a magnifying glass or other visual aid.

The particular materials and procedures, including the environment, for testing blind or partially sighted individuals vary with the degree of impairment. With respect to the testing environment, provisions must be made for adequate lighting, a quiet room free from distractions, and a relatively compact work space. Large type, materials in braille (if the examinee reads braille), and appropriate writing instruments (e.g., felt-tip pens or crayons rather than pencils) are also important. Other matters to be aware of when testing individuals whose vision is impaired are the following: (1) they may require more time than normally sighted persons; (2) multiple-choice questions that require too much concentration for the visually impaired should be avoided; (3) pretesting experience in touching the test materials should be provided.

The classroom teacher is often the first person to detect a visual impairment in a child. Among the signs of visual disabilities in schoolchildren are: holding a book too close to the eyes or holding the head to one side when reading; tilting the head forward when looking at objects; frowning or squinting when reading from a distance; confusing letters (such as o and a) or lines, or skipping words when reading aloud; failure of the eyes to work together; and complaints of double or blurred vision, headaches, or dizziness when doing close work (Fleming, 1973). A preliminary assessment of visual acuity may be obtained by means of a simple Snellen Chart or a more complex screening instrument (sight-screen, telebinocular, etc.). Color vision may be determined by the Ishihara Test for Color Blindness, the Dvorine Color Vision Test, or the Farnsworth Dichotomous Test for Color Blindness.

A variety of ability tests, both individually and group administered, have been adapted for use with visually handicapped people. For example, large-type or braille editions of the Scholastic Aptitude Test (SAT) and the Graduate Record Examinations (GRE) are available. Among the individually administered tests that have been used most extensively for this purpose are adaptations of the Stanford-Binet and Wechsler series.

Hayes-Binet and Perkins-Binet

The first Hayes-Binet test for the blind and partially sighted was a revision of the original (1916) Stanford-Binet Intelligence Scale. The second edition of the Hayes-Binet, known as the Interim Hayes-Binet, was published in 1942. Items not requiring the use of vision were selected from forms L and M of the Stanford-Binet, yielding six tests at years VIII–XIV and eight tests at the Average Adult level. A few special tests had to be devised to provide a sufficient number of items for years III–VII. Most of the resulting tests were oral in nature, with some consisting of braille materials. The split-half and test–retest reliabilities of the Interim Hayes-Binet were in the .90s, and correlations of the test with measures of school achievement were high.

A successor to the Interim Hayes-Binet—the Perkins-Binet Tests of Intelligence for the Blind—was published by the Perkins School for the Blind in Watertown, Massachusetts, in 1980. This age-level scale adaptation of the Stanford-Binet consists of verbal and performance items and is available in two forms for children aged 3 to 18 years. The ninety-four items on Form N were designed for children 4 to 18 years of age having no usable vision, and the ninety-nine items on Form U are for children 3 to 18 years old with usable vision. Like the Stanford-Binet, the items (including alternates) on the Perkins-Binet are grouped into year levels; the test also yields an overall mental age score and a deviation IQ. The Perkins-Binet was standardized on 2,153 legally blind youth selected from the register of the American Printing House for the Blind in 1962–1963. Of this 13 percent sample, 1,093 were enrolled in day schools and 1,060 in residential schools; 1,158 were males and 995 were females. None was considered severely emotionally disturbed or severely retarded or to have severe communication disorders or other serious handicaps.

Special training is needed to administer the Perkins-Binet. Because blind children are easily distracted by incidental noises, preparations for a quiet testing room are essential. Leading the child through the room prior to testing or permitting him or her to explore it, as well as providing interesting toys and other familiar materials, can also assist in making the child comfortable with the testing situation.

Ward and Genshaft (1983) made a number of technical recommendations for improved administration and scoring of the Perkins-Binet. According to these writers, the manual and test procedures are not clear on certain matters. Davis (1980) maintained that strict adherence to the printed instructions in the manual is not essential. As long as the item content is not changed, the examiner may translate the printed test directions so the examinee can understand them. Encouragement and support are effective when testing both handicapped and nonhandicapped children. When testing children with severe visual handicaps, in addition to verbally encouraging and praising the examinee, approval should be indicated by patting, touching, or clapping rather than by nodding and smiling.

The materials and norms on the Perkins-Binet are rather dated by this time, so the test is no longer as popular as it once was. It has not been adapted to the latest (fourth) edition of the Stanford-Binet and is no longer published by the Perkins School for the Blind. In its place, it is recommended that a combination of two subtests (Memory for Sentences and Memory for Digits) on Stanford-Binet-IV be used, supplemented perhaps by braille versions of other subtests (Delaney & Hopkins, 1987).

Haptic Intelligence Scale for Adult Blind

The Wechsler tests have also been adapted for use with blind and partially sighted children and adults. The most straightforward adaptation of the WISC-III or WPPSI-R is to administer the Verbal Scale and omit the Performance Scale subtests altogether. Sometimes used in conjunction with the WAIS–Verbal in testing visually impaired persons is a series of six specially designed performance tests known as the Haptic Intelligence Scale for Adult Blind. The six subtests are Digit Symbol, Object Assembly, Block Design, Object Completion, Pattern Board, and Bead Arithmetic. This test is appropriate for individuals 16 years and older and takes 60–90 minutes to administer. Partially sighted examinees are required to wear a blindfold while taking the test. The examinee uses tactile sensitivity rather than vision to accomplish such tasks as analyzing dot patterns, assembling puzzle parts, finding holes or missing sections, examining and reproducing pegboard patterns, and solving arithmetic problems on an abacus.

Other Tests for the Visually Impaired

Other adaptations and special instruments for assessing the intellectual functioning of visually impaired individuals have been constructed. Among these are single-task tests such as the Tactile Progressive Matrices, the Tactile Reproduction Pegboard, and the Stanford-Ohwaki-Kohs Block Design Intelligence Test for the Blind. The Stanford-Ohwaki-Kohs is a modified form of Kohs Block Design standardized on visually handicapped persons in the United States involving the sense of touch to identify and duplicate the designs. The test takes 1 to 2 hours to administer, and scores are converted to percentile ranks and IQs. Three test batteries for the visually handicapped that have received some attention are the Williams Intelligence Test for Children with Defective Vision, the Vocational Intelligence Scale for the Adult Blind, and the Blind Learning Aptitude Test.

The Blind Learning Aptitude Test (BLAT) (Newland, 1969) is an untimed, process-oriented test consisting of tactile items in an embossed (bas relief) format with dots and lines similar to those used in braille. The BLAT consists of six different kinds of behavioral tasks, which are adaptations of items on the Culture Fair Intelligence Test and the Raven Progressive Matrices (see Chapter 9). Covering the entire range of school grades (K–12), the BLAT was standardized on 961 blind students enrolled in residential schools in twelve states and fifty-five day schools throughout the United States. Although relatively small, the standardization sample was stratified by geographic region, age, sex, race, and socioeconomic status. Scores on the BLAT are expressed as *learning quotients* having a mean of 100 and a standard deviation of 15. The internal consistency reliability of the test, based on 961 cases, is .93, and the test–retest reliability in a sample of 93 children aged 10 to 16 years is .87. Little information on the empirical validity of the test is given in the manual, but its theoretical foundation appears to be sound. Reported concurrent validity coefficients are .74 with the Hayes-Binet and .71 with the WISC–Verbal. The magnitudes of these coefficients suggest that the BLAT overlaps to some extent with other measures of academic ability, but it also measures something different from other intelligence tests.

TESTING HEARING-IMPAIRED AND OTHER LANGUAGE-HANDICAPPED PERSONS

Difficulties in communicating with other persons may be receptive (sensory) or expressive (motor), or a combination of the two. A person with a sensory or brain disorder may have a problem understanding what is said or expressing what is well understood. *Aphasia*, a general term for a disability in using words, is also classified as either receptive or expressive. In *receptive aphasia*, the person is unable to understand spoken or written language. In *expressive aphasia*, the person cannot think of the right word to express an idea or use language meaningfully. Many tests for aphasia are available, including the Boston Diagnostic Aphasia Examination, the Minnesota Test for Differential Diagnosis of Aphasia, the Multilingual Aphasia Examination, and the Western Aphasia Battery. All four tests are appropriate for adults; the Western Aphasia Battery is also appropriate for adolescents, and the Multilingual Aphasia Examination for individuals aged 6–69.

Although it is true that difficulty in communicating is characteristic of mentally retarded individuals, it is obvious that mental retardation does not invariably accompany blindness, deafness, or brain disorders that lead to problems in communicating (see Report 8–1). For these reasons, the need for special intelligence tests for individuals with language handicaps was recognized quite early in the history of psychological testing. Most of these tests, such as the Pintner-Paterson Scale of Performance Tests and the Arthur Point Scale of Performance Tests, were nonverbal examinations requiring examinees to manipulate various objects or materials.

Leiter International Performance Scale and Arthur Adaptation

One early performance battery that is still being used to test the cognitive abilities of children with sensorimotor problems or other deficits that make it difficult for them to speak and read is the Leiter International Performance Scale. The Leiter was developed on ethnic Hawaiian school children and has been employed with a variety of other groups, including native Africans. In this sense, the Leiter is a cross-cultural test that was thought to be "culture-fair." The culture fairness of the Leiter has, however, been questioned, because large ethnic differences in scores have been found (Werner, 1965).

The Leiter consists of fifty-four nonverbal tasks arranged in an age-scale format. Although it is untimed, the test can be administered, without requiring verbal language, in 30–40 minutes to individuals from age 2 to adulthood. Instructions

---

Report 8–1

Deafness Is Not Retardation: A Case of Misdiagnosis

Robert was 7 years old. His mother had died when he was 2, and the identity of his father was unknown. Since his mother's death, Robert had been cared for by an aunt. At age 5, he was placed in a day-care center for severely retarded children. Robert was a friendly child who seemed eager to please others, and he responded enthusiastically to gestures of affection. However, Robert had no expressive language at all, and it was difficult for day-care staff to determine whether he understood any language. Nevertheless, he appeared to understand gestures and was able to follow a few simple directions. Most staff members never questioned the fact that Robert was retarded and appropriately placed in the facility.

The speech pathologist at the day-care center had insisted, shortly after Robert's arrival, that he should be evaluated by a psychologist and an audiologist. Having observed Robert closely, she was convinced that he was not retarded, but rather suffered from a severe hearing impairment. However, it took her nearly two years to overcome others' objections and secure referrals to appropriate professionals. Since Robert had no language, psychological evaluation was based on behavioral observations, ratings on objective behavior scales, and a nonverbal intelligence test. Results indicated that Robert was functioning in the normal range of ability. Audiological evaluation demonstrated that Robert did indeed have a severe hearing impairment. These studies eventuated in Robert's placement in a state school for the deaf where he was fitted with a hearing aid and given auditory training and training in manual communication. Robert made a good adjustment to this residential setting and flourished on the attention he received. He responded well to training in manual communication, and his development reflected normal intellectual ability. However, despite amplification with a hearing aid, Robert was unable to learn to communicate verbally.

---

may be given in pantomime, and items that are failed prior to establishing a basal age may be readministered. The basic task is to select blocks bearing symbols or pictures and place them in the appropriate recesses of a response frame equipped with an adjustable card holder. The tests include matching colors, shades, and forms or pictures; copying a block design; completing a picture; estimating numbers;

completing and memorizing series; recognizing age differences, spatial relations, and similarities between objects; and classifying animals by habitat.

The split-half reliabilities of the Leiter are in the low .90s. The test–retest reliabilities of a subsequent modification, the Arthur Adaptation of the Leiter International Performance Scale, for samples of handicapped children are in the .80s and .90s. In constructing the Arthur Adaptation of the Leiter, which was designed for children between 2 and 12 years and published in 1948, the few timed tests were omitted. The sixty items of the Arthur Adaptation also employ a response frame with an adjustable card holder, as well as two trays of response blocks and corresponding stimulus cards. Similar to the Stanford-Binet, a certain number of months credit is awarded for passing each of four subtests at each age level. Credits are then summed to yield a mental age, which is converted to a ratio IQ.

Scores on the Arthur Adaptation of the Leiter have moderate to high correlations with the WISC–Verbal ($r = .40$ to $.78$) and WISC–Performance ($r = .79$ to $.89$) scales. Furthermore, Leiter IQs average approximately 5 points lower than Stanford-Binet or WISC IQs. Another shortcoming of the Leiter is that the norms on both the original Leiter and the Arthur Adaptation are quite dated and limited. For example, the Arthur Adaptation of the Leiter was standardized in 1948 on 289 middle-class children from metropolitan areas in the midwestern United States. Other criticisms of the Leiter include outdated pictures, lack of clarity concerning the abilities measured by the test, and the small number of tests at each age level. For these and other reasons, such as the appearance of both tests, the Leiter is no longer administered as frequently as it was in the past.

Testing Hearing Impaired Persons

The deaf and hard-of-hearing are obviously not the only persons who experience difficulties with spoken language, but the sheer numbers of people with hearing impairments has created a need for special diagnostic and training methods. The extent to which deafness interferes with a child's learning and social functioning varies with the severity of the deficiency. Using as an index of the degree of deafness the number of *decibels* (db) (a measure of loudness, or sound pressure level) required for the person to hear in the better ear, four categories of hearing loss are recognized. Persons who can hear in the range of 0–30 db (the loudness of a whisper) have a *mild* hearing loss. If the sound pressure level must be in the 30–50 db range (normal house sounds) for the person to hear, the hearing loss is *moderate*. The hearing loss is *severe* when the sound pressure level must be in the 50–80 db range (ordinary conversation) for the person to hear. The hearing loss is *profound* if the sound pressure level must be 80–100 db (telephone ring or street traffic) in order for the person to hear, and *total* if the sound pressure level must be 100–130 db (loud thunder) to be heard.

The extent of hearing loss in each ear can be determined fairly accurately by means of an audiometer test and an audiogram plotted from the results. Alert observers, however, will note a number of informal signs of poor hearing in children: failure to pay attention when spoken to or asking the speaker to repeat words; hearing better when watching the speaker's face; confusing words having similar vowels but different consonants (e.g., *wood* and *hoot*); failure to articulate properly or omission of certain consonant sounds; frequent colds, earaches, runny ears, upper respiratory infections (sinusitis, tonsillitis), and allergies; and behavior problems or social withdrawal.

Poor hearing interferes with learning, and may be misdiagnosed as mental retardation, so it is important to obtain an accurate picture of the basic intellectual functioning of a hearing-impaired child. Because deaf children are usually more handicapped on verbal tests, early efforts to obtain accurate assessments of the intelligence of such children focused on tactile or manipulative-type tasks such as the those on the Arthur Point Scale. Subsequently, the Wechsler and other conventional intelligence tests were adapted for the deaf. One such adaptation was named, appropriately enough, the Adaptation of the WISC-R Performance Scale for Deaf Children.* Certain nonverbal group tests, such as the Revised Beta Examination, the Raven Progressive Matrices, and the Cattell Culture Fair Intelligence Test (see Chapter 9), have also been used for testing hearing-impaired persons. The Kaufman Assessment Battery for Children also contains a nonverbal scale for individuals between the ages of 4½ and 12½ years; the test is administered in pantomime or gesture and responded to nonverbally or motorically. The Arthur Adaptation of the Leiter International Performance Scale can also be administered to hearing-impaired children.

Other representative tests for the deaf and hard of hearing include the Nebraska Test of Learning Aptitude (Hiskey, 1966) and selected subtests of the Illinois Test of Psycholinguistic Abilities. As in testing the visually impaired, administering individual tests to hearing-impaired persons requires sensitive awareness of the examinee's handicap. For example, you (the examiner) should use facial expressions rather than voice tones to convey mood. Because facial expressions are significant to the deaf child, frowning, grimacing, and other signs of disapproval or dislike should be minimized. Gesturing, pantomiming, writing, signing, finger spelling, and drawing can also be used to communicate with deaf examinees. When speaking (reading instructions, asking questions, providing information or verbal reinforcement), you should make certain that the examinee is looking at your face.

The Nebraska Test of Learning Aptitude (NTLA),† which was designed to assess the learning abilities of hearing-impaired individuals between the ages of 3 and 16 years, consists of twelve nonverbal subtests administered with pantomimic directions to deaf children or verbal directions to normal children. The twelve subtests are Bead Patterns, Memory for Colors, Picture Identification, Picture Association, Paper Folding, Visual Attention Span, Block Patterns, Completion of Drawings, Memory for Digits, Puzzle Blocks, Picture Analogies, and Spatial Reasoning. The NTLA is an unspeeded point scale, yielding a *learning age* (*LA*) and a *learning quotient* (*LQ*) when the test is administered in pantomime or a mental age (MA) and

---

*This test, by R. J. Anderson and F. H. Sisco, is published by the Office of Demographic Studies, Gallaudet College, Washington, DC 20002.
†Available form Marshall S. Hiskey, 5640 Baldwin, Lincoln, NE 68507.

an intelligence quotient (IQ) when the test is administered verbally. The test is easy to administer and fairly popular among psychological examiners of the hearing impaired.

The NTLA was developed in 1941, and norms for hearing children were published in 1957. A revised edition, standardized on fifteen age-groups (1,079 deaf and 1,074 hearing children in ten states) between 2½ and 17 years, 5 months, was published in 1966. Although some reliability data are reported in the manual, neither the reliability nor the standardization of the NTLA is described clearly. With respect to its validity, correlations in the .70s and .80s have been found between the NTLA and the Stanford-Binet and WISC in small groups of children with normal hearing.

Illinois Test of Psycholinguistic Abilities (ITPA)

The authors of this test (Kirk & McCarthy, 1961) assumed that failure to respond to a stimulus may result from defective input, defective information processing by the brain, or defective output. Consequently, an analysis of learning difficulties may pinpoint a failure at one or more of these three stages. Three subtests are provided for each stage. At the input stage, for example, information may be visual, auditory, or tactile, so a separate subtest was constructed to measure the functioning of each of these modalities. Three subtests were also designed to measure the central processing of information from each of the three modalities, and additional subtests were constructed to measure motor and verbal output.

The ITPA, which was designed for children from 2 through 10 years of age, is not an easy test to administer. When the full test is administered, twelve scores, each having a mean of 36 and a standard deviation of 6, are obtained. When testing deaf or hard-of-hearing children, only the nonauditory and nonverbal subtests are administered.

The ITPA was standardized on 962 normal children and may be inappropriate for evaluating minority children or those of lower socioeconomic status. The reliabilities of the subtests are quite variable and generally low (.12 to .86).

Although the ITPA has been used extensively in the analysis of learning disabilities of the sort discussed later in the chapter, its effectiveness in this regard is questionable. At best, the test appears to be a fair measure of general mental ability rather than a means of obtaining an in-depth diagnosis of communication difficulties (Silverstein, 1978). The authors of the ITPA assumed that differences between subtest scores would be helpful in psychodiagnosis, but the subtests are insufficiently reliable to be used for this purpose. Furthermore, not only is the general overall score no better than a Stanford-Binet IQ, but the ITPA is more difficult to administer and usually requires more time than the former instrument.

Callier-Azusa Scale

Few standardized tests are appropriate for assessing the abilities of persons who are both deaf and blind. Most often used for this purpose are behavior rating scales or checklists such as the Callier-Azusa Scale (CAS), a behavior checklist for comparing the development of deaf and blind children aged from birth to 9 years on several areas (motoric, perceptual, language, daily living, socialization, etc.). Items on each of the sixteen subscales are checked only if "present fully and regularly." The CAS checklist may be completed on two or more occasions by teachers, parents, or other significant persons to evaluate developmental changes related to specific interventions (Stillman, 1974).

Test of Nonverbal Intelligence

One of the most popular of all intelligence tests used in the public schools is the Test of Nonverbal Intelligence (TONI). The second edition of this test (TONI-2) is widely used throughout the United States, and is the primary measure of intelligence on reevaluations in the New York City schools. Furthermore, its use is not limited to school-age children; it can be administered to individuals ranging in age from 5 to 85 years.

Like its predecessor, TONI-2 was designed to assess the intellectual, aptitude, and reasoning abilities of individuals with speech, language, or hearing impairments, non-English-speaking individuals, and those with brain injuries and/or academic disabilities. The fifty-five problem solving tasks on each of the two forms (A and B) require the examinee to determine the differences and similarities between figures, identify one or more problem-solving rules defining the relationships between the figures, and then select the correct response.

Except for the addition of a few items for gifted individuals, TONI-2 is quite similar to TONI. It is easy to administer (in pantomime) and score, and it was standardized on a nationwide sample of over 2,500 children and adults. Total scores are converted to standard quotients having a mean of 100 and a standard deviation of 15. The internal consistency reliabilities of the scores are in the .90s, and the alternative forms reliabilities in the .80s. Correlations with other tests of aptitude and achievement and construct validity studies indicate that the test is a good measure of academic ability. With regard to reviews of TONI-2, they have been both positive (Murphy, 1992) and negative (Watson, 1992). Watson criticizes the test for lack of clarity in certain sections of the manual, for its questionable description of a "nonlanguage" test, for its shaky theoretical distinction between "verbal" and "nonverbal," and for a paucity of (factor-analytic) studies pertaining to its construct validity.

PICTORIAL TESTS AND THE ORTHOPEDICALLY HANDICAPPED

Many children and adults have orthopedic impairments that interfere with their motor functioning. Included among these conditions are cerebral palsy, epilepsy, muscular dystrophy, and limb deficiencies due to genetic defects. The motor proficiency of children with serious motor dysfunctions and developmental handicaps can be assessed with instruments such as the Bruinicks-Oseretsky Test of

Motor Proficiency, but these provide little or no information concerning children's intellectual functioning. Because such individuals usually respond slowly and laboriously, scores on intelligence tests administered to the orthopedically handicapped often underestimate their cognitive abilities. It is possible in some cases to adapt tests such as the Stanford-Binet, the Wechsler series, and single-task tests such as the Porteus Mazes and the Raven Progressive Matrices to the orthopedically handicapped by removing time pressures and permitting the examinee to respond with head movements or pointing (Sattler, 1972; Theye, 1970). More popular in testing children with orthopedic handicaps, however, have been picture vocabulary tests and other pictorial intelligence measures requiring simple motor or verbal responses. These tests do not assess all aspects of intelligence, but they are usually valid measures of receptive vocabulary and are significantly correlated with scores on tests of scholastic aptitude and achievement. A limitation of pictorial intelligence tests of which the examiner must also be aware is that, because of their multiple-choice format, scores on these tests may be higher than justified by the examinee's true mental ability.

Perhaps the most popular of all picture vocabulary tests are the Columbia Mental Maturity Scale and the Peabody Picture Vocabulary Test. However, other pictorial tests, such as the Full-Range Picture Vocabulary Test and the Pictorial Test of Intelligence, also have proponents.

Columbia Mental Maturity Scale

The test materials on the Columbia Mental Maturity Scale (CMMS) consist of ninety-two items (a set of drawings) printed on 6- by 19-inch cards. The child (aged 3½ to 10 years) is asked to select from the series of drawings on each card the one drawing that does not belong with the others. In making the selection, the child employs perceptual discrimination and classificatory or general reasoning abilities involving color, shape, size, use, number, missing parts, and symbolic material. The ninety-two items on the scale are arranged in eight overlapping levels, but only fifty-one to sixty-five items are actually administered. Test administration time is 15 to 20 minutes, and directions are given in English or Spanish.

The CMMS was designed originally for testing cerebral-palsied children, but it can be administered to other children having impaired verbal or motor functioning (visually handicapped, speech impaired, hearing handicapped, mentally retarded), as well as hyperactive children. Raw scores are converted to age deviation scores, ranging from 50 to 150 with a mean of 100 and a standard deviation of 16. Percentile ranks, stanines, and maturity indexes may also be determined.

The latest (third) edition on the CMMS was standardized in the early 1970s on a national sample of 2,600 children in twenty-five states. The sample, which consisted of 100 boys and 100 girls each in thirteen 6-month age-groups between 3½ years and 9 years, 11 months, was also stratified by parental occupation, race, and geographic area. The split-half reliability coefficients of the CMMS range from .85 to .91, and the test–retest coefficients from .84 to .86. CMMS scores have moderate correlations (.62–.69) with scores on the Stanford-Binet and the Otis-Lennon Mental Ability Tests and modest correlations (.31-.61) with scores on the Stanford Achievement Test.

Criticisms of the CMMS include the fact that it is possible to obtain a score of 82 by chance alone, and a few fortunate guesses can result in an average score (Kaufman, 1978). Furthermore, the CMMS appears to be more a measure of concept formation ability than general mental ability.

Peabody Picture Vocabulary Test—Revised (PPVT-R)

The test materials on the PPVT-R are 175 pictorial plates, arranged in ascending order of difficulty by age level and containing four pictures each. The examiner presents a plate, says a word, and instructs the examinee to point to the picture on the plate that best illustrates the meaning of the word. The PPVT-R takes about 10 to 20 minutes to administer and score, and it can be used with a wide age range of examinees (2½ years to adulthood). Because verbal responses are not required, the test can be given to persons with speech impairments, cerebral palsy, or reading problems and to mentally retarded, withdrawn, or distractible children.

The two forms of the PPVT-R (L and M) were standardized in 1970 on a national sample of 4,200 persons from 2½ to 18 years of age and 800 adults aged 19 through 40. The sample was also selected by race, parental occupation, geographic region, and community size according to the 1970 U.S. Census. In addition, a study designed to equate PPVT-R scores with those of the original PPVT was conducted on 1,840 children aged 3 to 18 years.

In general, the psychometric characteristics of the PPVT-R are considered exceptional among picture vocabulary tests. The test norms are expressed as standard scores having a mean of 100 and a standard deviation of 15, percentile ranks, stanines, and age equivalents. The split-half reliabilities range from .73 to .91 for raw scores and .71 to .87 for standard scores. Test–retest coefficients by age-group range from .52 to .90 for raw scores and .54 to .90 for standard scores.

NEUROPSYCHOLOGICAL TESTING

Sometimes damage to the central nervous system is not detectable with CAT scans, EMR scans, PET scans, or other medical tests, but its effects are nevertheless manifested in behavioral disturbances and changes. Acquiring proficiency in diagnosing and treating deficits in neuropsychological abilities entails a long training program and extensive experience, and even then it is often as much of an art as a science.

Neuropsychological abilities include sensation, motor speed and strength, perception and perceptual-motor integration, language, attention, abstracting ability, flexibility of thinking, orientation, and memory (Grant & Reed, 1982). Brain-injured children experience deficits in one or more of these abilities. Thus, a brain-injured child is

> a ... child who before, during, or after birth has received an injury to or suffered an infection of the brain. As a result of such organic impairment, defects in the neuromotor system may be present or absent; however, such a child may show disturbances in perception, thinking, and emotional behavior, either separately or in combination. These disturbances prevent or impede a normal learning process. (Strauss & Lehtinen, 1947, p. 4)

Many different tests and test batteries that can contribute to the assessment of neuropsychological disorders are available. Several test publishers, including Psychological Assessment Resources, The Psychological Corporation, and Western Psychological Services, market entire series of older and newer tests for neuropsychological assessment. These single tests and test batteries have been designed specifically for neurological screening and/or the assessment of brain damage.

Because brain-injured children are typically more hyperactive, impulsive, distractible, and emotionally unstable than normal children, special preparations must be made when testing them. Such children should be told a few days in advance that they are going to be examined, and reassured concerning the procedures and purposes of the examination. Perceptual-motor deficits, coordination defects, short attention span, and uncooperativeness, which are more common in brain-injured children, contribute to difficulties in testing them. Consequently, such testing necessitates careful preparation, patience, and understanding on the part of the examiner. Because of the distractibility and problems with concentration, noise and other sources of disturbance in the testing room should be kept to a minimum when the child is being tested.

Perceptual–Memory Tests

As noted above, distortions of both perception and memory are characteristic of brain-injured persons. Among the single tests that tap perceptual and memory functions are the Bender Visual Motor Gestalt Test, the Memory for Designs Test, and the Benton Revised Visual Retention Test. These three tests are usually administered as supplements to individual intelligence tests or other longer psychological examinations.

The Bender Visual Motor Gestalt Test consists of nine geometric designs on 4- by 6-inch white cards. The examinee is directed to copy the designs, which are presented individually. The level of maturation of visual motor perceptions, which are associated with language ability and intellectual functions, is indicated by the responses. Notable departures of the copies from the originals, or errors, are interpreted in terms of perceptual deficits. Children 8 years or older and of normal intelligence usually make no more than two errors. Errors in making the drawings that suggest organic brain damage include shape distortions; rotating the design; problems with integrating the design; disproportionate, overlapping, or fragmented drawings; and perseverations. A restandardization of the Bender, including norms for ages 5 through 10 years, was published in 1975; the scores are highly correlated with IQ up to ages 9 to 10 (Koppitz, 1975; also see Lacks, 1984).

Screening instruments such as the Quick Neurological Screening Test—Revised, as well as the Stroop Neuropsychological Screening Test and the Wisconsin Card-Sorting Test, provide preliminary indexes to determine whether an individual should be referred for a complete neurological examination.

The Wisconsin Card-Sorting Test (by D. A. Grant & E. A. Berg; Psychological Assessment Resources) consists of a set of four stimulus cards and two sets of sixty-four response cards that display figures of varying forms, colors, and numbers. The examinee is told to place the response cards in front of one of the four stimulus cards; he or she is then told whether the response is right or wrong but not the sorting principle. The test covers the age range from 6½ to 80 years and can be administered in 20–30 minutes. It is used primarily to assess perseveration and abstract thinking, and scores are affected by brain lesions involving the frontal lobes. Although it is an improvement over previous card-sorting procedures for assessing abstract thinking abilities, the absence of reliability information and the inadequacy of the norms suggest that caution is advisable in using the Wisconsin Card-Sorting Test for clinical purposes (Egeland, 1985).

Other measures that have been used to detect brain damage are tests involving hidden figures, the detection of patterns, and sustained attention or concentration. In addition to these tests, instruments designed to identify or diagnose aphasia, problems with face recognition, form discrimination, and other specific neuropsychological disabilities are available. However, a comprehensive assessment of neuropsychological functioning requires administration of a battery of specialized tests.

Comprehensive Batteries for Assessing Memory

Deficits in memory and learning are diagnostic signs of specific learning disabilities, traumatic brain injury, neurological disorders, attention-deficit hyperactivity disorder (ADHD), and serious emotional disturbance. Because memory and learning are not unitary capacities, a battery of tests is often needed to identify the presence of specific deficits. These instruments do not take the place of tests such as the WISC-III or the K-ABC, which assess a wider range of cognitive functions, but they may be administered along with an individual intelligence test to provide supplementary data and diagnostic clues.

Two of the most popular memory assessment batteries for children are the Test of Memory and Learning (TOMAL) and the Wide Range Assessment of Memory and Learning (WRAML). These two batteries are similar in the age range for which they are appropriate (5–17 years for WRAML and 5–19 years for TOMAL), in their administration time (45 minutes), and in the memory and learning indexes for which they are scored. In addition, both batteries are well standardized and have high reliabilities and significant correlations with intelligence tests.

With respect to the age level, the Memory Assessment Scales (MAS) take up where the TOMAL and WRAML leave off. The MAS is appropriate for ages 18–90 and takes 40–45 minutes to administer. Like the TOMAL and WRAML, it measures both verbal and nonverbal (visual) memory functions and several additional memory and learning variables. The standardization sample for the MAS was somewhat smaller, and perhaps less representative of the target population, than that of the WRAML, but the reliability coefficients are comparable. Profiles of MAS scores for patients with neurological disorders such as dementia, closed head injury, left-hemisphere lesions, and right-hemisphere lesions are given in the manual.

Neuropsychological Test Batteries

Although conventional intelligence tests such as the WAIS-R and WISC-III are helpful in identifying neuropsychological deficits, a series of tests such as those making up the Halstead-Reitan Neuropsychological Test Battery, the Reitan-Indiana Neuropsychological Battery for Children, the Luria-Nebraska Neuropsychological Battery, or the Contributions to Neurological Assessment has traditionally been required to measure neuropsychologically based adaptive abilities that are not assessed by intelligence tests.

The Halstead-Reitan Neuropsychological Test Battery (available from Reitan Neuropsychology Laboratory) contains the first five tests listed in Table 8–3, but several of the remaining six psychometric procedures may also be included in the total battery. These tests and procedures tap a number of sensory abilities,

---

TABLE 8–3   Tests and Procedures of the Halstead-Reitan Test Battery

Category Test. The examinee tries to find the rule for categorizing pictures of geometric shapes. This test measures abstract reasoning and concept formation.

Tactual Performance Test. The blindfolded examinee places blocks in an appropriate cutout on an upright board with the dominant hand, then the nondominant hand, then both hands. This test measures kinesthetic and sensorimotor ability, as well as incidental memory.

Speech Sounds Perception Test. The examinee attempts to pick from four choices the written version of taped nonsense words. This test measures attention and auditory–visual synthesis.

Seashore Rhythm Test. The examinee indicates whether paired musical rhythms are the same or different. This test measures attention and auditory perception.

Finger Tapping Test. The examinee taps a telegraph-keylike lever as quickly as possible for 10 seconds. This test measures motor speed.

Grip Strength. The examinee squeezes a dynamometer as hard as possible; separate trials are given with each hand. This test measures grip strength.

Trail Making (Parts A and B). The examinee connects numbers (Part A) or numbers and letters in alternating order (Part B) with a pencil line under pressure of time. This test measures scanning ability, mental flexibility, and speed.

Tactile Form Recognition. The examinee tries to recognize simple shapes (e.g., triangle) placed in the palm of the hand. This test measures sensory-perceptual ability.

Sensory-Perceptual Exam. The examinee responds to simple bilateral sensory tasks (e.g., detecting which finger has been touched, which ear has received a brief sound). This test measures sensory-perceptual ability.

Aphasia Screening Test. The tasks on this test include naming a pictured item (e.g., fork), repeating short phrases, and copying. This test measures expressive and receptive language ability.

Supplementary. WAIS-R, WRAT-R, MMPI, or memory tests such as the Weschler Memory Scale or the Rey Auditory Verbal Learning Test may also be administered.

Source: Adapted by permission from Robert J. Gregory, *Psychological testing: History, principles, and applications.* Copyright © 1992 by Allyn & Bacon.

perceptual-motor speed and dexterity, expressive and receptive language functions, memory, concept formation, and abstract reasoning. Any of these abilities may be affected by damage to or dysfunction of the central nervous system or the sense receptors and muscles connected to it. A related battery of tests, the Reitan-Indiana Neuropsychological Battery for Children (Reitan, 1964), also includes a variety of sensorimotor and perceptual tests for several sensory modalities and response modes. Among the more complex tests included in the battery are the Category Test* and the Trail Making Test. On the Halstead-Reitan Category Test the examinee deduces general principles from information presented on slides. On the Trail Making Test, the examinee draws lines to connect numbered and lettered circles (from 1 to A, from 2 to B, and so on, alternating numbers and letters). Administration of all tests in the Halstead-Reitan Battery is time-consuming, requiring between 6 and 8 hours.

Based on the diagnostic techniques pioneered by A. R. Luria, the Luria-Nebraska Neuropsychological Battery (by C. J. Golden, A. D. Purisch, & T. A. Hammeke; Western Psychological Services) was designed to assess the following: cerebral dominance; tactile, visual, and motor functions; perception and reproduction of pitch and rhythm; receptive and expressive speech; reading, writing, and arithmetic; memory; concept formation; and other intellectual processes. Two forms are available; Form I has 269 items, and Form II has 279 items. Both forms can be scored by computer, but Form I can also be scored by hand. Like the Halstead-Reitan, the Luria-Nebraska is administered for more extensive neuropsychological screening for brain damage. Although the Luria-Nebraska takes only about one-third as much time to administer as the Halstead-Reitan, it has been criticized for relying too heavily on language skills and for failing to detect aphasia and certain other neuropsychological disorders adequately.

Contributions to Neuropsychological Assessment (by A. I. Benton, K. deS. Hamsher, N. R Varney, & O. Spreen; Psychological Assessment Resources) is a test battery that emphasizes a flexible, sequential approach to neuropsychological assessment. The specific tests administered are determined by the patient's complaint and the questions arising during the examination. The battery consists of twelve tests divided into two categories:

> *Tests of Orientation and Learning*
> Temporal Orientation
> Right–Left Orientation
> Serial Digit Learning
> *Perceptual and Motor Tests*
> Facial Recognition
> Judgment of Line Orientation
> Visual Form Discrimination

*A booklet version of this test, the Children's Category Test (CCT), is available from The Psychological Corporation. The CCT was designed to assess complex cognitive functions (concept formation memory, problem-solving abilities) in children aged 5 through 16 and thus to serve as a tool for diagnosing traumatic brain injury.

    Pantomime Recognition
    Tactile Form Perception
    Finger Localization
    Phoneme Discrimination
    Three-Dimensional Block Construction
    Motor Impersistence

These tests were developed over a period of 20 years and have been fairly extensively standardized and validated on brain-diseased or brain-injured patients.

Computer-Based Neuropsychological Assessment

During the past decade or so, advances in neurophysiology and cognitive psychology, coupled with improvements in computer technology and psychometric methodology, have led to an increased use of computers for administering, scoring, and interpreting neuropsychological tests. Neuropsychological testing has become faster, more flexible, and more focused; not only the accuracy of responses, but also their speed and even their intensity can be determined by means of computer-based assessment. The goal of such neuropsychological assessment is to detect the presence or absence of neurological disorders as well as the specific abilities and disabilities of the patient.

Among the many neuropsychological tests with computer-based versions are the Category Test and the Wisconsin Card Sorting Test (both from Psychological Assessment Resources). Computer software for components of the Halstead-Reitan Neuropsychological Battery and the Luria-Nebraska Neuropsychological Battery is also available.

Even more recent than tests that can be given by a human examiner or a computer are instruments that are administered exclusively by computer. An example of a test of this kind is MicroCog: Assessment of Cognitive Functioning. Designed to assess cognitive functioning in adults aged 18 to 80 years, MicroCog comes in a standard form requiring 50–60 minutes testing time and a brief form requiring 30 minutes. Nine interrelated areas of cognitive functions are assessed, including: Attention/Mental Control, Memory, Reasoning/Calculation, Spatial Processing, Reaction Time, Information Processing Accuracy, Information Processing Speed, General Cognitive Functioning, and General Cognitive Proficiency. MicroCog was standardized on 810 adults reportedly representative of the U.S. national population, with separate norms for nine age-groups as well as norms adjusted for educational level. Studies of the validity of MicroCog for various clinical groups (depression, dementia, schizophrenia, alcoholism, epilepsy, mixed psychiatric, lupus, etc.), as well as correlations with the WAIS-R, the Wechsler Memory Scale—Revised, and other neuropsychological tests, are reported in the manual.

Diagnosing Learning Disabilities

Not all children who score average or above on general intelligence tests do well in school. In addition to those who have pronounced physical handicaps, emotional disturbances, or low motivation are children of adequate intelligence who apparently have none of these problems but still experience difficulties in reading, arithmetic, spelling, writing, and/or other basic academic skills. Examples are the reading disability known as *dyslexia* and the impairment in learning arithmetic referred to as *dyscalculia*. The term *learning disability* or *specific learning disability* has been applied to such conditions, and the emphasis has been on identifying and diagnosing learning problems that cannot be explained by mental retardation, cultural deprivation, mental disorder, or sensory loss.

Research on learning disabilities and the construction of psychometric instruments for use in diagnosis and remediation programs were prompted by Public Law 94-142, the Education for All Handicapped Children Act, in 1975. This act mandated that handicapped children be evaluated for mental, behavioral, and physical disabilities and that appropriate educational opportunities be provided to them. Subsequent legislation (PL 99-457 and PL 102-119) provided funds for the states to implement the multidisciplinary evaluation of children who are delayed in cognitive, language, motor, socioemotional, or adaptive skills.*

As stated in the *Federal Register* of December 29, 1977, the diagnosis of learning disabilities must be multidisciplinary, including a teacher or other specialist knowledgeable in the field of the suspected handicap, the child's regular teacher, and at least one person qualified to conduct diagnostic evaluations of children by using valid psychometric instruments. To warrant a diagnosis of specific learning disability, a discrepancy between ability and achievement in one or more of the following areas must be found: oral expression, listening comprehension, written expression, basic reading skill, reading comprehension, mathematics calculation, or mathematical reasoning. Following team evaluation of the child, an *individualized education plan* (*IEP*), including long and short-term objectives and procedures for achieving them, was to be prepared.

Although eligibility criteria for providing learning disability services vary from state to state, one guideline for identifying learning disabled children in the state of California is that the child's ability level (as measured, for example, by a general intelligence test) should be at least 1.5 standard deviations above his or her level of achievement (as measured by a standardized achievement test). More complex regression models for defining a critical discrepancy between actual and expected achievement warranting a diagnosis of learning disability are discussed by Reynolds (1984–85).

Children diagnosed as learning disabled, whose actual performance levels do not keep pace with their estimated potential, are frequently inattentive and deficient in linguistic skills, most often in reading, which is a foundation skill for scholastic achievement. Classroom teachers may be able to detect such conditions

---

*Other congressional laws concerned with fair and nondiscriminatory treatment of the handicapped include PL 93-112, PL 101-476 (IDEA), and PL 101-336 (ADA). (Laws enacted by the U.S. Congress are designated by two numbers: the number in front of the dash refers to the particular session of Congress and the number after the dash refers to the order in which the law was enacted. Thus, PL 99-457 was the 457th law passed by the 99th Congress.)

through careful observation or administration of a group intelligence test and more specialized instruments such as the McCarthy Screening Test (The Psychological Corporation), the Pupil Rating Scale (Grune & Stratton), and the Slingerland Screening Tests for Identifying Children with Specific Language Disability (Western Psychological Services). However, the administration of a comprehensive battery of tests to determine the nature and extent of a child's learning disability and his or her educational needs requires the skills of a trained psychologist.

A variety of cognitive, perceptual, motor, and even affective measures may be included in a battery of tests for diagnosing learning disabilities. These include an individual intelligence test such as the SB-IV, WPPSI-R, or WISC-III, an achievement test battery such as the Peabody Individual Achievement Test—Revised, the Kaufman Test of Educational Achievement, or the Woodcock-Johnson Psycho-Educational Battery—Revised, and one or more special tests such as the Bender Visual Motor Gestalt Test or the Benton Visual Retention Test, the Goodenough-Harris Drawing Test, the Porch Index of Communicative Ability in Children, the Diagnostic Arithmetic Test, the Frostig Developmental Test of Visual Perception, the Gray Oral Reading Tests, and the Southern California Sensory Integration Tests. Because children with learning disabilities frequently have social and emotional problems as well, instruments designed to assess social and emotional functioning (e.g., Conners' Rating Scales, Personality Inventory for Children) may also be administered.

ADAPTIVE BEHAVIOR AND MENTAL RETARDATION

Physical and mental disorders are obviously *handicaps*, or potential limitations of functioning, but the degree of disability or impairment varies not only with the particular disorder but also with the individual. Although a person's life may be made more difficult by the presence of a physical handicap, for some people a handicap acts as a challenge that spurs them on to perform at a higher level. Such individuals adapt better than others to a disability, and by compensating (or overcompensating) for the condition, they may become even more successful than they might otherwise have been.

In diagnosing mental retardation, the American Association of Mental Deficiency (AAMD) recommends that diagnosticians take into account not only scores on intelligence tests but also academic and vocational attainments, motor skills, and socioemotional maturity. Thus, measures of adaptive behavior, which consists of the extent of independent functioning and maintenance as well as the ability to meet cultural demands for personal and social responsibility, are considered essential in diagnosing mental retardation. The concept of adaptive behavior has often been viewed as synonymous with that of *intelligent behavior*. However, current practice is to apply the term *adaptive behavior* to what a person typically does rather than what he or she is capable of doing under optimal conditions. Adults who adapt to their environment take reasonable care of their personal needs; they also work and engage in acceptable recreational and other leisure activities. Adaptive behavior among children and adolescents is behavior that leads to or prepares them for such activities in adulthood.

Adaptive behavior can be assessed by an informal analysis of a child's history and current behavior or by one of the standardized rating scales and tests listed in Table 8-4. These instruments, the great majority of which can be completed by interviewing a parent, a teacher, or another caregiver who has observed the child closely, cover a wide range of behaviors pertaining to personal and social adjustment.

AAMD Adaptive Behavior Scales

The two instruments in the second edition of this series cover the age range from 3 years through adulthood. The Adaptive Behavior Scale—Residential and Community: Second Edition (ABS-RC:2) evaluates the individual's ability to cope with the social demands of the environment. It was designed for mentally retarded or developmentally disabled adults in institutions as well as for assessing adaptive behavior in public school children. Among the applications of the ABS-RC:2 are determining a person's adaptive assets and liabilities, diagnosing developmental disabilities, documenting progress in intervention programs, and measuring adaptive behavior in research studies. Part I focuses on personal independence (important coping skills for daily living), whereas Part II deals with social behavior and manifestations of disorders of personality and behavior. Both parts may be completed, in 30-40 minutes, by someone who has a personal knowledge of the individual being rated or from information obtained by interviewing a close friend or relative. The ABS-RC:2 was standardized on 4,103 developmentally disabled persons. Internal consistency and test–retest reliabilities for Part I and the eight domain scores of Part II are all over .80.

TABLE 8–4   **Instruments for Assessing Adaptive Behavior**

AAMD Adaptive Behavior Scales—Residential and Community, Second Edition, by K. Nihira, H. Leland, & N. Lambert; © 1969, 1974, 1992; ages 3–adult; PAR & Publishers Test Service.

AAMD Adaptive Behavior Scales—School Edition, Second Edition, by N. Lambert, H. Leland, & K. Nihira; © 1969, 1974, 1975, 1992; ages 3–adult; PAR, Psychological Corporation, & Hawthorne.

Adaptive Behavior Evaluation Scales, by S. B. McCarney; ages 6–18; Hawthorne Educational Services.

Adaptive Behavior Inventory, by L. Brown & J. E. Leigh; © 1986; ages 5–18; pro.ed & Western Psychological Services.

Adaptive Behavior Inventory for Children, by J. R. Mercer & J. F. Lewis; © 1982; ages 5–11 years; Psychological Corporation.

Comprehensive Test of Adaptive Behavior, by G. L. Adams; © 1984; ages birth to 60 years; Psychological Corporation.

Normative Adaptive Behavior Checklist, by G. L. Adams; © 1984; birth to 21 years; Psychological Corporation.

T.M.R. School Competency Scales, by S. Levin, F. F. Elzey, P. Thormahlen, & L. F. Cain; ages 5–17; © 1976; Consulting Psychologists Press.

Vineland Adaptive Behavior Scales, by S. S. Sparrow, D. A. Balla, & D. V. Cicchetti; © 1984, 1985; birth–adulthood; American Guidance Service.

The AAMD Behavior Scales—School: Second Edition (ABS-S:2) was designed for children aged 3–16 years whose behavior suggests mental retardation, emotional disturbance, or other learning handicaps. The ninety-five items on the scale, which are answered by someone with detailed knowledge of the child's behavior, are divided into two parts covering twenty-one domains of adaptive behavior grouped into five factors. Personal independence in daily living tasks is evaluated by Part I, and personality and behavior disorders by Part II. The administrative and diagnostic manuals for the ABS-S:2 provide percentile norms tables, interpretive information on using the findings for diagnostic and placement purposes, and instructional planning profiles.

Vineland Adaptive Behavior Scales

This 1984 revision of the Vineland Social Maturity Scale comes in three editions: Interview Edition, Survey Form; Interview Edition, Expanded Form; and Classroom Edition. The Survey and Expanded forms assess individuals from birth to 18 years, 11 months, and low-functioning adults. The Classroom Edition is used with students aged 3 years to 12 years, 11 months. The Vineland assesses adaptive behavior in four domains (communication, daily living skills, socialization, and motor skills), with two to three subdomains under each skill. Scores on the four domains are combined to yield an Adaptive Behavior Composite. A fifth domain, Maladaptive Behavior, is assessed by the Survey and Expanded forms of the scale.

The Vineland Adaptive Behavior Scales were standardized on a representative national sample of 3,000 children selected according to the 1980 U.S. Census. Supplementary norms based on samples of mentally retarded, emotionally disturbed, visually handicapped, and hearing-impaired children are also provided. Various types of norms, including standard scores and error bands, percentile ranks, stanines, and age equivalents for each domain, are provided. The Expanded Form has the highest reliability and the Classroom Edition the lowest reliability. Computer software (Vineland ASSIST) is available for converting raw scores to norms and for preparing a narrative report of results.

Adaptive Behavior Inventory for Children

Another noteworthy adaptive behavior scale listed in Table 8–4 is the Adaptive Behavior Inventory for Children (ABIC). The ABIC was designed for children aged 5 to 14 years and is available in English or Spanish. The 242 questions concerning the child's behavior are asked in a 45-minute interview with a parent or principal guardian of the child. The inventory is divided into two sections; the first section is applicable to all children, whereas the questions in the second section are graded and administered according to the age of the child. The ABIC measures six areas of adaptive behavior (Family, Peers, Community, School, Earner–Consumer, and Self-Maintenance).

The ABIC was standardized on 2,085 California public school children, aged 5–12 years and three ethnic groups. Its reliability appears to be satisfactory, but it has been criticized for failing to take into account the influences of motivational and other nonsocioeconomic factors in assessing adaptive behavior. Be that as it may, the ABIC is probably as satisfactory as the AAMD Adaptive Behavior Scales and perhaps even the Vineland Adaptive Behavior Scales as a measure of adaptive behavior in the mentally retarded.

Other Adaptive Behavior Scales

A number of scales are oriented toward the adaptive behavior of specific subgroups, such as the trainable mentally retarded (e.g., T.M.R. School Competency Scales) or the severely or profoundly mentally retarded (e.g., Balthazar Scales of Adaptive Behavior). Adaptive behavior scales for blind children include an adaptation of the Vineland Social Maturity Scale (Maxfield & Buchholz, 1957) and the Developmental Checklists (Zimmerman & Bornstein, n.d.). A method of monitoring and developing life- and self-help skills in severely mentally retarded and multiple handicapped persons is provided by the Career Adaptive Inventory (Special Child Publications).

SUMMARY

Conventional intelligence tests such as the Stanford-Binet and Wechsler series can provide information concerning the mental abilities of handicapped persons. The Wechsler Verbal Scale is often administered to the blind, and the Wechsler Performance Scale to the deaf or otherwise linguistically handicapped. In addition, many special tests and test batteries have been designed to evaluate the abilities of handicapped individuals. Among the tests constructed specifically for evaluating the mental functioning of visually impaired persons are the Perkins-Binet Tests of Intelligence for the Blind, the Haptic Intelligence Scale for Adult Blind, and the Blind Learning Aptitude Test. The Perkins tests are an adaptation of the Stanford-Binet Intelligence Scale, and the Haptic scale is a set of performance tests used in conjunction with the WAIS-Verbal Scale.

Special measures for individuals with language disabilities include tests for aphasia, the Leiter International Performance Scale for persons with sensory or cultural defects in language, and the Arthur Adaptation of the Leiter. Representative intelligence tests designed for the deaf and hard of hearing are the Nebraska Test of Learning Aptitude and the Adaptation of the WISC-R Performance Scale for Deaf Children. The nonauditory–nonverbal portions of the Illinois Test of Psycholinguistic Abilities have also been administered to measure the cognitive abilities of the hearing impaired.

Many pictorial tests have been designed specifically to evaluate the intellectual functioning of children with orthopedic handicaps. These tests require the examinee to select a picture or other designated item from a set of illustrations in response to a question or instruction ("Where is the ...?", "Which one does not belong with the others?"). Among the most popular and well-standardized picture vocabulary or pictorial intelligence tests are the Columbia Mental Maturity Scale and the Peabody Picture Vocabulary Test—Revised.

Neuropsychological assessment involves administering a series of tests to determine the presence and location of organic brain disorders. Perceptual memory tests such as the Bender Visual Motor Gestalt Test and the Benton Revised Visual Retention Test, as well as the Wisconsin Card-Sorting Test and brief screening tests such as the Quick Neurological Screening Test—Revised and the Stroop Neurological Screening Test, can assist in the diagnosis. However, a thorough neuropsychological examination entails administering a battery of tests such as the Halstead-Reitan Neuropsychological Battery, the Luria-Nebraska Neuropsychological Battery, or the Contributions to Neuropsychological Assessment.

Learning disabilities, in which a significant discrepancy between intellectual ability and achievement cannot be explained by general mental retardation, sensory impairments, or neurological or emotional problems, are difficult to diagnose and even more difficult to remedy. Despite the presence of adequate intelligence, the child experiences difficulties in reading, arithmetic, spelling, writing, and/or other academic skills. Screening tests for learning disabilities include the McCarthy Screening Test, the Pupil Rating Scale, and the Slingerland Screening Tests. Various cognitive and perceptual-motor tests have been employed in diagnosing learning disabilities.

Mental retardation is diagnosed not only on the basis of scores on intelligence tests but also from observing a person's adaptive behavior. Adaptive behavior is determined by the degree to which a person can function independently and has the ability to meet personal and cultural demands. Illustrative of rating instruments for assessing adaptive behavior are the AAMD Adaptive Behavior Scales, the Vineland Adaptive Behavior Scales, and the Adaptive Behavior Inventory for Children. Special scales for assessing the adaptive behavior of severely and profoundly retarded children, the blind, and the severely handicapped are also available.

QUESTIONS AND ANSWERS

1. Define each of the following terms:

adaptive behavior	mental retardation
dyscalculia	neuropsychological disorder
dyslexia	nonlanguage test
haptic	nonverbal test
hearing impairment	screening test
learning disability	sensorimotor test

2. What is the difference between a nonverbal and a nonlanguage test of intelligence? Is it possible for a test to be nonverbal without being nonlanguage? Is it possible for a test to be nonlanguage without being nonverbal? Explain.
3. Name two tests that are appropriate for assessing the functioning intelligence of a child with:

   a. cerebral palsy or other motoric disorder

    b. a hearing impairment

    c. a visual impairment

    d. an oral language impairment

    e. a neurological disorder

    f. a poor understanding of the English language

4. Name two picture vocabulary tests of intelligence. What are the strengths and weaknesses of these kinds of tests? With what kinds of individuals and in what types of situations are they most likely to be used?

5. List and describe several tests of memory and the purposes for and/or circumstances under which they might be used.

6. Consult textbooks on physiological psychology, abnormal psychology, and neurology. Then list the behaviors and cognitive symptoms of various neuropsychological disorders. What contributions can psychological testing make in the diagnosis of such disorders?

7. Because the criteria by which specific learning disabilities are diagnosed, including the statistical procedure for determining the ability–achievement discrepancy, vary from state to state, would it be possible for a child to be learning disabled in one state and not in another? What consequences might this have for the child? For the governments and the people of the states?

8. Distinguish between specific learning disability, mental retardation, sensory defect, and neurological disorders in terms of behavior and psychological tests that can contribute to the diagnosis of each condition.

9. What is *adaptive behavior* and how can it be assessed?

SUGGESTED READINGS

Brown, A. L., & Campione, J. C. (1986). Psychological theory and the study of learning disabilities. *American Psychologist, 41,* 1059–1068.

Dean, R. S., & Gray, J. W. (1990). Traditional approaches to neuropsychological assessment. In C. R. Reynolds & R. W. Kamphaus (Eds.), *Handbook of psychological & educational assessment of children: Intelligence & achievement* (pp. 371–388). New York: Guilford Press.

DeStefano, L., & Thompson, D. S. (1990). Adaptive behavior: The construct and its measurement. In C. R. Reynolds & R. W. Kamphaus (Eds.), *Handbook of psychological & educational assessment of children: Personality, behavior, & context* (pp. 445–471). New York: Guilford Press.

Goldstein, G. (1990). Comprehensive neuropsychological assessment. In G. Goldstein & M. Hersen (Eds.), *Handbook of psychological assessment* (2nd ed., pp. 197–227). New York: Pergamon.

Harrison, P. L. (1990). Assessment with the Vineland Adaptive Behavior Scales. In C. R. Reynolds & R. W. Kamphaus (Eds.), *Handbook of psychological & educational assessment of children: Personality, behavior, & context* (pp. 472–488). New York: Guilford Press.

Naglieri, J. A., & Prewett, P. N. (1990). Nonverbal intelligence measures: A selected review of instruments and their use. In C. R. Reynolds & R. W. Kamphaus (Eds.), *Handbook of psychological & educational assessment of children: Intelligence & achievement* (pp. 348–370). New York: Guilford Press.

Reynolds, C. R. (1990). Conceptual and technical problems in learning disability diagnosis.

In C. R. Reynolds & R. W. Kamphaus (Eds.), *Handbook of psychological & educational assessment of children: Intelligence & achievement* (pp. 571–592). New York: Guilford Press.

Salvia, J., & Ysseldyke, J. E. (1988). *Assessment in special and remedial education* (4th ed., pp. 184–197). Boston: Houghton Mifflin.

Sullivan, P. M., & Burley, S. K. (1990). Mental testing of the hearing-impaired child. In C. R. Reynolds & R. W. Kamphaus (Eds.), *Handbook of psychological & educational assessment of children: Intelligence & achievement* (pp. 761–788). New York: Guilford Press.

Taylor, H. G., & Fletcher, J. M. (1990). Neuropsychological assessment of children. In G. Goldstein & M. Hersen (Eds.), *Handbook of Psychological assessment* (2nd ed., pp. 228–255). New York: Pergamon.

Chapter **9**

Group Tests of Intelligence

As discussed in Chapter 1, the first formal intelligence tests to be administered on a group basis—simultaneously to many examinees—were the Army Examination Alpha for literate and the nonverbal Army Examination Beta for illiterate or non-English-reading recruits. These two tests were administered to an estimated 1.7 million U.S. Army recruits during and shortly after World War I for purposes of military selection and classification.

As illustrated in Figure 9-1, the Army Alpha consisted of items involving analogies, arithmetic problems, number series completions, synonyms and antonyms, cube analysis, digit symbols, information, and practical judgment. It was the forerunner not only of later military tests such as the Army General Classification Test (AGCT), the Armed Forces Qualification Test (AFQT), and the Armed Services Vocational Aptitude Battery (ASVAB), but of many other group intelligence tests that came to be used in the public and private sector.

Two instruments based on experiences with the Army Alpha and Beta, the Otis Group Intelligence Scale and the National Intelligence Test, were published in 1918.

Test 1. Following Directions

"Attention! Look at 2, where the circles have numbers in them. When I say 'Go,' draw a line from Circle 1 to Circle 4 that will pass above Circle 2 and below Circle 3. Go!" (Allow not over 5 seconds.)

Test 2. Arithmetic Problems

10. If it takes six men three days to dig a 180-foot drain, how many will dig it in half a day?

Test 3. Practical Judgment

7. Why is wheat better for food than corn? Because
   0   it is more nutritious
   0   it is more expensive
   0   it can be ground finer

Test 4. Synonym-Antonym

26. Fallacy–verity .... same–opposite
36. Innuendo–insinuation .... same–opposite

Test 5. Disarranged Sentences

16. ninety canal ago built Panama years was the .... true–false
21. employ debaters irony never .... true–false

Test 6. Number Series Completion

11   13   12   14   13   15

81   27   9   3   1   1/3

Test 7. Analogies

17. lion–animal :: rose—smell   leaf   plant   thorn
36. tolerate–pain :: welcome—pleasure   unwelcome   friends   give

Test 8. General Information

21. The dictaphone is a kind of   typewriter multigraph phonograph adding machine
22. Mauve is the name of a   drink   color   fabric   food

FIGURE 9-1 Sample items from the Army Examination Alpha. (Excerpted from H. E. Garrett, Great experiments in psychology. New York: Century Co., pp. 33–36.)

These were the first group tests of intelligence designed for civilian, and especially educational, uses. They have long since been replaced by instruments such as those in Table 9-1, which is a representative list of commercially available group intelligence tests.

CHARACTERISTICS OF GROUP TESTS

Because group tests can be administered by one examiner to many people at the same time, they are more commonly used for mass testing in educational, military, and industrial/organizational contexts. Individual tests, on the other hand, are administered more frequently in one-to-one clinical or diagnostic situations. Thus, group tests have a broader range of applicability than individual tests.

Comparisons with Individual Tests

Compared with the complex skills required to administer an individual test, administrators of group tests need only to read the test directions correctly, keep the time accurately, make certain that cheating and disturbances are controlled, and collect and count the test papers at the end of the examination period. As in individual testing situations, they also need to be concerned about temperature, lighting, external noise, and other conditions that may affect the examinees' comfort and concentration.

Testing conditions tend to be more uniform in group testing that in individual testing. In group-testing situations examinees are also more likely to work at their own (hopefully comfortable) rate rather than feeling pressured by the examiner to answer every question promptly and accurately.

Rapport, a warm relationship between examinee and examiner, is less difficult to establish in an individual testing situation than in a group-testing one. The examinee is more inclined to cooperate and to do his or her best in such a face-to-face situation. This is more likely to be true when the examinee is told why he or she is being tested and is encouraged to do as well as possible. Furthermore, unexpected occurrences or uncontrolled circumstances are more readily detected and taken into account in interpreting the results of an individually-administered test.

Individual intelligence testing also provides a better opportunity to obtain useful information about a person. Fatigue and illness, motivational and emotional difficulties, and the manner in which a test problem is approached or solved are easier to observe when an individual test is administered. In fact, an individual intelligence test has many features of a standardized clinical interview. For this reason, it is expected that physically handicapped and emotionally disturbed persons will score higher on individual tests than on group tests of intelligence, or at the very least that their problems will be noted and taken into consideration when interpreting the test results.

The fact that individual testing permits more careful observations of examinees and greater assurance that they understand the test directions and are attempting to

TABLE 9–1   Representative Standardized Group Test of Mental Abilities

Cognitive Abilities Test, by R. L .Thorndike & E. P. Hagen; © 1993; levels 1 & 2 (grades K to 3), Levels
   A–H (grades 4 to 12); Riverside Publishing Company.
Comprehensive Ability Battery, by R. Hakistian & R. B. Cattell; © 1975–77; high school students and
   above; IPAT.
Culture Fair Intelligence Test, by R. B. Cattell & A. K. S. Cattell; © 1973; Scale 1 (4 to 8 years and
   educable mentally retarded); Scale 2 (8 to 14 years and average IQ adults); Scale 3, senior high,
   college, and high IQ adults); IPAT.
Draw a Person: A Quantitative Scoring System, by J. A. Naglieri; © 1988; ages 5–17 years; The
   Psychological Corporation.
Goodenough-Harris Drawing Test, by F. L. Goodenough & D. B. Harris; © 1963; ages 3 to 15 years; The
   Psychological Corporation.
Henmon-Nelson Tests of Mental Ability, by M. J. Nelson, T. A. Lamke, & J. L. French; © 1973; grades
   3–12 (Form 1), grades K–2 (Primary Battery); Riverside Publishing Company.
Kuhlmann-Anderson Intelligence Test, Eighth Edition, by F. Kuhlmann & R. G. Anders; ©1982; grades K
   to 12; Scholastic Testing Service.
Matrix Analogies Test—Short Form, by J. A. Naglieri; © 1985; ages 5 to 17 years; The Psychological
   Corporation.
Multidimensional Aptitude Battery, by D. N. Jackson; © 1984; ages 16 to 74 years; Sigma Assessment
   Systems.
Nonverbal Test of Cognitive Skills, by G. O. Johnson & H. F. Boyd; © 1981; ages 6 to 13 years; Charles E.
   Merrill.
Otis-Lennon School Ability Test—Sixth Edition, by A. S. Otis & R. T. Lennon; © 1982; grades K to 12; The
   Psychological Corporation.
Raven Progressive Matrices, by J. C. Raven; © 1938–86; Coloured Progressive Matrices (ages 5 to 11
   years, elderly persons, mentally and physically impaired persons, and non-English-speaking per-
   sons); Standard Progressive Matrices (6 to 80 years); Advanced Progressive Matrices (11 years to
   adulthood); The Psychological Corporation.
Revised Beta Examination, Second Edition, by C. E. Kellogg & N. W. Morton; © 1978; ages 16 to 59
   years; The Psychological Corporation.
Scholastic Assessment Test; high school and above; Educational Testing Service.
Scholastic Level Exam, by E. F. Wonderlic; rev. 1981; grades 11–15; Wonderlic.
Shipley Institute of Living Scale, by W. C. Shipley; © 1939–82, 1983; 14 years and older; Western
   Psychological Services.
Test of Cognitive Skills, 1981 Edition; © 1981; Level 1 (grades 2–3), Level 2 (grades 3–5), Level 3 (grades
   5–7), Level 4 (grades 7–9), and Level 5 (grades 9–12); CTB/McGraw-Hill.
Test of Cognitive Skills, Second Edition; © 1992; Level 1 (grades 2–3); Level 2 (grades 4–5); Level 3
   (grades 6–7); Level 4 (grades 8–9); Level 5 (grades 10–11); Level 6 (grades 11–12); CTB/McGraw-Hill.
Wide Range Intelligence and Personality Test, 1979 Edition, by J. F. Jastak; ages 9½ and over; Jastak &
   Slosson Educational Publishers.
Wonderlic Personnel Test, by E. F. Wonderlic; © 1939–1989; adults; Wonderlic.
Woodcock-Johnson Psycho-Educational Battery—Revised: Tests of Cognitive Ability, by R. W. Wood-
   cock & M. Bonner Johnson; © 1990; Riverside Publishing Company.

comply with them is a definite advantage of this type of testing. Because it might
seem that people will try harder on individual tests, one might expect that these
tests are more valid measures of cognitive abilities than group tests. It should be
remembered, however, that the examiner's behavior during a test may vary appreciably with the person being tested and the situation in which the test takes place.
For example, the nature of the social interaction between examiner and examinee

can have a stimulating or suppressing, or a positive or negative, effect on the latter's behavior. Because the administration procedure for an individual test is typically less standardized than that for a group test, there are more opportunities for the idiosyncrasies and biases of the examiner to influence both the examinee's responses and how those responses are scored.

Barring clerical errors, group tests can be scored more objectively, and hence more consistently and reliably, than individual tests. In addition, because of the relatively greater ease of obtaining large numbers of examinees to take a test as a group, the norms for group tests are often more representative than those on individual tests. Despite these advantages, however, group testing, particularly at the elementary school level, has not escaped criticism (Vernon, 1979a).

Format and Content

The multiple-choice format, which is most common in group tests, permits less flexibility or greater restrictiveness in responding than the open-ended response format of individual tests. The inflexibility in responding on group tests is also seen in the fact that examinees are expected to attempt all items rather than select a subset of items to answer.

Items on group tests may be arranged in various ways, usually as a series of separately timed subtests or in a spiral omnibus format. When a test consists of a series of separately timed subtests, the items within subtests are usually arranged in order of increasing difficulty. Illustrative of tests having this kind of item arrangement are the Test of Cognitive Skills and the Cognitive Abilities Test. A *spiral omnibus format* also requires that items be arranged in order of ascending difficulty. However, items of the same type or content appear throughout the test, intermingled with other types of items of similar difficulty, in a spiral of increasing difficulty levels. Examples of tests arranged in the spiral omnibus format are the Army Alpha, the Otis-Lennon Mental Ability Tests, and the Henmon-Nelson Tests of Mental Ability.

Items containing a variety of content can be placed in the objective format of a group test: vocabulary and reading comprehension, arithmetic and word problems; verbal similarities, differences, and sequences; sentence completions and arrangements; making inferences and deductions; discriminating differences; figural relationships and analogies; number series; sensing directions; and manipulating areas. Thus, group test items may be verbal or nonverbal, consisting of words, pictures, and other symbols; pictorial items are more common on tests in the lower primary grades. The method of answering items also varies with grade level: prior to the intermediate grades, answers are marked in the test booklet rather than on a separate answer sheet.

Depending on their purpose and design, certain types of group intelligence tests have been assigned special names, such as scholastic (or academic) aptitude tests and screening tests. A *scholastic* or *academic aptitude test* is a relatively long instrument designed specifically to measure aptitude for school work and is used most often as a selection or admissions device in educational settings. A *screening test* is a brief (10 to 20 minutes) instrument that is administered most often for initial selection purposes in employment contexts. An example is the Wonderlic Personnel Test. Screening tests are also used to determine what other (longer) tests may be appropriate. For example, some schools require every child who has attained an IQ of under 80 or over 120 on a group test to take an individual intelligence test to confirm or reject the classification indicated by his (her) IQ on the group test.

Administration and Scoring

Group intelligence tests can be administered to small groups of 10 to 15 children as young as 5 or 6 years old. When testing young children, examiners must make certain that the children understand the test directions, turn to the right page, start and stop on time, and so forth.

Administration of a paper-and-pencil (or booklet-and-pencil) group test of mental ability may be timed or untimed. Most of these instruments, however, are power tests. Power tests contain a sufficient number of items of appropriate difficulty to keep the examinees busy for a specified time period. The test may also be single level or multilevel, the latter being more common. Multilevel tests consist of a series of similar but progressively more difficult items at successively higher age or grade levels. Multilevel group tests with overlapping grade levels provide flexibility when testing children of different abilities. In *out-of-level testing*, a slower student can be administered a form of the test that was designed for students at a lower grade level.

Whether single level or multilevel, items on a group intelligence test may be arranged as a set of separate subtests or mixed up. When a separate subtest format has been selected, there are usually several subscores (one for each subtest) as well as a total score to be computed. On the other hand, when item types are alternated in a spiral omnibus format, typically only one overall, global score is computed. Raw scores, whether part or global, can then be changed to percentile ranks, standard scores, or other converted score units. Because reliability is directly related to the length of a test, it is usually advisable to compute only a total score on very short tests. A test needs to be fairly long in order to yield reliable scores on several parts.

Scores on group tests, even more than on individual tests, should be interpreted cautiously and against a background of other information (school grades, interview findings, observational results) about the person. Report 9–1 illustrates how the findings from a group intelligence examination may be reported and interpreted, along with other relevant information about the examinee. Interpretive profiles of scores can also be prepared by a test-scoring agency. Persons with very low scores should be followed up with further testing, preferably individual, before diagnostic or placement decisions are made.

Psychometric Characteristics

Although norms for group tests are based on larger sample sizes (hundreds of thousands of examinees for group tests compared with thousands of examinees for individual tests), the samples are not necessarily representative of the target populations. Group intelligence tests are usually standardized by grade level, often separately in the fall and spring. Unfortunately, many students at each grade level may choose not to take the test when given a choice or to make only a half-hearted attempt to do well. The probable consequence is that the norms will not be representative of the total population of students in the specified grades. Efforts need to be made by test publishers to ensure that their tests are standardized and restandardized adequately and that failure to include representative numbers of case segments of the target population does not result in inadequate or misleading norms.

The reliabilities of carefully constructed group and individual tests of mental abilities are usually satisfactory. Each format has different advantages in promoting high reliability. The multiple-choice format of group tests permits inclusion of a larger, and perhaps more representative, sample of content than individual tests, but examinees probably make greater efforts to do well on individual tests. Test–retest reliability coefficients, particularly over long time spans, tend to be higher for individual than for group tests. Hopkins and Bracht (1975) reported test–retest coefficients of .85–.90 between Stanford-Binet IQs from age 11 to 17–18 years, compared with .75 for verbal group tests and .60 for nonverbal group tests.

With respect to their construct validity, different group tests correlate in the .70–.90 range with each other and with scores on individual intelligence tests. The criterion-related (predictive and concurrent) validity of group tests of mental ability is seen in correlations of .40 to .70 between scores on these tests and school marks or scores on standardized achievement tests. As might be expected, verbal subtests tend to correlate more highly with verbal criteria, and numerical subtests with quantitative criteria.

MULTILEVEL GROUP TESTS

The rationale underlying construction of a multilevel intelligence test is to provide a series of overlapping, broad-range tests comparing the intellectual growth of children over a period of several years. Because the various levels of a test are not standardized on the same individuals at different ages but rather on different age-groups, equating test scores across age levels is not really possible. However, care in selecting equivalent samples of individuals at different ages, coupled with statistical procedures that permit computation of fairly comparable scores in different age-groups, can provide a basis for determining expected and unexpected changes in performance as a function of chronological age and factors intervening in time.

The Stanford-Binet Intelligence Scale and the Wechsler series of tests are popular examples of individually administered multilevel test batteries. Even more extensively administered than these individual tests are multilevel single-score group tests such as the Otis-Lennon School Ability Test, the Cognitive Abilities Test, and the Test of Cognitive Skills.

Report 9-1

Report of Group Intelligence Test Results

Name of Examinee: Jane N. Brown   **Sex**: Female
Birth Date: March 11, 1973   **Age**: 21 years, 11 months
Address: 12449 Mount Olive Street   **Education**: College senior
              Thousand Oaks, CA

Tests Administered: Otis-Lennon School Ability Test, Advanced Form R

Jane Brown, a young woman of approximately average height and weight (5'5", 120 pounds), volunteered to take the intelligence test because of a personal interest in her mental abilities and as a favor to the examiner. The test was administered as an assignment in Psychology 405 (Psychological Assessment) at Western College during the spring semester of 1994.

At the time of the examination, Jane was in her final semester as an accounting major at Western College. She reported her overall grade-point-average as 3.2. Jane indicated that she would like to attend graduate school in business eventually to work toward an M.B.A. degree, but that immediately after graduation she planned to work full time at an accounting firm in the Los Angeles area.

Jane's father is a college graduate, and her mother completed two years of college. Both the father and mother work in the family business, a tax-assistance firm. Jane has reportedly made good grades (B's and A's) through-out her school career, but she confessed that "I'm no scholar!" She seems to be very practical-minded in her interests, as indicated not only by her chosen major but also by her plans and other statements made to the examiner.

Jane showed moderate interest in the test questions and appeared re-laxed but involved during the testing process. She worked attentively and uninterruptedly during the entire 40 minutes. Testing conditions were good; no disruptions or other distractions occurred.

Otis-Lennon School Ability Test

The Otis-Lennon School Ability Test is the most recent in a series of tests going back to the Otis Group Intelligence Scale of the immediate post–World War I era (1918). The first Otis tests consisted of 240 items divided into ten separately timed subtests and was standardized on children in grades 4–12. Subsequent tests in the series included the Otis Self-Administering Tests of Mental Ability (1921), the Otis

Test Results and Interpretations

Jane completed all the test questions during the allotted time (40 minutes). She obtained the following scores on the Otis Lennon:

> Raw score = 65
> School Ability Index = 116
> Percentile Rank (18+ years group) = 84
> Stanine (18+ years group) = 7

These scores are approximately average for college seniors, indicating an overall intellectual ability in the "High Average" range for the general population. A brief analysis of the sixteen items that Jane answered incorrectly indicated that she has somewhat greater difficulty with nonverbal reasoning than with verbal reasoning. However, there is no significant pattern in the errors that she made; they are fairly random.

Conclusions and Recommendations

In a posttest interview, Jane indicated that she had done her best on the test and did not have to hurry to finish on time. She completed the test in 35 minutes and spent the last 5 minutes checking her answers. She indicated that the School Ability Index, which the examiner reported to her, was within 5 points of an IQ score that she made on an intelligence test she took in high school. She could not remember the name of the test.

Taking into account the conditions of testing, the examinee's observed behavior, and her statements after the test, the results are considered valid at this time. Jane's career plans and aspirations appear appropriate for her intellectual ability, although she will probably have to work fairly hard to obtain an M.B.A. from an accredited institution.

Laura F. Green
Senior Psychology Major
Western College

Quick-Scoring Mental Ability Tests (1937), and the Otis-Lennon Mental Ability Tests (1967).

Like its predecessors, the sixth edition of the Otis-Lennon School Ability Test (OLSAT), is composed of a variety of items designed to measure general mental ability. The items making up the two parallel forms of the test at each of seven levels from kindergarten through grade 12 are divided into five types: Verbal Comprehension, Verbal Reasoning, Pictorial Reasoning, Figural Reasoning, and Quantitative Reasoning. Seventy-five minutes working time is required.

Because OLSAT was standardized with the Stanford Achievement Test Series, Eighth Edition (Stanford 8) and administered with the Metropolitan Achievement Tests, Seventh Edition (MAT7), an achievement/ability comparison index (AAC) may be obtained by administering OLSAT with Stanford 8 or MAT7. AACs describe students' achievement in relation to the achievement of other students having the same measured ability. In addition, age-based scores, including a School Ability Index as well as percentile norms by grade and age and normal curve equivalents corresponding to raw scores, can be determined.

The reliability and validity of OLSAT appear quite satisfactory. Kuder-Richardson (internal consistency) coefficients are in the .90s, with test–retest reliabilities being somewhat lower. Correlations between OLSAT scores and school grades are moderate, the exact validity coefficient varying with the test level and the school subject.

Wonderlic Personnel Test

Based on the Otis Self-Administering Tests of Mental Ability is the Wonderlic Personnel Test, a brief (2–3 minutes for reading directions, 12 minutes for taking the test), fifty-item instrument. The questions on the Wonderlic, examples of which are given in Figure 9–2, are concerned with analogies, definitions, logic, arithmetic problems, spatial relations, word comparisons, and direction finding. The Wonderlic has been used extensively as a screening instrument in employment situations for many years, and is available in thirteen languages. Scores are related to job potential, educational potential, and training potential. The results of research conducted in military and organizational/industrial contexts indicate that the WPT is a fair and valid selection device for a wide range of jobs in the U.S. economy (*Cormier v. PPG Industries*). Internal consistency and alternate forms reliability coefficients reach .90 or higher; correlations of WPT scores with the WAIS-R are also in the low .90s. However, the interpretive guidelines and the potential for misuse of the cutting scores by undertrained personnel officers have been criticized (Schoenfeldt, 1985; Schmidt, 1985).*

Kuhlmann-Anderson Tests

The Kuhlmann-Anderson Measure of Academic Potential, Eighth Edition, is a modern adaptation of a multiscore intelligence test series initiated by Frederick Kuhlmann in the 1920s. Each of the seven levels of the Kuhlmann-Anderson (K—kindergarten; A—grade 1; BC—grades 2-3; CD—grades 3-4; EF—grades 5-6; G—grades 7-9; H—grades 9-12) takes 50 to 75 minutes to complete. The items consist of verbal and nonverbal cognitive tasks, being primarily nonverbal at the lower levels. Separate verbal, nonverbal, and full battery scores are expressed as

*Somewhat controversial is the practice of administering the Wonderlic Personnel Test to players drafted by the National Football League. Many professional football teams reportedly select players for particular positions on the basis of their Wonderlic scores (Plaschke & Almond, 1995).

Look at the row of numbers below. What number should come next?

8   4   2   1   1/2   1/4   ?

Assume the first 2 statements are true. Is the final one: (1) true, (2) false, (3) not certain?

The boy plays baseball. All baseball players wear
hats. The boy wears a hat.

One of the numbered figures in the following drawing is most different from the others. What is the number in that figure?

A train travels 20 feet in 1/5 second. At this same speed, how many feet will it travel in three seconds?

How many of the six pairs of items listed below are exact duplicates?

3421	1243
21212	21212
558956	558956
10120210	10120210
612986896	612986896
356471201	356571201

The hours of daylight and darkness in SEPTEMBER are nearest equal to the hours of daylight and darkness in

(1) June   (2) March   (3) May   (4) November

FIGURE 9-2 **Sample items from the Wonderlic Personnel Test.** (Reprinted by permission of Wonderlic Personnel Test, Inc.)

cognitive skills quotients (CSQs), standard scores, and percentile ranks and stanines by chronological age and grade levels.

The most recent (1982) norms for the Kuhlmann-Anderson are based on a large, heterogeneous sample of students. Split-half reliability coefficients are mostly in the low .90s, and test–retest coefficients vary from the low .80s to the low .90s. Scores on the Kuhlmann-Anderson are highly correlated with Stanford-Binet IQs and scores on other intelligence tests, as well as with school marks and standardized achievement test scores.

Cognitive Abilities Test

The Cognitive Abilities Test (CogAT) is a successor to the Lorge-Thorndike Intelligence Tests. The purpose of the fifth edition of CogAT is to assess abilities to reason and solve problems by using verbal, quantitative, and spatial (nonverbal) symbols. Designed for students in grades K through 12, the CogAT takes approximately 90 minutes to complete. It is a multilevel test, with Levels 1 and 2 for grades K-3 and levels A-H for grades 3-12. All levels consist of a Verbal Battery, a Quantitative Battery, and a Nonverbal Battery; each battery contains two subtests at levels 1-2 and three subtests at levels A-H (see Table 9-2). Working time for each subtest is 14 to 18 minutes at levels 1 and 2 (total of 98 minutes) and 8 to 12 minutes at levels A-H (total of 90 minutes). Raw scores on the Verbal, Quantitative, and Nonverbal batteries and a composite score are obtained. These scores may be converted to various types of norms (standard age scores, national grade and age percentile ranks, grade and age stanines, and normal curve equivalents) based on a 1992 national standardization.

Test of Cognitive Skills

The Test of Cognitive Skills (TCS) is a successor to the California Short-Form Test of Mental Maturity and the Short-Form Test of Academic Aptitude. The current (second) edition (TCS/2) of this test consists of four subtests (Sequences, Analogies, Memory, Verbal Reasoning) at six levels (2-3, 4-5, 6-7, 8-9, 10-11, and 11-12). A Primary Test of Cognitive Skills is available for testing in grades K through 1. The four subtests on the TCS/2 measure the following abilities:

Test 1, Sequences: Ability to comprehend a rule or principle implicit in a series of figures, letters, or numbers.
Test 2, Analogies: Ability to discern various literal and symbolic relationships.
Test 3, Memory: Ability to recall previously presented picture materials or nonsense words.
Test 4, Verbal Reasoning: Ability to reason deductively, analyze category attributes, and discern relationships and patterns.

TABLE 9-2   Subtests of the Multilevel Cognitive Abilities Test

	Levels 1-2	Levels A-H
Verbal Battery	Verbal Reasoning Oral Vocabulary	Verbal Classification Sentence Completion Verbal Analogies
Quantitative Battery	Relational Concepts Quantitative Concepts	Quantitative Relations Number Series Equation Building
Nonverbal Battery	Figure Classification Matrices	Figure Classification Figure Analogies Figure Analysis

Administration time for the four tests is 50 minutes at Levels 2–3 and 54 minutes at the other five levels.

Age or grade percentile, stanine, and standard score norms can be determined for each subtest of the TCS/2. In addition, the combined scores on all four subtests may be converted to a Cognitive Skills Index (CSI). Scores on the TCS/2 may also be used in combination with scores on the Comprehensive Tests of Basic Skills or the California Achievement Test to determine anticipated achievement at successive elementary and high school grade levels.

Multidimensional Aptitude Battery

The Multidimensional Aptitude Battery (MAB) is a group-administered adaptation of the WAIS-R for ages 16–74 years. Like the WAIS-R, the MAB consists of two scales (Verbal and Performance) containing five subtests each:

Verbal subtests	*Performance subtests*
Information	Digit Symbol
Comprehension	Picture Completion
Arithmetic	Spatial
Similarities	Picture Arrangement
Vocabulary	Object Assembly

The time limit on each subtest is 7 minutes, so the entire battery can be completed in about 1½ hours. IQs and standard scores on the Verbal, Performance, and Full Scale batteries, as well as subtest scale scores, age-corrected scale scores, and a narrative report of the scores and their interpretation, may be obtained from the computer-scoring service of Sigma Assessment Systems.

The MAB manual (Jackson, 1984) reports test–retest reliabilities over a period of 45 days as .95 for Verbal, .96 for Performance, and .97 for Full Scale scores. In a study of 500 individuals aged 16–20, internal consistency coefficients for Verbal, Performance, and Full Scale IQs were found to be in the high .90s. Correlations between MAB scores and WAIS-R IQs in a sample of 145 adults were .94 for Verbal, .79 for Performance, and .91 for Full Scale WAIS-R scores. Factor analyses of subtest scores on the MAB indicate that, like the WAIS-R, the test measures a general intelligence factor as well as separate verbal and performance factors.

ACADEMIC ABILITY AND SELECTION TESTS

Many group tests have been designed specifically to assess the ability to learn the kinds of tasks that are taught in school. The predictive validity coefficients of these *academic ability tests* (or *academic aptitude tests*), with criteria such as course marks or grade-point averages, are usually in the .50s and .60s.

Tests of academic ability are administered at every level of school—from the primary grades through undergraduate and graduate college years and by professional schools as well. As might be expected, these tests are more valid predictors of grades in English, mathematics, and other academic or basic skills courses than in art, physical education, shop, and similar less academic courses. Furthermore, they usually predict grades as well for minority and disadvantaged groups as for non-minority or nondisadvantaged groups (Breland, 1979; Reschly & Sabers, 1979; Schmeiser & Ferguson, 1978).

The use of academic ability tests is not restricted to school settings. Success in business and other employment situations often depends on the effective performance of activities of the sort pursued in academic contexts. Similar in verbal and numerical content to the academic ability tests discussed below are the Wesman Personnel Classification Test and the Personnel Tests for Industry (both available from The Psychological Corporation). A more comprehensive academic aptitude test battery administered to certain job applicants is the Professional and Administrative Career Examination (McKillip & Wing, 1980), which includes tests of verbal and numerical comprehension, deduction, induction, and judgment.

Scholastic Assessment Test

A number of different tests have been used over the years for college admissions purposes, including the American Council on Education Psychological Examination (ACE), the School and College Ability Test (SCAT), the College Entrance Examination Board's Scholastic Aptitude Test (SAT) (recently renamed the Scholastic Assessment Test), and the American College Testing Program Assessment (ACT).* The most widely used of these tests is the SAT, the earlier edition of which yielded two scores: Verbal (SAT-V) and Mathematical (SAT-M). Verbal analogies, antonyms, information, reading comprehension, and sentence completion items made up the Verbal section; arithmetic, algebra, geometry, charts and graphs, and logical reasoning items made up the Mathematical section. A short form of the SAT, the Preliminary Scholastic Aptitude Test (PSAT), has been available since 1959 for students who wish to practice for the SAT or for other reasons (early decision on college attendance or scholarship competition, for example).

Both the Verbal and Mathematical sections of the SAT were scored on a standard score scale having a mean of 500 and a standard deviation of 100, with the scores ranging from 200 to 800. To maintain continuity of meaning of the scores on new forms of the test constructed each year and to permit year-to-year comparisons of scores, the standard score scale of the SAT is based on the performance of the 1941 standardization group. However, the mean scores of today's high school students who took the SAT were somewhat lower than 500 on both the Verbal and Mathematical parts of the test.

From a psychometric viewpoint, the SAT is one of the most carefully designed of all tests of mental ability. Extensive research, involving hundreds of studies, has been conducted on this instrument. The reliability of the SAT is impressive: internal consistency coefficients are in the low .90s for SAT-V and SAT-M and in the mid-.90s for Total, and test–retest coefficients are in the high .80s and .90s. Median correlations between SAT-V and SAT-M are in the mid-.60s.

---

*The following description does not apply to the newer version of the Scholastic Assessment Test.

Correlations between SAT scores and college grade-point averages (GPA) are modest (median r in the .30s) and typically not as high as correlations between high school GPA and college GPA. A combination of SAT scores and high school GPA is more effective than either variable alone in predicting college GPA, the accuracy of prediction depending on the composition of the group and the particular college major or program.

The SAT is a better predictor at the extremes than in the middle of the score range. Students making very high SATs are quite likely to succeed in college, and those making very low SATs are quite likely to fail. The difficulty in predicting whether students in the middle of the SAT score range will succeed or fail is due to some extent to the influence of motivational and emotional factors, study skills, and other student activities on academic performance.

Effects of Coaching on SAT Scores

The question of whether special training or coaching on how to take the SAT has an effect on scores on this test has been a topic of discussion and research for many years. Results of earlier studies suggested that the effects of coaching are quite variable, depending on the similarity of the coached material to the test material, examinee motivation and educational level, and other factors. According to data reported some years ago by the College Entrance Examination Board (1971), short-term, intensive drill on items similar to those on the SAT does not lead to significant gains in scores, particularly on the verbal section. A number of people questioned this conclusion, one of whom, Stanley H. Kaplan, directs the largest test-coaching organization in the United States. Subsequently, the Federal Trade Commission (FTC) released a report of a study conducted in 1970 of the effects of a ten-week coaching program in three of the Kaplan Educational Centers. Admitting that the study had certain methodological flaws, the FTC concluded that performance on both the verbal and mathematical portions of the SAT can be improved by coaching courses. Reviewing the findings of the FTC investigation and other studies of coaching, Slack and Porter (1980) concluded that students can raise their SAT scores with training, that the scores are not good predictors of college grades, and that the test does not measure the capacity to learn.

After reanalyzing the data from the FTC investigation as well as Slack and Porter's (1980) review, Educational Testing Service (ETS) reported similar findings: inconsistent and negligible effects of coaching for students at two of the Kaplan schools and increases of 20 to 35 points for both verbal and mathematical scores at a third school. ETS acknowledged that significant increases in SAT scores can occur when coaching programs involve many hours of course work and assignments, but that at least part of the increases are attributable to differences in motivation and other personal characteristics (Fields, 1980). It is noteworthy that getting only two or three more items correct on the SAT increases the verbal or math scores as much as 20–35 points.

Other reviewers of the effects of coaching (Anastasi, 1981; Linn, 1982; Messick, 1980a) concluded that 8 to 12 hours of coaching can improve SAT scores by 10 points on the average, but only after 45 hours of coaching for the SAT-M and 200 hours of coaching for the SAT-V can gains as high as 30 points be expected. Not everyone has agreed with these estimates. For example, John Katzman, president of the test coaching organization Princeton Review, claimed to be able to increase students' SAT scores by as much as 200 points! The approach used by Katzman was to familiarize students with the standard test-wring techniques used by ETS so they can learn to think the way that ETS does and thereby outsmart the test (Biemiller, 1986). Furthermore, even students who do not take a coaching course may improve their scores by using a little test wiseness and perspicacity. It has been found, for example, that the answer options on certain reading passage items are so poorly designed that a substantial number of people can identify the right answer without even reading the passage on which it is based (Jacobson, 1993).

American College Testing Program Assessment (ACT)

More achievement oriented than the SAT is the second most popular college admissions test: the ACT. The ACT battery contains four Academic Tests: English, Mathematics, Natural Science, and Social Studies. Total testing time for the Academic Tests is 2 hours, 40 minutes. Scores are determined on the basis of these four content tests and a Composite of all four tests; unlike the SAT, the scores are not corrected for guessing. Each test is scored on a standard scale ranging from 1 to 36 (the Iowa Test of Educational Development, or ITED, scale). The standard deviation of these scores is approximately 5; the mean is approximately 16 for high school students and 19 for college aspirants. Like the SAT, the ACT has retained the original score scale, but the average scores on both tests have declined since the early 1960s.

The internal consistency reliability coefficients of the ACT are in the high .80s for the four Academic Tests and in the mid-.90s for the Composite score. A comparison of the content of the ACT with the item specifications for the four tests reveals a substantial degree of content validity. The predictive validity of the ACT, which is not significantly different for advantaged and disadvantaged students, varies with the specific tests and criterion. The Composite score correlates around .40 to .50 with college freshman GPAs. As indicated by the high correlation (in the .80s) between ACT Composite score and SAT-Total, there is a great deal of overlap in what these two tests measure.

Selection Tests for Graduate and Professional Schools

The most popular selection test for graduate school is the Graduate Record Examinations (GRE), which are administered several times each year at hundreds of locations throughout the United States and abroad. There are both scholastic aptitude (General Test) and specific subject matter (Subject Tests) portions on the GRE. The Subject Tests, which are 3-hour advanced achievement examinations in designated academic subjects, may be taken in any one of sixteen or so fields. The General Test, consisting of seven 30-minute sections, yields three scores—Verbal (GRE-V), Quantitative (GRE-Q), and Analytical (GRE-A). Scores on these three sections are based on the same standard score scale (200–800) as the SAT. The multiple-choice items for GRE-V, which consist of antonyms, analogies, sentence completions, and reading comprehension questions, are similar in format to those on the SAT-V. The GRE-Q is made up of quantitative comparison, discrete quantitative, and data interpretation questions, and the GRE-A is composed of analytical reasoning and logical reasoning items.

The GRE standard score scale is based on the performance of a reference group of 2,095 college seniors who took the examinations in 1952. Like the normative group, other psychometric aspects of the GRE are less impressive than those of the SAT. The internal consistency reliability coefficients (.93 for GRE-V and .90 for GRE-Q) are somewhat lower than those for the SAT-V and SAT-M scores, respectively. Furthermore, the validity of the GRE as a predictor of grades in graduate school is even poorer than the validity of the SAT as a predictor of undergraduate grades. This is due in large measure to the more restricted ability range of graduate than undergraduate students, combined with greater differences among the programs of study undertaken by graduate than undergraduate students. Like the SAT, high and low scores on the GRE are more predictive of high and low grades, respectively, than scores in the middle range.

Among professional school admissions tests similar in design and purpose to the SAT and GRE are the Medical College Admission Test (MCAT), the Law School Admission Test (LSAT), and the Graduate Management Aptitude Test (GMAT). Although these examinations are to some extent achievement oriented, certain sections are like those found on tests of academic aptitude. For example, the general aptitude score of the LSAT is based on verbal comprehension and reasoning ability. And the verbal, quantitative, and total scores on the GMAT are reminiscent of variables on other tests of academic ability.

Armed Services Vocational Aptitude Battery

Over the years, beginning with the Army Examinations Alpha and Beta in World War I, a variety of tests have been used to select and classify personnel in the U.S. armed services. During and after World War II millions of recruits took the Army General Classification Test (AGCT) to help classify them for skilled and unskilled jobs, to select those who could profit from further training, and to reject those who, because of low mental ability, were considered unfit for military service. Sometime after the war the AGCT was replaced by the Armed Forces Qualification Test (AFQT).

The Armed Services Vocational Aptitude Battery (ASVAB) became the uniform selection and classification test for the joint armed services during the 1970s. The current form of this battery (ASVAB, 18/19) consists of ten tests: General Science (GS), Arithmetic Reasoning (AR), Word Knowledge (WK), Paragraph Comprehension (PC), Numerical Operations (NO), Coding Speed (CS), Auto & Shop Information (AS), Mathematics Knowledge (MK), Mechanical Comprehension (MC), and Electronics Information (EI). Working time per test ranges from 3 minutes for NO to

36 minutes for AR, for a total of 144 minutes. Raw scores on each of these tests and three composites (Verbal Ability, Math Ability, Academic Ability) are converted to standard T scores and percentile score bands for reporting purposes.

Internal consistency reliability coefficients for the ASVAB range from .92 to .96 (U.S. Department of Defense, 1992, 1993). Alternate forms reliability coefficients range from .77 to .85 for the speeded tests (Numerical Operations and Coding Speed) and from .71 to .91 for the remaining (power) tests. Extensive information has been reported on the validity of the ASVAB with military personnel (U.S. Department of Defense, 1993; Welsh, Kucinkas, & Curran, 1990). Data on the validity of the battery extrapolated to high school and college students, to whom the test battery has been administered for career counseling purposes, are also available (U.S. Department of Defense, 1993, 1994).

NONVERBAL GROUP INTELLIGENCE TESTS

Performance tests designed as individually administered measures of the intellectual abilities of persons with language or cultural handicaps were discussed in Chapter 8. Similar instruments that can be administered on a group basis have been constructed for physically handicapped and culturally different individuals. The grandfather of these nonverbal tests was the Army Beta of World War I, which included tasks such as cube analyses, digit symbols, geometrical constructions, mazes, and picture completions. The Army Beta also proved useful in testing unskilled civilian workers, and it was updated, restandardized, and republished in 1978 as the Revised Beta Examination, Second Edition (see Figure 9-3).

Goodenough-Harris Drawing Test

Another example of a nonverbal test suitable for group or individual administration is the Goodenough-Harris Drawing Test. Unlike the Revised Beta Examination, which is a multiple-task test, the Goodenough-Harris requires only that the examinee perform the task of drawing a human figure. This test is a revision of the Goodenough Draw-a-Man Test, together with a similar Draw-a-Woman and an experimental Self-Drawing scale. The man and woman figures that the examinee is instructed to draw are scored for body and clothing details, proportionality among the various body parts (for example, head to trunk), and other characteristics, rather than according to artistic merit. The test is untimed, but it usually takes 10 to 15 minutes to complete. Norms for children from age 3 to 15 years are reported as standard scores and percentile ranks, separately by sex. Improvements in scoring the test were introduced by Naglieri in the Draw a Person: A Quantitative Scoring System test.

For many years, designers of intelligence tests have been besieged by the criticism that such instruments are loaded with tasks reflecting the cultural biases of Western society. It was hoped by Goodenough and Harris that their test would measure basic intelligence relatively free of cultural influences, but it has become

Mazes *ask examinees to mark the shortest distance through a maze without crossing any lines (1.5 minutes).*

Picture Completion *calls for drawing in a picture's missing parts (2.5 minutes).*

Coding *requires labelling figures with their corresponding numbers (2 minutes).*

Clerical Checking *requires marking pairs that are not alike (2 minutes).*

Paper Form Boards *involves fitting figures together to form squares (4 minutes).*

Picture Absurdities *involves identifying drawings that are wrong or foolish (3 minutes).*

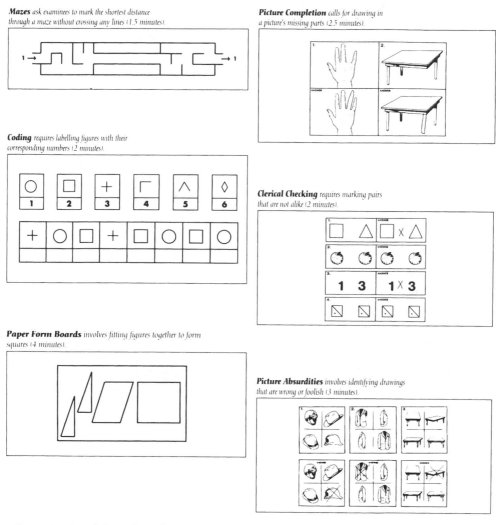

FIGURE 9-3 Sample items from the Revised Beta Examination, Second Edition. (From the Revised Beta Examination: 2nd Edition. Copyright © 1974, 1978 by The Psychological Corporation. Reproduced by permission. All rights reserved.)

clear that the task of drawing a human figure is significantly affected by specific sociocultural experiences. There have been several other noteworthy, but largely unsuccessful, attempts to develop a culture-free intelligence test, and subsequently the goal was modified to that of constructing a culture-fair test. On a culture-fair test of intelligence, an effort is made to include only items related to experiences common to a wide range of cultures. Consequently, items involving specific linguistic constructions and other culturally loaded tasks, such as speed of responding, are not included. In this sense, the Goodenough-Harris test was thought to be culturally fair. Two other widely used tests that have also been viewed as culturally fair are the Raven Progressive Matrices and the Culture Fair Intelligence Test.

Matrix Tests

The Raven Progressive Matrices may be administered on either an individual or a group basis. Developed in Great Britain as a measure of Charles Spearman's general intelligence factor and used as the major personnel selection test in the British military services during World War II, the original test consists of a series of sixty matrices involving figures and designs. Each matrix contains a blank section, and the examinee is directed to select the correct missing piece from eight choices.

The Raven test is available in two forms. The 1938 standard form, which is suitable for grades 8 through adulthood, can be obtained in five black-and-white sets of twelve pictures each. The 1947 form, the Raven Children's Coloured Matrices, is available in three sets for children aged 5½ to 11 years and for retarded adults. The Raven tests are untimed, but the 1938 form takes about 45 minutes and the 1947 form 25 to 30 minutes to administer. The percentile norms on both forms of the test were obtained on a sample of English schoolchildren and adults, but the samples were small and the norms are now dated. An Advanced Progressive Matrices for adolescents and adults is also available.

In addition to unrepresentativeness and datedness of its norms, the Raven Progressive Matrices has been criticized for a scarcity of information on its reliability and validity. The test–retest coefficients for older children and adults range from the high .70s to the low .90s on the standard form. Correlations with the Stanford-Binet and Wechsler tests range from .58 to .70. The test is obviously in need of updating, better standardization, and more complete information on reliability and validity.

Similar to but more recently developed than the Raven Progressive Matrices is the Matrix Analogies Test. It consists of nonverbal reasoning items organized into four groups: Pattern Completion, Reasoning by Analogy, Social Reasoning, and Spatial Visualization. The examinee (aged 5 to 17 years) is tested in 20 to 25 minutes on sixty-four abstract designs of the standard progressive matrix type, one design per page. The norms are based on a large, representative sample of individuals aged 5 to 17 years, 11 months. A short form of the test, the Matrix Analogies Test—Short Form, consisting of thirty-four items, is also available.

Culture Fair Intelligence Test

Perhaps more familiar to test users in the United States is the Culture Fair Intelligence Test. This series of tests is composed of three scales: Scale 1 for children aged 4 to 8 years and adult retardates; Scale 2 for children aged 8 to 14 years and adults of average intelligence; and Scale 3 for college students, executives, and others of above-average intelligence. As illustrated by the sample problems in Figure 9–4, each scale is composed of four subtests (series, classifications, matrices, and

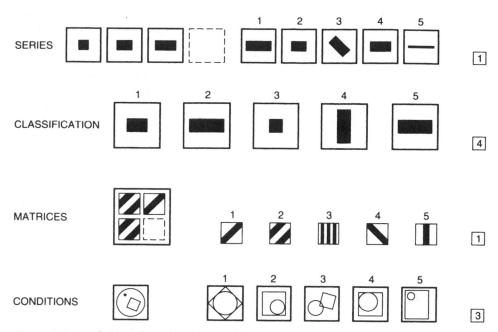

FIGURE 9-4 Sample items from the Culture Fair Intelligence Test. (Copyright © 1949, 1960, by the Institute for Personality and Ability Testing, Inc. All rights reserved. Reproduced by permission.)

conditions) for measuring the ability to perceive relationships. In addition to these four culture-fair subtests, Scale 1 contains four other subtests to measure cultural information and verbal comprehension. Testing time is 40 to 60 minutes for Scale 1 and 25 to 30 minutes for each of the two forms of scales 2 and 3.

Norms for the Culture Fair tests consist of mental ages and IQs on Scale 1 and percentile ranks by age and IQs on scales 2 and 3. The IQs are standard scores having a mean of 100 and a standard deviation of 15. Scale 1, which was published initially in 1950, was standardized on a small sample of American and British children. Scale 2 was standardized on slightly over 4,000 British and American children, who were almost certainly not representative of the total populations of children in these two countries. Although it was also small, the standardization sample for Scale 3 (3,140 American high school students divided equally among freshmen, sophomores, juniors, and seniors and a stratified job sample of young adults) was probably more representative of the target population.

Internal consistency reliability coefficients of the Culture Fair Intelligence Test are in the low .90s for Scale 1 and in the .70s for forms A and B separately or in the .80s for forms A and B of Scale 2 combined, in the .60s for forms A and B separately, and in the .70s for forms A and B of Scale 3 combined. Parallel forms coefficients for scales 2 and 3 are in the high .60s and low .70s; test–retest coefficients for the combined scores on the two forms (A and B) are in the .70s and .80s.

The Culture Fair Intelligence Test has been used in many different countries and correlated with a variety of criteria. Correlations with other intelligence tests range from .45 to .80 and from .22 to .59 with standardized achievement tests. Students' scores on the Culture Fair Intelligence Test have been related to teacher's ratings of students' behaviors and to grades in different school subjects. The scores have also been factor analyzed, yielding a general intelligence factor.

The Raven Progressive Matrices and the Culture Fair Intelligence Test represent commendable efforts to develop tests on which groups from different cultures score equally well. It is now recognized, however, that constructing test items whose content is independent of experiences that vary from culture to culture is probably impossible. A not uncommon finding is that middle-class Caucasian groups score higher on the culture-fair tests as well as on more verbal, "culturally loaded" intelligence tests. Even the Culture Fair Intelligence Test and similar instruments rely on skills—abstract thinking, problem solving, detecting relationships—that appear to be emphasized more in Western society than in other cultures. Therefore it is not surprising that middle-class children, who tend to absorb that culture to a greater extent than their working-class counterparts, score higher on both culture-fair and more verbal, culture-loaded intelligence tests. For example, the difference between the mean scores of blacks and whites on the Raven Progressive Matrices is approximately 20 points. This is almost 30 percent greater than mean black–white differences on other intelligence tests and would seem to put the case for this test as being culturally fair in serious jeopardy (C. B. Reynolds, personal communication, January 23, 1995). In any event, culture-fair tests are typically poor predictors of academic achievement, job performance, and other indicators of success in Western culture. They usually have lower validities for purposes of selection and placement than general ability tests containing more culturally relevant material.

SUMMARY

Group tests of intelligence were introduced during World War I, when the pioneering work of Arthur Otis led to the construction of the Army Group Examination Alpha and the Army Examination Beta. Revisions of these tests and other group intelligence instruments became popular in schools and industrial/organizational contexts after the war.

Group intelligence tests consisted principally of multiple-choice items arranged in a spiral omnibus format or as a series of separate subtests. In school situations, they have been used primarily as screening instruments, to be followed up with individual testing of examinees who made low scores. In business and industry, group intelligence tests have been used for selection and placement of employees.

Group tests can be administered more efficiently and scored more objectively than individual tests of intelligence. Group tests typically include a variety of content, thereby sampling the domain of intellectual abilities as well as or better than individual tests. A disadvantage of group tests is that because special efforts to establish rapport with examinees are not made, they may not be motivated to do their best. Furthermore, personality characteristics and behaviors observed when administering an individual test are not as likely to be detected and therefore will not be taken into account in interpreting performance when administering a group test to a large number of people.

Many group intelligence tests are standardized by grade level, separately during the fall and spring of the school year. Although efforts are often made to obtain a sample that is truly representative of the target population, the fact that some students are absent or otherwise decline to take the tests can result in unrepresentative norms. The norms are usually expressed as percentile ranks by grade or chronological age, or as standard scores (e.g., deviation IQs). The reliabilities of most such tests are usually satisfactory, but the validity information included in the test manual is often incomplete. Many validation studies are reported in professional journals after the test has been published.

Among the most popular and well-designed group tests of intelligence are multilevel instruments such as the Otis-Lennon School Ability Test, the Kuhlmann-Anderson Tests, the Cognitive Abilities Test, and the Test of Cognitive Skills. These tests yield one or more scores at each of several age or grade levels. Almost all of them represent revisions of earlier tests in the series and have good psychometric properties (norms, reliability, and validity). A particularly well-designed, multiscore group measure of intellectual functioning is the Multidimensional Aptitude Battery (MAB). Patterned after the Wechsler Adult Intelligence Scale—Revised, the MAB has high reliability and high correlations with WAIS-R IQs and other measures of intellectual potential.

Similar to group intelligence tests are academic ability tests, which are designed specifically to assess the ability to learn school-type tasks. Correlations between scores on academic ability tests and course marks or scores on standardized achievement tests are typically in the .50s and .60s. Applications of these tests are not limited to school situations; they are also used extensively for personnel selection purposes in business and industrial contexts.

The most popular academic ability test for selecting college freshmen is the Scholastic Assessment Test (SAT). Consisting of Verbal and Mathematical sections and a test of standard written English, the older version of the SAT was one of the most carefully designed of all tests of academic ability. Coaching appears to have a beneficial effect on SAT scores but perhaps not as much as students and coaches would like. Another noteworthy academic ability test is the American College Testing Program Assessment (ACT), but compared with the SAT it is oriented more toward achievement in specific school subjects.

Similar in structure and scoring to the SAT but at a higher level are the Graduate Record Examinations (GRE). These tests, which are used as screening instruments in selecting students for graduate school, consist of a General Test containing measures of Verbal, Quantitative, and Analytical abilities, as well as Subject Tests of achievement in particular college majors or fields. A number of other tests, which combine aptitude and achievement features, are used in selecting students for professional schools. Among these are the Medical College Admission Test (MCAT), the Law School Admission Test (LSAT), and the Graduate Management Aptitude Test (GMAT). The Armed Services Vocational Aptitude Battery (ASVAB) is used for selection and occupational placement purposes in the U.S. military and to some extent for career counseling in high schools.

QUESTIONS AND ACTIVITIES

1. Define each of the following terms used in this chapter:

academic ability tests	matrix test
cognitive skills	multilevel group test
culture-fair intelligence test	out-of-level testing
culture-free intelligence test	power test
drawing test	rapport
global score	scholastic (academic) aptitude
group test	screening test
individual test	spiral omnibus test

2. Compare the spiral omnibus format with the separate subtests format in group intelligence tests. What are the relative advantages and disadvantages of the two formats?
3. What intelligence test(s) would you recommend for use with each of the following individuals: (a) A 5-year-old child suspected of being mentally retarded; (b) a group of high school seniors; (c) a 10-year old child with cerebral palsy; (d) a group of South Sea island aborigines; (e) a normal, English-speaking adult; (f) a 7-year-old totally blind child; (g) an adult schizophrenic; (h) a group of culturally disadvantaged elementary school children.
4. Select one of the following categories of intelligence tests discussed in Chapters 5–9 and two representative instruments at the same level from the published tests in that category: individual pictorial tests, developmental scales for infants and young children, multilevel group intelligence tests, or nonverbal group intelligence tests. Obtain as much information on the two tests as you can from textbooks on testing, the *Mental Measurements Yearbooks*, and other sources (consult *Psychological Abstracts* and *Education Index* in particular). Write a comparative review of the two tests, focusing on test design and format, procedures for administering and scoring the tests, norms, reliability, validity, and research conducted with the tests. Draw appropriate conclusions regarding the relative merits of the two tests.
5. Are group intelligence tests more useful for individuals who are considering professional occupations or for those who are considering occupations in the skilled trades? Why?
6. Compare representative group intelligence tests with individual intelligence tests in terms of their theoretical (conceptual) bases, ease of administration and scoring, adequacy of standardization and types of norms, reliability, validity, and purposes for which they are used.
7. Consider the task of drawing a human figure. How can it be a test of intelligence when many highly intelligent people cannot draw well? How can it be a culture-fair test when drawing human figures is not practiced in all cultures? In fact, some cultures consider the construction of any image of a human figure to be a sin.

SUGGESTED READINGS

Aiken, L. R. (1985). Review of ACT Assessment Program. In J. V. Mitchell (Ed.), *The ninth mental measurements yearbook* (Vol. 1, pp. 29–31). Lincoln: University of Nebraska Press.

Anastasi, A. (1973). Culture fair testing. In L. R. Aiken (Ed.), *Readings in psychological and educational testing* (pp. 246–251). Boston: Allyn & Bacon.

Anastasi, A. (1985). Testing the test: Interpreting results from multiscore batteries. *Journal of Counseling and Development, 64,* 84–86.

Ebel, R. L. (1982). Evaluation and selection of group measures. In C. R. Reynolds & T. B. Gutkin (Eds.), *The handbook of school psychology* (pp. 873–890). New York: Wiley.

Reschley, D. (1990). Aptitude tests in educational classification and placement. In G. Goldstein & M. Hersen (Eds.), *Handbook of psychological assessment* (2nd ed., pp. 148–172). New York: Pergamon Press.

Vane, J. R., & Motta, R. W. (1990). Group intelligence tests. In G. Goldstein & M. Hersen (Eds.), *Handbook of psychological assessment* (2nd ed., pp. 102–119). New York: Pergamon Press.

Zeidner, M. (1988). Culture fairness in aptitude testing revisited: A cross-cultural parallel. *Professional Psychology: Research and Practice, 19,* 257–262.

Testing in Other Countries and Cultures

During the past 90 years, intelligence testing has been practiced primarily in Western European and North American countries and their possessions. Interestingly enough, it has not been in France, where Binet-type intelligence testing began, that these tests have proved most popular. In fact, compared with the degree of intelligence testing that has occurred in the United States and the United Kingdom, French psychologists have done relatively little to develop and extend Binet's pioneering efforts.

Even less positive has been the attitude in Russia (formerly the Soviet Union), which banned intelligence and personality tests in 1936. Soviet psychologists were critical of Western intelligence tests, although they were not opposed to learning from the "mistakes" of American and European psychologists. It was maintained that the United States, Great Britain, and other Western countries failed to test intelligence. Western intelligence tests were characterized as noncreative, lacking in feedback, and yielding unreplicable results (Shaw, 1980a, 1980b). Soviet psychologists also maintained that the notion of general mental ability espoused by British

247

and American psychometricians was misleading and that a sounder approach was the differential, diagnostic testing of specific abilities. American "clinical psychology" was described as being too preoccupied with standardized testing divorced from the clinic and not sufficiently concerned with qualitative psychological analysis (Zeigarnik, Luria, & Polyakov, 1977). In contrast to Western tests was the Soviet clinical method of assessment, which involved more complex, and hence less objective, techniques of the sort proposed by Vygotsky (1962, 1978).

Vygotsky's approach, which was highly praised by Russian educational psychologists and also pursued by certain Western psychologists (Brown & French, 1979), distinguished between a child's actual developmental level and his or her potential developmental level. By administering a standard task or problem to a child, actual developmental level is determined by the child's initial performance. Next, a series of "prompts" or hints is provided to ascertain the level of problem solving that the child was capable of reaching with assistance. The difference (or distance) between the child's actual (initially determined) developmental level and the level of potential development attainable under adult guidance or with peer collaboration is referred to as the *zone of proximal* (or *potential) development* for that child. To Vygotsky and his disciples, the technique of guided learning measures true intellectual potential more accurately than static tasks such as those of standardized intelligence tests.

The testing of intelligence or mental ability employing Vygotsky's procedure is actually a mini-learning process in which a succession of problems is presented and the child's zone of potential development is determined by noting the number of prompts or cues required with each succeeding trial. Effective transfer from trial to trial, indicated by a decreasing number of prompts, is indicative of a wide zone of potential development. By using a variety of tasks defined by task analysis procedures, the examiner can determine a zone of potential development for each type of task and thereby apply this procedure in the differential diagnosis of abilities. For example, of two children having a mental age of 8, one child may, with assistance by means of demonstration and instruction, be able to solve problems at the 12-year level whereas the other child cannot. The first child has a wider zone of potential development than the second one, who does not benefit from such assistance. Interestingly enough, children with learning disabilities usually require fewer cues and show better transfer of learning to other tasks than mildly retarded children (Brown & French, 1979; Stone, 1989).

Research based on Vygotsky's method (Feuerstein et al., 1987; Campione & Brown, 1987) has led to greater interest by American psychologists in *dynamic assessment* (Lidz, 1987), which focuses on the processes as well as the products of behavior and on the connections between assessment and intervention. Three approaches that have been employed in dynamic assessment are *learning potential assessment strategy* (*coaching*) (Budoff, 1987), *learning potential assessment device* (*mediation*) (Feuerstein, 1979), and *graduated prompting* (Campione & Brown, 1987). The first two approaches involve a test–teach–test sequence in which examinees are tested (pretested), then given practice on the test materials, and finally tested again (posttested). The change in the examinee's performance level from pretest to posttest is calculated as a measure of his or her learning potential. The second (mediation) approach is different from the first (coaching) in that the examiner interacts continuously with the examinee in order to maximize the probability that the latter will solve the problem. The third (graduate prompting) approach involves the use of a series of behavioral hints to teach the rules for successful completion of a test task. Unlike mediation, these prompts or hints—beginning with general prompts and proceeding to more specific prompts as needed—are generated from a predetermined script rather than from the examinee's responses.

USING AMERICAN INTELLIGENCE TESTS IN OTHER COUNTRIES AND CULTURES

Research on dynamic assessment is an illustration of the adaptation of assessment procedures developed in one country or culture to another country. Another example of such cross-cultural fertilization is found in the adoption and adaptation of American intelligence tests by other countries and cultures. Despite criticisms of Western-style intelligence tests, translations and adaptations of these tests have been employed in many non-English-speaking and other English-speaking countries. The Wechsler tests, for example, have been translated, adapted, and renormed in several countries. Examples are the Wechsler Adult Intelligence Scale (WAIS), Nederlandstalige bewerking (Netherlands); the Wechsler Intelligence Scale for Children—Revised (WISC-R), British edition; the Naylor-Harwood Adult Intelligence Scale (Australia); and Escala de Inteligencia Wechsler para Niños-Revisada de Puerto Rico.

Adapting American Tests to Spanish Language and Hispanic Culture

The Wechsler tests for children and adults have been translated and adapted for Spanish-speaking persons. These Spanish-American tests include the Escala de Inteligencia Wechsler Para Niños—Revisada (EIWN-R), the Escala de Inteligencia Wechsler Para Adultos (EIWA), and the Escala de Inteligencia Wechsler para Niños—Revisada de Puerto Rico (EIWN-R PR). Another illustration of a Spanish version of an American mental ability test is the Prueba de Aptitud Academia (PAR) (Angoff & Modu, 1973). This test, a Spanish-language adaptation of the Scholastic Aptitude Test (SAT), was developed for local use in Puerto Rico in the early 1970s.

Designed for a mixed population of Anglo- and Mexican American children (grades 1–6) is the Bicultural Test of Non-Verbal Reasoning (by A. S. Toronto, National Educational Laboratory Publishers). This is an individual pictorial test on which the child, who is presented with a series of picture stimuli, identifies a difference, a similarity, or an analogy by pointing to one of several line drawings.

Cross-Cultural Test Adaptation Technique

Adapting a test such as the WAIS-R or the SAT to another language and culture is a complex process involving more than a simple translation of test content.

Frequently employed is the process of *back translation*, in which the test is translated into the non-English language by one person or group and then translated back into English by a different person or group. This procedure affirms the correctness of the translation. Back translation is necessary but not always success-ful in creating an equivalent test in a language other than English. Certain English words may have no equivalents in the other language, there may be differences in dialects and regional differences in word meanings, and the level of difficulty and meanings of words may change in translation (Sattler, 1988).

Not the least of the problems encountered in a simple translation of a test from one language to another is the comparability of norms across cultures. To ensure greater parallelism of a test from one culture to another, a recommended procedure is to begin with a set of items (anchor items) appropriate for both the original group and, in translation, for the group for whom the test is being adapted. The anchor items are administered to both groups, and the anchor test scores provide a basis for converting the total scores on both tests to a common scale (Anastasi, 1988). It is obviously important to develop norms on the group for which the translated test is designed and to be aware of not only linguistic but also cultural differences between nationalities.

Culture-Fair Intelligence Tests

For many years, intelligence tests have been criticized for containing items that reflect the cultural biases of middle-class Western society. After a number of note-worthy, but unsuccessful, attempts to develop a culture-free intelligence test, the goal was modified to that of constructing a culture-fair test. As noted in the preceding chapter, in constructing a *culture-fair test* an effort is made to include only items related to experiences common to a wide range of cultures. Conse-quently, items involving specific linguistic constructions and other culture-loaded tasks (e.g., tasks involving and scored for speed of responding) are not included.

So-called culture-fair tests, which were designed to be fairer measures of general mental ability in language-handicapped and culturally different individuals, have been used with a variety of non-Western groups. Similar nonverbal tests have been designed for other countries, such as the Jenkins Nonverbal Test in Australia, the NFER-Nelson Non-Verbal Reasoning Test in England, the Non-Language Test of Verbal Intelligence in India, the New Guinea Performance Scale, and various tests in South Africa (see Table 10–1).

Culture-fair tests are not completely devoid of the effects of culture. Although the tests are nonverbal, cultural differences exist in areas other than language. Certainly nonverbal tests, which are viewed as more culturally fair, have done no better than more culturally loaded tests in predicting academic and vocational performance of persons of lower socioeconomic status or minority groups in the United States. With respect to group differences in performance on conventional and culture-fair tests, research has also shown that white children score higher than black children, middle-class children score higher than lower-class children, and older children score higher than younger children on culture-fair tests such as the

Coloured Progressive Matrices (Hall & Kaye, 1977) as well as on the more verbal Stanford-Binet Intelligence Scale. In fact, black children and children of lower socioeconomic status usually perform more poorly on nonverbal tests such as those on the WISC Performance Scale than on subtests such as those on the WISC Verbal Scale (Caldwell & Smith, 1968; Cole & Hunter, 1971). Culture-loaded, verbally oriented tests are also better predictors of most criteria of educational and job success in Western cultures. Summarizing a number of findings on this matter, Anastasi (1988) concluded that tests utilizing nonverbal content are probably no more culture fair than verbal intelligence tests. In fact, nonlanguage tests, which often demand analytic, abstract thinking of the sort encouraged in Western culture may be more culturally loaded than tests that rely heavily on written or spoken language.

Because the criteria of productivity and success defined by Western culture have permeated most developing countries, it can be argued that efforts to devise intelligence tests that are not reflective of behavior considered important in Western culture are not only futile but self-defeating. Verbal items and tests may actually be better suited as intercultural measuring instruments than any other kind. For example, in rural Africa intelligence is not usually measured by academic excellence (Tunga, 1979) nor by "quickness" (Wober, 1972). However, as environmental differences between Western and African cultures diminish, the concept of a distinctly African intelligence becomes more difficult to defend. Perhaps the most pragmatic approach to testing intelligence in African children is to adapt Western intelligence tests, which are highly verbal in nature, to African populations.

We shall return to the issue of intelligence testing in non-Western cultures later in the chapter. Meanwhile, standardized intelligence tests produced in English-speaking and other Western nations other than the United States will be inventoried. Although it is by no means exhaustive, such an inventory should provide some indication of what other countries have been up to in the field of intelligence testing.

TESTS INDIGENOUS TO OTHER COUNTRIES

In no other country has psychological testing flourished as much as in the United States, but the United Kingdom and the British Commonwealth countries have not been far behind. From the 1940s to the 1960s, intelligence tests were administered to all English children near the age of 11 years for purposes of placing them in different vocational training classes (Pellegrino & Varnhagen, 1985). Intelligence tests and test publishers abound in English-speaking countries (Tables 10–1 and 10–2), where the tests are used principally for educational selection, diagnosis, and placement.

In addition to devising their own psychometric instruments, almost all of the countries referred to in Tables 10–1 and 10–2 have imported and adapted American tests of various kinds for local administration. Two Commonwealth countries— Canada and Australia—make extensive use of intelligence testing in schools,

TABLE 10–1   Representative Intelligence Tests Published Outside the U.S.A.

Australia

ACER Advanced Test B40; ages 15+ years; Australian Council for Educational Research.
ACER Advanced Tests AL-AQ and BL-BQ; ages 15+ years; Australian Council for Educational Research.
ACER Higher Tests ML-MQ and PL-PQ; ages 15+ years; Australian Council for Educational Research.
ACER Intermediate Tests F and G; ages 10–15; Australian Council for Educational Research.
ACER Test of Reasoning Ability; upper secondary to adult; Australian Council for Educational Research.
ACER Tests of Learning Ability (TOLA); ages 8.6 to 13.2 years; Australian Council for Educational Research.
Jenkins Non-Verbal Test (1986 Revision); ages 3–8 years; Australian Council for Educational Research.
Non-Verbal Ability Tests; ages 8–adult; Australian Council for Educational Research.

Canada

Canadian Academic Aptitude Test; grades 8–9; Guidance Centre, University of Toronto.
Canadian Cognitive Abilities Test (CCAT), Form 7; grades K–3; Nelson Canada.
Canadian Intelligence Examination; ages 3–16; Ryerson Press.
Canadian Intelligence Test; ages 3 years and over; Ryerson Press.
Henmon-Nelson Ability Test, Canadian Edition; grades 3–12; Nelson Canada.
Non-Language Multimental Test; grades 2 and above; Institute of Psychological Research.
Safran Culture Reduced Intelligence Test; grades 1–6; published by C. Safran.

England

AH1X and Y Group Tests of Perceptual Abilty; ages 5–11 years; NFER-Nelson.
AH2/AH3 Group Tests of General Ability; ages 10 years–adulthood; NFER-Nelson.
AH4 Group Test of General Intelligence; 10 years–adults; NFER-Nelson.
AH5 Group Test of High Grade Intelligence; 13 years–university level; NFER-Nelson.
British Ability Scales; ages 2 years, 5 months to 8 years; 5–17 years; NFER-Nelson.
Children's Abilities Scales; 11 years–12 years, 6 months; NFER-Nelson.
Edinburgh Reasoning Series; ages 10 to 12 years; The Morrisby Organisation.
Educational Abilities Scales; ages 13+–14+ years; NFER-Nelson.
For Critical Reasoning Test (Verbal); all ages; The Morrisby Organisation.
General Ability Tests: Numerical, Perceptual, Verbal; all ages; The Morrisby Organisation.
Moray House Tests (MHT): Verbal Reasoning; MHT Junior 7 (ages 6½ to 10½ years); MHT 86, 87, 88, 80 or 90 (ages 10 to 12 years); MHT 12/1 or 12/2 (ages 10 to 13); MHT (Adv) 10 (ages 12 to 14 years); MHT (Adult) (ages 13½ to 17½ years).
NFER-Nelson Verbal Reasoning Test Series; Test 8 & 9 (ages 7 years, 3 months to 10 years, 3 months); Test 10 & 11 (ages 9 years, 3 months to 12 years, 3 months); Test 12 & 13 (ages 11 years, 3 months to 14 years, 3 months); NFER-Nelson.
NFER-Nelson Non-Verbal Reasoning Test Series; Test 8 & 9 (7 years, 3 months to 10 years, 3 months); Test 10 & 11 (9 years, 3 months to 12 years, 3 months); Test 12–14 (11 years, 3 months to 15 years, 3 months).
Non-Readers Intelligence Test (Third Edition) and Oral Verbal Intelligence Test; ages 6.7–14.11; children suspected of or diagnosed as educationally subnormal; Hodder & Stoughton.
Non-Verbal Reasoning Test Series; ages 7–15; poor readers; NFER-Nelson.
Raven's Progressive Matrices and Vocabulary Scales; Coloured Progressive Matrices and the Crichton Vocabulary Scales (ages 5 years to adult, elderly, or mentally retarded people); Standard Progressive Matrices and the Mill Hill Vocabulary Scale (6 years and over); Advanced Progressive Matrices (11 years and over); NFER-Nelson.
Williams Intelligence Test for Children with Defective Vision; blind and partially sighted ages 5–15 years; NFER-Nelson.

TABLE 10–1 *(Continued)*

India

Non-Language Test of Verbal Intelligence; ages 11–13; Statistical Publishing Company.

Ireland

Drumconda Verbal Reasoning Test 1; ages 10–13; Educational Research Centre.

The Netherlands

Snijders-Oomen Non-Verbal Intelligence Scale; Dutch children ages 2–6 to 7–0, 5–6 to 17–0; Swets Test Services.

New Guinea

New Guinea Performance Scale, by I. G. Ord; © 1961–1971; 17 years and over; Society for New Guinea Psychological Research and Publications.

New Zealand

Test of Scholastic Abilities; 9 years to 12 years, 5 months; 10 years, 6 months to 14 years, 5 months; 12 years, 6 months to 14 years, 11 months; New Zealand Council for Educational Research.

Scotland

Cotswold Tests; mental ability series 9, 10, 11, 12 for ages 10–10½; mental ability series C, D, E, F for ages 8½ to 9½; Robert Gibson.
Essential Intelligence Test; ages 8–12 years; Oliver & Boyd.

South Africa

General Scholastic Aptitude Test; ages 9 to 18 years; Human Sciences Research Council.
Group Tests for 5/6- and 7/8-year-olds; ages 5–8 years; Human Sciences Research Council.
Individual Intelligence: Northern Sotho (1990); 9 years to 19 years, 11 months; Human Sciences Research Council.
Individual Intelligence Scale for Tswana-Speaking Pupils; 9 years to 15 years, 11 months; Human Sciences Research Council.
Individual Intelligence: XHOSA (1988); ages 9 years to 19 years, 11 months; Human Sciences Research Council.
Individual Intelligence Scale for Zulu-Speaking Pupils (1990); ages 9 years to 19 years, 11 months; Human Sciences Research Council.

clinics, and employment situations, but many of the tests are imported from the United States and Great Britain. The Netherlands and the Republic of South Africa devise many of their own tests, also adapting some American and British tests for local use. In all of these countries, intelligence tests are used for purposes similar to those for which they are administered in the United States: identification of exceptional children (mentally retarded, mentally gifted, learning disabled, etc.) for special education and training, selection of students for higher education and professional schools, job selection and placement, clinical diagnosis, and other uses.

TABLE 10–2   Foreign Test Publishers and Addresses

The Associated Examining Board, Stag Hill House, Guildford, Surrey GU2 5XJ, England

Australian Council for Educational Research Ltd., 19 Prospect Hill Road Private Bag 55, Camberwell, Victoria 3124, Australia

Educational Research Centre, Test Department St. Patrick's College, 66 Richmond Road, Dublin 3, Ireland

Robert Gibson, Publisher, 17, Fitzroy Place, Glasgow, Scotland G3 7BR

Ginn & Co., Ltd., Elsinore House, Buckingham Street, Aylesbury, Bucks, England

Guidance Centre, Faculty of Education, University of Toronto, 10 Alcorn Avenue, Toronto, Ontario M4V 2Z8, Canada

Harrap Ltd., P.O. Box 70, 182 Holborn, London WC1V 7AX, England

Hodder & Stoughton Ltd., Mill Road, Dunton Greene, Sevenoaks, Kent TN13 2YA, England

Human Sciences Research Council, Private Bag X41, Pretoria 001, Republic of South Africa

Institute of Psychological Research, Inc., 34 Fleury Street West, Montreal, Quebec H3L 1S9, Canada

The Morrisby Organisation, 83 High Street, Hemel Hempstead, Hertfordshire HP1 3AH, England

Ramanath Kundu, Department of Psychology, University of Calcutta, 92, Acharya Prafulla Chandra Road, Calcutta-700009, India

Manual Moderno, Av. Sonora 206 Col Hipodromo 06100-Mexico, D.F.

National Foundation for Educational Research in England and Wales, National Institute for Personnel Research, P.O. Box 10319, Johannesburg, South Africa

Nelson Canada, 1120 Birchmount Road, Scarborough, Ontario M1K 5G4, Canada

New Zealand Council for Educational Research, P.O. Box 3237 (178 Willis St.), Wellington, New Zealand

NFER-Nelson Publishing Co., Ltd., Darville House, 2 Oxford Road East, Windsor, Berkshire SL4 1DF, England

Oliver and Boyd, Robert Stevenson House, 1-3 Baxter's Place Leith Walk, Edinburgh EH1 3AF, Scotland

Organizational Tests, Ltd., P.O. Box 324, Fredericton, N.B. E3B 4Y9, Canada

Ryerson Press, 330 Progress Avenue, Scarborough, Ontario, Canada M1P 2Z5

C. Safran, Calgary School Board, Calgary, Alberta, Canada

Shoukry D. Saleh, Department of Management Services, University of Waterloo, Waterloo, Ontario N2L 3G1, Canada

Saville & Holdsworth Ltd., The Old Post House, 81 High Street, Esher, Surrey KT10 9QA, England

Society for New Guinea Psychological Research and Publications, Papua, New Guinea

Statistical Publishing Society, Indian Statistical Institute, 203 Barrackpore Trunk Road, Calcutta 700 035, India

Swets Test Services (Swets & Zeitlinger, B.V.), Heereweg 347, P.O. Box 825, 2160 SZ Lisse, The Netherlands

The Test Agency Ltd., Cournswood House, North Dean, High Wycombe, Bucks HP14 4NW, England

University of London Press Ltd., St. Paul's House, Warwick Lane, London EC4P 4AH, England

Wolfe Personnel Testing & Training Systems, Inc., Box 1104-St. Laurent Station, Montreal, Quebec H4L 4W6, Canada

British Ability Scales

With the exception of the United States, a larger number of intelligence tests and research reports concerned with intelligence have been published in England than in any other country. Both group and individual tests have appeared in quantity in Great Britain since the early part of the century. Three of the most popular tests are Raven's Progressive Matrices, the Moray House Tests, and the AH Tests.

One of the most comprehensive and carefully developed of all intelligence test batteries is the British Ability Scales (BAS) (by C. D. Elliott, D. J. Murray, & L. S.

Pearson), a descendant of the British Intelligence Test. Several models or theories were taken into consideration in designing the BAS. The first phase in the development of the BAS took place during 1965–1970 at the University of Manchester under the guidance of Frank Warburton. The second phase, from 1973, was directed by Colin D. Elliott. Construction of the BAS incorporated the Rasch scaling procedure, which enables cognitive abilities to be expressed or estimated in norm-free (sample-free) interval units and new items to be added to a scale when desired.

The basic purposes of the BAS are to provide ability profiles for analyzing and diagnosing children's learning difficulties, to assess changes in abilities over time, and to identify, select, and classify children having learning disabilities. The age range of the scales is 2½ to 17½ years, but not all scales are appropriate throughout the entire age range. Selected age scales and parts of scales may be administered, depending on the child's level of development. The BAS is a flexible test battery: many scales have short forms to permit quick estimates of ability, and each scale can be administered on its own or in combination with other scales. A short-form IQ, based on four scales, may be obtained in as little as 15–20 minutes. The School Age Scales cover the age range from 5 to 17½ years, and the Supplementary Preschool and Early School Scales cover the age range from 2½ to 8 years.

Description of the BAS

The 1983 revised edition of the BAS consists of twenty-three scales grouped into six major areas: Speed of Information Processing (scale 1), Reasoning (scales 2–5), Spatial Imagery (scales 6–9), Perceptual Matching (scales 10–12), Short Term Memory (scales 13–17), and Retrieval and Application of Knowledge (scales 18–23). A twenty-fourth scale, Conservation (Length I, Length II, Number I, Number II, Area, Volume, Weight), based on Jean Piaget's theory of cognitive development, is also available. Although there are norms for the Conservation scale, the scale does not measure a unitary trait and is not included as part of the standard set of BAS tests.

Scale 1: Speed of Information Processing. The materials for this scale are four disposable booklets of simple number exercises, which differentiate between children's abilities in terms of time rather than power. The forty items on the scale cover the age range from 6 to 17½ years.

Scale 2: Formal Operational Thinking. The thirteen items on this scale consist of reasoning exercises based on illustrations of pairs of boys and girls. The scale covers the age range from 8 to 17½ years.

Scale 3: Matrices. The twenty-eight items on this scale require the examinee to draw the correct solution in the blank square of a matrix. The scale covers the age range from 5 to 17½ years.

Scale 4: Similarities. The examinee listens to three words (e.g., orange, strawberry, and banana) and explains why they are similar. The twenty-one items cover the age range from 5 to 17½ years.

Scale 5: Social Reasoning. The examinee evaluates stories told from the manual. Responses to the seven items, which cover the age range from 5 to 17½ years, are categorized in terms of four developmental stages.

Scale 6/7: Block Design—Level and Power. The examinee reconstructs two-dimensional patterns using blocks. Responses can be scored for accuracy (level) and for accuracy and speed (power). The sixteen items cover the age range from 5 to 17½ years.

Scale 8: Rotation of Letter-Like Forms. A small wooden doll is placed on the opposite side of the stimulus design from the examinee, who has to visualize how the design appears to the doll and then choose one of six alternatives. The ten items cover the age range from 8 to 14½ years.

Scale 9: Visualization of Cubes. The examinee is required to match patterned blocks to one of four alternative pictures. The eighteen items cover the age range from 8 to 17½ years.

Scale 10: Copying. The examinee is required to copy designs and letterlike characters while the stimulus is in front of him or her. The nineteen items cover the age range from 3½ to 8 years.

Scale 11: Matching Letter-Like Forms. The examinee must match a stimulus figure to one of six representations of it viewed from different angles. The fifteen items cover the age range from 4 to 9 years.

Scale 12: Verbal-Tactile Matching. The examinee is asked to select objects, from two bags, with certain characteristics and names. The nineteen items cover the age range from 2½ to 8 years.

Scale 13/14: Immediate Visual Recall/Delayed Visual Recall. A card containing pictures of twenty objects is shown for 2 minutes. The examinee must verbally recall the objects at once and again after 20 minutes. The nineteen items cover the age range from 5 to 17½ years.

Scale 15: Recall of Designs. After being shown a design for 5 seconds, the examinee draws it from memory. The nineteen items cover the age range form 5 to 17½ years.

Scale 16: Recall of Digits. A string of digits is presented at the rate of two digits per second, and the examinee is asked to repeat them in the correct sequence. The nineteen digit strings cover the age range from 2½ to 17½ years.

Scale 17: Visual Recognition. Drawings of toys and nonrepresentational figures are shown for 5 seconds. The examinee must then select the correct drawings from a number of alternatives shown on a second card. The seventeen items cover the age range from 2½ to 8 years.

Scale 18: Basic Number Skills. This scale was constructed by combining the original Basic Arithmetic and Early Number scales with twenty-eight new items. It focuses on the number skills that will lead to a basic competence in arithmetical calculations. The sixty-eight items cover the age range from 2½ to 14½ years.

Scale 19: Naming Vocabulary. Objects in the room or on picture cards are to be named by the examinee. The twenty items cover the age range from 2½ to 8 years.

Scale 20: Verbal Comprehension. The examinee is asked to carry out operations using toys in response to verbal commands. The twenty-seven items cover the age from 2½ to 8 years.

Scale 21: Verbal Fluency. This is a creativity test comprising a variety of activities: object naming, deducing consequences from events, and inkblot tests. The scale is scored solely on the number of distinct ideas produced by the examinee. The six items cover the age range form 3½ to 17½ years.

Scale 22: Word Definitions. The items on this scale are thirty-seven words to be defined; the examiner presents a word and asks what it means. The scale covers the age range from 5 to 17½ years.

Scale 23: Word Reading. The items on this scale are ninety words to be read aloud by the examinee. The scale covers the age range from 5 to 14½ years.

Perhaps the most novel scale on the BAS is scale 5, Social Reasoning. This scale is based to some extent on the work of Lawrence Kohlberg (1971) and other psychologists who conducted research on moral judgment and reasoning. The remaining twenty-two BAS scales represent a mixture of verbal and performance tests. Many of them, like the Social Reasoning scale, measure abilities not covered by other individual intelligence test batteries (such as speed of information processing, formal operational thinking, and verbal-tactile matching).

Scoring and Interpretation

Three types of scores, centiles and *T* scores based on children of the same age and a Rasch-based ability score independent of norms, enable the examiner to make ability estimates from each score, compare discrepancies among scores on different scales, calculate predicted scores, determine general, visual, verbal, and short-form IQs based on four or more scales, identify unusual item response patterns, and measure ability changes or growth over time.

With the exception of three scales (Social Reasoning, Recall of Designs, and Verbal Fluency), raw scores of 0 (incorrect) and 1 (correct) are assigned to item responses on each scale. On the Social Reasoning scale, responses are scored 0 (Prereasoning), 1 (Immediate Consequences), 2 (Partial Evaluation), 3 (Full Evaluation), or 4 (Generalized Comment) (see Table 10–3). On the Recall of Designs scale, possible scores are 0, 1, and 2; on Verbal Fluency, the number of responses (raw score) to each item is rescaled as 1 to 4.

The total raw score on each scale is converted to an ability score that is independent of the examinee's age. Other tables in *Manual 4, Tables of Abilities and Norms* (Elliott, Murray, & Pearson, 1983), permit conversion of each ability score to a *T* score and a centile score (percentile rank). *T* scores on certain scales may then be averaged and converted to IQs, and confidence intervals can be computed for the IQs. Only a general IQ can be computed for ages 2½ years to 4 years, 11 months, but general, visual, and verbal IQs can be computed for ages 5 years to 17 years, 5 months.

The scales used in computing general (Gen), visual (Vis), and verbal (Ver) IQs at specific age levels are indicated in Table 10–4. At the highest three age levels, scores on the scales for determining visual and verbal IQs are combined to yield a general IQ. Note also the superscript a's, indicating the scales that are administered on the short form of the test; scores on these scales may be used to compute short-form IQs.

TABLE 10–3   Scoring Criteria for BAS Social Reasoning Scale

Score —Pre-reasoning

The child is unable to comprehend what is required, or to provide a relevant response. This may be shown by no response, "I don't know," irrelevant responses, tenuously connected anecdotal responses, retelling the item without comment or responses which may sound sensible but which go beyond the incident described with no justification.

Score 1—Immediate Consequences

The child now responds relevantly, but only in terms of *immediate reactions or consequences*, often talking about the punishment or reward which one person in the item will get, or how he will feel. This may be shown by references to getting into trouble, being punished, being good or naughty, without further elaboration, being injured or breaking things. Anecdotes may be used and if relevant are acceptable. Sometimes statements about objects may be used to imply feelings which are not spelt out; e.g., it did matter—it was his best toy (item 2).

Score 2—Partial Evaluation

The child has now progressed to a broader grasp of *one side of the problem only*. This may be expressed either as value judgments about stealing, keeping promises, etc., statements of simple rules about behavior or practical solutions for solving the problem from one angle only. What is not apparent is a real view of both sides of the problem; one person is seen as being in the right or as being wrong.

Score 3—Full Evaluation

An attempt is made to find reasons and explanations for the actions of *both parties*. Some stereotyped judgments may be given, but unlike the stage 2 response, an attempt is made to see both or all sides of the problem. However, the stage-3 child is still immersed in the rights and wrongs of the particular problem and the people described, but may elaborate on the information provided to give a clearer picture of what really happens and why.

Score 4—Generalized Comment

At this stage the child ceases to be bound by the particulars of the problem, and is able to *see the problem as an example of general difficulties*. Stage-4 responses are mainly characterized by broader statements about types of situations and people, and less frequent response to the particular item although this may be referred to.

Source: C. D. Elliott, D. J. Murray, & L. S. Pearson, 1983. *British Ability Scales: Manual 3, Directions for Administration and Scoring* (Rev. Ed.). Windsor, Berks, England, NFER-Nelson.

BAS *Manual 4* also contains two tables for assisting in the interpretation of IQs. One of these tables provides percentile rank equivalents for obtained general, visual, and verbal IQs; the other table lists true score confidence bands (intervals) for these IQs. Procedures and tables for comparing scores on different scales are also provided in *Manual 4*. For each age level, a matrix of significant differences between the *T* scores for any two scales is given. Tables of the expected *T* scores on one scale, as predicted from the *T* score on another scale, are also available. Finally, a procedure for comparing a child's IQ with scores on the two scholastic attainment scales of the BAS (Basic Number Skills and Word Reading) is described.

TABLE 10–4   BAS Scales Used in Determining General (Gen), Visual
(Vis), and Verbal (Ver) IQ Estimates at Successive Age Levels

	Age level (years–months)				
Scale	2–6 to 3–5	3–6 to 4–11	5–0 to 7–11	8–0 to 13–11	14–0 to 17–5
1. Speed of Information Processing				Vis[a]	Vis[a]
2. Formal Operational Thinking					Ver
3. Matrices			Vis[a]	Vis[a]	Vis[a]
4. Similarities			Ver[a]	Ver[a]	Ver[a]
5. Social Reasoning					
6. Block Design—Level		Gen	Vis	Vis	Vis
7. Block Design—Power				Vis	Vis
8. Rotation of Letter-Like Forms				Vis	Vis
9. Visualisation of Cubes				Vis	Vis
10. Copying		Gen	Vis		
11. Matching Letter-Like Forms			Vis		
12. Verbal–Tactile Matching	Gen	Gen	Ver		
13. Immediate Visual Recall					
14. Delayed Visual Recall					
15. Recall of Designs			Vis	Vis	Vis
16. Recall of Digits	Gen[a]	Gen[a]	Ver[a]	Ver[a]	Ver[a]
17. Visual Recognition	Gen[a]	Gen[a]	Vis		
18. Basic Number Skills	Gen	Gen			
19. Naming Vocabulary	Gen[a]	Gen[a]	Ver[a]		
20. Verbal Comprehension	Gen[a]	Gen[a]			
21. Verbal Fluency					
22. Word Definitions			Ver	Ver	Ver
23. Word Reading					

[a]This scale is also included on the short form at this age level.

Standardization, Reliability, and Validity

As described in *Manual 2, Technical Handbook* (Elliott, 1983), the BAS was standardized on a sample of 2,435 British children. The standardization sample, which was stratified by geographic region, social class, and urban–rural residence, covered all areas of the United Kingdom. The school-age sample consisted of children in public, private, state, and FSN(M) schools; the preschool sample was randomly selected from area health authority registers.

In addition to details of the test standardization procedure, information on the reliability and validity of the BAS is reported in *Manual 2*. The mean internal consistency coefficients of the twenty-three BAS scales, averaged across age levels, range from .51 to .98 for the standardization sample. The mean internal consistency coefficients for the general, visual, verbal, and short-form IQs are .95, .94, .90, and .91, respectively. The test–retest coefficients (with alternate forms constructed from split halves of scales), obtained by retesting after 1 week sixty children aged 9 to 9 years, 5 months, range from .40 (Immediate Visual Recall) to .97 (Word Reading). The test–retest coefficient for the general IQ was .95. These coefficients are similar to those obtained with other individual intelligence tests, such as the WISC-III and the Stanford-Binet IV.

Evidence for the construct validity of the BAS is provided by the results of a principal components factor analysis described in *Manual 2*. These results appear to substantiate the distinctions between visual and verbal IQs, although there are appreciable scale loadings on a general (*g*) factor as well.

Correlations of short-form and general IQs with the two scholastic attainment scales vary with age level but are within the expected range. For example, at the age level 8–14 years, short-form IQ has a correlation of around .60 with the Basic Number Skills and Word Reading scales. The correlations of general IQ with these two scholastic achievement variables are somewhat higher, around .70.

Correlations of BAS short-form IQs with the WISC-R and the Wechsler Pre-school and Primary Scale of Intelligence (WPPSI) are modest, being higher with WPPSI IQs than with WISC-R IQs and higher with the Verbal and Full Scale IQs than with the Performance IQ on the respective Wechsler test. Also summarized in *Manual 2* are the results of several studies relating scores on the BAS to classroom observations, grammar school grades, and scores on reading tests. The BAS profiles of children with learning disabilities (hearing-impaired children and those with specific reading problems) have also been analyzed.

The results of research studies with the BAS contribute to the judgment that the BAS is a valid battery of tests of cognitive abilities. However, fewer empirical studies concerned with validating the BAS have been conducted than would seem necessary. In fact, Cronbach (1984, pp. 222–223) concluded that "the adequacy of the BAS measures cannot be judged on the basis of the limited technical studies so far reported." He also criticized the short form of the BAS as having the same defects as short forms of the Stanford-Binet and the Wechsler scales.

Exporting the BAS to the United States

In constructing the BAS, an effort was made to make the content of the items applicable outside the United Kingdom. In fact, the BAS has been adapted and standardized for use in the United States and published as the Differential Ability Scales (DAS) (see Chapter 5). Minor modifications in spelling (e.g., changing colour to color), phrasing, and other features of the test materials were made in adapting them to American usage. Some scales were eliminated and others were added.

The AH Tests

Perhaps the most comprehensive set of group intelligence tests published in England are the AH series of tests constructed by A. W. Heim, K. P Watts, and V. Simmonds. The AH1X and Y Group Tests of Perceptual Ability, which are parallel tests of nonverbal reasoning requiring 35–45 minutes to complete, were designed to assess the mental abilities of children aged 5–11 years, including those with reading difficulties or those whose first language is not English. The tests consist of multiple-choice, pictorial, and diagrammatic questions divided into four subtests: Series, Likes, Analogies, and Choices.

The AH2/AH3 Group Tests of General Ability, which were designed for children 10 years and over, are available as short forms (25 minutes) and long forms (42 minutes). Parallel tests on each form yield general reasoning scores in three areas (Numerical, Verbal, and Perceptual) as well as a total score. Additional tests in the AH series (AH4, AH5, AH6), for older children and adults, are also available.

The British Commonwealth and Other Countries

Australia

Among the most popular intelligence tests in Australia are the ACER Group Intelligence Tests (available from the Australian Council for Educational Research). Several versions of the tests are available at the lower and primary levels, the intermediate and higher levels, and the advanced level. Most popular of these are the ACER Intermediate Tests F and G, the ACER Higher Tests ML-MQ and PL-PQ, the ACER Advanced Tests B40, AL-AQ, and BL-BQ, and the ACER Tests of Learning Ability.

The ACER Tests of Learning Ability (TOLA), published in 1976, consist of two levels requiring 33 minutes testing time each: TOLA 4 for grade 4 or ages 8 years, 6 months to 11 years, 5 months, and TOLA 6 for grade 6 or ages 10 years, 3 months to 13 years, 2 months. Each level contains three separately timed subtests: Verbal Comprehension (vocabulary), General Reasoning (problem solving in a mathematical framework), and Syllogistic Reasoning (verbal analogies). The norms are stanines, IQ ranges, and percentile ranks based on a New South Wales sample.

The ACER Intermediate Tests F and G, published in 1982, consist of seventy-five items each (analogies, classification, synonyms, number and letter series, arithmetical and verbal reasoning questions, and proverbs). Testing time is 30 minutes for each form (F and G).

The ACER Advanced Test B40 (Revised) was designed for grades 11 through adulthood (15 years and over). It includes verbal and numerical reasoning items and takes 55 minutes to administer. The test was revised and restandardized and a new manual was published in 1983. Somewhat shorter measures of general intellectual ability in students aged 15+ years are the ACER Advanced Tests AL-AQ and BL-BQ, and the ACER Higher Tests ML-MQ and PL-PQ. The L forms of the tests (AL, BL, ML, PL) take about 15 minutes, and the Q forms (AQ, BQ, MQ, PQ) about 20 minutes, plus about 10 minutes for administering each section. The Advanced Tests were published in 1982 and the Higher Tests in 1981. Finally, the ACER Test of Reasoning Ability, a verbal test of general ability for use at the upper-secondary to adult levels, was published in 1990. The seventy numerical and verbal items in a multiple-choice format take approximately 1 hour to administer.

Canada

Because Canada is so geographically and economically close to the United States and politically and economically close to Great Britain, most intelligence tests administered in Canada are adaptations of American or British tests. Examples are the Canadian Cognitive Abilities Tests, the Henmon-Nelson Ability Test, Canadian Edition (published by Nelson Canada) Raven's Progressive Matrices and Vocabulary Scales, and the Mill Hill Vocabulary Scale (1982 Revision) (published by the Institute of Psychological Research). The Canadian norms for the Canadian Cognitive Abilities Tests are based on results from more than 180 schools in over 110 school districts selected from the ten provinces and the territories.

The Canadian Academic Aptitude Test for grades 8 and 9, which is part of the Canadian Test Battery, is published by the Ontario Institute for Studies in Education and distributed by the Guidance Centre. The test yields three scores: verbal reasoning, mathematical reasoning, and nonverbal reasoning. Several other Canadian intelligence tests are listed in Table 10–1.

India

The Non-Language Test of Verbal Intelligence is representative of the few intelligence tests published in India. Scores are assigned on the four parts of the test (analogy, classification, opposites, and picture arrangement), plus a total. The reliability coefficients of the test range from .50 to .70 for the separate parts and .91 for the total score, but the validity coefficients for predicting annual examination scores in five areas are low (.01–.41). A letter from the test authors indicates that the manual was revised in the early 1980s, but most of the test material appears to have been prepared in the 1960s. Some changes regarding presentation of the examples for each part of the test have been suggested in the latest manual.

The Netherlands

One of the most time-honored tests in the Netherlands is the Snijders-Oomen Non-Verbal Intelligence Scale. Designed for use with deaf children and also children with hearing difficulties and speech disturbances, this test is the lower level of a revision of the Nonverbal Intelligence Test for Deaf and Hearing Subjects (ages 3–16 years). There are five subtests: sorting (sorting objects and pictures), mosaic, combination (halves and puzzles), memory (the kitten house), and copying. Dutch and German editions of the test, which provides separate scores on the five subtests as well as a total score, are available. At a somewhat higher level is the Starren-Snijders-Oomen Non-Verbal Intelligence Scale. Eight subtests under the headings Form, Combination, Abstraction, and Immediate Memory are included. Deviation IQs and mental ages for Afrikaans-speaking pupils are provided. American, English, and German adaptations of the test are also available.

New Guinea

The New Guinea Performance Scale is based on the unpublished PIR Test used for screening in the Pacific Island Regiment. With minor modifications, it is the same as the Queensland Test, an older nonlanguage test published in Australia that attempts to attain culture fairness and relies greatly on short-term memory. There are six subtests on the New Guinea Performance Scale: Cube Imitation Test, Bead Threading Test, Passalong Test, Form Assembly Test, Observation Test, and Design Construction Test. The Passalong Test is a modification of a subtest of the Alexander Performance Scale, and the Design Construction Test is published separately as the Pacific Design Construction Test.

New Zealand

Because it is so close, geographically and culturally, to Australia, New Zealand has adapted a number of Australian tests for its own uses. Included among these are the New Zealand edition of the ACER Advanced Test B40 and the New Zealand revisions of the ACER Advanced Test BL-BQ and the ACER Higher Test PL-PQ. An example of a homegrown instrument is the Test of Scholastic Abilities. This test measures the verbal and numerical reasoning abilities considered necessary for academic success in the New Zealand school curriculum. The test has two forms (A and B), the age range of which is 9 years to 14 years, 11 months. The Test of Scholastic Abilities was revised in 1981; age, percentile rank, and stanine score norms are available.

Republic of South Africa

As witnessed by the older system of apartheid, linguistic and cultural differences among peoples living in South Africa are quite extensive. Not only English and Afrikaans, but also Northern Sotho, Tswana, Xhosa, and Zulu are the primary languages of large populations in this country. For this and other reasons, individual and group intelligence tests in different languages have been developed and used. In 1988 and 1990, a series of tests for ages 9 to 19 years, 11 months was published; the Individual Intelligence scales for children speaking Northern Sotho, Tswana, Xhosa, or Zulu. Similar in format to the Wechsler scales, these tests consist of a Verbal Scale and a Performance Scale containing five subtests each and yielding a Verbal IQ, a Performance IQ, and a Global IQ scored on a scale having a mean of 100 and a standard deviation of 15. Among the other intelligence tests developed in South Africa are the Junior and Senior South African Individual scales and the South African Individual Scale for the Blind.

CULTURAL, NATIONALITY, AND ETHNIC GROUP DIFFERENCES IN MENTAL ABILITIES

According to popular dogma, certain nationalities and ethnic groups possess specific personality and behavioral characteristics that distinguish them from other groups of people. Although these stereotypes contain an element of truth, they are usually overgeneralizations that have served as justifications for differential treatment or even mistreatment of particular national and ethnic groups. Nevertheless, social scientists have shown considerable interest in the relationships of cognitive variables to nationality and race.

Nationality

A number of early investigations concerned with group differences in intelligence focused on nationality. An influential study conducted in the 1920s concluded that Jewish, Scandinavian, and German immigrants (along with native-born Americans) had higher average intelligence test scores than other immigrant groups to the United States (Hirsch, 1926). Results such as these, which suggested that immigrants from countries in Northern and Western Europe were more intelligent than those from other countries, so impressed the psychologist H. H. Goddard that he lobbied for immigration laws that would restrict admission of all immigrants to the United States except those from Northern and Western Europe (Gould, 1981). Hirsch's (1926) findings, combined with those of Yerkes (1921), Brigham (1923), and others, were subsequently interpreted as being due to selective migration; significant nationality differences were not found when people were tested in their native countries and in their native languages. Brigham (1930), in particular, repudiated his statements concerning nationality differences on the Army Alpha and concluded that the methods used were wrong and that the tests measured familiarity with American language and culture rather than innate intelligence. A general finding of other studies of immigrants was that scores on American intelligence tests vary with the similarity between the examinees' native culture and that of the dominant American culture.

Cultural Variations in Specific Abilities

Despite the shortcomings of studies relating nationality to intelligence, it is still possible for cultural differences among nationalities to be related to mental abilities. Certainly the emphasis placed on specific skills varies with the particular culture, presumably resulting in greater adeptness in some abilities than in others. For example, children in certain national-cultural groups are oriented toward interpersonal relations skills (Hertzig et al., 1968). In other cultures, mechanical ability, interpersonal sensitivity, or even a highly specialized ability such as being able to send and receive Morse code may have great social value (Ford, 1957).

One variable that has a significant formative effect on specific cognitive abilities is education. Not only does education affect memory (Cole et al., 1971; Wagner, 1974) and the ability to perform abstract, symbolic tasks (Scribner & Cole, 1973), but mental abilities in general become more differentiated as a result of formal and informal education (Gibson et al., 1962). For example, it has been found that children growing up in isolated village communities do not have as well-developed memories as those who grow up in cities (Meacham, 1975; Wagner, 1974). Such urban–rural differences in mental abilities are, at least in part, undoubtedly influenced by differences in school attendance.

The relationships between education and mental abilities were also underscored by the results of an extensive study conducted in Peru (Stevenson, 1977). It was found that, regardless of race and social class, children who attended school performed better on four different learning and memory tests than those who did not attend. Not only did Stevenson find that education was positively related to all of the abilities that he studied, but education and culture also appeared to have a differentiating effect on the development of cognitive abilities. Thus, the correlations between tests of learning and memory were lower among children who attended school than among those who did not.

A classic study of the relationship of cultural differences in mental abilities was conducted by Lesser, Fifer, and Clark (1965). These investigators administered four tests measuring different aspects of intelligence (verbal, number, reasoning, and space abilities) to 3,200 six- and seven-year-old black, Chinese, Jewish, and Puerto Rican children living in ethnic neighborhoods in New York City. The tests were given in the child's dominant language by an examiner of the same cultural background. The profile of mean scores on the four ability tests varied with ethnic group. The order of scores, from highest to lowest, was as follows:

> Chinese: space, number, reasoning, verbal
> Jews: verbal, number, reasoning, space
> Blacks: verbal, reasoning, space, number
> Puerto Ricans: space, number, reasoning, verbal

Not all differences in mean test scores within or between ethnic groups were statistically significant. However, when the four ethnic groups were subgrouped by socioeconomic status, the ability profiles of the lower-class subgroups were parallel to but lower than those of the middle-class subgroups in each ethnic category. The main conclusion drawn from this study and from a follow-up study by Stodolsky and Lesser (1967) was that cultural background has a differentiating effect on mental abilities. However, these results have not been replicated by other studies (Flaugher & Rock, 1972; Hennessy & Merrifield, 1976; Sitkei & Meyers, 1969). These studies found highly similar structures of cognitive abilities in different ethnic groups, indicating that intelligence tests measure much the same abilities regardless of the ethnicity of the group tested.

Testing in Preliterate Societies

Among the many factors that have a bearing on differences in test scores associated with nationality, culture, and socioeconomic status is the manner in which a test is taken. For example, children of lower socioeconomic status are more likely to hurry through a test, marking answers at random (Anastasi & Cordova, 1953; Eells et al., 1951). Such rushing to be finished with difficult test material may be caused by lack of interest, lack of self-confidence, or feelings of inadequacy and anxiety. The consequence is a lower validity of the test when administered to such children.

Problems also arise when testing individuals in preliterate societies. Members of such societies may not share the Western cultural emphasis on speed (faster is superior), "minimal moves" (attaining a solution in the smallest number of steps represents superior performance), "no hands" (mental manipulations are superior to physical manipulations), and "something of one's own" (originality or creativity is superior to imitation or conformity) (Gill & Keats, 1980). Intelligence tests may not have the same meanings for people who live in different cultural settings. Many traditional societies associate intelligence with gradualness and patience, emphasizing cooperativeness, sociability, and a sense of honor more than Western culture does (Wober, 1974). Other societies may also place less emphasis on finding complete solutions or on formulating general principles in solving problems. And in certain societies rote learning and practical skills are rewarded more than criticalness and scholarly skills (Gill & Keats, 1980).

Greater emphasis is also placed on interpersonal considerations such as cooperativeness and deference in some cultures than in others. Compared with modern American and European culture, in more traditional societies children tend to be more respectful of parents and other authority figures as sources of knowledge. In a classic illustration of the importance of social sensitivity, traditional Zuñi culture placed such a premium on cooperativeness and concern for others that Zuñi children were often reluctant to compete or accept the rewards for victory lest they shame their peers. One teacher in a Zuñi school who sent a group of children to the blackboard with the instructions to work an assigned problem and face the class when they had finished discovered that no child turned around until all the others had finished.

The perception of test materials may also vary with the culture. For example, when shown a picture of a head having no mouth, Oriental immigrant children to Israel were more likely than Israeli children to say that the body was missing (Ortar, 1963). And a block design test of the sort found on the Wechsler scales was found to be useless in the New Guinea highlands: the examinees tried to use both the top and sides of the blocks when directed to make a two-dimensional design like the one arranged by the examiner (Ord, 1971).

When testing in developing countries, it is often necessary to modify the content and administration procedure of a test. In this regard, Cronbach (1990) listed a number of suggestions for obtaining more valid information on the abilities of people living in preliterate societies: (1) basing test content on words, stories, and objects familiar to the culture; (2) using objects rather than pictures; (3) minimizing the importance of quickness by not setting time limits or awarding time bonuses; (4) making the test a game and leading the examinee into the task by easy stages; (5) relying more on visual demonstration than on verbal directions; (6) administering all items of a given type before going on to another type of item; and (7) instructing examinees on how to take the test before actually administering it. In addition, individuals indigenous to the specific culture should be trained to serve as observers and examiners whenever possible. This can be accomplished more effectively by simplifying test instructions and being explicit and demonstrative in teaching test administration procedures. These modifications in standard testing procedure obviously create problems in comparing the abilities of people in different cultures, but the difficulties are usually offset by the gain in accuracy of information concerning the abilities of a particular culture.

Black–White IQ Differences

One of the most controversial issues in the measurement of mental abilities has been that of racial differences in IQ. A general finding of research on this topic is that although the mean IQ scores of Asian-Americans are usually equal to or greater than the mean IQ of Caucasian-Americans, the mean IQs of Native Americans, Hispanic-Americans, and black Americans average somewhat lower. Among the various group comparisons, major attention has been focused on black–white differences, a matter that is related to the heredity–environment controversy (see Chapter 12).

In a summary of the pre-1960 literature on black–white differences in abilities, Dreger and Miller (1960) concluded that, as a group, whites are superior to blacks in psychophysical, psychomotor, and intellectual functions, but that the differences are not as large in young children as in older children and adults. Many social scientists (Klineberg, 1963; Lee, 1951) have attributed the results of research on racial differences in mental abilities to differences in the cultural environments to which black and white children are subjected; others believe that the differences have a genetic basis (Eysenck, 1971; Jensen, 1969). After analyzing the results of research on black–white differences in intelligence, Jensen (1969) concluded that the frequency of genes carrying higher intelligence is lower in the black population as a whole than in the white. The consequence, he maintained, is that blacks, although equal to whites in rote learning ability, are poorer in abstract reasoning and problem solving.

One set of research findings cited by Jensen (1981) to counter a strictly environmentalist explanation of racial differences in intelligence is that Hispanic-American and Native American children who were living under even worse environmental conditions than blacks made higher mean scores on nonverbal intelligence tests than the latter group. Furthermore, despite the fact that their parents and grandparents were subjected to severe discrimination during the nineteenth and twentieth centuries, persons of Chinese and Japanese ancestry in the United States now excel Caucasians in mean nonverbal intelligence test scores, as well as in educational and occupational achievement, and are equal to Caucasians in verbal intelligence test scores. Finally, Jews, who themselves are no strangers to social discrimination, have consistently scored higher than other groups on verbal intelligence (Vernon, 1985). In many of these groups, however, there are cultural traditions and family characteristics that encourage high achievement even when the physical environment is bleak and the dominant society is hostile and unsupportive.

Despite the arguments of Jensen (1980), Herrnstein and Murray (1994), and others, the question of racial differences in intelligence is far from settled. Research findings indicate that whites outscore blacks by approximately one standard deviation on both the WAIS-R (Reynolds et al., 1987) and the Stanford-Binet: Fourth Edition (Thorndike et al., 1986b). There is, however, a great deal of overlap between the IQ distributions of the two ethnic groups. According to Vernon (1985), 15 percent of blacks obtain higher IQs than the average white, and 15 percent of whites score lower than the average black.

Although the difference in mean IQs of blacks and whites is significant, it is impossible to predict a person's IQ on the basis of skin color alone. Racial differences in intelligence can be attributed to an interactive combination of factors, including the inadequacies of intelligence tests, differences in environments, and genetic differences, but the relative importance of these three sources of variability has not been determined (Loehlin, Lindzey, & Spuhler, 1975). In any event, it would seem that a potentially more useful scientific and socially sensitive question than "What are the differences in mental abilities of blacks and whites?" is "What are the effects of environmental differences on the growth of mental abilities?" Research pertaining to this question is considered in Chapter 12 in the discussion of the heredity versus environment issue.

The Dove and the BITCH

It is well known that verbal intelligence tests tend to be somewhat biased toward middle-class Western culture, but efforts to develop tests that are equally fair to different cultures or subcultures have not been very successful. Nevertheless, it might be of interest to determine how well a group of middle-class white students would perform on the items listed in Figure 10-1. These items were taken from the Counterbalance General Intelligence Test, which was constructed by Watts social worker Adrian Dove to assess the intelligence of lower-class black Americans.

Similar in purpose to the Dove test is the BITCH-100 (Black Intelligence Test of Cultural Homogeneity), a multiple-choice instrument consisting of 100 vocabulary words selected by psychologist Robert Williams (1975) from the *Dictionary of Afro-American Slang* (Major, 1970). Among the words to be identified by the examinee are *apple alley*, *black draught*, *blood*, *boogie jugie*, and *boot* as they are used in black ghettos.*

The Counterbalance General Intelligence Test, the BITCH-100, and similar instruments are culturally biased in a reverse direction whenever members of the dominant American culture score lower than minority groups (see Box 10-1). Another problem with these instruments is that there is no conclusive evidence that they are effective in predicting any useful performance criteria or even that they consistently differentiate between ethnic or socioeconomic groups (e.g., Komm, 1978; Long & Anthony, 1974).

Japanese–American IQ Differences

Interest in the question of nationality and ethnic group differences in intelligence was stimulated anew some years ago with the finding of significantly higher mean IQs in Japanese than in American children (Lynn, 1982). It has been known for many years that children of Asian immigrants to the United States tend to score at least as high as Caucasian children in this country. Lynn (1982) reported that the

*From the Black Intelligence Test of Cultural Homogeneity, by Robert L. Williams. Used by permission of the author.

1. A "handkerchief head" is (a) a cool cat, (b) a porter, (c) an Uncle Tom, (d) a hoddi, (e) a preacher.
2. Which word is most out of place here? (a) splib, (b) blood, (c) gray, (d) spook, (e) black.
3. A "gas head" is a person who has a: (a) fast-moving car, (b) stable of "lace," (c) "process," (d) habit of stealing cars, (e) long jail record for arson.
4. "Down-home" (the South) today, for the average "soul brother" who is picking cotton from sunup until sundown, what is the average earning (take home) for one full day? (a) $.75, (b) $1.65, (c) $3.50, (d) $5, (e) $12.
5. "Bo Diddley" is a: (a) game for children, (b) down-home cheap wine, (c) down-home single, (d) new dance, (e) Moejoe call.
6. If a pimp is up tight with a woman who gets state aid, what does he mean when he talks about "Mother's Day?" (a) second Sunday in May, (b) third Sunday in June, (c) first of every month, (d) none of these, (e) first and fifteenth of every month.
7. "Hully Gully" came from: (a) East Oakland, (b) Fillmore, (c) Watts, (d) Harlem, (e) Motor City.
8. If a man is called a "blood," then he is a: (a) fighter, (b) Mexican-American, (c) Negro, (d) hungry hemophile, (e) Redman or Indian.
9. Cheap chitlings (not the kind you purchase at a frozen-food counter) will taste rubbery unless they are cooked long enough. How soon can you quit cooking them to eat and enjoy them? (a) 45 minutes, (b) two hours, (c) 24 hours, (d) one week (on a low flame), (e) one hour.
10. What are the "Dixie Hummingbirds?" (a) part of the KKK, (b) a swamp disease, (c) a modern gospel group, (d) a Mississippi Negro paramilitary group, (e) Deacons.
11. If you throw the dice and seven is showing on the top, what is facing down? (a) seven, (b) snake eyes, (c) boxcars, (d) little Joes, (e) 11.
12. "Jet" is: (a) an East Oakland motorcycle club, (b) one of the gangs in "West Side Story," (c) a news and gossip magazine, (d) a way of life for the very rich.
13. T-Bone Walker got famous for playing what? (a) trombone, (b) piano, (c) "T-flute," (d) guitar, (e) "Hambone."

FIGURE 10–1 Items from the Counterbalance Intelligence Test. The items were selected from a test developed by social worker Adrian Dove to measure intelligence as the term applies in lower-class black America. The answer to items 4 and 13 is d, the answer to item 6 is e, and the answer to item 11 is a; the answer to all other items is c. (From "Taking the Chitling Test," Newsweek, 7/15, © 1968 by Newsweek, Inc. All rights reserved. Reprinted by permission.)

Box 10–1

Cultural/Regional Uppercrust Savvy Test

As a spoof on the Dove Counterbalance General Intelligence Test and the BITCH-100, Herlihy (1977) designed the following Cultural/Regional Upper-crust Savvy Test (CRUST) for persons in the upper social class. Although knowing the answers to these questions might be of assistance in mixing with the upper class, the test seems more like a measure of social achievement than a measure of social intelligence.

1. When you are "posted" at the country club
   (a) you ride horses with skill
   (b) you are elected to the governance board
   (c) you are publicly announced as not having paid your dues
   (d) a table is reserved for you in the dining room.
2. An arabesque in ballet is
   (a) an intricate leap
   (b) a posture in which the dancer stands on one leg, the other extended backward
   (c) a series of steps performed by a male and a female dancer
   (d) a bow similar to a curtsy
3. The Blue Book is
   (a) the income tax guidelines
   (b) a guide to pricing used cars
   (c) a booklet used for writing essay exams
   (d) a social register listing 400 prominent families
4. Brookline is located
   (a) in suburban Boston
   (b) on Cape Cod
   (c) between Miami Beach and Fort Lauderdale
   (d) on the north shore of Chicago

---

difference in mean IQ between Americans and Japanese reared in their own countries is approximately 11 points in favor of the latter group. In fact, it has been estimated that at least 10 percent of the Japanese population, compared with only 2 percent of Americans and Europeans, have IQs of 130 or greater.

Several possible explanations have been offered for the IQ difference between Japanese and American children, a difference which has reportedly increased gradually since World War II. Assuming that the samples of Japanese and American children who were tested were equally representative of the specific populations

5. Beef Wellington is
   - (a) the king's cut of roast beef
   - (b) tenderloin in a pastry crust lined with pâte
   - (c) an hors d'oeuvre flavored with sherry
   - (d) roast beef with béarnaise sauce
6. Choate is
   - (a) a gelded colt used in fox hunts
   - (b) a prep school
   - (c) an imported brandy
   - (d) the curator of the Metropolitan Museum of Art
7. The most formal dress for men is
   - (a) white tie
   - (b) black tie
   - (c) tuxedo
   - (d) décolletage
8. *The Stranger* is
   - (a) the _____ family who moved into the neighborhood
   - (b) Howard Hughes
   - (c) a book by Camus
   - (d) an elegant restaurant in San Francisco
9. Waterford is
   - (a) a health sap for the hep set
   - (b) a "fat farm"
   - (c) hand-cut crystal from Ireland
   - (d) the Rockefeller family estate in upper New York
10. Dining "alfresco" means
    - (a) by candlelight
    - (b) a buffet supper
    - (c) at a sidewalk cafe
    - (d) outdoors

and that the tests were equally appropriate, the most obvious explanation concerns differences in child rearing and formal education practices in the two cultures. One biological explanation for the rise in IQ is that due to improvements in health and nutrition, Japanese children today are better off physically and mentally than their counterparts in the pre–World War II days. Another suggestion is that the IQ increase has been caused by heterosis (hybrid vigor) resulting from a decline in consanguineous (kinship) marriages as large numbers of Japanese have, since the 1940s, moved from small villages to large cities. Finally, Lynn (1987) proposed that differences in intelligence between Caucasians and people with Asian backgrounds are due to genetic differences in brain functioning. He maintains that in people of Asian backgrounds the left cerebral hemisphere evolved structures capable of processing visuo-spatial information. The result, according to Lynn, is that in Asians a higher proportion of cortical tissue is devoted to the processing of spatial information and thus a smaller proportion is available for processing verbal information. Consequently, linguistic communication in Japanese, as in reading and writing Kanji, involves spatial skills that normally depend on the right cerebral hemisphere. As reasonable as this explanation of the superior test scores of Japanese children may sound, however, Brody (1992) concluded that there is little or no persuasive evidence in favor of the theory.

SUMMARY

American tests of intelligence and special aptitudes have been translated into other languages and adapted to other countries and cultures. Efforts have also been made to construct culture-free tests, but the results have not been very successful. Nonverbal tests developed in Western culture appear to reflect the influence of that culture as much as verbal tests. Furthermore, nonverbal tests are poorer predictors of criteria of success (school grades, job ratings, etc.) in Western culture and even in the developing countries of Africa, Asia, and South America.

Intelligence tests are published in most Western nations and in certain Eastern countries as well. The most comprehensive of these tests is the British Ability Scales (BAS). The basic purpose of the twenty-three scales making up this instrument is to provide mental ability profiles of children aged 2½ to 17 years. These profiles are used to identify children with learning difficulties, analyze and diagnose those learning difficulties, select and classify such children, and assess changes in their abilities over time. The revised version of the BAS was developed using sophisticated psychometric procedures, such as item-response techniques, and is based on a variety of theories of cognitive development. The BAS was carefully standardized, has acceptable reliability, and provides for greater flexibility in the selection of subtests to administer than most other intelligence tests. Not only can the examiner choose which supplementary subtests to administer, but new items and subtests can also be added to the battery. Overall scores are expressed as general IQs for children aged 2½ to 4 years, 11 months, and as general, visual, and verbal IQs for children between the ages of 5 years and 17 years, 5 months.

The most popular intelligence tests published in Australia are the ACER Group Intelligence Tests. Although the great majority of intelligence tests administered in Canada are adaptations of American and British instruments, the Canadian Intelligence Examination and Canadian Intelligence Test are popular native products. Examples of intelligence tests published in other countries are the Non-Language Test of Verbal Intelligence (India), the Snijders-Oomen Non-Verbal Intelligence Scale (Netherlands), the Test of Scholastic Abilities (New Zealand), the Essential Intelligence Test (Scotland), and the Individual Intelligence scales (South Africa).

Various tests and procedures have been employed in investigations of national and ethnic differences in intelligence, yielding a body of controversial but interesting data. These studies have shown that the development of specific mental abilities and profiles of such abilities vary with the culture. However, formal education or schooling tends to improve mental abilities in general.

The manner in which intelligence test materials are perceived and responded to varies with the sociocultural status of examinees, and research on national and ethnic differences in intelligence must take such perceptual and behavioral differences into account. For example, the emphasis in Western culture on speed, efficiency, mental manipulation, and originality is not shared by all other cultures. Non-Western cultures may place more value on gradualness, patience, cooperation, and respect for authority. The testing of individuals in preliterate societies in particular requires adaptation of the test materials and procedures to the customs and folkways of the particular cultural group.

Despite hundreds of research studies concerned with the matter, the question of black–white differences in intelligence remains unresolved. In general, American blacks score significantly lower than American whites on IQ tests, but the question of the role of heredity, as opposed to environmental factors, in producing the differences continues to be debated. A similar controversy over the relative importance of biological and experiential factors in determining mental ability has resulted from the finding of significantly higher mean IQs among native Japanese than in Americans and other nationalities.

QUESTIONS AND ACTIVITIES

1. Discuss the meaning of each of the following concepts and how they are used in actual practice.

anchor items	heterosis
back translation	learning potential assessment device (mediation)
consanguineous marriage	learning potential assessment strategy (coaching)
dynamic assessment	zone of proximal (or potential) development
graduate prompting	

2. Administer the Counterbalance General Intelligence Scale (Figure 10–1) to different age, gender, and ethnic groups. Give 1 point for each item answered correctly. Compute the mean scores of the different age, gender, and ethnic groups. Are the differences among the group means significant by t tests or analysis of variance F tests? How should the statistical findings be interpreted?

3. Is it possible that the term "nonlanguage test" is a misnomer? Don't all tests involve some sort of symbolic, linguistic communication—with oneself and/or another person, even though it may be a nonverbal language?

4. Compare the British Ability Scales (BAS) with the Differential Ability Scale (DAS) in terms of content, age-groups, standardization, reliability, and validity.

5. In what countries, other than the United States, are intelligence tests most popular? Is there any relationship between the popularity of intelligence tests and the culture, customs, government, or economy of the country?

6. Design a research study to test the hypothesis that there are no significant differences between the mental abilities of blacks and whites. Don't be so concerned with the feasibility of the study, but make certain that extraneous (confounded) variables are controlled.

7. Why are the results of research on racial differences in intelligence such a political hot potato? In what ways do the responsibilities of the psychologist as a scientist and as a promotor of the welfare of society as a whole come into conflict with regard to the question of black–white differences in intelligence?

8. Is there a difference between "practical" and "academic" intelligence? How would you go about designing a test of "practical" intelligence? What would such a test look like, and what should it do?

9. Why do Japanese children score higher than American children on tests of intelligence designed in the United States?

SUGGESTED READINGS

Figueroa, R. A. (1990). Assessment of linguistic minority group children. In C. R. Reynolds & R. W. Kamphaus (Eds.), *Handbook of psychological & educational assessment of children: Intelligence & achievement* (pp. 671–696). New York: Guilford Press.

Gill, R., & Keats, D. M. (1980). Elements of intellectual competence: Judgments by Australian and Malay University students. *Journal of Cross-Cultural Psychology, 11,* 233–243.

Gottfredson, L. S. (1987). The practical significance of black–white differences in intelligence. *Behavioral and Brain Sciences, 10,* 510–512.

Gould, S. J. (1981). *The mismeasure of man.* New York: Norton.

Helms, J. E. (1992). Why is there no study of cultural equivalence in standardized cognitive ability testing? *American Psychologist, 47,* 1083–1101.

Jensen, A. R. (1985). The nature of the black–white difference on various psychometric tests: Spearman's hypothesis. *Behavioral and Brain Sciences, 8,* 193–263.

Lynn, R. (1991). Educational achievements of Asian-Americans. *American Psychologist, 46,* 875–876.

Lynn, R., & Hampson, S. (1986). The rise of national intelligence: Evidence from Britain, Japan, and the U.S.A. *Personality and Individual Differences, 7,* 23–32.

MacKenzie, B. (1984). Explaining race differences in IQ: The logic, the methodology, and the evidence. *American Psychologist, 39,* 1214–1233.

Reynolds, C. R., & Brown, R. T. (1984). Bias in mental testing: An introduction to the issues. In C. R. Reynolds & R. T. Brown (Eds.), *Perspectives on bias in mental testing* (pp. 1–39). New York: Plenum Press.

Zuckerman, M. (1990). Some dubious premises in research and theory on racial differences. *American Psychologist, 45,* 1297–1303.

Individual and Group Differences in Mental Abilities

Since their introduction during the first decade of this century, intelligence tests have been a part of numerous investigations concerned with the characteristics, causes, and effects of mental abilities. The findings of these investigations have prompted much speculation and controversy about the nature, development, decline, and modifiability of mental abilities. Questions and disagreements have led to research, and research to further discussion.

The research literature on individual and group differences in mental abilities is voluminous, and no attempt will be made to provide a comprehensive review in this chapter. These investigations, which were initiated by Francis Galton during the latter part of the nineteenth century, have been conducted with the realization that, although differences in mental abilities are to some extent inherited, individual initiative can help fulfill one's potentialities and even overcome the limitations imposed by biological makeup.

To a large extent, the aggregation of research studies on individual differences in mental abilities has been unsystematic and too often a reflection of convenient measuring instruments and methodology rather than profound contemplation and sound research design. Because of social sanctions against moving people like chess pieces, the majority of the findings reported in this chapter and in other treatments of individual differences (e.g., Minton & Schneider, 1980; Tyler, 1965; Willerman, 1979) are the harvest of correlational rather than experimental investigations. Consequently, it has rarely been possible to attribute causal explanations to the results, and the debate over which came first, the chicken or egg, remains unresolved in most instances. Although these findings are difficult to interpret in any conclusive sense, they are provocative and must be taken into account by theorists and others who are concerned with the structure and dynamics of intelligence.

DISTRIBUTION AND CLASSIFICATION OF INTELLIGENCE

Scores on intelligence tests, and IQ scores in particular, depend on what test is administered. A Wechsler (WISC-III or WAIS-R) IQ of 130, for example, is not exactly equivalent to a Stanford-Binet or Otis-Lennon IQ of 130. A person's score on an IQ test varies somewhat from test to test. Consequently, whenever the IQ is reported, it is important to include the name of the test on which it was obtained.

Despite variations from test to test in the meaning of an intelligence quotient, the shape of the IQ distribution for a well-standardized individual test of intelligence is approximately normal (bell-shaped). One reason why the distribution is not precisely normal is because of the low scores obtained by many children who have suffered accidents or diseases resulting in brain damage, resulting in a hump at the extreme lower end of the curve. In addition, because of assortative mating (mating among persons with similar characteristics), the distribution of intelligence test scores is often flatter than the normal curve. It has been argued that the flatness of the IQ distribution, which results from a larger number of very low and very high scores than in a normal distribution, is just what one would expect if intelligence is substantially influenced by heredity.

Mental Retardation

Alfred Binet's primary reason for constructing the first useful practical test of intelligence was to identify children who had little opportunity to make reasonable progress in regular classrooms. Therefore, it is not surprising that one of the most popular uses of general intelligence tests has been in diagnosing mental retardation.

According to the American Association on Mental Deficiency (AAMD):

> Mental retardation refers to significantly subaverage general intelligence functioning resulting in or associated with concurrent impairments in adaptive behavior and manifested during the developmental period. (Kidd, 1983, pp. 243–244)

Although this definition does not mandate the use of IQ tests in diagnosing mental retardation, intelligence test scores, along with measures of academic and vocational achievement, psychomotor skills, socioemotional maturity, and other *adaptive behaviors*, are taken into account in making the diagnosis. Adaptive behaviors may be assessed by an informal analysis of the person's history and present behavior or by administering a standardized instrument such as the Vineland Adaptive Behavior Scale or the AAMD Adaptive Behavior Scale (see Chapter 8). The psychological examiner fills out a Vineland or AAMD Adaptive Behavior scale from information supplied by a parent, a teacher, or another person who is well acquainted with the child's behavior.

Socially derogatory labels such as *moron*, *imbecile*, and *idiot*, which were once used to categorize different degrees of mental retardation, have been discontinued in the United States. In fact, there have been efforts to replace the term mental retardation with a perhaps less pejorative term such as *mental impairment* or *developmental disability*. In any event, various systems for classifying mental retardation have been proposed. One of the most widely used classification systems is that of the American Association of Mental Deficiency (AAMD) (Kidd, 1983):

> Mild mental retardation: IQ = 50–55 to approximately 70
> Moderate mental retardation: IQ = 35–40 to 50–55
> Severe mental retardation: IQ = 20–25 to 35–40
> Profound mental retardation: IQ = below 20 or 25

When a child's behavior is sufficiently impaired and judged to be due to deficits in reasoning and judgment, the limit of 70 on the mild mental retardation category may be extended upward to 75 or more if the test is sufficiently reliable. However, the term *marginal intelligence* is sometimes applied to IQs in the 70 to 85 range (Maloney & Ward, 1976).

The AAMD classification system, which is approved by some psychologists but considered confusing by others, is not uniformly adhered to throughout the United States. Although an IQ of 75 is generally accepted as the cutoff score, the definition and procedures for identifying mental retardation vary from state to state (Frankenberger, 1984). As advocated by Public Law 94-142 and by the AAMD, both adaptive behavior and IQ are usually considered in making the diagnosis.

Other systems of classifying the degree of mental retardation have been proposed by the National Association for Retarded Children (NARC) and the American Psychiatric Association (APA). The more functional NARC system consists of the following categories: marginally independent (IQ = 50 to 75); semidependent (IQ = 25 to 50); dependent (IQ = 0 to 25). The American Psychiatric Association (1994) lists three requirements for a diagnosis of mental retardation:

> Significantly subaverage intellectual functioning: an IQ of approximately 70 or below on an individually administered IQ test (for infants, a clinical judgment of significantly subaverage intellectual functioning).
>
> Concurrent deficits or impairments in present adaptive functioning (i.e., the person's effectiveness in meeting the standards expected for his or her age by his or her cultural group) in at least two of the following areas: communica-

tion, self-care, home living, social/interpersonal skills, use of community resources, self-direction, functional academic skills, work, leisure, health, and
safety.
> The onset is before age 18. (American Psychiatric Association, 1994, p. 50)

The four levels of severity in the APA system of classifying mental retardation are
comparable to those defined by the AAMD: mild mental retardation (IQ level 50–55
to approximately 70); moderate mental retardation (IQ level 35–40 to 50–55);
severe mental retardation (IQ level 20–25 to 35–40); profound mental retardation
(IQ level below 20 or 25).

Another classification system that is sometimes used in schools to emphasize
adaptive behavior rather than mental deficiency is *educable mentally impaired* for
children who are mildly retarded, *trainable mentally impaired* for those who are
moderately retarded, and *severely mentally impaired* for children who are severely
mentally retarded.

In the United States, mild mental retardation is associated with a number of
demographic variables related to low socioeconomic status: low educational level,
minority group membership, unemployment or low employment levels, poor
nutrition, poor health, and generally substandard living conditions. Heredity is
undoubtedly a significant factor in mild retardation, but the inadequate language
models, insufficient intellectual stimulation, and the unstructured and unpredictable environments in which a large percentage of these children live contribute
to the degree of retardation.

Descriptions of the characteristic behaviors of children in the four categories
designated by the American Psychiatric Association at three periods of development are given in Table 11–1. As shown in the table, expected behaviors vary with
both the degree of retardation and the chronological age of the person. The listed
behaviors are, of course, norms or averages, and the extent to which a particular
person's behavior corresponds to these norms varies with sociocultural background, other skills or characteristics possessed by the individual, and additional
circumstances.

The extreme retardation of persons falling in the severe and profound categories, and in some cases in the moderate category, may be caused by a variety of
disorders leading to central nervous system damage: major gene problems such as
galactosemia, gargoylism, phenylketonuria, and Tay-Sachs disease; genetic-dependent
conditions such as cretinism, hydrocephaly, and microcephaly; chromosomal ab-
normalities such as Down's syndrome and Klinefelter's syndrome; and intrauterine
infections, birth trauma (head injury, oxygen deprivation or oversupply), or diseases contracted during infancy (meningitis, encephalitis, lead poisoning, and
others). These conditions account for a relatively small percentage of the total
number of retarded children in the developed countries, where good maternal and
infant health care are the rule. In developing countries, where malnutrition is more
common and health care less adequate, disorders of malnutrition account for a
higher proportion of retarded individuals.

TABLE 11–1   Age-Related Behavioral Changes in the Mentally Retarded

Profound Mental Retardation (IQ below 20)

Preschool Age (0–5)
Extreme retardation in all areas; minimal sensorimotor abilities; requires nursing care.

School Age (6–21)
Obviously delayed in all areas of development; responds with basic emotions and may benefit from training in use of limbs and mouth; must be closely supervised.

Adult (21 and over)
May be able to walk and talk in a primitive way; benefits from regular physical activity; cannot take care of self, but requires nursing care.

Severe Mental Retardation (IQ = 20–34)

Preschool Age (0–5)
Pronounced delay in motor development; little or no speech; benefits from self-help (e.g., self-feeding) training.

School Age (6–21)
Usually walks unless locomotor disability present; can understand and respond to speech; can profit from training in health and other acceptable habits.

Adult (21 and over)
Follows daily routines and contributes to self-maintenance; needs direction and close supervision in controlled environment.

Moderate Mental Retardation (IQ = 35–49)

Preschool Age (0–5)
Most development noticeably delayed, particularly in speech; can be trained in variety of self-help activities.

School Age (6–21)
Learns to communicate and take care of elementary health and safety needs; learns simple manual skills but makes little or no progress in reading and arithmetic.

Adult (21 and over)
Performs simple unskilled or semiskilled tasks under supervised conditions; participates in simple games and travels alone in familiar places; incapable of self-maintenance.

Mild Mental Retardation (IQ = 50–70)

Preschool Age (0–5)
Slower than average to walk, feed self, and talk, but casual observer may not notice retardation.

School Age (6–21)
Learns perceptual-motor and cognitive skills (reading and arithmetic) on third- to sixth-grade level by late teens; can learn to conform socially.

Adult (21 and over)
Usually achieves social and vocational skills needed for maintaining self; requires guidance and help when under unusual economic or social stress.

Mental Giftedness

The most comprehensive longitudinal study of persons with high IQs was conducted by Lewis Terman and his associates. In this research program, 1,528 California boys and girls who were nominated by their teachers and had IQs of at least 135 on the Stanford-Binet Intelligence Scale were followed throughout their lives at 5- to 10-year intervals from 1921 onward. After Terman's death in 1956, the study was continued by M. H. Oden (1968) and Robert Sears (1977). The purpose of the study was to obtain information on the occupational success, physical and mental health, social adjustment, and other variables associated with high intelligence. Details on the childhood, education, personality, career(s), family, physical and mental health, and life stresses of the participants, as well as their adjustment to old age, were obtained from questionnaires.

The results of the Terman study seemed to contradict a number of popular myths concerning the gifted: that bright children are sickly, that they burn out early ("early ripe, early rot"), and that genius is akin to insanity. As children these gifted individuals were physically superior to other children: they were heavier at birth and remained heavier than the average child; they walked and talked earlier and matured at an earlier age than average; and their general health was better. Furthermore, they maintained their mental and physical qualities as adults. Follow-up data revealed that, compared with average adults, they earned more degrees, attained higher occupational success and salaries, had equivalent or better personal and social adjustment, achieved greater marital success, and were physically healthier (Terman & Oden, 1947, 1959). The greater occupational success of these mentally gifted individuals appears, however, to have been due to their higher educational attainments rather than their higher IQs per se. When educational level was controlled for, IQ scores obtained in childhood had no relationship to occupational achievement.

Terman's findings of better adjustment and a lower rate of mental disorders among the mentally gifted did not go unchallenged. Hughes and Converse (1962) suggested that the fact that the children were selected initially on the basis of teachers' ratings as well as IQ may have biased the sample in favor of better-adjusted persons. Terman's gifted children also tended to be of higher socioeconomic status, which is associated with better adjustment. They were also unrepresentative of the U.S. population at the time: less than 1 percent were Asian, African, or Native Americans (Friedman et al., 1995).

Subsequent research also posed questions concerning personality adjustment in the gifted. Webb and Meckstroth (1982) characterized gifted children as more inquisitive, active, and energetic, but also as being perceived as obnoxious, unruly, strong-willed, mischievous, unmanageable, and rebellious. These researchers noted that intellectually gifted children who are also highly creative are often troublesome to their parents and feel troubled themselves. Realizing that they are different from other children, they are presumably aware of the envy of their playmates and burdened by high expectations. Those who are particularly sensitive and under great stress to perform publicly may become depressed, use drugs, fail to perform up to their capacity, and occasionally drop out of society altogether.

There have been other investigations of mentally gifted children. Particularly noteworthy are the studies of mathematically precocious youth conducted by Julian Stanley and his colleagues (Keating, 1976; Stanley, Keating, & Fox, 1974). A special search was made for youngsters who by age 13 scored 700 or above on the Scholastic Aptitude Test–Mathematical (SAT-M). The children were then given various psychological tests and monitored while they took part in college mathematics courses.

As is true of other gifted children, those who are mathematically talented frequently learn complex material without being formally taught. Stanley and his coworkers also found that not only did these children benefit from college-level instruction in mathematics, but, despite initial fears that they would be unable to adjust to a college environment, they actually adapted quite well. Unlike some other findings concerning the mentally gifted and creative, the mathematically talented adolescents in Stanley's study tended to be personally well adjusted, and highly motivated (especially in mathematics!).

Creativity

Tests of intelligence or scholastic aptitude administered to school-age children usually do a fair job of predicting short-term school achievement and related criteria. These tests, however, were not designed to measure situational variables, lifelong determination, motivation, or nonscholastic talent of the sort that may influence creative performance. It is noteworthy that few, if any, of the intellectually gifted individuals studied by Terman attained the eminence of a Winston Churchill, an Albert Einstein, or an Ernest Hemingway. None was awarded a Nobel prize, and none became a famous composer, artist, or poet.

It is generally recognized that above-average intelligence is necessary but not sufficient for creative productivity. Beyond a minimum IQ of around 120, creative performance appears to depend more on motivation and special abilities than on general mental ability (MacKinnon, 1962). Therefore, investigations of creativity conducted since 1965 have focused on the identification of other cognitive and affective characteristics that distinguish creative from noncreative persons. For example, efforts have been made to develop measures of divergent, as opposed to convergent, thinking ability (Guilford, 1967). On measures of *convergent thinking*, such as problems of the sort found on intelligence tests, there is only one correct answer. In contrast, on tests of *divergent thinking*, examinees are presented with problems that have a number of possible solutions and are scored on the originality of their responses. Rather than having a fixed number of possible answers, items on tests of divergent thinking are open-ended. Unfortunately, this open-endedness leads to difficulties in scoring and determining the reliability and validity of these tests. Among the scoring procedures that have been advocated is evaluating answers for both the number of responses given by the examinee ("fluency") and their originality or uncommonness ("novelty").

Examples of "Creativity" Tests

The following are illustrative of items on so-called tests of creativity:

Consequences Test. Imagine all the things that might possibly happen if all national and local laws were suddenly abolished (Guilford, 1954).

Remote Associates Test. Find a fourth word that is associated with each of these three words: (a) rat-blue-cottage; (b) out-dog-cat; (c) wheel-electric-high; (d) surprise-line-birthday (Mednick, 1962).

Unusual Uses Test. Name as many uses as you can think of for: (a) a toothpick (b) a brick (c) a paper clip (Guilford, 1954).

Word Association Test. Write as many meanings as you can for each of the following words: (a) duck (b) sack (c) pitch (d) fair (Getzels & Jackson, 1962; copyright © 1962, John Wiley & Sons, Inc. Reprinted by permission).

Creativity Test Batteries

Two examples of creativity test batteries are the Structure-of-Intellect Abilities and the Torrance Tests of Creative Thinking. The tests on the Structure-of-Intellect Abilities (SOI), several of which are now published by Consulting Psychologists Press as Guilford's Measures of Creativity, are by-products of the factor-analytic research of J. P. Guilford and his coworkers on the nature of human intelligence (Guilford, 1967, 1974). Included in this battery are the Consequences and Unusual Uses tests, four Christensen-Guilford Fluency tests, other verbal tests such as Simile Interpretation, and nonverbal subtests such as Sketches, Making Objects, and Decorations. The majority of these tests can be administered at the junior high level and beyond, but the scoring is complex. The split-half reliabilities of the tests range from .60 to .90.

The Torrance Tests of Creative Thinking (TTCT) (from Scholastic Testing Service) consist of three picture-based exercises (Figural TTCT) and six word-based exercises (Verbal TTCT). An example of the kinds of items on the Verbal TTCT is to "Write out all the questions you can think of" about a given picture. On one part of the Figural TTCT, the examinee is asked to make a sketch from a basic line. The Verbal TTCT, which takes 45 minutes to complete, is scored on three mental characteristics: fluency, flexibility, and originality. The Figural TTCT, which takes 30 minutes to complete, is scored on five mental characteristics: fluency, originality, elaboration, titles, and closure. The TTCT was restandardized in 1980, and national percentile ranks and standard scores from grade 1 through college and adult level are given in the manual. Although a number of research studies have found the TTCT to be an unbiased indicator of giftedness (e.g., Esquivel & Lopez, 1988; Torrance, 1988), the reliabilities of the tests are quite variable and the results of validity studies are inconclusive (Hattie, 1980). Clearly, more work on the TTCT is needed before it can be used comfortably in applied settings as a measure of creativity.

The instruments that have been designed to assess creativity are intriguing, but it is important to heed the criticisms made by McNemar (1964) and other psychologists. Tests of creativity frequently have substantial correlations with IQ tests, and the former are apparently no more effective than the latter in predicting "creative performance." All things considered, a reasonable conclusion is that it remains to be demonstrated whether effective measures of creativity can be constructed. Until a test can be designed to predict performance on a generally accepted criterion of creativity, it would be well to follow McNemar's (1964) advice not to dispose of our general intelligence tests.

Characteristics of Creative People

Thomas Alva Edison held 1,093 patents, Albert Einstein published 248 papers, Pablo Picasso averaged over 200 works of art a year, and Wolfgang Amadeus Mozart composed more than 600 pieces of music by the time of his death at age 35. These cases illustrate the high inner drive or intrinsic motivation that creative people reportedly possess (Haney, 1985). Other affective and cognitive traits said to be characteristic of creative people are ideational fluency, flexibility, unconventionalism, social sensitivity, nondefensiveness, a greater willingness to concede faults, and close ties with parents (MacKinnon, 1962).

Based on the results of investigations by MacKinnon (1962) and Wallach and Kogan (1965), it would seem that creativity, especially when accompanied by high intelligence, is not a bad characteristic to possess from a mental health standpoint. However, in a study of prominent British artists (novelists, painters, playwrights, poets, and sculptors), Jamison (see Goodwin & Jamison, 1990) found that these individuals were much more likely than less creative people to have been treated for mood disorders (mania and depression). Similar results were found by Andreasen (1987) in a study of thirty faculty members in a writers' workshop: 80 percent exhibited depression or some other form of mood disorder, and 43 percent were diagnosed as manic-depressive. The meaning of these findings is not entirely clear, but at least they suggest that creative adults are no strangers to unhappiness and poor adjustment.

AGE-RELATED CHANGES IN INTELLIGENCE

Because of the popular misconception that a person's IQ is absolutely constant from year to year and test to test, it is important to stress the fact that IQs are not fixed or unvarying numbers. All intelligence tests are less than perfectly reliable; consequently, a person's score on one of these tests will change somewhat with time and testing conditions. It is true, however, that, given a relatively stable life situation and optimal testing conditions, scores on the Stanford-Binet, the WISC, and comparable intelligence tests are fairly stable during the school years. IQs obtained on group tests tend to be less stable than those on individual tests during early and middle childhood, but they become more stable during adolescence. A child's IQ on an individual intelligence test varies about 5 points on the average, although changes of 20 points or more can occur. However, large fluctuations in IQ are usually traceable to rather dramatic variations in health or living conditions. Occurrences such as a traumatic emotional experience or the removal of an emotional problem may also produce a dramatic change in IQ.

The older definition of the intelligence quotient as 100 times the ratio of mental age to chronological age implies that mental age must increase as chronological age increases if a child's IQ is to remain relatively stable from year to year. The same assumption applies to tests that do not employ a ratio IQ: raw scores and mental ages on intelligence tests should increase with age during childhood. The exact form of the function relating raw test scores or mental ages to chronological age depends, of course, on the specific test and the cognitive components measured by it.

Cross-Sectional and Longitudinal Studies

Conclusions from earlier studies of changes in general intelligence with age were almost always based on cross-sectional data (Doppelt & Wallace, 1955; Jones & Conrad, 1933; Yerkes, 1921). In an analysis of scores on the Army Examination Alpha administered to American soldiers during World War I, Yerkes (1921) found that average scores on this early group-administered test of intelligence declined steadily from the late teens through the sixth decade of life. In another early study, Jones and Conrad (1933) administered the Army Alpha to 1,200 New Englanders between the ages of 10 and 60 years. The general form of the curve relating mental ability to age in this investigation was a linear increase in scores from age 10 to 16, followed by a gradual decline to the 14-year level by age 55. Scores on the Wechsler Adult Intelligence Scale—Revised also indicate that mental ability peaks in youth, although at a somewhat older age than found in earlier studies. As shown in Figure 11–1, the mean sum of WAIS-R scaled scores reaches a peak in the early 20s, remains fairly constant from that point until the late 20s or early 30s, and then declines steadily throughout later life.

There are, of course, problems in attempting to interpret the results of these cross-sectional studies. Cross-sectional investigations compare people of different cohorts, that is, groups of people brought up in different environmental circumstances. Differences between cohorts in factors such as educational opportunity, which is closely related to intelligence test scores, make it difficult to match people of different ages. Consequently, it is impossible to compare different age groups on intelligence without confounding the effects of education and other test-related experiences with age. Compared with the results of cross-sectional studies, longitudinal studies show a smaller decline in mental test scores with age.

The steady rise in average educational and socioeconomic levels of Americans during the twentieth century must be taken into account when interpreting the apparent age decline in mental abilities. Because intelligence test scores are pos-

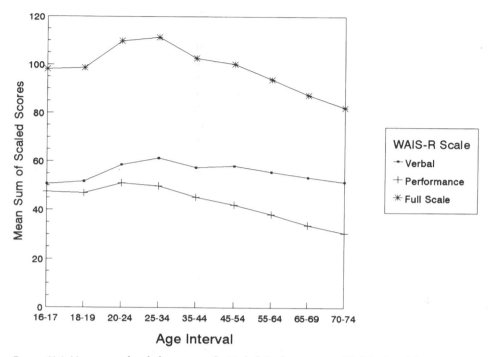

FIGURE 11-1 **Mean sum of scaled scores on the Verbal, Performance, and Full Scales of the WAIS-R at various age levels.** (The data from which this figure was constructed is from the Wechsler Adult Intelligence Scale—Revised. Copyright © 1981, 1955 by The Psychological Corporation. Reproduced by permission. All rights reserved.)

itively related to both educational level and socioeconomic status, it is understandable how older adults, who grew up during less intellectually stimulating times and had less formal education, might make significantly lower test scores than younger adults. Several longitudinal investigations have found that although intelligence test scores tend to remain fairly stable or to decrease slightly after early adulthood, in some cases the scores increase. It can be argued that, because longitudinal studies of intelligence have most often been conducted on college graduates or other intellectually favored groups, the findings do not necessarily apply to the general population (Bayley & Oden, 1955; Campbell, 1965; Nisbet, 1957; Owens, 1953, 1966). However, longitudinal investigations with people of average intelligence (Charles & James, 1964; Eisdorfer, 1963; Tuddenham, Blumenkrantz, & Wilkin, 1968) and with noninstitutionalized mentally retarded adults (Baller, Charles, & Miller, 1967; Bell & Zubek, 1960) have yielded similar findings. Botwinick (1977) summarized the results of these studies as indicating that intelligence continues to increase by small amounts during early adulthood and reaches a plateau between the ages of 25 and 30. Subsequently, people who are below average or fail to make adequate use of their abilities decline somewhat in intelligence, but individuals of above-average intelligence show no decline or may even improve until age 50.

Although the results of both cross-sectional and longitudinal studies reveal substantial declines in mental abilities during the 70s and 80s, Baltes and Schaie (1974) found that such abilities may continue to increase even after age 70. Similar results were obtained in the Duke Longitudinal Study (Busse & Maddox, 1985). These findings indicated that declines in intellectual abilities during older adulthood are not inevitable, except perhaps for people with cardiovascular disorders and certain other health problems or people living in deprived environments.

As the results of investigations by Schaie and Hertzog (1983), Busse and Maddox (1985), and others indicate, the magnitude of intellectual decline with aging varies with the task and the individual. As shown in Figure 11–2, for example, there is very little drop in mean scores on the Information, Vocabulary, or Arithmetic subtests of the WAIS-R with age, but mean scores on Picture Completion, Picture Arrangement, and Digit Symbol decline dramatically after midlife. The first three subtests involve well-learned verbal and quantitative abilities, but the last three are perceptual measures that require careful attention to detail and speed and are probably unfamiliar to the majority of older adults.

Specific Cognitive Abilities

General intelligence tests measure a combination of several cognitive abilities, and the pattern of change in performance with age depends on the specific ability being measured. For example, cross-sectional data reveal that scaled scores on the Verbal subtests of the Wechsler Adult Intelligence Scale remain fairly constant but that scaled scores on the Performance subtests decrease significantly with age (see Figures 11–1 and 11–2). The findings of other cross-sectional studies are similar: Scores on vocabulary and information tests typically show no appreciable changes with aging, but perceptual–integrative abilities and comprehension of numerical symbols decline more rapidly.

Both cross-sectional and longitudinal methods have shortcomings, and investigations combining the two approaches are required to reach valid conclusions regarding intellectual growth with age. One such study concerning the differential effects of aging on cognitive abilities was conducted by Schaie and Strother (1968). Fifty people in each 5-year age range from 20 to 70 were tested with the Primary Mental Abilities Test, and as many as could be located were retested 7 years later. The results varied with the specific ability, but some decline was found using both longitudinal and cross-sectional approaches. The greatest age-related decline in cognitive abilities was obtained with the cross-sectional method, a decline that also began earlier than with the longitudinal method. In a later longitudinal study, Baltes and Schaie (1974) found an age decline on the factor of "visuomotor flexibility" but no significant change in "cognitive flexibility." On the other hand, increases during the later years occurred in "crystallized intelligence" and "visualization," two other cognitive factors that were tested. It has also been noted that age-related declines are less likely to be found in vocabulary knowledge and similar skills dependent on previous learning than in performance on unfamiliar problems of logic and other skills requiring new learning. Similarly, Horn and Cattell (1967) found a greater

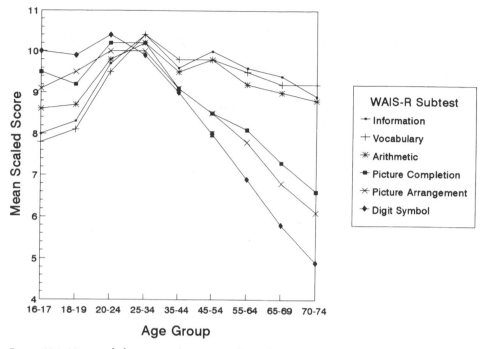

FIGURE 11-2 **Mean scaled scores on six WAIS-R subtests by age.** (The material in this figure is from the Wechsler Adult Intelligence Scale—Revised. Copyright © 1981, 1955 by The Psychological Corporation. Reproduced by permission. All rights reserved.)

decline in the ability to reason and solve problems involving visual and geometric stimuli ("fluid intelligence") than in verbal skills ("crystallized intelligence") (see also Kaufman, Reynolds, & McLean, 1989).

As the above results make clear, whether a decrease, no change, or even an increase in cognitive abilities is observed with age depends not only on the research methodology (longitudinal, cross-sectional, or variations on these methods) but also on the specific ability being measured and the individual being tested. Variations in mental ability during adulthood depend to some extent on the kinds of experiences relevant to test performance an individual has during these years. People who remain intellectually active show less decline in intelligence test scores than those who fail to continue in academic-type pursuits (Botwinick, 1967). Furthermore, even when older people do poorly on intelligence tests, they may possess highly specialized knowledge and skills in areas not covered by the tests. Those abilities may enable them to be even more competent than younger adults in dealing with the problems of everyday living.

There has been some, if not necessarily marked, disagreement among psychologists such as John Horn and Warner Schaie regarding the magnitude, quality, and generality of age changes in cognitive abilities. For example, Horn (1982; Horn & Donaldson, 1976) concluded that decrements in at least some of the important abilities making up intelligence are likely to occur if one lives long enough. In fact, he maintained that intelligence may begin to decline as early as the 20s and 30s. The decline becomes particularly noticeable during middle age, when it is more apparent in fluid intelligence than in crystallized intelligence.

Schaie (1983) recognized that there are differences between the cognitive abilities of older and younger adults, but that such differences are related more to variations in the experiences of young and old cohorts than to age or time of measurement. Although Schaie agreed that some age-related decline occurs, he maintained that it is much less than Horn and his colleagues asserted. To Schaie, the existence of interindividual variations in intelligence and its growth and decline, together with its multidimensionality, modifiability, and the interaction between age and cohort, leads to the conclusion that intelligence is a very plastic variable. A favorable environment—one with varied opportunities for intellectual stimulation—and the maintenance of a flexible lifestyle can help to sustain a high level of functioning intelligence in later life (Schaie, 1983; Schaie & Hertzog, 1986). Rather than simply accepting the apparent decline of intelligence in older adulthood, Schaie believes that psychologists should devote more attention to the subject of changing intelligence in a changing world and make an effort to enhance memory, abstract reasoning, and other cognitive abilities. With cognitive training, older adults can continue to learn and improve their performance on intelligence tests (Schaie & Willis, 1986; Willis, 1990).

Experiential and Biological Variables

Some years ago Wesman (1968) argued that older adults are not necessarily less intelligent than younger ones simply because they sometimes do poorly on tests designed for children and adolescents. Older adults may possess highly specialized knowledge and abilities that are not evaluated by conventional intelligence tests, abilities that enable them to be more competent than younger adults in dealing with the problems of everyday living. Unfortunately, skills that older adults can perform as proficiently as they did when they were young may have become obsolete in a rapidly changing, technologically advanced society. What is required, however, is not merely sympathy for older people whose cognitive abilities may be outmoded or inadequate but retraining and compensatory education that will enable them to function more effectively.

Personality variables such as cautiousness, anxiety, and depression can affect intellectual performance at any stage of life, but particularly in older adulthood (Reese & Rodeheaver, 1985). Social isolation resulting from retirement, the deaths of family members and friends, and the increased "interiority" or withdrawal associated with old age are also significant factors in intellectual decline. Physical factors such as poor health and deficiencies in vitamins and minerals may be even more important (Wurtman, 1979). Excessive use of alcohol and drugs, lack of exercise, and lack of practice on cognitive tasks can also lower intellectual achievement.

Studies of people in their seventies, eighties, and nineties have found a higher correlation between health and intelligence than between age and intelligence

(Birren, Cunningham, & Yamamoto, 1983; Palmore, 1970; Schaie & Gribbin, 1975). Generally speaking, brighter people are healthier in old age and live longer than the less bright. It has also been suggested that the relationship between mental ability and health in old age may be reflective of personality adjustment: better adjusted people are both brighter and healthier (Neugarten, 1976; also see Friedman et al., 1995). Certainly the feelings of depression and isolation that result from prolonged illness can contribute to a failure to bounce back to one's former level of intellectual functioning (Perlmutter et al., 1987).

Cognitive functioning in many older adults is affected by chronic brain syndrome (Ben-Yishay, Diller, Mandelberg, Gordon, & Gerstman, 1971; Overall & Gorham, 1972). The decline in cognitive abilities that is symptomatic of Alzheimer's disease is a case in point. This is no small matter: It has been estimated that nearly 20 percent of 75- to 84-year-olds suffer from Alzheimer's, a figure that increases to approximately 47 percent in 85-year-olds (Evans et al., 1989).

Even more common in later life is high blood pressure (hypertension), which may be accompanied by cardiovascular disease and stroke. The effects of chronic cardiovascular disease on mental functioning in old age have been demonstrated in a number of research investigations (e.g., Hertzog, Schaie, & Gribbin, 1978). A serious stroke, which is related to insufficient oxygen flow to the brain, can affect both intelligence and the motor skills required for speaking and walking.

In addition to hypertension and cardiovascular disease, emphysema, acute infection, poor nutrition, injuries, and surgery can temporarily or permanently affect intelligence in older adulthood by reducing the blood supply to the brain. Decreases in the speed and accuracy with which information is transmitted, coded, and stored in the brain occur with the aging of neurons in the central nervous system. A loss of neuronal tissue, changes in the metabolic rate of the brain, and a loss of circulatory capacity all lead to declines in cognitive functioning. But all is not lost when some brain neurons die; the surviving neurons continue growing. Coleman (1986) estimated that in middle-aged and older adults, on the average there is a growth of three million millimeters of dendrites in cortical neurons. This growth continues even during the 70s and 80s but apparently has ceased by the time the person reaches the 90s.

With respect to the remediation of intellectual decline, there is evidence for a causal connection between physical exercise and intelligence. In one investigation, a battery of cognitive tests was administered to groups of young and old men both before and after they participated in a program of physical exercise. Significant increases were found for both groups on measures of fluid mental ability but not on measures of crystallized mental ability (Elsayed, Ismail, & Young, 1980).

Terminal Drop

An apparent exception to the conclusion that intellectual abilities do not invariably decline in old age is a phenomenon referred to as the *terminal drop*, a decline in cognitive functioning (IQ, memory, cognitive organization), sensorimotor abilities such as reaction time, and personality characteristics such as assertiveness during the last few months or years of life. Prompting the initial research on terminal drop was the claim made by a nurse in a home for the aged that she could predict which patients were going to die soon merely by observing that they "seem to act differently" (Lieberman, 1965, p. 181). Subsequent research findings revealed declines in various areas of cognitive and sensorimotor functioning and the ability to cope with environmental demands in patients who died within a year after being tested (Granick & Patterson, 1972; Lieberman & Coplan, 1969; Reimanis & Green, 1971; Riegel & Riegel, 1972). Riegel and Riegel (1972) noted that the drop becomes evident as long as 5 years before death, but the results of more recent research indicate that it may not begin until about 2 years before death and occurs only on certain skills (White & Cunningham, 1988).

Studies of deceased men who had participated in a longitudinal study of aging conducted by Duke University researchers found no terminal drop on tests of physical functioning, but scores on intelligence tests tended to fall sharply a few months or years before death (Palmore, 1982; Palmore & Cleveland, 1976; Siegler, McCarty, & Logue, 1982). A decline was more likely to occur on nonspeeded tests such as vocabulary, which is apparently little affected by age until late in life, than on speeded tests of a perceptual or problem-solving nature. On the other hand, patients who did not show such declines in cognitive functioning and behavior did not die until a significantly longer period after being tested. According to Cooney, Schaie, and Willis (1988), declines in vocabulary test scores and other measures of crystallized ability are not typical of normal aging. Therefore, they argue, a drop in these abilities late in life may be indicative of disease or impending death. In any event, to the extent that it is a genuine phenomenon and not merely an artifact of inadequate research methodology, a terminal drop in intelligence is probably caused by cerebrovascular and other physiological changes during the last phase of life.

Changes in cognition are not the only feature of the terminal drop. Lieberman (1965) also noted that people who are approaching death become more preoccupied with themselves, not because of any conceit or egocentricity but rather in a desperate effort to keep from falling apart psychologically. Realizing that they are no longer able to organize and integrate complex sensory input efficiently and cannot cope with environmental demands adequately, they may experience feelings of chaos and impending doom and be less willing or able to exert themselves to perform up to their potential on psychological tests.

OTHER DEMOGRAPHIC VARIABLES

Intelligence test scores have been correlated with almost every demographic difference one can think of, including culture, education, ethnicity, fertility (family size), geography, nationality, occupation, ordinality (birth order), sex (biological gender), socioeconomic status, urban–rural residence, and a host personality, behavioral, and biological variables as well. Research on the relationships of intelligence to ethnicity, nationality, and culture was discussed in the last chapter. In this section we shall focus on a sample of other demographic variables.

Sex Differences

Occasionally, an investigator finds a difference between males and females in general intelligence, but it is usually insignificant.* The results of research indicate, however, that there are sex differences in specific cognitive and perceptual-motor abilities. Females tend to be superior to males in verbal fluency, reading comprehension, finger dexterity, and clerical skills; males tend to surpass females in mathematical reasoning, visuo-spatial ability, and speed and coordination of large bodily movements (Minton & Schneider, 1980). It is recognized that these findings are, at least in part, a function of differences in the ways in which boys and girls are treated in our society. For example, girls are usually expected to be more accomplished in linguistic and social skills, whereas boys are supposed to do better in mathematical, mechanical, and related problem tasks. In any event, differences between males and females in mathematical and spatial reasoning abilities have reportedly declined in recent years (Linn & Hyde, 1989).

The findings of an investigation by Witelson (1976) of twenty-five boys and twenty-five girls within each 2-year interval from ages 6 to 13 years indicate that the same brain structure may have different cognitive functions in boys and girls of the same age. On a test comparing object perception with the left and right hands, Witelson found no difference for girls, but boys obtained higher scores with the right than with the left hand. It was concluded that, in the case of boys, by the age of 6 the right cerebral hemisphere dominates the left in processing nonlinguistic spatial information. In girls, however, not until adolescence does the right hemisphere become dominant in processing spatial information. Although girls score lower than boys on tests of spatial ability, they also have a lower incidence of language problems. Perhaps, by being less specialized for a longer period of time, the brains of girls permit greater transfer of linguistic functioning from one hemisphere to the other. Consequently, damage to the left hemisphere is less debilitating.

Another source of information pertaining to the neurological bases of sex differences in cognitive abilities is found in the results of studies of the effects of brain lesions on intelligence test performance. Inglis and Lawson (1981) concluded that male patients who suffered left-hemisphere lesions declined significantly in WAIS Verbal IQ, whereas male patients with right-hemisphere lesions declined significantly in WAIS Performance IQ. On the other hand, female patients suffered declines in both Verbal and Performance IQs after left-hemisphere lesions. Women with right-hemisphere lesions, however, showed no significant changes on either

---

*Findings from statistical analyses by Richard Lynn (1994) indicate that males in America, Britain, and Sweden score about 4 IQ points higher than females in those countries. Lynn also maintains that men are slightly better at verbal skills and considerably better at spatial skills. See also Hedges and Nowell (1995).

IQ scale. Thus, the effects of lateralized brain lesions are apparently quite different for men than for women.

Not only sex (gender) but also sex hormones have been found to be related to cognitive abilities. For example, Money (1971) reported evidence of a relationship between high IQs and a genetically determined or accidental excess of androgens and progesterone during the prenatal period. A group of children and adults known to have received excessive sex hormones while still in the womb contained a greater than expected number of persons with high IQs. In another investigation, Hier and Crowley (1982) found a positive correlation between spatial ability and secretions of male sex hormones during puberty. The results of several investigations also suggest that testosterone slows development of the left hemisphere and enhances development of the right hemisphere of the brain, which is associated with the kinds of reasoning skills needed to solve mathematical problems (Christiansen & Knussman, 1987). Furthermore, it has been reported that women perform better on tests of motor coordination and verbal facility but poorer on tests of spatial reasoning during times of the month when the estrogen level in the blood is highest (Hampson, 1990; Kimura & Hampson, 1993).

Family Size and Birth Order

Many observers, from Francis Galton's time to the present, have noted the tendency for mentally duller persons to have larger families. More recent studies have confirmed the older finding that, on the average, intellectual ability declines as family size increases (Belmont & Marolla, 1973; Kellaghan & MacNamara, 1972; Zajonc, 1976). The negative correlation between family size and intelligence is not due entirely to socioeconomic differences between large and small families, because it remains significant even when socioeconomic differences between large and small families are taken into account. Such a finding might be a cause for concern among eugenicists were it not for the compensating fact that the death rate is also higher among people of lower intelligence. Thus, natural selection continues to favor those with greater adaptability—persons of higher intelligence.

Also commonly observed is the fact that high achievement is more often associated with firstborn than with later-born children in families. This finding has been reported in research articles dating back to the latter part of the nineteenth century. Summarizing the results of studies up through the mid-1960s, Altus (1966) concluded that firstborns constitute a greater percentage of the intellectually superior portion of the population than they do of the population as a whole. Firstborns also talk earlier and more clearly, learn to read earlier, and are better at problem solving and perceptual tasks than later-borns. One possible explanation for these differences is that parents usually treat firstborns (particularly boys) differently from later-borns. Both parents tend to be more attentive and stimulating to firstborn babies, spending more time with them, and encouraging and helping them more in tasks such as walking, talking, and reading at the appropriate age (Kilbride, Johnson, & Streissguth, 1977; MacPhee, Ramey, & Yeates, 1984). These differences in treatment are thought to be responsible for firstborns being more serious, responsible, studious, and competitive, while later-borns are more outgoing, relaxed, imaginative, and athletic.

Zajonc (1976) proposed a *confluence model* as a way of explaining both the finding that firstborns are brighter and the negative correlation between family size and IQ. According to this explanation, as the number of children in a family increases, the intellectual environment of the home declines. Thus, depending also on how births are spaced within a family, later-born children tend to grow up in a less intellectually stimulating home environment than earlier-born children. The model also states that intelligence is enhanced in children who grow up in families in which mean intelligence is high.

Consistent with the confluence model are research results such as those reported by Falbo and Cooper (1980). These investigators found, as predicted, that Peabody Picture Vocabulary Test (PPVT) scores were negatively correlated with family size ($r = -.43$) and positively correlated with the time parents spent with the child ($r = .34$). The fact that PPVT scores were also positively related to time spent with siblings ($r = .38$) would seem to be inconsistent with the confluence model. However, this finding may be explained by the observation that when interactions with siblings took place, over three-fourths of the time they were in the presence of the parents.

The confluence model has also been applied to explain the observed decline in Scholastic Aptitude Test (SAT) scores since the mid-1960s, a time when the baby boom children of the late 1940s and 1950s became high school seniors. The post–World War II baby boom resulted in many more families in which the average age difference between children was small. Long intervals between births presumably enhance the intellectual growth of children because in such families older children and adults are more likely to have time to talk with and teach younger children. Therefore, it appears reasonable that children who are reared in closely spaced families would tend to score lower on the SAT when they take the test in high school. Because the national birthrate began declining during the early 1960s, Zajonc predicted that the downward trend in scores on scholastic ability tests would continue until about 1980. As seen in Figure 11–3, Zajonc's prediction appears to have been confirmed. Mean total score on the SAT reached its lowest point (890) in 1980, but by 1994 it had risen to 902. This is, however, still an appreciable distance from the 1963 peak of 980.

The confluence model was criticized by Galbraith (1982), who found, contrary to what Zajonc would seem to have predicted, a slightly positive correlation between intelligence and family size in a large sample of Brigham Young University students. But Berbaum, Markus, and Zajonc (1982) maintained that these findings were atypical in that they were based on a special population—primarily that of Mormons, a religious group in which the family environment tends to be warmer or more caring than that of the average American family. Additional questions concerning the adequacy of the confluence model in accounting for population differences in intelligence were posed by Page and Grandon (1979), Brackbill and Nichols (1982), Steelman and Doby (1983), and Blake (1989). According to Blake (1989), earlier studies of the relationship between ordinal position and cognitive abilities

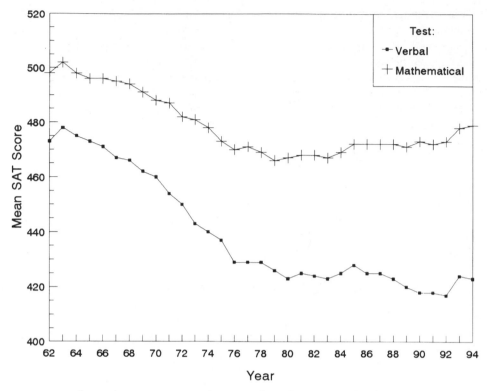

FIGURE 11-3 **Changes in mean SAT scores from 1962 through 1994.** Note that the mean scores are for the original SAT scale, not the new, recentered scale. (Data from College Entrance Examination Board.)

failed to control adequately for the fact that a disproportionate number of children from small families are present in any group of firstborns. Blake maintained that the relationship between birth order and intellectual attainment disappears when the number of children and family background factors are controlled for.

Occupational Status

In an open, competitive society such as ours, it is reasonable to expect that more highly intelligent people will enter occupations demanding greater cognitive ability. Likewise, persons of lower intelligence will tend to enter occupations requiring less cognitive ability. Related to this point is one of the most widely published findings in mental testing—differences in the mean scores on the Army General Classification Test (AGCT) of World War II inductees who had been employed in various civilian occupations (Harrell & Harrell, 1945). The mean AGCT scores computed on over seventy occupational groups showed accountants, lawyers, and engineers to be at the top. Teamsters, miners, and farmers were at the bottom, and other occupational groups were arranged in between in a hierarchy according to mean AGCT score. As might be expected, there was a wide range of scores within each occupation. For example, some truck drivers scored higher than some teachers, proving that the former are not necessarily the opposite of "wise guys." Nevertheless, the data clearly demonstrate the importance of the intelligence variable in the prediction of occupational membership. In general, intelligence test scores are reasonably good predictors of performance in a variety of occupations (Brody, 1992). However, the extent to which education, which is significantly related to both intelligence and occupational status, is responsible for the link between the last two variables is not entirely clear.

Cronin et al. (1975) maintained that the relationship between intelligence and occupational status is due to the fact that both variables are correlated with social class background. These researchers concluded that middle- or upper-class backgrounds are more likely than lower-class backgrounds to prepare children to do well on intelligence tests and in school work, thus paving the way for them to enter higher-status occupations. The effect sequence may also be like this: Scoring high on a test of intelligence or scholastic aptitude is usually a requirement for admission to a good college, and graduation from a good college or university (and/or a professional school in some cases) is a requirement for entering a more prestigious occupation.

Socioeconomic Status

One of the most consistent findings of research on individual and group differences in psychological characteristics is the positive correlation between IQ and socioeconomic status (SES), where SES is defined in terms of parental income, education, and occupation. Higher average IQs for children in higher social classes has been the rule in these studies, a distinction that holds on both conventional and culture-fair tests of intelligence (Spaeth, 1976). Whether social class differences in ability are primarily the results of heredity or environment is debatable, but it is generally agreed that a supportive home environment can exert a significant effect on cognitive abilities (Hunt, 1961; Skodak & Skeels, 1949).

Rural Versus Urban Residence

A variable that is related to both occupational membership and SES, as well as intelligence, is urban versus rural residence. Studies conducted in the United States during the first half of this century (see McNemar, 1942) found that children living in rural areas had significantly lower mean IQs than children living in urban areas. Although this urban–rural difference in mental ability still exists, it is not as pronounced in this country as it was a generation or two ago. Because of the media and other sources of information and intellectual stimulation, rural children of today are exposed to a wider range of environmental stimuli than their parents and grandparents were when they were growing up. Increased exposure to the wider culture has improved the vocabularies, level of knowledge, and general intellectual awareness of today's rural children. Furthermore, studies conducted among the

Venda of South Africa, the Malays and Chinese of Malaysia, and Nigerians support the conclusion that group differences in performance on intelligence tests reflect differences in social class and education rather than urban versus rural environment per se (Cronbach & Drenth, 1972; Scribner & Cole, 1973). The same could presumably be said for differences in the test scores of children living in different sections of metropolitan areas.

Homes of Children with Low IQs

Because socioeconomic status and educational level are closely related, it is difficult to conclude whether observed differences in IQs are due to differences in education or to some other variable associated with SES. Children who score low on intelligence tests tend not only to have less formal education but also to come from homes that are alienated from the dominant culture and are under greater than average economic stress. A language other than standard English is typically the primary means of communication in these homes, and the parents do not emphasize the importance of academic skills or know how to help their children learn them.

IQ, SES, and Educational Attainment

Despite the significant positive correlation between intelligence test scores and SES, the two variables are far from interchangeable. Consider, for example, the results of a study conducted by Thomas, Alexander, and Eckland (1979) of the relationships of these variables to school marks: it was found that the positive correlation between IQ and educational attainment remained significant even when SES was statistically controlled. On the other hand, when IQ was statistically controlled, the correlation between SES and educational attainment was slightly negative. These findings suggest that the correlation between IQ and school marks is not, as some psychologists have claimed, due primarily to differences in social class background. On the contrary, it seems that intellectual ability affects both SES and educational level. For this reason, it can be argued that a major reason why students from middle-class backgrounds are more likely than others to end up in the top half of their school classes is because they possess greater native ability.

Education and the Expectancy Effect

Cognitive abilities certainly have an effect on educational achievement, but education also influences abilities (Ceci, 1991). The effects of education on cognitive abilities are sometimes indirect, as revealed by studies of teacher expectations. The *looking-glass theory*—that people tend to adapt their behavior and self-perceptions to how they believe they are perceived by others—was proposed by the sociologist C. H. Cooley in 1909. More recently, investigations stemming from the observation that the expectations of researchers can affect their research findings were extended to the classroom situation. These investigations, which frequently involved socially disadvantaged children, were concerned with the role of teachers' expectations and attitudes in observed changes in the test scores and behaviors of students. The most famous, if highly controversial, experiment of this kind was conducted by Rosenthal and Jacobson (1968) in the elementary schools of a south San Francisco school district.

The purpose of the Rosenthal and Jacobson experiment was to determine the effects of telling teachers that certain pupils would show a "potential spurt" in intellectual growth during the ensuing school year. In September, verbal, reasoning, and total IQ scores for all the children in the school were obtained by having them take a nonverbal intelligence tests, the Tests of General Ability (TOGA). Then 20 percent of the children were labeled "potential spurters," ostensibly on the basis of their TOGA scores but actually at random, in a report to their teachers. The TOGA was readministered to all the children one semester, one year, and two years later. Comparisons were then made between the IQ gains of the experimental groups (potential spurters) and those of control groups of children who had not been labeled potential spurters. The experimental groups in grades 1 through 3 made greater average gains than the controls, but there were no differences between the experimentals and controls in grades 4 through 6. Mexican-American children and those in the medium-ability track showed the greatest initial gains in total IQ. Boys showed greater average gains in verbal IQ, and girls in reasoning IQ. The experimentals also showed greater gains in reading marks and were rated by their teachers as happier, more intellectually curious, and less in need of social approval than the controls.

Rosenthal and Jacobson were unable to identity specific teacher behaviors that produced the changes in IQs for the experimental groups, but they speculated that the teachers' higher expectations for these children were communicated by means of facial expressions, postures, touch, and other nonverbal cues. The findings of this experiment were not completely replicated by other investigators (e.g., Mendels & Flanders, 1973), and the experiment was criticized for a number of methodological flaws.

Subsequently, a meta-analysis of studies of the "expectancy effect" was undertaken by Raudenbush (1984). The results strongly supported the hypothesis that the more closely acquainted teachers are with their pupils, the smaller is the expectancy effect. It was also found that the expectancy effect was greater in grades 1 and 2 than in grades 3 through 6, but it became more pronounced in grade 7. Contrary to what might have been predicted, neither the type of IQ test (individual or group) nor the information given to the test administrators (none or expectancy-inducing information) seemed to influence the outcomes of the various studies in any significant way.

BIOLOGICAL FACTORS AND MENTAL ABILITIES

Modern scientists recognize that the brain is the organ of mental activity, but efforts to relate specific brain structures to cognitive abilities have not been very successful. Some of the smallest brains on record have been those of recognized geniuses (e.g., Walt Whitman and Anatole France), and some of the largest brains were those of severely retarded individuals. Still, research reviews have concluded that the overall size of the brain has a small positive correlation with mental ability (Broman et al., 1987; Jensen & Sinha, 1991; Stott, 1983; Willerman et al., 1989). In a study of 139 infants who had low birth weights (less than 1.5 kilograms), it was found that head circumference at 8 months after birth was a significant predictor of Stanford-Binet IQs at 3 years of age (Hack & Breslau, 1985). This remained true even when medical and sociodemographic variables, which were significant but poorer predictors than head circumference of later IQs, were statistically controlled. Although compensatory growth in the brain during the first 8 months after birth offset the lowering of later IQs in some infants, little catch-up brain growth was observed after 8 months. Thus it would appear that, at least in infants, head size may presage later intellectual status (see Wilson, 1985).

Cerebral Localization of Cognitive Functions

Although one might wish that it were possible to increase intelligence dramatically by surgical or chemical techniques, at present this is only science fiction. A popular hypothesis, that higher-order mental processes take place in the frontal lobes of the brain, has received some support from PET (positron emission tomography) scan data (Haier, 1991). Inconsistent with the frontal lobes/intelligence hypothesis is the finding that patients who had a prefrontal lobotomy, a brain operation used at one time for the treatment of chronic schizophrenia, showed no consistent changes in scores on intelligence tests. However, some postoperative deterioration in specific intellectual abilities was noted in these patients (DeMille, 1962).

Changes in certain cognitive abilities are associated with injury to specific areas of the brain. For example, damage to the left temporal lobe, which is in the dominant hemisphere for most people, disrupts verbal-symbolic performance more than perceptual-spatial performance. Damage to the right temporal lobe, on the other hand, affects perceptual-spatial performance more than verbal-symbolic performance. Also to be considered in assessing the effects of brain injury is the age of the patient. The cognitive development of a young child may be greatly affected by the same kind of brain injury that has no measurable effect on the abilities of an older person.

Response Times and Information Processing

Rather than attempting to link intelligence to a specific brain structure, some researchers have elected to search for evidence of differential functioning in the brains of individuals having different degrees of measured intelligence. Based on Eysenck's (1967) information-processing analysis of intelligence, Jensen and his coworkers (Jensen, 1982a, 1982b, 1985; Jensen, Schafer, & Crinella, 1981) described a series of investigations linking reaction time to scores on nonverbal measures of intelligence. Related studies were conducted by Seymour and Moir (1980), Sharma and Mehtani (1980), and Vernon (1981, 1983). One finding of these studies, which used subjects of various ages and intellectual abilities, is that the time required to make a choice among a set of stimuli varies directly with the complexity of the stimulus (bits of information represented by a perceptual display). A second finding is that reaction time varies inversely with intellectual ability as measured by standardized tests. These findings led Jensen and others to conclude that speed of information processing is the essential basis of the general intelligence factor (g).

Miller (1994) summarized research on response times and intelligence as showing that:

1. More intelligent people have faster reaction times.
2. Less intelligent people have more variable reaction times.
3. As the complexity of the task increases, the variability of choice reaction time increases more rapidly than median reaction time.
4. Reaction time declines with age.
5. The variability of reaction times increases more rapidly with increased task complexity in older than in young adults.
6. Relaxation times for white matter in the brain are shorter for more intelligent people than for less intelligent people.

This summary of the reaction time data, together with the findings that intelligence is subject to considerable genetic influence, that people with large brains (relative to their body size) are more intelligent, that more intelligent brains use less energy, and that intellectual performance declines with age, led Miller to hypothesize that much of the variance in intelligence is a reflection of differences in myelination of neural axons. Whether or not this hypothesis turns out to be correct, Francis Galton may be rolling in his grave with a smile on his face!

Diet and Chemicals

Malnutrition

It is reasonable to suppose that prenatal and postnatal nutrition affect intelligence, and research findings tend to support this hypothesis. For example, a recent research study found significantly higher WISC IQs at ages 7½ to 8 years in children who were born prematurely and had consumed mother's milk in the early weeks of life than in children who received no maternal milk (Lucas et al., 1992). Poor nutrition, particularly from 3 months before birth until 6 months after birth, is known to affect the growth of brain cells. The results of numerous studies document the effects of fetal and infant malnourishment on low intelligence (e.g., Stoch & Smythe, 1963) and the persistence of such effects (Zeskind & Ramey, 1981). Attempts to reverse the malnutrition-related deficit in intelligence by supplementing the diets of malnourished young children and exposing them to a caregiving environment have not been entirely successful in erasing the intellectual deficit, but such intervention can help to arrest the decline (Barba, 1981; Zeskind & Ramey, 1981).

Genetic Disorders and Diet

Very low intelligence is found in individuals having certain rare genetic disorders that are affected by diet. An example is phenylketonuria (PKU), a genetic disorder caused by failure to inherit a gene that directs production of an enzyme responsible for oxydizing phenylalanine. The result is an accumulation of phenylalanine in the blood and a drastic depression of intellectual abilities. PKU can be detected by a simple medical test at the time of birth and alleviated—and consequently the intelligence decline averted—when the child is placed on a phenylalanine-free diet.

PKU and certain other genetic disorders characterized by low intelligence, for example, Tay-Sachs disease and galactosemia, are transmitted by recessive genes. Tay-Sachs is associated with an accumulation of a fatty substance in the central nervous system, while galactosemia is associated with an accumulation of galactose in the blood. Like PKU, galactosemia is treatable by placing the patient on a special diet, one free of galactose in this case.*

Drugs

Drugs may, of course, have adverse as well as ameliorating effects of cognitive abilities, but the search for a "memory pill" or chemical has occasioned more scientific attention. Among the drugs or substances that at one time or another were thought to be associated with improvements in learning and memory are Gerovital, Dexedrine, glutamic acid, ascorbic acid, magnesium pemoline, vinpocetine, sex hormones, and various dietary and vitamin supplements. Evidence to substantiate such claims has been inconclusive at best. Although many drugs have seemed initially to enhance memory, the improvement is usually temporary or attributable to improvements in motivation and general health or to a "placebo effect." Some years ago, a compound known as Ribaminol, which was based on the RNA molecule, received a great deal of research attention. Preliminary findings with this drug, which was thought to accelerate protein synthesis in the brain, indicated that it had some effect on the short-term memories of hospitalized senile patients and college students. These results, however, were not confirmed by further tests (Botwinick, 1967). More recently, a drug known as deprenyl has been found to

*Diet may also have an effect on the intelligence of children with Down syndrome, a disorder associated with a third chromosome in position number 21 of the karyotype. In a study by Harrell et al. (1981), Down syndrome children who were given periodic dietary supplements consisting of vitamins A, C, D, and E and several minerals, including magnesium and calcium, gained an average of 10 IQ points. After reviewing studies concerned with the relationship between mental retardation and nutritional supplements, Schauss and Sommars (1982, p. 85) concluded that "there is much hope for children with developmental disabilities in nutritional studies that examine the possibility of brain regeneration."

improve the learning ability of rats. If deprenyl, believed to be a "nerve growth hormone," works in humans, it could be particularly useful in the treatment of Alzheimer's patients and other individuals with memory problems.

Exposure to Lead

Intelligence may be affected by either too little or too much of a substance. For example, evidence indicates that high levels of lead, which exists in housing, food, soil, and air, has a debilitating effect on intelligence. Needleman et al. (1978) observed slightly elevated levels of lead in children with low IQs. Similarly, in a study of 149 children aged 5 to 16 years, Thatcher et al. (1983) found a significant negative relationship between measures of intellectual functioning and level of lead concentration in the hair. The persistence of lead-related mental defect into adulthood was demonstrated in a reexamination of 132 of the 270 young adults who had initially been studied as primary school children. It was found that those with higher lead levels more often failed to graduate from high school and had increased absenteeism and reading disabilities and lower scores on tests measuring vocabulary, grammatical reasoning, fine motor skills, and eye–hand coordination (Needleman et al., 1990). These findings, combined with those of other investigators (e.g., Fulton et al., 1987; McMichael et al., 1988), provide support for the hypothesis that exposure to high levels of lead during early childhood has an adverse effect on intellectual development.

Climate and Season of Birth

It is possible that geographic region, season of birth, and other variables associated with climate can affect intellectual performance. However, to the extent that climate influences intellectual functioning, it appears to do so by decreasing motivation or activity level rather than by affecting cognitive abilities directly. In addition, diet is related to climate: malnutrition is more common in tropical countries, for example. Consequently, any relationship that exists between climate and intellectual performance may be due to nutrition rather than to climate per se.

Also related to climate, or at least to weather, is season of birth, which for the most part does not seem to be associated with intelligence. Mascie-Taylor (1980) found that a sample of working-class girls had higher performance IQs if they were born during the summer than the winter, but other relationships between season of birth and intelligence were not significant.

SUMMARY

Research on individual differences in mental abilities began in the last century with the work of Francis Galton, who, with his collaborator Karl Pearson, developed the method of correlation to quantify the direction and degree of relationship between variables. Since Galton's time, many demographic, psychological, and biological variables have been correlated with scores on intelligence tests. Considered as a whole, however, the results of these studies have failed to provide a systematic basis for understanding the nature and origins of mental abilities. What we have, primarily, is a collection of correlations between mental abilities and other characteristics that require explanation by any adequate theory of intelligence.

The distribution of intelligence test scores in the general population is roughly normal in shape, having a mean of approximately 100, a standard deviation of 15 or so, and varying with the specific test that is administered. Individuals who fall at the extreme low and high ends of this score distribution are referred to, respectively, as mentally retarded or mentally gifted, and much research has focused on both groups. Not only IQ but adaptive behavior and other characteristics play a role in the diagnosis of mental retardation. With respect to giftedness, creative performance is known to be not only a function of relatively high intelligence but also of motivation, special training, and perhaps other psychological abilities. Neither the mentally retarded nor the mentally gifted are free from problems of adjustment, but the former group has greater difficulties in this regard. For this reason, research and special programs have concentrated more on the retarded than the gifted.

Given a relatively stable home environment, adequate nutrition, and appropriate educational experiences, the IQ of an individual remains fairly stable after early childhood (within a standard error of approximately 5 points). The results of cross-sectional studies depict intelligence as rising into young adulthood and then declining gradually into old age; longitudinal studies find less decline with age. The rate of decline, or even rise in some cases, is a function of the kinds of activities engaged in by an individual throughout his or her lifetime; people who continue to pursue intellectual activities show less intellectual decline. The question of a terminal drop in intelligence (whether intelligence declines abruptly in the last weeks or months before death in old age) has not been answered satisfactorily.

Studies have revealed no consistent sex differences in general mental ability, but each sex tends to be superior to the other in certain specific abilities. Girls are better at rote memory, language-type tasks, perceptual speed and accuracy, and numerical computations. Boys are better at mathematical reasoning, visuo-spatial ability, mechanical ability, and speed and coordination of large bodily movements. The physiological bases of these sex differences are not well understood, but they are related to differences in the development and functioning of the left and right hemispheres of the brain.

Larger family size is in general associated with lower average IQs, and firstborn children tend to be brighter than later-born children. Zajonc's confluence model of the negative effects on intelligence of close spacing of children and the advantageous position of the firstborn child is an attempt to explain these facts.

Occupational status and socioeconomic status are positively correlated with each other and with intelligence, but it is not clear whether the advantages of being in a higher social class result in children with higher IQs or whether both higher IQs and higher social position are consequences of genetic factors. Other demographic variables associated with IQ scores are urban versus rural residence, educational level, nationality, and ethnicity. With respect to education, teachers attitudes concerning what children are capable of achieving ("teacher expectations") may also play a role in whether a child fulfills his or her potential.

Certain areas of the brain appear to be associated with specific cognitive functions, but the relationships of brain structures and functioning to general mental ability are complex and equivocal. Brain size, efficiency of energy utilization by the brain, extent of myelination of cerebral neurons, and other physicochemical characteristics of the brain have some relationship to measured intelligence.

Various hormones and drugs have been found to be associated with differences in cognitive abilities, but a pill guaranteed to improve memory or learning ability has not been discovered. When chemical substances have an effect on cognitive abilities, in many instances they do so by improving motivation or general health rather than abilities directly.

Although climate and season of birth are apparently unrelated to general mental ability, there is evidence for a significant relationship between nutrition and measured intelligence. Malnutrition, especially during the late prenatal or early postnatal period, can result in lower IQs. In addition, certain genetically based disorders (PKU, Tay-Sachs disease, and galactosemia, for example) associated with low IQs can be treated with special diets if detected soon enough.

QUESTIONS AND ACTIVITIES

1. Define each of the following terms used in this chapter:

adaptive behaviors	idiot
assortative mating	imbecile
confluence model	looking-glass theory
convergent thinking	marginal intelligence
developmental disability	moron
divergent thinking	severely mentally impaired
educable mentally retarded	terminal drop
expectancy effect	trainable mentally retarded

2. Because the method of diagnosing mental retardation, including the cutoff IQ, varies from state to state, it is possible for a child to be diagnosed as mentally retarded in one state and "borderline" or "low average" in another state. What consequences might this have for the child and for the state(s)?

3. Creativity is a topic in which almost all students are interested. Consequently, preparing an essay or research report on this topic should not be too distasteful an assignment for you. The paper or oral presentation should include such subtopics as the definition and assessment of creativity, the development of creativity in children and adults, the relationship of creativity to other cognitive and affective variables, and the characteristics of creative people.

4. Talk with a psychological examiner about his or her experiences in testing older adults. What particular problems are encountered in testing older adults, and what special techniques are used by examiners who work with this age group? On what types of items are older adults most likely to show deficits?

5. How does physical health affect cognitive abilities? Do people decline in intelligence or specific cognitive abilities when they become ill? Are there any physical disorders that are more likely to affect specific cognitive abilities?

6. Do you believe that the *terminal drop* is a bona fide phenomenon? Can you give examples from your own experience that support or fail to support the existence of a terminal drop in cognitive abilities?

7. What are the relative advantages and disadvantages of cross-sectional and longitudinal methods of investigating age-related changes in cognitive abilities? How can the effects of cohort, time of testing, familiarity with the test material, and sample attrition be controlled for in analyzing age changes in performance on cognitive tests?

8. What evidence is there for gender differences in general mental ability? In specific cognitive abilities? Read the article by Lynn (1994) and other recent sources (e.g., Hedges & Nowell, 1995) before making up your mind.

SUGGESTED READINGS

Ceci, S. (1991). How much does schooling influence general intelligence and its cognitive components? A reassessment of the evidence. *Developmental Psychology, 27,* 703–722.

Davis, G. A. (1989). Testing for creative potential. *Contemporary Educational Psychology, 14,* 257–274.

Hedges, L. V., & Nowell, A. (1995, July 7). Sex differences in mental test scores, variability, and numbers of high-scoring individuals. *Science, 269,* 41–45.

Jensen, A. R., & Sinha, S. N. (1993). Physical correlates of human intelligence. In P. A. Vernon (Ed.), *Biological approaches to human intelligence* (pp. 139–242). Norwood, NJ: Ablex.

Jones, D. M. (1989). Culture and testing. *American Psychologist, 44,* 360–366.

Lynn, R. (1994). Nutrition and intelligence. In P. A. Vernon (Ed.), *Biological approaches to human intelligence* (pp. 243–258). Norwood, NJ: Ablex.

Rothenberg, A. (1990). *Creativity and madness: New findings and old stereotypes.* Baltimore, MD: The Johns Hopkins University Press.

Schaie, K. W. (1994). The course of adult intellectual development. *American Psychologist, 49,* 304–313.

Shurkin, J. N. (1992). *Terman's kids.* Boston: Little, Brown.

Chapter 12

Theories and Issues in the Assessment of Mental Abilities

It should be clear from the previous eleven chapters of this book that *intelligence* is only a label for an aggregate of mental processes and behaviors that are described as *intelligent*. As is true of many scientific concepts, intelligence is a convenient fiction that assists psychologists in predicting and understanding the thoughts and actions of people. From their observations and deliberations about those thoughts and actions, some psychologists derive theories of intelligence, or rather theories of intelligent behavior.

Ever since Binet and Simon produced the first practical intelligence test, psychologists have tried to come to grips with a workable definition of the concept. Binet's definition emphasized judgment, understanding, and reasoning. Other definitions have described intelligence as the ability to think abstractly, the ability to learn, or the ability to adapt to one's environment. Each of these definitions has been criticized for one reason or another. Adaptability is obviously necessary for survival, but it is perhaps too broad as a synonym for intelligence. On the other hand, Lewis Terman's definition of intelligence as the ability to do abstract thinking appears to be too narrow: abstract thinking ability is an important aspect of intelligence but certainly not the only one. Finally, the popular conception of intelligence as the ability to learn is inadequate if intelligence tests are accepted as measures of intelligence. Scores on these tests are not very highly correlated with rate or speed of learning new tasks, although they are more closely related to the level or amount of learning of which a person is capable.

To traditional definitions of intelligence such as "the ability to learn and profit from experience" and "the ability to think or reason abstractly," Sternberg (1981, 1982) added two other components: "the ability to adapt to the vagaries of a changing and uncertain world" and "the ability to motivate oneself to accomplish expeditiously the tasks that need to be accomplished." Although current intelligence tests do a fair job of assessing the first two components—the ability to profit from experience and to think abstractly—there is, according to Sternberg, an obvious need for better measures of practical problem solving and motivation. Spurred on to a great extent by advances in computer technology and research on artificial intelligence, other recent theoretical approaches to intelligence have conceptualized it in terms of attentiveness, information processing, and planning (Naglieri, 1989; Naglieri, Das, & Jarman, 1990).

Rather than attempting to come up with a universally acceptable definition of intelligence, certain psychologists have suggested that it may be better to abandon the term altogether. If an alternative term is needed, one might use *general mental ability*, *scholastic aptitude*, or *academic ability*. The last two terms are a recognition of the fact that traditional intelligence tests are primarily predictors of success in school work. But however strong the opposition to the term *intelligence* may be, it is certainly less intense than opposition to the notion of IQ. Because of the controversy surrounding IQ and its implications of being a fixed measure of mental ability, even psychologists who have devoted their lives to the study of intelligence have expressed a willingness to abandon the concept of IQ (Vernon, 1979a). Certainly, the way in which IQs are now typically computed—as deviation scores—does not justify the term *quotient*, with its implication of being the result of a division process. If the term *intelligence* is retained, "intelligence index" or "intelligence estimate" would probably be more appropriate than "intelligence quotient."

One point that research findings and theories concerned with intellectual development have made clear is that the problem of understanding intelligence is part of the broader problem of discovering the psychological and physiological bases of cognition. Many procedures, ranging from simple problem-solving tasks and learning experiments in psychological laboratories to the simulation of complex learning and thinking processes on computers, can be brought to bear on the more general question of how knowledge is acquired and how thinking takes place. Meanwhile, the results of psychological assessment and studies of individual differences will continue to supply information to basic researchers in addition to contributing to the practical problem of predicting intelligent behavior.

THEORIES OF INTELLIGENCE

Theories of intelligence, or rather intelligent behaviors, have been characterized as based on psychometric, developmental, or information-processing models (Pellegrino & Varnhagen, 1985). The first two of these are traditional approaches, and the last is of more recent origin. The psychometric approach, which has resulted in many tests of intelligence and a variety of statistical methods for analyzing scores on those tests, stresses individual differences in cognitive abilities and a search for the causes of those differences. The developmental tradition, which stems from research on human developmental psychology, emphasizes uniformities, or interindividual similarities, in cognitive growth rather than individual differences. The information-processing approach, which stems primarily from research and theory in the physical sciences and their applications to human psychology, focuses on the brain as an information-processing system or machine that works more efficiently in some people than in others. No approach, however, has succeeded in providing a completely satisfactory explanation of how intelligence develops and changes, the causes of individual differences in intelligence, and the specific cognitive and physiological processes that are responsible for intellectual activity.

Theories Based on Factor Analysis

The statistical technique of factor analysis, which is discussed briefly in Chapter 2, was introduced by the British psychologist-statistician Charles Spearman. Spearman (1927) proposed a two-factor theory of intelligence, which he felt could explain the pattern of correlations in the group of cognitive tests he was analyzing. In its simplest form, the theory stated that performance on any cognitive task depends on a general factor (g) plus one or more specific factors ($s_1, s_1, s_3, ..., s_n$) unique to the particular task. Two tests that have been viewed as relatively pure measures of Spearman's g factor are Raven's Progressive Matrices and the Culture Fair Intelligence Test (see pp. 240–242).

Spearman was not alone in his belief in the explanatory power of a general intelligence factor. Alfred Binet and Lewis Terman made its existence an assumption of their work, and there is evidence that performance on the Stanford-Binet and similar tests can be explained largely in terms of g (McNemar, 1942). It has been suggested by certain psychometricians that intelligence should be defined as the first principal axis (factor) extracted from matrices of correlations between cognitive tests (Lohnes, 1973). The first factor typically dominates all other factors obtained from factor analyses of ability tests, and the common core of mental ability that it purportedly represents is primarily responsible for the reliability or stability of scores on most cognitive tests (Thorndike, 1975).

Criticisms of Spearman's two-factor theory have not been lacking, and many alternative factor theories have been proposed. The pioneer American psychologist E. L. Thorndike, for example, formulated a theory and devised a test—the CAVD (the letters stand for completions, arithmetic, vocabulary, and understanding of directions and discourse)—as an expression of his view that intelligence is a composite of many different abilities interconnecting in the brain. One proposal made by Thorndike for three kinds of intelligence (social, concrete, and abstract) was probably the first multifactor theory of cognitive abilities. This theory, however, was not based on the results of factor analyses of ability tests. It remained for L.

L. Thurstone and his coworkers to make the first serious assault on Spearman's two-factor theory.

Thurstone's Primary Mental Abilities

As a result of applying his centroid method of factoring and oblique rotation to the correlations between many different cognitive measures, Thurstone extracted seven important group factors. These *primary mental abilities*, as he labeled them, are:

Verbal meaning (V): Understanding ideas and word meanings, as measured by vocabulary tests.

Number (N): Speed and accuracy of performing arithmetical computations.

Space (S): The ability to visualize form relationships in three dimensions, as in recognizing figures in different orientations.

Perceptual Speed (P): The ability to distinguish visual details and the similarities and differences between pictured objects quickly.

Word Fluency (W): Speed in thinking of words, as in making rhymes or in solving anagrams.

Memory (M): The ability to memorize words, numbers, letters, and the like, by rote.

Inductive Reasoning (I): The ability to derive a rule from given information, as in determining the rule for a number series from only a part of the series.

Thurstone's multidimensional conception of mental abilities established a frame of reference for future factor-analytic research on intelligence in the United States, and his list of seven primary mental abilities was subsequently expanded to approximately twenty-five (Ekstrom, French, & Harman, 1979). Prominent among multifactor theorists were J. P. Guilford in the United States and Godfrey Thomson in the United Kingdom. British factor analysts continued to follow Spearman's lead in emphasizing a general intelligence factor (g), whereas American factor theorists were concerned more with group factors. It is noteworthy that in a further factor analysis of the seven primary mental ability factors, Thurstone found evidence of a second-order factor that could be interpreted as g. The results of many factor analyses of ability tests in both countries led British psychologists to represent intelligence as a general factor that could be broken down into more specific factors, whereas American psychologist emphasized specific (primary) abilities that could be combined to form more general abilities. This difference became associated with a greater emphasis on general aptitude testing in the United Kingdom as contrasted with differential aptitude testing in the United States.

Guilford's Structure-of-Intellect Model

Holding the record for the largest number of cognitive factors is J. P. Guilford's model of the structure of intellect (Guilford, 1967; Guilford & Hoepfner, 1971). In what was basically an extension of Thurstone's primary mental abilities theory,

Guilford proposed that performance on any cognitive task could best be understood by analyzing it into the kind of mental operation or process performed, the type of content or test material on which the mental operation is performed, and the resulting product of performing a particular operation on a certain type of test content. The original structure-of-intellect model contained 120 different factors, which were assumed to be independent, and for each of which Guilford and his associates set out to design a separate test. In a modification of his original model, Guilford conceptualized intelligence as consisting of five possible kinds of *operation* (cognition, memory, divergent thinking, convergent thinking, and evaluation), five types of *content* (figural auditory, figural visual, symbolic, semantic, and behavioral), and six *products* (units, classes, relations, systems, transformations, and implications). This implied the existence of $5 \times 5 \times 6 = 150$ possible intellectual tasks composing the structure of intellect. Although he initially assumed that these 150 factors were independent of each other, further research failed to support this assumption (Kelderman, Mellenberg, & Elshout, 1981). Guilford subsequently replaced the modified structure-of-intellect model of intelligence with a hierarchical ability model consisting of 150 first-order factors, 85 second-order factors, and 16 third-order factors (Guilford, 1981, 1985). This last model has not been thoroughly evaluated by research, but Brody (1992) concluded that it is not an acceptable alternative to a hierarchical model that includes a general factor (*g*) factor at the apex.

There have been other factor-analytic models of intelligence, but none has been viewed as completely satisfactory. An effort to combine the results of the various factorial conceptions of cognitive abilities into a logical whole is represented by Philip Vernon's hierarchical model, which has been more popular than the complex multifactor approach of Guilford.

Vernon's Hierarchical Model

Figure 12–1 is a diagram of the branching, hierarchical model of cognitive abilities proposed by Vernon (1960). A general cognitive factor (*g*) is at the top of the hierarchy, with two major group factors—verbal-educational (*v:ed*) and practical-mechanical-spatial (*k:m*)—at the next level. The *v:ed* and *k:m* factors are broken down further into a number of minor group factors. For example, *v:ed*

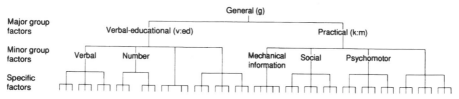

FIGURE 12-1 Vernon's hierarchical model of intellectual abilities. (After Vernon, 1960, p. 22. Courtesy of Methuen & Co., Ltd., Publishing.)

comprises abilities such as verbal fluency, numerical ability, and perhaps creativity. Some of the minor group factors under $k{:}m$ are mechanical comprehension, psychomotor ability, and spatial relations. At the bottom of the hierarchy are factors that are specific to particular tests.

In this hierarchical model of intelligence, the higher a factor is on the diagram, the broader it is or the wider the range of behaviors it encompasses. Consequently, Vernon's model retains Spearman's general intelligence factor while relegating Thurstone's primary mental abilities and Guilford's structure-of-intellect factors to a subordinate status under g. Integrated models of the sort represented by Vernon's hierarchy offer a plausible way of combining the findings and interpretations of various factor-analytic studies into a single theory.

Cattell's Fluid and Crystallized Intelligences

Donald Hebb (1949) distinguished between *Intelligence A*, the portion of overall intelligence that is due to heredity, and *Intelligence B*, the portion due to environment. Related to Hebb's distinction is R. B. Cattell's (1963) theory that general intelligence is composed of two "major general" factors: *fluid intelligence* (g_f) and *crystallized intelligence* (g_c). Cattell viewed these two types of intelligence as distinct but correlated. Both entail the ability to perceive relationships, but fluid intelligence is more biologically or genetically determined and consequently more nonverbal or culture-free. Compared with crystallized intelligence, fluid intelligence changes less over short time periods and is more adversely affected by brain injury. It is involved in many different areas of endeavor, being applied more extensively on tasks requiring adaptation to new situations. On the other hand, crystallized intelligence, which results from the action of fluid intelligence in a specific environmental or cultural context, is used more on tasks where habits have become fixed.

According to Cattell, fluid intelligence, as measured by culture-fair tests such as the Raven Progressive Matrices and the Culture Fair Intelligence Test, reaches a peak at around age 14 or 15. Crystallized intelligence, which expands by applying fluid intelligence to scholastic experiences, goes on developing until age 25 or 30. The Stanford-Binet Intelligence Scale and similar scholastic-type intelligence tests are considered better measures of crystallized than fluid intelligence.

Like Vernon's hierarchical model, Cattell's theory of fluid and crystallized abilities is a compromise between the theories of Spearman and Thurstone. From his extensive factor analyses of cognitive abilities tests, Cattell also found three less general factors: visual abilities (g_v), memory retrieval (g_r), and performance speed (g_s). In addition, the theory, which was extended by Horn (1979), depicts numerous oblique factors contributing to fluid and crystallized intelligence. A person's standing on twenty of these factors is assessed by The Comprehensive Ability Battery (by A. R. Hakistian & R. B. Cattell; Institute for Personality and Ability Testing). Another test based on the distinction between fluid and crystallized intelligence—the Kaufman Adolescent and Adult Intelligence Test (KAIT)—is described in Chapter 6.

Origins of Cognitive Factors

As is true of most psychological characteristics, the relative roles of heredity and environment in determining specific cognitive abilities—the factors of intellect revealed by factor analysis—is far from clear. Certain investigators have argued that specific factors, such as spatial and numerical abilities, are influenced by major sex-linked recessive genes (e.g., Stafford, 1972). Other investigators, observing that mental ability becomes more differentiated as a person matures, have concluded that cognitive factors are due to specific learning experiences.

Ferguson's (1956) *transfer hypothesis of ability differentiation* represents an attempt to explain how general mental ability gradually differentiates into a number of specific factors. The hypothesis states that the different abilities isolated by factor analysis are the results of overlearning and differential positive transfer in certain areas of experience. For example, the child who spends a greater portion of time in verbal pursuits such as reading and solving crossword puzzles will develop a more clearly differentiated verbal factor. And the child who spends a great deal of time studying mathematics and solving math puzzles develops a more clearly differentiated mathematical factor. Philip Very (1967) maintained that, because in our society girls are usually rewarded less than boys for mathematical endeavors, in high school boys are superior to girls in mathematical ability and have a more clearly differentiated mathematical factor.*

Developmental Theories

Research and theorizing on the nature and origins of intellectual abilities have not been limited to factor analysts and other psychometric psychologists. Experimental and developmental psychologists, as well as professionals in other disciplines, have formulated ideas concerning the relationships of intelligence to learning, thinking, problem solving, and other cognitive processes. Illustrative of these efforts are Jean Piaget's theory of cognitive development, Robert Sternberg's component process model, and computer models of problem solving.

Piaget's Theory of Cognitive Development

Jean Piaget's writings, which are a source of many observations and speculations pertaining to child development, represent more than a theory of intellectual growth. Piaget was actually an epistemologist as much as a psychologist: his writings are concerned not only with intelligence but also with the question of how human beings acquire knowledge and understanding about the world in which they live. In Piaget's epistemology, children are depicted as active, interacting

---

*Not all psychologists agree that sex differences in mathematical abilities can be explained entirely by environment. After examining several "environmental" explanations for the finding that "males" dominate the highest ranges of mathematical ability before they enter adolescence," Benbow and Stanley (1983, p. 1031) concluded that the reasons for this sex difference are unclear.

scientists who are constantly striving to make sense out of their experiences by organizing them, constructing hypotheses, and testing those hypotheses against their experiences. As a result, they generate practical knowledge that can be applied to future interactions with the environment.

Assimilation and Accommodation. According to Piaget, a child comes to know and understand the environment by interacting with it and adapting to it, a process referred to as *adaptation*, or *equilibration*. Equilibration involves both assimilation and accommodation. *Assimilation* consists of fitting new experiences into preexisting mental structures (*schemata*), and *accommodation* consists of modifying these schemata in the light of experience.

Young children assimilate whenever they take in or use (grasp, suck, explore, shake, probe, and so on) the environment. For example, when an infant tries to use one hand to grasp a glass container after having just grasped a rattle with that hand, he or she is attempting to assimilate the glass into a preexisting schema for grasping. If unsuccessful in grasping the glass with one hand, the infant will have to modify his or her behavior by employing both hands.

The process of accommodation occurs whenever the environment resists, moves, hurts, rewards, punishes, or, in other words, reacts. As the child matures, the grasping schema and other mental structures and the associated patterns of behavior become elaborated and refined in response to experience. Thus, a schema of an intelligent adult might be a philosophy of pacifism, which may need to be accommodated to external reality when the person is physically attacked. Finally, the tendency to combine elementary schemata into higher-order, integrated schemata is referred to as *organization*.

Periods of Intellectual Development. Piaget maintained that cognitive growth, which takes place by the actions of assimilation and accommodation in the external world, occurs in four periods containing a series of stages. These four periods constitute a hierarchy of development in that successful equilibrations in preceding periods are necessary for the individual to progress to succeeding ones. During the *sensorimotor* period, occurring between birth and 2 years of age, the child learns to exercise simple reflexes and coordinate various perceptions. In the *preoperational* period, between ages 2 and 7, the child acquires language and other symbolic representations of reality; this is a concrete, egocentric period of development. During the period of *concrete operations*, between 7 and 11 years, the child develops organized systems of operations by the process of social interaction, with a corresponding reduction in self-centeredness.* A child has reached the final period of cognitive development, that of *formal operations* (ages 11–15 years), when he or she can use logic and verbal reasoning and perform higher-level, more abstract operations.

This sequence of four periods is normally completed by age 15, and what

---

*Similar to the concept of an operation in mathematics, an *operation* in Piaget's theory is defined as any mental action that is reversible (can be returned to its starting point) and can be integrated with other reversible mental actions.

increases thereafter is not intelligence but achievement. In Piaget's system, intelligence, which he defined as the ability to solve new problems, supposedly declines slowly after age 15. For Piaget, the terminal age of intellectual growth is the same age as that at which Cattell maintains fluid intelligence is normally fully developed.

Although Piaget's theorizing has been more influential in educational planning and remediation than in the design of tests to predict academic performance or to assess cognitive disorders, a number of tests have been devised within the Piagetian framework. The major purpose of these instruments has been to determine a child's stage of cognitive development or the extent to which the child possesses one of the several mental processes described by Piaget: object permanence, operational causality, object relations in space, schemata development, means–end relations, and imitation. Among the more general-purpose instruments designed for these purposes are the Ordinal Scales of Psychological Development (Uzgiris & Hunt, 1975) and the Piaget Task Kit (by W. Stibal, Bureau of Educational Measurements). An individual test designed with the more limited aim of determining the degree to which young children understand the physical principle of conservation is the Concept Assessment Kit–Conservation (by M. L. Goldschmid & P. M. Bentler; Educational and Industrial Testing Service). An example of a test designed within a Piagetian framework for a specific population of psychiatric patients is the Cognitive Diagnostic Battery (by S. R. Kay; Psychological Assessment Resources). These and other Piagetian assessment devices are discussed in some detail by Clarizio (1982).

Cognitive Development in Adulthood

As noted above, according to Piaget, the entire sequence of cognitive development is normally completed by age 15; what increases thereafter is not intelligence but achievement. However, certain theorists have taken issue with this conclusion and have suggested that cognitive development continues throughout adulthood. These theorists maintain that adult thinking is accompanied by qualitatively different modes from the more formal thought processes of logical reasoning and problem solving. Research support for these theories is not plentiful, but they are intriguing and indicate the direction in which the topic of age changes in cognitive development is being pursued.

Following Riegel's (1973, 1976) argument that mature thought is characterized not by a search for a single "correct" solution but by an understanding that, paradoxically, things can be both true and not true, Pascual-Leone (1983) and Basseches (1984) maintained that there is an additional stage of reasoning in adulthood. This stage of *dialectical thought* involves movement or change and is made up of a continuous chain of thesis, antithesis, and synthesis:

> Dialectical thinking is an organized approach to analyzing and making sense of the world one experiences that differs fundamentally from formal analysis. Whereas the latter involves the effort to find fundamental fixed realities—basic elements and immutable laws—the former attempts to describe a fundamental process of change and the dynamic relationships through which this change occurs. (Basseches, 1984, p. 24).

An example of the dialectical thinking of adulthood is the realization that a quarrel may be nobody's "fault" and must be resolved by both opponents changing and adapting their demands to the situation. In contrast to thinking that is absolutist or even relativistic, dialectical thinking is characterized by an understanding that different viewpoints have merit and can be integrated into a workable solution. This type of thinking, which has also been referred to as *postformal thought* (Commons, Richards, & Kuhn, 1982; Commons, Richards, & Armon, 1984), recognizes that not only does the correct answer or solution to a problem vary with the situation and must be realistic to be reasonable but it also involves ambiguity and contradiction and is colored by emotion and other subjective factors.

The idea that qualitative changes in cognition continue during adulthood and that mature adult thinking involves an integration of emotion with logic has also been recognized by K. W. Schaie and his associates (Schaie, 1977/1978; Labouvie-Vief, 1985). According to Schaie, there are four stages of intelligence corresponding to four periods of development:

Childhood and adolescence: acquisitive stage
Young adulthood: achieving stage
Middle age: responsible and executive stage
Old age: reintegrative stage

Cognitive development during adulthood is characterized by a transition from the child's question "What should I know?" through the adult question "How should I use what I know?" to the older adulthood question "Why should I know?" The type of intelligence exhibited during the *achieving stage* considers the context of problem solving as well as the problem to be solved. This stage, which represents the application of term goals such as those involved in career and marriage decisions, is similar to that involved in school-type tasks but requires greater focus on the possible consequences of the problem-solving process. Next, the *responsible stage*, which requires applying cognitive skills in situations involving social responsibility, is typically manifested when an adult establishes a family and pays attention to the needs of his or her spouse and offspring. The last stage in Schaie's schema, the *reintegrative stage*, occurs when older adults acquire information and apply knowledge that is more a function of their interests, attitudes, and values than it was in earlier years. Thus, older people are reluctant to waste time on meaningless test questions that they perceive as irrelevant to their lives and are unwilling to make a great effort to solve a problem unless it is one that they face in their everyday lives.

Information-Processing Models and Theories

The rapid development of computer technology and communication systems during the past few years has led to a reevaluation and reconceptualization of the human brain as a kind of computing machine that operates along lines similar to those of a computer. Research in neurophysiology and cognitive psychology has also contributed to these *information-processing models* of human problem solving and thinking. The models are concerned with identifying the processes or operations by which information is encoded, stored, retrieved, and utilized by the brain in performing cognitive tasks of the sort presented by intelligence tests.

Rather than conceptualizing intelligence as a complex of mental structures or factors or as developing through a series of stages with different cognitive strategies being preferred at each successive stage, information-processing theorists attempt to provide a detailed, exhaustive description of the steps used by a person in solving a problem. In addition to data obtained from traditional correlational studies of individual differences, these theorists apply the findings of laboratory investigations of learning, thinking, and problem solving to develop and confirm theoretical propositions. Employing the functionally oriented language of representations, strategies, (planning, monitoring, shifting, etc.), and processes, the goal of many information-processing theorists is to simulate human cognitive performance on a computer and describe the cognitive processes in computer-oriented language.

Computer models of thinking and problem solving view the human brain's functioning as an information-processing system having a large storage capacity. The storage contains, among other things, complex programs or strategies that can be evoked by particular stimulus inputs. In these models, intelligence is analyzed in terms of variables such as storage capacity, speed of performing basic operations, and speed of access to storage, in addition to the number, variety, and complexity of programs on file in storage. An example of this kind of theorizing is the general information-processing model, or communication system for problem solving (SIPS), based on concepts provided by information theory and Guilford's structure-of-intellect model (Guilford & Tenopyr, 1968). Unfortunately, efforts to develop a realistic, workable computer model of human intellectual functioning have not been very successful. As pointed out by Vernon (1979b), it is extremely difficult to observe and measure the various stages or processes between the input and output of an information-processing system (initial filtering, short-term rehearsal, chunking, coding, and long-term storage, retrieval, and decoding). Intelligence is involved in all of these stages, as well as in controlling strategies derived from past experience.

Two mental processes that have been the subjects of theory and research on human information processing are attention and processing speed. Research on attention has been concerned with such questions as whether more intelligent people are able to mobilize and distribute their attention better than less intelligent people. For example, can more intelligent individuals shift their attention better when presented with two tasks at the same time? Although there is still some controversy over whether attention is a motivational rather than a cognitive variable, the results of a number of studies indicate that individuals with higher intelligence are more flexible in their attentiveness and can mobilize a greater amount of attention in performing a task (Eysenck, 1987; Hunt, 1980; Hunt & Lansman, 1983; Larson and Saccuzzo, 1989).

Another variable that has been studied from an information-processing perspective is processing speed. The fundamental question here is whether the brains of more intelligent people can process information faster than those of less intelligent people. Research has found small positive correlations between response time in performing mental tasks and measures of nonverbal intelligence (Carlson, Jensen, & Widaman, 1983; Vernon, 1987). Hunt (1983, 1987) also found that speed of performing tasks that required rapid access to memory had only a modest positive relationship with scores on reasoning and general comprehension tests. From these results it would seem that processing speed plays a relatively minor role in intelligent behavior.

The PASS Model

Attentional processes have been incorporated in the PASS (planning-attention-simultaneous processing-successive processing) model for intelligence (Naglieri & Das, 1990). PASS is based on Aleksandr Luria's theory that the cognitive activity of the human brain is divided into three functional units. The *first functional unit*, which is associated with the upper brain stem and the limbic system, is concerned with vigilance or attention and the discrimination among stimuli. Although not responsible for receiving and analyzing information, this unit is critical to cognitive processing because it provides a general state of readiness and a focus of attention. The *second functional unit*, which is associated with the posterior region of the cerebral hemispheres, including the visual (occipital), auditory (temporal), and general sensory (parietal) areas, is concerned with the reception, elaboration, and storage of information by means of simultaneous and successive processing. The *third functional unit*, which is associated with the anterior region of the cerebral hemispheres, particularly the prefrontal region, is responsible for the programming, regulation, and verification of cognitive activity. This unit regulates the activities of the first functional unit so behavior will be consistent with the individual's conscious goals and motives. In summary, the first functional unit is responsible for arousal and attention, the second for reception, analysis, and storage using simultaneous and successive reasoning processes, and the third for planning, regulating, and verifying mental activity (Naglieri & Das, 1990).

A diagram of the PASS cognitive processing model is given in Figure 12–2. As shown in the diagram, the model conceptualizes the three functional units of Luria's theory as operating on the individual's knowledge base. The knowledge base consists of all the information—in both long- and short-term memory—that is available to the individual at processing time. For processing to be effective this knowledge base must be integrated with the *planning* (third functional unit), *attention* (first functional unit), and *simultaneous and successive processes* (second functional unit) as they are demanded by the particular task. The result of processing, or *output*, involves speaking, writing, or other motoric activities.

Sternberg's Componential and Triarchic Theories

Another illustration of a theory of intelligence within the information-processing camp is Sternberg's triarchic theory. The idea that "intelligence consists of a set of developed thinking and learning skills used in academic and everyday problem-solving" (Sternberg, 1982, p. 20) is not new. The importance of experi-

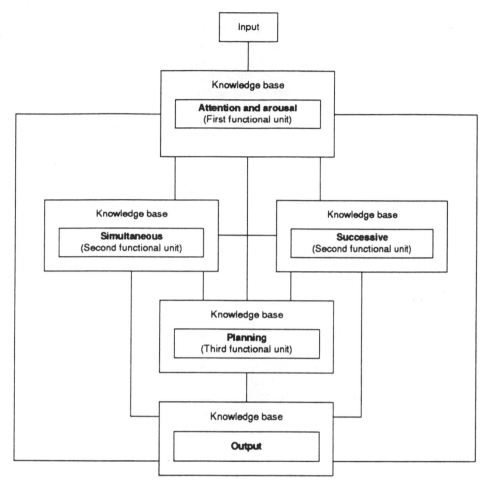

FIGURE 12-2 PASS cognitive processing model. (From Naglieri & Das, 1990, p. 315. Reprinted with permission.)

ence and learning in determining what test makers call intelligence has been emphasized by other psychologists (e.g., Wesman, 1968). The notion that test takers possess a set of cognitive processes that are involved in the intelligent behavior of solving test problems has also been developed by numerous researchers (e.g., Carroll, 1976; Hunt, 1983; Resnick, 1976). Among these skills, as listed by Sternberg (1982), are problem identification, process selection, representative selection, strategy selection, processing allocation, solution monitoring, sensitivity to feedback, translation of feedback into an action plan, and implementation of the action plan. What was novel in Sternberg's component process approach during the early 1980s was an attempt to delineate and make more precise the cognitive processes or mental components that are brought to bear in processing information, thinking abstractly, and solving problems.

According to Sternberg (1982), mental components, or cognitive processes for operating on information and solving problems, fall into five classes: metacomponents, performance components, acquisition components, retention components, and transfer components. The metacomponent processes involved in problem solving are used for executive planning and decision making. The decisions and plans made through the operation of these metacomponent processes are implemented by performance component processes, and learning of new information occurs through acquisition component processes. The retrieval of information that is stored in memory is carried out by retention components, and the carrying over of retained information from one situation to another is effected by transfer components.

Among the many components constituting intelligence in Sternberg's framework, two of the performance component processes—encoding and comparing—are critical to effective problem solving. In *encoding*, the examinee forms a mental representation of the essential elements of a problem. The encoded representations are then compared to find an answer. People who are able to encode and compare rapidly are more intelligent than those who require more time to carry out these processes.

Unlike the structural approach of factor-analytic models of intelligence, the component process approach provides a more functional analysis of the processes involved in problem solving. However, like traditional psychometric procedures, the emphasis is on diagnosis and remediation. Thus, an analysis of the component processes involved in a person's attack on specific problems results in a diagnostic profile of strengths and weaknesses in the various components. Poor strategy selection points to a metacomponent deficiency, inaccurate recall of relevant information reveals a retention component deficiency, and poor ability to generalize learned approaches to problem solving indicates a transfer component deficiency.

Sternberg revised and expanded his component process theory to include two subtheories in addition to the componential subtheory: an experiential subtheory and a contextual subtheory. In this *triarchic theory*, the componential subtheory was somewhat condensed to include metacomponents, performance components, and knowledge–acquisition components. The second part of the triarchic theory, the experiential subtheory, is concerned with the ability to formulate new ideas by combining seemingly unrelated facts or information. A high standing on this dimension indicates good ability at identifying critical information and combining seemingly unrelated facts. The third part of the theory, the contextual subtheory, is concerned with the ability to adapt to changing environmental conditions and to shape the environment in such a way that one's strengths are maximized and one's weaknesses are compensated for. A high standing on the contextual dimension indicates high practical intelligence.

In a later modification of his theory, Sternberg proposed the concept of *mental self-government*, which represents an attempt to combine the concept of intelligence with that of personality (Sternberg, 1988, 1989). The ways in which the three types of intelligence delineated by the triarchic theory—componential, experiential, and contextual—as brought to bear in solving everyday problems are characterized in this theory as *intellectual styles*. Whether or not a particular intellectual style works is said to depend on the extent to which it matches the person's intellectual ability, his or her preferred style, and the nature of the immediate problem to be solved. Like most theories of intelligence, Sternberg's triarchic theory is supported to some extent by the data (Sternberg, 1985, 1986) but it is by no means the final theoretical word on intelligence or cognition.

Gardner's Theory of Multiple Intelligences

Other theoretical approaches to intelligence have attempted to combine the results of research on individual differences with both factor-analytic and information-processing models. For example, Howard Gardner (1983) takes a *symbol systems* approach. He maintains that the distinctiveness of human cognition and information processing involves the deployment of various symbol systems, which are characteristic forms of perception, memory, and learning. Thus a person may be good at learning languages, but not at music, manipulation of the spatial environment, or in interpersonal interactions.

Elaborating on the symbol systems that humans employ, Gardner makes a case for seven forms of intelligence: linguistic, logical-mathematical, spatial, musical, bodily kinesthetic, and two forms of personal intelligence (intrapersonal and interpersonal). The first three forms on this list are measured by conventional intelligence tests, but the last four seem more like special aptitudes rather than intelligences. Bodily kinesthetic intelligence is seen more in athletes, craftsmen, dancers, and surgeons. Spatial intelligence is native to sculptors and surveyors, and musical intelligence to composers, musicians, and singers. Interpersonal intelligence is the ability to detect the moods of other people and to lead them, and intrapersonal intelligence involves knowledge of one's own feelings and understanding how to use that self-knowledge productively.

Defining intelligence as the "ability to solve problems or to create products that are valued in one or more cultural settings," Gardner cites findings from cross-cultural research to document the role of cultural values in determining the intellectual competencies developed by humans. Linguistic and logical-mathematical intelligences are most highly valued in Western culture, bodily kinesthetic intelligence is crucial in hunting cultures, and interpersonal intelligence is very important in highly ordered societies such as that of the Japanese. Spatial, bodily kinesthetic, and interpersonal intelligences have been more valued in apprenticeship systems, and linguistic and intrapersonal intelligences were most esteemed in old-fashioned religious schools.

Gardner finds support for his theory of multiple intelligences in a variety of sources, including neurological research. For example, injury to a particular area of the brain does not affect all cognitive abilities equally. Damage to the left cerebral hemisphere has a pronounced effect on linguistic intelligence but little if any effect on musical, spatial, or interpersonal intelligence. Damage to the right cerebral hemisphere affects musical, spatial, and interpersonal intelligences but leaves linguistic intelligence intact. And a patient who has become totally aphasic as a result of left-hemisphere damage, and hence can hardly speak or understand, may still be able to draw, sing, or even compose music very well. Apparently, the brain is wired differently for musical sounds and therefore analyzes them in a different way from linguistic sounds.

Gardner also draws on developmental research findings to demonstrate the independence of the seven intelligences. For example, a child's artistic ability is not related to his or her ability with language, logic, or dealing with people. The developmental basis of the theory is seen in the hypothesis that the forms of the seven intelligences change from infancy to old age. Logical-mathematical intelligence, for example, is said to decline fairly rapidly with age, whereas interpersonal intelligence shows a smaller age-related decrement.

In Gardner's (1983) view, by focusing on linguistic and logical-mathematical intelligences, American schools are wasting human potential. He feels that better educational programs should be initiated to develop the other forms of intelligence.

Like Guilford's factor theory, Gardner's theory of multiple intelligences, although not based as completely on the results of factor analysis, is a structure-of-intellect model rather than a process theory such as Sternberg's triarchic conceptualization. Gardner's theory has enjoyed wide popularity, especially among educators, but his ideas are based more on reasoning and intuition than on the results of empirical research studies. With respect to criticisms of the theory, Brody (1992) argues that the list of seven intelligences is arbitrary and that the omission of a general intelligence factor is simply wrong.

So which of the theories discussed above is the right one? Probably all of them are right to some extent, but certainly none of them is completely correct. For the present, it seems that information-processing theories offer the best chance for a logical and empirically based conception of cognitive abilities, but the situation could change with advances in neuropsychology as well as cognitive and developmental psychology. In any event, one thing is certain: other theories of intelligence will be forthcoming, and their value will be assessed in terms of how effective they are in predicting and explaining human learning and thinking.

ISSUES AND CONTROVERSIES IN INTELLIGENCE TESTING

Criticisms of intelligence testing during this century have ranged from the statistical to the political, from the stability of intelligence test scores to the educational and other social ramifications of relying on these scores in selection, placement, and counseling. In a summary of the critical literature through the 1970s, Vernon (1979a) concluded that despite the fact that many intelligence test items have been developed haphazardly and are frequently administered by poorly trained examiners, the tests measure a relatively stable component of human functioning.

Scores on intelligence tests can be affected by examiner bias, level of examinee motivation, practice or coaching, and expectancy effects. For these and other reasons, scores on the tests are not perfectly reliable: they change somewhat from testing to testing. Nevertheless, intelligence tests measure a general aptitude that goes beyond acquired information and skills, an aptitude that is not measured by achievement tests or other methods of cognitive assessment. Intelligence tests certainly do not tell psychologists, educators, parents, or other concerned persons everything they need to know about an individual in order to help him or her make informed educational and career choices. It has been shown, however, that when used in combination with other cognitive, affective, and psychomotor measures, scores on these tests contribute significantly to the prediction of behavior in a wide range of endeavors and situations. Not all would agree with this conclusion, but at least it has not been questioned to the same extent as other matters pertaining to the construction, administration, and uses of intelligence tests. Perhaps the most controversial issue of all concerns the origins of intelligence, and specifically the roles of heredity and environment in determining what intelligence tests measure.

Heredity and Environment

The question of the relative importance of heredity and environment in shaping intelligence is fundamentally concerned with the effects of child-rearing practices and more formal educational experiences, as opposed to genetic inheritance, on cognitive abilities. If it could be demonstrated that general mental ability is due primarily to genetic influences, then governmental support for education and training programs designed to develop the cognitive abilities of children would be more difficult to justify. Because of the greater diversity and complexity of environments and the wide variability of individual responses to the same environment, the effects of environment on intelligence have been harder to demonstrate than those of heredity.

Belief in the genetic determination of intelligence goes back at least as far as the time of Francis Galton in the late nineteenth century. Alfred Binet did not reject the idea that intelligence is genetically determined, but he was more interested in the possibility of modifying intellectual abilities by education, training, and environmental intervention (Eysenck, 1984). One of the staunchest early believers in the notion that intelligence is fixed by heredity was the psychologist H. H. Goddard, who advocated the reconstruction of society along IQ lines (Goddard, 1920, pp. v–vii):

> If mental level plays anything like the role it seems to, and if in each human being it is the fixed quantity that many believe it is, then it is no useless speculation that tries to see what would happen if society were organized so as to recognize and make use of the doctrine of mental levels. ... Testing intelligence is no longer an experiment or of doubted value. It is fast becoming an exact science. Greater efficiency, we are always working for. Can these new facts be used to increase our efficiency? We only await the Human Engineer who will undertake the work.

Most psychologists, child development specialists, and educational researchers would probably agree with the statement that general intelligence, or at least a predisposition to develop intellectually, is to some extent inherited (Snyderman & Rothman, 1987). The question of genetic differences in intelligence is still open, but certain genetics researchers consider intelligence to be a polygenic characteristic — one that is determined by the interaction of many minor genes rather than a single major gene.

Genetic Research Methods

The least ambiguous method of obtaining information concerning the effects of environment on mental ability is to conduct an experiment with pairs of identical twins, who have identical heredities. Some twin pairs would be separated at birth by assigning them to different experimentally contrived environments, while other twin pairs are kept together in the same environment. If greater differences in mental ability were found between twin pairs reared in different environments than between those reared in the same environment, the results would support the hypothesis that environment influences mental ability.

Because society will not permit even well-intentioned scientists to move children around like chess pieces, nonexperimental methods for determining the relative effects of heredity and environment have been employed. One approach is to compare, at various chronological ages, the IQs of identical twins who have been reared apart. In this way, heredity is effectively held constant while environment is varied, albeit in an unsystematic, uncontrolled manner. Furthermore, the IQs of individuals who have different heredities but live in similar environments, such as nonidentical siblings or unrelated children reared together, can be compared. Finally, comparisons can be made between the IQs of persons having different heredities and different environments, such as nonidentical siblings and unrelated individuals reared apart.

Despite the difficulty of locating pairs of identical twins who have been reared apart, several noteworthy investigations of this kind have been conducted (see Bouchard & McGue, 1981; Bouchard et al., 1990; Plomin, 1988, 1989). The results of these studies reveal that the correlation between the IQs of identical twins reared together is greater than that of identical twins reared apart, although both correlations are highly positive. The correlation coefficients listed in Table 12-1, which are the averages of results obtained from many different studies, demonstrate that the more similar the heredities of pairs of individuals, the more closely related are their intelligence test scores. These statistics also suggest that the effects of environment on the IQs of persons having different degrees of genetic similarity are not nearly as great as those of heredity. Findings such as these have been offered as evidence for the relatively greater importance of heredity than environment in determining intelligence.

Heritability Index

Population geneticists often express the results of studies of hereditary differences in terms of a *heritability index* (h^2), defined as the ratio of the test score

TABLE 12–1　Median Correlations between IQs
of Persons with Different Degrees of Kinship

Comparison	Median correlation
Identical twins reared together	.85
Identical twins reared apart	.67
Fraternal twins reared together	.58
Siblings reared together	.45
Siblings reared apart	.24
Half-siblings	.35
Parent and offspring (together)	.385
Parent and offspring (apart)	.22
Cousins	.145
Nonbiological siblings reared together	.29
Adoptive parent and offspring	.18

Source: T. J. Bouchard & M. McGue, 1981. Familial studies of intelligence: A review. *Science, 212*, p. 1056. Copyright 1981 by the American Association for the Advancement of Science and reprinted with
permission.

variance due to heredity to the test score variance due to both heredity and
environment. Although heritability estimates as high as .72 (Plomin, 1990) have
been reported, average estimates of h^2 for intelligence in the general population are
around .50. This means that an estimated 50 percent of the variance of IQs is
attributable to genetic factors. It should be cautioned that these numbers reveal
nothing about the relative importance of heredity and environment in determining
the intelligence of a specific individual; they apply only to populations.

Heredity–Environment Interaction

Even the strongest supporter of the genetic basis of intelligence, on the one
hand, and an extreme environmentalist, on the other, recognize that *both* heredity
and environment are important in the formation of cognitive abilities. *Environment* in this context refers not only to the psychosocial, or experiential, environment of the person, but also to the prenatal and postnatal biological environment
(nutrition, accidents, etc.). One interpretation of the research data bearing on this
matter is that heredity establishes a kind of upper limit to intelligence, a limit that is
attainable only under optimal environmental conditions (Weinberg, 1989). A corol-
lary to this proposition is that the higher the hereditarily determined upper limit
on a person's intelligence, the greater the potential effects of environment.

One can discuss heredity and environment as if they were independent influences, but the difficulty of separating their effects has been demonstrated in
research conducted by Sandra Scarr and her associates. The sample of individuals in
a study by Scarr and Weinberg (1976) consisted of 130 black and racially mixed
children who had been adopted into "advantaged" white families but whose biological parents had only average educations. The influence of an advantaged environ-

ment was seen in the fact that the adopted children scored above the overall averages for white children on tests of intelligence and achievement. But the influence of heredity was demonstrated by the finding that the biological children of the adoptive parents scored even higher on the tests than the adopted children.

The results of this study indicated that heredity and environment interact in shaping intelligence, but in discussing the findings of a later investigation Scarr emphasized the importance of the former variable. Summarizing the results obtained in comparing children adopted during the first few months of life with children reared by their natural parents, Scarr drew two conclusions: "(a) individuals differ genetically in ways that affect how much they learn from similar exposures to material, and (b) among whites in this culture there seem to be average genetic differences in IQ and test scores by social class" (Scarr & Yee, 1980, p. 20).

Cumulative Deficit

As the research of Scarr and others indicates, environment has a definite effect on measured intelligence. It might also be expected that the longer a child remains in a particular environment, the greater the effect of that environment on his or her intelligence. This expectation, as applied to intellectually impoverished environments, has been called the *cumulative deficit hypothesis*. Support for the hypothesis was obtained in a study by Jensen (1977) of 653 white children and 826 black children in a small rural town in southeastern Georgia. As predicted by the cumulative deficit hypothesis, Jensen found that the difference between the mean IQs of older and younger children in the black families increased with the number of years (from 1 to 7) separating the children. On the average, the sample of black children lost approximately 1 IQ point a year between the ages of 6 and 16, resulting in a cumulative loss of 5-10 IQ points.

Effects of Environmental Intervention in Young Children

To psychologists, two of the most important things to know about human characteristics are how amenable they are to change and how that change can be brought about (Tyler, 1965). The importance of mental stimulation in enhancing intellectual abilities was demonstrated in a number of older investigations (e.g., Goldfarb, 1955; Hunt, 1961). For example, Goldfarb (1955) found that institutionalized children who were deprived of stimulation made lower scores on intelligence tests than noninstitutionalized children. Subsequent studies (Bayley & Schaeffer, 1964; Bower, 1974; Bruner, 1975; Trevarthan, 1974) documented the importance of a close mother–child relationship to cognitive growth.

Some of the most frequently cited investigations in support of the effects of environmental intervention on IQ are those of Skeels (Skeels, 1966; Skeels & Dye, 1939). Skeels's findings, as well as those of other investigators (see Ramey & Campbell, 1984; Sprigle & Schaefer, 1985; Zigler, 1985), have often been cited in support of the impact of early environment on intellectual development. The results of these studies have been interpreted as demonstrating that environmental intervention or enrichment can raise the IQs of institutionalized or other "at-risk" children. But not all studies involving early environmental enrichment have resulted in IQ gains, and even when IQs have risen, the gains have not always persisted (Berrueta-Clement et al., 1984; Lazar & Darlington, 1982).

When pretest–posttest gains in IQ are associated with intervention programs, it is not always clear what is responsible for the change. There may be methodological flaws in the research design, statistical artifacts such as regression toward the mean, or misinterpretation of the findings. For example, Zigler et al. (1982) noted that a 10-point increase in IQ has been a common finding in evaluating preschool intervention programs such as Head Start. Rather than interpreting this result as necessarily due to real changes in intelligence, however, Zigler considered the possible influence of two other factors: familiarity with the test materials and motivation. When children are retested with the same intelligence test, there is some increase in scores due to practice or increasing familiarity with the test materials.* And continued improvement in scores from retest to posttest, as reported by Zigler et al. (1982), may be interpreted as being due to improvements in motivation as a consequence of participating in the program (in this case Head Start). Other than merely becoming more familiar with the test materials, IQ increases in an intervention program may be due to the fact that the program improves the children's test-taking skills. Just as children can learn how to learn—in other words, develop learning management or metacognitive skills—they can also learn how to take tests and extinguish their fear of them. Whatever the cause of IQ increases in intervention programs may be, it is generally acknowledged that the most effective programs are those that involve not only the children but also the parents or surrogate parents of the children.

Cognitive Training in Later Life

At the other end of the age spectrum, research conducted by Baltes, Schaie, and their coworkers (Plemons, Willis, & Baltes, 1978; Schaie & Willis, 1986; Willis, Blieszner, & Baltes, 1981; Willis, 1990) has demonstrated that people can continue to learn and improve their performance on intelligence tests in old age. Frequently, the interventions for attaining these improvements are fairly minor, often requiring merely that learners be provided with materials that they can study and practice on their own. The materials used in one intervention program (Project ADEPT), for example, required only five 1-hour sessions on the average (Baltes & Willis, 1982). The effects of such learning are not restricted to a specifically learned task but transfer to other, similar tasks as well. Unfortunately, there are methodological problems with much of the research on cognitive training. Thus, in some instances it is not clear whether the procedures actually reverse cognitive declines or simply teach new skills to the learners.

*"Ban Voided on IQ Tests for Black Pupils," *Los Angeles Times*, September 3, 1992, p. A3.

In addition to teaching specific cognitive skills or approaches to learning, pretraining in anxiety reduction may improve learning and remembering in later life (Yeasavage & Rose, 1984). Older learners must also accept the fact that certain abilities have declined with age but that by restricting the areas in which one is active, optimizing participation in a particular domain, and depending more on other skills to compensate for the loss of abilities, they can continue to perform effectively. Abilities do not decline uniformly with age, and everyone has a great deal of reserve capacity, as well as a wealth of experience and perhaps wisdom that can be utilized despite a decline in quickness and potential.

Legal Issues in Intelligence Testing

Whether intelligence tests are biased against minority groups and are thereby unfair selection measures in educational and employment contexts was the subject of lengthy legal dispute during the late 1960s and 1970s.

Legal Issues in Educational Testing

Major court cases concerned with the uses of intelligence tests in the schools were *Hobson v. Hansen* (1967), *Diana v. State Board of Education* (1970), *Guadalupe v. Tempe Elementary District* (1972), *Larry P. v. Riles* (1980), *Parents in Action on Special Education (PASE) v. Hannon* (1980), and *Georgia NAACP v. State of Georgia* (1985). In *Hobson v. Hansen* the court ruled that group tests of ability discriminate against minority children and hence cannot be used to assign students to different ability "tracks." In *Diana v. State Board of Education*, the court ruled that traditional testing procedures could not be used for the placement of Mexican-American children in educable mentally retarded (EMR) classes and that special provisions (e.g., bilingual assessment) must be used to test minority children. The court's decision in *Guadalupe v. Tempe Elementary District* was to have students tested in their primary language and to eliminate unfair portions of the test. Furthermore, it was decreed that IQ scores must be at least 2 standard deviations below the mean and that other determiners, such as measures of adaptive behavior, must be included in making decisions as to whether children should be classified as mentally retarded.

In his book *Bias in Mental Testing*, Jensen (1980) asserted that neither verbal nor nonverbal tests of intelligence are biased in any meaningful way against native-born minorities in the United States. He pointed out that tests of intelligence and other cognitive abilities have predictive validity for all ethnic groups and that the tests are not responsible for differences among these groups. As reflected in the decision in the case of *Larry P. v. Riles* (1980), Judge Robert Peckham of the federal district court of San Francisco disagreed with Jensen. After concluding that IQ tests denied the five black plaintiffs in a class action suit equal protection under the law, Judge Peckham ordered a continuation of his earlier ban on IQ testing for the placement of blacks in classes for EMR children in California schools. Thus, it was ruled that individually administered tests of intelligence are biased against blacks and that the California State Department of Education should not use these tests for educational diagnosis or placement. Contributing to this decision was the fact that a disproportionate number of black children had been assigned to EMR classes, which Judge Peckham labeled "dead-end education." Consequently, it was stipulated that the proportion of black children in EMR classes must match their proportion in the general population of school children. In 1986, Judge Peckham reissued his ruling prohibiting the use of IQ tests in the public schools of California, even when parental consent has been obtained. The court's decision in *Larry P.*, however, did not ban the use of all intelligence tests in California public schools; intelligence test scores could still be used under certain conditions.

Less than a year after the decision in *Larry P. v. Riles* was handed down, another federal judge, John F. Grady, rendered a very different decision in a similar case in Illinois. In this case, *Parents in Action on Special Education (PASE) v. Hannon* (1980), it was decreed "that the WISC, WISC-R, and Stanford-Binet tests, when used in conjunction with the statutorily mandated '[other criteria] for determining an appropriate educational program for a child' (under Public Law 94-142) ... do not discriminate against black children" (p. 883). As a result, intelligence tests continue to be administered for special class placement in Illinois public schools and in the schools of many other states. Similar to the decision in *PASE v. Hannon*, the court ruled in *Georgia NAACP v. State of Georgia* that intelligence tests do not discriminate against black children. Also contrary to the ruling in the *Larry P.* case, it was concluded in the Georgia decision that the presence of disproportionate numbers of black children in EMR classes does not constitute proof of discrimination. Finally, in 1992 Judge Peckham lifted his ban on intelligence testing in California public schools on the grounds that it was unfair to black parents who wanted the tests to be used in the class placement of their learning disabled children. This ruling effectively nullified the earlier (1986) prohibition against the use of intelligence tests in the public schools of California. As a review of these and other court cases concerned with the use of intelligence tests in the schools indicates, judicial decisions pertaining to the issue have varied from state to state and with the political climate of the times.

Although the use of intelligence tests may sometimes encourage discrimination and even contribute to a self-fulfilling prophecy in which a person becomes what he or she is labeled as being, a number of psychologists and educators maintain that there are advantages to using intelligence tests for class placement purposes. Many children who are considered by teachers as being in need of special education are found not to be so when such tests are administered. In fact, if the tests were not used, more minority children would probably be assigned to special education classes. And even those who are placed in such classes because of low test scores often profit from special education to such an extent that their IQs are raised and they become ineligible for those services. Finally, one might ask what happens to children who need special education but are not identified when intelligence tests are not used. How many children who fall farther behind every year do so because they are deprived of an appropriate education by being taught in regular classes?

Legal Issues in Employment Testing

The fairness of intelligence tests and other psychometric devices for purposes of job selection, placement, and promotion is equally as important as the use of such devices in schools and colleges. The legal issue concerning the use of intelligence tests for employment selection purposes stems from Title VII of the Civil Rights Act of 1964. During that same year, the question of whether a test that was being used for employee selection purposes was racially discriminatory was debated in the case of *Myart v. Motorola* (1964). Coming in the wake of this case, the Civil Rights Act specifically prohibited discrimination in employment on the basis of race, national origin, or religion.

A Supreme Court ruling on Title VII occurred in the case of *Griggs et al. v. Duke Power Company*. The case challenged Duke Power Company's requirement that in order to gain advancement in the organization, an employee had to make a specified minimum score on a specially constructed test of mental ability. The difficulty of that test, which none of the black or white applicants for advancement was able to pass, is indicated by the following problem (Kaplan & Saccuzzo, 1993, p. 616):

> In printing an article of 24,000 words, a printer decides to use two sizes of type. With the larger type, a printed page contains 900 words. With the smaller type, a page contains 1200 words. The article is allotted 21 full pages in the magazine. How many pages must be in small type?*

The majority opinion of the Supreme Court in this case was that "if an employment practice which operates to exclude Negroes cannot be shown to be significantly related to job performance, the practice is prohibited" (*Griggs v. Duke Power Company*, p. 60). But Chief Justice Burger also stated (p. 11):

> Nothing in the [Civil Rights] Act precludes the use of testing or measuring procedures; obviously they are useful. What Congress has forbidden is giving these devices and mechanisms controlling force unless they are demonstrably a reasonable measure of job performance. Congress has not commanded that the less qualified be preferred over the better qualified simply because of minority origins. Far from disparaging job qualifications as such, Congress has made such qualifications the controlling factor, so that race, religion, nationality, and sex become irrelevant.

The intent of the decision in *Griggs v. Duke Power Company* and subsequent court cases (*United States v. Georgia Power, Albemarle Paper Co. v. Moody, Washington v. Davis*, etc.) was to require employees to demonstrate that the skills measured by their selection tests and other hiring procedures were job related. The decisions prompted a reexamination, and in some situations a discontinuance, of certain tests that were being used in employee selection and promotion.

*The answer can be obtained by constructing and solving two simultaneous linear equations ($900L + 1,200S = 24,000$ and $L + S = 21$). Substituting $L = 21 - S$ into the first equation and solving for L yields 4; than solving the second equation with $L = 4$ yields $S = 17$.

Convinced that Title VII of the Civil Rights Act was not being properly enforced and that discrimination in employment against minorities and women was continuing, a revision of the Civil Rights Act—the Equal Employment Opportunity Act—was passed in 1972. The Equal Employment Opportunity Commission (EEOC) mandated by this second act subsequently prepared a set of "Uniform Guidelines on Employee Selection Procedures" to be followed by employers, labor organizations, and employment agencies. These procedures were designed to ensure if an employment selection device adversely affects members of any racial, ethnic, or sex group at a higher rate than another group, it must be validated according to the guidelines laid down by the act and that alternative employment procedures having less adverse effects are unavailable (EEOC, 1973). The guidelines further stated that a test or other valid predictor of performance cannot be judged to be a valid predictor of performance if it does not account for at least half of the reliably measurable skills and knowledge pertaining to the job.

Further clarification of the EEOC guidelines led to the concept of *adverse impact*, which follows the *four-fifths rule*. According to this rule, a condition of adverse impact exists if an applicant group has a selection rate that is less than four-fifths (80 percent) of that of other groups. The question of adverse impact occurred in the case of *Cormier v. PPG Industries*, in which an updated and revised edition of the Wonderlic Personnel Test was found to be valid and fair.

The EEOC revised its guidelines for employee selection once again in 1978, but the newer guidelines are not as strict as the original version in requiring employers to conduct differential validity studies. Like their predecessors, the revised guidelines are designed to require employers to justify the use of tests and other selection procedures that exclude disproportionate numbers of minority group members and women. Three validation methods on which employers may rely are described in the revised guidelines: criterion-related validity, content validity, and construct validity. Unfortunately, the guidelines are not clear on how large the validity coefficients must be. Furthermore, although the revised guidelines state that the use of tests is legitimate when the scores are related to job performance, they do not specify what is meant by "job-related criteria."

SUMMARY

Intelligence is a multifaceted concept that has been defined in various ways, ranging from the strictly operational definition of "whatever is measured by an intelligence test" to more abstract, complex conceptions. The question of the meaning of intelligence is intertwined with the broader problem of determining the psychophysiological basis of cognition and thought.

Factor analysis, a set of mathematical procedures for determining the dimensionality of an aggregate of measurements, has been applied to the analysis of intelligence test scores for many years. Among the theories or models of cognitive abilities stemming from the results of factor analyses are Spearman's two-factor theory (consisting of a general factor plus several specific factors for each test),

Thurstone's multifactor theory of seven primary mental abilities, Guilford's structure-of-intellect model, and Vernon's hierarchical model (a general factor at the first level, verbal-educational and practical-mechanical-spatial factors at a second level, and a number of minor group factors at a third level).

Cattell's theory of two kinds of intelligence, fluid and crystallized, is also based on the results of factor analysis and is related to Hebb's Intelligence A and Intelligence B. The relative roles of heredity and environment in differentiating factors of intellect are not clear, though Cattell's fluid intelligence is considered to be more genetically than environmentally determined and his crystallized ability is the result of fluid ability acting on the environment. Ferguson proposed that different mental factors result from overlearning and differential positive transfer in certain areas of experience.

An influential developmental theory of intelligence is Piaget's conception that cognition develops from the actions of assimilation and accommodation on the external world. By interacting with the environment, the growing child develops schemata, or mental structures, to serve as explanatory maps and guides to behavior. In the development of cognition, children normally mature intellectually through a series of progressive stages: sensorimotor, preoperational, concrete operational, and formal operational. Piaget believed that the growth of intelligence ceases at around age 15, but a number of researchers have questioned this conclusion. They maintain that intelligence continues to develop throughout adulthood and is characterized by dialectical or postformal thinking.

Information-processing models of problem solving and thinking are concerned with identifying the cognitive processes or operations by which the brain deals with stimulus input in learning and thinking. Research on attention and processing speed has received particular emphasis from an information-processing perspective.

The PASS (planning, attention, simultaneous processing, successive processing) model of intelligence is based on Luria's theory that cognitive activity in the brain can be described in terms of three functional units. The validity of PASS, and a test battery developed from the theory, is still under scrutiny.

In his component process approach to intelligence, Sternberg conceptualized the brain as an information-processing (and problem-solving) organ. He initially hypothesized five classes of component processes by which the brain operates on information and solves problems. Among the various components in these five classes, encoding and comparing are especially critical for effective problem solving. In an extension of his component process theory, Sternberg proposed a triarchic theory that includes three subtheories: a componential subtheory, an experiential subtheory, and a contextual subtheory. In the notion of mental self-government, Sternberg has tried to combine the concepts of intelligence and personality; he describes how different intellectual styles lead to different methods of solving everyday problems.

Gardner's proposal that there are many different kinds of intelligence is reminiscent of factor theories, but it actually owes more of a debt to Piaget and information-processing models of intellect. Gardner makes a case for seven forms of intelligence: linguistic, logical-mathematical, spatial, musical, bodily-kinesthetic, interpersonal, and intrapersonal. He argues that Western culture has overemphasized the first two forms, but in many societies and circumstances the other five forms of intelligence are more important and valued.

Among the various issues and controversies surrounding intelligence testing for a good part of this century, the most debated has been that of the relative contributions of heredity and environment in shaping mental abilities. Evidence from dozens of investigations underscores the relationship of heredity to general mental ability while not denying that both heredity and environment are important and interactive in their effects on intelligent behavior. This issue has been particularly controversial because of its association with the question of racial differences in intelligence.

Although the findings of numerous investigations have led to the conclusion that in an assortatively mating population, the heritability coefficient (proportion of variance in the intelligence test scores of the general population accounted for by heredity) is as high as .72, it is recognized that the biological and psychosocial environments also have important influences on intelligence. Studies of the effects of environmental enrichment, as in Head Start and other intervention programs, have found significant differences in mean IQs in intervention groups when compared with controls. Schaie and his coworkers have also reported some success in improving the intelligence test scores, memories, and learning abilities of older adults by means of special training programs.

A number of court cases have been concerned with the use of intelligence testing in educational and employment contexts. The practices of assigning children to special classes for the mentally retarded and of selecting employees on the basis of biased tests have been of particular concern. Decisions made in these cases are not entirely consistent with one another and are often based more on political factors than on scientific data and sound judgment. It is reasonable to conclude, however, that the judicial decisions have resulted in greater caution in using intelligence tests to categorize children as mentally retarded and in the section and placement of minority groups and women in employment situations.

QUESTIONS AND ACTIVITIES

1. Define each of the following terms used in this chapter:

accommodation	dialectical thought
adaptation	encoding
adverse impact	equilibration
assimilation	fluid intelligence
concrete operations	formal operations
crystallized intelligence	four-fifths rule
cumulative deficit hypothesis	heritability index

information-processing models   primary mental abilities
intellectual styles   schemata
mental self-government   sensorimotor period
operation   symbol systems
polygenic characteristic   transfer hypothesis of ability differentiation
postformal thought   triarchic theory
preoperational period

2. Prepare an essay paper or oral report on one of the following topics: racial and national differences in intelligence; improving intelligence through special education and training; the social ethics of intelligence testing; the future of intelligence testing.
3. Ask your instructor to divide the class at random into an even number of small groups of equal size, and then randomly assign half the groups to a "mostly hereditary" condition (Condition H) and half the groups to a "mostly environmental" condition (Condition E). Finally, pit each of the Condition H groups against one of the Condition E groups (this should also be done randomly), and have the students collect as much information as they can in preparation for a defense of their assigned position on the issue of whether intelligence is determined mostly by heredity or mostly by environment. Regardless of how he or she really feels, the student should take the position indicated by the group to which he or she is assigned. Each group should debate its counterpart in the opposite condition for approximately 30 minutes, after which the audience or other students should declare one group the winner. What group dynamic factors were associated with the win? Did taking a position opposite to your initial (pre-assignment) attitude toward the issue change your attitude in any way? The following simple bipolar scale, scored from 1 to 7 and administered as a pretest and again as a posttest may provide crude quantitative information on any change in attitude.

Directions: Check the place on the line that corresponds most closely to your opinion concerning the relative influences of heredity and environment in determining a person's intelligence.

A Person's Intelligence Is Determined:

Entirely by Heredity ———————————————————————— Entirely by Environment

4. The statistics in Table 12–1 indicate that the median correlation between the IQs of fraternal twins reared together is .58 and the median correlation between the IQs of identical twins reared together is .85. A suggested formula for computing the heritability coefficient (h^2) is

$$h^2 = (r_i - r_f)/(1 - r_f^2),$$

where r_i is the correlation between the IQs of identical twins and r_f the correlation between the IQs of fraternal twins. Using this formula with the data given in Table 12–1, compute and interpret the obtained value of h^2.
5. A criticism of factor analysis is that it encouraged the nineteenth-century viewpoint that the mind is composed of a set of mental faculties or separate abilities, as opposed to being an integrated, dynamic whole. Comment on this criticism.
6. Compare the theories of Robert Sternberg and Howard Gardner in terms of their: (1) reasonableness, (2) consistency with research findings, (3) practical utility, and (4) social responsibility. Defend your choice.

SUGGESTED READINGS

Herrnstein, R. J., & Murray, C. (1994). *The bell curve*. New York: The Free Press.

Horn, J. (1989). Models of intelligence. In R. L. Linn (Ed.), *Intelligence: Measurement, theory, and public policy* (pp. 29-73). Urbana, IL: University of Illinois Press.

Kornhaber, M., Krechevsky, M., & Gardner, H. (1990). Engaging intelligence. *Educational Psychologist, 25*, 177-199.

Larson, G. E., & Saccuzzo, D. P. (1989). Cognitive correlates of general intelligence: Toward a process theory of g. *Intelligence, 13*, 5-32.

Lerner, B. (1989). Intelligence and law. In R. L. Linn (Ed.), *Intelligence: Measurement, theory, and public policy* (pp. 172-192). Urbana, IL: University of Illinois Press.

Lohman, D. F. (1989). Human intelligence: An introduction to advances in theory and research. *Review of Educational Research, 59*, 333-373.

Thompson, L. A. (1993). Genetic contributions to intellective development in infancy and childhood. In P. A. Vernon (Ed.), *Biological approaches to the study of human intelligence* (pp. 95-138). Norwood, NJ: Ablex.

Weinberg, R. A. (1989). Intelligence and IQ: Landmark issues and great debates. *American Psychologist, 44*, 98-104.

Looking Forward

Like specialists in other disciplines, psychologists are often dissatisfied with the rate of progress in their profession. Occasionally they may speculate about how things might have been if Alfred Binet or other measurement pioneers had not come along and unwittingly set the course for psychological and educational assessment in the twentieth century (see Sternberg & Davidson, 1990). Looking forward instead of backward, they may also "dip into the future" and try their hand at predicting how the situation may have changed in 20, 50, or even a 100 years.

Realizing that short-term predictions are usually more accurate than long-term ones, futurists in the psychological assessment profession tend to be rather conservative in this regard: they prefer to make forecasts that are no more than 20 or so years in advance. This is undoubtedly wise because scientific progress is at least as much a function of the (nearly unpredictable) political and social climate of the times as it is of advances in science and technology. It is unlikely that even Nostradamus could have predicted how influential the intelligence test devised by Binet and Simon over 90 years ago would come to be in educational, clinical, and industrial/organizational contexts during the twentieth century.

Projections of what intelligence testing will be like in the next century were hazarded some years ago by Thorndike (1975), by several writers in the September 1979 issue of the journal *Intelligence*, and by Glaser (1981). More recently, Vernon (1990), Brody (1992), and Matarazzo (1992) have also tried their hands at prog-

335

nostication. These seers agree that among the continuing developments and changes related to the measurement of intelligence and other cognitive abilities during the next 20 years will be technological and methodological advances, progress in discovering the physiological and biochemical bases of intelligence, more sophisticated theories and research on learning and thinking, and clarification of legal and social issues pertaining to psychological assessment.

TECHNOLOGY AND METHODOLOGY

Some of the most dramatic changes in the construction, administration, scoring, and interpretation of psychological tests and techniques that have taken place during the past few years are the results of the expanding uses of digital computers and associated technology. Computers assist in test development by computing item-response statistics, norms, derived scores, and reliability and validity coefficients. Test item pools for interactive or adaptive (sequential, tailored, or routing) tests can also be assembled by computer through applications of item-response techniques and methodologies such as latent trait theory, item characteristic curve theory, and the Rasch model. Exploratory and confirmatory factor analyses, path analysis, structural equation modeling, and other advanced statistical procedures that contribute to an understanding of the meaning of test scores and the results of research employing tests can all be carried out efficiently and effectively on high-speed computers. Programming computers to administer and score objective tests is a fairly straightforward process, but computer-based administration and scoring of open-ended or interlocking questions is more difficult. Computer-based administration of many of the subtests on the Wechsler series has been possible for many years, but administration and scoring of tests on which response scoring requires making a subjective judgment of accuracy are not as easy to program. However, fifth-generation computers with their parallel circuitry and voice-activation should make the process easier and eventually the cumbersome typewriter keyboard will no longer be the primary input device.

The greater flexibility of computers in the future may result in the replacement of multiple-choice questions by free-response test items. Such machines will be capable of generating open-ended questions and, by being programmed to recognize a set of key words and phrases, of evaluating the typed or spoken answers. The expert systems of artificial intelligence with their natural language-processing capabilities will facilitate the analysis of complex verbal responses. Computers having this capacity will be able to recognize many different answers and score them intelligently. By using various input and output devices such as audio- and video-cassettes, light-, heat-, and touch-sensitive screens, joysticks, dials, and psychophysical transducers, it will be possible to administer a variety of assessment devices and speedily interpret the responses of both normal and handicapped examinees on a wide range of psychological variables. In the schools of the future, computers will also administer interactive diagnostic tests, keep a record of each examinee's performance, and track errors to identify patterns and problems. Feedback will be immediate and on-screen, confirming right answers, correcting wrong answers, and suggesting instructional materials that can correct errors and improve performance.

Even more difficult than administering and scoring tests is interpretation of the results by a computer. Dozens of computer-based test interpretation (CBTI) programs designed to score and interpret the results of tests of cognitive abilities, neuropsychological functions, and personality characteristics are now in use. Many companies offer CBTI and reporting services, as well as hardware and software for computer-based testing.

Despite the advantages of fast and accurate processing of information, adaptability to individual differences in abilities, and prompt scoring and interpretation of results, the use of computers in psychological assessment has encountered some serious problems. Among these problems are (1) the cost of the system, (2) the inadequacy of the software, (3) the inappropriateness of computer-based administration with certain groups of people (young children, the mentally retarded, severely mentally ill individuals, etc.), and (4) the maintenance of confidentiality of results. There is also a tendency to endow computer-generated test reports with greater status than they deserve, to view the narrative reports as "written in stone" even when their validity has not been adequately demonstrated. Believing that interpretations generated by computers are necessarily valid is an illustration not only of the "power of the machine" fallacy but also of the *Barnum effect*—accepting as true descriptions and interpretations phrased in generalities, truisms, and other statements that sound specific to a given person but may actually apply to anyone. Future psychologists must be careful of becoming too enamored of the technology of testing. Human experts will still be needed to monitor the computers and fine-tune the machine-generated interpretations of test results.

PHYSIOLOGICAL SUBSTRATES OF INTELLIGENCE

The mind is a function of an anatomical structure called the brain, and the mind cannot work when the body is dead or nonexistent. This is the credo of monism, the philosophical position that the mind and body are one. It is a position held by most biologists and probably by most psychologists as well. To the monistic psychologist, intelligence is an operation of the mind, and like the mind it has biological roots. From those biological roots—the substrates of perception, memory, planning, and problem solving—the mind develops from experience. Therefore, exploring the physiological and biochemical correlates of intelligent thought and behavior should improve our knowledge of the structure and functioning of intelligence and perhaps provide us with better methods of measuring it.

Research on the physiological bases of cognitive abilities is not new. Although not labeled as such, the *neural efficiency model*—that intelligent behavior is a reflection of the speed and efficiency with which the neurophysiological processes underlying the performance of such behavior occur—goes back to the time of Francis Galton. Efforts to measure those processes by means of reaction time, sensory discrimination, and other tests based on nineteenth-century associationistic theory were, however, not very successful, and in any case they were superseded by the Binet-Simon Intelligence Scale and similar tests consisting of school-type tasks.

Due to a combination of factors, among which are advances in brain-imaging techniques (MRI and PET scans) and legal battles concerning the bias of paper-and-pencil tests of intelligence, in recent years there has been an upsurge of scientific interest in physiological variables related to intelligence. Among the variables that have been examined are average evoked potentials, cerebral glucose metabolism, nerve conduction velocity, regional cerebral blood flow, serum uric acid level, serum calcium level, and vital capacity. Of these, the most direct support for the neural efficiency model of intelligence has been obtained in the PET-scan research of Roger Haier and his associates on cerebral glucose metabolic rates (CGMRs) (Haier, 1991; Haier, Siegel, MacLachlan et al., 1992; Haier, Siegel, Tang et al., 1992).* CGMRs may not only provide a physiological correlate of intelligence but also indicate what regions of the brain are active during different types of tasks, thereby having a potential diagnostic function for learning-disabled individuals (Vernon, 1990). Other physical correlates of intelligence include general stature, myopia, and even oldtimers like choice reaction time, sensory discrimination, and inspection items (see Vernon, 1990; Matarazzo, 1992).

Because these physiological indices are significantly correlated with scores on conventional intelligence tests, it is possible that the former might even prove to be better than the latter as measures of mental ability. In this regard, Vernon (1990) has argued that it would be possible to devise a nonverbal intelligence test based on a weighted combination of physiological and physical measures that would be less subject to many of the psychometric and political–social problems that have plagued paper-and-pencil tests. Matarazzo (1992) also foresees additional technological advances in the near future in neurophysiological, neurochemical, and neuromolecular indicators of intelligence. Be that as it may, it is very unlikely that these measures will replace traditional tests of intelligence in the foreseeable future. Physiological and biochemical indicants of cognitive abilities will undoubtedly continue to be intriguing and hopefully informative to researchers, but the apparatus and procedures for generating these indicants is probably too cumbersome and complex to take the place of the efficiently administered and scored instruments that are now available. For this reason it is expected that physiological measures will complement rather than supplant traditional paper-and-pencil performance tests of intelligence. New measures of cognitive abilities based on neurophysiological and biochemical indicators will also be devised, and they could radically change the way in which we view human intelligence.

---

*The CGMR, an index of the rate at which glucose is metabolized in the brain, is determined by measuring the accumulation of an intravenously injected positron-emitting radioactive substance (2-deoxyglucose) in a particular area of the brain.

TEST DEVELOPMENT AND THEORIES

The use of intelligence tests by various countries for purposes of educational selection and placement has declined noticeably in the past two or three decades. Among the reasons for the decline are extensive public criticism of the validity and usefulness of intelligence tests, discontinuance of ability grouping and the track system in the schools, and the increased popularity of standardized achievement tests. Although intelligence tests usually have a broader *bandwidth* than achievement tests, in certain circumstances the latter have greater *fidelity;** that is, they are better predictors of subsequent achievement than tests of intelligence or special aptitudes (Vernon, 1985).

Little is to be gained in terms of increases in reliability and validity by attempting to improve the structure of existing paper-and-pencil tests, although greater efforts to standardize the tests more often and on more representative samples may improve their usefulness. Be that as it may, intelligence tests will undoubtedly continue to serve many of the same functions in the twenty-first century as they have in the twentieth. In educational settings, these functions include the diagnosis of mental retardation and learning disabilities, as well as admission to postsecondary schools and training programs. With respect to special children, if the sizes of mainstreamed classes could be made small enough (ten or twelve students), then special class sections for the mentally retarded, the learning disabled, or the gifted might be unnecessary. However, the cost of very small, heterogeneous classes in which each child would be treated as special is probably prohibitive. In addition to their uses in education, intelligence tests will continue to be administered for purposes of personnel selection in the military and business–industrial organizations and psychodiagnosis in clinical contexts.

Diagnostic Testing

A critically needed improvement in the assessment of cognitive abilities is for assessment instruments to be constructed that are more diagnostic in nature. Consequently, it is likely that less emphasis will be placed on static, single score tests that measure performance on one variable at a particular point in time, and more emphasis will be placed on dynamic, multivariable test batteries designed to appraise and predict performance on multiple variables and in a variety of situations. Furthermore, these diagnostic tests will probably be of the criterion-referenced (absolute assessment) rather than the norm-referenced (relative assessment) type.

Examples of the above are seen in the development of diagnostic tests that measure not only what students know or can do at a certain time, but that also assist

---

Bandwidth refers to the range of criteria predictable by a test. Tests having broad bandwidths can predict a wider range of criteria than tests have narrower bandwidths. *Fidelity*, which is similar to validity, refers to the accuracy with which a test predicts a particular criterion. Whereas the bandwidth of a test is broad or narrow, its fidelity is high or low.

them in mastering new fields of knowledge. These diagnostic tests are individualized and adaptive, including a brief challenge examination, probes to identify the component skills of an area in which the student has problems, construction of a profile of the student's strengths and weaknesses, and presentation of remedial instruction. Tests of this type are aimed primarily at helping people learn and succeed rather than simply yielding scores for institutional decision making. By guiding instruction and self-development on a continuing basis rather than merely comparing the performances of different examinees, they serve individuals more than institutions.

Cognitive Theories

Traditional intelligence tests were constructed on an empirical rather than a theoretical basis. Consisting of a representative sample of questions about what an individual presumably should know from experience, as well as the application of that knowledge to simple problems, the tests were able to predict future achievement. There seemed to be little connection, however, between test development and theories of the sort considered in Chapter 12. In fact, psychologists are still unable to agree on an acceptable definition of the concept—intelligence—they have presumably been measuring all these years.

Concerning the relationship between tests and theories of intelligence, it has been pointed out that:

> In terms of scientific validity, the tests do seem to be inadequate. They bear little or no relationship to the theories we have examined and thus lack an adequate theoretical foundation or superstructure. Nevertheless, the items on intelligence tests have proven their practical value, such as the prediction of school achievement. Thus, while not conforming to any theoretical notions per se, the tests do relate to the types of performances that almost everyone agrees reflect the operations of intelligence, that is, school achievement. It is in terms of these practical effects that tests are designated "successful." (Maloney & Ward, 1976, pp. 224–225)

Although they will not necessarily replace the empirically based Wechsler series or the Stanford-Binet, during the early years of the next century we shall see an increasing number of theory-based instruments of the sort represented by the Kaufman Assessment Battery for Children, the Kaufman Adolescent and Adult Intelligence Test, and the Cognitive Assessment System. Newer tests based on information-processing and neurophysiological models will be constructed with the recognition that human beings are active, planning, strategy-learning and strategy-playing organisms that learn and shift strategies and plans in attempting to adapt to and cope with the environment. Traditional intelligence tests are static, making a measurement at one point in time and under one set of conditions. Future tests, in contrast, will be more dynamic, involving multiple assessments across time and abilities. Unlike traditional tests that focus more on the product and the final outcome, newer tests will focus on the process of thinking, on the steps involved in reaching the final outcome. The availability of the newer tests in multiple languages and the provision of separate norms for different demographic groups will also make these tests more useful with a wide range of individuals.

OTHER ISSUES AND DEVELOPMENTS

An issue of enduring concern in intelligence testing is the use of the term *IQ*. This term seems particularly inappropriate with tests such as those in the Wechsler series, in which the scores are not quotients based on ratios. IQ should be abolished and replaced with labels more specific to the tasks making up intelligence tests (vocabulary, general information, analogical reasoning, quantitative skills, and syllogistic reasoning, for example). A person's score would be calculated on each of these separate tasks rather than as a combined index of ability. Even if it is retained, IQ should not be used as the primary basis on which a decision concerning a child's educational future is made. Observations of the child's behavior, both within and outside the school environment, should also be taken into account in planning instructional options for the child (Weinberg, 1989).

Not only IQ but even the term *intelligence* may ultimately fall by the wayside. However, the latter term seems so deeply ingrained in the English language that it is not likely to disappear for some time.

Group Intelligence Tests

Another question pertaining to the persistence of the old is that of the value of group intelligence testing. Though group tests may continue to be useful as controlling or matching variables in psychological research, certain authorities would not be disappointed to see group intelligence tests that were designed for elementary school children fall into disuse (Resnick, 1979; Vernon, 1979). According to Vernon (1979a), group intelligence tests are so often administered by untrained persons, and therefore frequently misscored and misinterpreted, that they are responsible for misclassifying large numbers of children. Even individual tests such as the Stanford-Binet-IV, the WISC-III, and the WPSSI-Revised, although they are more reliable than most group tests, may provide an overstatic picture of the mental abilities of developing children.

Measures of Practical Intelligence

Evaluating cognitive abilities in the context of how a person relates to society is a growing concern. Adapting to the world is largely dependent on the ability to manage oneself and other people (Sternberg, 1984). For this reason it is likely that better tests will be developed to measure practical social competence. In addition to research on the ability to deal successfully with other people, better studies of how intelligence functions in everyday problem situations, as in managing one's own affairs, are needed. Because traditional intelligence tests, with their emphasis on speed of responding, often encourage impulsiveness rather than the reflective-ness required to adapt successfully, better measures of reflective thinking and problem solving, rather than rapidity of solution, are also required.

Legal Issues

Many psychologists believe that the social questioning and criticism indicated by litigation concerning psychological tests during the last two or three decades have served a useful purpose. To these psychologists, criticism of the status quo in psychological testing has stimulated research, theorizing, and improvements in test design and usage. Other psychologists have concluded, however, that the resolu-tion of issues concerning the fairness of intelligence tests or the soundness of special education policies should not take place in courts of law (Elliott, 1987; Reschly, Kicklighter & McKee, 1988; Sattler, 1988). They point out that scientific questions concerning the validity of intelligence tests are far from identical to the public policy questions concerning these instruments that are aired in the courts. Whether of value or not, the court decision in the case of *Larry P. v. Riles*, and similar outcomes when tests have been put on trial, dampened the enthusiasm for intelligence testing in many educational and occupational contexts.

Still, psychological testing and psychological testers learned something from their encounters with the courts during the 1960s and 1970s: they became more legally sophisticated and more sensitive to ethical issues pertaining to psychological assessment. For these reasons juridical exchanges of the sort that occurred several years ago with respect to the uses and misuses of intelligence tests are unlikely to be repeated with the same passion and confusion.

Research on Individual Differences

Research on the causes and correlates of individual differences in cognitive abilities, and particularly the effects of specific experiences on those differences, will continue and improve in the first part of the twenty-first century. With respect to the heredity–environment controversy, it will not be laid to rest. However, more emphasis will be placed on tests as measures of abilities that develop through experience rather than being inherited from one's forebears.

Intelligence tests (by whatever name) and other measures of cognitive abilities will continue to be employed in studies of human development and the effects of treatment or other interventions on behavior. If nothing else, the Head Start pro-gram should have taught us that there are methodological, social, and political pitfalls in well-meaning efforts to improve the cognitive abilities of children. With respect to physical treatments, biochemical research may succeed in discovering or synthesizing a substance that produces reliable increases in the intellectual func-tioning of mentally retarded individuals and those with impaired memories. But the discovery of an "intelligence pill" that is guaranteed to elevate the abilities of normal children and adults does not appear to be on the horizon.

QUESTIONS AND ACTIVITIES

1. Define each of the following terms used in this chapter:

bandwidth	diagnostic testing
brain-imaging techniques	fidelity
cerebral glucose metabolic rate (CGMR)	neural efficiency model
cognitive theories	practical intelligence

2. Retake the inventory in exercise 8 of the "Questions and Activities" in Chapter 1. Compare your answers to the inventory now with those that you gave at the beginning of the course.

3. After studying this textbook and consulting other sources as well as your own personal experiences and feelings, what predictions would you make concerning the future of intelligence testing and psychological testing in general?

4. Look up *intelligence*, *IQ*, *cognition*, and related terms in the *Readers Guide*, the *New York Times Index*, and other popular reference sources. What conclusions concerning the current status of intelligence testing can you draw from the titles of the articles cited in these sources?

5. How have digital computers in general, and microcomputers in particular, changed the nature of psychological testing and assessment during the past two decades? What further changes in testing are likely to result from continuing developments in technology and in the methodology of psychological assessment?

SUGGESTED READINGS

Brody, N. (1992). *Epilogue: The future of intelligence*. In *Intelligence* (2nd ed., pp. 349–356). San Diego, CA: Academic Press.

Jones, L. V., & Appelbaum, M. I. (1989). Psychometric methods. *Annual Review of Psychology*, *40*, 23–44.

Matarazzo, J. D. (1992). Psychological testing and assessment in the 21st century. *American Psychologist*, *47*, 1007–1018.

Matarazzo, J. D. (1990). Psychological assessment versus psychological testing: Validation from Binet to the school, clinic, and courtroom. *American Psychologist*, *45*, 999–1017.

Vernon, P. A. (1990). The use of biological measures to estimate behavioral intelligence. *Educational Psychologist*, *25*(3 & 4), 293–304.

Glossary

Ability test   A test that measures the extent to which a person is capable of performing a certain task or occupation.

Academic aptitude   The ability to learn school-type tasks; also called *scholastic aptitude*. Many intelligence tests are basically measures of academic aptitude.

Accommodation   In Piaget's theory of cognitive development, the modification of schemata as the result of experience.

Achievement   The degree of success or accomplishment in a given area or endeavor; a score on an achievement test.

Adaptive behavior   The extent to which a person is able to interact effectively and appropriately with the environment.

Adaptive testing   Testing procedure, usually computer-based, in which the specific items presented vary with the estimated ability or other specified characteristics of the examinee and his or her responses to previous items.

Age equivalent score   See *Age norm*.

Age norm   Median score on an aptitude or achievement test made by children of a given chronological age.

Age scale   A test, such as the Stanford-Binet, on which items are grouped by age level. Test items on the Stanford-Binet that two-thirds to three-fourths of a representative group of children of a given age passed were grouped at that age level.

Alternate-forms reliability   An index of reliability determined by correlating the scores of individuals on one form of a test with their scores on another form.

Alzheimer's disease   Degenerative neurological disorder of middle to old age characterized in particular by loss of memory.

Analogies test   A test that requires the examinee to determine a relationship, similarity, or difference between two or more things. Example: "Roses are to red as violets are to (a) blue, (b) green, (c) orange, (d) yellow."

Anchor test   A common set of items on each of several forms of a test used to equate scores on the several forms.

Apgar rating   A rating score, determined at 1 minute and at 5 minutes after birth, for evaluating neonates. A rating of 9 to 2 is assigned to measurements of heart rate, respiration, muscle tone, reflexes, and color. A sum of ratings between 7 and 10 is normal for newborns.

Aphasia   Disorder characterized by disability in using words (expressive aphasia) or in understanding the meanings of words (receptive aphasia).

Aptitude   Capability of learning to perform a particular task or skill. Traditionally, aptitude was thought to depend more on inborn potential than on actual practice.

Aptitude test   A measure of the ability to profit from additional training or experience, that is, become proficient in a skill or other ability.

Arithmetic mean   A measure of the average or central tendency of a group of scores. The arithmetic mean is computed by dividing the sum of the scores by the number of scores.

Assessment   Appraising the presence or magnitude of one or more personal characteristics. Assessing human behavior and mental processes includes such procedures as observations, interviews, rating scales, checklists, inventories, projectives techniques, and tests.

Assimilation   In Piaget's theory of cognitive development, the process of fitting new experiences into preexisting mental structures.

Assortative mating   Nonrandom mating between individuals possessing similar characteristics.

Audiometer   An instrument for measuring auditory acuity that presents pure tones of varying intensities and frequencies in the normal range of hearing. Hearing is tested in each ear, the results being plotted as an audiogram, a graph of the examinee's auditory acuity at each frequency and for each ear.

Average   Measure of central tendency of a group of scores; the most representative score.

Bandwidth   Cronbach's term for the range of criteria predictable from a test; the greater the number of criteria that a test can predict, the broader its bandwidth. See *Fidelity*.

Basal age   The highest year level on an intelligence test, such as older editions of the Stanford-Binet, at and below which an examinee passes all subtests.

Base rate   Proportion of individuals having a specified condition who are identified or selected without the use of new selection procedures.

Battery of tests   A group of aptitude or achievement tests measuring different things but standardized on the same population, thus permitting comparisons of a person's performance in different areas.

Bimodal distribution   A frequency distribution having two modes (maximum points). See *Frequency distribution*; *Mode*.

Ceiling age   The minimum age or year level on a test, such as the Stanford-Binet, at which an examinee fails all subtests. See *Basal age*.

Central tendency   Average, or central, score in a group of scores; the most representative score (e.g., arithmetic mean, median, mode).

Classification   The use of test scores to assign a person to one category rather than another.

Cluster sampling   Sampling procedure in which the target population is divided into sections or clusters, and the number of units selected at random from a given cluster is proportional to the total number of units in the cluster.

Coaching Short-term instruction designed to improve the test scores of prospective test takers. The instructional activities include practice on various types of items and test-taking strategies.

Coefficient alpha An internal consistency reliability coefficient, appropriate for tests composed of dichotomous or multipoint items; the expected correlation of one test with a parallel form containing the same number of items.

Coefficient of equivalence A reliability coefficient (correlation) obtained by administering two different forms of a test to the same group of examinees. See *Test–retest reliability*.

Coefficient of internal consistency Reliability coefficient based on estimates of the internal consistency of a test (for example, split-half coefficient and alpha coefficient).

Coefficient of stability A reliability coefficient (correlation) obtained by administering a test to the same group of examinees on two different occasions. See *Test–retest reliability*.

Coefficient of stability and equivalence A reliability coefficient obtained by administering two forms of a test to a group of examinees on two different occasions.

Cognition Having to do with the processes of intellect; remembering, thinking, problem solving, and the like.

Cognitive assessment Measurement of intellective processes, such as perception, memory, thinking, judgment, and reasoning. See *Affective assessment*.

Cognitive style Strategy or approach to perceiving, remembering, and thinking that a person seems to prefer in attempting to understand and cope with the world (e.g., field independence–dependence, reflectivity–impulsivity, or internal–external locus of control).

Communality Proportion of variance in a measured variable accounted for by variance that the variable has in common with other variables.

Component processes Sternberg's theory that cognitive processes or mental components fall into five classes: metacomponents, performance components, acquisition components, retention components, and transfer components.

Componential intelligence Sternberg's theory concerning the mental mechanisms that are responsible for intelligent behavior.

Composite score The direct or weighted sum of the scores on two or more tests or sections of a test.

Concrete operations stage In Piaget's theory of cognitive development, the stage (7–11 years of age) during which a child develops organized systems of operations by the process of social interaction, with a corresponding reduction in self-centeredness.

Concordance reliability Several raters or scorers make numerical judgments of a characteristic or behavior shown by a large sample of people. Then a *coefficient of concordance*, an index of agreement among the judgments of the scorers or raters, is computed.

Concurrent validity The extent to which scores obtained by a group of people on a particular psychometric instrument are related to their simultaneously determined scores on another measure (criterion) of the same characteristic that the instrument is supposed to measure.

Confidence interval A range of values within which one can be fairly certain (usually 95 or 99 percent confident) that an examinee's true score (or difference between scores) on a test or score on a criterion variable falls. See *Standard error of estimate*; *Standard error of measurement*.

Construct validity The extent to which scores on a psychometric instrument designed to measure a certain characteristic are related to measures of behavior in situations in which the characteristic is supposed to be an important determinant of behavior.

Content validity The extent to which a group of people who are experts in the material with which a test deals agree that the test or other psychometric instrument measures what it was designed to measure.

Convergent thinking Using facts and reason to produce a single correct answer.

Correction for guessing A formula, applied to raw test scores, to correct for the effects of random guessing by examinees. A popular correction-for-guessing formula requires subtracting a portion of the number of items the examinee answers incorrectly from the number he or she answers correctly.

Correlation Degree of relationship or association between two variables, such as a test and a criterion measure.

Correlation coefficient A numerical index of the degree of relationship between two variables. Correlation coefficients usually range from -1.00 (perfect negative relationship), through .00 (total absence of a relationship), to $+1.00$ (perfect positive relationship). Two common types of correlation coefficients are the product-moment coefficient and the point-biserial coefficient.

Creativity test A test that assesses original, novel, or divergent thinking.

Criterion A standard or variable with which scores on a psychometric instrument are compared or against which they are evaluated. The validity of a test or other psychometric procedure used in selecting or classifying people is determined by its ability to predict a specified criterion of behavior in the situation for which people are being selected or classified.

Criterion-referenced test A test that has been designed with very restricted content specifications to serve a limited range of highly specific purposes. The aim of the test is to determine where the examinee stands with respect to specified objectives. See *Norm-referenced test*.

Criterion-related validity The extent to which a test or other assessment instrument measures what it was designed to measure, as indicated by the correlation of test scores with some criterion measure of behavior.

Cross-validation Readministering an assessment instrument that has been found to be a valid predictor of a criterion for one group of persons to a second group of persons to determine whether the instrument is also valid for that group. There is almost always some shrinkage of the validity coefficient on cross-validation, since chance factors spuriously inflate the validity coefficient obtained with the first group of examinees.

Crystallized intelligence   R. B. Cattell's term for mental ability (knowledge, skills) acquired through experience and education.

Cultural deprivation   Concept that experiences or upbringing in one culture may retard one's intellectual functioning in another culture, as reflected by low scores on intelligence or other ability tests designed in the second cultural context.

Culture-fair test   A test composed of materials to which all sociocultural groups have presumably been exposed. Thus, the test should not penalize any socio-cultural group because of lack of relevant experience. Attempts to develop culture-fair tests have not been very successful.

Demographic variable   Age, sex, ethnicity, socioeconomic status, educational level, and other characteristics used to classify individuals as members of a particular group or population.

Derived score   A score obtained by performing some mathematical operation on a raw score, such as multiplying the raw score by a constant and/or adding a constant to the score. See *Standard scores*; *T scores*; *z scores*.

Developmental quotient (DQ)   An index, roughly equivalent to a mental age, for summarizing an infant's behavior as assessed by the Gesell Developmental Sched-ules.

Deviation IQ   Intelligence quotient (IQ) score obtained by converting raw scores on an intelligence test to a score distribution having a mean of 100 and a fixed standard deviation, such as 16 for the Stanford-Binet or 15 for the Wechsler tests.

Divergent thinking   Creative thinking that involves more than one solution to a problem.

Down's syndrome (mongolism)   A disorder characterized by a flattened skull; thickened skin on eyelids; short, stubby fingers and toes; coarse, silky hair; short stature; and moderately low intelligence. An extra chromosome is found in the twenty-first position in karyotypes of Down's syndrome cases.

Dynamic assessment   A test–teach–test approach to assessment in which the examinee is tested (pretested), then given practice on the test materials, and finally tested again (posttested). The change in performance level from pretest to posttest is a measure of learning potential. See *Zone of proximal development*.

Dyscalculia   Disorder in which one has difficulty performing simple arithmetic operations or number manipulations.

Dyslexia   Disorder in which one experiences difficulty reading silently or aloud (e.g., reading backwards).

Educable mentally retarded (EMR)   Children characterized by a mild degree of mental retardation (IQ = 51–69). Such children are capable of obtaining a third- to sixth-grade education and can learn to read, write, and perform elementary arithmetic operations.

Equilibration   In Piaget's theory of cognitive development, the process by which a child comes to know and understand the environment by interacting with it. Equilibration includes the processes of assimilation and accommodation.

Equipercentile method   Traditional method of converting the score units of one test to the score units of a parallel test. The scores on each test are converted to percentile ranks, and a table of equivalent scores is produced by equating the score at the pth percentile on the first test to the score at the pth percentile on the second test.

Equivalent forms   See *Parallel forms*.

Estimated learning potential (ELP)   An estimate of a child's ability to learn, derived from measures obtained in the System of Multicultural Pluralistic Assessment (SOMPA). The ELP takes into account not only the child's IQ on the Wechsler Intelligence Scale for Children—Revised or the Wechsler Preschool and Primary Scale of Intelligence but also family size, family structure, socioeconomic status, and degree of urban acculturation.

Evaluation   To judge the merit or value of an examinee's behavior from a composite of test scores, observations, and reports.

Exceptional child   A child who deviates significantly from the average in mental, physical, or emotional characteristics.

Expectancy effect   Effect of teacher expectations on the IQ scores of pupils; more generally, the effect of a person's expectations on another person's behavior.

Expectancy table   A table giving the frequency or percentage of examinees in a certain category (score interval) on a predictor variable (test) who would be expected to fall in a certain category (score interval) on the criterion variable.

Experiential intelligence   According to Sternberg, the ability to cope effectively with novel tasks.

Face validity   The extent to which the appearance or content of the materials (items and the like) on a test or other psychometric instrument is such that the instrument appears to be a good measure of what it is supposed to measure.

Factor   A dimension, trait, or characteristic of personality revealed by factor analyzing the matrix of correlations computed from the scores of a large number of people in several different tests or items.

Factor analysis   A mathematical procedure for analyzing a matrix of correlations between measurements to determine what factors (constructs) are sufficient to explain the correlations.

Factor loadings   In factor analysis, the resulting correlations (weights) between tests (or other variables) and the extracted factors.

Factor rotation   A mathematical procedure applied to a factor matrix for the purpose of simplifying the matrix for interpretation purposes by increasing the number of high and low factor loadings in the matrix. Factor rotation may be either orthogonal, in which case the resulting factors are at right angles to each other, or oblique, in which the resulting factor axes form acute or obtuse angles with each other.

Fairness   On an aptitude test, the extent to which scores are unbiased, that is, equally predictive of the criterion performance of different groups.

False negative   Selection error or diagnostic decision error in which an assessment procedure incorrectly predicts a maladaptive outcome (e.g., low achievement, poor performance, or psychopathology).

False positive   Selection error or diagnostic decision error in which an assessment procedure incorrectly predicts an adaptive outcome (e.g., high achievement, good performance, or absence of psychopathology).

Fidelity   The narrowness of the bandwidth of a test or other measuring instrument. A test with high fidelity is a good predictor of a fairly narrow range of criteria. See *Bandwidth*.

Fluid intelligence   R. B Cattell's term for inherent, genetically determined mental ability, as seen in problem-solving or novel responses.

Formal operations   The final stage (11–15 years) in Piaget's cognitive development sequence, in which the child can now use logic and verbal reasoning and perform higher-level, more abstract mental operations.

Four-fifths rule   Selection rule that any procedure resulting in a selection rate for any race, gender, or ethnic group that is less than four-fifths (80%) of that of the group having the highest rate has an adverse impact and is consequently illegal.

Frequency distribution   A table of score intervals and the number of cases (scores) falling within each interval.

g factor   The single general factor of intelligence postulated by Spearman to account for the high correlations between tests of intelligence.

General cognitive index (GCI)   Standard score on the McCarthy Scales of Children's Abilities having a mean of 100 and a standard deviation of 16.

Generalizability theory   A theory of test scores and the associated statistical formulation that conceptualizes a test score as a sample from a universe of scores. Analysis of variance procedures are used to determine the generalizability from score to universe value, as a function of examinees, test items, and situational contexts. A generalizability coefficient may be computed as a measure of the degree of generalizability from sample to population.

Grade norm   The average of the scores on a test made by a group of children at a given grade level.

Group test   A test administered simultaneously to a group of examinees by one examiner. See *Individual test*.

Heritability index (h^2)   Ratio of the test score variance attributable to heredity to the variance attributable to both heredity and environment.

Hierarchical model   Vernon's branching model of intelligence, which consists of a general factor at the highest level, two major group factors—verbal-educational and practical-mechanical-spatial—at the second level, and a number of minor group factors at a third level.

In-basket technique   A procedure for evaluating supervisors or executives in which the candidate is required to indicate what action should be taken on a series of memos and other materials of the kind typically found in a supervisor's or executive's in-basket.

Individual test   A test administered to one examinee at a time.

Informed consent   A formal agreement made by an individual, or the individual's guardian or legal representative, with an agency or another person to permit use of the individual's name and/or personal information (test scores and the like) for a specified purpose.

Intelligence   Many definitions of this term have been offered, such as "the ability to judge well, understand well, and reason well" (Binet) and "the capacity for abstract thinking" (Terman). In general, what is measured by intelligence tests is the ability to succeed in school-type tasks.

Intelligence quotient (IQ)   A derived score, used originally in scoring the Stanford-Binet Intelligence Scale. A ratio IQ is computed by dividing the examinee's mental age (MA), as determined from a score on an intelligence test, by his or her chronological age (CA), and multiplying the resulting quotient by 100. A deviation IQ is computed by multiplying the z score corresponding to a raw score on an intelligence test by the standard deviation of the deviation IQs and adding 100 to the product.

Intelligence test   A psychological test designed to measure an individual's aptitude for scholastic work or other kinds of activities involving verbal ability and problem solving.

Internal consistency   The extent to which all items on a test measure the same variable or construct. The reliability of a test computed by the Spearman-Brown, Kuder-Richardson, or Cronbach-alpha formulas is a measure of the test's internal consistency.

Interrater (interscorer) reliability   Two scorers assign a numerical rating or score to a sample of people. Then the correlation between the two sets of numbers is computed.

Interval scale   A measurement scale on which equality of numerical differences implies equality of differences in the attribute or characteristic being measured. The scale of temperature (Celsius, Fahrenheit) and, presumably, standard score scales (z, T), are examples of interval scales.

Intraclass reliability   Several raters or scorers make a numerical judgment of a characteristic or behavior of a person. Then an *intraclass coefficient*, an index of agreement among the numbers assigned by the various judges, among the scores is computed.

IQ constancy   The assumption, made on the Wechsler tests, that the IQ remains constant with aging even though raw intellectual ability may shift and decline.

Item   One of the units, questions, or tasks of which a psychometric instrument is composed.

Item analysis   A general term for procedures designed to assess the utility or validity of a set of test items.

Item characteristic curve   A graph, used in item analysis, that depicts the proportion of examinees passing a specified item against the total test score.

Item difficulty index   An index of the easiness or difficulty of an item for a group of examinees. A convenient measure of the difficulty of an item is the percentage (p) of examinees who select the correct answer.

Item discrimination index   A measure of how effectively an item discriminates between examinees who score high on the test as a whole (or on some other criterion variable) and those who score low.

Item-response (characteristic) curve   Graph showing the proportion of examinees who get a test item right, plotted against an internal (total test score) or external criterion of performance.

Kuder-Richardson formulas   Formulas used to compute a measure of internal consistency reliability from a single administration of a test having 0–1 scoring.

Leaderless group discussion (LGD)   Six or so individuals (e.g., candidates for an executive position) are observed while discussing an assigned problem to determine their effectiveness in working with the group and reaching a solution.

Learning disability   Difficulty in learning to read, write, spell, or perform arithmetic or other academic skills by a person whose score on an intelligence test (IQ) is average or above.

Linear regression analysis   Procedure for determining the algebraic equation of the best-fitting line for predicting scores on a dependent variable from one or more independent variables.

Local norms   Percentile ranks, standard scores, or other norms corresponding to the raw test scores of a relatively small, local group of examinees.

Measurement   Procedures for determining (or indexing) the amount or quantity of some construct or entity; assignment of numbers to objects or events.

Median   Score point in a distribution of scores below and above which 50 percent of the scores fall.

Mental age (MA)   An examinee's derived score on an intelligence test such as the Stanford-Binet. An examinee's mental age corresponds to the chronological age of a representative sample of children of the same chronological age whose average score on the test was equal to the examinee's score. See *Intelligence quotient*.

Mental age grade placement   An index of the grade level at which a person is functioning mentally.

Mentally gifted   A person who is significantly above average in intellectual functioning, variously defined as an IQ of 130 or 140 and above.

Mentally retarded   A person who is significantly below average in intellectual functioning, indicated by low IQ scores (70 or 75 or lower) and poor adaptability to the environment.

Mode   The most frequently occurring score in a group of scores.

Multilevel test   A test designed to be appropriate for several age levels; a separate test is constructed for each level.

Multiple-choice item   A test item consisting of a stem (statement, question, phrase, or the like) and several response options (usually three to five), only one of which is correct.

Multiple-correlation coefficient (R)   A measure of the overall degree of relationship, varying between -1.00 and $+1.00$, of several variables with a single criterion variable. For example, the multiple correlation of a group of scholastic aptitude tests with school grades is typically around .60 to .70, a moderate degree of correlation.

Multiple-regression analysis   Statistical method for analyzing the contributions of two or more independent variables in predicting a dependent variable.

National norms   Percentile ranks, standard scores, or other norms based on a national sample. See *Local norms*; *Norms*.

Neuropsychological assessment   Measurement of cognitive, perceptual, and motor performance to determine the locus, extent, and effects of neurological damage.

Nominal scale   The lowest type of measurement, in which numbers are used merely as descriptors or names of things, rather than designating order or amount.

Nonverbal test   A test that does not necessitate the use of spoken or written words but requires the examinee to construct, manipulate, or respond to test materials in other nonverbal ways.

Norm group   Sample of people on whom a test is standardized.

Normal distribution   A smooth, bell-shaped frequency distribution of scores, symmetrical about the mean and described by an exact mathematical function. The test scores of a large group of examinees are frequently distributed in an approximately normal manner.

Normalized scores   Scores obtained by transforming raw scores in such a way that the transformed scores are normally distributed with a mean of 0 and a standard deviation of 1 (or some linear function of these numbers).

Norm group   Sample of people on whom a test is standardized.

Norm-referenced test   A test whose scores are interpreted with respect to norms obtained from a (it is hoped, representative) sample of examinees. See *Criterion-referenced test*.

Norms   A list of scores and the corresponding percentile ranks, standard scores, or other transformed scores of a group of examinees on whom a test has been standardized.

Objective test   A test scored by comparing the examinee's responses to a list of correct answers (a key) prepared beforehand, in contrast to a subjectively scored test. Examples of objective test items are multiple-choice and true-false questions.

Oblique rotation   In a factor analysis, a rotation in which the factor axes are allowed to form acute or obtuse angles with each other. Consequently, the factors are correlated.

Odd-even reliability   The correlation between total scores on the odd-numbered and total score on the even-numbered items of a test, corrected by the Spearman-Brown reliability formula. See *Spearman-Brown formula*.

Omnibus test   A test consisting of a variety of items designed to measure different aspects of mental functioning. The Otis-Lennon School Ability Test and the Henmon-Nelson Tests of Mental Ability are omnibus tests. See *Spiral omnibus test*.

Operation   In J. P. Guilford's structure-of-intellect model, one of five possible types of mental processes (cognitive, memory, divergent thinking, convergent thinking, evaluation). In Piaget's theory of cognitive development, any mental action that is reversible (can be returned to its starting point) and integrated with other reversible mental actions.

Ordinal scale   Type of measurement scale on which the numbers refer merely to the ranks of objects or events arranged in order of merit (e.g., numbers referring to order of finishing in a contest).

Orthogonal rotation In factor analysis, a rotation that maintains the independence of factors, that is, the angles between factors are kept at 90 degrees and hence the factors are uncorrelated.

Out-of-level testing Administering a test designed primarily for one age or grade level to examinees below or above that level.

Parallel forms Two tests that are equivalent in the sense that they contain the same kinds of items of equal difficulty and are highly correlated. The scores made by examinees on one form of the test are very close to those made by them on the other form.

Parallel forms reliability An index of reliability determined by correlating the scores of individuals on parallel forms of a test.

Percentile The pth percentile is the test score at or below which p percent of the scores fall.

Percentile band A range of percentile ranks within which there is a specified probability that an examinee's true score on a test will fall.

Percentile norms A list of raw scores and the corresponding percentages of the test standardization group whose scores fall below the given percentile.

Percentile rank The percentage of scores falling below a given score in a frequency distribution or group of scores; the percentage corresponding to the given score.

Performance test A test on which the examinee is required to manipulate various physical objects; performance tests are contrasted with paper-and-pencil tests. Examples are the Performance Scale of the Wechsler Intelligence Scale and the Arthur Point Scale of Performance.

Pluralistic model In the System of Multicultural Pluralistic Assessment (SOMPA), a combination made up of the Student Assessment Materials and the Parent Interview. A child's score on the various measures are interpreted by comparing them with the scores of other children having a similar sociocultural background.

Point-biserial coefficient Correlation coefficient computed between a dichotomous variable and a continuous variable; derived from the product-moment correlation coefficient.

Point scale A test on which points (0, 1, or 2, for example) are assigned for each item, depending on the accuracy and completeness of the answer. All items with similar content are grouped together on such a scale.

Power test A test with ample time limits so all examinees have time to attempt all items. Many of the items are difficult, and they are often arranged in order of difficulty from easiest to hardest.

Predictive validity Extent to which scores on a test are predictive of performance on some criterion measure assessed at a later time; usually expressed as a correlation between the test (predictor variable) and the criterion variable.

Preoperational period In Piaget's theory of cognitive development, the egocentric period of development (3–7 years) when the child acquires language and other symbolic representations.

Quartile A score in a frequency distribution below which either 25 percent (1st quartile), 50 percent (2nd quartile), 75 percent (3rd quartile), or 100 percent (4th quartile) of the total number of scores fall.

r   A symbol for the Pearson product-moment correlation coefficient.

Random sample   A sample of observations (e.g., test scores) drawn from a population in such a way that every member of the target population has an equal chance of being selected in the sample.

Range   A crude measure of the spread or variability of a group of scores computed by subtracting the lowest score from the highest score.

Rapport   A warm, friendly relationship between examiner and examinee.

Rasch model   One-parameter (item difficulty) model for scaling test items for purposes of item analysis and test standardization. The model is based on the assumption that indexes of guessing and item discrimination are negligible parameters. As with other latent trait models, the Rasch model relates examinees' performances on test items (percentage passing) to their estimated standings on a hypothetical latent ability trait or continuum.

Ratio IQ   An intelligence quotient obtained by dividing an examinee's mental age score on an intelligence test (such as the older Stanford-Binet) by his or her chronological age and multiplying the quotient by 100. See *Deviation IQ*.

Ratio scale   A scale of measurement, having a true zero, on which equal numerical ratios imply equal ratios of the attribute being measured. Psychological variables are typically not measured on ratio scales, but height, weight, energy, and many other physical variables are.

Raw score   An examinee's unconverted score on a test, computed as the number of items answered correctly or the number of correct answers minus a certain portion of the incorrect answers.

Readiness test   A test that measures the extent to which a person possesses the skills and knowledge necessary to learn a complex subject.

Regression equation   A linear equation for forecasting criterion scores from scores on one or more predictor variables; a procedure often used in selection programs or actuarial prediction and diagnosis.

Regression toward the mean   Tendency for test scores or other psychometric measures to be closer to the mean on retesting; the more extreme is the original score, the closer it will be to the mean on retesting.

Reliability   The extent to which a psychological assessment device measures anything consistently. A reliable instrument is relatively free from errors of measurement, so the scores obtained on the instrument are close in numerical value to the true scores of examinees.

Reliability coefficient   A numerical index, between .00 and 1.00, of the reliability of an assessment instrument. Methods for determining reliability include test–retest, parallel-forms, and internal consistency.

Representative sample   A group of individuals whose characteristics are similar to those of the population of individuals for whom a test is intended.

Scatter diagram   A cluster of points plotted from a set of X-Y values, in which X is the independent variable and Y the dependent variable.

Schema   In Piaget's theory of cognitive development, a mental structure (grasping, sucking, shaking, and so on) that is modified (accommodated) as a result of experience.

Scholastic aptitude test   Any test that predicts the ability of a person to learn the kinds of information and skills taught in school. The abilities measured by these tests (e.g., the Scholastic Aptitude Test) are similar to those measured by general intelligence tests.

Scoring formula   A formula used to compute raw scores on a test. Common scoring formulas are Score = Number Right and Score = Number Right − Number Wrong/$(k − 1)$, where k is the number of answer options per item.

Screening   A general term for any selection process, usually not very precise, by which some applicants are accepted and other applicants are rejected.

Secure test   A test administered under conditions of tight security to make certain that only persons who are supposed to take the test actually take it, and that copies of test materials are not removed from the examination room(s) by examinees.

Selection   The use of tests and other devices to select those applicants for an occupation or educational program who are most likely to succeed in that situation. Applicants who fall at or above the cutoff score on the test are selected (accepted); those who fall below cutoff are rejected.

Selection ratio   The proportion of applicants who are selected for a job or training (educational) program.

Semi-interquartile range (Q)   A measure of the variability of a group of ordinal-scale scores, computed as half the difference between the first and third quartiles.

Sensorimotor stage   The first stage in Piaget's theory of cognitive development (0–2 years), during which the child learns to exercise simple reflexes and to coordinate various perceptions.

Sequential processing   Mental process in which a series of items is processed sequentially, in serial order. An example of a sequential task is attempting to recall a series of numbers. See *Simultaneous processing*.

Sequential testing   Testing procedure in which an examinee's answers to previous items determine which items will be presented next; also referred to as *adaptive* or *tailored testing*.

Simultaneous processing   Mental process in which several bits or pieces of information are synthesized or integrated simultaneously. See *Sequential processing*.

Skewness   Degree of asymmetry in a frequency distribution. In a positively skewed distribution, there are more scores to the left of the mode (low scores), as in a test that is too difficult for the examinees. In a negatively skewed distribution, there are more scores to the right of the mode (high scores), as in a test that is too easy for the examinees.

Snellen chart   A chart containing letters of various sizes, designed to measure visual acuity at a distance.

Spearman-Brown formula   A formula for estimating what the reliability of a test would be if it were increased in length by a specified amount by adding more items of the same general type. See *Split-half coefficient*.

Special children   Children having physical, psychological, cognitive, or social problems that make the fulfillment of their needs and potentials more difficult than for average children.

Specificity   The proportion of the total variance of a test that is due to factors specific to the test itself.

Specific learning disability   See *Learning disability*.

Speeded test   A test consisting of a large number of fairly easy items but having a short time limit so that almost no one completes the test in the allotted time. Many tests of clerical, mechanical, and psychomotor ability are speeded.

Spiral omnibus test   A test consisting of a variety of items arranged in order of ascending difficulty. Items of a given type or content appear throughout the test, intermingled with other types of items of similar difficulty, in a spiral of increasing difficulty.

Split-half coefficient   An estimate of reliability determined by applying the Spearman-Brown formula for $m = 2$ to the correlation between two halves of the same test, such as the odd-numbered items and the even-numbered items.

Standard deviation   The square root of the variance; used as a measure of the dispersion or spread of a group of scores.

Standard error of estimate   The standard deviation of obtained criterion scores around the predicted criterion score; used to estimate a range of actual scores on a criterion variable for an individual whose score on the predictor variable is equal to a specified value.

Standard error of measurement   An estimate of the standard deviation of the normal distribution of test scores that an examinee would theoretically obtain by taking a test an infinite number of times. If an examinee's obtained test score is X, then the chances are two out of three that he or she is one of a group of people whose true scores on the test fall within one standard error of measurement of X.

Standard scores   A group of scores, such as z scores, T scores, or stanine scores, having a desired mean and standard deviation. Standard scores are computed by transforming raw scores to z scores, multiplying the z scores by the desired standard deviation, and then adding the desired mean to the product.

Standardization   Administering a carefully constructed test to a large, representative sample of people under standard conditions for the purpose of determining norms.

Standardization sample   The subset of a target population on which a test is standardized.

Standardized test   A test that has been carefully constructed by professionals and administered with standard directions and under standard conditions to a representative sample of people for the purpose of obtaining norms.

Stanine   A standard score scale consisting of the scores 1 through 9, having a mean of 5 and a standard deviation of approximately 2.

Statistic   A number used to describe some characteristic of a sample of test scores, such as the arithmetic mean or standard deviation.

Stratified random sampling   A sampling procedure in which the population is divided into strata (e.g., men and women; blacks and whites, lower class, middle class, upper class), and samples are selected at random from the strata; sample sizes are proportional to strata sizes.

Subtest   A portion or subgroup of items on a test (e.g., a group of items measuring the same function or items at the same age level or difficulty level).

***T* scores**   Converted, normalized standard scores having a mean of 50 and a standard deviation of 10. Z scores are also standard scores with a mean of 50 and a standard deviation of 10, but in contrast to T scores they are not normalized.

Target population   The population of interest in standardizing a test or other assessment instrument; the norm group (sample) must be representative of the target population if valid interpretations of (norm-referenced) scores are to be made.

Taylor-Russell tables   Tables for evaluating the validity of a test as a function of the information contributed by the test beyond the information contributed by chance.

Test   Any device used to evaluate the behavior or performance of a person. Psychological tests are of many kinds—cognitive, affective, and psychomotor.

Test anxiety   Anxiety in a testing situation.

Test–retest reliability   A method of assessing the reliability of a test by administering it to the same group of examinees on two different occasions and computing the correlations between their scores on the two occasions.

Trainable mentally retarded (TMR)   Children in the moderately retarded range of IQs (approximately 36–50), who usually cannot learn to read and write but can perform unskilled tasks under supervision.

Transfer hypothesis (of ability differentiation)   Ferguson's hypothesis that the different abilities isolated by factor analysis are the results of overlearning and differential positive transfer in certain areas of learning.

True score   The hypothetical score that is a measure of the examinee's true knowledge of the test material. In test theory, an examinee's true score on a test is the mean of the distribution of scores that would result if the examinee took the test an infinite number of times.

Validity   The extent to which an assessment instrument measures what it was designed to measure. Validity can be assessed in several ways: by analysis of the instrument's content (*content validity*), by relating scores on the test to a criterion (*predictive* and *concurrent validity*), and by a more thorough study of the extent to which the test is a measure of a certain psychological construct (*construct validity*).

Validity generalization   The application of validity evidence to situations other than those in which the evidence was obtained.

Variability   The degree of spread or deviation of a group of scores around their average value.

Variable   In contrast to a constant, any quantity that can assume more than one state or numerical value.

Variance   A measure of variability of test scores, computed as the sum of the squares of the deviations of raw scores from the arithmetic mean, divided by one less than the number of scores; the square of the standard deviation.

Verbal test   A test with verbal directions requiring oral or written word and/or number answers.

z **score**   Any one of a group of derived scores varying from $-\infty$ to $+\infty$, computed from the formula $z = $ (raw score $-$ mean)/standard deviation, for each raw score. In a normal distribution, over 99 percent of the cases lie between $z = -3.00$ and $z = +3.00$.

Zone of proxmial (potential) development   Vygotsky's term for the difference (distance) between a child's actual developmental level—his or her completed development as assessed by a standardized test—and his or her potential development—the degree of competence he or she can attain with assistance.

Appendix A

Standardized American Individual Intelligence Tests

Arthur Adaptation of the Leiter International Performance Scale, by G. Arthur; © 1952; ages 3–12 years; Western Psychological Services and Stoelting.

Arthur Point Scale of Performance Tests: Form I, by G. Arthur; © 1925–1943; ages 4 years to adulthood; Stoelting.

Bayley Scales of Infant Development—Second Edition, by N. Bayley; © 1993; ages 3–30 months; The Psychological Corporation.

Blind Learning Aptitude Test, by T. E. Newland; © 1971; blind, ages 6–20 years; U.S. Department of Education & University of Illinois Press.

Brazelton Neonatal Assessment Scale, by T. B. Brazelton; © 1973, 1984; 3 days–4 weeks; J. B. Lippincott.

Cattell Infant Intelligence Scale, by P. Cattell; © 1940–1960; ages 3–30 months; The Psychological Corporation.

Cognitive Diagnostic Battery, by S. R. Kay; ages 2 and older; PAR.

Columbia Mental Maturity Scale, Third Edition, by B. B. Burgemeister, L. H. Blum, & I. Lorge; © 1954–1972; ages 3½–9 years, 11 months; The Psychological Corporation.

Detroit Tests of Learning Aptitude, Third Edition (DTLA-3), by D. D. Hammill; © 1993; ages 6–17 years; PAR; pro.ed; Jastak.

Detroit Tests of Learning Aptitude—Primary (DTLA-P:2), by D. D. Hammill & B. R. Bryant; ages 3–6 years; PAR; pro.ed.

Detroit Tests of Learning Aptitude—Adult (DTLA-A), by D. D. Hammill & B. R. Bryant; ages 16–79 years; pro.ed; Jastak.

Differential Ability Scales, by C. D. Elliott; © 1990; ages 2.6–17.11 years; The Psychological Corporation.

Escala de Inteligencia Wechsler para Adultos, by D. Wechsler; adapted and translated by R. F. Green & J. H. Martinez; © 1964, 1968; ages 16 years and over; The Psychological Corporation.

Escala de Inteligencia Wechsler para Niños, by D. Wechsler; © 74, 1982; ages 5–15 years; The Psychological Corporation.

Full-Range Picture Vocabulary Test, by R. B. Ammons & H. S. Ammons; © 1948; ages 2 years and over; Psychological Test Specialists.

Goodenough-Harris Drawing Test, by F. L. Goodenough & D. B. Harris; © 1963; ages 3–15; Harcourt Brace Jovanovich.

Haptic Intelligence Scale for the Blind, by H. C. Shurrager & P. S. Shurrager; © 1964; adults; Psychology Research.

Hiskey-Nebraska Test of Learning Aptitude, by M. S. Hiskey; 1966; ages 3–18 years; Union College Press.

Kahn Intelligence Test: 1975 Revision, by T. C. Kahn; © 1975; ages 1 years and over; Psychological Test Specialists.

Kaufman Adolescent & Adult Intelligence Test, by A. S. & N. L. Kaufman; © 1993; ages 11–85+; American Guidance Service.

Kaufman Assessment Battery for Children, by A. S. & N. L. Kaufman; © 1983; ages 2½–12½ years; American Guidance Service.

Kaufman Brief Intelligence Test, by A. S. & N. L. Kaufman; © 1990; ages 4–90; American Guidance Service.

Leiter Adult Intelligence Scale, by R. G. Leiter; © 1949–1964; adults; Stoelting.

Leiter International Performance Scale, by R. G. Leiter; © 1929–1952; ages 2 years and over; PAR; Stoelting.

McCarthy Scales of Children's Abilities, by D. McCarthy; © 1970–1972; ages 2½–8½ years; The Psychological Corporation.

Matrix Analogies Test—Expanded Form, by J. A. Naglieri; © 1985; ages 5–17 years; The Psychological Corporation.

Matrix Analogies Test—Short Form, by J. A. Naglieri; © 1985; ages 5–17 years; The Psychological Corporation.

Nonverbal Test of Cognitive Skills, by G. O. Johnson & H. F. Boyd; © 1981; ages 6–13; Charles E. Merrill.

Peabody Picture Vocabulary Test—Revised, by L. M. Dunn; © 1959–1981; ages 2½ to adulthood; American Guidance Service.

Perkins-Binet Tests of Intelligence for the Blind, by C. J. Davis; © 1980; blind and partially sighted; ages 3½–18 years; Perkins School for the Blind.

Pictorial Test of Intelligence, by J. L. French; © 1964; ages 3–8 years; Houghton Mifflin.

Proverbs Test, by D. P. Gorham; © 1954–1956; grades 5 and over; Psychological Test Specialists.

Quick Screening Scale of Mental Development, by K. M. Banham; © 1963; ages 6 months–10 years; Psychometric Affiliates.

Quick Test, by R. B. Ammons & C. H. Ammons; © 1958–1962; ages 2 years–adult; Psychological Test Specialists.

Ring and Peg Tests of Behavior Development; 1975 Edition, by K. M. Banham; © 1975; ages birth–6 years; Psychometric Affiliates.

Smith-Johnson Nonverbal Performance Scale, by A. J. Smith & R. E. Johnson; © 1977; ages 2–4 years; Western Psychological Services.

Stanford-Binet Intelligence Scale. Fourth Edition, by R. L. Thorndike, E. Hagen, & J. Sattler; © 1985; 2 years through adult; Houghton Mifflin.

Visual-Verbal Test: A Measure of Conceptual Thinking, by M. J. Feldman & J. Draskow; © 1959; adults; Western Psychological Services.

Wechsler Adult Intelligence Scale—Revised, by D. Wechsler; © 1981; ages 16 years and over; The Psychological Corporation.

Wechsler Intelligence Scale for Children—Third Edition, by D. Wechsler; 1991; ages 6–16.11 years; The Psychological Corporation.

Wechsler Preschool and Primary Scale of Intelligence—Revised, by D. Wechsler; © 1980; ages 3–7½ years; The Psychological Corporation.

Woodcock-Johnson Psycho Educational Battery, Part One: Tests of Cognitive Ability, by R. H. Bruinicks et al.; © 1985; 3 years–adult; DLM Teaching Resources; CPPC.

Appendix B

American Suppliers of Intelligence Tests and Related Materials

Addison-Wesley Testing Service, 2725 Sand Hill Road, Menlo Park, CA 94025.

American Association on Mental Deficiency, 5201 Connecticut Avenue, N.W., Washington, DC 20015.

American College Testing Program (ACT), P.O. Box 168, Iowa City, IA 52243.

American Guidance Service (AGS), 4201 Woodland Road, P.O. Box 99, Circle Pines, MN 55014-1796. Tel. 800/328-2560.

American Orthopsychiatric Association, Inc., 1790 Broadway, New York, NY 10019.

Behavior Science Systems, Inc., P.O. Box 1108, Minneapolis, MN 55440.

Consulting Psychologists Press, Inc. (CPP), 3803 East Bayshore Road, P.O. Box 10096, Palo Alto, CA 94303. Tel. 800/624-1765.

CPPC, 4 Conant Square, Brandon, VT 05733. Tel. 800/433-8234.

CTB/McGraw-Hill, 20 Ryan Ranch Road, Monterey, CA 93940. Tel. 800/538-9547.

Denver Developmental Materials, P.O. Box 20037, Denver, CO 80220.

DLM Resources, One DLM Park, Allen, TX 75002. Tel. 800/527-4747.

EdITS (Educational and Industrial Testing Service), P.O. Box 7234, San Diego, CA 92167. Tel. 619/222-1666.

Educational Testing Service (ETS), P.O. Box 6736, Princeton, NJ 98540.

GED Testing Service, One Dupont Circle, N.W., Washington, DC 20036.

Harcourt Brace Jovanovich, 757 Third Avenue, New York, NY 10017.

Hawthorne Educational Services Inc., 800 Gray Oak Drive, Columbia, MO 65201. Tel. 800/542-1673.

Hiskey, Marshal S., 5640 Baldwin, Lincoln, NB 68507.

Houghton Mifflin, 110 Tremont Street, Boston, MA 02107.

IPAT (Institute for Personality and Ability Testing), P.O. Box 1188, Champaign, IL 61824-1188. Tel. 800/225-4728.

Jastak Associates, P.O. Box 3410, Wilmington, DE 19804-0250. Tel. 800/221-WRAT.

LADOCA Publishing Foundation, 5100 Lincoln Street, Denver, CO 80216.

MetriTech, Inc., P.O. Box 6479, Champaign, IL 61820. Tel. 217/398-4868.

National Educational Laboratory Publishers, Inc., 813 Airport Boulevard, Austin, TX 78702.

Personnel Press, 191 Spring Street, Lexington, MA 02173.

pro.ed, 8700 Shoal Creek Boulevard, Austin, TX 78757-6897. Tel. 512/451-3246.

PAR (Psychological Assessment Resources, Inc.), P.O. Box 998, Odessa, FL 33556. Tel. 800/331-TEST.

Psychological Corporation, The, 555 Academic Court, San Antonio, TX 78204-2498. Tel. 800/228-0752.

Psychological Test Specialists, Box 9229, Missoula, MT 59807.

Psychometric Affiliates, Box 807, Murfreesboro, TN 37133-0807. Tel. 615/898-2565.

Publishers Test Service, CTB/McGraw-Hill, 20 Ryan Ranch Road, Monterey, CA 93940. Tel. 800/538-9547.

Reitan Neuropsychology Laboratories, 2920 South 4th Avenue, Tucson, AZ 85713-4819. Tel. 602/882-2022.

Riverside Publishing Company, The, 8420 Bryn Mawr Avenue, Chicago, IL 60631. Tel. 800/323-9540.

Scholastic Testing Service, Inc. (STS), 480 Meyer Road, P.O. Box 1056, Bensenville, IL 60106-1617. Tel. 708/766-7150.

Science Research Associates (SRA), 155 N. Wacker Drive, Chicago, IL 60606.

Sigma Assessment Systems, Inc., P.O. Box 610984, Port Huron, MI 48061-0984. Tel. 800/265-1285.

Slosson Educational Publications, Inc., P.O. Box 280, East Aurora, NY 14052-0280. Tel. 800/828-4800.

Special Child Publications, P.O. Box 33548, Seattle, WA 98133.

SRA/London House, 9701 Higgins Road, Rosemont, IL 60018. Tel. 800/221-8378.

Stoelting, Oakwood Centre: 620 Wheat Lane, Wood Dale, IL 60191. Tel. 708/860-9700.

U.S. Employment Service, Division of Program Planning and Operations, U.S. Department of Labor, 601 D Street, N.W. Washington, DC 20213.

U.S. Military Entrance Processing Command Testing Directorate, 2500 Green Bay Road, North Chicago, IL 60064.

Western Psychological Services (WPS), 12031 Wilshire Boulevard, Los Angeles, CA 90025-1251. Tel. 800/648-8857.

Wonderlic Personnel Test, Inc., 1509 N. Milwaukee Avenue, Libertyville, IL 60048-1380. Tel. 800/323-3742.

References

Aiken, L. R. (1991). Detecting, understanding, and controlling for cheating on tests. *Research in Higher Education, 32*, 725–736.

Aiken, L. R. (1994). *Psychological testing and assessment* (8th ed.). Needham Heights, MA: Allyn & Bacon.

Als, H. (1984). Newborn behavioral assessment. In W. J. Burns & J. V. Lavigne (Eds.), *Progress in pediatric psychology* (pp. 1–116). New York: Grune & Stratton.

Als, H., Tronick, E., Lester, B. M., & Brazelton, T. B. (1979). Specific neonatal measures: The Brazelton neonatal behavioral assessment scale. In J. Osofsky (Ed.), *Handbook of infant development* (pp. 185–215). New York: Wiley.

Altus, W. D. (1966). Birth order and its sequelae. *Science, 151*, 44–49.

American Educational Research Association, American Psychological Association, & National Council on Measurement in Education (1985). *Standards for educational and psychological testing*. Washington, DC: American Psychological Association.

American Psychiatric Association. (1994). *Diagnostic criteria from DSM-VI*. Washington, DC: Author.

American Psychological Association, Committee on Professional Standards, & Committee on Psychological Tests and Assessment (1986). *Guidelines for computer-based tests and interpretations*. Washington, DC: American Psychological Association.

American Psychological Association (1992). Ethical principles of psychologists and code of conduct. *American Psychologist, 47*, 1597–1611.

Ames, L. B. (1967). Predictive value of infant behavior examinations. In J. Hellmuth (Ed.), *Exceptional infant. Vol. 1: The normal infant* (pp. 207–239). Seattle, Straub & Hellmuth.

Ames, L. B., Gillespie, B. S., Haines, J., & Ilg, F. L. (1979). *The Gesell Institute's child from one to six: Evaluating the behavior of the preschool child*. New York: Harper & Row.

Anastasi, A. (1981). Coaching, test sophistication, and developed abilities. *American Psychologist, 36*, 1086–1093.

Anastasi, A. (1988). *Psychological testing* (6th ed.). New York: Macmillan.

Anastasi, A., & Cordova, F. A. (1953). Some effects of bilingualism upon the intelligence test performance of Puerto Rican children in New York City. *Journal of Educational Psychology, 44*, 1–19.

Andreasen, N. C. (1987). Creativity and mental illness: Prevalence rates in writers and their first-degree relatives. *American Journal of Psychiatry, 144*(10), 1288–1292.

Angoff, W. H., & Modu, C. C. (1973). *Equating the scales of the Prueba de Aptitud Academica and the Scholastic Aptitude Test*. Princeton, NJ: College Entrance Examination Board, Research Report 3.

Armstrong, K. (1993). *A history of God*. New York: Ballantine Books.

Baker, H. J., & Leland, B. (1967). *Detroit Tests of Learning Aptitude (examiner's handbook)*. Indianapolis: Bobbs-Merrill.

Baller, W. R., Charles, D. C., & Miller, E. L. (1967). Midlife attainment of the mentally retarded: A longitudinal study. *Genetic Psychology Monographs, 75,* 235–329.

Baltes, P. B., & Schaie, K. W. (1974). The myth of the twilight years. *Psychology Today, 7*(10), 35–40.

Baltes, P. B., & Willis, S. L. (1982). Plasticity and enhancement of intellectual functioning in old age: Penn State's Adult Development and Enrichment Program (ADEPT). In F. I. M. Craik & S. E. Trehub (Eds.), *Aging and cognitive processes* (pp. 353–389). New York: Plenum.

Bannatyne, A. (1974). Diagnosis: A note on recategorization of the WISC scaled scores. *Journal of Learning Disabilities, 7,* 272–274.

Barba, C. V. (1981). Mental development after dietary intervention: A study of Philippine children. *Journal of Cross-Cultural Psychology, 12,* 480–488.

Basseches, M. (1984). *Dialectical thinking and adult development*. Norwood, NJ: Ablex.

Bauman, M. K. (1974). Blind and partially sighted. In M. V. Wisland (Ed.), *Psychoeducational diagnosis of exceptional children* (pp. 159–189). Springfield, IL: Charles C. Thomas.

Bayley, N. (1933). Mental growth during the first three years. *Genetic Psychology Monographs, 14,* 1–92.

Bayley, N. (1949). Consistency and variability in the growth of intelligence form birth to 18 years. *Journal of Genetic Psychology, 75,* 165–196.

Bayley, N. (1993). *Bayley Scales of Infant Development—Second Edition manual*. San Antonio, TX: The Psychological Corporation.

Bayley, N., & Oden, M. M. (1955). The maintenance of intellectual ability in gifted adults. *Journal of Gerontology, 10,* 91–107.

Bayley, N., & Schaefer, E. S. (1964). Correlations of maternal and child behaviors with the development of mental abilities. *Monographs of the Society for Research in Child Development, 29*(6).

Beal, J. A. (1991). Methodological issues in conducting research on parent-infant attachment. *Journal of Pediatric Nursing, 6,* 11–15.

Bell, A., & Zubek, J. (1960). The effect of age on the intellectual performance of mental defectives. *Journal of Gerontology, 15,* 285–295.

Belmont, L., & Marolla, F. A. (1973). Birth order, family size, and intelligence. *Science, 182,* 1096–1101.

Ben-Yishay, Y., Diller, L., Mandelberg, I., Gordon, W., & Gerstman, L. (1971). Similarities and differences in block design performance between older normal and brain-injured persons. *Journal of Abnormal Psychology, 78,* 17–25.

Benbow, C. P., & Stanley, J. C. (1983). Sex differences in mathematical reasoning ability: More facts. *Science, 222,* 1029–1030.

Berbaum, M. L., Markus, G. B., & Zajonc, R. B. (1982). A closer look at Galbraith's closer look. *Developmental Psychology, 18,* 174–180.

Bernheimer, L. P., & Keogh, B. K. (1988). Stability of cognitive performance of children with developmental delays. *American Journal of Mental Retardation, 92,* 539–542.

Berrueta-Clement, J. R., Schweinhart, L. J., Barnett, W. S., Epstein, A. S., & Weikart, D. P. (1984). *Changed lives: The effects of the Perry Preschool Program on youth through age 19*. Ypsilanti, MI: High/Scope Educational Research Foundation.

Biemiller, L. (1986, January 8). Critics plan assault on admissions tests and other standard exams. *Chronicle of Higher Education,* pp. 1, 4.

Binet, A., and Henri, V. (1896). La psychologie individuelle. *L'Année Psychologique*, *2*, 411–465.

Binet, A., & Simon, T. (1905). Methodes novelles pour le diagnostic du niveau intellectuel des anormaux. *L'Année Psychologique*, *11*, 191–244.

Birren, J. E., Cunningham, W. R., & Yamamoto, K. (1983). Psychology of adult development and aging. *Annual Review of Psychology*, *324*, 543–575.

Bitterman, M. E. (1965). Phyletic differences in learning. *American Psychologist*, *20*, 396–410.

Bitterman, M. E. (1975). The comparative analysis of learning. *Science*, *188*, 699–709.

Black, R., & Dana, R. H. (1977). Examiner sex bias and Wechsler Intelligence Scale for Children scores. *Journal of Consulting and Clinical Psychology*, *45*, 500.

Blake, J. (1989). *Family size and achievement*. Berkeley, CA: University of California Press.

Bloom, A. S., Allard, A. M., Zelko, F. A. J., Brill, W. J., Topinka, C. W., & Pfohl, W. (1988). Differential validity of the K-ABC for lower functioning preschool children versus those of higher ability. *American Journal of Mental Retardation*, *93*(3), 273–277.

Boor, M., & Schill, T. (1968). Subtest performance on the WAIS as a function of anxiety and defensiveness. *Perceptual and Motor Skills*, *27*, 33–34.

Boring, E. G. (1923, June). Intelligence as the tests test it. *New Republic*, *35*, 35–36.

Botwinick, J. (1967). *Cognitive processes in maturity and old age*. New York: Springer.

Botwinick, J. (1977). Intellectual abilities. In J. E. Birren & K. W. Schaie (Eds.), *Handbook of the psychology of aging* (pp. 580–605). New York: Van Nostrand Reinhold.

Bouchard, T. J., Jr., Lykken, D. T., McGue, M., Segal, N. L., & Tellegen, A. (1990). Sources of human psychological differences: The Minnesota Study of Twins Reared Apart. *Science*, *250*, 223–228.

Bouchard, T. J., Jr., & McGue, M. (1981). Familial studies of intelligence: A review. *Science*, *212*, 1055–1059.

Bower, T. G. R. (1974). *Development in infancy*. San Francisco: W. H. Freeman.

Bowman, M. L. (1989). Testing individual differences in Ancient China. *American Psychologist*, *44*, 576–578.

Brackbill, Y., & Nichols, P. L. (1982). A test of the confluence model of intellectual development. *Developmental Psychology*, *18*, 192–198.

Bracken, B. A. (1985). A critical review of the Kaufman Assessment Battery for Children (K-ABC). *School Psychology Review*, *14*, 21–36.

Bradbury, P. J., Wright, S. D., Walker, C. E., & Ross, J. M. (1975). Performance on the WISC as a function of sex of E, sex of S, and age of S. *Journal of Psychology*, *90*, 51–55.

Brazelton, T. B. (1973). *Neonatal behavioral assessment scale*. Philadelphia: Lippincott.

Brazelton, T. B. (1984). *Neonatal behavioral assessment scales* (2nd ed.). Philadelphia: Lippincott.

Breland, H. M. (1979). *Population validity and college entrance measures*. New York: College Entrance Examination Board.

Brigham, C. C. (1923). *A study of American intelligence*. Princeton, NJ: Princeton University Press.

Brigham, C. C. (1930). Intelligence tests of immigrant groups. *Psychological Review*, *37*, 158–165.

Brody, N. (1992). *Intelligence* (2nd ed.). San Diego, CA: Academic Press.

Broman, S. H., Nichols, P. L., Shaughnessy, P., & Kennedy, W. (1987). *Retardation in young children*. Hillsdale, NJ: Erlbaum.

Brooks-Gunn, J., & Weinraub, M. (1983). Origins of infant intelligence testing. In M. Lewis (Ed.), *Origins of intelligence: Infancy and early childhood* (2nd ed., pp. 25–66). New York: Plenum.

Brown, A. L., & French, L. A. (1979). The zone of potential development: Implications for intelligence testing in the year 2000. *Intelligence, 3*, 255-273.

Bruner, J. S. (1975). Poverty and childhood. *Oxford Review of Education, 1*, 31-50.

Buckhalt, J. A. (1991). Wechsler Preschool and Primary Scale of Intelligence—Revised. *Journal of Psychoeducational Assessment, 9*, 271-279.

Budoff, M. (1987). The validity of learning potential assessment. In C. S. Lidz (Ed.), *Dynamic assessment: An interactional approach to evaluating learning potential* (pp. 52-81). New York: Guilford.

Burstein, A. (1976). Schizophrenic patterns on the WISC and their validity for white, black, and Hispanic children. *Dissertation Abstracts International, 37*, 875A-876A. University Microfilms No. 76-17, 894.

Busse, E. W., & Maddox, G. (1985). *The Duke longitudinal studies of normal aging*. New York: Springer.

Caldwell, M. B, & Smith, T. A. (1968). Intellectual structure of southern Negro children. *Psychological Reports, 23*, 63-71.

Campbell, D. P. (1965). A cross-sectional and longitudinal study of scholastic abilities over twenty-five years. *Journal of Counseling Psychology, 12*, 55-61.

Campbell, D. T., & Fiske, D. W. (1959). Convergent and discriminant validation by the multitrait-multimethod matrix. *Psychological Bulletin, 56*, 81-105.

Campione, J. C., & Brown, A. L. (1987). Learning ability and transfer propensity as sources of individual differences in intelligence. In P. H. Brooks, R. D. Sperber, & C. McCauley (Eds.), *Learning and cognition in the mentally retarded* (pp. 265-294). Baltimore, MD: University Park Press.

Carlson, J. S., Jensen, C. M., & Widaman, K. F. (1983). Reaction time, intelligence and attention. *Intelligence, 7*, 329-344.

Carroll, J. B. (1976). Psychometric tests as cognitive tasks: A new "structure of intellect." In L. Resnick (Ed.), *The nature of intelligence*. Hillsdale, NJ: Lawrence Erlbaum.

Carvajal, H., Gerber, J., Hewes, P., & Weaver, K. (1987). Correlations between scores on Stanford-Binet IV and Wechsler Adult Intelligence Scale—Revised. *Psychological Reports, 61*, 83-86.

Carvajal, H., Hardy, K., Smith, K., & Weaver, K. (1988). Relationships between scores on Stanford-Binet IV and Wechsler Preschool and Primary Scale of Intelligence. *Psychology in the Schools, 25*, 129-131.

Cattell, R. B. (1963). Theory of fluid and crystallized intelligence: A critical experiment. *Journal of Educational Psychology, 54*, 1-22.

Ceci, S. (1991). How much does schooling influence general intelligence and its cognitive components? A reassessment of the evidence. *Developmental Psychology, 27*, 703-722.

Chaille, S. E. (1887). Infants: Their chronological progress. *New Orleans Medical and Surgical Journal, 14*, 893-912.

Charles, D. C., & James, S. T. (1964). Stability of average intelligence. *Journal of Genetic Psychology, 105*, 105-111.

Chasnoff, I. J., Burns, K. A., & Burns, W. J. (1987). Cocaine use in pregnancy: Perinatal morbidity and mortality. *Neurotoxicology and Teratology, 9*, 291-293.

Children's Defense Fund (1976). *Your rights under the Education for All Handicapped Children Act P.L. 94-142*. Washington, DC: Author.

Chinn, P. C., Drew, C. J., & Logan, D. R. (1975). *Mental retardation: A life cycle approach*. St. Louis: Mosby.

Christiansen, K., & Knussman, R. (1987). Sex hormones and cognitive functioning in men. *Neuropsychobiology, 18*, 27-36.

Clarizio, H. F. (1979). SOMPA—A symposium continued: Commentaries. *School Psychology Digest, 8,* 207–209.

Clarizio, H. F. (1982). Piagetian assessment measures revisited: Issues and application. *Psychology in the Schools, 19,* 421–430.

Cohen, J. (1957). The factorial structure of the WAIS between early adulthood and old age. *Journal of Consulting Psychology, 21,* 283–290.

Cohen, R. J., Swerdlik, M. E., & Smith, D. K. (1992). *Psychological testing and assessment* (2nd ed.). Mountain View, CA: Mayfield.

Cole, M., Gay, J., Glick, J. A., & Sharp, D. W. (1971). *The cultural context of learning and thinking.* New York: Basic Books.

Cole, S., & Hunter, M. (1971). Pattern analysis of WISC scores achievement by culturally disadvantaged children. *Psychological Reports, 29,* 191–194.

Coleman, P. D. (1986, August). *Regulation of dendritic extent: Human aging brain and Alzheimer's disease.* Paper presented at the 94th annual meeting of the American Psychological Association, Washington, DC.

Coles, C. D., Smith, I. E., Falek, A. (1987). Prenatal alcohol exposure and infant behavior: Immediate effects and implications for later development. *Advances in Alcohol and Substance Abuse, 6,* 87–104.

College Entrance Examination Board (1971). *Report of the Commission on Tests.* New York: Author.

Commons, M. L., Richards, F. A., & Armon, C. (Eds.). (1984). *Beyond formal operations: Late adolescent and adult cognitive development.* New York: Praeger.

Commons, M. L., Richards, F. A., & Kuhn, D. (1982). Systematic and metasystematic reasoning: A case for levels of reasoning beyond Piaget's stage of formal operations. *Child Development, 53,* 1058–1069.

Connor, F. P., Hoover, R., Horton, K., Sands, H., Sternfield, L., & Wolinsky, G. F. (1975). Physical and sensory handicaps. In N. Hobbs (Ed.), *Issues in the classification of children* (Vol. 1, pp. 239–260). San Francisco: Jossey-Bass.

Cooney, T. M. Schaie, K. W., & Willis, S. L. (1988). The relationship between prior functioning on cognitive and personality dimensions and subject attrition in longitudinal research. *Journal of Gerontology, 43,* 12–17.

Cooper, D., & Fraboni, M. (1988). Relationship between the Wechsler Adult Intelligence Test—Revised and the Wide Range Achievement Test—Revised in a sample of normal adults. *Educational and Psychological Measurement, 48,* 799–803.

Coren, S. (1994). *The intelligence of dogs.* New York: Ballantine.

Costello, J., & Dickie, J. (1970). Leiter and Stanford-Binet IQ's of preschool disadvantaged children. *Developmental Psychology, 2,* 314.

Cronbach, L. J. (1984). *Essentials of psychological testing* (4th ed.). New York: Harper & Row.

Cronbach, L. J. (1990). *Essentials of psychological testing* (5th ed.). New York: Harper & Row.

Cronbach, L. J., & Drenth, P. J. D. (Eds.). (1972). *Mental tests and cultural adaptation.* The Hague: Mouton.

Cronin, J. Daniels, N., Hurley, A., Kroch, A., & Webber, R. (1975). Race, class, and intelligence: A critical look at the IQ controversy. *International Journal of Mental Health, 3*(4), 46–132.

Damerin, F. (1978). Review of Cattell Infant Intelligence Scale. In O. K. Buros (Ed.), *The eighth mental measurements yearbook* (pp. 296–297). Highland Park, NJ: Gryphon Press.

Das, J. P. (1984). Simultaneous and successive processes and K-ABC. *Journal of Special Education*, *18*, 229–238.

Davis, C. J. (1980). *Perkins-Binet Tests of Intelligence for the Blind*. Watertown, MA: Perkins School for the Blind.

Davis, J. A., & Smith, T. W. (1994). *General social surveys, 1972–1994* [machine-readable data filc]. Principal Investigator, James A. Davis: Director and Co-Principal Investigator, Tom W. Smith. NORC ed. Chicago: National Opinion Research Center, producer, 1994; Storrs, CT: The Roper Center for Public Opinion Research, University of Connecticut, distributor.

Dean, R. S. (1977). Patterns of emotional disturbance on the WISC-R. *Journal of Clinical Psychology*, *33*, 486–490.

De Jesus, N. H. (1978). Effects of ethnicity of examiner and language of test instructions on the test performance of Latino children. *Dissertation Abstracts International*, *39*, 2678B. University Microfilms No. 78-23, 893.

Delaney, E., & Hopkins, T. (1987). *Examiner's handbook: An expanded guide for Fourth Edition users*. Chicago: Riverside Publishing.

Delugach, R. R. (1991). Review of Wechsler Preschool and Primary Scale of Intelligence—Revised (WPPSI-R). *Journal of Psychoeducational Assessment*, *9*, 280–290.

DeMille, R. (1962). Intellect after lobotomy in schizophrenia. *Psychological Monographs*, *76*(16), 1–18.

Diana v. State Board of Education, C-70 37 RFT (N.D. Cal 1970).

Doppelt, J. E., & Wallace, W. L. (1955). Standardization of the Wechsler Adult Intelligence Scale for older persons. *Journal of Abnormal and Social Psychology*, *51*, 312–330.

Doyle, K. O., Jr. (1974). Theory and practice of ability testing in Ancient Greece. *Journal of the History of the Behavioral Sciences*, *10*, 202–212.

Dreger, R. M., & Miller, K. S. (1960). Comparative psychological studies of Negroes and whites in the United States. *Psychological Bulletin*, *57*, 1–5.

Edwards, G. A. (1966). Anxiety correlates of the WAIS. *California Journal of Educational Research*, *17*, 144–147.

Eells, K. (1951). *Intelligence and cultural differences*. Chicago: University of Chicago Press.

Egeland, B. (1985). Review of Wisconsin Card Sorting Test. In J. V. Mitchell (Ed.), *The ninth mental measurements yearbook* (pp. 1746–1747). Lincoln: University of Nebraska Press.

Eisdorfer, C. (1963). The WAIS performance of the aged: A retest evaluation. *Journal of Gerontology*, *18*, 169–172.

Ekstrom, R. B., French, J. W., & Harman, H. H. (1979). Cognitive factors: Their identification and replication. *Multivariate Behavior Research Monographs*. Ft. Worth: TX: Society for Multivariate Experimental Psychology.

Elliott, C. D. (1983). *British Ability Scales: Manual 2, Technical handbook*. Windsor, Berks., England: NFER-Nelson.

Elliott, C. D., Murray, D. J., & Pearson, L. S. (1983). *British Ability Scales: Manual 4, Tables of abilities and norms*. Rev. ed. Windsor, Berks., England: NFER-Nelson.

Elliott, R. (1987). *Litigating intelligence*. Dover, MA: Auburn House.

Elsayed, M., Ismail, A. H., & Young, R. S. (1980). Intellectual differences of adult men related to age and physical fitness before and after an exercise program. *Journal of Gerontology*, *35*, 383–387.

Emory, E. K., Tynan, W. D., & Dave, R. (1989). Neurobehavioral anomalies in neonates with seizures. *Journal of Clinical and Experimental Neuropsychology*, *11*, 231–240.

Equal Employment Opportunity Commission (1973, Aug. 23). *The uniform guidelines of employee selection procedures*. Discussion draft. Washington, DC: Author.

Esquirol, J. E. D. (1838). *Des maladis mentales considérées sons les rapports médical, hygiéneique et medicolegal*. Paris: Bailliére.

Esquivel, G. B., & Lopez, E. (1988). Correlations among measures of cognitive ability, creativity, and academic achievement for gifted minority children. *Perceptual and Motor Skills, 67*, 395-398.

Evans, D., Funkenstein, H., Albert, M., Scherr, P., Cook, N., Chown, M., Herbert, L., Hennckens, C., & Taylor, D. (1989). Prevalence of Alzheimer's disease in a community population of older people. *Journal of the American Medical Association, 262*, 2551-2556.

Eysenck, H. J. (1967). Intelligence assessment: A theoretical and experimental approach. *British Journal of Educational Psychology, 34*, 197-201.

Eysenck, H. J. (1971). *The IQ argument*. New York: Library Press.

Eysenck, H. J. (1984). Recent advances in the theory and measurement of intelligence. *Early Child Development and Care, 15*, 97-115.

Eysenck, H. J. (1987). Speed of information processing, reaction time, and the theory of intelligence. In P. A. Vernon (Ed.), *Speed of information-processing and intelligence* (pp. 21-67). Norwood, NJ: Ablex.

Falbo, T., & Cooper, C. R. (1980). Young children's time and intellectual ability. *Journal of Genetic Psychology, 137*, 299-300.

Ferguson, G. A. (1956). On transfer and the abilities of man. *Canadian Journal of Psychology, 10*, 121-131.

Feuerstein, R. (1979). *The dynamic assessment of retarded performers: The learning potential assessment device, theory, instruments, and techniques*. Baltimore: University Park Press.

Feuerstein, R., Rand, Y., Jensen, M. R., Kaniel, S., & Tzuriel, D. (1987). Prerequisites for assessment of learning potential: The LPAD model. In C. S. Lidz (Ed.), *Dynamic assessment: An interactional approach to evaluating learning potential* (pp. 35-51). New York: Guilford.

Fields, C. M. (1980, June 9). SAT score improvements laid to "motivation." *Chronicle of Higher Education, 20*(15), 4.

Flaugher, R. L., & Rock, D. A. (1972). Patterns of ability factors among four ethnic groups. *Proceedings of the 80th Annual Convention of the American Psychological Association, 7*, 27-28.

Fleming, J. W. (1973). *Care and management of exceptional children*. New York: Appleton-Century-Crofts.

Ford, J. B. (1957). Some more on the Samoans. *American Psychologist, 12*, 751.

Forns-Santacana, M., & Gomez-Benito, J. (1990). Factor structure of the McCarthy Scales. *Psychology in the Schools, 27*, 111-115.

Frankenberger, W. (1984). A survey of state guidelines for identification of mental retardation. *Mental Retardation, 22*, 17-20.

Franklin, M. R., & Stillman, P. L. (1982). Examiner error in intelligence testing: Are you a source? *Psychology in the Schools, 19*, 563-569.

Friedman, H. S., Tucker, J. S., Schwartz, J. E., Tomlinson-Keasy, C., Martin, L. R., Wingard, D. L., & Criqui, M. H. (1995). The aging and death of the "Termites." *American Psychologist, 50*, 69-78.

Fulton, M., Thomson, G., Hunter, R., Raab, G., Laxen, D., & Hepburn, W. (1987). Influence of blood lead on the ability and attainment of children in Edinburgh. *Lancet, 1*, 1221-1226.

Gaines, T., & Morris, R. (1978). Relationships between MMPI measures of psychopathology and WAIS subtest scores and intelligence quotients. *Perceptual & Motor Skills, 47,* 399–402.

Galbraith, R. C. (1982). Sibling spacing and intellectual development: A close look at the confluence models. *Developmental Psychology, 18,* 151–173.

Galton, F. (1869). *Hereditary genius.* London: Macmillan.

Galton, F. (1883). *Inquiries into human faculty and its development.* London: Macmillan.

Gardner, H. (1983). *Frames of mind: The theory of multiple intelligences.* New York: Basic Books.

Geary, D. C., & Whitworth, R. H. (1988). Dimensional structure of the WAIS-R in a simultaneous multi-sample analysis. *Educational and Psychological Measurement, 48,* 945–959.

Georgia State Conferences of Branches of NAACP v. State of Georgia. Eleventh Circuit Court of Appeals, No. 84-8771 (1985).

German, D. (1983). Analysis of word finding disorders on the Kaufman Assessment Battery for Children (K-ABC). *Journal of Psychoeducational Assessment, 1,* 121–133.

Gesell, A., & Amatruda, C. S. (1941). *Developmental diagnosis.* New York: Paul B. Hoeber.

Getzels, J. W., & Jackson, P. W. (1962). *Creativity and intelligence: Explorations with gifted students.* New York: Wiley.

Gibson, E. J., Gibson, J. J., Peck, A. D., & Osser, H. A. (1962). A developmental study of the discrimination of letterlike forms. *Journal of Comparative and Physiological Psychology, 55,* 897–906.

Gill, R., & Keats, D. M. (1980). Elements of intellectual competence: Judgments by Australian and Malay university students. *Journal of Cross-Cultural Psychology, 11,* 233–243.

Glaser, R. (1981). The future of testing: A research agenda for cognitive psychology and psychometrics. *American Psychologist, 36,* 923–936.

Glueck, B. C., & Reznikoff, M. (1965). Comparison of computer-derived personality profile and projective psychological test findings. *American Journal of Psychiatry, 121,* 1156–1161.

Goddard, H. H. (1920). *Human efficiency and levels of intelligence.* Princeton, NJ: Princeton University Press.

Goldfarb, W. (1955). Emotional and intellectual consequences of psychologic deprivation in infancy. In E. Hoch & J. Zubin (Eds.), *Psychopathology in childhood* (pp. 105–119). New York: Grune & Stratton.

Good, R. H., & Lane, S. (1988). *Confirmatory factor analysis of the K-ABC and WISC-R: Hierarchical models.* Paper presented at the annual meeting of the American Psychological Association, Atlanta, GA.

Goodwin, F. K., & Jamison, K. R. (1990). Manic-depressive illness, creativity, and leadership. In *Manic-depressive illness* (pp. 332–367). New York: Oxford.

Gould, S. J. (1981). *The mismeasure of man.* New York: W. W. Norton.

Granick, S., & Patterson, R. D. (1972). *Human aging, II: An eleven year follow-up biomedical and behavioral study.* Washington, DC: U.S. Government Printing Office.

Grant, D., & Reed, R. (1982). Neuropsychological testing. In W. C. Wiederholt (Ed.), *Neurology for non-neurologists* (pp. 143–155). New York: Academic Press.

Gregory, R. L. (1992). *Psychological testing: History, principles, and applications.* Boston: Allyn & Bacon.

Griggs et al. v. Duke Power Company. 401 U.S. 424, 3FEP175 (1971).

Graziano, W. G., Varca, P. E., & Levy, J. C. (1982). Race of examiner effects and the validity of intelligence tests. *Review of Educational Research, 52,* 469–498.

Guadalupe v. Tempe Elementary School District, Stipulation and Order (January 24, 1972).

Guicciardi, G., & Ferrari, G. C. (1896). I testi mentali per l'esame degli alienati. *Revista sperimentale di Freneatria, 22,* 297–314.

Guilford, J. P. (1954). A factor analytic study across the domains of reasoning, creativity, and evaluation, I. Hypothesis and description of tests. *Reports from the Psychology Laboratory.* Los Angeles: University of Southern California.

Guilford, J. P. (1967). *The nature of human intelligence.* New York: McGraw-Hill.

Guilford, J. P. (1974). *Structure-of-intellect abilities.* Orange, CA: Sheridan Supply.

Guilford, J. P. (1981). Higher-order structure-of-intellect abilities. *Multivariate Behavioral Research, 16,* 411–435.

Guilford, J. P. (1985). The structure-of-intellect model. In B. B. Wolman (Ed.), *Handbook of intelligence: Theories, measurements and applications* (pp. 225–266). New York: Wiley.

Guilford, J. P., & Hoepfner, R. (1971). *The analysis of intelligence.* New York: McGraw-Hill.

Guilford, J. P., & Tenopyr, M. L. (1968). Implications of the structure-of-intellect model for high school and college students. In W. B. Michael (Ed.), *Teaching for creative endeavor* (pp. 25–45). Bloomington: Indiana University Press.

Gutkin, T. B. (1979). WISC-R scatter indices: Useful information for differential diagnosis? *Journal of School Psychology, 17,* 368–371.

Gutkin, T. B., & Reynolds, C. R. (1981). Factorial similarity of the WISC-R for Anglos and Chicanos referred for psychological services. *Journal of School Psychology, 18,* 30–39.

Gyurke, J. S. (1991). The assessment of children with the Wechsler Preschool and Primary Scale of Intelligence—Revised. In B. A. Bracken (Ed.), *The psychoeducational assessment of preschool children* (2nd ed., pp. 86–132). Needham Heights, MA: Allyn & Bacon.

Gyurke, J. S., Stone, B. J., & Beyer, M. (1990). A confirmatory factor analysis of the WPPSI-R. *Journal of Psychoeducational Assessment, 8,* 15–21.

Hack, M., & Breslau, N. (1985). Very low birth weight infants: Effects of brain growth during infancy on intelligence quotient at 3 years of age. *Pediatrics, 77,* 196–202.

Haier, R. J. (1991). Cerebral glucose metabolism and intelligence. In P. A. Vernon (Ed.), *Biologic approaches to the study of human intelligence.* Norwood, NJ: Ablex.

Haier, R. J., Siegel, B. V., MacLachlan, A., Soderling, E., Lottenberg, S., & Buchsbaum, M. S. (1992). Regional glucose metabolic changes after learning a complex visuospatial-motor task: A positron emission tomographic study. *Brain Research, 570,* 134–143.

Haier, R. J., Siegel, B. V., Tang, C., Abel, L., & Buchsbaum, M. S. (1992). Intelligence and changes in regional cerebral glucose metabolic rate following learning. *Intelligence, 16*(3–4), 415–426.

Hall, V. C., & Kaye, D. B. (1977). Patterns of early cognitive development among boys in four subcultural groups. *Journal of Educational Psychology, 69,* 66–87.

Hammill, D. D. (1985). *Detroit Tests of Learning Aptitude (DTLA-2).* Austin, TX: pro.ed.

Hammill, D. D. (1991). *Detroit Tests of Learning Aptitude, Third edition examiner's manual.* Austin, TX: pro.ed.

Hampson, E. (1990). Variations in sex-related cognitive abilities across the menstrual cycle. *Brain and Cognition, 14,* 26–43.

Haney, D. A. (1985, February 3). Creative people: Their inner drive awes researchers. *Los Angeles Times,* pp. I2, 9.

Harlow, H. F. (1949). The formation of learning sets. *Psychological Review, 56,* 51–65.

Harlow, H. F. (1958). The evolution of learning. In A. Roe & G. G. Simpson (Eds.), *Behavior and evolution* (pp. 269–290). New Haven: Yale University Press.

Harrell, R. F. Capp, R. H., Davis, D. K., Peerless, J., & Ravitz, L. R. (1981). Can nutritional supplements help mentally retarded children? An exploratory study. *Proceedings of the National Academy of Sciences, 78,* 574-578.

Harrell, T. W., & Harrell, M. S. (1945). Army General Classification Test scores for civilian occupations. *Educational and Psychological Measurement, 5,* 229-342.

Harvis, P. E., & Barth, J. T. (1994). *The Halstead-Reitan Neuropsychological Battery: A guide to interpretation and clinical application.* Odessa, FL: Psychological Assessment Resources.

Hattie, J. (1980). Should creativity tests be administered under test-like conditions? An empirical study of three alternative conditions. *Journal of Educational Psychology, 72,* 87-98.

Hayden, D. C., Frulong, M. J., & Linnemeyer, S. (1988). A comparison of the Kaufman Assessment Battery for Children and the Stanford-Binet IV for the assessment of gifted children. *Psychology in the Schools, 25,* 239-243.

Hebb, D. O. (1949). *The organization of behavior.* New York: Wiley.

Hedges, L. V., & Nowell, A. (1995, July 7). Sex differences in mental test scores, variability, and number of high-scoring individuals. *Science, 269,* 41-45.

Hennessy, J. J., & Merrifield, P. R. (1976). A comparison of factor structures of mental abilities in four ethnic groups. *Journal of Educational Psychology, 68,* 754-759.

Henning, J. J., & Levy, R. H. (1967). Verbal-performance IQ differences of white and Negro delinquents on the WISC and WAIS. *Journal of Clinical Psychology, 23,* 164-168.

Herbert, W. (1982). Intelligence tests: Sizing up a newcomer. *Science News, 122,* 280-281.

Herlihy, B. (1977). Watch out, IQ myth: Here comes another debunker. *Phi Delta Kappan, 59,* 298.

Herring, J. P. (1922). *Herring revision of the Binet-Simon tests: Examination manual—Form A.* London: World Book Co.

Herrnstein, R. J. (1973). *IQ in the meritocracy.* Boston: Little, Brown.

Herrnstein, R. J., & Murray, C. (1994). *The bell curve.* New York: The Free Press.

Hertzig, M. E., Birch, H. G., Thomas, A., & Mendez, Q. A. (1968). Class and ethnic differences in the responsiveness of preschool children to cognitive demands. *Monographs of the Society for Research in Child Development, 33*(1, Serial No. 117).

Hertzog, C., Schaie, K. W., & Gribbin, K. (1978). Cardiovascular disease and changes in intellectual functioning from middle to old age. *Journal of Gerontology, 33,* 872-883.

Hier, D. B., & Crowley, W. F., Jr. (1982). Spatial ability in androgen-deficient men. *New England Journal of Medicine, 306,* 1202-1205.

Hinde, K. A. (1970). *Animal behaviour* (2nd ed.). New York: McGraw-Hill.

Hindley, C. B. (1965). Stability and change in abilities up to 5 years: Group trends. *Journal of Child Psychology and Psychiatry, 6,* 85-99.

Hirsch, N. D. M. (1926). A study of natio-racial mental differences. *Genetic Psychology Monographs, 1,* 231-406.

Hiskey, M. (1966). *Hiskey-Nebraska Test of Learning Aptitude.* Lincoln, NB: Union College Press.

Hobson v. Hansen, 269 F. Suppl. 401 (D.D.C. 1967).

Hodges, W., & Spielberger, C. (1969). Digit span: An indication of trait or state anxiety? *Journal of Consulting and Clinical Psychology, 33,* 430-434.

Hooper, S. R., & Hynd, G. W. (1982). *Differential diagnosis of subtypes of developmental dyslexia with the Kaufman Assessment Battery for Children.* Paper presented at the annual convention of the National Academy of Neuropsychologists, Atlanta, GA.

Hopkins, K. D., & Bracht, G. H. (1975). Ten-year stability of verbal and nonverbal IQ scores. *American Educational Research Journal, 12,* 469-477.

Horn, J. L. (1979). The rise and fall of human abilities. *Journal of Research and Development in Education, 12,* 59-78.

Horn, J. L. (1982). The theory of fluid and crystallized intelligence in relation to concepts of cognitive psychology and aging in adulthood. In F. I. M. Craik & S. Trehub (Eds.), *Advances in the study of communication and affect: Volume 8: Aging and cognitive processes* (pp. 237-278). New York: Plenum.

Horn, J. L., & Cattell, R. B. (1966). Refinement and test of the theory of fluid and crystallized intelligence. *Journal of Educational Psychology, 57,* 253-276.

Horn, J. L., & Cattell, R. B. (1967). Age differences in fluid and crystallized intelligence. *Acta Psychologica, 26,* 107-129.

Horn, J. L., & Donaldson, G. (1976). On the myth of intellectual decline in adulthood. *American Psychologist, 31,* 701-719.

Huey, E. B. (1910). The Binet scale for measuring intelligence and retardation. *Journal of Educational Psychology, 1,* 435-444.

Hughes, H. H., & Converse, H. D. (1962). Characteristics of the gifted: A case for a sequel to Terman's study. *Exceptional Children, 29,* 178-183.

Humphreys, L. G. (1985). Review of the System of Multicultural Pluralistic Assessment. In J. V. Mitchell (Ed.), *The ninth mental measurements yearbook* (pp. 1517-1519). Lincoln: University of Nebraska Press.

Hunt, C. B. (1980). Intelligence as an information processing concept. *British Journal of Psychology, 71,* 449-474.

Hunt, E. (1983). On the nature of intelligence. *Science, 219,* 141-146.

Hunt, E. (1987). The next word on verbal ability. In P. A. Vernon (Ed.), *Speed of information-processing and intelligence* (pp. 347-392). Norwood, NJ: Ablex.

Hunt, E., & Lansman, M. (1983). Individual differences in intelligence. In R. Sternberg (Ed.), *Advances in the psychology of human intelligence.* Hillsdale, NJ: Lawrence Erlbaum Associates.

Hunt, J. McV. (1961). *Intelligence and experience.* New York: Ronald Press.

Inglis, J., & Lawson, J. S. (1981). Sex differences in the effects of unilateral brain damage on intelligence. *Science, 212,* 693-695.

Intelligence and its measurement: A symposium. (1921). *Journal of Educational Psychology, 12,* 123-147, 195-216.

Irons, D. (1981). The effect of familiarity with the examiner on WISC-R Verbal, Performance, and Full Scale scores. *Psychology in the Schools, 18,* 496-498.

Jackson, D. N. (1984). *Multidimensional Aptitude Battery manual.* Port Huron, MI: Research Psychologists Press.

Jacobson, R. L. (1986, July 2). Selective colleges' use of SAT is unshaken by controversy. *Chronicle of Higher Educaiton,* p. 8.

Jacobson, R. L. (1993, June 16). Researcher finds admissions tests vulnerable to attempts by students to answer "passageless" reading questions. *The Chronicle of Higher Education,* pp. A33-34.

Jensen, A. R. (1969). How much can we boost IQ and scholastic achievement? *Harvard Educational Review, 39,* 1-123.

Jensen, A. R. (1977). Cumulative deficit in IQ of blacks in the rural south. *Developmental Psychology, 13,* 184-191.

Jensen, A. R. (1980). *Bias in mental testing.* New York: Free Press.

Jensen, A. R. (1981). *Straight talk about mental tests.* New York: Free Press.

Jensen, A. R. (1982a). Reaction time and psychometric *g.* In H. J. Eysenck (Ed.), *A model for intelligence.* Berlin: Springer-Verlag.

Jensen, A. R. (1982b). The chronometry of intelligence. In R. J. Sternberg (Ed.), *Advances in research in intelligence*. (Vol. 1). Hillsdale, NJ: Erlbaum.

Jensen, A. R. (1984). The black–white difference on the K-ABC: Implications for future tests. *Journal of Special Education, 18*, 377–408.

Jensen, A. R. (1985). Methodological and statistical techniques for the chronometric study of mental abilities. In C. R. Reynolds & V. L. Willson (Eds.), *Methodological and statistical advances in the study of individual differences*. New York: Plenum.

Jensen, A. R., Schafer, E. W., & Crinella, F. M. (1981). Reaction time, evoked brain potentials, and psychometric g in the severely retarded. *Intelligence, 5*, 179–197.

Jensen, A. R., & Sinha, S. N. (1991). Physical correlates of human intelligence. In P. A. Vernon (Ed.), *Biological approaches to the study of human intelligence* (pp. 139–242). Norwood, NJ: Ablex.

Jones, H. E., & Conrad, H. S. (1933). The growth and decline of intelligence: A study of a homogeneous group. *Genetic Psychology Monographs, 13*, 223–298.

Kahn, J. V. (1983). Sensorimotor period and adaptive behavior development of severely and profoundly mentally retarded child. *American Journal of Mental Deficiency, 88*, 69–75.

Kalat, J. W. (1983). Evolutionary thinking in the history of the comparative psychology of learning. *Neuroscience and Biobehavioral Reviews, 7*(3), 309–314.

Kamphaus, R. W., & Reynolds, C. R. (1987). *Clinical and research applications of the K-ABC*. Circle Pines, MN: American Guidance Service.

Kaplan, R. M., & Saccuzzo, D. P. (1993). *Psychological testing: Principles, applications, and issues* (3rd ed.). Pacific Grove, CA: Brooks/Cole.

Kaufman, A. S. (1975a). Factor structure of the McCarthy Scales at five age levels between 2½ and 8½. *Educational and Psychological Measurement, 43*, 135–147.

Kaufman, A. S. (1975b). Factor analysis of the WISC-R at eleven age levels between 6½ and 16½ years. *Journal of Consulting and Clinical Psychology, 43*, 135–147.

Kaufman, A. S. (1978). Review of Columbia Mental Maturity Scale. In O. K. Buros (Ed.), *The eighth mental measurements yearbook*, (Vol. 1., pp. 299–301). Highland Park, NJ: Gryphon Press.

Kaufman, A. S. (1982). The impact of WISC-R research for school psychologists. In C. R. Reynolds & T. B. Gutkin (Eds.), *The handbook of school psychology* (pp. 156–177). New York: Wiley.

Kaufman, A. S. (1983). Test review: WAIS-R. *Journal of Psychoeducational Assessment, 1*, 390–319.

Kaufman, A. S. (1984). K-ABC and giftedness. *Froeper Review, 7*(2), 83–88.

Kaufman, A. S. (1990). *Assessing adolescent and adult intelligence*. Boston: Allyn & Bacon.

Kaufman, A. S. (1994). *Intelligent testing with the WISC-III*. New York: Wiley.

Kaufman, A. S., & DiCuio, R. F. (1975). Separate factor analyses of the McCarthy Scales for groups of black and white children. *Journal of School Psychology, 13*, 10–18.

Kaufman, A. S., & Kaufman, N. L. (1975). Social class differences on the McCarthy scales for black and white children. *Perceptual and Motor Skills, 41*, 205–206.

Kaufman, A. S., & Kaufman, N. L. (1977). *Clinical evaluation of young children with the McCarthy Scales*. New York: Grune & Stratton.

Kaufman, A. S., & Kaufman, N. L. (1983a). *Kaufman Assessment Battery for Children: Administration and scoring manual*. Circle Pines, MN: American Guidance Service.

Kaufman, A. S., & Kaufman, N. L. (1983b). *Kaufman Assessment Battery for Children: Interpretive manual*. Circle Pines, MN: American Guidance Service.

Kaufman, A. S., Kaufman, N. L., & Goldsmith, B. (1984). *Kaufman Sequential or Simultaneous (K-SOS)*. Circle Pines, MN: American Guidance Service.

Kaufman, A. S., & McLean, J. E. (1986). K-ABC/WISC-R factor analysis for a learning disabled population. *Journal of Learning Disabilities, 19,* 145–153.

Kaufman, A. S., Reynolds, C. B., & McLean, J. E. (1989). Age and WAIS-R intelligence in a national sample of adults in the 20- to 74-year age range: A cross-sectional analysis with education level controlled. *Intelligence, 13,* 235–253.

Keating, D. P. (Ed.). (1976). *Intellectual talent: Research and development*. Baltimore, MD: Johns Hopkins University Press.

Keith, T. Z., & Bolen, L. M. (1980). Factor structure of the McCarthy Scales for children experiencing problems in school. *Psychology in the Schools, 17,* 320–326.

Keith, T. Z., & Novak, C. G. (1987). Joint factor structure of the WISC-R and K-ABC for referred school children. *Journal of Psychoeducational Assessment, 5*(4), 370–386.

Kelderman, H., Mellenberg, C. J., & Elshout, J. J. (1981). Guilford's facet theory of intelligence: An empirical comparison of models. *Multivariate Behavioral Research, 16,* 37–61.

Kellaghan, T., & MacNamara, J. (1972). Family correlates of verbal reasoning ability. *Developmental Psychology, 7,* 49–53.

Kidd, J. W. (1983). The 1983 A.A.M.D. definition and classification of mental retardation: The apparent impact of the CEC-MR position. *Education and Training of the Mentally Retarded, 18,* 243–244.

Kilbride, H. W., Johnson, D. L., & Streissguth, A. P. (1977). Social class, birth order, and newborn experience. *Child Development, 48,* 1686–1688.

Kimura, D., & Hampson, E. (1993). Neural and hormonal mechanisms mediating sex differences in cognition. In P. A. Vernon (Ed.), *Biological approaches to the study of human intelligence,* (pp. 375–397). Norwood, NJ: Ablex.

King, L. A., & King, D. W. (1982). Wechsler short forms: A brief status report. *Psychology in the Schools, 19,* 433–438.

Kirk, S. A., & McCarthy, J. J. (1961). The Illinois Test of Psycholinguistic Abilities: An approach to differential diagnosis. *American Journal of Mental Deficiency, 66,* 399–412.

Klineberg, O. (1963). Negro–white differences in intelligence test performance. *American Psychologist, 18,* 198–203.

Knight, B. C., Baker, E. H., & Minder, C. C. (1990). Concurrent validity of the Stanford-Binet: Fourth Edition and the Kaufman Assessment Battery for Children with learning disabled students. *Psychology in the Schools, 27*(2), 116–120.

Knobloch, H., & Pasamanick, B. (Eds.). (1974). *Gesell and Amatruda's developmental diagnosis* (3rd ed.). New York: Harper & Row.

Knobloch, H., Stevens, F., & Malone, A. (1987). *Manual of developmental diagnosis: The administration and interpretation of the Revised Gesell and Amatruda Developmental and Neurologic Examination*. Houston, TX: Developmental Evaluation Materials, Inc.

Kohlberg, L. (1971). Stages of moral development as a basis for moral education. In C. M. Beck, B. S. Crittenden, & E. V. Sullivan (Eds.), *Moral education: Interdisciplinary approaches*. New York: Newman Press.

Komm, R. A. (1978). A comparison of the Black Intelligence Test of Cultural Homogeneity with the Wechsler Intelligence Scale for Children (Revised), as measured by a conventional achievement test within a black population at different social class levels. *Dissertation Abstracts International, 39,* 6041A–6032A. (University Microfilms No. 79-05059).

Koppitz, E. M. (1975). *The Bender Gestalt Test for young children: Research and application, 1963-1973*. New York: Grune & Stratton.

Koronakos, C., & Arnold, W. J. (1957). The formation of learning sets in rats. *Journal of Comparative and Physiological Psychology, 50*, 11-14.

Krohn, E. J., & Lamp, R. E. (1989). Concurrent validity of the K-ABC and Stanford-Binet—Fourth Edition for Head Start Children. *Journal of School Psychology, 27*(1), 59-67.

Krohn, E. J., Lamp, R. E., & Phelps, C. G. (1988). Validity of the K-ABC for a black preschool population. *Psychology in the Schools, 25*, 15-21.

Kuhlmann, F. (1912). A revision of the Binet-Simon system for measuring the intelligence of children. *Journal of Psycho-Asthenics, Monograph Supplement, 1*(1), 1-4.

Kunce, J. T., Ryan J. J., & Eckelman, C. C. (1976). Violent behavior and differential WAIS characteristics. *Journal of Consulting and Clinical Psychology, 44*, 42-45.

Labouvie-Vief, G. V. (1985). Intelligence and cognition. In J. E. Birren & K. W. Schaie (Eds.), *Handbook of the psychology of aging* (2nd ed., pp. 500-543). New York: Van Nostrand Reinhold.

Lacks, P. (1984). *Bender-Gestalt screening for brain dysfunction*. San Antonio, TX: The Psychological Corporation.

Larry P. v. Riles, 495 F. Supp. 926(N.D. Cal. 1979), appeal docketed, No. 80-4027 (9th Cir., Jan. 17, 1980).

Larson, G. E., & Saccuzzo, D. P. (1989). Cognitive correlates of general intelligence: Toward a process theory of *g*. *Intelligence, 13*, 5-32.

Laurendeau, M., & Pinard, A. (1962). *Causal thinking in the child: A genetic and experimental approach*. New York: International Universities Press.

Laurendeau, M., & Pinard, A. (1970). *The development of the concept of space in the child*. New York: International Universities Press.

Laurent, J., Swerdlik, M., & Ryburn, M. (1992). Review of validity research on the Stanford-Binet Intelligence Scale: Fourth Edition. *Psychological Assessment, 4*, 102-112.

Lazar, I., & Darlington, R. B. (1982). Lasting effects of early education: A report from the Consortium for Longitudinal studies. *Monographs of the Society for Research in Child Development, 47* (2-3, Serial No. 195).

Lee, E. S. (1951). Negro intelligence and selective migration: A Philadelphia test of the Klineberg hypothesis. *American Sociological Review, 16*, 227-233.

Lesser, G., Fifer, G., & Clark, D. (1965). Mental abilities of children from different social classes and cultural groups. *Monographs of the Society for Research in Child Development, 30* (4, Serial No. 102).

Lichtenstein, R., & Martuza, V. (1984). Review of Kaufman, A., & Kaufman, N. The Kaufman Assessment Battery for Children. *Journal of Educational Measurement, 21*, 408-417.

Lidz, C. S. (1987). *Dynamic assessment: An interactional approach to evaluating learning potential*. New York: Guilford.

Lieberman, M. A. (1965). Psychological correlates of impending death: Some preliminary observations. *Journal of Gerontology, 20*, 71-84.

Lieberman, M. A., & Coplan, A. S. (1969). Distance from death as a variable in the study of aging. *Developmental Psychology, 2*, 71-84.

Linfert, H. E., & Hierholzer, H. M. (1928). *A scale for measuring the mental development of infants during the first years of life*. Baltimore, MD: Williams & Wilkins.

Linn, M. L., & Hyde, J. S. (1989). Gender, mathematics, and science. *Educational Researcher, 18*(8), 17.

Linn, R. L. (1982). Admissions testing on trial. *American Psychologist, 37*, 279-291.

Lippmann, W. (1922). The mental age of Americans, etc. *New Republic, 32*, 213–215, 246–248, 275–277, 297–298, 328–380, *33*, 9–11, 145–146.

Lippmann, W. (1923). Mr. Burt and the intelligence tests, etc. *New Republic, 34*, 263–264, 295–296, 322–323.

Loehlin, J. C., Lindzey, G., & Spuhler, J. N. (1975). *Race differences in intelligence*. San Francisco: Freeman.

Lohnes, P. R. (1973). Evaluating the schooling of intelligence. *Educational Researcher, 2*(2), 6–11.

Long, P. A., & Anthony, J. J. (1974). The measurement of mental retardation by a culture-specific test. *Psychology in the Schools, 11*, 310–312.

Lucas, A., Morley, R., Cole, T. J., Lister, G., & Leeson-Payne, C. (1992). Breast milk and subsequent intelligence quotient in children born preterm. *The Lancet, 339*, 261–264.

Luria, A. R. (1966). *Higher cortical functions in man*. New York: Basic Books.

Lynn, R. (1982). IQ in Japan and the United States shows a growing disparity. *Science, 297*, 222–223.

Lynn, R. (1987). The intelligence of the mongoloids: A psychometric, evolutionary and neurological theory. *Personality and Individual Differences, 8*, 813–844.

Lynn, R. (1994). Sex differences in intelligence and brain size: A paradox resolved. *Personality and Individual Differences, 17*, 257–271.

MacFarlane, J. W. (1953). The uses and predictive limitations of intelligence tests in infants and young children. *Bulletin WHO, 9*, 409–415.

MacKinnon, D. W. (1962). The nature and nurture of creative talent. *American Psychologist, 17*, 484–495.

MacPhee, D. Ramey, C. T., & Yeates, K. O. (1984). Home environment and early cognitive development: Implications for intervention. In A. W. Gottfried (Ed), *Home environment and early cognitive development. Longitudinal research* (pp. 343–369). Orlando, FL: Academic.

Major, C. (Ed.). (1970). *Dictionary of Afro-American slang*. New York: International.

Maloney, M. P., & Ward, M. P. (1976). *Psychological assessment: A conceptual approach*. New York: Oxford University Press.

Martin, C. J. (n.d.). *Kaufman Assessment Battery for Children: Usefulness of the mental processing scales for provision of normative and diagnostic data in a population of hearing impaired children*. Circle Pines, MN: American Guidance Servce.

Mascie-Taylor, C. G. N. (1980). Season of birth, IQ components, and personality traits. *Journal of Genetic Psychology, 137*, 151–152.

Matarazzo, J. D. (1972). *Wechsler's measurement and appraisal of adult intelligence* (5th ed.). Baltimore: William & Wilkins.

Matarazzo, J. D. (1985). Review of the Wechsler Adult Intelligence Scale—Revised. In J. V. Mitchell (Ed.), *The ninth mental measurements yearbook* (pp. 1703–1705). Lincoln: The Buros Institute of Mental Measurements, University of Nebraska.

Matarazzo, J. D. (1992). Psychological testing and assessment in the 21st century. *American Psychologist, 47*, 1007–1018.

Maxfield, K. B., & Buchholz, S. (1957). *A social maturity scale for blind preschool children: A guide to its use*. New York: American Foundation for the Blind.

McCall, R. B. (1979). The development of intellectual functioning in infancy and the prediction of later IQ. In J. D. Osofsky (Ed.), *Handbook of infant development* (pp. 707–741). New York: Wiley.

McCarthy, D. A. (1972). *Manual for the McCarthy Scales of Children's Abilities*. New York: The Psychological Corporation.

McDermott, P. A., Fantuzzo, J. W., & Glutting, J. J. (1990). Just say no to subtest analysis: A critique on Wechsler theory and practice. *Journal of Psychoeducational Assessment*, *8*, 290–302.

McKillip, R. H., & Wing, H. (1980). Application of a construct model in assessment for employment. In *Construct validity in psychological measurement: Proceedings of a colloquium on theory and application in education and employment*. Princeton, NJ: Educational Testing Service.

McMichael, A. J., Baghurst, P. A., Wigg, N. R., Vimpani, G. V., Robertson, E. F., & Roberts, R. J. (1988). Port Pirie cohort study: Environmental exposure to lead and children's abilities at the age of four years. *New England Journal of Medicine*, *319*, 468–475.

McNemar, Q. (1942). *The revision of the Stanford-Binet scale*. Boston: Houghton Mifflin.

McNemar, Q. (1964). Lost: Our intelligence? Why? *American Psychologist*, *19*, 871–882.

McTurk, R. H., & Neisworth, J. T. (1978). Norm referenced and criterion based measures with preschoolers. *Exceptional Children*, *44*, 34–47.

Meacham, J. A. (1975). Patterns of memory ability in two cultures. *Developmental Psychology*, *11*, 50–53.

Mednick, S A. (1962). The associative basis of the creative process. *Psychological Review*, *69*, 1220–1232.

Mendels, G. E., & Flanders, J. P. (1973). Teacher's expectations and pupil performance. *American Educational Research Journal*, *62*, 321–327.

Mercer, J. R., & Lewis, J. F. (1979). *System of Multicultural Pluralistic Assessment*. Cleveland: The Psychological Corporation.

Messick, S. (1980a). Test validity and the ethics of assessment. *American Psychologist*, *35*, 1012–1037.

Messick, S. (1980b). Meaning and values in test validation: The science and ethics of assessment. *Educational Researcher*, *18*(2), 5–11.

Messick, S. (1988). The once and future issues of validity: Assessing the meaning and consequences of measurement. In H. Wainer & H. Brown (Eds.), *Test validdty* (pp. 33–45). Hillsdale, NJ: Erlbaum.

Messick, S. (1989). Meaning and values in test validation: The science and ethics of assessment. *Educational Measurement*, *18*(1), 5–11.

Miller, E. M. (1994). Intelligence and brain myelination: A hypothesis. *Personality and Individual Differences*, *17*, 803–832.

Minton, H. L., & Schneider, F. W. (1980). *Differential psychology*. Monterey, CA: Brooks/Cole.

Mishra, S. P. (1983). Effects of examiners' prior knowledge of subjects' ethnicity and intelligence on the scoring of responses to the Stanford-Binet scale. *Psychology in the Schools*, *20*, 133–136.

Mishra, S. P., & Brown, K. (1983). The comparability of WAIS and WAIS-R IQs and subtest scores. *Journal of Clinical Psychology*, *39*, 754–757.

Money, J. (1971). Psychosexual development: Maternalism, nonpromiscuity and body image in fifteen females with precocious puberty. *Impact of Science on Society*, *1*, 45–60.

Murphy, K. R. (1992). Review of the Test of Nonverbal Intelligence, Second Edition. In J. J. Kramer & J. C. Conoley (Eds.), *The eleventh mental measurements yearbook* (pp. 969–970). Lincoln, NE: Buros Institute of Mental Measurements.

Myart v. Motorola, 110 Cong. Record 5662–64 (1964).

Myers, B. J. (1982). Early intervention using Brazelton training with middle-class mothers and fathers of newborns. *Child Development*, *53*, 462–471.

Naglieri, J. A. (1982). Two types of tables for use with the WAIS-R. *Journal of Consulting & Clinical Psychology*, *50*, 319–321.

Naglieri, J. A. (1989). A cognitive processing theory for the measurement of intelligence. *Educational Psychologist, 24*, 185–206.

Naglieri, J. A., & Das, J. P. (1990). Planning, attention, simultaneous, and successive (PASS) cognitive processes as a model for intelligence. *Journal of Psychoeducational Assessment, 8*, 303–337.

Naglieri, J. A., Das, J. P., & Jarman, R. F. (1990). Planning, attention, simultaneous, successive cognitive processes as a model for assessment. *School Psychology Review, 19*, 423–442.

Naglieri, J. A., & Haddad, F. A. (1984). Learning disabled children's performance on the Kaufman Assessment Battery for Children: A concurrent validity study. *Journal of Psychoeducational Assessment, 2*, 49–56.

Naglieri, J. A., & Harrison, P. L. (1979). Comparison of McCarthy General Cognitive Indexes and Stanford-Binet IQs for educable mentally retarded children. *Perceptual and Motor Skills, 48*, 1251–1254.

National Society for the Study of Education. (1922). *Intelligence tests and their use. The twenty-first yearbook*. Bloomington, IL: Public School Publishing.

Needleman, H. L., Gunnoe, C., Leviton, A., & Perie, H. (1978). Neuropsychological dysfunction in children with "silent" lead exposure. *Pediatric Research, 12*, 1374. (Abstract)

Needleman, H. L., Schell, A., Bellinger, D., Leviton, A., & Allred, E. N. (1990). The long-term effects of exposure to low doses of lead in childhood. *New England Journal of Medicine, 322*(2), 83–88.

Neugarten, B. L. (1976). The psychology of aging: An overview. *Master lectures in developmental psychology* (cassette tape). Washington, DC: American Psychological Association.

Newland, T. E. (1969). *Manual for the Blind Learning Aptitude Test: Experimental edition*. Urbana, IL: T. Ernest Newland.

Nisbet, J. D. (1957). Intelligence and age: Retesting after twenty-four years' interval. *British Journal of Educational Psychology, 27*, 190–198.

Oakland, T. (1979). Research on the Adaptive Behavior Inventory for Children and the estimated learning potential. *School Psychology Digest, 8*, 63–70.

Oden, M. H. (1968). The fulfillment of promise: 40-year follow-up of the Terman gifted group. *Genetic Psychology Monographs, 77*(1), 3–93.

Oehrn, A. (1895). Experimentelle Studien zur Individual psychologie. *Psychologische Arbeiten, 1*, 95–152.

Ord, J. G. (1971). *Mental tests for pre-literates*. London: Ginn.

Ortar, G. (1963). Is a verbal test cross-cultural? *Scripta Hierosolymitana (Hebrew University, Jerusalem), 13*, 329–235.

Osgood, R. L. (1984). Intelligence testing and the field of learning disabilities: A historical and critical perspective. *Learning Disabilities Quarterly, 7*, 343–348.

Otis, A. S., & Lennon, R. T. (1989). *OLSAT: National norms booklet*. San Diego, CA: Harcourt Brace Jovanovich.

Overall, J. E., & Gorham, D. (1972). Organicity versus old age in objective and projective test performance. *Journal of Consulting & Clinical Psychology, 39*, 98–105.

Owens, W. A., Jr. (1953). Age and mental abilities: A longitudinal study. *Genetic Psychology Monographs, 48*, 3–54.

Owens, W. A., Jr. (1966). Age and mental abilities: A second adult follow-up. *Journal of Educational Psychology, 57*, 311–325.

Page, E. B., & Grandon, G. M. (1979). Family configuration and mental ability: Two theories contrasted with U.S. data. *American Educational Research Journal, 16*, 257–272.

Palmore, E. (Ed.). (1970). *Normal aging*. Durham, NC: Duke University Press.

Palmore, E. (1982). Predictors of the longevity difference: A 25-year follow-up. *Gerontologist*, *225*, 513-518.

Palmore, E., & Cleveland, W. (1976). Aging, terminal decline, and terminal drop. *Journal of Gerontology*, *31*(1), 76-86.

Parents in Action on Special Education (PASE) v. Joseph P. Hannon, No. 74C 3586 (N.D. Ill. 1980).

Parker, K. C. H., Hanson, R. K., & Hunsley, J. (1988). MMPI, Rorschach, and WAIS: A meta-analytic comparison of reliability, stability, and validity. *Psychological Bulletin*, *103*, 367-373.

Pascual-Leon, J. (1983). Growing into human maturity: Toward a metasubjective theory of adult stages. In P. B. Baltes & O. G. Brim, Jr. (Eds.), *Life-span development and behavior* (Vol. 5, pp. 118-156). New York: Academic Press.

Pellegrino, J. W., & Varnhagen, C. K. (1985). Intelligence: Perspectives, theories, and tests. In T. Husén & T. N. Posthlethwaite (Eds.), *The international encyclopedia of education* (Vol. 5, pp. 2611-2618). New York: Wiley.

Perlmutter, M., Adams, C., Barry, J., Kaplan, M., Person, D., Verdonik, F. (1987). Aging and memory. In K. W. Schaie & K. Eisdorfer (Eds.), *Annual review of gerontology and pediatrics* (Vol. 7, pp. 57-92). New York: Springer.

Peterson, J. (1925). *Early conceptions and tests of intelligence*. New York: World Book.

Phares, E. J. (1992). *Clinical psychology: Concepts, methods, and profession* (4th ed.). Belmont, CA: Brooks/Cole.

Plaschke, B., & Almond, E. (1995, April 21). Has NFL draft become thinking man's game? *Los Angeles Times*, pp. C1, C6.

Plemons, J. K., Willis, S. L., & Baltes, P. B. (1978). Modifiability of fluid intelligence in aging: A short-term longitudinal training approach. *Journal of Gerontology*, *33*, 224-231.

Plomin, R. (1988). The nature and nurture of cognitive abilities. In R. J. Sternberg (Ed.), *Advances in the psychology of human intelligence* (Vol. 4, pp. 1-33). Hillsdale, NJ: Erlbaum.

Plomin, R. (1989). Environment and genes: Determinants of behavior. *American Psychologist*, *44*, 105-111.

Plomin, R. (1990). *Nature and nurture: An introduction to human behavior genetics*. Pacific Grove, CA: Brooks/Cole.

Plotnik, R. J., & Tallarico, R. B. (1966). Object-quality learning-set formation in the young chicken. *Psychonomic Science*, *5*, 195-196.

Prechtl, H., & Beintema, D. (1964). *The neurological examination of the full term newborn infant*. London: Heineman.

Purvis, M. A., & Bolen, L. M. (1984). Factor structure of the McCarthy Scales for males and females. *Journal of Clinical Psychology*, *40*, 108-114.

Ramey, C. T., & Campbell, F. A. (1984). Preventive education for high-risk children: Cognitive consequences of the Carolina Abecedarian project. *American Journal of Mental Deficiency*, *88*, 515-523.

Rapaport, D., Gill, M. M., & Schafer, R. (1968). *Diagnostic psychological testing* (rev. ed.). New York: International Universities Press.

Raudenbush, S. W. (1984). Magnitude of teacher expectancy effects on pupil IQ as a function of the credibility of expectancy induction: A synthesis of findings from experiments. *Journal of Educational Psychology*, *76*, 85-97.

Reese, H. W., & Rodeheaver, D. (1985). Problem solving and complex decision making. In J. E. Birren & K. W. Schaie (Eds.), *Handbook of the psychology of aging* (2nd ed., pp. 474-499). New York: Van Nostrand Reinhold.

Reimanis, G., & Green, R. F. (1971). Imminence of death and intellectual decrement in the aging. *Developmental Psychology, 5,* 270-272.

Reitan, R. M. (1964). *Manual for administering and scoring the Reitan-Indiana Neuropsychological Battery for Children (aged 5 through 8).* Indianapolis: Indiana University Medical Center.

Reitan, R. M. (1966). A research program on the psychological effects of brain lesions in human beings. In N. R. Ellis (Ed.), *International research in mental retardation, 1* (pp. 153-218). New York: Academic Press.

Reschly, D. J., & Kicklighter, R., & McKee, P. (1988). Recent placement of litigation part III: Analysis of differences in Larry P., Marshal and S-1, and implications for future practices. *School Psychology Review, 17,* 39-50.

Reschly, D. J., & Sabers, D. L. (1979). Analysis of test bias in four groups with the regression definition. *Journal of Educational Measurement, 16,* 1-9.

Resnick, L. B. (Ed.). (1976). *The nature of intelligence.* New York: Lawrence Erlbaum.

Resnick, L. B. (1979). The future of IQ testing in education. *Intelligence, 3,* 241-253.

Reynolds, C. R. (1984-85). Critical measurement issues in learning disabilities. *The Journal of Special Education, 18*(4), 452-476.

Reynolds, C. R. (1985). Review of the System of Multicultural Pluralistic Assessment. In J. V. Mitchell (Ed.), *The ninth mental measurements yearbook* (pp. 1519-1521). Lincoln: University of Nebraska Press.

Reynolds, C. R. (1987). Playing IQ roulette with the Stanford-Binet, 4th ed. *Measurement and Evaluation in Counseling and Development, 20,* 139-141.

Reynolds, C. R., Chastain, R. L., Kaufman, A. S., & McLean, J. E. (1987). Demographic characteristics and IQ among adults: Analysts of the WAIS-R standardization sample as a function of the stratification variables. *Journal of School Psychology, 25,* 323-342.

Reynolds, C. R., Kamphaus, R. W., & Rosenthal, B. L. (1988). Factor analysis of the Stanford-Binet Fourth Edition for ages 2 years through 23 years. *Measurement and Evaluation in Counseling and Development, 21,* 52-63.

Riegel, K. F. (1973). Dialectic operations: The final period of cognitive development. *Human Development, 16,* 346-370.

Riegel, K. F. (1976). The dialectics of human development. *American Psychologist, 31,* 689-701.

Riegel, K. F., & Riegel, R. M. (1972). Development, drop, and death. *Developmental Psychology, 6,* 306-319.

Rome, H. P., Mataya, P., Pearson, J. S., Swenson, W., & Brunnick, T. L. (1962). Symposium on automation techniques in personality assessment. *Proceedings of the Staff Meetings of the Mayo Clinic, 37,* 61-82.

Rosenblith, J. F. (1961). *Manual for behavioral examination of the neonate as modified by Rosenblith from Graham.* Providence, RI: Brown Duplicating Service.

Rosenthal, R., & Jacobson, L. (1968). *Pygmalion in the classroom.* New York: Holt, Rinehart & Winston.

Ryan, J., Prefitera, A., & Powers, L. (1983). Scoring reliability on the WAIS-R. *Journal of Consulting and Clinical Psychology, 51,* 149-150.

Saigh, P. A. (1981). The effects of positive examiner verbal comments on the total WISC-R performance of institutionalized EMR students. *Journal of School Psychology, 19,* 86-91.

Sameroff, A. J. (Ed.). (1978). Organization and stability of newborn behavior: A commentary on the Brazelton Neonatal Behavior Assessment Scale. *Monographs of the Society for Research in Child Development, 43* (5-6, Serial No. 177).

Samuels, W. (1977). Observed IQ as a function of test atmosphere, tester expectation, and race of tester: A replication for female subjects. *Journal of Educational Psychology, 69*, 593–604.

Sandoval, J. (1985). Review of the System of Multicultural Pluralistic Assessment. In J. V. Mitchell (Ed.), *The ninth mental measurements yearbook* (pp. 1521–1525). Lincoln: University of Nebraska Press.

Sattler, J. M. (1972). *Intelligence test modifications on handicapped and non-handicapped children*. Washington, DC: Department of Health, Education, and Welfare.

Sattler, J. M. (1988). *Assessment of children* (3rd ed.). San Diego: Jerome M. Sattler.

Sattler, J. M., & Gwynne, J. (1982). White examiners generally do not impede the intelligence test performance of black children. *Journal of Consulting and Clinical Psychology, 50*, 196–208.

Sattler, J. M., Hillix, W. A., & Neher, L. A. (1970). Halo effect in examiner scoring of intelligence test responses. *Journal of Consulting and Clinical Psychology, 34*, 172–176.

Sattler, M. M., & Winget, B. M. (1970). Intelligence testing procedures as affected by expectancy and IQ. *Journal of Clinical Psychology, 26*, 446–448.

Scarr, S., & Weinberg, R. A. (1976). I.Q. test performance of black children adopted by white families. *American Psychologist, 31*, 726–739.

Scarr, S., & Yee, D. C. (1980). Heritability and educational policy: Genetic and environmental effects on IQ, aptitude and achievement. *Educational Psychologist, 15*, 1–22.

Schaie, K. W. (1977/1978). Toward a stage theory of adult cognitive development. *Aging and Human Development, 8*, 129–138.

Schaie, K. W. (1983). The Seattle Longitudinal Study: A twenty-one year exploration of psychometric intelligence in adulthood. In K. W. Schaie (Ed.), *Longitudinal studies of adult psychological development* (pp. 64–135). New York: Guilford.

Schaie, K. W., & Gribbin, K. (1975). Adult development and aging. *Annual Review of Psychology, 26*, 65–96.

Schaie, K. W., & Hertzog, C. (1983). Fourteen-year cohort-sequential analyses of adult intellectual development. *Developmental Psychology, 19*, 531–543.

Schaie K. W., & Hertzog, C. (1986). Toward a comprehensive model of adult intellectual development: Contributions of the Seattle Longitudinal Study. In R. J. Sternberg (Ed.), *Advances in the psychology of human intelligence* (Vol. 3, pp. 79–118). Hillsdale, NJ: Lawrence Erlbaum.

Schaie, K. W., & Strother, C. R. (1968). A cross-sequential study of age changes in cognitive behavior. *Psychological Bulletin, 70*, 671–680.

Schaie, K. W., & Willis, S. L. (1986). Can decline in adult cognitive functioning be reversed? *Developmental Psychology, 22*, 223–232.

Schauss, A. G., & Sommars, E. (1982). Children's mental retardation study is attacked: A closer look. *International Journal for Biosocial Research, 3*(2), 75–98.

Schmeiser, C. B., & Ferguson, R. L. (1978). Performance of black and white students on test materials containing content based on black and white cultures. *Journal of Educational Measurement, 15*, 193–200.

Schmidt, F. L. (1985). Review of Wonderlic Personnel Test. In J. V. Mitchell, Jr. (Ed.), *The ninth mental measurements yearbook* (Vol. 2, pp. 1755–1757). Lincoln, NE: The Buros Institute of Mental Measurements, University of Nebraska.

Schroeder, H. E., & Kleinsasser, L. D. (1972). Examiner bias: A determinant of children's verbal behavior on the WISC. *Journal of Consulting and Clinical Psychology, 39*, 451–454.

Schoenfeldt, L. F. (1985). Review of Wonderlic Personnel Test. In J. V. Mitchell, Jr. (Ed.), *The ninth mental measurements yearbook* (Vol. 2, pp. 1757–1758). Lincoln, NE: The Buros Institute of Mental Measurements, University of Nebraska.

Scribner, S., & Cole, M. (1973). Cognitive consequences of formal and informal schooling. *Science, 182,* 553–559.

Sears, R. R. (1977). Sources of life satisfactions of the Terman gifted men. *American Psychologist, 32,* 119–128.

Seguin, E. (1907). *Idiocy: Its treatment by the physiological method.* New York: Bureau of Publications, Teachers College, Columbia University. (Reprinted from the original edition of 1886.)

Seymour, P. H., & Moir, W. L. (1980). Intelligence and semantic judgment time. *British Journal of Psychology, 7*(1), 53–61.

Sharma, R. S., & Mehtani, D S. (1980). Reaction time: Is it a function of intelligence? *Psychological Studies, 25*(2), 105–107.

Sharp, S. E. (1898). Individual psychology: A study of psychological method. *American Journal of Psychology, 10,* 329–391.

Shaw, K. (1980a, June 6). West has failed totally to test intelligence. *Times (London) Educational Supplement,* 3338:15.

Shaw, K. (1980b, November 7). Western IQ tests can be useful: Soviet Union. *Times (London) Educational Supplement,* 7359:13.

Siegler, I. C., McCarty, S. M., & Logue, P. E. (1982). Wechsler Memory Scale scores, selective attribution, and distance from death. *Journal of Gerontology, 37,* 176–181.

Silverstein, A. B. (1978). Note on the construct validity of the ITPA. *Psychology in the Schools, 15,* 371–372.

Silverstein, A. B. (1982a). Pattern analysis as simultaneous statistical inference. *Journal of Consulting and Clinical Psychology, 50,* 234–240.

Silverstein, A. B. (1982b). Two- and four-subtest short forms of the Wechsler Adult Intelligence Scale—Revised. *Journal of Consulting & Clinical Psychology, 50,* 415–418.

Simon, A. J., & Bass, L. G. (1956). Toward a validation of infant testing. *American Journal of Orthopsychiatry, 26,* 340–350.

Sitkei, E. G., & Meyers, C. E. (1969). Comparative structure of intellect in middle- and lower-class four-year-olds of two ethnic groups. *Developmental Psychology, 1,* 592–604.

Skeels, H. M. (1966). Adult status of children with contrasting early life experiences: A follow-up study. *Monographs of the Society for Research in Child Development, 31* (3, Serial No. 105).

Skeels, H. M., & Dye, H. B. (1939). A study of the effects of differential stimulation of mentally retarded children. *Proceedings of the American Association of Mental Deficiency, 44,* 114–136.

Skodak, M., & Skeels, H. M. (1949). A final follow-up study of one hundred adopted children. *Journal of Genetic Psychology, 75,* 85–125.

Slack, W. V., & Porter, D. (1980). The Scholastic Aptitude Test: A critical appraisal. *Harvard Educaitonal Review, 50,* 154–175.

Slate, J. R., & Jones, C. H. (1990). Student error in administering the WISC-R: Identifying problem areas. *Measurement and Evaluation in Counseling and Development, 23,* 137–140.

Smith, D. K., St. Martin, M. E., & Lyon, M. A. (1989). A validity study of the Stanford-Binet: Fourth Edition with students with learning disabilities. *Journal of Learning Disabilities, 22,* 260–261.

Sneed, G. A. (1976). An investigation of examiner bias, teacher referral reports, and socioeconomic status with the WISC-R. *Dissertation Abstracts International, 36,* 4367A. (University Microfilms No. 75-29, 943).

Snyderman, M., & Rothman, S. (1987). Survey of expert opinion on intelligence and aptitude testing. *American Psychologist, 42,* 137-144.

Society for Industrial and Organizational Psychology, Inc. (1987). *Principles for the validation and use of personnel selection procedures* (3rd ed.). College Park, MD: Author.

Sostek, A. M. (1978). Review of the Brazelton Neonatal Assessment Scale. In O. K. Buros (Ed.), *The eighth mental measurements yearbook* (Vol. 1, pp. 208-209). Highland Park, NJ: Gryphon Press.

Spearman, C. E. (1927). *The abilities of man.* London: Macmillan.

Spaeth, J. L. (1976). Characteristics of the work setting and the job as determinants of income. In W. H Sewell, R. M. Sauser, & D. L. Featherman (Eds.), *Schooling and achievement in American society* (pp. 103-131). New York: Academic Press.

Sperry, R. W. (1968). Hemisphere deconnection and unity in conscious awareness. *American Psychologist, 23,* 723-733.

Sprigle, J. E., & Schaefer, L. (1985). Longitudinal evaluation of the effects of two compensatory preschool programs on fourth- through sixth-grade students. *Developmental Psychology, 21,* 702-708.

Stafford, R. E. (1972). Hereditary and environmental components of quantitative reasoning. *Review of Educational Research, 42,* 183-201.

Stanley, J. C., Keating, D. P., & Fox, L. H. (Eds.). (1974). *Mathematical talent: Discovery, description, and development.* Baltimore: Johns Hopkins University Press.

Steelman, L. C., & Doby, J. T. (1983). Family size and birth order as factors in the IQ performance of black and white children. *Sociology of Education, 46,* 101-109.

Sternberg, R. J. (1981). Testing and cognitive psychology. *American Psychologist, 36,* 1181-1189.

Sternberg, R. J. (1982). Thinking and learning skills: A view of intelligence. *Education Digest, 47,* 20-22.

Sternberg, R. J. (1984). The Kaufman Assessment Battery for Children: An information analysis and critique. *Journal of Special Education, 18,* 269-279.

Sternberg, R. J. (1985). *Beyond IQ: A triarchic theory of human intelligence.* Cambridge: Cambridge University Press.

Sternberg, R. J. (1986). *The triarchic mind: A new theory of human intelligence.* New York: Viking.

Sternberg, R. J. (1988). Mental self-government: A theory of intellectual styles and their development. *Human Development, 31,* 197-224.

Sternberg, R. J. (1989). Domain-generality versus domain-specificity: The life and impending death of a false dichotomy. *Merrill-Palmer Quarterly, 35,* 115-130.

Sternberg, R. J., & Davidson, J. E. (1990). Introduction to special issue. *Educational Psychologist, 25,* 175.

Stevenson, H. W. (1977, March). *The effect of schooling on memory and cognitive processes of urban and rural children in Peru.* Paper presented at the meeting of the Society for Research in Child Development, New Orleans.

Stillman, R. (1974). *Assessment of deaf-blind children: The Callier-Azusa Scale.* Paper presented at the Intercom '74, Hyannis, MA.

Stoch, M. B., & Smythe, P. M. (1963). Does undernutrition during infancy inhibit brain growth and subsequent intellectual development? *Archives of Disorders of Childhood, 38,* 546-552.

Stodolsky, S., & Lesser, G. (1967). Learning patterns in the disadvantaged. *Harvard Educational Review*, *37*, 546–593.

Stone, C. A. (1989). Improving the effectiveness of strategy training for learning disabled students: The role of communicated dynamics. *Remedial and Special Education*, *10*(1), 35–42.

Stott, D. H. (1983). Brain size and "intelligence." *British Journal of Developmental Psychology*, *1*(3), 279–287.

Strauss, A. A., & Lehtinen, L. E. (1947). *Psychopathology and education of the brain-injured child*, Vol. 1. New York: Grune & Stratton.

Swenson, W. M., & Pearson, J. S. (1964). Automation techniques in personality assessment: A frontier in behavioral science and medicine. *Methods of Information in Medicine*, *3*, 34–36.

Taking the chitling test (1986, July 15). *Newsweek*, *72*(3), 51–52.

Terman, L. M., & Childs, H. G. (1912). Tentative revision and extension of the Binet-Simon Measuring Scale of Intelligence. *Journal of Educational Psychology*, *3*, 61–74, 133–143, 198–208, 277–289.

Terman, L. M., Dickinson, V. E., Sutherland, A. H., Franzen, R. H., Tupper, C. R., & Fernald, G. (1922). *Intelligence tests and school reorganization*. Yonkers-on-Hudson: World Book.

Terman, L. M., & Merrill, M. A. (1973). *Stanford-Binet Intelligence Scale: 1972 norms edition*. Boston: Houghton Mifflin.

Terman, L. M., & Oden, M. H. (1947). *Genetic studies of genius: The gifted child grows up* (Vol. 4). Stanford, CA: Stanford University Press.

Terman, L. M., & Oden, M. H. (1959). *The gifted group at mid-life: Genetic studies of genius. V.* Stanford, CA: Stanford University Press.

Terrell, F., Terrell, S. L., & Taylor, J. (1981). Effects of type of reinforcement on the intelligence test performance of retarded black children. *Psychology in the Schools*, *18*, 225–227.

Thatcher, R. W., Lester, M. L., McAlaster, R., Horst, R., & Ignasias, S. W. (1983). Intelligence and lead toxins in rural children. *Journal of Learning Disabilities*, *16*, 355–359.

Theye, F. W. (1970). Violation of standard procedure on the Wechsler scales. *Journal of Clinical Psychology*, *26*, 70–71.

Thomas, G. E., Alexander, K. L., & Eckland, B. K. (1979). Access to higher education: The importance of race, sex, social class, and academic credentials. *School Review*, *87*, 133–156.

Thorndike, E. L. (1911). *Animal intelligence*. New York: Macmillan. (Original work published 1898.)

Thorndike, R. L. (1975). Mr. Binet's test 70 years later. *Educational Researcher*, *4*(5), 3–6.

Thorndike, R. L. (1990). Would the real factors of the Stanford-Binet Fourth Edition please come forward? *Journal of Psychoeducational Assessment*, *8*, 412–435.

Thorndike, R. L., Hagen, E. P., & Sattler, J. M. (1986a). *The Stanford-Binet Intelligence Scale: Fourth Edition, Guide for administering and scoring*. Chicago: Riverside Publishing Company.

Thorndike, R. L., Hagen, E. P., & Sattler, J. P. (1986b). *The Stanford-Binet Intelligence Scale: Fourth Edition, Technical manual*. Chicago: Riverside Publishing Company.

Tinbergen, N. (1951). *The study of instinct*. New York: Oxford University Press.

Torrance, E. P. (1988). The nature of creativity as manifest in its testing. In R. J. Sternberg (Ed.), *The nature of creativity: Contemporary psychological perspectives* (pp. 43–75). Cambridge, England: Cambridge University Press.

Trentham, L. L. (1975). The effect of distractions on sixth-grade students in a testing situation. *Journal of Educational Measurement*, *12*, 13–18.

Trevarthan, C. (1974). Conversations with a two-month-old. *New Scientist*, *62*(896), 230–235.

Tronick, E. Z. (1987). The neonatal behavioral assessment scale as a biomarker of the effects of environmental agents on the newborn. *Environmental Health Perspectives*, *74*, 185–189.

Tronick, E., & Brazelton, T. B. (1975). Clinical uses of the Brazelton Neonatal Behavioral Assessment. In B. Friedlander, G. Sterritt, & G. Kirk (Eds.), *Exceptional infant* (Vol. 3, pp. 137–156). New York: Brunner/Mazel.

Trueman, M., Lynch, A., & Branthwaite, A. (1984). A factor analytic study of the McCarthy Scales of Children's Abilities. *British Journal of Educational Psychology*, *54*, 331–335.

Tsushima, W. T., & Bratton, J. C. (1977). Effects of geographical region upon Wechsler Adult Intelligence Scale results: A Hawaii–mainland United States comparison. *Journal of Consulting & Clinical Psychology*, *45*, 501–502.

Tuddenham, R. D., Blumenkrantz, J., & Wilkin, W. R. (1968). Age changes in AGCT: A longitudinal study of average adults. *Journal of Counseling & Clinical Psychology*, *32*, 659–663.

Tunga, N. (1979). Contemporary differences between African and Western concepts of intelligence. *Revue de psychologie applique*, *29*(1), 53–61.

Tyler, L. E. (1965). *The psychology of human differences*. Englewood Cliffs, NJ: Prentice Hall.

U.S. Department of Defense. (1992). *Counselor's manual for the ASVAB*. North Chicago, IL: U.S. Military Entrance Procesing Command.

U.S. Department of Defense. (1993). *ASVAB 18/19 technical manual*. North Chicago, IL: U.S. Military Entrance Processing Command.

U.S. Department of Defense. (1994). *Technical manual for the ASVAB 18/19 career exploration program*. North Chicago, IL: U.S. Military Entrance Processing Command.

Uzgiris, I. C. (1983). Organization of sensorimotor intelligence. In M. Lewis (Ed.), *Origins of intelligence: Infancy and early childhood* (2nd ed., pp. 135–189). New York: Plenum.

Uzgiris, I. C., & Hunt, J. McV. (1975). *Assessment in infancy: Ordinal scales of psychological development*. Urbana, IL: University of Illinois Press.

Vernon, P. E. (1960). *The structure of human abilities* (Rev. ed.). London: Methuen.

Vernon, P. E. (1969). *Intelligence and cultural environment*. London: Methuen.

Vernon, P. E. (1970). Intelligence testing and the nature/nurture debate, 1928–1978: What next? *British Journal of Educational Psychology*, *49*, 1–14.

Vernon, P. E. (1979a). Intelligence testing and the nature/nurture debate, 1928–1978: What next? *British Journal of Educational Psychology*, *49*, 1–14.

Vernon, P. E. (1979b). *Intelligence: Heredity and environment*. San Francisco: W. H. Freeman.

Vernon, P. E. (1981). Reaction time and intelligence in the mentally retarded. *Intelligence*, *5*, 345–355.

Vernon, P. E. (1983). Speed of information processing and general intelligence. *Intelligence*, *7*, 53–70.

Vernon, P. E. (1985). Intelligence: Heredity-environment determinants. In T. Husen & T. N. Posthlethwaite (Eds.), *The international encyclopedia of education* (Vol. 5, pp. 2605–2611). New York: Wiley.

Vernon, P. A. (1987). New developments in reaction time research. In P. A. Vernon (Ed.), *Speed of information-processing and intelligence* (pp. 1–20). Norwood, NJ: Ablex.

Vernon, P. A. (1990). The use of biological measures to estimate behavioral intelligence. *Educational Psychologist*, *25*(3 & 4), 293–304.

Very, P. S. (1967). Differential factor structures in mathematical ability. *Genetic Psychology Monographs, 75*, 169–207.

Vygotsky, L. S. (1962). *Thought and language* (E. Hanfmann & G. Vakar, Trans.). Cambridge, MA: The M.I.T. Press. (Original work published 1934).

Vygotsky, L. S. (1978). (M. Cole, V. John-Steiner, S. Scribner, & E. Souberman, Eds. and Trans.). *Mind in society: The development of higher psychological processes.* Cambridge: Harvard University Press.

Wachs, T. D. (1975). Relation of infants' performance on Piaget scales between twelve and twenty-four months and their Stanford-Binet performance at thirty-one months. *Child Development, 46*, 929–935.

Wagner, D. A. (1974). The development of short-term and incidental memory: A cross-cultural study. *Child Development, 45*, 389–396.

Walker,, N. W. (1981). Modifying impulsive responding to four WISC-R subtests. *Journal of School Psychology, 19*(4), 335–339.

Wallach, M. A., & Kogan, N. (1965). *Modes of thinking in young children.* New York: Holt, Rinehart & Winston.

Wallbrown, F. H., Blaha, J., & Wherry, R. J. (1973). The hierarchical factor structure of the Wechsler Preschool and Primary Scale of Intelligence. *Journal of Consulting and Clinical Psychology, 41*, 356–362.

Ward, M. E., & Genshaft, J. (1983). The Perkins-Binet Test: A critique and recommendations for administration. *Exceptional Children, 49*, 450–452.

Warren, J. M. (1973). Learning in vertebrates. In D. A. Dewsbury & D. A. Rethlingshafter (Eds.), *Comparative psychology: A modern survey.* New York: McGraw-Hill.

Watson, T. S. (1992). Review of the Test of Nonverbal Intelligence, Second Edition. In J. J. Kramer & J. C. Conoley (Eds.), *The eleventh mental measurements yearbook* (pp. 970–972). Lincoln, NE: Buros Institute of Mental Measurements.

Webb, J. T., & Meckstroth, B. (1982). *Guiding the gifted child.* Columbus: Ohio Psychology Publishing Co.

Wechsler, D. (1939). *The measurement of adult intelligence.* Baltimore: Williams & Wilkins.

Wechsler, D. (1958). *The measurement and appraisal of adult intelligence* (4th ed.). Baltimore: Williams & Wilkins.

Wechsler, D. (1975). Intelligence defined and undefined. *American Psychologist, 30*, 135–139.

Wechsler, D. (1981a). The psychometric tradition: Developing the Wechsler Adult Intelligence Scale. *Contemporary Educational Psychology, 6*, 82–85.

Wechsler, D. (1981b). *WAIS-R manual.* New York: The Psychological Corporation.

Wechsler, D. (1989). *Manual for the Wechsler Preschool and Primary Scale of Intelligence—Revised.* San Antonio, TX: The Psychological Corporation.

Wechsler, D. (1991). *Wechsler Intelligence Scale for Children—Third Edition manual. San Antonio: The Psychological Corporation.*

Weinberg, R. A. (1989). Intelligence and IQ: Landmark issues and great debates. American Psychologist, 44, 98–104.

Weiss, L. G. (1995). WISC-III IQs: New norms raise queries. *Assessment Focus, 1*(2), 1, 5. San Antonio, TX: The Psychological Corporation.

Welsh, J. R., Kucinkas, S. K., & Curran, L. T. (1990). *Armed Services Vocational Aptitude Battery (ASVAB), Integrative review of validity studies (AFHRL-TR-90-22).* Brooks Air Force Base, TX: Air Force Human Resources Laboratory.

Werner, E. E. (1965). Review of the Arthur Adaptation of the Leiter International Performance

Scale. In O. K. Buros (Ed.), *The sixth mental measurements yearbook* (pp. 814–816). Highland Park, NJ: Gryphon Press.

Wesman, A. G. (1968). Intelligent testing. *American Psychologist, 23*, 2567–2574.

Whipple, G. M. (1910). *Manual of mental and physical tests* (Vols. 1–2). Baltimore, MD: Warwick & York.

White, N., & Cunningham, W. R. (1988). Is terminal drop pervasive or specific? *Journal of Gerontology: Psychological Sciences, 43*, P141–P144.

Willerman, L. (1979). *The psychology of individual and group differences*. San Francisco: W. H. Freeman.

Willerman, L., Schultz, R., Rutledge, J. N., & Bigler, E. (1989). *Magnetic resonance imaged brain structures and intelligence*. Paper presented to the 19th annual meeting of the Behavior Genetics Association, Charlottesville, VA.

Williams, R. L. (1975). The BITCH-100: A culture-specific test. *Journal of Afro-American Issues, 3*, 103–116.

Williamson, W. D., Wilson, G. S., Lifschitz, M. H., Thurbers, S. A. (1990). Nonhandicapped very-low-birth-weight infants at one year of age developmental profile. *Pediatrics, 85*, 405–410.

Willis, S. L. (1990). Introduction to the special section on cognitive training in later adulthood. *Developmental Psychology, 26*, 875–878.

Willis, S. L., Blieszner, R., & Baltes, P. B. (1981). Intellectual training research in aging: Modification of performance in the fluid ability of figural relations. *Journal of Educational Psychology, 75*, 41–50.

Willmott, M., & Brierley, H. (1984). Cognitive characteristics and homosexuality. *Archives of Sexual Behavior, 13*, 311–319.

Wilson, R. S. (1985). Risk and resilience in early mental development. *Developmental Psychology, 21*, 795–805.

Wissler, C. (1901). The correlation of mental and physical tests. *Psychological Review Monograph Supplement 3*, No. 6.

Witelson, S. F. (1976). Sex and the single hemisphere: Specialization of the right hemisphere for spatial processing. *Science, 193*, 425–427.

Wober, M. (1972). Culture and the concept of intelligence: A case in Uganda. *Journal of Cross-cultural Psychology, 3*, 327–328.

Wober, M. (1974). Towards an understanding of the Uganda concept of intelligence. In J. W. Berry & P. R. Dasen (Eds.), *Culture and cognition: Readings in cross-cultural psychology*. London: Methuen.

Wolf, T. H. (1973). *Alfred Binet*. Chicago: University of Chicago Press.

Wurtman, R. J. (1979). Symposium of choline and related substances in nerve and mental disease, Tucson, AZ. (Reported by H. M. Schmeck in *New York Times*, January 9, 1970, p. C1ff.)

Yeasavage, J. A., & Rose, T. (1984). The effects of a face-name mnemonic in young, middle-aged, and elderly adults. *Experimental Aging Research, 10*, 55–57.

Yerkes, R. M. (Ed.). (1921). Psychological examining in the United States army. *Memoirs of the National Academy of Sciences, 15*.

Ysseldyke, J. E., & Samuel, S. (1973). Identification of diagnostic strengths and weaknesses on the McCarthy Scale of Children's Abilities. *Psychology in the Schools 10*, 304–315.

Zajonc, R. B. (1976). Family configuration and intelligence. *Science, 192*, 227–236.

Zeigarnik, B. V., Luria, A. R., & Polyakov, Y. F. (1977). On the use of psychological tests in clinical practice in the U.S.S.R. *Intelligence, 1*, 82–93.

Zeigler, H. P. (1961). Learning set-formation in pigeons. *Journal of Comparative and Physiological Psychology*, *54*, 252–254.

Zeskind, P. S., & Ramey, C. T. (1981). Preventing intellectual and interactional sequelae of fetal malnutrition: A longitudinal transaction, and synergistic approach to development. *Child Development*, *52*, 213–218.

Zigler, E. (1967). Familial mental retardation: A continuing dilemma. *Science*, *155*, 292–298.

Zigler, E. (1985). Assessing Head Start at 20: An invited commentary. *American Journal of Orthopsychiatry*, *55*, 603–609.

Zigler, E., Abelson, W. D., Trickett, P. K., & Seitz, V. (1982). Is an intervention program necessary in order to improve economically disadvantaged children's IQ scores? *Child Development*, *53*, 340–348.

Zimmerman, I. L., & Woo-Sam, J. M. (1973). *Clinical interpretation of the Wechsler Adult Intelligence Scale*. New York: Grune & Stratton.

Zimmerman, R., & Bornstein, S. (n.d.). *Developmental Checklist*. Boston: Boston Center for Blind Children.

Author Index

Subject Index

Tests and Instruments Index

XINJIANG

THE SILK ROAD: ISLAM'S OVERLAND ROUTE TO CHINA

XINJIANG

THE SILK ROAD: ISLAM'S OVERLAND ROUTE TO CHINA

PETER YUNG

HONG KONG OXFORD NEW YORK
OXFORD UNIVERSITY PRESS
1986

Oxford University Press

Oxford New York Toronto
Petaling Jaya Singapore Hong Kong Tokyo
Delhi Bombay Calcutta Madras Karachi
Nairobi Dar es Salaam Cape Town
Melbourne Auckland

and associated companies in
Beirut Berlin Ibadan Nicosia

Library of Congress Cataloging-in-Publication Data

Weng, Wei-ch'üan, 1949 –
    Xinjiang, the Silk Road.

    1. Sinkiang Uighur Autonomous Region (China) —
Description and travel — Views.   2. Silk Road —
Description and travel — Views.   I. Title.
DS793. S62W43   1986   915.1'6'00222   86-18106
ISBN 0-19-584121-2

Designed by Peter Cook
Produced by PPA Design Limited, Hong Kong
Colour separations by Dai Ichi Seihan, Hong Kong
Printed in Hong Kong by Paramount Printing Co., Ltd.
Published by Oxford University Press, Warwick House, Hong Kong

CONTENTS

ACKNOWLEDGEMENTS

6

This book is dedicated to my son Jimmy Chun-Yin

In the preparation of this book I am particularly grateful to the following: Wu Jiang; John Chan; Andy Tong; Ivy Ng; Rebecca Yuen; Apple Chu; China News Service; China Film Corporation; the Government of the Xinjiang Uygur Autonomous Region; and the People's Liberation Army. And I am specially indebted to Miss Farida Wahab for her painstaking work in translating the text.

PREFACE

'About a hundred miles to the north are sand mountains spanning almost a thousand miles ... The sand is a shimmer of the dawn's glow. Come dusk and the quiet of evening, and there are sounds like armies clashing in battle which reach the ears of the villagers in the foothills.'

T HESE ghostly noises of battle in the night are recorded in the archives of an ancient village in Barkol Kazak Autonomous County in northern Xinjiang province. Legend has it that during a raging battle in this area between Han Chinese and Hun soldiers, a sandstorm blew up and engulfed the armies. Locals today still claim to hear the cries of the soldiers. The story was previously banned by the Communists as pure superstition, but has been recently revived and since China initiated her 'open-door' policy in 1979, has been once again related to travellers.

It was such folklore that inspired me to make a film on a related theme: a contemporary Chinese archaeologist, in his search for the precise location of the battle in the legend, unearths some remains of the buried armies. From studying ancient weapons, he hopes to gain insights into the military customs and tactics of that bygone age. Beset by many dangers and enmeshed in a series of adventures, he finally fulfils his self-appointed task with the aid of an old Kazak huntsman, born and bred in the desert.

For the past decade or so photography and filming have been my passport to travels in far-flung places, and in 1981-2 they proved to be the key

Portrait of a lady/Tang/ unearthed in 1972 at the Hastana Graves.

8

Painting on paper of the life of a landlord/Jin/ unearthed in 1964 at the Hastana Graves.

to penetrating Xinjiang province in western China. With the authorization and assistance of the government of the Xinjiang Uygur Autonomous Region and the People's Liberation Army, I was able to wander virtually where I pleased, even in military zones which are usually closed to travellers. To collect material for my proposed script, I amassed information on the Kazak and Tajik who inhabit the area I was interested in, and I learned a great deal about their customs and habits.

In the course of my research I travelled widely in the Kazak and Tajik autonomous counties, the homes of the legendary horsemen of Xinjiang. Under special arrangements made for me by the authorities, I was able to visit a model herdsman's round felt-covered tent, known as a yurt. Roaming at will, the guide-interpreter and I also encountered more primitive examples of the herdsmen's life in those wild regions. One of the photographs we took, of a family with five children, ranging in age from a few months to four years, shows clearly the extremely low standard of living, in sharp contrast with the model home specially laid on for visitors. But whether it is a matter of an arranged visit, or of just dropping in casually, the Kazak are extremely hospitable people. They invariably insist that you stay for a cup of milk tea with cheese, flatbread and cakes. Though they may not slaughter a whole sheep in your honour — as some books lead one to believe — their sincerity and warmth are beyond compare.

In our search for a suitable actress for the female lead in our film, we visited various performing troupes and film studios, including the one at Qapqal near the Soviet frontier. We finally discovered our actress — the young housekeeper at a small guesthouse on the outskirts of Ili. After a few film tests we decided she was ideal for the role.

Finding an elderly Kazak hunter with an eagle for the lead role was more difficult, and yet the Kazak strongly objected to the idea of someone from even a neighbouring clan impersonating them. We ended up by clipping photos of old herdsmen from newspapers and magazines and sending them out to the personnel departments of every locality in the county. We had to cross mountain ranges and ford scores of watercourses in order to inspect the most likely candidates. By this trial-and-error method we finally tracked our man down in a place named Mori. He had never even left his home district to visit the local township — let alone Ürümqi or Beijing!

After casting, location-hunting proved the next most difficult problem. Our search covered the barren desert along the ancient Silk Road, the course of which is followed today by the chief highway across Xinjiang. The actual distance from Hami to Turpan and on to Kashgar (Kashi) did not take us long to traverse: it was problems of food supply, lack of horses, scorching heat and bitter cold that made our task so arduous. In the end, we settled for a 1,500-kilometre stretch of desert linking the eastern part of the Junggar Basin with the borders of Mongolia, following the northern route around the Tianshan.

The fascinating thing about this belt of country is its three-coloured pattern. It begins with a stretch of lush pasture, which is overtaken by moving sand dunes, merging into hundreds of miles of desert composed of pebbles and sandy ground.

Another location was the Turpan Depression, a land of harsh climate and vast desert, and containing the famous Flaming Mountains. As we drove through the depression, the heat was intense, the desert

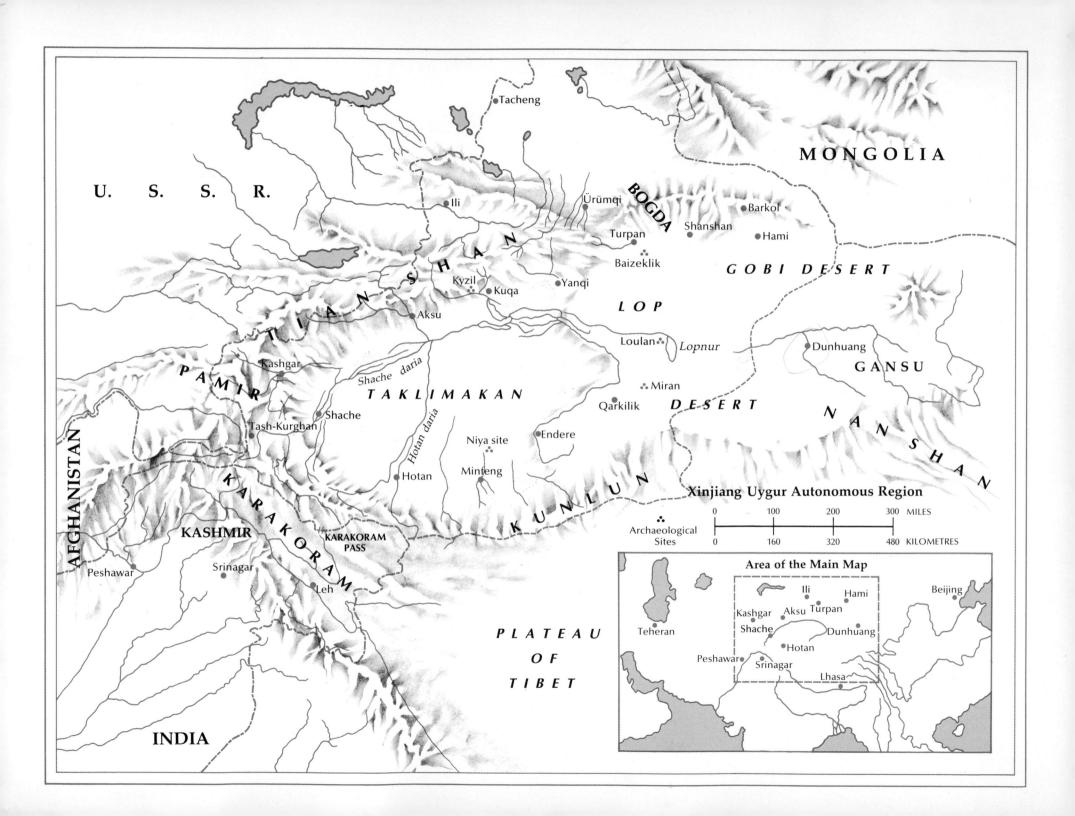

Tacheng

MONGOLIA

U. S. S. R.

BOGDA

Ili

Ürümqi

Barkol

Shanshan

Hami

TIAN SHAN

Turpan

Baizeklik

GOBI DESERT

Kyzil

Kuqa

Yanqi

LOP

Aksu

Loulan

Lopnur

Dunhuang

PAMIR

Kashgar

Shache daria

TAKLIMAKAN

GANSU

Miran

Shache

Qarkilik

DESERT

Tash-Kurghan

Hotan daria

Endere

NAN SHAN

Niya site

AFGHANISTAN

Hotan

Minfeng

KUNLUN

KARAKORAM

Xinjiang Uygur Autonomous Region

KASHMIR

KARAKORAM
PASS

Archaeological
Sites

| 0 | 100 | 200 | 300 | MILES |

Peshawar

Srinagar

Leh

| 0 | 160 | 320 | 480 | KILOMETRES |

Area of the Main Map

PLATEAU

OF

TIBET

Ili

Hami

Beijing

Kashgar

Aksu

Turpan

Shache

Dunhuang

Teheran

Hotan

Peshawar

INDIA

Srinagar

Lhasa

was like an ocean, and our jeep seemed to float across its vast expanse.

With its high temperatures and extremely low rainfall, the climate of the Turpan area acts as a natural preservative for historic relics and ancient cities. Of all the archaeological sites in the area, I was most interested in the underground Hastana Graves.

At the graves I was shown round by a grave-watchman. I was escorted first along a slanting passage to a typical coffin-chamber, a small enclosure whose walls had spaces for storing burial objects. They were empty, however, and the watchman told me that the contents had been removed for inspection by specialists at museums in Xinjiang and Beijing.

The main grave-chamber, the total area of which was about 10 square metres, had an earth platform about 1 metre high with rooms opening off to the left and right. The frescoes had been freshly repainted, but the corpse had also been taken to a museum. The old man then led me along a long passage to another chamber, a small room dug out of the bare earth and about 4 square metres in size. A plank, covered with a dirty, worn straw mat, was laid across a pair of wooden benches. Heaps of rags were piled in every corner and there was dust everywhere. The old man drew back the straw mat to disclose an incomplete, slightly bent and naked corpse. It was a most distressing sight.

My other main purpose in Turpan was to visit the ruins of the ancient cities of Jiaohe and Gaochang, and the Thousand Buddha Caves at Baizeklik, near Gaochang. Dug out from a man-made platform on a

12

cliff, the Thousand Buddha Caves are known to the Uygur as 'the place decorated with paintings'. Alas, the Buddhist statues and wall paintings of the caves are no longer intact. Faces have been mutilated with sharp instruments, either by local farmers who fear the 'evil eye', or by Muslim iconoclasts who believed that it was sinful to portray human figures. The walls of some of the caves are marked by the tools of European explorers and archaeologists who removed the best paintings at the beginning of the century. According to their own records, the German archaeologist, Albert von Le Coq, and his assistant Bartus alone took away 400 cases of artefacts and frescoes from these caves and from Jiaohe and Gaochang. Other adventurers took much of the rest.

All these areas in Xinjiang were to be the setting for the docudrama filmed in 1982, with Kazak 'warriors' riding horses supplied by the Chinese Liberation Army. Since 1983 I have been working on a documentary about the effects of wind in the desert, and on a feature film about espionage along the Silk Road in the Han dynasty. Both projects have once again taken me the length and breadth of Xinjiang in search of material.

During those years of wandering along the Silk Road, I never forgot that I was a photographer and my mind revolved round the idea of a book to be compiled from the thousands of shots that I would take. Everywhere I wandered I found new and fascinating shots, and the surprise and delight I felt never gave way to disillusionment or tedium.

Mural in Cave No. 9 at Baizeklik.

A<small>T</small> the command of Pope Innocent IV, a Franciscan missionary named John of Plano Carpini set out in 1246 for Karakorum, the capital of the Mongol empire. The journey was to take him across thousands of miles of deserts, steppes and wild mountain ranges. His mission: to establish diplomatic relations with the empire. At that time — the mid-thirteenth century — the Mongols were the most feared conquerors in the world and were regarded by Europeans as savages.

In anticipation of long and arduous travelling ahead, John and his companions had their arms and legs tethered with rope to prepare them for the endurance test of successive days and nights on horseback. North of the Caspian Sea, they crossed into the enormous land empire founded by the Mongol conqueror, Genghis Khan (1167-1227). They rode around the clock, their horses being changed five or six times a day by their Mongol escorts. They continued until they reached the Aral Sea, proceeding from there to the little-known lands of Central Asia, or Tartary, as it was called in Europe.

They pushed on past swamps and salt-water lakes into lands inhabited by the Uygur, a Turkic people who were on the brink of being converted to Islam. At last the travellers reached Lake Balkash in the northwest of China. Skirting the Altay Mountains, they arrived at Karakorum after a journey of only a few months — reflecting the efficiency of the Mongol system of post-horses which united an empire larger than any the world had seen before. They remained there for four months and witnessed the coronation of the Emperor Guyuk Khan, the grandson of Genghis Khan.

Forage account of horse stable/Tang/unearthed in 1973 at the Hastana Graves.

On their return to the Vatican, the Franciscans compiled a report on their travels, which may seem fanciful in some of its details, as the following extract demonstrates:

'After the son of Genghis Khan succeeded to the throne, he built a city on the territory of the Black Khitan, near Lake Alakol, and called it Emi'n. South of this city is a vast desert. We were informed with the utmost earnestness that this desert was inhabited by savages deprived of the gift of speech. Their legs had no joints, so that, if they fell over and had no one to help them, they could not stand up again. But they were intelligent enough to make blankets and clothing from camel-hair to cover themselves against the bitter winds. If attacked by the Mongols, they defended themselves with bows and arrows and used grass to bind their wounds before making their escape.'

The vast desert to the south of Emi'n is known as the Taklimakan, which lies in the Tarim Basin. Fables and legends abound regarding this huge desert. Not a word of praise or admiration for it has ever been uttered by the numerous merchants, adventurers, diplomats and pious missionaries who have had occasion to pass through it. Since time immemorial it has been regarded as a place of evil.

The famous Chinese pilgrim, Xuanzang, who travelled from Chang'an (present-day Xi'an) to India in search of Buddhist scriptures, describes the desert in his journal, *Records of Western Lands:*

'One enters the desert from the northwest. Not a drop of water nor a blade of grass may be seen. The road stretches on to an unseen destination; you look for the horizon, but the vastness appears to have no end ... The wind erupts in forceful, whipping gales, churning the sand and hurling rocks. Whoever is engulfed by it stands at death's door; the end is certain.'

The Taklimakan is an ocean of massive, shifting sand dunes covering an area greater than that of Great Britain. Some of the dunes tower to a height of 300 metres, while others of 50 to 80 metres are common. Severe sandstorms are frequent occurrences.

These sudden, terrifying storms are known to the natives as *karaburan* or 'black hurricanes'. The German archaeologist, Albert von Le Coq, author of *Buried Treasures of Chinese Turkestan* (1928), describes such a storm witnessed by him in the early 1900s:

> 'Quite suddenly the sky goes dark, the sun becomes a dark-red ball of fire seen through the fast-thickening veil of dust . . . and a moment after, the storm bursts with appalling violence upon the caravan. Enormous masses of sand, mixed with pebbles, are forcibly lifted up, whirled round and dashed down on man and beast, the darkness increases and strange, clashing noises mingle with the roar and howl of the storm, caused by the violent contact of great stones as they are whirled up through the air. The whole happening is like hell let loose . . . '

More than 2,000 years ago, in accounts written during China's Han dynasty (206-220 AD), the Taklimakan was known as the 'moving sands'. According to one such account, 'wind-whirled sand chokes the sky and dyes it a blinding yellow, the bare sand dunes devoid of cover for man or beast'. All the dunes are slaves of the wind, changing position, shape and size unpredictably and unceasingly.

The Chinese were familiar even then with the geography and terrain of the desert which marked the western confines of their empire. Emperor Han Wudi sent an explorer named Zhang Qian on a secret mission to Xiyu, the Western Region, beyond the so-called Yumenguan, or Jade Gate, near Dunhuang in present-day Gansu province to contact the ancient people now called Indoscythians. Wudi had learned that the Indoscythians had been defeated by the Xiongnu, or Huns, some years earlier and had been forced to move to the west, near Amu Daria. There, they were waiting to avenge their defeat. The aim was to obtain their agreement to form a military alliance and wipe out the Xiongnu who were perpetually making war on China.

By the Tang dynasty (618-907 AD) the Western Region was considered to extend as far as Persia and Turkey in the west, and India in the south. Genghis Khan extended the frontiers to Eastern Europe and southern Russia. Included was the territory now known as Xinjiang, which became a Chinese province in 1884, and which, in 1955, was officially named the Xinjiang Uygur Autonomous Region, with its regional capital in Ürümqi. Previously known as Chinese Tartary or Eastern Turkistan, Xinjiang has an area of more than 1.6 million square kilometres, accounting for one-sixth of China's total land area.

As a result of Zhang Qian's two diplomatic missions to the Western Region in 183 and 119 BC, economic and cultural links were forged between China and Central Asia, clearing the way for the creation of the so-called Silk Road between East and West. (In fact, the term Silk Road was coined by a German scholar only about a century ago.) Merchants plying this route traded not only in silk, but also in tea, iron, and a host of other commodities.

The Silk Road consisted of two separate routes: the northern and the southern. Both began in the city now known as Xi'an in the province of Shaanxi. They traversed Dunhuang and passed by Yumenguan on the way to Loulan, in the vicinity of Lopnur. There, one route branched off northwards to

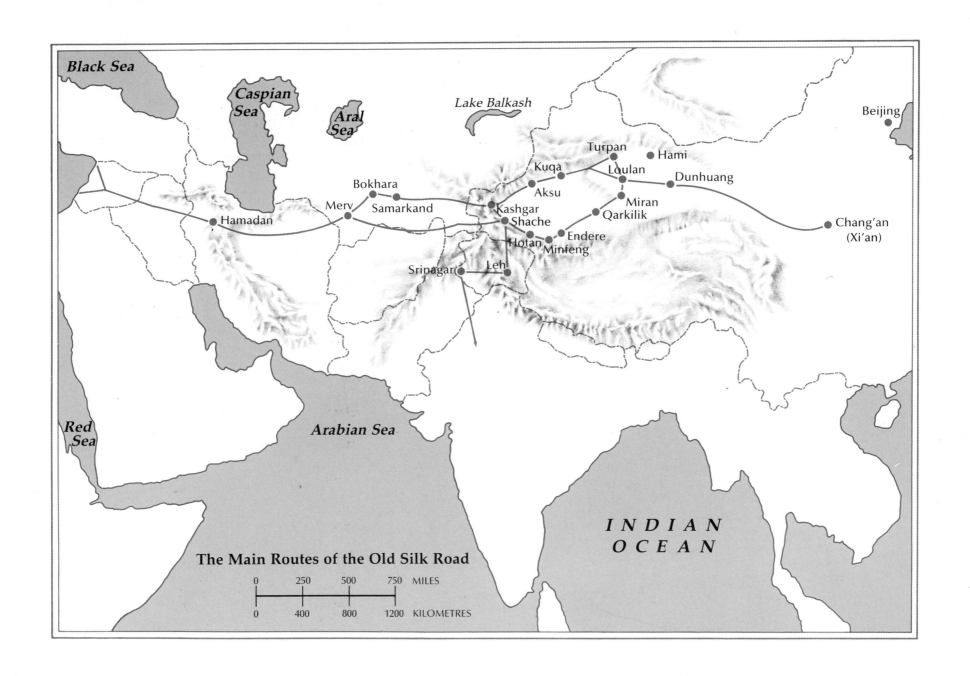

Black Sea

Caspian Sea

Aral Sea

Lake Balkash

Beijing

Turpan

Hami

Kuqa

Loulan

Dunhuang

Bokhara

Aksu

Miran

Merv

Samarkand

Kashgar

Qarkilik

Chang'an (Xi'an)

Hamadan

Shache

Endere

Hotan

Minfeng

Srinagar

Leh

Red Sea

Arabian Sea

INDIAN OCEAN

The Main Routes of the Old Silk Road

| 0 | 250 | 500 | 750 | MILES |

| 0 | 400 | 800 | 1200 | KILOMETRES |

pass between the southern foothills of the Tianshan and the lush oases of the Taklimakan Desert's northern rim, which included the cities of Turpan, Kuqa, Aksu, and finally Kashgar.

The southern route turned southwest at Loulan to skirt the northern foothills of the Kunlun Mountains, and then wound along the southern rim of the Taklimakan with its string of oases — past Miran, Qarkilik (Ruoqiang), Endere, Hotan (Khotan), Yarkand (Shache) — and met up with the northern route to cross the High Pamir to Kokand, Samarkand, Bokhara and Merv, and then on through Iran and Iraq to the Mediterranean, with its sea lanes to Rome.

There is also the northern Tianshan route. This runs north of Hami to climb the foothills of the Tianshan and leads to Barkol in northern Xinjiang, with its seemingly endless flat pastures and deserts. A succession of ancient beacon towers runs continuously west to Ili, from where, after crossing the High Pamir, the route reaches Lake Balkash.

In the seventh century the importance of the 6,500-kilometre long Silk Road began to decline as trade between China and the West shifted to the sea routes, which proved to be safer. By the sixteenth century the Silk Road had become obsolete.

The Xinjiang Uygur Autonomous Region is bordered on three sides by mountains. The Altay Mountains form the northern boundary, while the western and southwestern limits are marked by the High Pamir and the Karakoram Mountains, linking the region to the Soviet Union, Afghanistan, Pakistan and India. The Kunlun Mountains delimit its southern extension and link it with Tibet. The entire area is traversed by the Tianshan, which stretch for almost

Painting of a lady playing chess/Tang/unearthed in 1972 at the Hastana Graves.

1,600 kilometres and create a natural north-south division of the region.

Northern Xinjiang lies close to Siberia, hence the bitter cold of its climate. It consists mainly of pastures, where nomadic tribes such as the Kazak make up the core of the population and engage in pasturage.

In southern Xinjiang lies the blusteringily hot Taklimakan Desert. This covers about one-fifth of the entire area of Xinjiang and, because of its great size, most routes through Central Asia must cross or skirt it. Along the foothills of the Tianshan lie the oasis towns, sometimes known as the 'little fertile fields of the desert'. These walled towns are the cradles of a civilization based on agriculture and animal husbandry, and the people's life-style differs greatly from that of the nomadic herdsmen.

Xinjiang is a multi-national, multi-religious and multi-lingual region composed of Kazak, Tajik, Tatar, Uzbek, Xibe, Kirgiz, Mongol, Hui, Manchu, Russ, Han Chinese and Uygur peoples. The Uygur are the most numerous, numbering some 6 million, or nearly half the total population. Of all the indigenous nationalities of Central Asia, the Uygur have the most highly developed civilization.

Emperor Jingai of the Han dynasty (reigned 156-140 BC) advanced the following policy with regard to Xinjiang: 'To move people and soldiers to the borderland; certain segments of the population to carry on collective, specialized production, to develop the economy and culture of the region, and to guard the frontier'. This policy is remarkably similar to the formation of the 'production and construction corps' for border areas proposed by the late Chairman Mao

Zedong in 1949. As a result of this official policy, together with the settlement of Han Chinese in the area, the Han population in Xinjiang now constitutes some 5.3 million, or about 40 per cent of the total. By 1983 the total membership of these corps was put at 2.25 million, or almost half of the entire Han population of Xinjiang. As well as being inhabited by the Han and the Uygur, the northern region is home to some 900,000 Kazak, 26,000 Tajik, 12,000 Uzbek, 4,000 Tatar, and 2,900 Russ.

From ancient times Xinjiang has served as a bridge for the exchange of culture between Chinese Central Asia and the West. It was also the conduit through which major religions were absorbed into China. Buddhism was introduced from India in the first century AD through the outposts of Hotan and Kuqa, and became firmly rooted in Xinjiang before spreading eastward. Indeed, by the eighth century a total of 169 pilgrimages to India had been made by Chinese in search of Buddhist scriptures. Seven centuries of Buddhist influence notwithstanding, Xinjiang then entered an entirely new phase — one that would last through to the present day.

*Clay heads/Tang/
unearthed in 1960 at the
Hastana Graves.*

In AD 651 a ruler of Arabia sent an ambassador to China, who was received by Emperor Gaozong. The ambassador told of Arab customs and described their faith — the relatively new religion of Islam.

During the Tang dynasty relations between the Chinese and the Arabs grew apace. Numerous Arab traders made their way to China by coastal navigation along the shores of the Gulf, India and the Malayan Peninsula to Guangzhou (Canton) and other coastal cities of the Chinese empire where they traded such wares as jewellery, spices and glass. Later Arab traders also took the overland route along the Silk Road via Persia, Xinjiang and the Chinese capital of Chang'an (present-day Xi'an).

Contacts between the two civilizations led to the introduction of Islam to China. From the seventh to the tenth century, Xinjiang and parts of China were dominated by Buddhism, Zoroastrianism, Manichaeism and Nestorian Christianity, to say nothing of Daoism, Confucianism and primitive animism. In the late tenth century Uygur merchants travelled to Arabia, became converted to Islam, and returned to spread the new faith in Xinjiang.

The Arabs also dispatched missionaries to China. These missionaries entered Xinjiang through Kashgar, and helped to spread Islam to Yarkand and Hotan. In the twelfth century Islam reached Kuqa, a stronghold of Buddhism, and gradually replaced Buddhism and Zoroastrianism as the principal religion of the Uygur. In the north of Kuqa is a gravestone dedicated to an Arab missionary who spread the Islamic faith in China from 1241 to 1264.

Shortly afterwards the whole of Xinjiang, including the eastern area around Turpan, had been converted to Islam. During his western campaign, the Mongol conqueror Genghis Khan captured many Muslims and brought them back to China. Among them were the Khorezm, whose descendants intermarried with Chinese to create the Muslim community known as Hui, who inhabit the present-day Ningxia Hui Autonomous Region and other parts of northern and northwestern China including Beijing. But the driving force in the introduction of Islam were the Uygur, who were favoured with great trust at the high point of the Mongol empire and who made determined attempts to spread the Muhammadan faith. Largely as a result of their efforts, Islam remains little diminished in Xinjiang today despite the passage of the centuries and the Communist revolution.

The continuing strength of Islam is epitomized in the buildings of Xinjiang: besides the flat-roofed mud huts similar to those of the Middle East, almost everywhere in the populated areas are towering minarets and domed square buildings topped with crescent moons. These are the mosques and tombs of Islam, the crescent moon being the symbol of the Muhammadan faith. The walls of the buildings bear intricate mosaics, of blue and jade-green decorative ceramic tiles, set off by carved geometric patterns and engraved pillars. The domed roofs are usually made of mud tiles and have small wooden window-frames. Common enough in the towns, the mosques are also the focal point of the life and activity of the rural villages.

According to a survey made recently by the Chinese Islamic Association, ten ethnic

Brocade with the design of a small pearl-studded roundel containing a bird/Tang/unearthed in 1959 at the Hastana Graves.

minorities follow the Muslim religion: the Hui, Uygur, Kazak, Tatar, Tajik, Kirgiz, Uzbek, Dongxiang, Salar and Baoan. According to the 1982 national population census more than half of China's total Muslim population of some 14 million live in Xinjiang.

The Xinjiang Muslims belong to both the Shiite and Sunni sects, as well as to the esoteric and colourful Sha'fee sect popular with the Uygur and the Uzbek. The majority of Uygur, Hui, Uzbek and Tatar are Sunni, as indeed are 80 per cent of the world's Muslims. The Tajik and Kirgiz are mainly Shiites, like the Iranians.

Some Muslims of Xinjiang bow to the Holy Tomb, a custom derived from the Sha'fee sect in Central Asia. By so doing the Muslim is paying his respects to the holy spirit and asking for mercy and blessing from Allah. The practice can be seen in the fifth, sixth, eighth and ninth months of the year.

Similar worship of a tomb is carried out in Kashgar by some single and married women who come from far and near to visit the tomb of Abakh Hoja, a seventeenth-century Muslim leader, and of his granddaughter Xiang Fei, who was a concubine and later the wife of Emperor Qianlong (reigned 1736-95). Women touch the wall of the tomb, voicing their problems and hopes in the search for peace and joy.

Of the 14 million Chinese Muslims, the Uygur Muslims in Xinjiang alone account for over 5 million of these, hence their close link to Islam.

The Uygur trace their origins to the ancient Turkic nomadic herdsmen called Tölö, who lived in the area between Siberia's Lake Baikal and Lake

Balkash in northern China. The Tölö subdued the Huns, who previously dominated the area, and were nicknamed 'Big Wheels' because of the huge wheels on their carts. The world Tölö is a Chinese derivation from Turk, the Turks being active in the silk trade between East and West which began a century or two before Christ.

During the early seventh century AD the Uygur emerged as a political unit symbolized by their name, which means 'unity'. They embraced several different groups of ethnic herdsmen whose numbers shrank or swelled with the vicissitudes of history. The Uygur maintained quite close ties with the Chinese Tang dynasty and its rulers in the seventh and eighth centuries and on occasion even served under them in wartime.

The Uygur exported horses, jade, spices, herbal medicines and glass to China in exchange for silk, steel artefacts, tea and precious metals. These the Uygur traded via the Silk Road to Western Asia and the Mediterranean. The Uygur's position straddling the trade routes brought them economic prosperity and a rich culture, helping to identify them as a separate entity among the welter of Turkic and other tribes in central Asia.

From the ninth to the twelfth century the Uygur gradually abandoned their life-style as nomadic herdsmen and adopted a more settled, agricultural mode of existence. Finding it increasingly difficult to survive in the harsh conditions and amidst the more backward ethnic groups of northern Xinjiang, they established their cities in the Turpan Depression and the oases of southern Xinjiang, which became their permanent homes. An inscription excavated from Kara-Balsaghun and dating from the eighth or ninth century describes the transformation of the Uygur: 'These people who were known to drink blood like savages have turned to eating the crops of the earth. They who used to indulge in bloodshed are now adherents of benevolence.'

The Uygur cultivated contacts and intermarried with the indigenous peoples of southern Xinjiang, such as the people of Hotan and Kuqa, and even the Tibetans and Mongols whom they had subjugated in the past. Through trade with other parts of Central Asia and Europe, the Uygur extended their influence and incorporated many other ethnic groups of the region into their community.

From the seventh to the sixteenth century the Uygur spoken and written language became a *lingua franca* of Central Asia, and at the rise of the Mongol empire the Uygur were entrusted with the administration of large areas. The Mongol written language was derived from Uygur script (itself a form of ancient Sogdian), and even today Uygur language and other Turkic tongues are so close that films made in Xinjiang can be shown in Istanbul without dubbing.

From evidence unearthed in the Thousand Buddha Caves at Baizeklik near Turpan and at Dunhuang in Gansu province, as well as from excavated books and documents written in Uygur, it is evident that the Uygur helped to transmit to Europe the printing techniques invented by the Chinese. The Uygur thus played an important role not only in trade but also in East-West scientific and cultural exchange. Their music, dance and dress are a combination of colours and styles derived from places as far distant as Greece and Egypt. Their culture flourished as early as the period from the eighth to the eleventh century, and at that time their two large cultural and academic centres in southern Xinjiang were Kashgar in the west

Deed for selling slave, written in ancient Uygur/Yuan/unearthed in 1953 at Turpan.

and Turpan in the east. Even today Kashgar and Turpan are still Uygur strongholds.

At first sight Kashgar strikes one as a cosmopolitan city of regular design. Rows of trees give shade along the roads both inside and outside the city, and form a towering barrier against the sand. Streams running at the sides of the wide, open roads bring a refreshing coolness to the city. On the main streets stand monolithic, Russian-style buildings, but in behind them high mud walls conceal peaceful courtyards where family life is conducted.

An old Uygur man, bearded, with skin as pale as that of a European, and wearing a square skull-cap known as a *doppa*, plods along the road on a mule. A group of worshippers make their way to the mosque. Beside them trundles a wooden mule-cart with two wheels, its passenger a fat, sleeping woman who is shaded from the sun by a colourful canopy.

At roadside stalls buyers and sellers haggle in a tongue which bears no resemblance to any Chinese dialect. It is Uygur — common throughout Xinjiang. Kashgar's numerous mosques and Muslim graves give the impression of a Middle Eastern city, although this is really China. The presence of many Han Chinese serves as a reminder that China is indeed a multi-national state.

The Uygur, especially those of Kashgar, have proven able businessmen from ancient times, and Kashgar has long been an important centre of trade. Reports of travellers who visited Xiyu, the Western Region, include the following: 'The ten-square-mile city is virtually paved with goods and different wares. People swarm around like bees, hoping to find some rare gems amongst the merchandise, whilst around them farm products pile up in profusion.'

Apart from the advantages of their geographical position, the Uygur have depended heavily on the heritage of a race of people known as the Sogdians of Samarkand. The Sogdians were early settlers in the Kashgar region. In the Tang dynasty the Buddhist pilgrim Xuanzuang reported that the written and spoken language used in that region was Sogdian.

The Sogdians were an ancient people related to the Persians, who were prominent in trade, and they were ranked with the Phoenicians as masters of commerce in classical times. Their children were taught reading and arithmetic from the age of five, and making money was regarded as a highly respectable occupation. New-born babies had to wear coins as ornaments so that they should never be far from money. By the end of the Tang dynasty the Sogdians had been largely absorbed by the Uygur who adopted their script. Inevitably, the Uygur imbibed some of the Sogdian business acumen, as can be seen today in the Kashgar bazaar, a fascinating mart of commerce.

In the bazaar almost any daily necessity can be found for sale or being fabricated on the spot. Elegant, hand-made musical instruments are displayed side by side with knives of all sizes. Workers pound padded coverlets or make painstaking gem inlays with grindstones in tiny workshops. Blacksmiths and their apprentices hammer out farm implements and horseshoes, the red fury of the forge matching the clank of hammer and steel. Next door an old craftsman hammers out the copper bowls for which Kashgar has long been famous, while his neighbours haggle over their Hotan carpets. An old man tries to sell a bright red apron dangling from his arm, and Han Chinese buy up plastic bags which still

Cotton cloth with pattern dyed by the wax-resist technique/Han/unearthed in 1959 at Niya.

reek of the chemicals they once contained. Kazak horsemen finger inlaid wooden saddles.

Almost every Uygur male in Kashgar wears a hat — the mark of correct etiquette. This explains the corner of the bazaar which is devoted entirely to hats. The choice is extensive: embroidered Muslim skull-caps, velvet hats lined with sheepskin and bordered with fur, the collapsible felt hats of the Kazak, and even simple cotton and nylon caps.

It would be unpardonable to visit this key location on the Silk Road and not to look at any silk! On Sundays in particular, when the masses pour into the bazaar, many of the women wear silk, from the veils on their faces to their tight-ankled trousers. This is the silk unique to the areas around Kashgar and Hotan. Much of it is made by the tie-and-dye method, a legacy of the Tang dynasty, which gives the material the traditional, complex patterns which were always a feature of the clothing of the Xiyu Uygur. Kashgar silk is known for its elaborate patterns and many colours, whilst that of Hotan tends towards bold designs in fewer colours.

At the bazaar bordering on Kashgar's central square a young man who looks like a tourist from Hong Kong is suddenly accosted by two Uygur youths in traditional headgear. After a brisk exchange, they dart into a nearby building, a small tailor's workshop. To the whir of sewing-machines, with the sunlight streaming in from a window in the roof, a pile of foreign exchange certificates is exchanged for a bundle of Chinese *renminbi*. Each party quickly checks the amount and they separate. A black market currency transaction has just taken place in broad daylight. Almost any tourist who steps on to the square is approached by a member of some ethnic minority offering to exchange currency at nearly two-to-one against the normal rate. The locals say that with the present open-door policy it is only they who risk being arrested, and that foreigners have nothing to fear.

The Uygur business sense is in evidence in other parts of China also. Around the major hotels in Beijing the Uygur operate black market currency rackets. It is said that in 1984 and 1985, in Guangzhou in southern China, Uygur businessmen from Kashgar were doing a roaring trade in television sets and cars. By offering high black market rates, they acquired large sums of foreign exchange which they channelled to the Special Economic Zones in Guangdong province to buy luxuries.

The other Uygur stronghold in southern Xinjiang, in the east, is Turpan, which lies in the Turpan Depression, China's Land of Extremes. One of the extremes which mark this part of Xinjiang is that it contains the lowest point in the whole of China, the salt-saturated Lake Aydingkol which lies 154 metres below sea level. The weather in the depression is also characterized by extremes of temperature, with maximums in July of around 47°C (the highest temperature recorded is 49.6°C) and minimums in January of below -10°C. The average maximum ground temperature is over 70°C, but a blistering 82.3°C was recorded in 1974. This explains why Turpan is known as the Land of Fire.

Turpan is also a most unusually windy spot: the wind strength averages force 8 to 9, but hurricanes are frequent and may last for days — eight days is the record. The wind is capable of lifting stones of up to 4 centimetres in diameter from the ground so that yet another nickname for Turpan is the Storehouse of Winds.

The Turpan Depression was once a focus of conflict between the Han empire and the Xiongnu, the barbaric, horse-riding race thought to be related to the Huns who invaded Europe centuries later. Nowadays it is an economic, political and cultural centre of China's western domains.

About 80 per cent of the population of the Turpan Depression are Uygur, who circulate many legends about the area. One of these is the legend of the Flaming Mountain, known as the Red Mountain in Uygur. It is said that in ancient times a wicked dragon used to fly regularly to Turpan to eat a virgin and a boy sacrificed by the people of the region. If they were not supplied, the dragon would destroy crops and houses and kill men and livestock. A brave young man petitioned the king to be allowed to subdue the dragon. Wielding a double-edged sword, he fought fiercely with it for three days. Eventually he cut it in two at the Qixiao (Heptagonal) Well. The dragon was still struggling even though it was soaked in its own blood and so the youth chopped it up into ten pieces. The dragon was transformed into the Red Mountain, and the ten cuts became the ten gorges of the mountain. In reality the cuts in the 'dragon's body' were caused by slow movements of the earth's crust. Rainwater and huge amounts of melted snow from the Tianshan burst forth as springs to form fertile oases. For over a thousand years these oases have been yielding such products as grapes, melons and cotton.

Xinjiang's economy depends heavily on these numerous desert-rim oases. There are about one thousand of them, covering an area of some 70,000 square kilometres; Turpan is one of the largest. In Turpan some of the oases are irrigated by water from the ten gorges of the Red Mountain, and others by the rainwater runoff and melting snows of the Tianshan. Most of this water arrives by underground watercourses, which were described by Lin Zexu, China's Imperial Commissioner during the Anglo-Chinese Opium War, when he was inspecting Turpan in 1845 following his official disgrace: 'Along the way I saw many holes in the ground, and when I asked what they were called I was told they are named *ka*. These wells conduct the water from the high ground to the plain in a south-north direction. Water running through underground caverns —what an extraordinary phenomenon!'

These man-made underground channels, known as *karez* in Uygur, rely on a gradient to move the water from one point to another. A *karez* well consists of four parts: a vertical well, an underground channel, a surface channel, and a small pool or reservoir. The vertical well is for ventilation and clearance of dirt and rubble which forms sizeable mounds beside the opening. Eventually the water, which is up to 30 metres underground when it begins its journey to the oasis, trickles forth naturally at the edge of the irrigated area.

Some authorities believe that *karez* channels were copied from the system in use in Shaanxi province in the Han dynasty. Others claim that the system originated in Persia. What is known for certain is that the Uygur were familiar with this technology four or five centuries ago and expanded its use greatly during the Qing dynasty (1644-1910). There are almost one thousand *karez* with a total of some 3,000 kilometres of channels — longer than the Grand Canal linking Beijing and Hangzhou. A typical channel is 3 kilometres long and the longest is 10 kilometres. In addition, the numerous vertical wells have been built only at the cost of much labour and expenditure. Even in the hot, windy, dusty Turpan Depression, where the evaporation rate is high, the *karez* system has made it possible to irrigate farmland all year round, making the oasis a good as well as a well-known agricultural region.

Brocade with the design of a small pearl-studded roundel containing a deer/Tang/unearthed in 1959 at the Hastana Graves.

The irrigation systems allow crops and fruits to be grown. In and around Turpan one of the most profuse fruits is the grape, which came originally to Xinjiang from Western Asia and the Mediterranean. Vines were cultivated in Turpan as many as 2,000 years ago. There are three kinds of grape: the seedless white grapes which are dried to make the famous Turpan raisins; the mare's milk grapes which are eaten in their natural state; and the Kashgar and rose fragrance grapes which are used to make wine.

The huts in which the grapes are dried to make raisins are box-like brick structures about 3 metres high and 4 to 5 metres wide. The bricks are laid in such a way that many gaps are left as ventilation holes, and the roofs are trellises from which the bunches of grapes are hung. Each trellis can carry about 100 kilograms of grapes. The trellises are not exposed to direct sunlight, but hot draughts of air come up from the holes in the walls, drying the grapes naturally in thirty to forty days. The resulting raisins are pale and soft and contain over 60 per cent of sugar.

The other important fruit grown in the Turpan Depression, in Shanshan country, is the Hami or musk melon. The legendary reason why the Hami melon is so called is that a former ruler of Hami presented a tribute to the Qing Emperor Kangxi (reigned 1662-1722) in the form of this type of melon. The emperor found it delicious, and so from then on the ruler of Hami presented this kind of musk melon as a tribute every year. Another reason for the name of the melon is that although the melons are grown elsewhere, the majority of those that are exported are sent from Hami. With its crisp sweet flesh ranging from orange to white in colour, the Hami melon contains abundant carbohydrates and vitamins, and the traditional Chinese *Compendium of Materia Medica* says that the fruit is 'good for quenching thirst and curing discomfort caused by heat'.

In and around Turpan the Uygur live in mud-brick houses with rectangular gardens planted with flowers, trees, calabashes, and vines which, in summer, bear clusters of pale green, translucent grapes. The flat roofs of their houses may be used to dry melons and other fruits for preservation, and may also be used to store fodder during winter.

Skylights open into the houses through the flat roofs. Inside most of the houses is an adobe *kang* platform about 50 centimetres high, covered with a rug, and on which people both sit and sleep. In cold weather the platform may be heated by the stove underneath. In the walls are niches for food, utensils and small items of decoration, and one wall may be decorated with a hanging rug. Visitors are invariably welcomed with milk tea and delicious bread called 'biao, of different sizes, and either plain or stuffed with savoury mutton and onions.

The Uygur are very hospitable, and I have been invited several times to wedding celebrations, the most impressive of which was in Turpan itself. The ceremony was held at the bridegroom's place of work, the office of a public bus service. Though the ceremony was not elaborate, it was highly authentic. A folk-singer performed an instrumental solo, and an old man at his side occasionally beat a drum as accompaniment. The singer, with his straightforward and uninhibited performance, excited the audience. A small boy danced to the rhythm of the song, while other people joined in and clapped. The dance rhythm grew faster as we watched, more people joined in, and the spectators clapped vigorously throughout. Then two dancers gave

Brocade with design of trees, paired birds and lambs/Gaochang/unearthed in 1972 at the Hastana Graves.

33

a humorous performance which caused the spectators to convulse with laughter.

Later we shared a large pot of 'finger rice' — rice rolled into balls in the hand and eaten with fingers rather than with chopsticks in the Han Chinese fashion. The dish is called *pailuo* in Chinese, which is derived from the Persian name for the dish of sweet rice flavoured with vegetables, fruit and meat (better known in the West as pilaff or pilau). The main ingredients are husked rice, mutton, carrots, raisins and onions. Cooking oils are mutton fat or vegetable oil such as cotton oil. Sometimes frozen meat such as chicken, duck and goose are used, but these are modern additions. Some guests poured yoghurt over the finger rice, saying that it reduced the greasiness of the food, stimulated the appetite and aided digestion.

With its high temperatures and extremely low rainfall, the climate of the Turpan area acts as a natural preservative for historic relics and ancient cities. For this reason more than half of the historic sites in Xinjiang are in the Turpan area. Among these are the ancient ruined cities of Gaochang and Jiaohe, the Thousand Buddha Caves at Baizeklik, and the ancient graves of Hastana.

Unfortunately, at the beginning of the century, caravan-loads of priceless ancient artefacts and wall paintings from sites such as the ruined cities of Gaochang and Jiaohe, and the Thousand Buddha Caves at Baizeklik were taken away to museums in the West, where a number are on display today. Only when the nation is at peace, and people live in harmony with a higher standard of living, will the culture and art of the country be better appreciated and protected.

THE KAZAK: HORSEMEN OF NORTHERN XINJIANG

Iɴ the past the areas surrounding the oases of Xiyu, the Western Region, were inhabited by wild, horse-riding who gradually came under the civilizing influence of the settled areas. But at times these barbarian nomads would attack the settlements and massacre or subjugate the inhabitants. One tribe, the Huns, even defeated the Roman, Chinese and Indian empires for brief periods.

The reason for these savage attacks would nowadays be called ecological: the constant expansion of the desert due to wind movements gradually diminished the area of pastureland suitable for horses and other livestock. The tribes were therefore forced to expand their territory or go under. But as well as this natural pressure to expand their territory, there was also a human factor behind the attacks, essentially a question of leadership. Aware that horseback-riding was the most irresistible way of waging war in the steppes, a great leader might attempt to bring all the scattered tribes under his own domination. Such a unified force of cavalry and archers would almost inevitably prevail in battle against settled, agricultural peoples. With no fighting force and no knowledge of the military aspects of the terrain, the settlers could only wait passively for death or enslavement.

The strategy of the Mongol leader, Genghis Khan, was to mobilize a huge army of cavalry at the shortest possible notice, and use it to make ruthless attacks on his victims. The speed and force of the attack easily overcame soldiers using West Asian and Roman

Mural in Cave No. 13 at Kyzil.

tactics — fighting on foot with swords and shields. Within a mere twelve years of warfare, Genghis Khan established his rule from the Pacific to the Black Sea and over the whole of Russia.

The cultural and religious differences between the nomads of Central Asia were for the most part only slight. The fighting tactics and lifestyles of the Mongols had changed little in a thousand years since those of the Huns of more than 2,000 years ago. Today's Kazak and Tajik have basically retained the traditions and customs of the Mongols and even of the Huns, except that they are followers of Islam rather than of Manichaeism.

Despite their former ferocity, these nomadic herdsmen are by no means uncivilized. They have long had their own customs and rituals. Living off the pastures, they have been forced to travel great distances to feed and water their livestock, which has brought them into contact with many of the great civilizations of history. Archaeological finds have shown that the Huns had contact with the Syrians and the Chinese, whilst the medieval Turkic peoples, especially the Uygur, had high cultural and scholastic standards.

Because the nomads have to seek water and pasturages, the tribal structure of their communities has remained important up to the present day. The groups vary in size and are based chiefly on blood relationships and marriage ties. But past movements and changes have ensured that the tribes are intermingled to a considerable extent. Thus, while moving around or assembling their herds, related clans often work side by side.

The great nomadic kingdoms of the past had their centres of power in the Pamir,

Berlin

Moscow

Black Sea

Caspian Sea

Aral Sea

U. S. S. R.

Lake Baikal

Lake Balkash

Karakorum

Bokhara

Emi'n

Tacheng

MONGOLIA

Barkol

Ili

Ürümqi

Aksu   Kuqa   Hami

INNER   MONGOLIA

Kashgar   Turpan

PAMIR

XINJIANG

AFGHANISTAN

Shache

Beijing

Hotan   Minfeng   Qarkilik   Dunhuang   GREAT

KOREA

JAPAN

Tokyo

PAKISTAN

WALL

Xi'an

TIBET

CHINA

Shanghai

NEPAL

Hangzhou

PACIFIC OCEAN

INDIA

Guangzhou

BURMA

Hong Kong

LAOS   VIETNAM

China and Central Asia

| 0 | 200 | 400 | 600 | 800 | MILES |

| 0 | 320 | 640 | 960 | 1280 | KILOMETRES |

northern Xinjiang and Mongolia. Today, these areas have been designated 'autonomous' areas by the Chinese Government, for instance, for the Kazak, Tajik, Mongol and Kirgiz.

The Xinjiang Uygur Autonomous Region is divided into five autonomous prefectures, six autonomous counties and eight districts. Besides the Changji Huizu Autonomous Prefecture, the Yanqi Huizu Autonomous County, and the Qapqal Xibe Autonomous County, all the others are home to nomadic tribes. For example, there are two Mongol, one Kirgiz and one Kazak autonomous prefectures, and one Mongol, one Tajik and two Kazak autonomous counties.

After the Uygur and the Han, the next most populous minority in northern Xinjiang is the Kazak. They are better known to the Westerner as Cassacks or Cossaks.

Around the end of 300 BC, the Huns united all the nomadic tribes of the northern deserts of Central Asia under a single leadership. The region which now makes up Xinjiang and western Gansu fell under their control. In the process, they forced a tribe called the Wusun to move away from Gansu and take up their abode in the Ili Valley in northern Xinjiang. These people were the forefathers of the Kazak.

But, most important, the Kazak were the assimilation of Mongolian blood; they were gradually absorbed into the nomadic tribes of Central Asia in the sixteenth century. In fact, the 900,000 Kazak to be found in China today constitute only a portion of the entire Kazak population of Central Asia. The others live across the Soviet border.

Like most of the nomadic herds-men of Central Asia, the Kazak are 'followers of rich pastures', herding horses, goats, sheep, cattle and camels. They live in the round felt-covered tents known as yurts which have a light trellised frame that is easily assembled and dismantled. The frame is made from branches of the red willows which grow in the pasturelands. The yurt has two parts: a domed roof and a round body. The roof is constructed first, from branches bent into a dome. The bodywork is then put up in the form of a trellis, and matted grass is put round it. This frame is then covered with multi-coloured patterned felts which are secured with thick strips of felt. An opening covered with a flag or rug is left in the roof to provide ventilation and light.

The doorway is rectangular and shielded with a rug. Inside the yurt the arrangements are invariably the same. To the top right is the sleeping area for adults, and before it is the storage area for cooking utensils and provisions. To the top left is the sleeping area for the younger members of the family, beside which is kept the riding and hunting equipment. Directly opposite the door are saddles and garment-chests, the area in front of the latter being reserved exclusively for guests. The stove is in the centre of the floor-space, immediately beneath the roof-opening.

In the more remote areas, yurts tend to have low roofs and are equipped with only the most basic necessities. The slender framework is covered with only a thin layer of woollen carpet, and there is no allowance for fastidious taste or fancy decoration. Life is made the more difficult by the herdsmen's ignorance of birth-control. Families live a hand-to-mouth existence, dependent on just a few heads of sheep. When the parents are out with the herds, the children have to look after themselves since there are virtually no kindergartens or schools. Children have the chance of only a few hours'

Interior of a Kazak yurt.

tuition every month, and the teachers themselves are mobile. Parents have to take their children to the temporary classrooms which may be as far as 12 kilometres away.

In the winter the Kazak repair the roofs of their mud-huts on the pasturelands and remain there till the spring. The huts protect them from winter winds and snowstorms. Over the past century the herdsmen of northern Xinjiang have taken to agriculture both as a full-time occupation and in combination with pasturage, as a result of the losses of livestock from snowstorms, other natural disasters and the depredations of war. Over the past thirty-five years with the 'farming and fighting' policy of the People's Liberation Army, there have arisen production and planning units, and institutes for the study of agricultural technology. The practical applications of the findings of such institutes have in turn been demonstrated to the herdsmen, greatly stimulating their agricultural production. In recent years retired farmer-soldiers have developed fur and fishing industries near the pasturages, which have had considerable effect on the economic and even the political scene. The development of agriculture and pasturage has helped to raise the living standards of the nomadic herdsmen, but it has also had an irreversible impact on their traditional life-style.

As well as engaging in agriculture and pasturage, the Kazak make handicrafts such as patterned hats and garments, saddles and tools, rugs, tapestries and steel items for everyday use, all with their unique patterns and designs. These, however, are made solely for family use and not for sale. Using mainly a brilliant red combined with an equally bright green, women embroider patterns on the walls of their tents and on carpets. The patterns on the wall-hangings behind the bed match those on the garment-chest. The

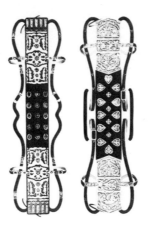

*Designs on bed canopy
and design on horse girth.*

white coverings for the clothes, the pillows, and even the bags used for keeping odds and ends are all colourfully decorated, and the wooden beds, ornaments and other objects are carved with patterns of flowers and grass. Even the thick strips of felt used to tie together the frames of the yurts and to secure the multi-coloured patterned felts covering the domed roofs have human or animal patterns made from white and black sheep's wool. The colours and designs of objects in the yurts of the clan-leaders tend to be more exotic and grandiose.

The Kazak are not only outstanding warriors, but are also renowned hunters. In the past, having to face fierce animals such as the wolf, fox, bear and panther, they were forced to engage in savage combat with them. Today, with firearms, their task is easier, but they still regard eagles and hunting dogs as indispensable aids to combat. Most of the older generation of Kazak hunters can still be seen sitting proudly in their silver-chased saddles with eagles perched on their wrist, scanning the surroundings for prey. The culture and history of the Kazak is closely bound up with the business of hunting, which has been perpetuated in folksong and local lore.

Milk and meat — mostly mutton — form the main part of the Kazak diet. The Kazak also make milk products such as rock-hard cheese. They derive a large proportion of necessary fats from the milk, and vitamins and minerals from the sheep. The Kazak brew their tea with milk to make their favourite drink, which helps to make up nutrients not found in the rest of their diet. Small pieces of batter fried in sheep's fat are served as snacks with the milk tea.

The Kazak are warm-hearted, hospitable people and will offer visitors these foodstuffs; if it is a festival day, they will also offer fermented mare's milk. A day before the feast, the innards are removed from a slaughtered sheep, the carcass is washed, and then put in an enormous pot to boil, providing a delicious meal. First the clan-head offers thanks to Allah. Then the entire sheep's head is passed among the guests, who slice off pieces of meat from the cheek with their small knives, and hand these morsels to the clan elders. An ear is cut off and given to the young people. The guest then slices off a piece of meat for himself, and the head is returned to the host. The young people serve the broth from the cooking-pot. Then the meat is passed around on a tray and eaten with the fingers. In the past these trays were hollowed out from blocks of wood by hand, and then adorned with tiny, carved patterns. All eating and drinking utensils, including the tubs where mare's milk is kept, were traditionally made of wood. Unfortunately wood has now been largely replaced by enamel, which at least is better than plastic.

When there is a birth, a wedding or an Islamic festival, the herdsmen hold large horse-riding contests. In one such trial a group of children around the age of ten compete in bareback-riding over three courses which take several hours to finish. In the intermission entertainment is provided by wrestling matches and games of 'catch the maiden'.

This highly popular game is played as follows: first, the young men and girls choose partners and walk slowly towards an appointed spot. As they walk, the boy teases and jokes with the girl, who is not permitted to become angry. But on the return journey the girl continually whips, or pretends to whip, her partner in revenge — sometimes so hard that he is knocked off his feet. The excited spectators encourage them. Such games provide the perfect setting for love to blossom in, or so the Kazak say!

THE TAJIK: NOMADS OF THE HIGH PAMIR

Silk cloth printed with hunting scene/Tang/ unearthed in 1972 at the Hastana Graves.

'This is said to be the highest place in the world . . . a plain between two mountains with a lake from which flows a very fine river . . . This plateau, the name of which is Pamir, extends fully twelve days' journey, during which there is no habitation or shelter.'

Marco Polo was referring to the High Pamir, sometimes called 'the roof of the world' (an appellation also applied to Tibet). The two mountains mentioned by Marco Polo are the huge, rocky masses of the Kongur Peak, the second highest mountain in the world (7,719 metres), and the Muztagata Peak, also known as the Father of the Ice Mountain (7,546 metres).

The High Pamir have been home to generations of Tajik, and the summit of the Pamir, the westernmost frontier of China, is known in Tajik as Tash-Kurghan (Taxkorgan), meaning Stone Castle. Today the town of Tash-Kurghan has only one street about 30 metres in length! It accommodates the only shop, post office, hospital, school and government office in the entire area.

The name Tajik dates from the eleventh century, when it was used by the Turkic peoples of Xinjiang to designate anyone who spoke the language of Eastern Iran and followed Islam. Before that, in the second and third centuries AD, the kingdom of Tash-Kurghan had arisen as a stronghold of Buddhism. Monasteries abounded and there were large numbers of monks and nuns. The golden age of the kingdom lasted about 500 years.

Deep red silk skirt with printed floral pattern/ Tang/unearthed in 1972 at the Hastana Graves.

Scattered along the Pamir range are lush pastures dotted with yurts occupied by Tajik herdsmen and herds of sheep and cattle — all nestling in the shadow of the snow-capped mountains. Some of the settlements have square, flat-roofed houses, the sturdy walls of which are composed of stone slabs, the crevices stuffed with straw, and the roofs made of branches covered with grass and mud. In the middle of the roof is an opening, and there is a single window. The door opens to the east. Despite their low ceilings, the houses are spacious inside: earth mounds form platforms on the floor, covered with woollen rugs to provide snug seats.

In the summer the fields are laden with crops of green beans and barley, which are planted every spring by the Tajik, despite the bitter cold. That done, the Tajik drive their herds up to higher plateaux. They live in their yurts and graze their animals until the end of autumn, returning to their villages with the onset of winter. This is the pattern of semi-nomadic life for the 26,000 people in the area.

Most Tajik families span three generations. The young are obliged by etiquette to greet the old whenever they meet. With relatives, handshakes must be performed. In the gesture of greeting, the man places his hand on his chest and bows, while the woman clasps both her hands before her and also bows. Marriages among Tajik and members of other nationalities are rare, and are countenanced only with Uygur and Kirgiz. Marriages between relatives — except between brother and sister — are allowed, regardless of age. Everything is arranged by the parents, and the usual wedding gifts are farm animals, gold and silver. On the wedding day a large number of friends and relatives are invited, and the bridegroom, accompanied by his best man, goes to the bride's house for the religious ceremony.

The Tajik are Muslims, and their life-style has always been closely connected with their religion and its various customs. The birth of a child is an important occasion: if the baby is male, three loud shouts are given or three shots are fired to bless the child and encourage it to grow up brave and intelligent. If it is a girl, a broom is placed on her head to ensure she will be a good housewife when she grows up. Friends and relatives come to congratulate the parents and sprinkle flour on the baby's head for luck.

According to a Tajik legend, the eagle was the symbol of the tribe which lived in the locality. Their most popular musical instrument is a small flute made from the bones of the eagle's wings and very similar to the three-holed flute used by the Kazak. In the Tajik's favourite dance the eagle was very much present. In the dance they imitate the eagle spreading its wings prior to flight. The Kazak also have a dance in which they imitate the eagle swooping down from the sky on its prey, whether it be a fox or a rabbit.

Both the Tajik and the Kazak are famous for their skill on horseback. At festivals and weddings the Tajik organize contests similar to those of the Kazak. Two teams of first-rate horsemen vie with one another to grab the carcass of a sheep whose head, limbs and innards have been removed. The team that manages to gain control of it and put it down at a place designated as the goal wins the match. The only difference between the Tajik and Kazak version of the sport is that the Tajik usually hold the reins of their horses in their mouths while they chase after the carcass.

The diet of the Tajik is little different from that of the Kazak: both like milk tea, fermented milk and dry cheese. Both tribes live in the same type of yurt, and share the same kinds of sport and music. Thus, it can be said that the legendary Kazak and Tajik horsemen of Xinjiang are close in brotherhood.

Amongst the Tajik of Tash-Kurghan we encountered hospitality similar to that offered by the Kazak. People were willing and helpful, especially the children, as this episode illustrates.

Not far to the south of Tash-Kurghan is a former citadel on high ground called the Princess's Tower. Tradition has it that it was dedicated to a Chinese princess who married a member of the Tash-Kurghan royal family. The tower is referred to in one of the works of Sir Aurel Stein, the great British explorer and archaeologist who made several visits to Xinjiang in the early 1900s. A Chinese archaeologist whom I met in Kashgar, however, told me that Stein's description of the citadel is not accurate. The archaeologist claimed that within the walls of the citadel there were a number of dried-up ponds and in one of these grew a copse of unusual-looking trees. If Stein had seen them himself, he would surely have mentioned them in his book.

I was told that the citadel was at a height of 1,000 metres above where we stood, and to reach it involved an arduous and dangerous climb which should be attempted only by someone with experience and the right equipment. I immediately made up my mind that this was an experience I would not miss. First, however, I had to obtain the permission of the authorities, since the citadel was a strategic point only about 3 kilometres from the Afghan border. The authorities agreed to send soldiers to accompany me.

Early one morning I set out on one of the most dramatic journeys of my life. The road

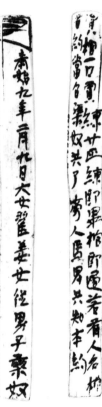

was white and icy as it had snowed the night before, and the temperature was -5°C. After a two-hour journey I arrived at an army base not far from the Princess's Tower, which the soldiers pointed out to me, perched atop a solid cliff of reddish-brown rock.

After an early lunch we set out. But after a short while the driver announced that our jeep would not be able to cross the Daira River which lay across our route, and that we should give up. Having come half-way, and thinking our goal only about an hour's climb from where we were, I refused to turn back and insisted on proceeding on foot. The soldiers returned to their base to fetch horses for me. But I did not want to wait, and continued with the guide-interpreter supplied by the army and my art director.

On the way we ran into two children, aged ten and eleven, and asked them if they could guide us to the Princess's Tower. In the course of my travels I have learned that the best guide is a local person, who will show you the way just for the fun of it, and will refuse any reward. The children were like this. It turned out that the interpreter had never been to the tower himself, so we left him contentedly puffing a cigarette at the foot of the mountain.

With the two children as guides, watching every step I took, we proceeded up the mountain. The cliff sloped at an unbelievably steep angle. It was slippery and the sand and soil were loose, contributing to the danger. The rarified atmosphere made the going tough. At several points I was so afraid that I suggested we try another route. After several hours, however, we reached the summit, and scaling a ruined wall of mud bricks, we entered the citadel itself. I realized then that the Princess's Tower was surrounded on three sides by sheer cliffs. Below the wall on one side

Inscribed wooden tablet/Jin/unearthed in 1966 at the Hastana Graves.

a waterfall gushed forth, the water flowing into the caves and fissures of the mountain until it eventually reached the Daira River.

The vast High Pamir could be seen from the citadel and there was a good view of the towering ranges marking the border with Afghanistan. A group of nomadic herdsmen were sauntering along a mountain road with bundles of firewood. At last I understood why the kingdom of Tash-Kurghan, meaning Mountain Road in the ancient language of Eastern Iran, was so called in the second and third centuries AD.

Inside the citadel, apart from a ruined wall of mud bricks — of the same type as those used by the Han Chinese 2,000 years ago to construct their garrison towns in the desert — there was nothing to be seen but the dried-up ponds and trees with unusually-shaped branches.

As I sat there on the 'roof of the world', gazing in all directions, I pondered how infinitely small man was by comparison with this magnificent landscape. At the same time, however, I reflected that man could overcome any obstacles when he exercised his strength and endurance, his ceaseless will to struggle, and his inextinguishable passion for life. For thousands of years people had lived here. Why had this citadel been built so high up here on the summit of this cliff? Was it to escape some danger or enemy? Or was it, as I felt it to be at that moment, as a hermitage, isolated from society, where one could attain nirvana?

XINJIANG DISCOVERED

The Xinjiang Uygur Autonomous Region, previously known as Chinese Tartary or Eastern Turkistan, is renowned for its spectacular desert scenery, such as the Flaming Mountains near Turpan (left), and for the hospitality of the Uygur people (above).

Desert accounts for one-third of Xinjiang's total land area, the largest desert being the Taklimakan (opposite). Sudden, severe sandstorms, known to the natives as karaburan *or 'black hurricanes', are frequent occurrences (right).*

Being a central land mass with high mountain ranges and arid desert land (above), Xinjiang receives little rainfall. This type of climate acts as a natural preservative for historic relics and ancient cities, such as the Buddhist city of Kuqa (left) which was established in the early fifth century.

The Silk Road, the major thoroughfare for the exchange of goods between China, the Middle East and Europe, passed through Xinjiang. Throughout the region camels are still considered one of the most convenient means of transportation (left and opposite).

Of Xinjiang's ancient cities, the best known today are the ruins of Gaochang (left) and Jiaohe (above) in the Turpan Depression. Among the ruins can still be seen the remains of streets, workshops and Buddhist temples.

The Thousand Buddha Caves at Kyzil near Kuqa (right) constitute the largest cave complex in China after the Mogao Caves near Dunhuang in Gansu province. Alas, the Buddhist statues and wall paintings of the caves are no longer intact (above). At the beginning of the century caravan-loads of priceless ancient artefacts and wall paintings were taken away to museums in the West.

Xinjiang is bordered on three sides by mountains, and traversed by the Tianshan range which creates a natural north-south division of the region. Northern Xinjiang borders on Siberia and consists mainly of pastures (right), while southern Xinjiang is made up of blistering hot desert (above).

When it leaves the desert, the Silk Road runs into dramatic mountain ranges (left). Although the Silk Road had several branches, all met eventually with the High Pamir. One of the summits of the Pamir is known in Tajik as Tash-Kurghan, meaning Stone Castle (above). In the town of Tash-Kurghan, perched atop a steep cliff, is a stone citadel known as the Princess's Tower (overleaf).

In the seventh century the importance of the Silk Road began to decline as trade between China and the West shifted to the sea routes. But because of Xinjiang's unusual landscape features, such as the Flaming Mountains (above) and the 'roof of the world' (right), the Silk Road remains a fascinating route for any traveller in China.

As well as its mountains and deserts, Xinjiang contains a number of lakes, such as the well-known Tianchi (Heavenly Lake), not far from Ürümqi, where the Fairy Queen of the West is said to have washed her feet.

XINJIANG:
STRONGHOLD OF ISLAM

The largest oasis town in southern Xinjiang is Kashgar (above), which at first sight strikes one as a cosmopolitan city of regular design. Rows of trees give shade along the roads both inside and outside the city, and form a towering barrier against the sand (right).

Kashgar's numerous mosques (left) and Muslim graves give the impression of a Middle Eastern city, although this is really China. The presence of many Han Chinese and People's Liberation Army (opposite) serves as a reminder that China is indeed a multi-national state.

*Islam was introduced to China from Arabia in the late tenth century through Kashgar, and soon became firmly rooted in Xinjiang. The tomb of Abakh Hoja (*above *and* right), *a seventeenth-century Muslim leader, and of his granddaughter Xiang Fei, who was a concubine and later the wife of Emperor Qianlong, draws worshippers from far and near.*

Kashgar has the largest mosque in China, the Id Kah Mosque (above) with a total area of 168,000 square metres, and room for 8,000 worshippers. Mosques are also the focal point of the life and activity of the rural villages (right).

The Xinjiang Muslims belong to both the Shiite and Sunni sects, as well as to the Sha 'fee sect popular with the Uygur and the Uzbek. The Sha 'fee Muslims in Xinjiang bow to the Holy Tomb to ask for mercy and blessing from Allah (above and left).

According to the 1982 national population census, more than half of China's total Muslim population of some 14 million live in Xinjiang. Of the 14 million Chinese Muslims, the Uygur Muslims (left and above) in Xinjiang alone account for over 5 million of these.

As the one-child policy does not apply to the ethnic minorities of China, the streets of towns like Kashgar are full of children. It is a custom among Uygur girls, even the very young (right) and (opposite), to link their eyebrows with a painted line, an effect which can be most attractive.

Besides the flat-roofed mud huts of Xinjiang, similar to those of the Middle East (left), almost everywhere in the populated areas are mosques decorated with pillars and geometric carving (opposite).

The Uygur's staple food is a kind of bread called biao, *similar to Indian* naan *bread. They come in different sizes, and may be plain or stuffed with savoury mutton and onions (left). The bread is baked on the walls of a deep clay over similar to the Indian* tandoor *oven (above).*

Two of the main preoccupations are eating and sitting around. Many stalls serve hand-pulled noodles with a spicy vegetable and mutton stew (right and opposite).

The Uygur love singing and dancing, and will perform almost anywhere and at any time. Most cities and counties have their own performing troupes (opposite) although many performances are spontaneous and uninhibited (left).

Almost every Uygur male wears a hat — the mark of correct etiquette. This explains the corner of the Kashgar bazaar which is devoted entirely to hats (opposite). Women wear colourful textiles, many of them silks, which are sold at stalls in the Kashgar bazaar (right).

In the Kashgar bazaar almost any daily necessity can be found for sale or being fabricated on the spot (opposite). Blacksmiths and their apprentices hammer out farm implements and horseshoes, the red fury of the forge matching the clank of hammer and steel (left).

The Uygur art of medicine, well known throughout Central Asia, is a combination of the tribe's own remedies and traditional Chinese ones (opposite). A haircut by a Uygur barber is usually a simple process since most Uygur men come only to have their heads shaved (above).

The Uygur have depended heavily on a race of people known as the Sogdians who were ranked with the Phoenicians as masters of commerce in classical times. Their children were taught arithmetic from the age of five — all for the purpose of trade. Inevitably the Uygur, even the young, have imbided some of the Sogdian business acumen.

Besides Kasghar in the west, the other Uygur stronghold in southern Xinjiang, in the east, is Turpan, which lies in the Turpan Depression, China's Land of Extremes (overleaf).

Transportation of most produce and goods within Xinjiang is by lorry or truck. Soldiers, however, are accustomed to moving on foot (above and opposite).

Most homes are basic, with little or no mechanical equipment to help with the daily chores.

The Kazak:
Horsemen of Northern Xinjiang

The fascinating thing about the area of northern Xinjiang between the Junggar Basin and Mongolia is its three-coloured pattern. It begins with a stretch of rich lush pasture, which is overtaken by moving sand dunes, merging into hundreds of miles of desert composed of pebbles and sandy ground (left). Today, much of this territory has been made into autonomous areas by the Chinese government for the Kazak, Tajik, Mongol and Kirgiz (above).

*Because the nomads have to seek water and pasturage, the tribal structure of their communities has remained important up to the present day. Thus, while moving around or assembling their herds, related clans often work side by side (*above *and* right).*

After the Uygur and the Han, the next most populous minority in northern Xinjiang is the Kazak. They are better known to the West as Cassacks or Cossaks. The Kazak are not only outstanding horsemen, but are also good wrestlers (left and above).

As well as engaging in agriculture and pasturage, the Kazak make handicrafts such as patterned hats and garments, saddles and tools, wall-hangings and rugs for everyday use, all with their unique patterns and designs (above and right).

In the more remote areas of northern Xinjiang, yurts tend to have low roofs and are equipped with only the most basic necessities. Life is made all the more difficult by the herdsmen's ignorance of birth-control. When the parents are out with the herds, the children have to look after themselves since there are virtually no kindergartens or schools (above and left).

The Kazak are 'followers of rich pastures', herding horses, goats, sheep and camels. They live in the round felt-covered tents known as yurts which have a light trellised frame that is easily assembled and dismantled. After the frame has been erected, it is covered with felts which are secured with thick strips of felt (left *and* opposite).

When there is a birth, a wedding or an Islamic festival, the Kazak hold large horse-riding contests. In one such trial a group of children around the age of ten, coming from all directions, compete in bareback-riding over three courses which take several hours to finish (**left**, **above** and **overleaf**). In the intermission entertainment is provided.

The other most popular horse-riding sport among the herdsmen is 'grab the carcass'. Two teams of first-rate horsemen vie with one another to grab the carcass of a sheep whose head, limbs and innards have been removed. The team that manages to gain control of it, and put it down at a place designated as the goal, wins the match (left, above and overleaf).

This beautiful lady, the young housekeeper at a small guesthouse in the outskirts of Ili, is the female lead in my film (opposite). The young actor (left) belongs to the Ili performing troupe.

*The Kazak are renowned hunters. Most of the older generation of Kazak hunters can still be seen sitting proudly in their silver-chased saddles with eagles perched on their wrist, scanning the surroundings for prey (*right *and* opposite*).*

The Kazak are warm-
hearted, hospitable people.
The 900,000 to be found
in China today constitute
only a portion of the
entire Kazak population
of Central Asia. The
others live across the
Soviet border.

The Tajik:
Nomads of the High Pamir

The journey from Kashgar to Tash-Kurghan, regional capital of the High Pamir, sometimes called 'the roof of the world', takes six to eight hours (opposite). Groups of nomadic herdsmen saunter along the mountain roads — Tash-Kurghan originally meant Mountain Road (left).

Here and there are lush pastures with herds of sheep and cattle nestling in the shadow of the snow-capped Pamir (above). Some of the settlements have square, flat-roofed houses which have been home to generations of Tajik (right).

The town of Tash-Kurghan has only one street about 30 metres in length. It accommodates the only shop, post office, hospital, school and government office in the entire area (above *and* right).

Most Tajik families span three generations (opposite). *The young are obliged by etiquette to greet the old whenever they meet. With relatives, handshakes must be performed. In the gesture of greeting, the man places his hand on his chest and bows, while the woman claps both hands before her and also bows.* (left).

The Tajik's flat-roofed
houses, despite their low
ceilings, are spacious
inside. Earth mounds form
platforms on the floor
which are covered over
with woollen rugs to
provide snug seats (left).
Marriages are arranged by
the eldest (above).

The birth of a child is an important occasion: if the baby is male, three loud shouts are given or three shots are fired to bless the child. If it is a girl, a broom is placed on her head to ensure she will be a good housewife when she grows up (left). Despite the bitter cold, due to the high altitude, the bicycle is still an important form of transportation (opposite).

This is said to be the highest place in the world ... a plain between two mountains with a lake from which flows a very fine river ... This plateau, the name of which is Pamir, extends fully twelve days' journey, during which there is no habitation or shelter' (Marco Polo) (overleaf).

In his writings Marco Polo mentions the huge, rocky masses of the Kongur Peak
(above), the second highest mountain in the world (7,719 metres), and the
Muztagata Peak (right), also known as the Father of the Ice Mountain (7,546
metres).

Faced with the awe-inspiring grandeur of the High Pamir, one cannot but feel the insignificance of man's place in nature (right *and* opposite).

LIST OF NAMES

Official Chinese names (pinyin romanization)	Other common names and spellings	Official Chinese names (full form)	Ancient Chinese names
Aksu		阿克蘇	姑墨
Altay	Altai	阿爾泰	
Altay Shan	Altai Mountains	阿爾泰山	金山
Aydingkol	Lake Ayding	艾丁湖	
Baikalkol	Lake Baikal	貝加爾湖	北海
Baizeklik	Bezeklik	伯孜克里克	
Balkashkol	Lake Balkash	巴爾喀什湖	夷播海
Baoan	Paoan	保安	
Barkol		巴里昆	鎮西府
Beijing	Peking	北京	北平、燕京
Bogda Feng	Bogda Peak	博格達峯	金莎嶺
Bokhara		布哈拉	安息
Chang'an	Ch'ang-an	長安	
Changji Huizu	Ch'ang-chi Hui-tsu	昌吉回族	
Dongxiang	Tung-hsiang	東鄉	
Dunhuang	Tun-huang	敦煌	
Emi'n	Emil	葉密立	額敏
Endere		且末	安得悅
Gansu	Kansu	甘肅	
Gaochang	Kao-ch'ang, Karakhoja	高昌	西州
Guangdong	Canton	廣東	
Guangzhou	Canton	廣州	
Hami	Kumul	哈密	
Han		漢	
Han Wudi	Han Wu-ti	漢武帝	
Hangzhou	Hangchow	杭州	
Hastana Mu	Astana Graves	阿斯塔那古墓	武城
Hotan	Khotan	和田	于闐
Hui		回	
Huoyan Shan	Flaming Mountains	火焰山	
Ili		伊犁	伊列
Jiaohe	Yarkhoto	交河	
Junggar Pendi	Dzungarian Basin	準噶爾盆地	
Kangxi	K'ang-hsi	康熙	
Karakorum	Karakoron	和林	哈剌和林
Karakoram Shan	Karakoram Mountains	喀喇崑崙山	
Kashi	Kashgar	喀什	疏勒
Kazak	Kazakh	哈薩克	烏孫
Kirgiz	Kirghiz	柯爾克孜	乞里吉思
Kokand	Khokand	浩罕	可汗那
Kongur Feng	Kongur Peak	公格爾峯	
Kunlun Shan	Kun-lun Mountains	崑崙山	
Kuqa	Kucha	庫車	龜茲
Lin Zexu	Lin Tse-hsu	林則徐	
Lopnur	Lop-nor	羅布泊	鹽澤

I pondered how infir
man was by compari
magnificent landscape a
At the same ti
that man could ove
when he exercised hi
his ceaseless w
inextinguis

*I pondered how infinitely small
man was by comparison with this
magnificent landscape and mountain ranges.
At the same time, I reflected
that man could overcome any obstacles
when he exercised his strength and endurance,
his ceaseless will to struggle, and his
inextinguishable passion for life.*

LIST OF NAMES

Official Chinese names (*pinyin* romanization)	Other common names and spellings	Official Chinese names (full form)	Ancient Chinese names
Aksu		阿克蘇	姑墨
Altay	Altai	阿爾泰	
Altay Shan	Altai Mountains	阿爾泰山	金山
Aydingkol	Lake Ayding	艾丁湖	
Baikalkol	Lake Baikal	貝加爾湖	北海
Baizeklik	Bezeklik	伯孜克里克	
Balkashkol	Lake Balkash	巴爾喀什湖	夷播海
Baoan	Paoan	保安	
Barkol		巴里昆	鎮西府
Beijing	Peking	北京	北平、燕京
Bogda Feng	Bogda Peak	博格達峯	金莎嶺
Bokhara		布哈拉	安息
Chang'an	Ch'ang-an	長安	
Changji Huizu	Ch'ang-chi Hui-tsu	昌吉回族	
Dongxiang	Tung-hsiang	東鄉	
Dunhuang	Tun-huang	敦煌	
Emi'n	Emil	葉密立	額敏
Endere		且末	安得悅
Gansu	Kansu	甘肅	
Gaochang	Kao-ch'ang, Karakhoja	高昌	西州
Guangdong	Canton	廣東	
Guangzhou	Canton	廣州	
Hami	Kumul	哈密	
Han		漢	
Han Wudi	Han Wu-ti	漢武帝	
Hangzhou	Hangchow	杭州	
Hastana Mu	Astana Graves	阿斯塔那古墓	武城
Hotan	Khotan	和田	于闐
Hui		回	
Huoyan Shan	Flaming Mountains	火焰山	
Ili		伊犂	伊列
Jiaohe	Yarkhoto	交河	
Junggar Pendi	Dzungarian Basin	準噶爾盆地	
Kangxi	K'ang-hsi	康熙	
Karakorum	Karakoron	和林	哈剌和林
Karakoram Shan	Karakoram Mountains	喀喇崑崙山	
Kashi	Kashgar	喀什	疏勒
Kazak	Kazakh	哈薩克	烏孫
Kirgiz	Kirghiz	柯爾克孜	乞里吉思
Kokand	Khokand	浩罕	可汗那
Kongur Feng	Kongur Peak	公格爾峯	
Kunlun Shan	Kun-lun Mountains	崑崙山	
Kuqa	Kucha	庫車	龜茲
Lin Zexu	Lin Tse-hsu	林則徐	
Lopnur	Lop-nor	羅布泊	鹽澤

Official Chinese names (*pinyin* romanization)	Other common names and spellings	Official Chinese names (full form)	Ancient Chinese names
Loulan	Lou-lan	樓蘭	
Man		滿	
Merv		馬里	木鹿城
Minfeng	Manfung, Niya	民豐	尼雅
Miran		米蘭	小鄯善
Mongol	Mongolian	蒙古	蒙兀
Mori		木壘	獨山城
Muztagata	Mustagh-ata Peak	慕士塔格峯	
Nei Mongol	Inner Mongolia	內蒙古	
Ningxia	Ninghsia	寧夏	
Pamir		柏米爾	葱嶺
Qapqal Xibe		察布查爾錫伯	
Qianlong	Ch'ien-lung	乾隆	
Qinggis Han	Genghis Khan	成吉思汗	鐵木眞
Ruoqiang	Qarkilik, Charklik	若羌	鄯善
Russ	Russia	俄羅斯	
Salar		撒拉	
Samarkand		撒馬爾罕	康居
Shaanxi	Shaansi	陝西	
Shache	Shache, Yarkand, Yarkant	莎車	莎車國
Shanshan	Pichan, Piqan	鄯善	闐展城
Song Lizong	Song Li-tsung	宋理宗	
Tajik	Tadjik	塔吉克	大食
Taklimakan Shamo	Taklamakan Desert	塔克拉瑪干沙漠	
Tang Gaozong	T'ang Kao-tsung	唐高宗	
Tarim Pendi	Tarim Basin	塔里木盆地	
Tatar	Tartar	塔塔爾	韃靼
Taxkorgan	Tash-Kurghan	塔什庫爾干	褐盤陀國
Tianshan	Ti'en Shan, Heavenly Mountains	天山	
Turpan	Turfan	吐魯番	高昌
Turpan Pendi	Turfan Depression	吐魯番盆地	
Uygur	Uighur	維吾爾	回鶻
Uygur Zizhiqu	Uighur Autonomous Region	維吾爾自治區	
Uzbek	Ozbek	烏兹別克	
Wulumuchi	Ürümqi, Urumchi, Tihwa	烏魯木齊	迪化
Xi'an	Sian	西安	長安
Xiang Fei	Hsiang Fei	香妃	容妃
Xibe	Sibo	錫伯	
Xinjiang	Sinkiang	新疆	
Xiongnu	Hsiung-nu, Huns	匈奴	
Xiyu	Hsi-yu, the Western Region	西域	
Xuanzang	Hsuan-tsang	玄奘	
Yanqi Huizu	Yen-ch'i Hui-tsu	焉耆回族	
Yumenguan	Yu-men-kuan, the Jade Gate	玉門關	
Zhang Qian	Chang Ch'ien	張騫	

Note on Cameras

T HE past ten years have not seen many changes in the photographic equipment and techniques that I employ. But this has not prevented me from making progress. Experience and a deeper understanding of photography have helped more than anything to perfect my skill as a photographer.

Because I am both short and slight, I try to avoid being buried in photographic equipment when I set off on an assignment. I usually carry a Nikon FTN (almost twenty years old) and one Nikon FE, as well as four lenses (24mm, 55mm micro, 85 mm, and 200 mm.) I never take a tripod. The FTN is invariably loaded with black-and-white film, and the FE with colour transparency. In recent years, on assignments to remote and undeveloped areas, I have taken a Nikon FE2 with a 300 mm lens and loaded with high-speed colour film.

I always try to remind myself that the camera and lenses are only aids for the human eye. Nowadays with advanced photographic technology, there is no need to worry about films being over-exposed or other technical details. The most important thing is to develop confidence in your equipment, so that when you come across the right moment and the right quality of light, you are in complete control of the camera.

160